mposium:
venty Years
UAQ

urban affairs quarterly

volume 21, number 1 / september 1985

SAGE PUBLICATIONS

urban affairs quarterly

SAGE Publications / *Beverly Hills / London / New Delhi*

urban affairs quarterly

volume 21, number 1 / september 1985

contents

Symposium:
Twenty Years of UAQ

Editor's Introduction 3

Crossing Urban Boundaries: *The Mission of* Urban Affairs Quarterly
ALBERT HUNTER 5

The American City: *A National Priority or an Expendable Population?*
MARILYN GITTELL 13

Urban Affairs: *A Look into the Past and the Future*
ROBERT L. LINEBERRY 20

The Urban Condition: *"Plates" Beneath City Surfaces and a New Research Agenda*
MARGARET T. GORDON 25

Other Articles

Corporate Strategies and the Decline of Transit in U.S. Cities
J. ALLEN WHITT
GLENN YAGO 37

Same City, Different Worlds: *Examining Gender- and Work-Based Differences in Perceptions of Neighborhood Desirability*
ANNE B. SHLAY
DENISE A. DiGREGORIO 66

Suburban Municipalities: *The Changing System of Intergovernmental Relations in the Mid-1970s*
MARK SCHNEIDER
JOHN LOGAN 87

Employment in Service Activities and Inequality in Metropolitan Areas
JOEL I. NELSON
JON LORENCE 106

Book Review Essays

Planners and the Public
JOHN FORESTER 126

Public Property and Private Power
JAMES R. ALEXANDER 129

Urban Displacement Research: *Local, National, International*
W. DENNIS KEATING 132

MANUSCRIPTS should be submitted to the editors in care of Professor Albert Hunter, **URBAN AFFAIRS QUARTERLY,** Center for Urban Affairs and Policy Research, Northwestern University, Evanston, Illinois 60201. Include *five* (5) copies of the manuscript. Full-length manuscripts should not exceed 25 pages total and research notes should not exceed 10 pages total (*including* footnotes, references, and tables or figures). All text, footnotes, and references should be typewritten with one-inch margins and double-spaced. All references to the author's previous work should be omitted in the text. Footnotes and bibliographic citations should follow the current **UAQ** style. Copies of the style sheets may be obtained from the editors or the publisher. A brief biographical paragraph describing each author's current affiliation, research interests, and recent publications should be submitted, and an abstract of approximately 100 words should accompany each copy of the manuscript.

Manuscripts will not be returned to authors. Please keep copies for your own needs. The editors assume that manuscripts are for the exclusive consideration of **UAQ** and have not simultaneously been submitted elsewhere.

BOOKS FOR REVIEW should be sent to Professor Bryan D. Jones, Book Review Editor, **URBAN AFFAIRS QUARTERLY,** Department of Political Science, Wayne State University, Detroit, Michigan 48202. Potential contributors of book review essays are encouraged to correspond with the book review editor before submitting manuscripts.

The Editor and Publisher are grateful to the Center for Urban Affairs and Policy Research, Northwestern University, for providing facilities and ancillary services for URBAN AFFAIRS QUARTERLY.

URBAN AFFAIRS QUARTERLY is published four times annually—in September, December, March, and June—by Sage Publications, Inc., 275 South Beverly Drive, Beverly Hills, CA 90212.

Subscriptions: Regular institutional rate $60.00 per year. Individuals may subscribe at a one-year rate of $25.00. Add $6.00 for subscriptions outside the United States. Orders from the U.K., Europe, the Middle East, and Africa should be sent to London address (below). Orders from India should be sent to the New Delhi address (below). Noninstitutional orders **must** be paid by personal check.

Second class postage paid at Beverly Hills, California. ISSN 0042-0816

This journal is abstracted or indexed in **Sage Urban Studies Abstracts, Human Resources Abstracts, Educational Administration Abstracts, Sociological Abstracts, Abstracts for Social Workers, ABC POL SCI, Sociology of Education Abstracts, Urban Affairs Abstracts, Sage Public Administration Abstracts, International Political Science Abstracts, Ethnic Studies Bibliography, Public Affairs Information Service, Ekistic Index, Current Contents, Social Science Citation Index,** and **United States Political Science Documents,** and is available on microfilm from University Microfilms, Ann Arbor, Michigan.

Back Issues: Information about availability and prices of back issues may be obtained from the publisher's order department (address below). Single-issue orders for 5 or more copies will receive a special adoption discount. Contact the order department for details. Write to London office for sterling prices.

Inquiries: Address all correspondence and permissions requests to SAGE PUBLICATIONS, Inc., 275 South Beverly Drive, Beverly Hills, California 90212. Inquiries and subscriptions from the U.K., Europe, the Middle East, and Africa should be sent to SAGE PUBLICATIONS Ltd, 28 Banner Street, London EC1Y 8QE, England. From India, write to SAGE PUBLICATIONS INDIA Pvt. Ltd, P.O. Box 4215, New Delhi 110 048 India. Other orders should be sent to the Beverly Hills office.

Advertising: Current rates and specifications may be obtained by writing to the Advertising Manager at the Beverly Hills office (address above).

Claims: Claims for undelivered copies must be made no later than three months following month of publication. The publisher will supply missing copies when losses have been sustained in transit and when the eserve stock will permit.

Change of Address: Six weeks' advance notice must be given when notifying of change of address. Please send old address label along with the new address to insure proper identification. Please specify name of journal. POSTMASTER: Send change of address to: Urban Affairs Quarterly, c/o 275 South Beverly Drive, Beverly Hills, CA 90212.

SYMPOSIUM
Twenty Years of *UAQ*

This issue marks the twentieth anniversary of the first publication of *Urban Affairs Quarterly*. Two decades of dedication to urban research attests to the continuing centrality of the subject and of the journal itself. To mark the event, I have asked the previous editors of the journal to reflect on the past and future, a common but worthwhile activity on such occasions. The editors of the journal have been Marilyn Gittell (1964-1971), Peter Bouxsein (1971-1974), Louis H. Masotti (1974-1980), Robert L. Lineberry (1980-1982), Margaret T. Gordon (1981-1984), and Albert Hunter (1980 to date). (Peter Bouxsein and Louis H. Masotti were regrettably unable to contribute to this symposium due to previous commitments.)

I encourage the readers also to pause and reflect on where we have been and where we go from here. I offer the readers my own brief reflections on the continuing mission of *UAQ*, and have asked past editors to address three more specific questions:

(1) What have been the major factors affecting the conditions of American urban areas over the past two decades, and what trends and projections do you foresee over the next two decades into the twenty-first century?
(2) What have been the most significant policy initiatives by governments at both the federal and local level over the past two decades, both successes and notable failures, and what policy initiatives do you foresee as being required at these different levels to deal with the future needs of American cities?
(3) What are the needed areas of research that social scientists should undertake in addressing the future conditions of cities and informing policymakers with respect to possible alternative policy initiatives?

Beginning with the March 1986 issue, the editorship of *UAQ* will move to the Center for Metropolitan Studies at the University of Missouri at St. Louis. The new editors will be Dennis R. Judd and Donald Phares. All future manuscripts should be sent to the new editors c/o The Center for Metropolitan Studies, University of

Missouri-St. Louis, 8001 Natural Bridge Road, St. Louis, MO 63121; telephone (314) 553-5273.

At this time it is also fitting and appropriate to extend our gratitude to all who have assisted *UAQ* over the years in varying capacities: from associate to managing editors, to members of the editorial board, to authors, reviewers, and readers. A journal is a collective activity and a collective expression of interest. From the editor's perspective it is gratifying to see that there exists among us that rare but still honorable collectivity—a community of scholars. Thank you.

—The Editor

CROSSING URBAN BOUNDARIES
The Mission of *Urban Affairs Quarterly*

ALBERT HUNTER
Northwestern University

The headlines of the *New York Times* in September of 1965 were describing riots in numerous cities of the United States and reporting the national debate over the war on poverty, its related model cities program, the establishment of the Department of Housing and Urban Development, and other federal, state, and local governmental programs and services designed to deal with the urban ills of the time: poverty, unemployment, inadequate housing, violence and crime, racial segregation, and the continuing decay of central cities. It was the beginning of the urban crisis. We had lived through the more specific fears of the Cuban missile crisis, and looming over the horizon were the as yet unheard of energy and fiscal crises.

In universities and research centers throughout the country scholars also were once again turning their attention to these enduring social problems of cities, with the hope and promise, shared by political leaders and governmental administrators who provided abundant research funds, that the social sciences could contribute not only to an accurate definition of the problems, but also to the design and administration of programs to deal effectively with those problems. As well, private foundations entered the urban arena, establishing their own programs and supporting numerous urban research centers that became a firmly entrenched part of the academic landscape by the end of the decade. Having reached crisis proportions, urban affairs were at the top of the national agenda. Within this context there appeared a critical need to provide for the dissemination of the rapidly accumulating knowledge on, in, and about cities—knowledge of basic research and applied programs that would cross disciplinary boundaries within the academy, and also cross back and forth from the academy to policymakers in city halls, state capitols, and Washington itself.

URBAN AFFAIRS QUARTERLY, Vol. 21 No. 1, September 1985 5-12

In September of 1965 Volume 1, Number 1 of *Urban Affairs Quarterly* appeared to fulfill that role. And although the content of its mission has changed over the ensuing two decades as the crises themselves have unfolded and altered, the task of *UAQ* has remained unchanged. The faith and commitment continues that urban problems and policies must be addressed by the highest quality research that the social sciences can provide. This twentieth anniversary issue of *UAQ* exemplifies this mission, a mission of crossing boundaries. It is both a milestone marking the movement across the past two decades of urban affairs as Americans moved into the last half of the twentieth century and a signpost pointing to the next two decades that will see it launched and targeted on its way into the twenty-first century. If the last century was one during which we came to live in an urban world, the next is likely to be one in which we come to live on urban worlds.

CROSSING FROM AFFAIRS THAT ARE URBAN TO URBAN AFFAIRS

For years social scientists have continued to debate the very role that cities have played and continue to play in social life and, more specifically, the role that cities and things defined as urban should play in theory and research. Was the urban crisis in reality simply a series of overlapping social problems that just happened to be located in cities, or was there something more specific about the very organization and operation of our cities that contributed to the crises of the day?

Perhaps this debate is most succinctly summarized in the distinction between cities as settings and cities as subjects. It is difficult, if not impossible in nations that are as urbanized as those of the Western world, to think of any major social phenomenon that does not take place in cities. Therefore, the designation of phenomena as urban can be a relatively meaningless categorization insofar as it includes almost everything and therefore becomes a superfluous adjective. It is as if the prevailing theoretical distinction and comparison were still that of an earlier era in which "urban" was most readily contrasted with "rural," and that urban economists, urban geographers, urban historians, urban political scientists, and urban sociologists were naturally to be contrasted with their counterparts—rural economists, rural geographers, rural historians, and so on. Given the prevailing urbanization of people and their institutions at the close of the twentieth century, an urban focus must mean more than the mere happenstance that something is located in a city. To define as urban affairs all that goes on in cities is to miss the real social and theoretical potential and power of the urban concept.

What is that powerful potential? To paraphrase Lewis Mumford, it lies in the recognition that cities are the largest and most complex physical and symbolic artifacts constructed by human beings to organize their collective life. The pyramids of the pharaohs and the Stonehenge of the druids pale in comparison to the scale of the modern metropolises of Cairo and London. This recognition has three central characteristics: (1) Cities are physical constructions, or, in today's parlance, "built environments," grounded landscapes (cityscapes) on which are enacted the dramas of modern social life; (2) they are symbolic representations of the institutionalized values and power by which people organize their collective existence; and (3) perhaps most importantly, they are artifacts in the true sense that they are socially constructed by people and therefore hold the promising potential of being subject to conscious manipulation, alteration, planning, and control. In short, cities are the concrete embodiment of the assertion that people produce their own history. Therefore, urban affairs are best seen as those phenomena that are most directly linked to these three enduring social and theoretical characteristics of cities. In the language of the modern social sciences, things are urban to the degree that these characteristics of cities are seen as critical independent or dependent variables, as causes or consequences in theoretical explanations of modern social life.

CROSSING ACADEMIC BOUNDARIES

Each of these three characteristics of cities also can be seen as a central concern of specific academic disciplines—of planners with their processes of design, of economists with their land and housing markets, of political scientists and sociologists with their institutions, and of policy analysts and public administrators with their attempts to discharge the public trust. Over the years each of the traditional academic disciplines has carved out its own theoretical conception and has brought its own research methods to bear on cities as a subject of analysis.

Given the increasing specialization and organizational development of these disciplines, replete with their own professional associations and journals, the increasing risk is that the Roshamon effect will prevail, with each discipline seeing a different reality and carving up the beast in its own image. The intellectual result could easily be not only an increasing inability to communicate with one another within the academy, but as well to sound to concerned outsiders more like the tower of babble rather than the tongues of angels. Therefore, a journal such as *Urban Affairs Quarterly* that purposefully crosses traditional academic boundaries in pursuit of its subject of investigation runs the risk of being dismissed in more narrow, traditional circles of the academy as a less pure pursuit of knowledge in that it is "applied" to a single subject.

However, such a journal provides a unique service, not only to the subject of its investigations, cities themselves, but to the knowledge of the academy, in that it presents the possibility of creative cross-fertilization among disciplines that can lead to new empirical and theoretical insights. In this sense the many who have been connected with and concerned about the subjects of investigation published over the past two decades in *Urban Affairs Quarterly* are uniquely positioned at the intersection of two demanding constraints: to provide the best that their disciplines can offer in empirical and theoretical insights and to speak to others different than themselves who also are interested in the subject of investigation—cities. One must serve more than one master, and do so with the best that can be offered. This is the continuing challenge that the readers, reviewers, and writers of *Urban Affairs Quarterly* have appropriately come to expect and demand from one another.

CROSSING THE POLICY BOUNDARY

The urban crisis of the 1960s was the context within which *Urban Affairs Quarterly* first appeared, and ensuing crises under other labels (e.g., energy, fiscal) have kept cities at the center of the national policy agenda, even though that agenda may eschew the label of "urban."

It is as if the crises of an earlier era were either solved or mysteriously disappeared through the waving of the magic wand of benign neglect. However, to say that the urban crisis is no longer with us is to confuse labels with reality. Not only within government but also in foundations and even within the academy itself "urban" is not the same "sexy" label that it was in the 1960s. A number of alternative foci of intellectual interest have risen to center stage and now compete with urban interests for funds, people, energy, and effort.

For example, "policy analysis," "evaluation research," and "applied programs" now deal with many of the same issues previously addressed under the urban label and the urban agenda. However, where these newer endeavors often differ from the old is in their focus on a particular "method" of addressing different agendas. This is in contrast to the specific subject-oriented approach to urban phenomena that "urban affairs" explicitly connotes. Furthermore, these method-focused interests often contain as a core assumption the idea that government, at various levels and in various policies and programs, is the actor on the urban scene best able to deal with these issues. As a consequence, if there is government retrenchment it would appear on the surface that there are fewer "affairs" of concern that deal directly with cities, when in fact urban affairs continue to multiply outside the more limited scope of the scientist's method or microscope.

By focusing on methods and a predefined narrow set of actors, rather than on the specific subject of cities themselves, such analyses may lose sight of the numerous impacts that other social processes and players may be having on cities, and on the impacts that the changing spatial and social organization of cities may be having on these other issues. In short, the continuing need for a grounded subject matter of investigation requires that a journal such as *Urban Affairs Quarterly* continue to point to the ways in which urban populations and institutions are affected by external factors, and, in turn, how these other factors are themselves influenced by the most basic of urban affairs.

What to academics is the grounded subject of investigation is to urban policymakers and administrators the very ground on which they walk, talk, and act. Or, to paraphrase Norton Long, cities are the gameboard on which they play. The role of the social scientist, then, is to discover the "rules" by which that game is being played, and to inform policymakers to make them better players. However, the interchange between academic researchers and urban policymakers is more of a mutual exchange of information than a one-sided scientist/subject or ruler/subject relationship. Indeed, the interchange of personnel between academic and policymaking positions attests to both the increasing power and influence of the former and the increasing sophistication and professionalization of the latter. It is important, therefore, that a conduit exist for the flow of information across that boundary, and *Urban Affairs Quarterly* is such a conduit. Although it is primarily a journal speaking with the voice of academics, the very nature of the research published in these pages is either implicitly or explicitly "policy relevant." Not necessarily in the narrow sense of speaking only to and about specific urban policies and programs, but in the broader sense of keeping policymakers informed of the latest theoretical developments and empirical trends that can provide them with greater insight and understanding, if not specific ways of acting. In short, it is as if *Urban Affairs Quarterly* were the hyphen in Plato's ideal of the "philosopher-king."

CROSSING CITY BOUNDARIES: FROM POLIS TO METROPOLIS TO TERRAPOLIS

Although the problems that defined the urban crisis of the 1960s (e.g., riots, race relations, and renewal) were seen to be centered in the nation's "central cities," the ensuing research of subsequent decades pointed to the need for a larger conceptual focus beyond the boundaries of central cities to provide an adequate understanding and explanation of these crises.

In the 1950s urban analysts discovered the suburbs, but for the most part saw them more as relatively isolated "little communities," whereas research of the 1970s increasingly focused more appropriately on the integrated reality of the metropolitan area as a whole. The slums of the central city and the suburbs beyond the city's rim were seen not simply as different categories of community, but as interdependent parts of a larger metropolitan structure. Whether specific analyses looked at issues of racial segregation, vacancy chains in housing, the shifting location of industry, jobs, and the ecological form of structural unemployment, or the efficiency and equity of distribution of various governmental services, their theoretical explanations (if not always their empirical indicators) were framed at the metropolitan level. This represented, of course, not simply a shift in intellectual styles, but a shifting reality of the way in which the nation's urban areas were being restructured.

The metropolitan restructuring demanded a new theoretical accounting. We were no longer simply an urban nation (a threshold passed in 1920, when a majority of the nation's population was classified as urban), but were rapidly becoming a metropolitan nation. The complexity of governmental policies and programs emanating from municipal, county, state, and federal levels and the intergovernmental relations that ensued may be seen as attempts to deal with the increasing metropolitan character of the nation's new urban form.

In reviewing the past two decades of *UAQ* this metropolitan transformation is strikingly evident in the articles published and books reviewed. It includes not only the more explicit demographic, ecological, and economic analyses of metropolitan populations and institutions, but an increasing focus on "urban affairs" as a specific concern of state and federal policy. From the earlier model cities and CAPs through revenue sharing to CDBGs and UDAGs, to state IRBs and the newly proposed federal (and already in place state) "enterprise zones," the growing list of acronyms begins to rival the alphabet soup of the New Deal, and attests to the degree to which "urban affairs" have in fact crossed beyond city boundaries and become national affairs.

Nowhere is this shift more clearly seen than in the phenomenon of sunbelt/frostbelt, which at the national level parallels the metropolitan level issues of differences in community growth and decline. This metropolitan issue also is captured in the issues of demetropolitanization of populations and institutions that has more recently emerged, an issue seemingly in direct contrast to the contemporary "gentrification" of inner-city neighborhoods—two opposing population flows that demand an integrated theoretical understanding that accounts for both. The reality of the regionally interdependent metropolitan structure of the nation requires a more systematic and explicit exploration of these linkages among levels, and an awareness on the part of researchers and policymakers alike that no matter how parochial the theoretical problem or the governmental policy, contemporary "urban affairs" must be seen to lie within these interlocking parameters.

There is, of course, a clearly emerging "ultimate" urban structure that extends beyond the boundaries of nation-states themselves to a recognition that the world as a whole can be analyzed as an interdependent metropolitan system. From this perspective nation-states can be seen as an intermediate (though significant) geopolitical category between specific metropolitan areas and the world system of interdependent metropolitan areas, or terrapolis. These metropolitan interdependencies are evident when U.S. mayors and governors fly to Tokyo or Stuttgart to negotiate for a plant location in their area, or when CEOs of American corporations headquartered in Detroit, Dallas, or Denver fly to Paris, Prague, or Peking to negotiate with local leaders for flows of capital, technology, or personnel. A more purely symbolic example of this world level of metropolitan interdependency is the International World's Fair Commission's selection of Seville and Chicago as the joint sites of the 1992 World's Fair.

A recognition of this world system level of metropolitan interdependencies requires among academics a new form of theory and research that extends beyond the usual comparisons drawn in "cross cultural" or "comparative" urban research. Although much research is needed on specific metropolitan areas in different nations and regions of the world to explore the full range of variation that exists, it is no longer simply sufficient to treat these as categorical variations or "types." This is similar to earlier research that simply looked at slums and suburbs as different types of communities. Rather, worldwide metropolitan variations should be explored as resulting to a degree from the positional interdependencies that given metropolitan areas have within the world system of metropolitan areas—terrapolis. The use of "terra" as the prefix to this next level of urban structure is purposefully parochial—for as we move into the twenty-first century, other specific worlds may have to be labeled as variations on a newly emerging urban form. I leave it to the reader's imagination to take him or her as far as he or she wants to go, with every expectation that a copy of *Urban Affairs Quarterly* will accompany him or her on the journey.

THE AMERICAN CITY: A National Priority or an Expendable Population?

MARILYN GITTELL
City University of New York

We have come a long way in the last two decades—from a national priority to address the urban crisis, to benign neglect, to disdain for cities and their needs. The initiation of *Urban Affairs Quarterly* was a reflection of the national mood in the 1960s, an acceptance of the responsibility that faced us as a society to confront the needs of our cities through national urban policies. Developments in the 1950s provided the rationale; most notable was the Supreme Court decision in the Brown case, which established with the use of social science data that, whatever the mythology of our democratic system, large segments of the population were suffering from discriminatory policies and practices. We finally were forced to admit as a society that 30 to 40 million people were living in poverty, and that lower-income and minority people were denied equal access to housing, education, and health care.

The single most important change that occurred in the early 1960s was the acceptance of the fact that it was necessary for the national government to develop policies that would redistribute the benefits of the system; that as a society we had to work at making the political system more inclusive; and that public policies would include preferential treatment to compensate for past abuses. This change in attitude was the source of support for a new perspective on the importance of cities and their populations in the nation's future. Some have said that the emergence of the United States as *the* world power was instrumental in creating this national sense of responsibility to correct inequities. Thurow has attributed this more altruistic ideology to the general expansion of the economy, and there is evidence that historically the democratic ideology in America, the concern with equality, is tied directly to economic progress (Thurow, 1981; Potter, 1954).

URBAN AFFAIRS QUARTERLY, Vol. 21 No. 1, September 1985 13-19

Still others would credit national leadership and or movement politics with the setting of a new purpose and direction. More structural analyses suggest that the growth of professionalism, changes in technology, and centralization were contributing factors to the expansion of government programs. It is likely that all of these and other variables combined to produce a decade of dramatic change in public attitudes and policies and a determination to address the needs of American cities. It is only now in retrospect that we can look to that era and marvel at the comparatively radical policies it made acceptable. Until the 1960s federal programs were reinforcement for state programs, in the 1960s they changed to establish and fulfill national goals. The centerpiece of the changes were the Great Society programs, which directed resources to the urban areas.

Lyndon Johnson, in 1965, announced to Congress that cities were to play the most vital role in the future of the country. From 1964 to 1969 federal assistance for cities increased at five times the rate it did for nonurban areas. Finally, the cities in the United States were being treated as essential to the country's progress. Two major changes, the acceptance of public responsibility for achieving a more equitable society and an affirmation of the central role of cities in American life, made the 1960s policies a radical departure from earlier policies, although still within the parameters of American ideology (i.e., few direct federal service programs and a limited welfare state concept).

Federal policies were shaped to assure that both goals would be pursued. The emphasis on categorical grants and their specificity in addressing low-income populations was reflected in the new legislation in housing, education, and health. The antipoverty legislation, now almost universally disparaged, was an adventurous approach to the political and social problems that had to be addressed. Its original conception, fashioned on the demonstrated experience of the Ford Foundation Grey Areas Project, provided for political organization and participation of excluded populations in the development of new service delivery systems in the cities. Comprehensive neighborhood services and programs would be developed in city neighborhoods by local citizens, as a means of training and engaging lower-income and minority populations who had been excluded from the political system. City bureaucracies and elected officials who had ignored these groups would be bypassed and these new structures would build new constituency power. Even though city officials immediately organized to amend the legislation to prevent the shift in responsibility away from the city government, the legislation was flexible enough to allow implementation in different cities to produce some significant results.

Community action agencies in cities throughout the country, especially in the early years, became concerned with services and developed innovative programs. Their encouragement and use of community-based organizations for service delivery made for more responsive programs in many communities. Perhaps equally important was the training of cadres of new leaders in lower-income areas, who have since become important participants in city politics.

Several major pieces of federal legislation in that era reflect the pursuit of these new national goals best. The initiation of a federal presence in education with the passage of the Elementary and Secondary Education Act (ESEA) of 1965 was a significant step, even though federal aid was never a significant percentage of the total dollars spent on education. The Act provided funding particularly for school districts with minority and impoverished children. The aid formula guaranteed that federal funds would be concentrated on inner-city schools. More important than direct funding was the impact of the federal thrust, the opening up of large city school systems to public review. Federal school desegregation legislation and affirmative action requirements provided new standards of expectations and performance from city agencies that had never existed before. Lower-income and minority parents, many of whom were organized under the provisions of the antipoverty legislation, made increased demands on the system and were encouraged to participate in the development of school policies under mechanisms provided in the federal legislation.

The 1965 and 1968 Housing Acts also required that a majority of all housing units had to be made available to low- and moderate-income families, and at least 20% had to be designed for low-income families. The rent supplement provisions and expanded payments for individual housing assistance were intended to provide the option for lower-income populations in urban areas to live outside of public housing projects. Model cities legislation in 1966 coordinated the allocation of resources for particular areas within a city, concentrating efforts in the communities in most desperate need. Similarly, the 1962 Manpower Development and Training Act and subsequent manpower legislation established more direct public responsibility for the unemployed, particularly the structurally unemployed. By 1965, seven of ten MDTA graduates had been placed in jobs for which they had been trained and the drop-out rate for the program was less than for the high schools.

By strict evaluation standards, Headstart and Job Corp must be viewed as the most successful programs of that era. Children who participated in Headstart before the age of six were about 60% less likely to be assigned to special education classes, about 45% less likely to be held back a grade, they increased their IQs and were more likely to pursue higher education. It should not be forgotten that Headstart was one of the neighborhood-based, participatory programs that was planned to bypass the existing city school systems. Job Corp also was neighborhood-based and relied on community organizations. Some of the more important and long-lasting results of many of the other programs, however, may not have been measured. Certainly, the seemingly uniform condemnation of the programs of the 1960s is not justified by the evidence (Schwarz,1983).

Not to be ignored in the contribution of the 1960s policies were the most redistributive programs of direct transfers, which increased medical care for the poor and provided food stamps for the hungry. The national policy commitment to cities and deprived populations in the 1960s is characterized by the assertion in the Demonstration Cities and Metropolitan Development Act of 1966 that "Congress hereby finds and declares that improving the quality of urban life is the most critical domestic problem facing the United States."

Although the Nixon and Ford eras moved away from the central national commitment to cities and even attempted to downplay the concept of an urban crisis by a policy of benign neglect, their policies were not radical departures from the 1960s. The 1970s saw more of a reliance on state and local governments, less emphasis on the need to redistribute the benefits of the society, and less reliance on federal intervention to direct state and city efforts. Nixon did offer the family assistance plan, which would have replaced existing dependency programs and could have moved the country to a more realistic support system for the poor without the trappings of a bureaucratic welfare system. In 1969, his call for a new federalism offered overhauling of the manpower programs to increase state and city discretion, and restructuring of the Office of Economic Opportunity to reduce the "experimental" programs. He also proposed and succeeded in getting revenue sharing that reduced federal discretion and resulted in somewhat reduced aid for cities.

Community-based organizations no longer were viewed as desirable alternatives for the delivery of local services or agencies that should be directly receiving federal funds. Regional centers for the administration of federal programs were established in an effort to reduce the role of the Washington bureaucracy. National goals were abandoned and consolidation of programs and revenue sharing were the new priorities. Funding for many of the federal programs increased significantly, although the emphasis changed. From 1969 to 1977, functional changes in the allocation of federal funds saw a significant increase in support for natural resources and environment, general government aid, law enforcement, education, and health care. Commerce and transportation and public assistance became a reduced percentage of the total allocation of federal aid. Congress was instrumental in the support for many of the new programs, particularly in the environmental area.

Overriding economic conditions, particularly inflation, stimulated at least some of the changes in the late 1970s to reduce government programs and spending in cities. Although Carter tried to once again establish a national commitment to urban areas and to issues of equity, he was never able to guide the nation or Congress to enact any of his major policies in this area. By the end of his term he had already initiated the major reductions in public assistance programs and was concerned with reforming the federal categorical grant system following the trend of the Nixon and Ford eras. General purpose assistance grants, however, had been reduced considerably as compared to the Nixon approach, and transfer programs were appreciably increased. Carter did not announce an urban policy until 1978, and it stressed revitalization of neighborhoods and economic development. None of these measures was adopted.

The most widely accepted interpretations of the impact of the 1960s and 1970s programs and policies on cities is decidedly negative. Emphasis is placed on the fiscal outlays that cities were required to make to meet federal program demands, which produced large increases in public employment roles and expenditures for programs they could not afford given their restrictive tax bases, and which ultimately bankrupted them. Another criticism is the backlash argument, which holds that the expenditures on compensatory programs aroused the distress of the middle class, because their taxes were raised excessively to support those programs. Still another widely held view is that none of the programs worked and/or they were corrupted by poverty pimps, who were the only people to reap the rewards.

Certainly there was public dissatisfaction with the economic changes that came at the end of the 1970s, not the least of which was inflation. Also, nativism, if not overt racism, and perceived threats to the traditional distribution of power emerged to challenge redistributive politics. Fiscal crises in several large cities, which reflected enormously increased expenditures for larger bureaucracies and vastly increased pension and welfare benefits, became the excuse for abandonment of equity goals. More significantly, the thrust of the 1960s for direct and broadened participation in the political system through decentralization and community control was seen as a cause of the problem rather than a solution. The solution was to create a more centralized, less participatory structure, removed even from accepted democratic controls.

The Municipal Assistance Corporation in New York City heralded a new era of private sector domination of American cities. No longer were we to be concerned with the special needs of the poor, blacks, or women, who had been excluded from the system. The new concerns were economic, and economic problems are best dealt with by private industry. This traditional strain in American politics of privatization was to embark on a new adventure. If it was necessary to explain how the problems of the disadvantaged were to be addressed, and that was certainly less of an issue than it had been, the trickle-down theory sufficed. The poor would only benefit if the economy of the city was turned around.

The new era saw the creation of business partnerships in every major city, which would serve as the benevolent overseers of progress. Reductions in city services and city work forces in large cities throughout the country reduced budgets and taxes. The creation of economic development agencies was encouraged and the Federal Budget Act of 1981 provided additional tax advantages to real estate developers in cities to build large office buildings and hotels and to gentrify neighborhoods. Cities began to compete for businesses to locate or relocate and to outbid one another in tax concessions that more often than not went to local industry.

Federal policies under Reagan confirmed the new order. C.E.T.A. became J.T.P.A. and private industry councils ran the new manpower programs with new tax concessions for hiring. Community-based organizations and the unemployed most in need were abandoned as performance standards required creaming practices in order to maintain funding. Enterprise zones were the solution offered to distressed city areas. City economic development agencies, which are shadow governments outside the direct control of city councils, are not concerned with the poor or the unemployed; their constituency is business. Planners who used to care about the "city beautiful" now display their love for large-scale office buildings and upper-income apartment buildings. Their historical desire to escape public control is answered by these city development corporations, which issue debt for enterprises without public referendum and grant tax abatements to real estate developers for projects that earn large profits.

It is exciting to see some of the physical changes in some of the old city neighborhoods, if your interest is in new buildings and not people. Meanwhile, the poor in cities have increased dramatically, the feminization of poverty has accelerated, the drop-out rate in high schools for blacks and hispanics is about 75%, unemployment for black youth is over 50%, teen-age births have reached new highs, infant mortality has increased, and deindustrialization has reduced the number of jobs in large cities.

Projections in every major city suggest that only the most bottom-level service, janitorial, and clerical jobs will increase in the next decade.

The research has already been done to demonstrate the nature of the problem, the leadership of the country has even determined the solution and what we can expect from the American city of the future. It will take a new radical movement in the 1990s to make any significant change in the current direction. It will take some better evaluation of what was worthwhile in the efforts of the 1960s. And it will require a new social consciousness and a reaffirmation of democratic principles to guide public policies. A good beginning would be a national campaign for income security for every person, establishing a commitment to at least that common need. From that beginning, perhaps we can once again see cities not as private enterprises but as the public corporations their historical origins intended them to be.

REFERENCES

POTTER, D. (1954) People of Plenty. Chicago: Univ. of Chicago Press.

SCHWARZ, J. E. (1983) America's Hidden Success: A Reassessment of Twenty Years of Public Policy. New York: Norton.

THUROW, L. (1981) The Zero-Sum Society. New York: Penguin.

URBAN AFFAIRS
A Look into the Past and the Future

ROBERT L. LINEBERRY
University of Kansas

It is difficult to believe that a twenty-year time span takes us back only to 1965, the date of the founding of *Urban Affairs Quarterly,* and a most significant time otherwise for American urban history. One demographic transformation—the sorting out of people in the metropolis by race—was by then all but complete. Until 1940 three-quarters of all American blacks lived in the South. By 1965 large central cities—Newark, Cleveland, Atlanta, Washington, D.C., Gary, and others—were at or near a tipping point, at which a white majority was turning into a black one. Whites had fled the cities and walled themselves in suburban enclaves. Just over a decade before the Supreme Court had ordered the racial integration of the public schools. Cities today still confront the agonizing implications of that decision and a stream of subsequent ones requiring desegregation of schools and workforces. The year 1965 was the first one with large-scale racial demonstrations that turned episodically into racial violence.

Twenty years ahead will take us to 2005. Your guess is as good as mine. We presume that *UAQ* will still be a striving and thriving academic journal at that time, and we hope that the cities can say the same about themselves.

In my opinion, the most important transformations shaping the city during the past twenty years are those associated with demography, fiscal "deforestation," the changing international economy, and a more nebulous change in our own sense of self and our communitarian obligations.

Cities have reaped the whirlwind of demographic changes, as the denuding of white populations has been nearly complete in many cities. Despite scattered regentrification, the demographic makeup of the cities appears to be locked in for the next twenty years, with a single excep-

URBAN AFFAIRS QUARTERLY, Vol. 21 No. 1, September 1985 20-24

tion: There is reason to believe that a new American melting pot will dramatically add non-Western citizens to the urban population. One estimate by the Census Bureau reported that if present trends continue, by the middle of the next century we will likely have a nonwhite majority in America. Part of this comes from differential birthrates. But more comes from the legal and illegal immigration from Latin America and East Asia. The "Little Italies" of the late nineteenth century will become the "Little Manilas" of the twenty-first. The first black mayor or the first hispanic mayor was everywhere an achievement for urban minority groups. So will be, I presume, the first Thai or Filipino mayor.

The "fiscal deforestation" of the city is well known, although by many other names. As rain forests are stripped bare in the tropics, the urban fiscal base has often been stripped bare in America. There now is an ideological aversion to increments in public spending on social programs. For the city, the 1950s were times when political issues, particularly related to the rights of minorities, were at the top of the urban agenda; the 1960s were times when social issues took top spot; and the 1970s were times when economic issues displaced political and social issues. There is little momentum for scrapping social programs, but not much more for sustaining them. In a time of pinched economic resources, social programs take a back seat to the daily grind of competing for jobs and industry.

This competition is not made easier by a shifting international economy. A hundred years ago Memphis and St. Louis, Baltimore and Philadelphia, and Houston and Galveston might vie for economic supremacy. Today they all vie with Hong Kong, Singapore, and Tokyo. Staggering wage disparities between American and foreign workers, coupled with the easy flow of capital across national borders, put Memphis *and* St. Louis at a competitive disadvantage. Now our trade is shifting from Western Europe to the Pacific Rim. With that shift will come further changes in the fortunes of various cities.

Last, the previous twenty years have seen a well-known explosion of special or single-interest groups in the cities and the nation. Perhaps they have also seen an explosion of self-interest. Our national thread has always been "don't tread on me" and these special or single interest groups have picked up the strand. They are in Washington and the neighborhoods. They come from all races, both sexes, and every economic stratum. For one thing, they make it more difficult to deal with the fiscal deforestation. Groups reluctant to give an inch are equally reluctant to give up their favorite programs or pay taxes for someone else's. This is the sort of social rigidification of which the distinguished economist Mancur Olson speaks in his provocative (if arrogant) book, *The Rise and Fall of Nations.*

It is undeniable that cities will be shaped in the next two decades by a high-tech transformation and the shifting sands of energy supplies. More, though, may have been made about the possibilities of the "sci-fi" city than is warranted by the facts. The dreams of the 1950s about high-flying monorails have yielded mainly to debates about the funding of Amtrak and buses. Cities are likely to muddle through with their infrastructure deteriorating, but essentially similar to that of two decades ago.

No doubt there are other transformations at work in the modern metropolis. These, however, will suggest a few lines of change afoot in the city over a forty-year time span.

URBAN POLICY INITIATIVES

There has been an explosion of policy initiatives in the past two decades. Indeed, the creation of *UAQ* coincides with the foundation of new programs in neighborhood redevelopment, affirmative action, aid to the downtrodden, support for urban infrastructures, aid to urban schools, and, slightly later, revenue sharing. At the urban level we have experimented with neighborhood councils, policy review boards, industrial revenue bonds, citizen watches, minority hiring, and a score of other new policies.

It is next to impossible to sort these into neat boxes, one called "successes," the other labeled "failures." The debate about the success of these programs goes on and the evidence is not hard on either side. It is clear that the aggregate effect of these on the distribution of American income is negligible. The careful work of Reynolds and Smolensky at the University of Wisconsin makes it clear that what they call "net fiscal incidence" (i.e., the net impact of government spending and taxing on the distribution of income) changed little between the 1960s, when the explosion of federal social policy began, and the 1970s. This does not, of course, prove that the programs did not "work." Indeed, perhaps things would have gone worse without them. Aggregate impacts are, in any event, extremely hard to demonstrate.

Over the long run those federal, state, and local policies related to economic development are likely to have significant impacts on the distribution of economic and, thereby, social opportunities in the cities. Cats chase mice, and cities chase economic development. According to one estimate, there are now some 18,000 offices, boards, or commissions in our country charged with hustling, begging, borrowing, or pirating firms to states and localities. Just as the aggregate effect of social policies is hard to measure, the aggregate effect of these economic development efforts is hard to pin down. On one hand, they may simply shuffle around firms and factories, shifting, through their generous subsidies, private sector costs to the public sector. On the other, they may spur economic development in hard-pressed regions and communities.

It is clear that those local economic initiatives will increasingly be shaped by the trends in the international economy I have mentioned above. Two decades ago the flamboyant Los Angeles Mayor Sam Yorty was criticized for his worldly junkets, and the saying was that "Los Angeles is the only city in the United States which has its own foreign policy." Now almost every city has its own forcign policy, and those that do not are almost hopelessly left out of the economic running. It is easy to see how industrial revenue bonds may help Pittsburgh compete with Peoria, but it is harder to understand how they will keep American industries from moving jobs and production abroad.

One commonplace solution for this problem is some sort of national industrial policy. Part of the demand for this is based on a misperception of what the Japanese in fact do, as Ezra Vogel among others has pointed out. But part of it reflects a genuine concern that other nations have far richer links between government and industry than we do. This industrial policy—rather like urban policy—is impaled on the horns of an ugly political dilemma: Do we aid "sunrise" industry, which might help us compete effectively in world markets, or do we aid "sunset" industries, which have historically been vital to our economy? The urban policy analogy, of course, is this: Do we spend more money helping the old and decaying cities or invest in the urban frontier areas? Few believe that the current political climate, riddled as it is with rigidities and single-issue groups, will be able to resist pressures and choose between the computer industry and the steel industry.

Urban policy has come a long way in the last two decades. Although the cities per se have a lower place on our national agenda, it would be wrong to think that the problems in the cities have disappeared from the policy process.

URBAN RESEARCH AGENDA

As urban research has matured, it has also fragmented. When I entered the urban field nearly twenty years ago, the sociology model, based on the "Chicago school," was firmly entrenched. Now it no longer dominates urban research in political science, and it competes with other research paradigms, for example, network analysis in sociology. Nor is the familiar elitist-pluralist debate completely alive and well, and perhaps that is for the better.

For a time the principal direction of much urban research flew under the several flags called "policy research" or "policy analysis." Today policy studies have themselves become so large that they have little distinct core, save that they are not expressly micropolitical or behavioral in orientation. Research on "the politics of" education, crime, and so forth continues to be done in an interdisciplinary vein, and some of it is very good indeed. As a field, however, policy analysis has multiple paradigms and a soft center, a sort of subject matter without a clear method or theory.

Unquestionably, the most important emergent field in urban studies today has been variously described as "political economy" or "neo-Marxist" analysis. Some of this is European in origin, and other parts of it come from American scholars. Among its several other attributes, it rejoins history with political science and sociology, and most of it is open to quantitative, empirical work. There is every likelihood that this genre of research will continue to grow in the next twenty years.

There also should be a place for work that links cities to the larger world economy. Paul Peterson's *City Limits,* one of the best recent works on the city, is largely confined to the American experience, but its theoretical reach is potentially broader. American metropolitan areas will come more and more to share patterns of dependency that characterize Third World cities and nations. There is excellent work in those areas, much of which would be intellectually stimulating to American urbanists.

REFERENCE

PETERSON, P. (1981) City Limits. Chicago: Univ. of Chicago Press.

THE URBAN CONDITION
"Plates" Beneath City Surfaces and a New Research Agenda

MARGARET T. GORDON
Northwestern University

What is daily life like for the average person in one of our nation's big cities? What are the underlying factors or forces that seem to be setting the parameters for what individuals see as their options? I used these two questions to prompt reflections on the "urban condition." The results are no doubt affected by my own experiences of living and working in a range of places, including the heart of one of our largest cities (New York City), a suburb of a large, midwestern city (Evanston, near Chicago), two southeastern towns (Chattanooga, Tenn., and St. Petersburg, Fla.), a large town in Denmark (Aarhus), and rural southern Nigeria (Nsukka).

Sadly, I have concluded that at the moment only the rich have the possibility of a pleasant and comfortable life in large U.S. cities, and even they appear to be threatened daily by a barrage of assaults to the senses. Many people, if not most, choose to leave if they can, or at least opt to live outside the city. This option is more available to the relatively well off. They often work in the city or come into the city on occasion to take advantage of those aspects of city life they do enjoy, but then retreat to the quieter, cleaner, greener, safer suburbs. People, especially women, who live in cities or spend much time in them take for granted a certain amount of danger—for themselves and for their belongings—and develop protective strategies for coping with it. Although this may seem more true in the older northern and eastern cities, where the signs of urban infrastructure

---

AUTHOR'S NOTE: *These comments were written while I was on leave from Northwestern University and in residence as Senior Fellow at the Gannett Center for Media Studies, Columbia University.*

URBAN AFFAIRS QUARTERLY, Vol. 21 No. 1, September 1985 25-36

decay are more obvious than in the newer, still expanding sunbelt cities, both systematic and anecdotal data suggest that daily existence for the nonwealthy majority in all but a few of our cities is increasingly difficult, threatening, unhealthy, stressful, expensive, and, more often than not, generally overwhelming.

Although the constellation of economic factors that resulted in uncommonly high (for the United States) inflation and interest rates during the late 1970s and early 1980s would appear to be the major culprit for many of the most obvious urban ills, I believe there are some other factors that may offer more basic explanations and suggest additional remedies.

URBAN PLATES

Daniel Yankelovitch, in his 1981 book *New Rules,* discusses "plates of culture," a concept derived from studies of the movements of the Earth's crust. The planet's surface is believed to be composed of several large sections or "plates" that are in constant motion, sometimes crashing or rubbing together and resulting in rifts, faults, volcanos, and mountains. Yankelovitch, without going into much detail, suggests the concept may be applied to our culture. One such "plate of culture"—the "new ethic of commitment"—becomes a major theme of his book. In what follows, I have borrowed this concept of "plates" to discuss several issues that I believe underlie the surface problems in our cities.

There are at least three "plates" that have endured over time and that now shape our urban environments: failure of courage to deal with racism, cancerous individualism, and short-term thinking. These plates seem now to be permanent fixtures of our social structure and prominant features of our cityscapes. Four others I focus on below represent more recent fissures or breaks in the city landscapes, but seem in danger of joining the others as permanent plates, as causes of our urban ills. These four are nonaccountability of leaders, diversity of peoples and information, loss of faith, and the ever-present nuclear threat.

Each of these actualized and emerging "urban plates" informs and shapes my view of the urban condition. Some may also affect the "national condition," but their profiles seem especially sharp in our cities.

FAILURE OF COURAGE TO DEAL WITH RACISM

The first urban plate is what I regard as a failure of courage to deal with racism in our nation, or with the resulting psychological, social, and political barriers erected between and among peoples of different racial and cultural heritages. This failure has had enormous costs for our nation as well as for our cities' institutions and businesses, churches, and schools. Flight of city residents, businesses, and industry to suburban and rural areas has weakened urban tax bases, and schools once dominated by the majority (whites) are now populated primarily by a range of minority groups (usually nonwhite). In many suburban and rural areas it is still unusual to see a nonwhite person. Alliances have grown up along the cleavages and are now more dangerous and difficult to break down than they would have been at an earlier time.

This plate is particularly acute for cities for two reasons. First, those who dominate the business and governmental structures of cities often choose not to live there and so are less concerned with some of the problems. Second, there are enough people from each of several ethnic groups to support distinct institutions (churches, schools, restaurants, etc.) thus making it less rewarding to ignore differences and/or keep barriers low.

CANCEROUS INDIVIDUALISM

The second of my plates is what Robert Bellah and his colleagues have called cancerous individualism. In *Habits of the Heart* (1985) they argue that the individualism so much vaunted in the early chapters of our history may have grown cancerous. After interviewing 200 middle-class citizens—because "that is where power in American society, for good or for bad, still resides"—they conclude that Americans feel alone, disappointed, and disillusioned about public life. Bellah comments, "Over time, and especially since World War II, the traditions of atomistic individualism have grown stronger, while the traditions of the individual in society have grown weaker. The sense of cohesive community is lost."

Yankelovitch, in *New Rules,* seems to suggest that it has become stylish and easy to focus on people and issues close to home. He argues that our world is now "turned upside down," and that we Americans have loosened our attachment to the ethic of self-denial and deferred gratification that undergirded eras of productivity and growth.

Although Yankelovitch concludes that we are now leaving behind the excesses of the "me generation," he does not perceive a return to the traditional ethic of self-denial but, rather, an emergence of a new "ethic of commitment" to a life that supports self-fulfillment through enduring commitments primarily to relationships, but also to career and mere survival.

John Kenneth Galbraith (1984) is less charitable and characterizes us now as "the heartless society." He argues that an enormous proportion of our population has lost so much faith that millions have become completely alienated from the political process, giving over control to those who are not yet alienated. The nonalienated, he says, are the rich and the upwardly mobile, those who still feel they are "making it." Now in political control, Galbraith says, they are making decisions in their own best interests, heartlessly uncaring about the millions of alienated, discouraged disadvantaged. Nowhere are these sentiments more evident than in our cities.

SHORT-TERM THINKING

Third, our business and political leaders have seemed unwilling to think or act in the long term; that is, to genuinely consider the consequences of their actions or inaction for future generations. We have helped them to ignore their responsibilities to the future by believing that the next generation of citizens will have the creativity and resourcefulness to find or generate the resources needed then for solutions. Meanwhile, we have proceeded using the resources created through centuries as if there were no tomorrow.

The problems created by this kind of thinking are particularly evident in our larger, older cities, where infrastructure maintenance and repairs have been allowed to lapse in favor of flashier, more popular efforts. It is also exacerbated by our election process, which makes accountability an issue every two or four years, but rarely for longer periods.

POLITICAL NONACCOUNTABILITY

The first of the new emerging plates is political nonaccountability, nationwide "teflonism." During the past several years there seems to have developed an increasing lack of willingness among politicians at all levels to be either responsible or accountable for healing our urban ills. It seems to be increasingly rare for campaigns to highlight the need for solutions to urban problems. Neither Ronald Reagan nor his Democratic challenger, Walter F. Mondale, focused on problems of cities in 1984, and few on the campaign trail even asked any questions that would make the candidates uncomfortable about the omission. M. Carl Holman, president of the National Urban Coalition, fears that the federal government's lack of sympathy for the plights of cities and city dwellers may reflect a lack of interest, or tiredness, among the general population. "You say 'cities,' and people think, 'blacks, Hispanics, poor,'" Holman said. Politicians, at least, seem to have concluded that urban problems are unsolvable and that discussing such issues as urban poverty, affordable housing, and declining health of urban dwellers puts them in a no-win position. We have let them get away with that.

DIVERSITY OF PEOPLES AND INFORMATION

A second emerging plate that I view as affecting the urban condition is the diversity of peoples and the diversity of information to which we are all exposed. The diversity of peoples means there are different cultures, values, interests, and commitments vying for attention. Furthermore, there is a diversity of information such that any given individual has an almost infinite number of choices. And yet each of us can attend to and absorb only a finite amount of information. The diversity of options means that it is likely that fewer and fewer people are attending to any one, and that the public is becoming ever more fragmented. It is now the rare occasion that there is a truly "national audience," despite the best efforts of the networks. (Some analysts believe big media spectaculars viewed by 50 million or more are the closest we have come in recent years to political and social unity.) This state of affairs has important consequences for our political life and for the difficulty of leadership. How can a leader reach all the people and be sure that all the people get the same message?

All this affects the urban condition, first, because most media messages originate in our nation's large cities and, second, because it is in the largest cities where the diversity is greatest.

LOSS OF FAITH

The third emerging plate—loss of faith in leaders and in nation—is related to the second. Perhaps because of the diversity (and presumed difficulty of reaching agreement or consensus) of peoples living in our cities, it difficult for any one person to satisfy or unify the interests. In their efforts to satisfy as many as possible, leaders and would-be leaders have become too willing to say what seems tactical or political, rather than what is true or what is courageous. As pointed out in a recent *Columbia Journalism Review* article by Marro (1985), we have come to expect some level of deception from officials who are engaged in political posturing, face-saving, and dealing with the consequences of honest errors, bad judgments, and legitimate security concerns. Public knowledge of such posturing and deception, and the fact that such behavior is routine, undermines our faith in local and federal leaders and in our nation.

There also has been a marked decline since 1966 in the respect and confidence the public has in the major institutions in this country. Surveys conducted for several years by the Gallup organization, Harris Polls, and the National Opinion Research Center all show that the general public has less faith in the military, big business, the courts, the media, organized religion, organized labor, and medicine. The pollsters measured confidence in many ways—respect for leaders of institutions, perceptions of power, moral practices, need for regulation, change over time, legitimacy, fairness—with clear, consistent patterns in the results. After reviewing these trends, Lipset and Schneider (1983) conclude that there is a substantial discrepancy between the institutions and the public that must be addressed.

EVER-PRESENT NUCLEAR THREAT

A final emerging "plate" underlying current urban conditions is the nearly constant threat of a nuclear war that, although it would take only moments to wage, would destroy us all or leave us in such a condition that we would no longer wish to live. Although perhaps not an issue most people think or worry about on a daily basis, it is one that lurks on the back burners of people's minds and it does seem to have special impact on the youth of today, many of whom doubt that they will live to grow up and have children, careers, and grandchildren. This concern affects their willingness to sacrifice, to make long-term commitments, and to invest in the future. Several surveys in recent years have documented this trend. Anecdotal evidence is also available from a high school English teacher who for several years has asked his students to write an essay answering the question, "Should we have hope?'' The percentage of the class that has concluded ''no'' has increased markedly in recent years. He says the students reason that people are basically selfish, leading to confrontation, and today's weapons are too totally destructive and allow no room for human emotion or error.

Although a nuclear attack would be devastating for the entire country, I assume the human and physical destruction would be worse in cities than in rural areas.

PLATE MOVEMENT

It is the continuous movement of these seven (and perhaps other) actual and emerging plates just below the surfaces of our society that has resulted in eruptions or rifts between or among two or more of them and produced the problems and the anomalies we see on the streets in our cities—crime and fear of crime, poverty of the many and wealth of the few, unemployment and yuppies, deteriorating structures and infrastructures next to and under new high-rise apartment and office buildings, the homeless not far from boarded-up apartment buildings and hotels, sick people who cannot afford to go to hospitals with empty beds, and people who want to be part of a community but feel they have been taught it's wise to mind their own business.

Unless we are willing to do whatever may be necessary to interrupt the development and flow of these plates, their movements will continue, and there will continue to be eruptions and rifts obvious on the surfaces of our cities.

OLD AND NEW INITIATIVES

None of the urban policy initiatives of recent years at the federal or state levels have done anything to affect the development or movement of these plates. I believe that all—from urban renewal to enterprise zones—have represented attempts to deal with fires from fissures and volcanos—to continue the metaphor—and I believe the proof is in the problems now confronting us. It is my belief that too few people have benefited from these programs, and that we are left with too many disenfranchised poor who have little or no sense of control over their lives. Analyses of the one effort to receive more than passing attention during the Reagan administration, enterprise zones, indicate that because zones are designed to function through a set of tax incentives, they appeal only to the larger corporations and entities. Thus, zones also benefit the less needy rather than the more needy. Rather than catalogue the failures, let us turn to why so many federal initiatives, often begun with the greatest hope, have turned sour.

I believe there are several reasons for the failures, some related to the "plates" discussed above, that can be derived from experiences with specific programs. First, and probably foremost, the solutions to problems were often designed without the input and understanding of the people most affected. Second, programs designed at the federal or state level were too often attempted to be implemented uniformly, with little or no consideration given to local variations or differences that made the proposed solutions acceptable or not. Third, the policy-makers designing programs too often were proposing what was tactical or political at the moment, but not what was the result of careful, considered planning. Fourth, the solutions were often effective only in the short term, with negative long-term consequences outpacing the original problems. Fifth, initiatives were too often unable to be adapted to changing conditions and environments. Sixth, initiatives too often bred complacency rather than creativity. And, finally, the policies too often have been contradictory.

HOPE

Do I believe there is hope for cities? Absolutely. Despite all the problems, I also see a great deal of vitality and strength. There are a great many local-level initiatives that spark excitement and represent a determination and spirit to halt the development and movement of the plates. They are taking place in well-defined areas where the people making the decisions are also the ones affected by the proposed changes or "solutions." I believe our greatest hope lies in these initiatives. People are ingenious at devising ways to use elements of their environments to accomplish their own ends, and local urban leaders, elected and unelected, have labored to overcome the discouraging lack of concern for cities at the state and federal levels. They have fought back with determination in all kinds of ways in an effort to keep cities from deteriorating further and to reinvigorate local development and commitment. As Bellah and his colleagues noted, individuals seem to have a yearning, a "hankering, a nostalgia for face-to-face community." Together with local foundations, social agencies, and community organizations, many have launched activities that they hope will "make a difference."

Children from a poor neighborhood in New York City staged entertainment and bake sales, raising pennies, dimes, nickels, and quarters, for grain for what they termed the "really hungry" in Ethiopia. The not-for-profit organization, Save the Children, aided the children in arranging for the grain to be delivered. Inspired, ABC television sent a film crew to Ethiopia when the grain arrived, and later showed the children the footage and taped their responses. A "special" shared the emotional moments with the nation, and in the days following resulted in 10,000 telephone calls per day to Save the Children, thousands of new donations, and requests for help in starting similar programs in other cities. Those young New Yorkers also developed a sense of efficacy about social life and conditions that they had never before felt. Some talked about turning their efforts toward their neighborhood.

In Chicago Mayor Harold Washington announced in late 1984 an "Affirmative Information Program," by which the city was to provide neighborhood organizations with information on such topics as housing-code violations, arson, and zoning regulations that they need in making plans for their areas. Previously, such information had been generally inaccessible to the public.

Citizens' groups throughout the United States also are taking a more active role in trying to reduce the level of violence in American cities. For example, the National Alliance Against Violence, a New York City group, trained police in four cities—New York, Chicago, Minneapolis, and Oakland—to work with local citizen organizations in informing them about the dangers of possessing handguns. The idea spread, and police chiefs in thirteen additional cities are now interested in participating in the program, and school systems and church organizations are using program materials in their curricula.

A Boston physician specializing in adolescent medicine became alarmed by the numbers of young victims of violence she was treating and started a program now spread to several other cities in which videotapes and street theater are used in classrooms to help students learn nonviolent ways of expressing feelings.

Although these and other local efforts may seem too limited, too scattered, or too dependent on a charismatic person to be generally effective, they are happening by the hundreds across the nation. I believe they are representative of citizens' determination and optimism that negative trends can be reversed when the local conditions of people's lives are improved. I believe they can be empowering and ultimately more effective than the large-scale, expensive, imposed programs of the past.

This is not to say that the federal and state governments have no responsibilities to deal with these problems. I don't believe they have the right to simply ignore cities, as the Reagan administration appears to have done. Among other things, it seems to me that governments have the responsibility to identify and support mechanisms that empower, and through which the costs of solving the problems are shared equally.

TOWARD A REVISED RESEARCH AGENDA

What does all this suggest for an urban research agenda? Much that I have had to say has to do with values, ethics, and accountability—not the usual urban research topics. Nonetheless, I believe that my views suggest at least three directions for new research.

NEW, MORE APPROPRIATE RESEARCH METHODS

This first strand represents both frustration about how little we seem to really know (with much confidence) about the dynamics of urban life and a plea for new ways to gather data that take account of both the complexity and humanness of our subject. By and large, most social scientists still use the scientific tools originally developed for physical and life sciences, and we often knowingly violate the assumptions implicit in those methods. It is time for a concerted, sustained effort to develop more suitable tools for our subject.

SPECIAL ATTENTION TO UNINTENDED CONSEQUENCES

The second strand of research I would urge is one designed to identify, monitor, and evaluate both the unintended and intended consequences of urban policies and programs at all levels—local, state, and federal. I believe that concerted attention to the unintended consequences of earlier efforts would have alerted us to problems when it would have been easier to solve them.

PROCESSES AND PRODUCTS OF PLATE MOVEMENT

The third emphasis focuses more on the substance of what I have referred to as urban plates moving under the surfaces of our cityscapes and the resultant eruptions and rifts. We need new conceptualizations and understanding of processes and trends, research that leads to policy options, and notions of how to interrupt developments judged to be undesirable.

For example, I believe we need courageous research on racism and how and why it works the way it does in our cities. It is my view that most researchers view race as a "variable," and ignore racism as a destructive process. Although it is a topic that has been around the social and policy sciences for many years, we have done little (especially in recent years) to contribute to its elimination or to solving the problems it causes. We need new conceptualizations that allow us to make much needed progress.

A second substantive line of research might key off of Yankelovitch's "cultural plate," the "ethic of commitment," and focus on the processes of productivity and growth and how they relate to the new commitment and accountability. If substantial numbers of people in our cities are changing in the ways Yankelovitch suggests, we need better understanding than we now have of how the process is working and what its consequences are. We might address such issues as the relationship between productivity and greed, the role of envy, and what is believed to constitute reasonable profit on investments.

A third new emphasis might be on communication and community; that is, the relationship between available communication channels or outlets and the sense of community or cohesiveness possible within and among geographical areas. The ownership and control of media channels, issues of access to media, accountability, and credibility of sources and channels all are topics relatively unexplored in urban social science.

Still another focus should be on modern leadership styles appropriate to cities of today. It is my impression that we view leadership and politics traditionally, despite the evidence that leaders are created and maintained in new and different ways from those in the past. Television has been especially important in the change, but the process is not well examined or understood. Studies of accountability among leaders and institutions might lead to changes that, in turn, could lead to a narrowing of the "confidence gap."

Finally, we might want to examine the processes that seem to take us ever closer to nuclear war; we need work with the clear goal of identifying and articulating policy proposals our leaders can accept that will move us gradually away from war. One approach might be to study the effects of worry on everyday life, and on overall levels of productivity and commitment. Another might be to focus on the processes in those societies in which every human act is regarded as a social act, because all human behavior is regarded as having consequences for other people. In such societies there is more emphasis on interrelatedness and less on individual achievement and rights.

In summary, I believe it is not only possible but urgent that we identify and construct an urban research agenda that recognizes both that our urban problems are symptoms and that solutions are most thoroughgoing and lasting when the people most affected are involved in designing them.

REFERENCES

ARENDT, H. (1985) "Public happiness or a share in public power." Kettering Rev. (Winter): 20-25.

BELLAH, R., R. MADSEN, W. M. SULLIVAN, A. SWINDLER, and S. TIPTON (1985) Habits of the Heart. Berkeley: Univ. of California Press.

BOK, D. (1985) "The university and the public beyond its walls." Kettering Rev. (Winter): 46-52.

GALBRAITH, J. K. (1984) "The heartless society." New York Times Magazine (September 2): 20-24.

HARRIS, W. W. (1977) "Television's image of the city: the Jamaica plain case." Ph.D. dissertation, Massachusetts Institute of Technology.

LIPSET, S. M. and W. SCHNEIDER (1983) The Confidence Gap: Business, Labor, and Government in the Public Mind. New York: Free Press.

MARRO, A. (1985) "When the government tells lies." Columbia Journalism Rev. (March/April): 29-41.

YANKELOVITCH, D. (1981) New Rules: Searching for Self-Fulfillment in a World Turned Upside Down. New York: Random House.

The urban transportation systems that carry us around are not solely the result of technological innovation or efficiency. They are also a product of the rising and sinking political and market power of industrial interest groups, the changing relations among social classes, the politics of urban development struggles, and the inherent dynamics of the economic system. We attempt to show how these factors, particularly corporate control of transportation policy, have profoundly shaped urban streetcar, automobile, bus, and rail transport in the United States during this century. We conclude that this private dominance over urban transportation policy has often led to narrow, profit-seeking behavior that has thwarted the development of more effective public transit.

CORPORATE STRATEGIES AND THE DECLINE OF TRANSIT IN U.S. CITIES

J. ALLEN WHITT
University of Louisville

GLENN YAGO
State University of New York at Stony Brook

In the United States two related ideas tend to dominate our thinking about urban transit systems. The overwhelming reliance on private automobile is seen as the result of millions of individual transit consumers freely choosing the mode of transportation that offers them the most satisfaction and efficiency of movement. These conventional ideas of technical efficiency and consumer choice also are used to account for the less successful fate of competing modes of transit. If the streetcar or bus does not attract as many riders as the automobile, it is because these other ways of getting around town have lost out in the transit marketplace in a fair and open contest of efficiency and satisfaction.

These popular explanations of why we rely on the automobile to the virtual exclusion of other modes also are given support by established scholarly authority. For example, following in the long line of

URBAN AFFAIRS QUARTERLY, Vol. 21 No. 1, September 1985 37-65

such a tradition, Meyer and Gomez-Ibanez (1981) argue that the private automobile is so popular and technically superior that it has been, and will continue to be, the preferred mode of urban transport, and that we must learn to adapt our cities to the automobile.

In this article we develop an alternative perspective to the technological efficiency/popular choice point of view. We have come to this alternative perspective as a result of our independent research on the history of urban transportation (Yago, 1983; Whitt, 1982). We argue that there is an important, largely neglected dimension to the creation and change of transportation systems. This dimension is the political-economic dimension which profoundly affects the character of urban transit systems, above and beyond simple technological availability, the state of consciousness at city hall, and free public choice. In addition to the classical market forces of supply and demand, there are other important institutions that operate to constrain those forces in significant ways. To understand why particular systems of transport achieve dominance, or wither, it is necessary to understand: (1) the inherent dynamics of the market economic system; (2) the historic rise and fall of the political-economic power of industrial interest groups; (3) changing relations among social classes; and (4) the struggles over urban development and land use schemes.

We cannot review all of these issues here. Our aim will be to demonstrate some of the links among economic development, social class formation, city growth, and transportation. In particular, we wish to show that urban transportation development in the United States in many ways has been under the strong influence or control (directly or indirectly) of profit-seeking corporations. Our point is that corporate control has affected public choices, contributed to transit problems, and retarded the development of more effective public transit.

It is important to point out that we are not arguing the issue of public transportation versus private automobiles. We are not saying that cars should give way to mass transit in our cities because such transit is more efficient. Rather, we are raising the issue of why the United States—almost alone among industrialized countries of the world—relies almost exclusively on automobiles to move people in our cities. We would argue that an effective urban transportation system should consist of a balanced and coordinated system of mass transit, private autos, and other modes; not the present overwhelming dominance of one mode. In other words, how do we account for the peculiar situation evident in American cities? To attempt an answer, we must look at the historical record.

At the close of World War I, Delox Wilcox, the country's earliest and most prominent transportation engineer, recognized how transportation was subordinated to the individual transit operator's interest and how that situation led to the decline of electrical railway systems.

> It must be admitted that in the development of the street railway systems and the corporations that controlled them in this country, *the idea of public service has generally been incidental.* The driving force, the motive that has negotiated franchises, consolidations, and mergers, has been for profit only [Wilcox, 1919: 34; emphasis added].

More than half a century later, Bradford C. Snell, U. S. Senate Antitrust Committee Counsel, noted in his study of U. S. surface transportation that the highly concentrated corporate power of automobile firms and their diversification into various areas of transportation manufacturing "may have retarded the development of mass transportation, and, as a consequence may have generated a reliance on motor vehicles incompatible with metropolitan needs" (Snell, 1974: A47).

Both Wilcox and Snell recognized an underlying force, the corporate profit motive, that we will argue has contributed to the decline of public transportation in the United States. Profit-seeking by both street railway magnates and automobile corporations often has proved damaging to the rational organization of city space for both social and economic needs. State intervention generally has been limited to accommodating the hegemonic interest of particular industrial groups engaged either in transit operation, as in the beginning of the twentieth century, or in transportation equipment production later in the century. Government traditionally has been limited to planning which is local, limited in scope, short range, and ad hoc; it commonly has not addressed the larger issue of the overall relation between transportation and city development. Government, we hold, has been ineffective in defending and advancing the common public interest in transportation. Corporate leaders have been allowed to engage in internal class organization and private planning in order to thrash out their common corporate interests in urban transportation, and to dominate policy and development issues.

Transportation development has been continuously subordinated to large corporate control, but the specific industrial groups exercising that control have changed with the shifting composition and concentration of corporate capital.

What follows is an exploration of the development of national transportation policy as it has been subordinated to the interests of large corporations within the United States. We are concerned with policy changes, corporate intervention in policy formation, and the influence of corporate power on the decline of public transportation, both through direct intervention in planning and through the creation of economic and political institutional frameworks that minimized the opportunities for transit development.

ECONOMIC BACKGROUND AFFECTING NATIONAL TRANSPORTATION POLICY

The historical circumstances of capital accumulation in the United States have played a substantial role in the formation of business interests in transportation.

Before World War I, the capitalist class in the United States on the whole was characterized by intraclass competition, rather than coalition. Although the patterns of industrial development were apparent by the Civil War, the development of legal structures for corporations, the role of state intervention in providing the basis for economic consolidation, and the development of market infrastructure all developed by the turn of the century. This allowed the United States to produce a more competitive manufacturing system with greater technical diversity than in Europe (Averitt, 1968).[1] Corporate financing was primarily internal, with banks entering the industrial stock market only in the late 1870s. In this more competitive situation, the possibilities for innovative transportation technology rose dramatically. Whether in the more rapid electrification of streetcars, or in the motorization of transportation, the rate at which surplus-absorbing outlets for capital accumulation were provided was very rapid in the United States.[2] Nor was there much reliance on existing corporate giants for technological innovation. The technical convergence of growth in the automobile, oil, and rubber industries, as well as the internal expansion of cities during this period, made capital accumulation highly dynamic, and the realignment of industrial power was profound.

The initial emergence of the auto-oil-rubber nexus as representative of an industrial strategy for economic growth was the outcome of historical circumstances specific to the United States. Auto production began in earnest nearly a decade after the first merger movement in the petroleum, rubber, and steel industries began the process of monopolization (Kennedy, 1941: 135; Bunting, 1972). Auto expansion and the reorganization of corporate growth strategy was financed by the largest U.S. banks during the 1920s (Seltzer, 1928; Chandler, 1968; Edwards, 1966). These economic conditions provided a powerful base for its integration of financial and industrial automotive interests, the market expansion of basic industries (e.g., the indigenous steel and oil industries), and the stimulation of consumer demand. The decline of older rail-linked industrial groups such as coal, electric machinery manufacturing, and utilities lessened competition with auto interests and allowed the close linkage between motorization and economic growth. As contrasted with the European case, the weaker involvement of the state in accumulation at both local and national levels of government and the absence of organized labor and popular demands for transit services allowed the unhindered pursuit of motorization as a corporate strategy for industrial expansion.

THE GROWTH PERIOD OF PUBLIC TRANSPORTATION IN THE UNITED STATES

After the Civil War, the limitations of horsedrawn trolley systems became readily apparent (Ward, 1971: 131-134). After an initial period of growth, the market for trolley systems became saturated—demand for the geographically limited transit technology was satisfied. Under these conditions the rapid innovation of the electrification of trolley lines with low per unit cost and increasing supply capability became possible and desirable. More important, the electrification of urban transportation corresponded with the growth of the electrical manufacturing industry; the most important industry of the period 1888-1900 (Passer, 1953; McKay, 1976). Urban transportation in the form of electric trollies became part of the universal growth in public utilities investment during this period.

Electrification meant transit growth. For most of the period between 1890 and 1918, urban transportation ridership grew faster than the urban population. The streetcar network pushed cities toward their peripheries as population and industry expanded. Land speculators and transit owners spoke with one voice (and were sometimes the same person) encouraging this expansion (Wilcox, 1921: 67-100). Urban transportation was viewed by transit owners and city planners as a "moral influence" in removing people from unhealthy environments in inner cities (Tarr, 1973; McShane, 1975; Warner, 1976).[3] Because of the increased cost of investment, electrification encouraged the consolidation and concentration of transit ownership among local companies. A conglomeration of land-owning, public utilities, and financial interests (e.g., transit trusts such as Yerks in Chicago and Doherty or Mellon on the East Coast) came to dominate public transportation.[4] Similarly, the private railroads also attempted to discourage the growth of streetcar lines either by taking ownership of such lines or by developing competitive lines to drive commuter traffic away from the electrics. Rate wars and "line wrecking" were common business strategies that hampered fiscally sound urban transportation (Forbes, 1905: 35). The resulting tendency toward the monopolization of street railways by land and public utility interests and by steam railroads set the stage for electrical transportation's decline.

Although the street railway building booms of 1890-1908 were well financed, the transit monies often were pocketed through overcapitalization, corrupt accounting practices, or overextended transit lines that were unprofitable—except, of course, for land speculation and investment. The combination of corruption and poor management resulted in a total credit collapse between 1916 and 1923, when over a third of the transit companies in the United States went bankrupt (Smerk, 1975: 135). During this period capital moved toward the more profitable, less politically problematic field of automobile investment. As one major transportation financier testified before the Federal Electrical Railway Commission (FERRC) in 1919: "We insiders are selling out just as fast as we can, and when ten years are up, you won't find your Uncle Dudley or any one of us that will own a share of stock or bond in electrical transit" (FERRC, 1920: 1058).

Simultaneously with "cut throat competition," the political activity of the producers and consumers of transportation services also discouraged investment in public transit. Between 1916 and 1920, the transit industry experienced the highest level of strike activity in its history (Kuhn, 1951: 26-27). Labor costs in the transit industry increased faster than average industrial wages (Schmidt, 1935). These higher labor costs, along with wartime inflation affecting material costs, drove the ratio of operation costs to gross income of transit firms from

50% to 77%. As unionized transit workers made gains in their ability to strike, transit lines made less profit. During this early period the right to operate public transportation was granted by local government to private entrepreneurs. In the late nineteenth century citizens and consumers formed popular movements to constrain transit operating companies through their local franchise charters. As a result, the power of those transit companies was curbed and, unintentionally, these restraints helped to establish monopoly barriers to new entrants into public transportation. Franchises often prescribed the use of certain types of equipment, thus restricting innovation, and frequently they required line extensions, street maintenance, and street construction. Such practices usually served to benefit existing firms that were able to meet concomitant costs. Automobiles also benefited by extensive street construction. Finally, flat-rate fares in some franchises subsidized suburban development relative to inner-city travel.

Attempts by transit trusts to circumvent or renegotiate franchise agreements lead to overcrowding and the abandonment of lines due to service cutbacks by operators. This situation eventually lead to popular calls for public ownership. Between 1898 and 1920, every major U. S. city was the scene of legal battles, referenda over rate hikes, public ownership campaigns, and investigations of transit corruption.[5] In this politically volatile climate the corporate liberals of the National Civic Federation (NCF) intervened to consider the transit problem. As reported by August Belmont, owner of New York's transit properties and president of the Federation, the NCF's investigation determined that public ownership would be less efficient than adequate regulation (Jensen, 1956). But regulation for whom?

The government policy that resulted from NCF recommendations was typical of urban reform during the corporate liberal period. Regulation removed the political struggle over transportation from the public sphere of city politics to the forums of appointed, business-oriented, public utility and public service commissions at the state level. This was the first step in insulating transportation decisions from public pressure by the de facto disenfranchisement of the urban population. Transportation planning by appointed state-level organizations was substantially different from direct public participation in transportation policy decision making on local transportation councils and referenda.

Typically, students of urban transportation have attempted to isolate a single cause for the origin of transit's decline, particularly focusing on corruption, poor business practices, the lack of technological innovation, overcrowded service, land use dispersion, and the rise of the automobile.

However, all of these factors are linked in the change from public to private transportation organization. This change involved not merely the technological shift from rail to rubber wheel vehicles; it encompassed basic relations of labor and capital, the production of transportation equipment, and the cost of job-related travel for the working class.

By shifting from public to private transportation technology, business avoided rising labor and construction costs. Organized public transit workers could be left to attrition, and the production of automobiles and streets could be accomplished with unorganized labor. Where private companies were obligated by public franchises to lay track, the federal government would construct roads. The cost of transportation infrastructure could thereby be socialized.

The shift to private transportation would remove the volatile political issue of urban transportation from the political agenda. Consumer movements over rate hikes, public ownership, and transit corruption would be unlikely to form. Finally, the shift from public to private transportation ensured the transfer of capital investment from an increasingly restricted area of local transit operations to a more expansive one, that of national transportation equipment production.

CORPORATE STRATEGY AND STATE POLICY: THE FALL OF MASS TRANSPORTATION

Although the corporate abuse of the "local transit trusts," capital flight from transportation, the movement toward state regulation, and the reorganization and new composition of leading corporate capital did much to start mass transportation's decline, it did not ensure its demise. During the 1920s, when public transit stagnated, an ambiguous relationship between private and public transportation developed. After the initial rash of abandonments and receiverships following World War I, conditions within the transit industry stabilized. Receiverships fell from 9% to 7% annually and remained below 18% until the Depression. Moreover, the reduction in riders and track miles could be interpreted as the first rational shrinkage in railway networks to a more financially viable economic scale (Dewees, 1970: 564-565). In addition, the decline in ridership may well have been the result of new, more honest accounting practices that became dominant as the result of state regulations during the 1920s.

The idea that more autos resulted in less public transit, an idea prominent in Federal Railway Commission testimonials and among modern historians, seems a gross oversimplification. If the ridership between 1918 and 1927 for major U. S. cities is disaggregated, we find an increase in ridership for some major cities (St. Louis saw a 3.1% gain in ridership; Chicago, a 10.1% gain; and New York City, a 37% gain; see Barrett, 1976: 418-419; memo of the effect of the automobile on patronage, APTA File .075.441). Decreases in public transportation were felt mostly by cities with less than 500,000 population (Dewees, 1970: 569).

There was an inverse relationship between automobile density and city size. In cities in which bus and rail modernization were undertaken, traffic surveys showed public transit trips increasing at a higher rate than autogenerated trips—17% compared to 25%. A sharp decline in public transportation had been arrested. Despite financial disasters and rising fares, rail transit was surviving and was cheaper than the operation of buses. Aggregate data from trade sources have shown that comparative costs and profit analysis of motor buses, electric buses, and electric streetcars during this period support the contention that existing transportation operations with bus and streetcar facilities were more economically efficient than solely bus operations (St. Clair, 1981: 579-600).

Even though transit operations retreated from the financial brink, the impact of earlier mismanagement by local transit monopolies was devastating for the equipment manufacturers (Hilton and Due, 1960). The railway equipment industry had peaked, and the absence of significant levels of new private or public investment meant that an already limited market contracted further. Meanwhile, other supplier and related industries also were in eclipse or transformation. The coal, electrical manufacturing, steel, and public utilities industrial complex, which comprised the leading growth sectors of the pre-World War I economy, changed (Duncan and Lieberson, 1970). As a newly regulated industry, public utilities were buffeted by investigations and scandals leading to the Holding Company Act of 1934. Coal and steel reoriented their production toward the growing auto and construction sectors. And electrical machinery manufacturing shifted from capital to consumer goods production. Relatively, the overall position of these industries declined.

Meanwhile, economic centralization and concentration in new growth sectors—auto, oil, and rubber—proceeded. The automobile industry provides a prime example of the concentration and centralization of capital with the rise of market oligopolies. Although the automobile was initially developed in Germany and France in the late nineteenth century (Flink, 1970: 12), the first successful commercial automobile in the United States was introduced in 1893 (Motor Vehicle Manufacturers Association of the U.S., 1974: 11). At first the industry was small and consisted of a multitude of dynamic, highly competitive firms. For example, Flink (1970: 302) estimates that over 500 companies engaged in the manufacturing of automobiles in the United States between 1900 and 1908. However, some firms lost out while their more successive competitors grew, and the industry soon began to show signs of rising concentration. As early as 1912, only seven companies accounted for over half of the U. S. production of autos. In 1908, there were 253 active automobile manufacturers in the United States; by 1920, there were only 108. Just nine years later there were 44. The industry was characterized by aggressive reorganization and acquisition by key firms such as General Motors (Yago, 1980; other Department of Justice documents on GM Antitrust suit). In the context of increasing concentration within the automobile industry, the resiliency of mass transportation, along with declines in automobile demand, produced a crisis requiring a response in corporate strategy. Although new financing and reorganization within large automotive companies had been achieved (Chandler, 1968), there remained problems of competing transportation modes. From 1923 on, the new car market was saturated (Weiss, 1961; Kennedy, 1941; Seltzer, 1928). Alfred Sloan, Henry Ford, Charles W. Nash, the National Automobile Chamber of Commerce, and others agreed that the problem required a more rapid turnover of automobiles (Flink, 1977: 145-152). General Motors led the way with strategies for frequent style changes, extensive advertising, franchise distribution, and cheap financing. Despite these changes, stabilization of the automobile market remained a threat to the industry and to suppliers associated with it. The oil and rubber industries faced overproduction and falling prices; housing construction went into decline.[6]

Corporations required long-range plans to neutralize public transportation effectively and thereby promote demand. Early automotive industrialists such as Bill Durant and Henry Ford were incapable of establishing the cross-industrial coalitions that would be necessary to accomplish such a task (Chandler, 1968; Flink, 1976). The following scenario seems likely. The spectacular investment in street railways during boom years had created large, "sunk," fixed capital costs that by the 1920s could be used at reduced expense and were thereby more competitive; this aided the mini-recovery of mass transportation in major cities during this period. Simultaneously, capital that was invested in street railways was devalued through lower productivity and use. Although the automobile industry attempted to overcome the old, fixed capital investment in street railways by promoting federally subsidized road investment ("new" fixed capital investment), thereby facilitating automotive traffic, rail transit remained a serious constraint on the expansion of automobiles and related industries, which were the centers of capital accumulation during this period.

The transportation technology that first allowed the decentralization in expansion of cities became a burden to later additional expansion. Continued urban expansion was essential in order for cities to fulfill their function as loci of economic activity and of increased capital accumulation. For this to happen, the U. S. population had to be put in cars.

It soon became obvious that the mere manipulation of conditions internal to the auto industry was insufficient to accomplish this crucial task. Ford was wrong. Solely by producing cheap automobiles, the United States would not be motorized. By 1927, Chevrolet had overtaken Ford due to Sloan's successful strategies of product diversification, marketing, and auto purchase financing (Flink, 1976; Chandler, 1968). But Sloan was also wrong: Refinements in automobile production and distribution could not accomplish full motorization. The competition from public carriers would not disappear. The stagnation of automobile demand, overproduction, and general indicators of economic crisis all led the automobile industry and its partners to develop a new corporate strategy: destruction of urban rail transit. This was accomplished by ripping up rails and replacing streetcars with buses, and by simultaneously displacing thousands of transit passengers into automobiles.[7]

The auto-oil-rubber coalition firms used various methods to promote conversion from electrical transit to buses: direct acquisition of electrical transit operating companies (as in the case of Motor Transit Corporation and National City Lines); the establishment of noncompetitive supply contracts; investments by corporate officers or managers in other transit lines; financial pressure through banks; direct or indirect loans; and trade association activities. The long and complicated history of this transformation of urban transportation is detailed elsewhere (Snell, 1974; Yago, 1980).

The consequences of the conversion were disastrous for mass transportation. In order to finance bus modernization, route abandonment became common as a cost-cutting measure, leaving many riders with no alternative to the automobile. This also hastened declining ridership by shrinking the area served by public transportation. Generally, buses were also less appealing to passengers. Moreover, bus operations were less economically efficient than mixed modal systems (St. Clair, 1981).

Local transit monopolies declined and were supplanted by a national corporate coalition of automobile-oil-rubber oligopolies. The fragmented nature of locally owned transit systems in the United States facilitated the successful penetration of this corporate strategy into local transportation development. The lack of coordination between transit systems nationally and regionally allowed the isolation of key transit systems, their conversion to buses, and the subsequent decline of rail transit. As noted earlier, industrial groups that might have opposed this corporate strategy either were now dependent on this growth coalition or had little remaining power. For example, other transportation equipment producers, such as Dr. Thomas Conway, the Brill Company, Westinghouse, and other streetcar lines, opposed conversions. Throughout the 1930s Conway called meetings to defend rail lines and to popularize the use of modernized streetcars that would reduce operating costs. However, the attempts of equipment producers and users to inform and convince civic associations, city governments, and transit groups concerning the merits of modernized streetcar equipment were quashed by the superior economic and political power of General Motors and its allied companies. The elimination of the competition electric transit posed for buses and private automobiles was a boon for motorization. As auto, truck, and bus dominance was promoted by corporate actions and spread throughout the urban areas of the United States, it became progressively more difficult for transit consumers' preferences to call forth alternatives to motor vehicles. Economist Matthew Edel shows how those persons who do not wish to drive and who would prefer good public transportation are caught in a bind of increasingly restricted choice:

> The relation of each driver to others can be described by what game theorists call the *prisoner's dilemma,* after the case of two suspects, each of whom is told separately by the district attorney that the other will confess, in which case his sentence may be harsh, each will confess to keep his risk small. In any prisoner's dilemma situation, one course can yield everyone the best result, if everyone follows it. But if not everyone follows it, then those who do make the attempt suffer a great loss. Unless there is some mechanism for ensuring that others will make the attempt, it is therefore rational to accept a suboptimal outcome and not try for the best possible result. This is the case with the automobile. For each individual it may be irrational not to drive, unless enough others also stop driving and demand good public transit.
>
> In this situation, to seek a psychological explanation for why individuals drive is to ask the wrong question. The problem is not why individuals drive, given the options open to them. It is why the options in American cities involve few alternatives to life in residential neighborhoods that require automobiles be used for work, shopping, and other necessary activities [Edel, 1973: 117].

The actions of the auto interests greatly compounded this dilemma, leading to the growth to overwhelming dominance of the private auto. Given restricted effective choice, the insulation of transportation policymaking from mechanisms of citizen participation, it is now difficult if not impossible to determine what the "true" preferences of transit consumers may be. Behavior becomes an unreliable indicator. Although many of us probably would prefer not to drive, we do drive as we no longer have any reasonable alternative.

STATE POLICY: THE GRADUAL SHIFT TOWARD MOTORIZATION

State intervention into transportation policy dates back to World War I. However, until World War II transportation policy was merely an element of other policy areas such as national defense, public service, economic recovery, and urban planning. State intervention before World War I was primarily concerned with decreasing the time and cost of travel for conveying goods to market and people to work. Street railways were supportive of federally aided line extensions. But state subsidization was for construction costs alone. Line extensions, although quite useful for the factories involved, were not financially sound, and streetcar companies were locked into serving these costly and often failing lines through existing franchise agreements.

Other more indirect measures were taken that inhibited public transit, perhaps unintentionally. Restrictive franchise agreements forced streetcar companies to bear heavy tax burdens. In 1917-1918, rail taxes used in road building reached $2.25 million (FERRC, 1920: 425). Similarly, regulatory statutes created an impressive environment for rail transit. Bus companies often required less stringent public franchises or none at all, and thereby were exempt from various tax and imposed arrangements, as they did not need the exclusive access to rights-of-way. State regulatory policies and the beginnings of highway building often led to offsetting the lower operating costs of rail transit, which still had higher land acquisition and fixed investment costs.

It was not until the New Deal, when Roosevelt extended aid to urban highways in 1934 and 1936, that highway policy became an important part of personal transportation and urban planning policy. Although the New Deal was severely constrained in the amount of financial support it could give to highway development, the notion of physical infrastructural support was firmly established. The National Resources Planning Board, the Reconstruction Finance Corporation, and the Bureau of Public Roads all acted to construct constraints and biases of planning that would come to facilitate motorization after World War II.[8] Local and regional planning authorities were encouraged to draft proposals for highway projects with federal assistance. The records of the National Resources Planning Board show that chambers of commerce, manufacturers associations, and other business organizations encouraged individual states and local communities to build roads through making recommendations to state planning commissions. These organized groups dominated the recommendations to planning agencies. State legislation increased tax supports for municipal road building, and planners and engineers argued that these roads be built parallel to railroad rights-of-way. Under the direction of the National Resources Planning Board, development commissions within state planning commissions were oriented toward urban development and transportation planning. Automobile, oil, and rubber company representatives typically were overrepresented on these transportation planning boards (Yago, 1982).[9]

On the local level, measures were initiated to reduce the expense and inconvenience of private auto ownership. The task of regulating traffic was interpreted as the task of increasing traffic flows. Parking regulations were adapted to the needs of auto usage (Barrett, 1976: 400-401). Unlimited automobile accommodation through new taxes, improved roads, expanded parking facilities, extensive surveys, and systems of regulation became the goal of local planning policy. In the process, the neglect of public transportation development and maintenance became institutionalized. The impetus for such regulations came from the emerging profession of urban and traffic planners, automobile interests, motor clubs, and central city business interests that were worried about how regulations might harm central city shopping. Planning served as a response to situations and problems, not as a method for anticipating them. This notion of problem solving, so dominant in the urban planning tradition in the United States, was plainly exemplified by local transportation policy. Moreover, it left urban development particularly vulnerable to the corporate strategy of opposing mass transportation. Everything was done by state policy to promote the automobile, nothing to constrain it.

What developed was a largely unsystematic, almost accidental relationship between cities and transportation systems. Instead of comprehensive, long range, publicly determined goals for city and regional development (with plans for transportation systems that complement and facilitate overall urban development), we have cities that grow haphazardly and transportation facilities that provide inadequate service for many residents of the metropolitan area (Meyer et al., 1965; Ornati, 1968; Davies and Albaum, 1974). Although the structure of urban areas could be planned, for example, to minimize the need for unnecessary travel, the opposite condition came to exist. To the extent that there has been any urban planning, that planning has involved a virtual surrender to the automobile. As Flick (1975: 164) observes:

> Thus, instead of attempting to discourage the use of private passenger cars in cities, politicians and city planners adopted the expensive and ultimately unworkable policy of unlimited accommodation to the motor car. That American life would conform to the needs of automobility rather than vice versa was obvious by the early 1920's.

The industrial coalition that gave birth to bus conversions and motorization also organized the highway lobby that informally developed national transportation policy. As the Automobile Manufacturers Association (Memo of AMA Committee on Highway Economics, November 1, 1959, GM files R-89) points out:

> From the beginning of the automobile industry in the U.S., vehicle manufacturers have recognized their direct stake in highway development and financing policies. Both through industry-wide programs and through leadership by industry executives, continuous activities have been carried out through the years.

On the state level the National Highway Users Conference, with 2800 lobbying groups, decisively affected the creation of model state highway trust funds that were free from competition with other state budgetary items. Through lobbying, campaign contributions, control of various lobbying organizations, and the influence of corporate representatives on decision-making bodies, highway building was insulated fiscally and politically from opposition.

A series of conferences in the 1950s and 1960s sponsored by the auto industry through the Automotive Safety Foundation (founded by the Automobile Manufacturers Association) and the National Committee on Urban Transportation (and later the Joint Committee on Highways) specified the issues to be considered by state and local officials, traffic engineers, and city planners in the process of transportation planning. Technically, transportation planning reinforced and expanded the patterns of auto domination that had been established by the mid-1950s (Holmes, 1973: 381-383). Through federal financing and profit planning conferences, state highway agencies were relieved of fiscal, legislative, administrative, and planning constraints in the implementation of freeway, primary and secondary route, and feeder route construction. This plethora of technical solutions provided state highway engineers with enormous power to counter any coalition of municipalities or civic groups committed to policy alternatives.

Highway planning was in essence an attempt to reorganize transportation policy at higher levels of government and, in successive stages, to remove it from the sphere of public decision making.[10] Because the 1962 and 1965 Highway Acts called for "comprehensive, cooperative, and continuous planning," (the so-called "3C" process) the Bureau of Public Roads was able, through various directives and instructional memoranda, to ensure that planning would be concentrated in and controlled by the Bureau and state highway offices. The language of participatory planning was reinterpreted to emphasize the technical factors rather than the social effects of highway construction. Public hearings were not intended as "popular referenda," but as trial balloons for testing local opposition, developing highway support, and constructing a political strategy for any proposed highway (Morehouse, 1965).[11] This stands in great contrast to the tradition of participatory planning, a practice that has a long and generally successful history in many other countries. Moreover, in the United States as the 3C process of transportation planning (through a metropolitan planning organization) became institutionalized, the locus of planning control slipped from city hands.

At the state level, agency control over transportation planning was dominated largely through these provisions. Since the turn of the century, transit planning by city governments has been generally replaced by regional and state transportation planning agencies, agencies that stress intercity and suburban service. A recent study by the U.S. Department of Transportation indicates that in 24 out of 30 communities examined, the initiative for route selection, project staffing, and planning was taken by state rather than local agencies working through metropolitan planning bodies (U.S. Department of Transportation, 1976). The increased public opposition to highway construction in the 1960s resulted in several court decisions that tended to reinforce centralized planning. These decisions focused on procedural rather than substantive issues. The courts determined that construction could be halted if highway planners had made some mistake in the procedures. However, the power of the community in public hearings, the social and economic impact of highways, and other issues were left untouched by the courts.[12]

In addition to the planning biases of federal legislation, economic biases have abounded. The apportionment formulae allowing for heavy federal subsidization of highway construction make other transportation modes inconceivable. Less obvious is an antiurban bias. Until recently (1978) states have not been permitted to receive more than 12.5% of apportionment funds for other transportation modes (Mantel, 1971: 177-123). In the federal government's computation of cost and benefits of auto transportation, the valuations of land, pollution, residential dislocation, induced traffic congestion, energy waste, and other social costs were excluded.

SUMMARY

A major determinant of national transportation policy as it has affected cities has been the corporate profit-making strategies of the auto-oil-rubber industrial complex, strategies that are designed to broaden market areas and to provide the physical infrastructure necessary to sell the commodities these and closely related industries produce. Transportation policy also has involved local and regional efforts to obtain capital to increase the development of land, to foster industrial construction and new housing so as to establish new bases to increase profits. Thus, capital at the national level involved in the most monopolized sectors of production and similar interests at local and regional levels involved in more speculative, less directly productive areas have been unified politically and economically in motorizing transportation.

In large measure, transportation policy reflects a profit-making and spatial planning interest of capital accumulation. Historically, the profit-making function of transportation had dominated national developments. Such policy has been developed within corporate circles, expanded through public policy bodies, supported by corporations, and transmitted into state policy. As rail transit became a fetter on expanded production and new industries, and on profit making in urban land and housing, pressures arose from the corporate sector to supplant rail with motorization policies. Although electrical transit had been the climax of industrial growth associated with other industries (coal, steel, electrical machinery), it became an obstacle to the emergence of an ascendent industrial group associated with the automobile, oil, and rubber industries. This new group took steps to constrain transportation policy by its own investment decisions, by its influence on the emerging economic structure, and by engaging in political struggles against older corporate interests associated with rail transit. Having created structural influences, corporate control over transportation policy was greatly strengthened through the participation of corporate leaders and allies in high levels of government dealing with transportation.

CONSEQUENCES OF PRESENT TRANSIT POLICY

Kapp (1963) vividly demonstrates how many serious social costs are generated by private production processes. He defines social costs as "all direct and indirect losses sustained by third persons or the general public as a result of unrestrained and unregulated economic activities."

Such costs may take the form of immediate monetary losses, damages to human health, deterioration of property values, the premature depletion of natural resources, and the impairment of less tangible human values (such as aesthetic losses). There are several ways that we can examine the applicability of the theory of social costs to the political economy of urban transportation.

Every federal administration over the past 40 years has celebrated the objective of safe, cheap, and efficient transportation as the goal of transportation policy. Let us examine the federal government's policy criteria for urban transportation. During the last two decades consumers, as taxpayers, have begun to cast a jaundiced eye upon highway-dependent transportation, questioning why the goals of cheap, safe, and efficient transportation have not been met, in spite of steadily rising costs. Without effective mass transit, the proportion of personal transportation consumption expenditures have more than tripled (from 4.5% to 17.0%) in the last 70 years. The energy crisis ensures that these trends will continue. Transportation increasingly has become a private consumption item absorbed through rising auto purchase and operation and maintenance costs. Moreover, the resulting infrastructural investment in highways is a costly and rapidly expanding burden. It is becoming evident that the commitment to highway transportation with a concomitant neglect of public transportation exacts great fiscal and social costs. Direct federal expenditures since 1956 for the national highway program total between $200 and $300 billion; highway lobbyist Peter Koltnow, former president of the Highway Users for Safety and Mobility and former head of the Transportation Research Board, predicts it will take even more than that amount to repair and maintain those same roads. Federal highway expenditures have not diminished the fiscal burden of unbalanced transportation on cities and states. Since World War II state and local highway debts have risen from $3.6 billion to $24 billion.

Overemphasis on highways generates many other fiscal burdens as well—police and safety services, local road construction and maintenance, and snow removal are a few. In 1973, the Federal Highway Administration conservatively estimated that 30%, or $7 billion, of direct highway expenses were not covered by highway user revenues or tolls. This does not include indirect costs of auto accidents, energy waste, and environmental damage associated with overdependence on highway traffic and resulting urban sprawl. Nor does it cover the expense of the expansion of social support services, declining urban taxes, and the abandonment of real estate that accompany the low-density land use of the auto age.

Not only do we spend more money traveling, it often takes more time and energy to get where we are going. Although transportation policy promoted motorization to overcome the barriers of space through decreased travel time, in many ways it created land use patterns that imposed new, special limits to mobility. The average time required to travel to work—the trek constituting most urban travel—generally remains about the same despite faster cars. In those urban centers that are more dependent on the automobile than public transportation, the average travel time to work has increased (Voorhees and Bellomo, 1970: 121-135; Guest, 1975: 220-225). Moreover, average blue-collar workers and the poor, consisting largely of minority populations, take longer to travel to work than they did after World War II (Greytak, 1970). Projections show average travel time to work increasing 15% to 20% by the year 2000.

That our highway transportation system wastes natural resources and fuel also is readily demonstrable. The motor vehicle industry alone consumes a substantial amount of the total U. S. steel, aluminum, lead, iron, rubber, and zinc production. As auto production and profits are based largely on obsolescence (annual style changes and lower annual years of use), resource depletion will increase, thus escalating future transportation costs. Environmental Protection Agency projections indicate resource reserves necessary for current levels of auto production will dissipate by the year 2000. Costlier extraction processes and new technologies will boost travel costs even further.

Transportation's share of petroleum consumption has increased over 50% since World War II. Cars, trucks, and buses consume 80% of the gasoline used in transportation, resulting in a tripling of gasoline use since 1950 (Office of Technology Assessment, 1975; 17-24). In Western European countries, by contrast, only 25-30% of their petroleum consumption goes for transportation, because of better public transportation, more fuel-efficient cars, and the maintenance of high gasoline prices. Public transportation, transit-coordinated land use planning, conservation, and alternative fuel uses account for those countries lower per capita energy requirements than in the United States.

Our present transportation system also compromises our personal safety. Since World War II deaths from traffic accidents have catapulted from insignificance to the third major cause of mortality; for young people (15-34) it has become the major cause of death. Disabilities from motor vehicle accidents have increased for all age groups. Drivers regularly ignore the speed limits imposed during the 1973 oil crisis and casualties continue. Although consumer groups (reflecting public attitudes as expressed in opinion polls) have fought for seatbelts, safer construction, and airbags, safe travel has declined along with public transportation alternatives.

The future of automobile safety looks grim. Since auto usage began in the United States, well over 2 million people have been killed in accidents. Because mortality increases with decreased auto weight and increased travel distance, the reduction of car weight and increased fuel efficiency (downsizing) will likely result in increased mortality figures. In the rush to dominate the new small car market, the developmental response to energy shortages, producers sometimes have cut corners on safety. Environmental quality diminishes with the pursuit of current transportation policy as well. Air pollution provides a continued area of controversy among consumers, federal regulators, and the auto industry.

In short, it has become clear to many observers that urban transportation has become unnecessarily expensive, wasteful, and dangerous. Transportation policy largely has ignored the needs of the poor, elderly, young, disabled, and minorities. Access to employment, recreation, and urban services are thus distributed unequally. The effects on industrial policy and industrial decline in the automobile industry have been enormous.

HIGH-TECHNOLOGY RAIL SYSTEMS: NEW CONTRADICTIONS

Our analysis of the political economy of transportation has focused largely on corporate interests and strategies at the national level. We have done this to contrast certain aspects of transit development in the United States with transit development in European countries. Transportation systems also have strong and specific locational impacts, and local corporations, real estate interests, and other groups play active roles in shaping metropolitan transportation policies and systems. As the work of Harvey (1973), Molotch (1976), and others demonstrate, the struggle to obain locational advantages and to maximize ground rents is the essence of metropolitan politics, in transit as in many other matters. Although we have not analyzed them here, such local struggles to control transportation policies, technologies, and routes are—in addition to the events we have examined—important not only in shaping transit at the local level, but also in influencing the strategies that are pursued at the national level.

A national-level analysis based on corporate actions and an analysis of local corporations and groups who compete for locational advantage and profits are both needed for a full understanding of the political economy of transportation in the United States. For example, part of the reason for the attempted resurgence of rail transit in the near past has been a recent coalition between business at the local level (e.g., corporate headquarters operations in the central business district [CBD], banks) and others at the national or regional level (aerospace and other high-tech firms).

Another important factor is the impact the long-dominant automobile is having on central cities. The story is a familiar one. Traffic often comes to a standstill as hoards of individuated, private, mostly single-passenger vehicles fight for freeway space during rush hours. Noise and exhaust fumes fill the air. The suburbs recede even further away as more and more land is covered with concrete to satisfy the needs of the auto. Land also is taken off tax rolls by this process. The fiscal status of cental cities further declines. Affluent commuters face longer and longer journeys and increasing delays. The inner-city poor are trapped in their neighborhoods and cannot get to employment opportunities. Corporations are also affected. Traffic tie-ups hurt downtown property values and retail sales. Decentralization of population and fragmentation of governmental units, brought about in part by automobility, make corporate management in urban areas difficult. At the local level, big businesses become worried about the possible and actual decline of CBD property values and the political challenge of poor urban minorities.

More farsighted corporate planners, trying to respond to these contradictions, come to realize that the auto-highway system may have reached the practical extent of its possible development in urban areas, and that the situation has often begun to decline—the auto is making things worse. What was once seen as highly useful for developing corporate and urban America is now seen as much less useful and often damaging.

Various urban redevelopment schemes and governmental reorganization plans are put forth to rescue urban land values and availability, and pacification programs are initiated to cool out protest of the urban underclass. In the 1960s and 1970s ambitious high-tech rail transit systems such as the Bay Area Rapid Transit (BART) system in San Francisco and the Metro in Washington, D.C., have been built, fundamentally, we would argue, as political tools for urban redevelopment and pacification. They are particularly initiated and supported, not by grass-roots citizens' groups, but by big corporations in the center city as a way to try to halt skid rows, to make suburb-to-central-city commuting easier for corporate executives and functionaires, to reinforce centralized dominance of headquarters firms and financial institutions, and to boost CBD property values (Whitt, 1982).

These expensive new systems are designed to try to reduce labor conflict and expenses by being as fully automated as possible. The aerospace industry, long subject to political fluctuations in government demand, sees them as attractive markets for products. Banks stand to make a lot of money by buying the bonds used to construct them. The public is told that these new systems will ease air pollution, reduce traffic congestion, benefit low-income groups, and make it easier to get around in the city. The actual effects usually are minimal as, in our view, the prime *raison d'etre* for rail transit as currently conceived is urban growth and private corporate profit, not making life better for urban residents in general.

All of this leads to important contradictions. Urban business leaders want these systems to enhance capital accumulation, central city political hegemony, and corporate legitimacy. But voters sometimes do not see the "need" for them and often balk at paying higher taxes. Conflicts sometimes divide elements of the business community too over additional auto-related development versus mass transit, over how to pay for costly transit development, and over where routes will be laid and thus which local property owners will most benefit. A particularly sore spot in the business community is whether to tap highway funds in significant ways. The "highway lobby" still has a lot of clout, although it is somewhat diminished. The biggest contradiction is financial: Voters often cannot be persuaded to pay more taxes, government has traditionally been most reluctant to subsidize transit development, and the private corporations who stand to gain have a hard time—even if willing—raising the large amounts of capital needed.

At present, the result is a stalemate: After two decades of talk about new transit systems, and the construction of several, new construction of urban transit has virtually halted. These expensive projects cannot be financed without governmental subsidies, and the Reagan administration is strongly opposed to such aid. New proposals for urban transit systems will get nowhere, at least in the foreseeable future. Meanwhile, automobile dominance is unabated and the contradictions facing urban areas and central city firms grow worse. We interpret the historical record as suggesting the following general conclusions and policy implications.

The seemingly never-ending cycle of problems and contradictions in transportation continues. Within the present organization of urban transportation, the pursuit of profit satisfies private interests, and only on a short-run basis. The very "success" of private profitability in transit undermines its own foundation. New plans, investments, and problems must always be dealt with. In this context, the "solution" of one problem leads to another. In the process, this corporate drive for profits fails to serve the needs of commuters and cities for more rational, coordinated, efficient public transportation. The example of many European cities shows that this state of affairs need not exist. Our cities too often have become costly, ugly patchworks of wasteful automobiles, decaying neighborhoods, unplanned sprawl, and expensive but ineffective high-tech tools for profit. Without a significant degree of public control and grass-roots participation, continued corporate dominance over transit policy and development will lead merely to the usual profit-seeking, contradictory policies and the maintenance of anemic, minimal systems of public transport. More avenues for public participation in transit policymaking would be appropriate, as would a greater degree of publicly sponsored planning emphasizing an integration of such considerations as urban development and growth, transportation needs, social costs, and environmental impacts. In this regard, comparative studies suggest that much may be gained by emulating examples that exist in other countries.

NOTES

1. Kolko (1978: 2-12) has argued convincingly that rapid economic growth occurred in the United States without the existence of centralized financial and capital control

as many have assumed. He maintains that decentralization and local and regional authority were far more characteristic of the U.S. economy prior to 1900.

2. In the cases of both electrification and automobilization, the process of innovation was faster in the United States than in Germany. Public transportation was fully electrified in the United States by 1895, with full German electrification not occurring until the turn of the century (McKay, 1976: 35-84). The same process appears to have occurred in automobilization (Kramer-Bardoni et al., 1971: 19-24).

3. It also was a convenient way to displace social conflict. Henry Ford was noted for the aphorism, "We shall solve the problems of the city by leaving the city." The point is that technological changes in transportation equipment made possible more rapid capital accumulation and affected the disorganization of the working class over commonly conceived problems of production and consumption. The spatial dislocation of working populations through transportation and urban physical changes separated the arenas of production and consumption struggles, thus diminishing the possibility of class struggle over such issues (Katznelson, 1976: 28).

4. The expansion of the electrical transit system often was not in the interests of rational transportation development, but advanced profit making by transit operators, land speculators, and banks. Ralph S. Bauer's testimony before the Federal Electrical Railroad Commission (1920: 1622) is illustrative of this point. Bauer, President of the Lynn, Massachusetts Board of Trade, noted:

> I found that a little later on in the nineties, banking interests in the Northeast became interested in the street railway problem, and believed that by consolidating these competing companies there could be evolved from such consolidation a unit system which would pay tremendous profits. . . . I further found that the ground hogs in the different communities—the land speculators—had brought certain influences to bear on the local governments which compelled the street railway to build extensions into property for the sake of adding rental and sales values to pasture land, and the politicians in charge of the localities in those times brought sufficient influence to bear on the railways to compel them to build the kind of extensions *which would never profit producing lines.*

5. Contrary to some current interpretations, the movement for public ownership of transit, utilities, ice manufacturing, and so on at the turn of the century was not simply a "petit-bourgeois" movement of the Progressive Era. Yago's archival research concerning the "Traction Question" in Chicago indicates working-class community mobilization (of community groups, Socialist and People's parties, religious groups), in alliance with many small business interests in the community, against what was called "the exploitation of people's needs" such as food, transportation, and electricity (Vickers, 1934; Goodwyn, 1976). Information on popular oppositional movements regarding transit during this period is available for the following urban areas: San Francisco (Bean, 1968), New Orleans (Jackson, 1969), Baltimore (Crooks, 1968), Detroit (Holli, 1969), Cincinnati (Miller, 1960), Philadelphia (Warner, 1976), and Milwaukee (MacShane, 1975). Cheape (1980) presents additional evidence of these referenda and

mass protests in Boston, New York, and Philadelphia; and how these demands were transformed into regulatory management procedures in a bureaucratic framework.

6. Regarding descriptions of the market saturation problems of the major accumulation growth industries of this period (auto, oil, rubber, etc.), see Weiss (1961), Flink (1975: 148-160), and Sloan (1962: 208).

7. The most important break in the story of the decline of public transit has been the investigation by Bradford Snell (1984). Much of the present discussion is based on Snell's thorough study. He has pointed the way to the critical questions concerning transit's decline in the United States.

Snell's hypothesis has been widely contested. The regularity with which unsubstantiated claims are made about the technological superiority of highway transportation modes is astounding; it appears in both popular and scientific works. Dunn (1981: 75) states, "But the economics of the declining transit industry would have dictated much of this switch [from streetcars to buses] in any case, since buses were cheaper to purchase and operate (in the short run) than trolleys." Concerning automobiles, Altschuler (1980: 21) argues, "In the course of achieving this overwhelming dominance, the automobile appears to have become the less expensive mode for most purposes, as well as the more rapid, convenient, and flexible." Neither Dunn nor Altschuler provides any evidence for these claims. In fact, the evidence from Germany and the United States, detailed by Yago (1980, 1983), appears to support just the opposite. Most recently, St. Clare (1981: 600) examined aggregate data from trade sources to compare costs and profits of motor buses, electric buses, and electric streetcars. He concludes that the "motor buses were consistently the least economical transit vehicle during the period 1935-1950." This includes consideration of both capital and operating costs and is the most definitive study of comparative modal costs.

8. The Reconstruction Finance Corporation was quite active in supporting bus conversion programs during the 1930s (APTA Files, 900.01, 308.01, various city files). As part of modernization and public service, the use of these subsidized loans aided the corporate strategy of bus conversions. See also U. S. National Resources Committee (1940).

9. For example, the National Advisory Committee on a National Highway Program consisted of General Lucius D. Clay, Chairman, Continental Can; Stephen D. Bechtel, President, Bechtel Corporation; David Beck, President, International Brotherhood of Teamsters; S. Sloan Colt, President, Bakers' Trust Company; and W. A. Roberts, President, Allis Chalmers Manufacturing Company.

10. The federal government financed but did not actually construct the highways as in Germany. This "pork barrel" nature of the U.S. strategy allowed for state highway departments to dispense with federally contracted monies as a way to curry support for highway spending. This maximized support and control for highway building and ultimately for planning centralization.

11. This bureaucratic control of highway planning to dedemocratize it is reflected in numerous policy memoranda (BPR Policy and Procedure Memo, 20-8, August 10, 1956; see also Morehouse, 1965). This is consistent with findings of urban political scholars who have shown the loss of administrative power by large urban populations through organizational changes and control within the state bureaucracy.

12. In most recent court cases judges have tended to emphasize procedural rather than substantive issues of transit planning. If a community could discover where a particular impact statement had failed to be filed or some hearing procedure overlooked, there was the possibility of halting highway construction. But over the substantive

matters of what impact statements should consider or what the power of the community is in hearings, the court has tended to constrain any democratization of transit planning. In highway hearings, rights of cross-examination are not required, nor does an accurate court-like record need to be maintained. The courts have upheld that federal highway officials' decisions need not be reviewed (Morningside Lennox Park Association v. State Highway Department); that federal officials have the final say in determining whether procedures and plans were sufficient and proper (D.C. Federation of Civic Association v. Volpe); and that planning need not be intermodal (Citizens for Mass Transit Against Freeways v. Brinegar).

REFERENCES

ALTSCHULER, A. (1980) Urban Transportation Policy. Cambridge, MA: MIT Press.

AVERITT, R. (1968) The Dual Economy. New York: Norton.

BARRETT, P. F. (1976) "Mass transit, the automobile, and public policy in Chicago, 1900-1930." Ph.D. dissertation, University of Illinois.

BEAN, W. (1968) Boss Ruef's San Francisco. Berkeley: Univ. of California Press.

BUNTING, D. (1972) "Rise of large American corporations, 1896-1905." Ph.D. dissertation, University of Oregon.

CHANDLER, A. D., Jr. (1968) Strategy and Structure. Garden City, NY: Doubleday.

———and H. DAEMS (1974) "The rise of managerial capitalism and its impact on investment strategy in the Western world and Japan," pp. 1-34 in H. Daems and H. Van der Wee (eds.) The Rise of Managerial Capitalism. The Hague: Martinus Nijhoff.

CHEAPE, C. (1980) Moving the Masses. Cambridge, MA: Harvard Univ. Press.

CROOKS, J. B. (1968) Politics and Progress: The Rise of Urban Progressivism in Baltimore, 1895-1911. Baton Rouge: Louisiana State Univ. Press.

DAVIES, C. S. and M. ALBAUM (1976) "The mobility problem of the poor in Indianapolis." Antipode 1: 67-86.

DEWEES, D. (1970) "The decline of the American street railways." Traffic Q. 24 (September): 563-582.

DUNCAN, B. and S. LIEBERSON (1970) Metropolis and Region in Transition. Beverly Hills, CA: Sage.

DUNN, J. A. (1981) Miles to Go. Cambridge, MA: MIT Press.

EDEL, M. (1973) Economies and the Environment. Englewood Cliffs, NJ: Prentice-Hall.

EDWARDS, C. D. (1966) Dynamics of the U.S. Automobile Industry. Columbia: Univ. of South Carolina Press.

Federal Electric Railways Commission [FERRC] (1920) Commission Proceedings. Washington, DC: Government Printing Office.

FLINK, J. J. (1975) The Car Culture. Cambridge, MA: MIT Press.

——— (1970) America Adopts the Automobile, 1895-1910. Cambridge, MA: MIT Press.

FORBES, H. C. (1905) Public Safety and the Interurban Road vs. the Railroad Monopoly in Massachusetts. Cambridge: Cambridge Univ. Press.

GOODWYN, L. (1976) Democratic Promise: The Populist Movement in America. New York: Oxford Univ. Press.

GREYTAK, D. (1970) Residential Segregation, Metropolitan Decentralization, and the Journey to Work. Springfield, VA: National Technical Information Center.
GUEST, A. M. (1973) "Urban growth and population densities." Demography 10, 1: 53-69.
HARVEY, D. (1973) Social Justice and the City. Baltimore: Johns Hopkins Univ. Press.
HILTON, G. N. and J. E. DUE (1960) The Electric Interurban Railways in America. Stanford, CA: Stanford Univ. Press.
HOLLI, M. (1969) Reform in Detroit: Hazen Pingress and Urban Progress. New York: Oxford Univ. Press.
HOLMES, E. H. (1973) "The state of the art in urban transportation planning." Transportation 4: 379-402.
JACKSON, J. J. (1969) New Orleans in the Guilded Age: Politics and Urban Progressivism, 1880-1896. Baton Rouge: Louisiana State Univ. Press.
JENSES, G. (1956) "The national civic federation: American business in an age of social change and reform, 1900-1910." Ph.D. dissertation, Princeton University.
KAPP, K. W. (1963) The Social Costs of Business Enterprise. Bombay: Asia Publishing.
KATZNELSON, I. (1976) "The patterning of class in the U.S." Presented at the annual meeting of the American Political Science Association, Chicago.
KENNEDY, E. D. (1941) The Automobile Industry. New York: Reynal & Hitchkock.
KOLKO, G. (1978) Main Current in Modern American History. New York: Harper & Row.
KRAEMER-BADONI, T. (1971) Zur sozio-oekonomischen Bedutung des Automobils. Frankfurt/Main: Suhrkamp.
KUHN, A. (1952) Arbitration in Transit. Philadelphia: Univ. of Pennsylvania Press.
MacSHANE, C. (1975) "American cities and the coming of the automobile in the 19th century." Ph.D. dissertation, University of Wisconsin-Madison.
MANTEL, E. H. (1971) "Economic biases in urban transportation planning and implementation." Traffic Q. 25: 177-230.
McKAY, J. (1976) Tramways and Trolleys: The Rise of Urban Mass Transit. Princeton, NJ: Princeton Univ. Press.
MEYER, J. R. and J. A. GOMEZ-IBANEZ (1981) Autos, Transit, and Cities. Cambridge, MA: Harvard Univ. Press.
MEYER, J. R., J. F. KAIN, and M. WOHL (1972) The Urban Transportation Problem. Cambridge, MA: Harvard Univ. Press.
MILLER, J. A. (1960) Fares Please! New York: Dover Press.
MOLOTCH, H. (1976) "The city as a growth machine: toward a political economy of place." Amer. J. of Sociology 82 (September): 309-332.
MOREHOUSE, T. A. (1965) "The determinants of federal policy for urban transportation planning under the federal highway act of 1962." Ph.D. dissertation, University of Minnesota.
Office of Technology Assessment (1975) Energy, The Economy, and Mass Transit. Washington, DC: Government Printing Office.
ORNATI, O. (1968) Transportation and the Poor. New York: Praeger.
PASSER, H. (1953) The Electrical Manufacturing Industry. Cambridge, MA: Harvard Univ. Press.
SCHMIDT, E. P. (1935) "The development of the street railway." Ph.D. dissertation, University of Wisconsin-Madison.
SELTZER, L. H. (1928) A Financial History of the American Automobile Industry. Boston: Houghton-Mifflin.

SLOAN, A. P., Jr. (1962) My Years with General Motors. Garden City, NY: Doubleday.
SMERK, G. (1975) Urban Transportation Policy. Bloomington: Indiana Univ. Press.
SNELL, B. C. (1974) American Ground Transport. Washington, DC: Subcommittee on Antitrust and Monopoly of Judiciary Committee, U.S. Senate.
ST. CLARE, D. J. (1980) "The motorization and decline of urban transit, 1935-50." J. of Econ. History 41 (September): 579-600.
TARR, J. (1973) "From city to suburb: the 'moral' influence of transportation technology," pp. 202-212 in A. B. Callow, Jr. (ed.) American Urban History. New York: Oxford Univ. Press.
U. S. Department of Transportation (1976) Urban System Study. Washington, DC: Government Printing Office.
U. S. National Resources Committee (1940) Urban Government. Vol. 1: Supplementary Report of the Urbanism Committee. Washington, DC: Government Printing Office.
VICKERS, L. (1934) "Fare structures in the transit industry." Ph.D. dissertation, Columbia University.
VOORHEES, A. M. and S. BELLAMO (1970) "Urban travel and city structure." Highway Research Record 322: 121-135.
WARD, D. (1971) Cities and Immigrants: A Geography of Change in Nineteenth Century America. New York: Oxford Univ. Press.
WARNER, S. M., Jr. (1976) Streetcar Suburbs. New York: Atheneum.
WEISS, L. (1961) Economics and American Industry. New York: John Wiley.
WHITT, J. A. (1982) Urban Elites and Mass Transportation: The Dialectics of Power. Princeton, NJ: Princeton Univ. Press.
WILCOX, D. F. (1921) Analysis of the Electrical Railway Problem. New York: author.
——— (1919) "Solving the traction problem from the public point of view." Presented at the 10th anniversary of the New York State Conference of Mayors and City Officials, Schnectady, NY, June 12.
YAGO, G. (1983) The Decline of Transit. New York: Cambridge Univ. Press.
——— (1980) "Corporate power and urban transportation," pp. 296-323 in M. Zeitlin (ed.) Classes, Class Conflict, and the State. Cambridge, MA: Winthrop.

J. Allen Whitt is Associate Professor of Sociology at the University of Louisville. His major areas of research include urban politics, corporate elites, transportation, and work organization. Recent publications include Urban Elites and Mass Transportation: The Dialectics of Power *(Princeton University Press, 1982) and* Organizational Democracy *(Cambridge University Press, forthcoming) with Joyce Rothschild-Whitt.*

Glenn Yago is Director of the Economic Research Department at the State University of New York at Stony Brook. His research on urban transportation, housing, and economic development has been published in the Annual Review of Sociology, Comparative Social Research, *and the* International Journal of Urban and Regional Research. *His book,* The Decline of Transit, *was published in 1984 by Cambridge University Press.*

Studies of residential location typically have treated the household unit as an undifferentiated whole and have not accounted for divergent needs and desires between male and female household members. Using the factorial survey technique, this article examines different preferences for neighborhood characteristics between men and women, focusing on women with varying family and labor market responsibilities. Based on a sample of 177 Syracuse, New York, metropolitan residents, this article shows the desires of men, housewives, single women, and employed women for varying combinations of neighborhood attributes. Findings show that men's desires for neighborhoods suit them well for the typical suburb, whereas women's desired neighborhood characteristics are found both in suburbs and in central cities. Women expressed contradictory desires, wanting the density, residential homogeneity, and racial and socio-economic composition of suburbs, but with the diversity and proximity of services found in cities. These findings suggest that for women suburbs need to include higher densities, public services, and transportation, but should retain much of their residential ambience.

SAME CITY, DIFFERENT WORLDS
Examining Gender- and Work-Based Differences in Perceptions of Neighborhood Desirability

ANNE B. SHLAY
DENISE A. DiGREGORIO
Cornell University

Urban policy has debated the implications of metropolitan spatial distributions for many households that vary by race, ethnicity, income, and family life cycle. Yet the "household" is treated as an undifferentiated whole; the assumption appears to be that all household members—both men and women—have similar housing desires and needs, and therefore neighborhood choices reflect compatible interests between members of the same household. Studies of housing choice

AUTHORS' NOTE: *We are grateful to Peter H. Rossi and Dee Weber-Burdin for critical research insights, to William Putsis for energetic research assistance, to a team of frozen interviewers, to Jennifer Gerner, Joseph A. Kahl, and two anonymous*

URBAN AFFAIRS QUARTERLY, Vol. 21 No. 1, September 1985 66-86

rarely acknowledge that locational decisions may reflect power differentials within the household between male and female members.

Critics now argue that current housing distributions reflect patriarchal dominance and mitigate against women's participation in the labor market (Markusen, 1981). These critics question the suitability of different housing arrangements for women and ask whose interests are best served by these patterns. They propose that, distinct from men, women's residential location severely affects their opportunities; lower-density, residentially homogeneous suburbs hamper women, whereas central city density and mixed land use liberate women (Wekerle et al., 1980; Hayden, 1981; Stimson et al., 1981; Hayden, 1984).

With flexible transportation, women's residential location within homogeneous suburbs restricts their ability to travel, limits employment accessibility, and maintains traditional divisions of labor within the household (Cichocki, 1980; Fava, 1980; Saegert and Winkel, 1980; Lopata, 1981; Saegert, 1981). Employed women tend to reside closer to work than men in part because women retain primary household responsibilities and have more time constraints (White, 1977; Madden and White, 1980; Madden, 1981).[1] By living in suburbs, women are more restricted to work near these areas. Moreover, women's reliance on public transportation, their lack of access to cars, and suburbs' exclusion of mixed land use may restrict women to the home or permit only minimal labor force participation (Michelson, 1977; Rosenbloom, 1978; Freeman, 1981). Suburbs provide men easy access to employment and a private domestic retreat maintained by women but work against women's attempts to combine family and career (Saegert, 1981).

Central city residential locations provide women with necessary amenities (Saegert, 1981; Hayden, 1984). Urban density, public transportation, and a larger employment base allow women more flexibility. Employed women cite public transportation as a major reason for living in central cities (Michelson, 1977). Single-parent women tend to live in central cities because they depend on public transit as well as access to public services, employment, and affordable rental housing (Freeman, 1981). Single-parent women's poverty and their family responsibilities attract them to cities. Cities open up options for women to more easily manage labor market and household responsibilities.

---

reviewers for key commentary, and to Sabella J. Bradley for typing the manuscript with good humor under time constraints. This study was funded by U.S.D.A. Hatch Grant 420. An earlier draft of this article was presented at the annual meeting of the American Sociological Association, August 1983.

Although cities lessen problems for women working outside the home, they tend to be viewed as aggravating problems with work inside the home. Crime, traffic, and the general trouble associated with city life raise potential dangers for children. Men tend to like suburbia for residence and place high value on the suburban house as a financial investment (Michelson, 1977). Research suggests that although women find suburbs less satisfying for their individual opportunities, they find suburbs more amenable for contented family lives (Michelson, 1977; Saegert, 1981). According to Saegert (1981), cities and suburbs represent polarized worlds and contradictory realities for women who wish to maximize opportunities for themselves and care for their families.

Also called into question is the organization of household production. Women's work at household production may be inefficient (Hayden, 1979, 1980, 1981, 1984). Collective household facilities such as communal kitchens and daycare are absent or distant from most neighborhoods (Michelson, 1983; Hayden, 1984). Regardless of the location, individualized household production facilities contribute to women's difficulties in working both at home and at a paid job. A central city location eases women's work outside the home, but may not change the nature of household labor. Full-time suburban homemakers may have little choice in seeking employment given the organization of daily housework as well as the physical constraints of suburbs.

Women's spatial needs and time constraints suggest that women and men desire different types of neighborhoods. Without changes in housing design and service delivery systems, women may desire neighborhoods that maximize their abilities to do their work, either in the home, in the labor market, or in both. Men may desire neighborhoods that reflect their absence from the home during the day and their presence for leisure and family activities.

This article looks at these differences in neighborhood perceptions. It examines the desirability of particular neighborhood characteristics for individuals who vary by gender and by family and employment responsibilities. This article disaggregates the household unit and looks at those neighborhood characteristics that are considered more or less desirable by men, by women, by homemakers, by single women, and by employed women. Through the lens of the factorial survey technique, we demonstrate that women and men may live in the same city but desire very different neighborhood worlds.

DESIGN AND DATA BASE

The factorial method is designed to unravel judgments of complex and multi-dimensional phenomena (Rossi and Nock, 1982). This technique combines the orthogonality found in experimental designs with the richness and diversity found in survey techniques. Characteristics describing a complex phenomenon are randomly assigned to short stories or vignettes. Respondents evaluate the vignettes as complete packages. Using standard linear regression techniques, the independent influence or weighting placed by respondents on each characteristic can be assessed. Because these characteristics are randomly assigned to the vignettes, the characteristics are uncorrelated and independent of one another. Vignettes approximate descriptions of real-world phenomena, but are free from the multicollinearity found in the real world. Respondents' weightings of each characteristic, therefore, represent abstract and unconstrained preferences for characteristics associated with the particular phenomena.

This study uses the factorial survey technique to show how men and women evaluate different neighborhood characteristics that are not necessarily found together within housing markets. This technique allows people to express desires for combinations of neighborhood characteristics that may seem contradictory or empirically unavailable (e.g., high-density suburbs with good public transportation). The abstract preferences for different combinations of local characteristics represent the types of neighborhoods repondents might choose if they could.

Neighborhood vignettes contained statements involving these dimensions: racial, socioeconomic, family, and housing composition; political jurisdiction; neighborhood age and density; travel time to work; access to friends, relatives, public transportation, and other amenities; and adjacent nonresidential land use. For example, one vignette might describe a neighborhood located in the central part of a city, one hour from work with no public transportation, one-fourth black, and composed mostly of single people with an average income of $25,000. Each of these descriptors of the neighborhood served as levels along which each vignette could vary.

For each vignette respondents were asked, "How desirable is this for you as a place to live?" and provided a rating along an 11-point scale on which low values indicated an undesirable situation and high values indicated a desirable situation. These scaled measures represent overall preferences for particular combinations of neighborhood characteristics. The influence of neighborhood characteristics on the variation in the neighborhood desirability rating is independent preference for particular neighborhood attributes. Each respondent rated 20 neighborhood vignettes and was surveyed about his or her household's socioeconomic and housing characteristics, neighborhood situation, family life cycle stage, and composition.

In January 1982, a sample of white respondents was selected from Onondaga County, New York, which contains the city of Syracuse and its metropolitan periphery.[2] Households were randomly selected from blocks contained within four census tracts: a high-income suburban tract containing mostly owner-occupied housing; a middle-income suburban tract containing a mixture of rental and owner-occupied housing; a low-income central city tract containing mostly rental housing; and a middle-income central city tract containing a mixture of rental and owner-occupied housing. Approximately equal numbers of households were sampled per tract by weighting the total number of desired households by the number of households per block relative to the total number of households within the tract area. One respondent was interviewed per household. These procedures yielded 177 respondents, each rating 20 neighborhood vignettes, providing over 3500 units of analysis.

THE SAMPLE

Due to socialization, family responsibilities, and differential market treatment (e.g., women on average earn less money than men), women and men differ along a series of socioeconomic and family dimensions. This article argues that these social and economic differences among men and women influence local needs and therefore affect their preferences for neighborhoods. Table 1 examines these differences among the sample of respondents.

Table 1 compares the socioeconomic, family, and housing characteristics for the households of male and female respondents. Comparisons of household characteristics are made among women who are full-time homemakers (married, not employed), single (unmarried, employed or unemployed), and labor market participants (employed, married or single). Although not mutually exclusive categories, these comparisons among households show the socioeconomic characteristics accompanying varying labor market and family responsibilities for these women.[3]

TABLE 1
Respondents' Characteristics by Gender and Women's Marital and Employment Status

	MEN	WOMEN			
	All	All	Single	Married, Not Employed	Employed
Income (% each category)*					
$1-$14,000	20	45	76	34	38
$14,001-$28,000	44	27	17	36	29
$28,001+	36	27	6	30	33
	(52)	(117)	(45)	(50)	(45)
Family Composition					
% Not married	40	37	–	–	49
	(55)	(122)	–	–	(47)
% With children less than 18 years old in household	25	58	33	79	36
	(55)	(122)	(45)	(53)	(47)
% Parents	60	78	56	94	57
	(55)	(122)	(45)	(53)	(47)
Mean number of people in household	2.73	3.25	2.11	4.11	2.53
SD	1.47	1.99	1.72	2.30	1.50
	(55)	(122)	(45)	(53)	(47)
Housing and Locational Characteristics					
% Owners	55	54	20	70	55
	(55)	(122)	(45)	(53)	(47)
% Residing in Single Family Neighborhoods	31	31	7	42	32
	(55)	(122)	(45)	(53)	(47)
% City Residents	49	49	78	38	45
	(55)	(122)	(45)	(53)	(47)
% Using automobiles for transportation to work	68	–	57	–	64
	(34)	–	(23)	–	(47)
Mean number of cars in household	1.57	1.44	.64	1.81	1.43
SD	.84	1.08	.68	1.14	.79
	(53)	(113)	(36)	(53)	(44)

NOTE: Ns are in parentheses.
*Percentage totals may not equal 100% due to rounding.

In the aggregate, women's household characteristics appear similar to men's. Although women's households tended to be poorer, larger, and to have more children than men's households, proportionately as many women were married, homeowners, suburbanites, and owned at least one car.

Differences among men and women are revealed more sharply by disaggregating women by their employment and marital status. Households of single women tended to be poorer than other households; over 75% of these women earned less than $14,000 annually. More single women rented housing in the central city and relied on public transportation than did other women. Many did not own a car. Although one-third of these single women lived alone, another third had young children at home.

The households of married, full-time homemakers tended to be larger than other households. Most of these women had dependent children at home and the majority lived in their own suburban single-family home. Employed women, representing both married and single women, were neither simply renters nor homeowners. Like men, employed women lived in either the suburbs or the central city.

These differences in the socioeconomic, family, and housing characteristics of sample respondents mirror the diversity and flux in women's roles, responsibilities, and locations. Many of these single women raised children on low incomes in the central city. Half of the employed women had husbands and were parents. The large suburban households of the full-time homemakers reflect the characteristics of the more traditional American nuclear family. The remainder of this article examines how these differences may influence the way people evaluate the desirability of neighborhoods.

FINDINGS AND DISCUSSION

To examine differences in respondents' perceptions of neighborhoods, the model employed in this research expresses each stratum's ratings of the desirability of neighborhood situations as a function of the characteristics describing each situation. Ordinary least squares were employed using the following model:

$$D_i = b_o + b_i N_{il} + \ldots b_k N_{ik} + e_i$$

D_i = the neighborhood desirability rating given to vignette i;
N_{ik} = the neighborhood characteristic contained in vignette i for every k respondent;
e_i = random error.

Each vignette characteristic is expressed in binary form. Within each dimension of attributes (e.g., travel time to work), one variable is omitted to avoid linear dependence. Separate equations were estimated for each stratum. The value of each coefficient, therefore, is the weight placed by respondent types (e.g., single women versus men) on the desirability of each neighborhood characteristic compared to the omitted characteristic within each dimension.

GENDER- AND WORK-BASED DIFFERENCES IN NEIGHBORHOOD DESIRABILITY

Do women desire public transportation more than men? Are men more concerned with neighborhood status? Do women with labor market responsibilities place more value on living closer to work than men and housewives? Or do employed women's preferences converge with those of men? Are housewives more concerned about neighborhood amenities for their children? Do single women want to live in the central city? Table 2 addresses these issues.

Table 2 presents five equations that model the effects of neighborhood characteristics on perceptions of neighborhood desirability. The first equation shows the values placed by men on neighborhood characteristics. The second equation shows the values placed by all women on neighborhood characteristics. The remaining equations show the values placed by single women, married unemployed women, and employed women on these same characteristics. At the bottom of each equation is the mean desirability rating of neighborhood vignettes for each stratum along with the associated standard deviations.

A central city location is argued to be more desirable for women, particularly for women who are in the wage labor market (Michelson, 1977; Freeman, 1981; Saegert, 1981). These women, however, were indifferent to the location of vignette neighborhoods. Neither housewives, nor employed, nor single women, nor men desired an urban or suburban location over a rural area ($p > .05$).

Rather than expressing desires or antipathies for location, each stratum paid close attention to particular neighborhood characteristics that might describe the specific features of a central city or suburban neighborhood. Both men and women desired to live close to work, within no more than 30 minutes travel time. Employed women placed most importance on local workplace accessibility and rated neighborhoods 1.58 points higher if they were less than 10 minutes from employment. Housewives without employment responsibilities placed little emphasis on travel time to work.

Although single women cared less than employed women about workplace accessibility, they rated the availability of public transpor-

(text continues on page 78)

TABLE 2
Respondent's Evaluation of Neighborhoods (Dependent = Neighborhood Desirability Ranking)

	MEN	WOMEN All	WOMEN Single	WOMEN Married, Not Employed	WOMEN Employed
Location[2]					
Central Part of City	-.40	-.21	.35	-.43	-.44
	(.24)	(.16)	(.28)	(.25)	(.26)
Outlying Part of City	.10	.17	.21	.17	-.03
	(.24)	(.16)	(.28)	(.23)	(.26)
Small Town	-.06	.07	.15	-.04	.08
	(.24)	(.16)	(.27)	(.24)	(.26)
Suburb	.08	.12	.21	-.30	.32
	(.23)	(.16)	(.28)	(.23)	(.26)
Distance to Work[3]					
10 Minutes from Work	.55*	.60*	.92*	-.07	1.53*
	(.23)	(.16)	(.28)	(.24)	(.26)
20 Minutes from Work	.35	.64*	.35	.52*	1.22*
	(.23)	(.16)	(.27)	(.24)	(.25)
30 Minutes from Work	.46*	.57*	.57*	.17	1.38*
	(.23)	(.15)	(.27)	(.23)	(.25)
45 Minutes from Work	.09	.09	.24	-.13	.44
	(.23)	(.16)	(.27)	(.24)	(.26)
Public Transportation[4]					
No Public Transportation	-.17	-.76*	-1.07*	-.70*	-.52*
	(.18)	(.12)	(.22)	(.19)	(.20)
Some Public Transportation	-.10	-.26*	-.48*	-.41*	.07
	(.18)	(.12)	(.22)	(.18)	(.20)
Neighborhood Amenities[5]					
Close to a School	.51	.50	-.71	.78	1.14*
	(.43)	(.30)	(.52)	(.45)	(.51)
In an Area with no Schools	.25	-.38	-1.13*	-.06	-.32
	(.44)	(.29)	(.55)	(.41)	(.52)
Close to Worship Place	.68	.32	.03	.57	.60
	(.42)	(.28)	(.48)	(.43)	(.46)
No Places of Worship	-.04	-.47	-1.00*	-.17	-.04
	(.45)	(.29)	(.49)	(.44)	(.48)
Near a Park	.77	.56*	.32	.88*	.68
	(.43)	(.28)	(.49)	(.42)	(.47)
In an Area with No Parks	.19	-.28	-.78	-.03	-.04
	(.45)	(.30)	(.51)	(.43)	(.50)
Near a Day-Care Center	.46	.35	.10	.62	.33
	(.44)	(.30)	(.54)	(.44)	(.51)
No Day-Care Centers	.83*	.05	.14	.20	.17
	(.41)	(.28)	(.51)	(.44)	(.46)
Close to Shopping	.65	.50	.06	.53	1.00*
	(.43)	(.28)	(.49)	(.42)	(.46)
Not near Shopping	-.15	-.23	-.37	-.26	.59
	(.44)	(.29)	(.49)	(.44)	(.47)

TABLE 2 (Continued)

	MEN	WOMEN All	WOMEN Single	WOMEN Married, Not Employed	WOMEN Employed
Close to Parents' Home	.74 (.44)	.76* (.29)	.60 (.52)	1.07* (.45)	.52 (.50)
Far From Parents' Home	.17 (.43)	.20 (.28)	-.34 (.47)	.42 (.43)	.86 (.48)
Near where Friends Live	1.03* (.46)	.61* (.30)	1.05* (.52)	.21 (.43)	1.32* (.51)
Far from Friends	.02 (.44)	-.35 (.28)	-.57 (.49)	-.06 (.42)	-.45 (.48)
Can Walk to Sibling	-.02 (.44)	.27 (.29)	-.06 (.49)	.42 (.44)	.63 (.46)
Near Closest Relatives	.95* (.45)	.88* (.29)	.95 (.52)	.64 (.42)	1.61* (.47)
Racial Composition[6]					
All White	-.11 (.36)	-.10 (.26)	-.29 (.46)	.19 (.40)	-.28 (.43)
All Black	-2.15* (.37)	-1.97* (.28)	-2.43* (.50)	-1.60* (.40)	-1.90* (.47)
Mostly White	.56 (.39)	.36 (.27)	-.02 (.47)	.80* (.39)	.18 (.47)
Mostly Black	-1.30* (.40)	-1.87* (.28)	-2.25* (.46)	-1.62* (.43)	-2.01* (.45)
Half Black	-.85* (.38)	-1.19* (.28)	-1.65* (.51)	-.85* (.40)	-1.03* (.48)
Half White	-.25 (.40)	-.34 (.28)	-.59 (.49)	.20 (.40)	-.80 (.47)
One-fourth Black	-.42 (.39)	-.92* (.26)	-1.66* (.45)	.07 (.38)	-1.52* (.43)
One-fourth White	-.63 (.40)	-.84* (.27)	-1.00* (.48)	-.27 (.39)	-.73 (.47)
A Few Whites	-.27 (.42)	-1.39* (.28)	-1.83* (.51)	-.90* (.39)	-1.30* (.48)
A Few Blacks	.25 (.38)	.05 (.27)	-.03 (.47)	.51 (.39)	.10 (.45)
Integrated Neighborhood	-.15 (.39)	-.49 (.27)	-1.04* (.46)	.03 (.41)	-.23 (.44)
One White Family	-1.37* (.39)	-1.50* (.27)	-1.79* (.48)	-1.00* (.39)	-1.37* (.47)
One Black Family	.47 (.39)	.15 (.27)	-.19 (.46)	.18 (.41)	.38 (.47)
Three White Families	-.49 (.39)	-1.23* (.26)	-2.03* (.44)	-.53 (.38)	-1.47* (.42)
Family Life Cycle Composition[7]					
Families with Children	-.01 (.30)	.49* (.22)	.31 (.38)	.76* (.34)	.21 (.34)
Mostly Single People	-.26 (.32)	.01 (.22)	.33 (.39)	-.23 (.34)	.24 (.36)

(continued)

TABLE 2 (Continued)

	MEN	WOMEN			
		All	Single	Married, Not Employed	Employed
Mixture of Families	.01 (.31)	.89* (.22)	.97* (.37)	.92* (.35)	.63 (.35)
Has Few Younger Children	-.21 (.31)	.25 (.22)	-.03 (.38)	.55 (.34)	.09 (.36)
Has Few Older Residents	-.31 (.32)	.33 (.21)	.24 (.37)	.69* (.33)	.15 (.34)
Mostly Young Couples	-.21 (.32)	.67* (.22)	.34 (.38)	1.03* (.34)	.22 (.36)
Mostly Teenage Children	-.17 (.32)	.24 (.22)	.12 (.38)	.50 (.35)	.12 (.35)
Retired Residents	-.10 (.32)	.15 (.22)	-.20 (.38)	.32 (.34)	-.18 (.35)
Neighborhood Average Income Compositions[8]					
$5,000	-2.41* (.28)	-1.10* (.20)	-.58 (.35)	-1.62* (.30)	-.84* (.32)
$10,000	-1.69* (.29)	-.35 (.20)	.34 (.36)	-.90* (.31)	.25 (.33)
$15,000	-1.11* (.28)	-.26 (.20)	-.25 (.34)	-.39 (.29)	-.32 (.32)
$20,000	-1.00* (.29)	-.17 (.20)	.03 (.35)	-.60* (.30)	.25 (.32)
$25,000	-.64* (.29)	-.06 (.20)	.22 (.36)	-.59 (.31)	.25 (.31)
$30,000	-.39 (.29)	.01 (.20)	.39 (.38)	-.35 (.30)	.22 (.33)
$35,000	-.29 (.28)	.07 (.20)	.56 (.35)	-.60* (.30)	.20 (.33)
Neighborhood Housing Composition[9]					
Single Family Homes	-.04 (.32)	-.39 (.22)	-.35 (.39)	-.43 (.32)	.08 (.36)
Mostly Apartments	-.40 (.33)	-.53* (.21)	-.41 (.37)	-.87* (.32)	-.10 (.35)
Single-Family Homes and Apartments	-.19 (.33)	.06 (.21)	-.16 (.36)	.39 (.33)	.04 (.35)
Townhouses (mostly) Apartments (a few)	-.29 (.33)	-.33 (.21)	-.33 (.37)	-.33 (.32)	-.31 (.36)
Townhouses (a few) and Apartments	-.11 (.31)	-.73* (.21)	-.69 (.36)	-.56 (.31)	-.55 (.35)
Single-Family Homes and Townhouses	.17 (.32)	-.05 (.21)	-.09 (.36)	.09 (.32)	.16 (.37)
Single-Family and Two-Family Homes	-.14 (.32)	-.22 (.21)	-.00 (.37)	-.13 (.31)	-.24 (.35)
Two-Family Homes and Apartments	-.23 (.32)	-.18 (.22)	.08 (.38)	-.12 (.32)	.13 (.37)
Non-Residential Characteristics[10]					
Has Many Small Businesses	.03 (.34)	-.06 (.23)	.65 (.42)	.26 (.36)	-.30 (.36)

TABLE 2 (Continued)

	MEN	WOMEN All	WOMEN Single	WOMEN Married, Not Employed	WOMEN Employed
Near an Industrial Park	-.23 (.35)	-.49* (.23)	-1.02* (.42)	-.24 (.37)	-.50 (.35)
Near a Small Factory	-.11 (.39)	.17 (.25)	.35 (.42)	-.02 (.39)	.21 (.39)
Near a Large Factory	-.66 (.34)	-.58* (.23)	-.95* (.37)	-.60 (.36)	-.56 (.37)
Near Heavy Industry	-.66 (.35)	-.86* (.25)	-1.27* (.42)	-.53 (.38)	-1.17* (.42)
Near an Office Complex	.66* (.33)	-.39 (.25)	-.36 (.50)	-.43 (.35)	-.54 (.42)
Home for Psychologically Disturbed	-.08 (.35)	-.46* (.23)	-.58 (.40)	-.24 (.32)	-.75* (.37)
Home for Mentally Retarded	-.00 (.35)	.47* (.23)	.40 (.42)	.39 (.35)	.48 (.40)
Home for Juvenile Delinquents	-.36 (.34)	-.84* (.22)	-.78 (.42)	-.79* (.32)	-.93* (.38)
Home for Released Prisoners	-.02 (.35)	-.51* (.24)	-.58 (.40)	-.60 (.36)	-.23 (.40)
Neighborhood Age[11]					
New Neighborhood	.03 (.15)	-.08 (.10)	-.22 (.17)	-.26 (.15)	.00 (.16)
Density[12]					
Densely Populated	-.24 (.15)	.02 (.10)	.11 (.18)	-.17 (.15)	.12 (.17)
C	5.53* (.59)	4.93* (.42)	5.72* (.72)	5.14* (.61)	3.65* (.70)
R^2 =	.22	.19	.26	.21	.25
N =	1100	2432	896	1057	939
Neighborhood Desirability Scale					
Mean Ranking	4.30	4.06	4.33	4.10	3.98
Standard Deviation	2.58	2.65	2.82	2.54	2.67

NOTE: Shown are the B coefficients and their associated standard errors in parentheses. Scale runs from 1 to 11, where 1 is totally undesirable and 11 is extremely desirable. Omitted variables are as follows: 2—Located in a rural area; 3—60 minutes from work; 4—Good public transportation; 5—Far from closest relative; 6—Three black families; 7—Single adults in their 20s and 30s; 8—Average income $40,000; 9—Townhouses and two-family homes; 10—Blank text; 11—Old neighborhood; 12—Sparsely populated.
*Significant at the .05 level.

tation higher than any other stratum. Neighborhoods without public transportation (compared to those with "good public transportation") lost over one point. Employed women and housewives expressed less concern with living near good public transit but did not desire neighborhoods without this service. Men expressed no desire for neighborhoods with any public transportation. Clearly, gender and accompanying home and work responsibilities influence these men and women's desires for traveling ease to and from their home.

Both men and women desired a close social network within their immediate environment. Yet the composition of these networks differed among men and women. Housewives desired their parents nearby, perhaps to help with the children. Single women and men both preferred to live near friends. Employed women desired the most complete, immediately available network; they desired both their friends and their closest relatives to live close to home.

One reportedly important neighborhood feature, day care, was ignored by women (Michelson, 1983). No female stratum desired to live close to a day care center. By contrast, men strongly desired not to live near day care facilities ($b = .83$). Perhaps men's antipathy to day care proximity reflects what one researcher suggests as an underlying desire by men to have women stay at home with the children (Saegert, 1981).

Nonetheless, housewives desired proximity to a park, probably for their children. Employed women, with many time constraints, emphasized the importance of living close to schools and shopping. Single women, many with dependent children, disliked neighborhoods far from schools or religious institutions. Men did not care about living near any of these facilities. Their homes' proximity to recreational, shopping, or religious facilities did not influence their rating of vignette neighborhoods' desirability.

A neighborhood's family composition was important to housewives; they strongly discriminated among what types of families were desirable neighbors. These women rated neighborhoods higher if they contained mostly young couples, a mixture of families, few older residents, or were dominated by families with children. These women preferred to live near some married neighbors who had or soon might have children; that is, neighbors like themselves. Single women preferred a more heterogeneous neighborhood and desired to live among a mixture of family types. Employed women evaluated local family composition like men; they were indifferent to the types of surrounding families.

Density is regarded as an important attribute for women, as higher land use densities reduce travel time and provide proximate services such as shopping and public transportation. However, neighborhood vignette descriptors are uncorrelated with one another, so that density per se is not associated with location, travel time to work, or proximity to shopping or public transportation. Although these women overall desired neighborhood characteristics empirically associated with higher land use densities, they did not wish to live in neighborhoods of higher densities. Generally, women desired not to live in neighborhoods containing mostly apartments and did not react to neighborhoods described as either sparsely or densely populated ($p > .05$). Women were attracted to the amenities that accompany density, but also desired the land use characteristics of more suburban areas. This was not true for men. Concerned with living close to work, men were indifferent to both local amenities and local residential land use.

Researchers suggest that women may find more opportunities living among a mixture of residential and nonresidential land uses (Markusen, 1981; Saegert, 1981; Hayden, 1984). Yet these women did not desire to live in neighborhoods among business and industry. Although they desired to be close to work, they did not want this work near their homes. These seemingly contradictory desires are allowed clear expression through the factorial survey technique; women may want quiet, clean, and unpolluted neighborhoods for themselves and their families (as in suburbs) but also want workplace proximity and services (as in cities). Men expressed no concern with the closeness of industry or small business, although they preferred to be close to an office complex.

Indifferent to a neighborhood's physical or familial character, men were most concerned about the neighborhood's socioeconomic composition. Compared to women, men placed dramatic importance on the average income levels of neighborhood residents. Poor neighborhoods (incomes of $5,000) were rated approximately 2.4 points lower than wealthy neighborhoods (incomes of $40,000). For men, each additional $5,000 average income increment increased the neighborhood's desirability, but these men rated any neighborhood lower if its average income level was less than $30,000. Men's sensitivity to neighborhood income may reflect, in part, their concern with residence as an investment.

Women were far less attuned to neighborhood income levels. Unconcerned with neighborhood's socioeconomic status, single women were indifferent to local income levels. Almost equally undiscriminating, employed women did not want to live among very poor people (income = \$5,000), but did not distinguish among graduations in the income composition of neighborhood areas. More like men, housewives desired to live in middle-to high-income neighborhoods.

All of these white respondents, however, desired the dominance of their race in their neighborhoods and did not want to live among many blacks. Men and housewives appeared tolerant of racially mixed neighborhoods as long as whites constituted at least half of the area. Single and employed women expressed the strongest desires for racial homogeneity. These women rated neighborhoods with more than a few blacks about one point lower compared to white neighborhoods.

These different preferences for neighborhoods' socioeconomic and racial composition are important. Men and homemakers expressed more tolerance for the inclusion of some blacks in their neighborhood but also expressed more antipathy for living among lower-income people. These two strata were less concerned with what race they lived among as long as that race was of a particular income level. For men and for the full-time housewives of men, class more than race distinguished a good neighborhood from a bad neighborhood. For single and employed women, class was not a major criterion to discriminate among neighborhoods. For these women, neighborhoods containing some blacks were far less desirable regardless of these black households' incomes.

These neighborhood vignettes did not contain descriptors that directly characterized the level of safety or crime within a neighborhood. Respondents' dislike of group homes in their neighborhood may serve as an indicator of these concerns because, in the public's mind, a group home's proximity has been associated with crime increases within local areas (Witkin, 1981). Overall, each group of women desired not to live near group homes for either juvenile delinquents, released prisoners, or the psychologically disturbed. Nonetheless, women rated neighborhoods containing group homes for the mentally retarded higher than neighborhoods without these institutions. Women were concerned with the location of potential law breakers within their neighborhoods. They were not opposed to living among the physically debilitated as represented by mentally retarded people. Apparently, women reacted to the types of people in group homes rather than group homes per se in their evaluations of neighborhoods. Men, seemingly unconcerned with safety or crime, did not rank neighborhoods either higher or lower if they contained group home facilities.

These findings show those neighborhood characteristics that dominated men's and women's judgments of neighborhood desirability. As important as those characteristics emphasized by each stratum are those that each group ignored. Men evaluated neighborhoods by their income and racial composition and by their proximity to work. Men did not pay attention to neighborhoods' land use or family composition and were unconcerned with public transportation availability. Neighborhood status and travel to and from their homes dominated men's judgments; men cared little about amenities that affect daily life within these areas. Men's desires suit them well for the typical middle-class suburb.

Housewives' desires for neighborhood status mirrored men's desires. Yet housewives' judgment processes included more than merely prestige; they desired facilities and playmates for their children in a low-density environment with good public transportation. Housewives desired citified suburbs, neighborhoods with the benefits of the city without city density or troubles.

Single women's evaluations were antithetical to men's and housewive's evaluations. They desired diversity in family composition but vehemently rejected living among black families. Unconcerned with socioeconomic status or density, single women desired nearby public transportation and institutional facilities. Single women's desires reflect preferences for city neighborhoods without black neighbors.

Employed women's concerns with getting quickly from home to work dominated their neighborhood evaluations. Class and housing composition were unimportant for these women. They desired primarily white residential areas but were not concerned with density, the availability of public transportation, or surrounding families. Employed women's preferences, like single women, fit central city neighborhoods, although employed women might also like suburbs that are proximate to where they work.

Zero-order correlations between the pairs of regression coefficients associated with each neighborhood characteristic for each stratum provide summary measures of the general similarities or differences in neighborhood evaluations between each group. The correlation between men's and housewives' preferences ($r = .74$) shows that the pattern of male preferences was most similar to housewive's preferences. Men's preference patterns differed more from employed women ($r = .64$) and most from single women ($r = .51$).

The high correlation between men's and housewives' preferences patterns suggest that full-time homemakers may more systematically exhibit the desires of their husbands. Conversely, employed and single women's deviations from men's patterns show that labor market participation and head-of-household status do not produce convergence in men's and women's locational preferences but produce more divergence from male patterns. Women and men agree most about what constitutes desirable or undesirable neighborhoods when women do not have labor market responsibilities and when their primary work is to care for their homes, their children, and their husbands.

CONCLUSION AND IMPLICATIONS

The men and women in this study evaluated neighborhood characteristics easily discerned individually within real-world metropolitan areas but rarely found together. Unlike investigations of actual locational decisions, the factorial survey technique allows respondents to express empirically contradictory desires and to design their ideal neighborhood without real-world constraints. In the vignette world respondents could ignore neighborhood status and focus on the things they need, such as public transportation, work place accessibility, family compatibility, and safety. They could desire white neighborhoods and still desire central city amenities. They could prefer suburban-like densities and still want urban public services and diversity. Hence, from this study we can begin to assess the dimensions of neighborhoods that women desire to bring together, to build new neighborhoods not for men, not for children, but for everyone.

The real-world, high-status, homogeneous suburb, devoid of public facilities, fits the wishes of men with wives who stay at home and take care of their families. But suburbs cannot easily house women with changing responsibilities or enable change in men's responsibilities and activities. Suburbs are safe, quiet, and socially comfortable—characteristics desired by some women. Yet they are not easily traversed and impede women who wish or need to work. To be manageable locations for women, suburbs require proximate public services and employment like cities, but for women suburbs cannot become cities. Women with families desire residential spaces near friends, neighbors, and relatives. For women suburbs need to encourage density that fiscally supports public services and attracts business, but does not allow overt intrusions on residential spaces.

To raise their families, yet keep a job, women require that urban amenities be brought to the suburb. Careful relaxation of zoning restrictions, attention to public transportation, business incentives, and public mandates that make a local priority of planning for women as well as "families" can begin to create suburbs that permit more flexible workroles but do not deny family responsibilities and spatial desires. Seemingly contradictory desires can be planned and developed within suburbs if local governments and residents choose to encourage these changes.

The density, diversity, and accessibility provided by real-world central city neighborhoods also may provide poor spaces for women. Cities are not the "natural" location for women if women must fear for the safety of their children and themselves. City neighborhoods may provide many of the physical supports desired by women within the labor market and by single-parent women, but they may not provide the seclusion, safety, and community desired by women for their families. As suburbs should allow more urbanization within their political boundaries, cities should focus more on creating safe residential neighborhoods, like suburbs.

To be sure, central city areas attract more problems than suburbs because of the same amenities that attract single women to these areas: transportation, housing, and employment. Cities incur more burdens than suburbs because urban amenities facilitate the lives of so many kinds of people. But cities, like suburbs, make development choices. Cities compete for the location of business and industry and provide massive public support for maintaining downtown infrastructure and for redeveloping business districts. Similar intensities of energy, money, and imagination need to be redirected to create and maintain residential spaces for families, not simply upwardly mobile young couples or those who are wealthy. To make women's needs an urban priority, cities need to think about creating safe residential environments as much as suburbs need to work on attracting density and diversity.

Yet obstacles to change exist among women. The intense racism found in this study by all women and expressed most strongly by single and employed women suggests that white women may choose to support neighborhood designs and densities that exclude racial minorities (e.g., the current suburb). They may work harder at keeping minorities out of their central city neighborhoods than at including the requisite physical and social amenities that will help them. In short, white women may choose racial segregation over those community and housing needs that allow women more freedom to travel, to work, and to raise children.

Currently, metropolitan areas provide best those suburban neighborhoods that create the highest satisfaction for a minority of households—those of men with wives at home. Women are faced with competing desires for neighborhoods, wanting packages of neighborhood amenities that often do not coexist in the same spatial areas. But before new neighborhoods can be built to create satisfaction for everyone, women's desires for white racial dominance must be tackled. Further research needs to address the roots and remedies of racism among white working women with nontraditional households.

NOTES

1. Research shows that women's work trips are shorter than men's by time and distance. The explanation for gender commuting differences is unclear. Research has not yet untangled the relationships among residential locational decisions, work locational decisions, and the value of commuting time, especially for women with both home and labor force responsibilities (Madden and White, 1980).

2. The sampling strategy deliberately selected census tracts containing only white residents. Blacks were excluded from the sample to eliminate race as a competing factor with income, housing, family type, and gender in explaining residential evaluations, given the small size of the total sample.

3. Sample size limitations do not permit analyses that compare women by employment status independent of marital status or family responsibilities. Differences in characteristics among women varying in employment status regardless of marital status or among women varying in marital status regardless of employment status should be viewed as suggestive of the influences of these roles and responsibilities. Future research should provide more detailed analyses of the effects of women's family and employment responsibilities on local needs and desires.

REFERENCES

CICHOCKI, M. K. (1980) "Women's travel patterns in a suburban development," pp. 151-163 in G. R. Wekerle et al. (eds.) New Space for Women. Boulder, CO: Westview.

FAVA, S. (1980) "Women's place in the new suburbia," pp. 129-149 in G. R. Wekerle et al. (eds.) New Space for Women. Boulder, CO: Westview.

FREEMAN, J. (1981) "Women and urban policy," pp. 1-19 in C. R. Stimpson et al. (eds.) Women and the American City. Chicago: Univ. of Chicago Press.

HAYDEN, D. (1984) Redesigning the American Dream: The Nature of Housing, Work, and Family Life. New York: Norton.

———(1981) The Grand Domestic Revolution: A History of Feminist Designs for American Homes, Neighborhoods, and Cities. Cambridge, MA: MIT Press.

———(1980) "Redesigning the domestic workplace," pp. 101-121 in G. R. Wekerle et al. (eds.) New Space for Women. Boulder, CO: Westview.

———(1979) "Charlotte Perkins Gilman and the kitchenless house." Radical History Rev. 21 (Fall): 225-247.

LOPATA, H. Z. (1981) "The Chicago woman: a study of patterns of mobility and transportation," pp. 158-166 in C. R. Stimpson et al. (eds.) Women and the American City. Chicago: Univ. of Chicago Press.

MADDEN, J. F. (1981) "Why women work closer to home." Urban Studies 18 (June): 181-194.

———and M. J. WHITE (1980) "Spatial implications of increases in the female labor force: a theoretical and empirical synthesis." Land Economics 56 (November): 432-446.

MARKUSEN, A. R. (1981) "City spatial structure, women's household work and national urban policy," pp. 20-41 in C. R. Stimpson et al. (eds.) Women and the American City. Chicago: Univ. of Chicago Press.

MICHELSON, W. (1983) "Maternal employment, community context and pressures: the case of child care." Presented at the annual meeting of the Society for the Study of Social Problems, Detroit, August.

———(1977) Environmental Choice, Human Behavior, and Residential Satisfaction. New York: Oxford Univ. Press.

ROSENBLOOM, S. (1978) Women's Travel Issues: Research Needs and Priorities. Washington, DC: Department of Transportation, Research and Special Programs Administration.

ROSSI, P. H. and S. L. NOCK (1982) Measuring Social Judgments: The Factorial Survey Approach. Beverly Hills, CA: Sage.

SAEGERT, S. (1981) "Masculine cities and feminine suburbs: polarized ideas, contradictory reality," pp. 93-108 in C. R. Stimpson et al. (eds.) Women and the American City. Chicago: Univ. of Chicago Press.

———and G. WINKEL (1980) "The home: a critical problem for changing sex roles," pp. 41-63 in G. R. Wekerle et al. (eds.) New Space for Women. Boulder, CO: Westview.

STIMPSON, C. R., E. DIXLER, J. NELSON, and K. B. YATRAKIS (1981) Women and the American City. Chicago: Univ. of Chicago Press.

WEKERLE, G. R., R. PETERSON, and D. MORLEY (1980) New Space for Women. Boulder, CO: Westview.

WHITE, M. J. (1977) "A model of residential location choice and commuting by men and women workers." J. of Regional Sci. 17 (April): 41-52.

WITKIN, G. (1981) "But not in my neighborhood." Planning 47 (May): 23-26.

Ann Shlay is Assistant Professor of Consumer Economics and Housing in the College of Human Ecology at Cornell University. She currently is researching credit flows within metropolitan areas from 1980 to 1983 with the Woodstock

Institute, and is completing a study of growth coalitions promoting Chicago's 1992 World's Fair. She recently has published in the Journal of Urban Affairs.

Denise A. DiGregorio is a Ph.D. candidate in the Department of Sociology at Cornell University. She is studying the outcomes of social movements by examining the ratification process of the Equal Rights Amendment.

The mid-1970s was a period of rapid expansion in intergovernmental aid. With this expansion, two major issues emerged. One concerned targeting—the extent to which these new monies went to communities with the most need. A second issue focused on the growing fiscal dependency of local governments on higher levels of government. In this article we investigate the distribution of intergovernmental aid across suburbs in the mid-1970s and identify types of suburbs that came to rely increasingly on transfer funds. The research shows that higher-income suburbs significantly increased the absolute levels of aid they received, but their reliance on aid did not increase dramatically. In contrast, suburban municipalities housing the growing number of black and low-income suburbanites became the most fiscally dependent during this time period. The implications of the growing fiscal dependency of large numbers of disadvantaged suburbs for the implementation of the New Federalism are discussed.

SUBURBAN MUNICIPALITIES The Changing System of Intergovernmental Relations in the Mid-1970s

MARK SCHNEIDER
State University of New York at Stony Brook
JOHN LOGAN
State University of New York at Albany

The system of fiscal federalism built on intergovernmental transfer payments was marked by rapid expansion during the early and mid-1970s. The early 1970s saw a spurt in the growth of direct federal transfer payments to local governments. By fiscal year 1973, federal transfers in constant dollars increased by almost one-third over the fiscal year 1971 level. Additional federal monies found their way to local governments through "pass along" provisions of federal aid to state governments. After slowing considerably in 1974 and 1975, federal aid increased again in 1976 and 1977. Many states also enacted their own programs increasing transfer payments to local governments (see, for example, ACIR, 1980, 1982; Wright, 1982; Bowman 1981; Puryear and Ross, 1978).

URBAN AFFAIRS QUARTERLY, Vol. 21 No. 1, September 1985 87-105

Expanded intergovernmental aid raised several major policy issues. Two were especially important. First, there was debate over the degree to which increased intergovernmental aid was targeted to local governments with the most need. In 1972, under heavy pressure from an urban coalition, Democrats in control of Congress rewrote general revenue sharing from the program of state aid proposed by the Nixon administration to a program of aid to virtually all general purpose local governments. In 1974, the suburban part of that urban coalition showed its power by radically expanding the Community Development Act to include suburban government participation in federal programs that had been overwhelmingly oriented to the central city. One effect of these political decisions was to spread the benefits of intergovernmental aid to more and more communities, especially middle- and upper-income communities, which previously had not received federal aid (Nathan et al., 1975; Nathan, 1978; Conlan, 1981; Barfield, 1982; NAHRO, 1977). The failure of many new intergovernmental aid programs to target directly on low-income communities was one issue of the changing intergovernmental system.

A second issue concerned the effects of increased aid on the capacity of local governments to manage their own affairs. Analysts noted that local governments were becoming increasingly dependent fiscally on monies from higher levels of government to balance their books and to fund their services. The debate over fiscal dependency expanded to encompass a growing concern for "policy dependency"—the argument that local governments were losing the ability to control their own policy decision processes (Lovell, 1981).

The issue of fiscal dependency became dramatically more concrete after 1977, when the federal government and many state governments began to impose severe cutbacks in intergovernmental aid. Several factors produced such reductions. Most visible was a growing fiscal conservatism especially evident at the state level (Danziger and Ring, 1982; Pascal et al., 1979). In 1978 alone as many as 44 separate tax and expenditure limitation proposals were considered in 27 different states (Eribes and Hall, 1981). When coupled with continuing "stagflation" in the economy, the new fiscal conservatism succeeded in slowing and even reversing the growth in transfer payments. Transfer payments from the national to subnational governments declined in 1979, showed no growth in 1980, and are scheduled to be cut substantially through the 1980s. Such gyrations produced substantial management problems for local governments (see, e.g., Levine and Rubin, 1980; Behn, 1982). Although most investigations of the consequences of changes in intergovernmental aid focus on central cities, suburbs also were affected by the fiscal federalism of the 1970s. In this article we examine the distribution of growing intergovernmental aid between 1972 and 1977 across a large sample of suburbs classified by race and income and then investigate some implications of the growing fiscal dependency of specific types of suburbs.

SUBURBAN DIVERSITY

Research on the problems of suburban government has been neglected in part because of the stereotypical image of suburbia as affluent and crisis-free. But this image is substantially outdated. Fiscal disparities between suburbs exist, and many suburban municipalities face disproportionately high service demands in relation to their resources and are thus highly vulnerable to fiscal strain (see Schneider and Logan, 1981, 1982; Hill, 1974; Branfman et al., 1974).

Two demographic trends have reinforced the emerging fiscal disparities between suburban communities. First, increasing numbers of blacks now reside in suburbia. But because of discrimination and unequal economic resources, blacks are steered mostly into the worse-off suburban communities. Frequently these are inner suburbs being abandoned by whites, or they may be suburbs that have traditionally been defined as minority communities. In either case, black suburbs often resemble central cities in their low socioeconomic status, high density, aging housing stock, and high service needs combined with a weak local fiscal base (Farley, 1970; Connolly, 1973; Guest, 1978). In the early 1970s, black suburbs managed their fiscal situation through high dependency on intergovernmental transfers, high debt, and high taxes (Schneider and Logan, 1982; Rose, 1976). How did the system of increased transfer payments affect the fiscal situation and service levels of black suburbs between 1972 and 1977?

Paralleling the increasing suburbanization of blacks, suburbs now house a wider range of income groups. Social classes are also highly segregated across suburbs. Motivated in part by the desire to avoid the fiscal drag that lower-income families represent, suburbs have incentives to engage in exclusionary growth policies. Such strategies have a direct impact on government finances in those suburbs in which the poor are concentrated, creating a system of government that Hill describes as "separate and unequal" (Hill, 1974; also see Branfman et al., 1974; Danielson, 1976). The most recent evidence from California suggests that in times of fiscal hardships, exclusionary growth policies also will increase (Dowall, n.d.; Chapman and Kirlin, 1979).

Suburbs with a large low-income population in the early 1970s had high service and expenditures, especially for social services such as housing and hospitals. These costs were paid through reliance on transfer payments and high levels of debt (Schneider and Logan, 1981). In these respects their fiscal situation resembled that of black suburbs. Similar to our investigation of black suburbs, we examine how poor suburbs were affected by the rapidly changing system of intergovernmental aid of the mid-1970s.

SAMPLE AND DATA SOURCES

In this article we investigate changing suburban municipal service and revenues between 1972 and 1977, a period of rapidly expanding intergovernmental aid. Our sample consists of 577 suburban municipalities with a population greater than 10,000 in 1977, for which the Census of Governments published information on revenues and expenditures. These communities were drawn from 29 different SMSAs.[1] The SMSAs in our sample frame were among the 100 largest SMSAs in 1970, subject to the two following constraints: No more than 3 SMSAs were included in the sample from a single state; and there were at least 4 incorporated suburban municipalities in the region.

Data on intergovernmental revenues and expenditures come from the 1972 and 1977 Census of Governments. We also have used these data to construct measures of the mix of services local governments offer and their levels of functional responsibility (see Liebert, 1976, for a discussion of the importance of the concept "functional responsibility"). The "Common Index" measures the number of basic services communities offer from the following: police, fire, sanitation, parks, highways, general control, and general government. It has a possible range of 0 to 7. The "Social Index," with a range of 0 to 4, measures the number of social services (welfare, health and hospitals, education, and housing) to which the local government provides budgetary support. To measure the extent of these outlays we report the current per capita operating expenses of local governments for common and social services. Although expenditure data do not translate into measures of the quality of a service, they do provide us with information about the degree to which different types of services command scarce local budgetary resources.

Data on community taxes and tax base come from local sources, such as state comptrollers or state municipal finance divisions. To compensate for differences in assessment practices, nominal tax rates and assessed value have been corrected by equalization ratios used by states or counties. This provides estimates of true value and effective tax rate. All dollar figures reported for 1977 are adjusted for inflation between 1972 and 1977 (an increase of 44.8% in the Consumer Price Index). Most data are reported per capita. Given that population data are from the 1970 and 1980 Census of Population and that the Census of Government was conducted in 1972 and 1977, we have assumed a linear growth in population between 1970 and 1980 and estimated 1972 population as the 1970 community population plus 20% of the change in population between 1970 and 1980. The 1977 population is estimated in the same way but using a 70% increment.

We classify suburbs according to their racial and class composition at the opening of the period. In 1970, 466 suburbs (81%) in our sample were more than 95% white and are classified as "white suburbs." For want of a better term, the remaining suburbs we have called "black suburbs." We recognize that this may be a misnomer as the population of many of these communities in fact consists of a majority of whites. Yet most blacks living in suburbs live in these so-called black suburbs. Furthermore, compared to most suburbs that have no black population at all, the racial composition of black suburbs is clearly different from the majority of suburban communities.

Among black suburbs, we distinguish two further categories: "stable black" communities (n = 60), which are those that increased less than 5% in their black proportion during the 1960s, and "growing black" suburbs (n = 35), which experienced more rapid black population growth. Although these categories of "stable" and "growing" are based on the 1960-1970 period, differences between them remained consistent during the 1970s. For example, the average increase in the percentage of blacks in stable black suburbs was 13% between 1970 and 1980, whereas the increase for growing black communities was 61%. It should be noted that 16 suburbs fail to fall into any of these three racial categories. These communities had declining black population concentrations. However, because of their small number and lack of similarity in other community characteristics, we have dropped them from this part of the analysis.

We also have classified suburbs according to their income composition in 1970 as measured by the U.S. Bureau of the Census. We first divided the suburban population of each SMSA into six roughly equal income groups, ranging from the poor (families with incomes less than $6,000 annually), to four categories of middle income, to the affluent (families with incomes greater than $25,000). Using a measure called the Location Quotient (LQ), we compared the actual distribution of income groups in each suburb with what could have been expected by chance (Berry and Horton, 1970; Schneider and Logan, 1981). Suburbs with an overly large concentration of low-income families (an LQ for the lowest income category greater than 2.0) are classified as "poor suburbs." We have identified 53 poor suburbs in our sample. Suburbs with a disproportionate concentration of high-income families are classified as "affluent suburbs." There were 58 such communities in our sample. The remaining suburbs are classified as "middle"—a residual category of suburbs with a wide range of income levels represented.

We present the changing distribution of service expenditures and intergovernmental revenues across these types of suburbs during the period 1972-1977. Although we have a national sample of suburban municipalities, we recognize that there are major differences in regional patterns of functional responsibility, levels of expenditures, taxes, and growth. For example, it is well known that in the Northeast local governments have responsibility for a more extensive range of services than suburban municipalities in the Sunbelt. Patterns of intergovernmental aid also vary significantly between regions (see, for example, Schneider, 1980). In the first stage of this investigation we employ a two-way analysis of variance design in which both community type and SMSA location are entered into our analysis. This technique controls for differences in regional patterns of government finance and services as they are found in each SMSA.

Given this background, we now inspect the experiences of different types of suburbs between 1972 and 1977 and how they were affected by growing intergovernmental aid.

FISCAL IMPLICATIONS FOR POOR SUBURBS

Table 1 reports the changing fiscal and service patterns for suburbs classified along income lines. In the mid-1970s poor suburbs received

TABLE 1
Changing Fiscal Situations of Suburbs, 1972-1977

	Poor Suburbs (N = 53)	Middle Suburbs (N = 466)	Affluent Suburbs (N = 58)	Significance (F-Test)
Transfer Payments[a]				
1972	$46	$26	$26	.001
1977	62	45	31	.006
Transfer Percent				
1972	21%	19%	16%	.001
1977	33	25	19	.005
True Value (in thousands)				
1972	$7.3	$8.4	$11.7	.001
1977	7.8	9.7	12.7	.001
Tax Rate (per $100 of true value)				
1972	$1.20	$1.02	$ 1.19	.004
1977	1.19	.90	1.02	.001
Debt				
1972	$167	$177	$126	.05
1977	176	160	92	.05
Total Expenditures				
1972	$197	$155	$175	n.s.*
1977	195	160	172	.05
Operating Expenditures				
7 Common Functions[b]				
1972	$97	$76	$100	.001
1977	97	90	105	.001
4 Social Functions[c]				
1972	$24	$10	$ 6	.05
1977	27	14	14	n.s.
Functional Responsibility[d]				
7 Common Functions				
1972	6.7	6.6	6.8	.02
1977	6.8	6.6	6.5	n.s.
4 Social Functions				
1972	.60	.29	.21	.001
1977	1.52	1.08	.95	.001

SOURCES: U.S. Bureau of the Census (1972, 1977); rate reports from state tax commissions, state and county boards of equalization, and assessors offices.

*Not significant at the .05 level.

a. All per capita figures use estimates of 1972 or 1977 population. All 1977 dollar figures are adjusted for change in the CPI between 1972 and 1977.

b. Common functions include highways, police, fire, parks and recreation, sanitation, general control, general government, services provided by over 80% of communities in our sample.

c. Noncommon social functions include education, welfare, hospitals, and housing.

d. The indices of functional responsibility are the number of functions on which a community spends money, regardless of the level of funding The index of common functions has a range of 0 to 7; the social index has a range of 0 to 4.

the highest absolute levels of transfer payments and were the most reliant on intergovernmental transfers. Transfer payments increased from 21% to 33% of total revenues—the most rapid growth in dependency on outside funding. However, the absolute dollar amounts of intergovernmental aid increased faster in middle-income suburbs, indicating the dilution of intergovernmental aid brought about by the policy changes of the New Federalism.

In order to better evaluate the dependence of communities on aid, we must take into account other characteristics of local budgets. We have already noted that poor suburbs were most reliant on aid. Poor suburbs also had relatively high expenditure levels. In this measure they were similar to the most affluent suburbs (for similar evidence on the "U-shaped" distribution of expenditures, see Levy et al., 1974; Sanger, 1981). But affluent suburbs supported their high service levels mostly from a strong local property tax base. They also spent proportionately less of their funds for social services and more on the common functions of government. Poor suburbs, by contrast, maintained their higher expenditures by heavily taxing their weak local fiscal base. In contrast to declining effective tax rates in other suburbs, tax rates in poor suburbs remained high. Finally, note that only poor suburbs experienced an actual increase in debt measured in constant dollars. For low-income suburbs, reliance on outside funding is a part of a clear pattern of fiscal weakness.

Between 1972 and 1977, middle-class suburbs reduced both tax rates and debt levels. Yet at the same time they were able to substantially reduce their expenditure gap with other types of suburbs. Growing participation in intergovernmental transfers made possible this neat fiscal trick. In constant dollars, transfer payments to middle-income suburbs grew by 73% compared to 35% for poor suburbs and only 19% for affluent suburbs. Thus, middle-class suburbs benefited substantially from revenue sharing and other aid programs.

FISCAL IMPLICATIONS FOR BLACK SUBURBS

Table 2 reports the changing fiscal and service pattern between 1972 and 1977 of suburbs categorized by racial composition. Similar to poor suburbs, black suburbs received relatively high absolute amounts of external assistance during the 1970s. Black suburbs also dramatically increased their reliance on aid from other governments during the

TABLE 2
Changing Fiscal Situations of White and Black Suburbs, 1972-1977

	White Suburbs (N = 466)	Stable Black Suburbs (N = 60)	Growing Black Suburbs (N = 35)	Significance (F-Test)
Transfer Payments				
1972	$26	$39	$53	.001
1977	41	66	84	.001
Transfer Percent				
1972	19%	19%	23%	.04
1977	24	29	35	.001
True Value (in Thousands)				
1972	$8.7	$8.5	$7.7	n.s.*
1977	10.1	8.6	7.7	.01
Tax Rate (per $100 of true value)				
1972	$1.00	$1.25	$1.41	.001
1977	.88	1.18	1.37	.001
Debt				
1972	$165	$186	$209	n.s.
1977	143	206	189	.05
Total Expenditures				
1972	$150	$202	$234	n.s.
1977	152	218	230	.001
Operating Expenditures				
7 Common Functions				
1972	$75	$100	$108	.001
1977	88	115	101	.001
4 Social Functions				
1972	$ 7	$18	$ 51	n.s.
1977	10	33	46	.001
Functional Responsibility				
7 Common Functions				
1972	6.6	6.7	6.7	n.s.
1977	6.6	6.8	6.5	n.s.
4 Social Functions				
1972	.24	.53	.75	.001
1977	1.03	1.44	1.59	.001

SOURCES: U.S. Bureau of the Census (1972, 1977); rate reports from state tax commissions, state and county boards of equalization, and assessors offices.
NOTE: See notes for Table 1.

1972-1977 period. Among stable black suburbs, the percentage of their total revenues coming from transfer payments increased from 19 to 29% and for growing black suburbs from 23 to 35%. In contrast, white suburbs, although also increasing their reliance on transfers, moved up only from 19 to 24%. This pattern is duplicated in the per capita dollar figures for transfer revenues.

Substantial differences existed between black suburbs and white suburbs in the level of services provided and in their dependency on intergovernmental aid. In 1977, black suburbs had significantly higher expenditures than did white suburbs. Furthermore, the mix of services provided black suburbs is different than that provided white ones. Both stable black and growing black suburbs provided a greater number of social services than did white suburbs (the Social Index is significantly higher for black suburbs both in 1972 and 1977), and they spent more money on these services than did white suburbs. Adjusting for inflation, stable black suburbs increased their funding for social services at a faster rate than any other type of community.

Aside from intergovernmental aid, how did black suburbs support local services? Looking first at the local property tax base, we find that the adjusted per capita true value of property in black suburbs remained relatively stable, whereas the value of property in white suburbs increased by about 16%. As a result of their weak fiscal base, in both 1972 and 1977 black suburbs maintained consistently higher taxes than white suburbs.

In 1972, black suburbs had higher debt levels than white suburbs, although not significantly so. In constant dollars, white suburbs were able to reduce their debt levels by about 13% between 1972 and 1977. In contrast, growing black suburbs reduced their debt by only 10% and even more important, stable black suburbs had an increasing debt level, up about 11% in 5 years. By 1977, differences in debt levels were statistically significant.

In short, compared to suburbs that are predominantly white, suburbs housing the growing population of blacks are supporting significantly higher service levels, despite a poorer local tax base. In the process they became more heavily dependent on intergovernmental transfer payments.

MULTIVARIATE DYNAMIC ANALYSIS

The previous analysis documented basic patterns in the changing fiscal position and service levels of suburbs classified along race and class lines. However, the analysis of variance approach leaves several important questions unanswered. First, we find that both the racial and the income characteristics of suburbs affect the changing fiscal situation of suburbs. But we have not sorted out the independent effects of either demographic variable. Most notably, we know that black population concentration and low income levels in suburbs coincide, leading to possible redundancy in the above findings.

The relationships between racial composition and intergovernmental aid raises a particular problem. Many intergovernmental aid formulas are driven by income levels of communities, and racial characteristics do not explicitly enter into formula allocations. Thus, the relationship between racial composition and aid may be the result of the lower income level of black suburbs, not the result of any independent role of race.

It is also possible that other community characteristics, such as density or the employment base of suburbs, are systematically related to income and racial composition of suburbs and are affecting the relationships between demographic characteristics and the fiscal situation of suburbs. Guest (1978) and Schneider and Logan (1982) have shown systematic relationships between racial composition and community characteristics such as distance from central city, density, employment concentration, and community median income. Municipal budgets also are known to be affected by these characteristics (see, e.g., Logan and Schneider, 1981).

To estimate the independent effects of race and income and to measure change more directly, we use a multivariate lagged endogenous model. In this analysis the 1977 value of each dependent variable is modeled as a function of its previous value, measured in 1972. To control for SMSA effects, we used a set of dummy variables representing metropolitan regional location.

We include the following control variables in our regression models: (1) community population, 1970; (2) change in population, 1970-1980; (3) density (number of people per square mile); (4) distance of suburb from central city (measured as the linear distance in miles between the inner boundary of each suburb and its central city); and (5) employment ratio (the number of workers in a suburb divided by its total population—a variant of the more traditional employment/residents ratio).

In the previous analysis of variance design we employed categories of communities based on income and racial composition. The discontinuities in the relationship between income categories and the dependent variables suggest that the relationship between income and fiscal/service characteristics may not be linear. Similarly, observed differences between stable and growing black suburbs suggest that, in addition to the size of the resident black population, rates of change in black population may also affect the fiscal situation of suburbs. To measure possible nonlinearity in effects of the income variable, we include not only the median income of each community but also its squared value. To model the independent effect of changing black population composition, we include not only the percentage of the population of each community that is black in 1970 but also the rate of change in black population composition between 1970 and 1980. Results of these regressions are reported in Table 3.

FISCAL IMPLICATIONS FOR BLACK SUBURBS: A MULTIVARIATE ANALYSIS

First, Table 3 shows that black population composition of suburbs is significantly related both to intergovernmental transfer payments and to a higher reliance on such payments. Despite the lack of explicit recognition of black population in aid formulae, transfer payments per capita increased faster in suburbs with larger black populations than in suburbs with fewer blacks. These transfer payments also represented an increasingly large proportion of the revenues of black suburbs, indicating a growing fiscal dependency in the suburbs to which blacks have access.

Black population concentration also is related to other indicators of deteriorating fiscal condition in communities, even after controlling income levels. For example, larger community black population concentration is associated with more rapidly increasing debt and with more rapidly increasing property tax rates. Black population concentration also is associated with more rapid increases in total expenditures, and there is a strong effect of black population concentration on the index of social functions.

These findings confirm the results based on the analysis of variance reported earlier: There is a strong effect of suburban racial composition on local community treasuries—almost invariably in the direction of increasing fiscal problems.

TABLE 3

Changing Fiscal and Service Levels in Suburbs, 1972-1977

1977 Variable =	Constant +	1972 value (+ SMSA) +	Employment rate +	Population 1970 (in thousands) +	Population Δ 1970-1980 +	Density +	Distance +	Percent Black 1970 +	Percent Black 1970-1980 +	Median Income* 1970 +	Median Income* 1970 squared	R^2
Transfer payments = per capita	19.4	+0.645[a] (0.066)	+36.4 (6.69)	+0.158 (0.07)	-17.1 (4.4)	-0.0099 (0.004)		+132.3 (18.5)				51
Transfer percent =	0.42	+0.407 (0.033)	- 0.04 (0.01)		- 0.033 (0.009)			+ 0.129 (0.039)		-0.023 (0.01)	+0.004 (0.000)	65
True value = per capita (in thousands)	-1.14	+0.827 (0.02)	+ 1.46 (0.74)		- 2.80 (0.35)	-0.001 (0.0004)				+0.58 (0.20)	+0.01 (0.004)	87
Tax rate =	24.9	+0.389 (0.03)	-13.6 (6.45)			+0.02 (0.004)		+ 99.7 (18.0)				84
Debt =	66.1	+0.351 (0.04)	+101.1 (30.8)	+0.75 (0.33)	-51.6 (21.7)	-0.057 (0.022)		+252.8 (81.5)				33
Total expenditures = per capia	42.8	+0.538 (0.06)	+176.8 (24.3)		-53.4 (15.3)			+276.0 (64.2)		+6.42 (2.0)		41
Social Expenditures = per capita	-72.3	+1.17 (0.10)	+78.2 (17.8)							+4.14 (1.5)		33
Common Expenditures = per capita	15.7	+0.97 (0.06)	+100.5 (9.06)		-32.4 (5.19)			+ 66.9 (22.6)		+2.61 (0.69)		69
Social Index	0.48	+0.37 (0.07)	+ 0.007 (0.000)					+ 1.15 (0.37)				45
Common Index	4.4	+0.39 (0.05)	+ 0.003 (0.000)			+0.01 (0.004)						27

SOURCES: U.S. Bureau of the Census (1972, 1977); True value and tax rate reports from state tax commissions, state and county boards of equalization, and assessors offices.

NOTE: See notes for Table 1.

a. These are unstandardized regression coefficients. The numbers below are the standard errors of the estimates.

FISCAL IMPLICATIONS FOR POOR SUBURBS: MULTIVARIATE ANALYSIS

We find no relationship between income levels and changing levels of per capita aid; communities at all income levels participated in the expanding intergovernmental aid available in the mid-1970s. But Table 3 describes a curvilinear relationship between income and dependence on transfer payments: For communities at both ends of the income spectrum the percentage of local revenues coming from intergovernmental aid increased more rapidly than for communities in the middle of the income distribution.

The data in Table 3 also confirm the importance of personal income levels on the fiscal fortunes of suburban governments. The relationship between high income concentration and the strengthening of local community tax base is particularly important. Elsewhere we have shown that during the course of the 1960s, rich families concentrated disproportionately in communities with strong tax bases. This migration pattern had the effect of increasing the service and tax options available to upper-income suburbanites (Schneider and Logan, 1982). The data in Table 3 confirm the opposite side of that fiscal coin: In the mid-1970s wealthy suburbanites improved the local fiscal base of suburbs in which they concentrated, allowing them even further latitude in choosing service and tax levels.

DISCUSSION

These data show important patterns in fiscal federalism between 1972 and 1977. The most important empirical findings document the extent to which intergovernmental aid in the mid-1970s was not targeted on low-income suburbs. The clear winners in the competition for intergovernmental dollars in this period of the New Federalism were middle-income suburbs. Although all suburbs received more intergovernmental aid, the largest proportional gains were made by middle-income suburbs, an increase of over 70% in the five-year period. Our analysis shows that the expanding intergovernmental pie of the mid-1970s helped more affluent suburbs reduce debt levels and cut tax rates. Moreover, when affluent suburbs increased service expenditures, it was usually to support common functions—governmental activities most likely to benefit a broad middle-class constituency.

Lower-income communities also received more intergovernmental dollars during this period. But compared to the effects of this money in higher-income suburbs, the effects for poor suburbs were less beneficial. First, low-income suburbs became much more dependent on intergovernmental aid than did other types of suburbs. Second, increased intergovernmental aid did not result in an improved local fiscal situation. In contrast to the experience of wealthier suburbs, poor suburbs were not able to decrease their tax rates or their debt levels.

The situation in black suburbs resembled the evolving situation in poor suburbs. Similar to poor suburbs, reliance on intergovernmental aid increased rapidly—twice as fast in black suburbs as in white ones. And these intergovernmental flows did not improve the fiscal situation of black suburbs—the taxes in black suburbs did not decrease at the same rate as those of white suburbs, and the debt levels in black suburbs also remained much higher than those of white suburbs.

CONCLUSIONS

The findings we have presented indicate several questions for further research. First, the independent role of black population composition on suburban finance deserves further consideration. The racial composition of suburbs has a strong effect on levels of intergovernmental transfer payments, independent of income levels. This is a surprising finding in that many intergovernmental aid programs are based on formulae in which community income but not minority racial measures are included. We suggest a possible explanation for this result.

Although formula-based entitlement programs were the fastest growing and most visible federal aid programs in the 1970s, categorical aid programs continued to account for most of the actual dollar aid going to local governments (see, for example, Wright, 1982). Black suburbs may have higher needs and preferences for a broader range of programs than can be supported by intergovernmental aid. It is likely that the placement of these nonentitlement grants is more responsive to racial composition of suburbs than are the entitlement programs. In addition, in suburban regions many of the formula grants themselves are made to consortia of local governments, organized at the county level. Within the broad political constraints of these consortia, monies can be allocated to different communities using criteria other than the strict formulae that determined the dollar allocations from the federal government. In this case decision makers at the county level may direct extra resources to local governments with a visible and perhaps well-organized minority community. Given the nature of our data this possibility cannot be satisfactorily resolved, leaving this issue as an important topic of further research.

Second, our analysis has treated the municipalities in our sample as a national aggregate. Variations between SMSAs and larger geographical regions have been controlled in the research design we employed. Yet because of significant differences in functional responsibility and funding patterns, the solutions municipalities choose in response to cutbacks may vary across regions. This too is an issue for future research.

Third, and perhaps most important, is the need for continued study of the impact of the ongoing changes in fiscal federalism on suburbs. The research in this article has documented changes between 1972 and 1977, a period during which the face of fiscal federalism was dramatically altered by rapid increases in the flow of federal monies to state and local governments. Much of this growth in transfer payments reflected the shift to revenue sharing and block grant programs based on entitlements. Additional federal monies found their way to local governments through provisions imposed on states. Some states themselves developed new and expanded intergovernmental transfer programs.

Despite reservations about the mandates associated with them (Lovell, 1979), most suburban governments willingly accepted these new funds to increase service levels, to develop programs, and/or to reduce taxes.

However, the new fiscal conservatism and continuing problems in the American economy have led to cutbacks in the intergovernmental fiscal "safety net" to which local governments have grown accustomed, and these cutbacks have helped produce fiscal distress in many municipalities.

The distribution of the fiscal problems of suburban municipalities will reinforce the cutbacks being imposed by the federal government on aid programs that benefit individuals. The initial effects of cutbacks in federal aid have been borne mostly by low-income individuals, especially the working poor and minorities, while the treasuries of state and local governments have been affected less adversely than originally anticipated (Nathan et al., 1982). Often local governments have simply "ratified" cutbacks by the federal government—that is, they have not used their own funds to make up for federal cutbacks. Furthermore, many local governments have in the short run been able to count on increased state aid to avoid fiscal strain. But the huge fiscal surplus that enabled California to bail out its local governments is depleted, and transfers in other states, such as Massachusetts, have been paid for by a massive curtailment of state services. Money in the federal grants "pipeline" also eased short-term adjustment problems. But in the long run local governments will have to reduce expenditures as transfer payments become harder and harder to come by.

Our data suggest that it is the suburbs with the most disadvantaged populations that are most at risk. Ongoing research in Massachusetts documents the risk. Karl Kim has shown wide variation in the degree to which different services are being cut as municipalities face fiscal constraints brought on by Proposition 2-1/2. In particular, the cutbacks being enacted by low-income suburbs are more severe than those experienced by higher-income communities (Kim, 1982).

Although Kim's findings match projections based on our national sample, only a fuller analysis of the 1982 Census of Governments will delineate the full impact on different communities of the cutbacks imposed since 1977.

At present, however, our data suggest that unless the distributional impact of cutbacks is more clearly factored into policies restricting intergovernmental aid, it is low-income and minority communities, places where residents are already feeling cutbacks in aid programs to individuals, that will have the most difficult fiscal problems resulting from shrinking intergovernmental transfer programs.

NOTE

1. The SMSAs included are as follows: Allentown, PA; Anaheim, CA; Buffalo, NY; Chicago, IL; Cincinnati, OH; Cleveland, OH; Columbus, OH; Dallas, TX; Denver, CO; Detroit, MI; Fort Lauderdale, FL; Grand Rapids, MI; Houston, TX; Kansas City, MO; Los Angeles, CA; Miami, FL; Milwaukee, WI; Newark, NJ; New York, NY; Paterson, NJ; Philadelphia, PA; Phoenix, AZ; Pittsburgh, PA; Portland, OR; St. Louis, MO; Salt Lake City, UT; Seattle, WA; and Tampa, FL.

REFERENCES

Advisory Commission on Intergovernmental Relations (1982) Significant Features of Fiscal Federalism, 1980-1981. Washington, DC: Government Printing Office.

———(1980) Recent Trends in Federal and State Aid to Local Governments. Washington, DC: Government Printing Office.
BARFIELD, C. E. (1982) Rethinking Federalism: Block Grants and Federal, State, and Local Responsibilities. Washington, DC: American Enterprise Institute.
BEHN, R. H. (1980) "Leadership in an era of retrenchment." Public Administration Rev. 40 (November/December): 603-626.
BERRY, B. and F. HORTON (1970) Geographic Perspectives on Urban Systems. Englewood Cliffs, NJ: Prentice Hall.
BOWMAN, J. (1981) "Urban revenue structures: an overview of patterns, trends, and issues." Public Administration Rev. 41 (January): 131-143.
BRANFMAN, E., B. COHEN, and D. TRUBEK (1974) "Measuring the invisible wall: land use controls and residential patterns of the poor," pp. 57-82 in D. Listokin (ed.) Land Use Controls: Present Problems and Future Reform. New Brunswick, NJ: Rutgers University, Center for Urban Policy Research.
CHAPMAN, J. and J. J. KIRLIN (1979) "Changes in government land use policies: and unforeseen response to the Jarvis-Gann initiative." Urban Interest 1 (January): 81-86.
CONLON, T. J. (1981) "Back in vogue: the politics of block grant legislation." Intergovernmental Perspective 7: 8-17.
CONNOLLY, H. X. (1973) "Black movement into the suburbs: suburbs doubling their black population during the 1960s." Urban Affairs Q. 9 (September): 91-111.
DANIELSON, M. (1976) The Politics of Exclusiveness. New York: Columbia Univ. Press.
DANZINGER, J. N. and P. S. RING (1982) "Fiscal limitations: a selected review of recent research." Public Administration Rev. 42, 1: 47-55.
DOWALL, D. (n.d.) "The suburban squeeze: land policies in the San Francisco Bay area." Berkeley: University of California Institute of Urban and Regional Development. (unpublished)
ERIBES, R. A. and J. S. HALL (1981) "Revolt of the affluent: fiscal controls in three states." Public Administration Rev. 41 (January): 107-121.
FARLEY, R. (1970) "The changing distribution of Negroes within metropolitan areas: the emergence of black suburbs." Amer. J. of Sociology 75 (January): 512-529.
GUEST, A. M. (1978) "The changing racial composition of suburbs, 1950-1970." Urban Affairs Q. 14 (December): 195-206.
HILL, R. C. (1974) "Separate and unequal: governmental inequality in the metropolis." Amer. Pol. Sci. Rev. 68 (December): 1557-1568.
KIM, K. E. (1982) "Post 2 1/2 changes: municipal appropriations levels." Impact 2 1/2, 37.
LEVINE, C. and I. RUBIN [eds.] (1980) Fiscal stress and public policy. Beverly Hills, CA: Sage.
LEVY, F., J. MELTSNER, and A. WILDAVSKY (1974) Urban Outcomes. Berkeley: Univ. of California Press.
LIEBERT, R. (1976) Disintegration and Political Action. New York: Academic.
LOVELL, C. (1981) "Evolving local government dependency." Public Administration Rev. 41 (January): 189-202.
LOVELL, C. H., R. KNEISEL, M. NEIMAN, A. Z. ROSE, and C. A. TOBIN (1979) Federal and State Mandating on Local Governments: An Exploration of Issues and Impacts: Final Report to the National Science Foundation. Riverside: University of California.

National Association of Housing Rehabilitation Officers NAHRO (1977) Newsletter 20, 1.
NATHAN, R. P. (1978) Block Grants for Community Development. Washington, DC: U.S. Department of Housing and Urban Development.
———A. D. MANVEL, and S. E. CALKINS (1975) Monitoring Revenue Sharing. Washington, DC: Brookings Institution.
NATHAN, R. P., P. M. DEARBORN, C. A. GOLDMAN, and ASSOCIATES (1982) "Initial effects of the fiscal year 1982 reductions in federal domestic spending," pp. 315-350 in J. W. Ellwood (ed.) Reductions in U.S. Domestic Spending: How They Affect State and Local Governments. New York: Transaction Books.
PASCAL, A., M. D. MENCHIK, J. M. CHAIKEN, P. L. ELLICKSON, W. E. WALKER, D. N. DETROY, and A. E. WISE (1979) Fiscal Containment of Local and State Government. Santa Monica, CA: Rand.
PURYEAR, D. L. and J. P. ROSS (1978) "Tax and expenditure limitations: the fiscal context." Presented at the HUD Conference on Tax and Expenditure Limitations, University of California, Santa Barbara, December.
ROSE, H. (1976) Black Suburbanization: Access to Improved Quality of Life or Maintenance of the Status Quo. Cambridge, MA: Ballinger.
SANGER, M. B. (1981) "Are academic models of urban service distributions relevant to public policy? Lessons from New York." Policy Studies J. 9 (Summer): 1011-1020.
SCHNEIDER, M. (1980) "Resource reallocation and the fiscal condition of metropolitan communities." Social Sci. Q. 61 (December): 545-566.
———and J. R. LOGAN (1982) "Suburban racial segregation and black access to local public resources." Social Sci. Q. 63 (December): 762-770.
———(1981) "Fiscal implications of class segregation." Urban Affairs Q. 17 (September): 23-36.
WRIGHT, D. S. (1982) Understanding Intergovernmental Relations. Monterey, CA: Brooks/Cole.

Mark Schneider is Associate Professor of Political Science, State University of New York at Stony Brook. He has published numerous articles on patterns of suburban growth. His recent research has explored the size of suburban government.

*John Logan is Associate Professor of Sociology and Public Affairs at SUNY, Albany. In addition to a series of studies of suburban politics and community development, he is completing a book—*Urban Fortunes: A Reconstruction of Urban Sociology*—in collaboration with Harvey Molotch.*

This article explores the influence of various service industries on male earnings inequality within the 125 largest metropolitan areas in the United States. The data indicate that service sector employment increases inequality. Contrary to past literature suggesting that service growth proliferates low-paying occupational positions that increase inequality, however, multiple regression analyses demonstrate that increasing inequality is more a function of high-paying jobs in "producer services"—the service sector providing financial resources as well as technical and legal expertise to the business community. Greater concentrations of producer services in metropolitan areas increase the proportion of workers with exceedingly high incomes without affecting median incomes. Consequently, when producer services are extensive in an area, earnings distributions are more skewed and unequal.

EMPLOYMENT IN SERVICE ACTIVITIES AND INEQUALITY IN METROPOLITAN AREAS

JOEL I. NELSON
University of Minnesota

JON LORENCE
University of Houston

Numerous studies in the urban literature have identified factors contributing to earnings inequality across metropolitan areas. These studies offer considerable insight into the structure of economic opportunity. Although a variety of critical factors have been noted, one important characteristic is the economic activity of the metropolis—specifically, the level of employment in manufacturing. Using such traditional dependent variables as inequality in male earnings or family income, the role of manufacturing in reducing inequality has been documented repeatedly. Haworth et al. (1978), for example, analyzed 79 SMSAs

AUTHORS' NOTE: *The research for this project was supported by the Agricultural Experiment Station, University of Minnesota. This article may be identified as paper 14,221, scientific journal series, Agricultural Experimental Station, University of Minnesota.*

URBAN AFFAIRS QUARTERLY, Vol. 21 No. 1, September 1985 106-125

in 1970 and showed manufacturing to be inversely related to male and family income inequality. Murray (1969) and Frech and Burns (1971) also reported an inverse relationship between manufacturing and male income inequality for 1950 and 1960 SMSA data. Similar findings have been noted by Hirsch (1982), Burns (1975), Danziger (1976), Farbman (1975), and Garofalo and Fogarty (1979).

The typical explanation offered for these findings is that because manufacturing tends to be more productive and unionized than other industrial sectors, manufacturing raises wages and thereby reduces dispersion in earnings. This explanation, convincing as it may sound, is incomplete in failing to specify which "other industrial sectors" compare less favorably with manufacturing wages. In the developmental literature on nations (Moore, 1963; Kuznets, 1955) the absence of manufacturing implied the presence of agriculture; and indeed, in that context, manufacturing offered more favorable wages than low-paying jobs commonly identified with employment in the primary sector. But comparisons between manufacturing and agriculture are implausible in metropolitan communities.

Across metropolitan communities manufacturing varies inversely with services. The presence of one implies the absence of the other.[1] But if manufacturing reduces inequality by reducing low-wage opportunities, it does not follow that services necessarily increase inequality by increasing low-wage opportunities. The matter is more complicated. One vision of service activity may indeed be of low-paid retail clerks, delivery personnel, and the never-ending legion of fast food workers. But another vision of services is reasonable as well—the one contained in Thompson's (1968: 109) summarizing comment, "with true metropolitan standing, ever more esoteric services are acquired and supported over ever greater distances (e.g., administrative, legal, financial), probably turning the income distribution toward greater inequality." This vision points to inequality as a function not of low-wage jobs but of high-wage white-collar pyramids—to the scores of businessmen, bankers, lawyers, and other professional service providers who predominate in major metropolitan areas. Each of these visions—of inequality emanating from the top or bottom of the occupational hierarchy—has quite different implications for understanding the link of inequality to services (and to manufacturing).

Unfortunately, research on services and inequality as well as an overarching theory to guide such research are nonexistent.[2] This void in the urban literature is made more critical in light of the predominance of service activities in the economy. In 1970, the census reported that 58% of the male labor force in metropolitan areas was engaged in service jobs (U.S. Bureau of the Census, 1972b: 420). By 1980, this had risen to 61% (U.S. Bureau of the Census, 1983: 87). Yet recent literature is mute on the role of service workers in determining inequality. This article reports an exploratory study of the relationship between service employment and inequality in metropolitan communities. Using census data on the 125 largest metropolitan areas, we examine precisely why male earnings are more unequal in metropolises with high levels of labor force involvement in the service sector.

BACKGROUND LITERATURE

Little is known about the impact of the service sector on the distribution of economic rewards. This is an important omission in the urban literature in that work activities generally are thought to influence inequality, and inequality itself describes in large part the differential access individuals have to securing scarce and valued resources. Judgments, however, vary widely as to how service activities and income inequality might be related. Some writers link growth in service activities to the general homogenization of the stratification structure; in this view income inequality declines as service employment expands (see a review of this position in Blumberg, 1980: 9-64). Others, such as Blau (1980), estimate that service activities and income inequality probably are unrelated. Still others speculate that recent growth in income inequality is in part a function of rapid increases in highly paid professional and technical workers, particularly those employed in professional and finance service sector industries (Henle, 1972: 23). Stanback has supplemented the latter position by suggesting that service industries dichotomize the occupational structure—that, unlike manufacturing, "a middle tier of jobs is missing" (Stanback, 1979: 107); this position implies that service industries increase inequality by proliferating job opportunities for both the poor and affluent. More recently, Maume (1983) suggested that services increase the range of skill levels and hence increase the magnitude of inequality.

Unfortunately, a larger theoretical framework useful for deducing a cogent set of testable hypotheses does not exist. Instead, there is a diverse literature on a variety of issues related to services and income. At first glance this literature broadly suggests that services generate inequality by increasing the percentage of low-wage workers. As Fuchs

(1968: 6) noted, "persons employed in the service sector earn significantly less than those employed in industry." Direct examination of census statistics bears out Fuch's observation. Although there is considerable variation in the earnings of service workers, those employed in the service sector earn on the average $600 per year less than workers in the manufacturing sector. This differential is sustained even within occupational categories. For example, managers in manufacturing earn about $2600 more than those in services, whereas skilled blue-collar workers earn $1250 more (U.S. Bureau of the Census, 1973b: 778-779). Furthermore, these differences appear to affect the income opportunities of workers across communities. Lincoln and Friedland (1977), for example, have shown that in nonmetropolitan communities median family income decreased as the precentage of workers in wholesale trade, retail trade, and personal services increased. Although the correlation between the percentage of workers in the remaining service industries and median income was positive, in no case was any of these correlations above .08.

These findings suggest that service activities lower income opportunities for workers. Others have suggested that services increase income opportunities except for skilled labor. In summarizing work on metropolitan hierarchies, Maume (1983: 415) suggested that "in larger service-based cities, a compensatory wage payment will be paid to attract skilled labor, but will not be paid to unskilled labor. This, of course, gives rise to income inequality." At the same time, it must be emphasized that there is considerable variation in the occupations that constitute the service sector. Greater proportions of low-paid workers in fast food outlets, hospitals, and hotels may indeed lower average community income as well as increase the negative skew of a community's income distribution. But business executives, accountants, lawyers, and other professionals also may be classified as service workers. These latter occupations hardly qualify as examples of depressed income opportunities. Most past research examining economic dispersion implicitly assumes that overall economic inequality is due to differences between individuals at the lower end of an earnings distribution. However, overall economic inequality also can be due to earnings differences between median and affluent earners. This raises an unexamined question as to whether income inequality is more a function of disparities arising from the incomes of the rich at the upper end of the income distribution or of the poor at the lower end. If inequality is primarily a result of upper-income disparities, then whether or not services generate lower-income opportunities may be superfluous to the influence of service sector employment on inequality.

Several factors suggest a possible error in emphasizing disparities due to the lower end of the earnings distribution when trying to account for income inequality. Although metropolitan areas have been popularly described as residential havens for the poor, this description ignores the predominantly white-collar labor force characteristic of the metropolis. In large metropolitan areas skilled professional and managerial workers draw substantial wages commensurate with their technical skills and bureaucratic responsibilities. Given the considerable variation in the employment of such workers across metropolitan areas (Galle, 1963), the distribution of income and the level of income inequality likewise may vary considerably. Various observers in fact have related high-income earners to inequality in the metropolis. Urban economist, Wilbur Thompson (1968: 106-109) in part describes the metropolis as residences for the "gifted and ambitious," for the "name corporation with its executive suite," as the "home of the very rich"—all of which turn "the income distribution . . . toward greater inequality."

More recently, the influence of high incomes on inequality has been raised in the debate on urban hierarchies. Haworth et al. (1978) suggest that inequality is high in big cities because of the large salaries given to workers whose domain expands as city size increases—school superintendents or newspaper editors, for example (see also Hirsch, 1982). Consistent with this view are findings showing that the larger the metropolis, the lower the income levels of families at the 10th and 25th percentiles but the higher the income levels of families at the 75th and 90th percentiles and the higher the coefficient of inequality as well (Garofalo and Fogarty, 1979).

These observations do not suggest that income inequality is dominated by disparities from upper strata income; they do suggest, however, the possible error in considering inequality as wholly a reflection of lower-income opportunities. Consequently, in trying to understand the connection between services and inequality, attention also should be given to the influence of service sector employment on generating highly paid occupational positions.

THE FINANCIAL SECTOR

A prime candidate for producing overall inequalities because of the upper end of the income distribution is the "finance, insurance, and real estate" service category listed by the census as the highest paid of all industrial sectors (U. S. Bureau of the Census, 1973b: 778-779). That this sector is associated with high wages should not be surprising given the priority placed on financial activities in a capitalistic economy. That is, institutions at the heart of the decision-making process in the business sector—banks, insurance firms, large real estate conglomerations—have broad implications for resource allocation; they consequently may be key control mechanisms in the economy (Stephens, 1980; Wright, 1976; Poulantzas, 1975; Carchedi, 1975). In Browning and Singlemann's (1978: 489) view, these kinds of financial service activities cater to "producers and to individuals who control property in its various forms," and, according to Braverman (1974: 301), such activities, particularly as embodied in financial institutions, "are accorded a place at the pinnacle of the social division of labor." To the extent that these activities are important to the economy, they will draw on highly skilled professional and managerial employees who command substantial wages (see Greenfield, 1966; and Stanback et al., 1983, for a review of the importance of this general sector of the econony).

The potential disparity in wages brought about by such highly paid workers is one way to link services to inequality and a complementary alternative to the more common emphasis on low-income workers. There are several indications in past literature that finances and related activities are indeed associated with metropolitan income inequality in the manner suggested. Danziger (1976: 474), for example, notes that certain "industries offer trade-offs between equality and income levels. Finance, insurance and real estate . . . are associated with high but unequally distributed incomes." Thompson (1968: 107), likewise, has observed that income inequality is in part a function of "the ancillary business services that call for the highest professional skills (e.g., corporation lawyers and financial counselors)." More recently, Stanback et al. (1983: 71) also have commented on the inequality contrasts set up by high-income workers in financial and administrative jobs.

We do not intend to detract from the possibility that services generate lower-income opportunities and that this in turn influences income inequality. The predominance of services in the metropolis indicates, after all, proportionately fewer jobs in manufacturing and ordinarily lower wages for workers. Nonetheless, to the extent that Thompson and others are correct in conceiving of income inequality as in part differentiated at the upper-income end, financial activities—and the other services possibly associated with them—may be an important factor in linking inequality to service sector employment in metropolitan areas.

METHODS

SAMPLE AND DATA

The sample for this study is drawn from the 125 largest SMSAs in the United States in 1970, those with more than one-quarter of a million residents. Published secondary sources of the 1970 and 1980 U. S. Census provided the data base for the study. The consolidation of Dallas and Fort Worth reduced the number of SMSAs to 124 for 1980. Past research in the urban literature on industry and inequality has used either family income or male income as the source for measuring the dependent variable. For several reasons the latter was selected for this analysis. Given that our research focuses on how service industries influence the distribution of economic rewards, individual instead of family or household inequality was chosen because economic rewards are derived from an individual's position in the labor force.

Although one's standard of living may be greatly influenced by a spouse's contribution to income, it is difficult to disentangle the effects of industrial and occupational employment on family income because family members often work in different industrial and occupational positions. The focus on male earners is necessitated by the desire for comparability with previous research on individual earnings dispersion in the metropolis that has focused almost exclusively on males. Further analyses are required to determine if the processes reported for males are comparable for females. Males employed in agriculture were excluded due to their scant representation in metropolitan labor markets.

INEQUALITY

Thiel's information-based inequality coefficient was used to measure the overall dispersion in male earnings (U. S. Bureau of the Census, 1972a: Table 175; 1983: Table 222). The principle underlying this measure is that income shares proportional to population shares reflect equality. Perfect equality exists if each proportional segment of the population has the same income. Thiel's measure of inequality was chosen because it has more desirable statistical properties than other measures of overall economic dispersion (see Allison, 1978).[3] Inequality measures often require estimates of means within income categories. Consequently, the means of the open-ended earnings interval were estimated by assuming that Pareto distributions fit the open-ended intervals. For the closed earnings intervals, midpoints were used as means.[4]

Because a summary inequality measure often can conceal information providing further insights about the nature of economic inequality, two additional measures describing metropolitan earnings distributions were calculated. First, the ratio of median earnings over the 5th percentile (the point in an earnings distribution at which 5% of the individuals have the lowest earnings) was computed. This ratio (P50/P5) indicates negative skewedness or the difference in earnings between the least affluent and median metropolitan male earners. Computing the ratio (P95/P50) of the earnings at the 95th percentile (the point in a distribution at which 5% of the individuals have the largest earnings) over the median indicates the degree of positive skew, or the gap between median and affluent earners. A larger ratio between the upper end and the center of a metropolitan earnings distribution indicates that the more affluent individuals have a greater economic advantage over median earners than exists for high earners in another metropolitan area. Applications of this procedure are given by Lydall (1968) and Garofalo and Fogarty (1979).

THE SERVICE SECTOR

To measure service sector employment, we drew on a conceptually more coherent scheme than was available from the census. Several typologies are given in the literature, although they all use remarkably similar distinctions (Foote and Hatt, 1953: 365; Bell, 1976: 117; Browning and Singlemann, 1978: 491). To increase the continuity in this literature, we selected one of these schemes, specifically, the typology offered by Browning and Singlemann (1978, 1980). Four types of service activities are distinguished:

(1) personal services (e.g., entertainment, repairs, eating and drinking)
(2) social services (e.g., medical, education, government)

(3) producer services (e.g., banking, legal services, communication, accounting, other business services)[5]
(4) distributive services (e.g., wholesale trade, retail trade, and transportation)

We also followed Browning and Singlemann's characterization of the transformative sector that includes all forms of manufacturing, construction, and utilities. To measure involvement in these sectors, we coded male labor force participation as given in the census (U. S. Bureau of the Census, 1972a: Table 188; 1983: Table 231). The rationale for disaggregating the service sector is simply that different components of this broad sector likely have different effects on earnings inequality.

ADDITIONAL VARIABLES

Service sector employment does not influence inequality in a vacuum. Consequently, we included control variables that might be related to service sector employment in one way or another. Each of these variables has been used in previous research on metropolitan income inequality and is derived from the general assumption that earnings distributions are a function of individual characteristics and institutional forces operating in an ecological context. The individual characteristics were race or percentage black (U. S. Bureau of the Census, 1972a: Table 175; 1983: Table 219), variance of the age distribution of male civilian employees (U. S. Bureau of the Census, 1972a: Table 164, 1983: Table 221), and median education (U. S. Bureau of the Census, 1972a: Table 197, 1983: Table 237). The institutional forces were the level of structural unemployment as measured by the percentage unemployed (U. S. Bureau of the Census, 1973a: Table 3, 1982: Table 213) and labor union concentration (U. S. Bureau of the Census, 1971: Table 2, 1982). For the latter measure we followed Lincoln's (1978) approximation of labor union presence by dividing the total number of organizations in an SMSA into the number of nonprofit labor organizations (i.e., employee associations, labor unions, and other organizations advancing labor interest).[6] Finally, the ecological factors were region (e.g., non-South = 0; South = 1 using the standard census regional classification) and population size (U. S. Bureau of the Census, 1973a: Table 3, 1981: Table 20). Given the obvious relevance of average earnings in a metropolitan area to the consideration of service sector employment, we included median earnings as an additional control variable (U. S. Bureau of the Census, 1972a: Table 175, 1983: Table 222).

FINDINGS

Table 1 reports the zero-order correlations between the transformative sector, the service sector, the component parts of the service sector, several indicators of points and distances on the income distribution, and the Thiel coefficient of inequality. Because the service and transformative sectors are so highly correlated (r = −.980 for 1970 and r = −.910 for 1980) there is little surprise in the finding that services and inequality are also highly related. The correlations of .585 and .674 for 1970 and 1980, respectively, indicate that metropolitan areas with extensive employment in service activities are also likely to have more unequally distributed incomes.

As previously noted, past literature suggests that the negative relationship of manufacturing to inequality is partly a consequence of the higher wages workers in manufacturing receive. An inference from this literature is that services reduce inequality by decreasing workers' wages. The data in Table 1, however, question whether this assumption is appropriate for metropolitan areas. Specifically, the correlations in Table 1 indicate that the income disparities that result from comparing the upper-income percentile and the median (P95/P50) and the lower-income percentile and the median (P50/P5) are about equally affected by both the service and transformative sectors in 1970; in 1980, the correlations of these two sectors with the P50/P5 is minimal. Consequently, an emphasis on lower-income opportunities alone may be misplaced. More important, however, each of these measures of positive and negative skew are differently related to the overall index of inequality. The correlation between overall inequality and P95/P50 is .920 in 1970 and .669 in 1980, whereas the correlation between P50/P5 and inequality is only .281 in 1970 and −.129 in 1980. Overall inequality appears to be due to greater earnings disparities between the highest and median earners than between the median and lowest earners.

To further estimate the influence of affluent and poor earners on inequality, it is possible to determine the proportion of overall in-

TABLE 1

Zero-Order Correlations for Transformative and Service Sectors and Inequality Measures for Males in Metropolitan Areas

				Correlations										
Varibles	Year	$\overline{X}$	S.D.	2	3	4	5	6	7	8	9	10	11	12
1. Transformative Sector	1970	42.9	10.9	-.980	-.771	-.433	-.711	-.717	-.537	-.500	-.477	-.268	-.619	-.258
	1980	39.9	9.6	-.910	-.718	-.478	-.633	-.488	-.677	-.343	-.028	.105	.448	.425
2. Service Sector	1970	56.0	10.5		.818	.533	.723	.649	.585	.550	.473	.325	-.589	-.232
	1980	56.4	9.0		.823	.530	.678	.524	.674	.425	-.006	-.023	-.389	-.392
3. Producer Services	1970	11.6	3.0			.371	.413	.565	.746	.694	.390	.570	-.365	-.038
	1980	12.8	3.2			.353	.398	.415	.735	.655	-.085	.275	-.139	-.200
4. Personal Services	1970	5.3	2.7				.073	.161	.209	.185	.078	.116	-.106	-.051
	1980	5.9	2.9				.106	.072	.343	.229	-.150	-.009	-.058	-.194
5. Social Services	1970	15.3	5.3					.195	.334	.392	.489	.271	-.489	-.109
	1980	16.1	4.6					-.020	.328	.129	.315	-.127	-.544	-.286
6. Distributive Services	1970	23.8	4.2						.365	.260	.230	-.013	-.515	-.377
	1980	21.6	3.3						.370	.144	-.241	-.146	-.119	-.308
7. Total Inequality	1970	.3	.1							.920	.281	.672	-.393	.199
	1980	.3	.1							.669	-.129	.010	-.457	-.542
8. P95/P50	1970	3.0	.5								.158	.801	-.229	-.108
	1980	2.7	.23								-.031	.630	-.010	-.025
9. P50/P5	1970	7.9	1.1									.231	-.715	.209
	1980	9.4	.9									.308	-.391	.429
10. P95	1970	23538.6	4538.8										.135	.496
	1980	39619.4	5860.8										.508	.757
11. P5	1970	1012.9	153.7											.513
	1980	1580.9	177.4											.659
12. Median Income	1970	7926.5	838.0											
	1980	14868.0	1714.8											

NOTE: N = 125, 1970; N = 124, 1980.
*p < .05
**p < .025
***p < .001

equality due to the upper and lower ends of the earnings distribution. The effect can be assessed by computing a measure similar to Bowley's coefficient of skewedness (Mincer, 1974: 110). The measure is a ratio defined by the following expression: (P95 - P50)/(P95 - P5) × 100. Although the procedure is crude, it provides an approximation of positive skewedness for the entire metropolitan male earnings distribution. The mean ratio of positive skewedness for 1970 is 68.6 (S.D. = 4.6) and for 1980 is 64.7 (S.D. = 3.6) indicating that approximately two-thirds of overall inequality is due to differences between affluent and median earners rather than between median and poor earners. The correlation between this skewedness score and the Thiel measure of inequality is .915 and .673 for 1970 and 1980, respectively, indicating that overall inequality increases with positive skewedness. There is little question that earnings inequality in the metropolis is dominated by disparities created by exceedingly high earners.

The data also suggest which service sectors, as defined by Browning and Singlemann, most clearly affect the P95/P50 and hence inequality in the overall distribution of income. The correlations reveal that the relationship of producer services to the P95/P50 earnings ratio is substantially stronger than the next most highly related sector: social services for 1970 and personal services for 1980. An anomaly is the more substantial relationship of the 95th percentile to producer services in 1970 than in 1980. As for dispersion at the lower end (P50/P5), social services are clearly the most critical correlate; this may be more a consequence of other factors commonly associated with social services (e.g., poverty that causes the need for social workers and other public employees) than with the social service sector per se actually generating a more negatively skewed earnings distribution.[7] As to the interrelationship among these sectors, producer services are more highly correlated with the personal, social, and distributive sectors than these sectors are with one another. The data consequently suggest the major role of producer services in understanding why services and inequality are inversely related in the metropolis.

To explore this suggestion more thoroughly, we report in Table 2 analyses regressing the various income disparity and percentile measures on the four service sectors and select control variables.[8] These analyses provide a test of whether producer services are related to inequality more strongly and independently of the other service sectors and the control variables such as race, size of SMSA, and so forth. The first column of the table shows that the producer services sector has the

TABLE 2
Standardized Coefficients for Male Earnings Inequality Measures Regressed on Service Sector Industries and Control Variables

	Dependent Variables											
Independent Variables	(1) Total Inequality		(2) P95/P50		(3) P50/P5		(4) P95		(5) P5		(6) Median Income	
	1970	1980	1970	1980	1970	1980	1970	1980	1970	1980	1970	1980
Producer Services	.590***	.414***	.561***	.515***	.103	-.174	.512***	.227*	-.016	-.002	.018	-.120
Personal Services	-.046	.021	-.074	-.021	-.035	-.152*	-.082	-.113	.019	.026	-.012	-.119*
Social Services	-.005	-.113	.110	-.209**	.126	.117	-.006	-.474***	-.233***	-.556***	-.212***	-.461***
Distributive Services	-.214**	-.034	-.227**	-.182**	-.011	-.042	-.335***	-.248***	-.213**	-.127	-.214**	-.174**
Variation in Age	.108*	.128**	.018	-.026	.219**	-.077	-.122*	-.185**	-.313***	-.160*	-.196***	-.217***
Percent Black	.060	.007	.040	.124	-.087	.105	.063	.285***	.101	.167	.080	.248***
Population Size (Log)	.240***	.049	.158**	.143	-.046	-.061	.332***	.284***	.235***	.262**	.276***	.229***
Percent Unemployed	-.026	.206**	-.090	.037	.286***	.463***	-.067	.008	-.246***	-.409***	.057	.003
Proportion of Labor Organizations	-.114*	-.292***	-.124	-.254**	-.095	-.082	-.036	.021	.173**	.329***	.061	.253**
Median Education	.190**	.293***	.133	.154	.527***	.559***	.265***	.431***	-.259***	-.004	.319***	.441***
Median Income	-.129	-.367***	---	---	---	---	---	---	---	---	---	---
South	.353***	.249**	.346***	.011	.081	-.082	.008	-.285**	-.415***	-.310**	-.518***	-.342***
R^2	.784	.797	.707	.572	.564	.516	.671	.660	.660	.53	.728	.711

NOTE: N = 125, 1970; N = 124, 1980.
*p < .05
**p < .025
***p < .001

most substantial relationship to overall inequality of all the service sectors. Because producer services is the only service sector showing a positive and statistically significant relationship with inequality, we reiterate our former contention: Producer services are largely responsible for the overall relationship between service activities and inequality in the metropolis.

Furthermore, producer services also appear to be somewhat more highly related to inequality than most of the control variables associated with traditional explanations of inequality. Consistent with past literature, region (South/North) is related significantly to greater inequality. However, the relationship between median education and inequality is positive. This finding contradicts the traditional hypothesis advanced in past literature that characteristics related to the level of economic development—such as median education—are strongly and negatively related to inequality (Rubinson, 1976; Lenski, 1966; Kuznets, 1955; Cutright, 1967). Developmental theory suggests that upgraded educational skills reflect mobility opportunitics for thc lower strata. Fulfilling these opportunities is the mechanism for reducing income differences between lower and middle strata, thus reducing income inequality. Reduced income inequality in the metropolis does not appear, however, to be a simple consequence of upgraded educational skills. This is congruent with our interpretation of the data in Table 1 that metropolitan income inequality does not reflect income disparities created by the lower strata.

Further analyses of metropolitan inequality are presented in columns 2 through 6 of Table 2. These columns report the standardized coefficients associated with the independent variables and the different points and contrasts in the income distribution. Noteworthy are the coefficients relating producer services to the contrast between upper and median income (P95/P50) and to the upper-income percentile itself (P95). These coefficients are shown in columns 2 and 4. The more extensive the labor force involvement in producer services, the higher the income level of the 95th percentile and the greater the disparity between median and upper earners. The coefficient relating producer services to the 95th percentile, however, appears to be substantially weaker in 1980 than in 1970. Columns 2 and 4 also indicate that distributive services (and social services in 1980) have a more modest relationship to lower scores on the P95 and the P95/P50. Given the correlation between producer and distributive services ($r = .565$ and .415), one sector offsets the other's connection to inequality, but not to the point of reducing completely the relationship between inequality and the overall measure of services.

We mentioned previously that producer services may increase the earnings level of the 95th percentile because of the increase in professional and managerial employees and the generally high wages they receive. This anticipation is derived from the general contention advanced in past literature that certain types of activity in the industrial sector are carried out by persons with particular occupational training that in turn has implications for the way rewards are distributed (Blau, 1974; Bloomquist and Summers, 1982; Hawley, 1968). That this view has merit in the present context is indicated by the zero-order correlations: Employment in producer services is highly related to the percentage of professionals and managers in the labor force ($r = .720$ in 1970 and .758 in 1980) and in turn the percentage of professionals and managers is related to the earnings level of the 95th percentile ($r = .708$ and .435 for 1970 and 1980, respectively). Furthermore, entering the percentage of professionals and managers into the regression reported in column 4 reduces the coefficient associated with producer services to a nonsignificant level. Occupation appears to be an important link intervening between producer services and high earners.

The data in columns 3, 5, and 6 indicate that producer services are unrelated either to median income or to the lower-income percentile measures. However, social services in 1970 and 1980 are consistently and negatively related to the median and to the 5th percentile; but as both the median and the 5th percentile appear to be lowered simultaneously, these two sectors do not significantly affect the income disparities at the lower end of the distribution (P50/P5). For the control variables, parallel effects on the median, P5, and P50/P5 are shown for variation in both age and median education for 1970. For this time period, the largest effect on the P50/P5 is with education, which is related to an increase in median income and a decline in the P5. This latter relationship probably reflects the absence of manufacturing in metropolitan areas with high education. The correlation between median education and the transformative sector is −.420 (1970). In 1980, none of the control variables is consistently related to P50/P5, P5, or median income. Incidentally, personal services—the lowest paid of all service activities and the sector popularly associated with minimal income opportunities for the lower strata—has no discernible effect on any disparity measure of the income distribution for 1970 and is weakly related for 1980 to only the P50/P5 ratio.

CONCLUSION

There is little question from the data that services are related to inequality in our sample, and, further, that producer services are chiefly responsible for linking inequality to the general category of service employment. The variability in income inequality across metropolitan areas is dominated by disparities from the upper end of the income distribution, from upper-strata income. Where employment in producer services is extensive, the P95/P50 ratio rises and so does inequality.

It is not our contention, however, that individuals working in the producer service sector are the only ones profiting from rising incomes. Our data suggest that as employment in producer services increases, so do the separate 95th income percentiles of individuals employed in the transformative, the producer, and the wholesale portion of the distributive sector. That producer services may have some "lateral effects" in a metropolis—effects whereby high incomes spread across other industrial sectors—has been suggested elsewhere. For example, in describing the impact of financial activities for the city of New York, a recent *New York Times* (1983: 12) article noted,

> A financial center involves the buying and selling of securities, the making of loans, the managing of assets, the manipulating of currencies, all of this served by a financial press, lawyers, accountants, and public relations people.
>
> But . . . it also needs entertainment and cultural activities to make people want to visit the city. Felix G. Rohatyn, a partner in the investment banking firm of Lazard Freres and Company, said: "We use the restaurants, the hotels, the high-priced barber shops and buy a lot of tickets for the New York Rangers, the Jets and the theater. And we support the operas and the museums."

New York is unquestionably an extreme case of a financial center, more on a par with London, for example, than with the metropolitan areas in our analysis with extensive employment in producer services: San Francisco, Atlanta, Washington, D.C. Nonetheless, these lateral effects, spilling over high incomes from one sector to another, likely involve in microcosm some of the processes described by the *Times* in all metropolitan areas high in producer service employment. More detailed earnings breakdowns by industrial and occupational groups, however, are necessary to pinpoint precisely how other sectors might benefit from producer services.

NOTES

1. Duncan et al. (1960), for example, have noted that when there is extensive manufacturing in a community, other industrial activities are unlikely to take root.

2. An exception to this void in the literature is Danziger's (1976) research relating aspects of the service sector, other measures of the industrial structure, and general characteristics of the community to income inequality. There is, however, a difficulty in interpreting Danziger's results (see Danziger, 1976: 473, Table 2). In his major regression analysis of inequality, all segments of the industrial structure—manufacturing, service, construction, mining, and so forth—are negatively related to inequality. This is either a simple error in reporting, a reflection of colinearity among the independent variables, or some complexity not immediately apparent. Whatever the situation may be, Danziger's results are not clearly interpretable. Brief mentions of the relationship between services and inequality are given by Hirsch (1982) and Maume (1983); in the latter's study, service employment, however, is combined in the analysis with a variety of related indicators.

3. The findings would have been similar had the more popularly used Gini coefficient been chosen instead; the correlation between the Thiel and Gini coefficients was .995.

4. The only exception to this was the exceedingly broad category of $25,000-49,999 for 1980, in which simple interpolation was used.

5. Included in the "producer services" sector are men employed in "repair services." Although these individuals should be placed in the "personal service" sector in order to conform to the Browning and Singlemann typology, published census data for metropolitan areas do not provide a detailed enough industrial sector breakdown enabling one to disentangle "repair services" from "other business services."

6. Although a better measure of labor's strength might be obtained by coding the proportion of individuals belonging to a union or covered by collective bargaining, these data are not systematically available for all metropolitan areas. Given that categories of organizations are not presented by SMSA in 1980, organizational information was aggregated for counties within the metropolitan boundaries.

7. Contrary to past literature (Fogel and Lewin, 1974; Durden and Schwarz-Miller, 1982), government employment does not appear to increase equality. When public administration is analyzed separately from Browning and Singlemann's general category of social services in 1970 for example, the measure is correlated positively with inequality ($r = .274$); but controlling for the other variables in Table 2 reduces this association to statistical nonsignificance.

8. Given the colinearity between the transformative and service sectors, it is risky to sort out simultaneously the differential effects of employment in these sectors on inequality. Consequently, a variable controlling for transformative activities was not included.

REFERENCES

ALLISON, P. D. (1978) "Measures of inequality." Amer. Soc. Rev. 43 (December): 865-880.

BELL, D. (1976) The Coming of Post-Industrial Society. New York: Basic Books.

BLAU, P. M. (1980) "Implications of growth in services for social structure." Social Sci. Q. 61 (June): 3-22.

———(1974) "Presidential address: parameters of social structure." Amer. Soc. Rev. 39 (October): 615-635.

BLOOMQUIST, L. and G. SUMMERS (1982) "Organization of production and community income distribution." Amer. Soc. Rev. 47 (June): 325-338.

BLUMBERG, P. (1980) Inequality in an Age of Decline. New York: Oxford Univ. Press.

BRAVERMAN, H. (1974) Labor and Monopoly Capital. New York: Monthly Review Press.

BROWNING, H. and J. SINGLEMANN (1980) "Industrial transformation and occupational change in the U.S., 1960-1970." Social Forces 59 (September): 246-264.

———(1978) "The transformation of the U.S. labor force: the interaction of industry and occupation." Politics and Society 8: 481-509.

BURNS, L. S. (1975) "The urban income distribution." Regional Sci. and Urban Economics 5 (December): 465-485.

CARCHEDI, G. (1975) "On the economic identification of the new middle class." Economy and Society 4 (February): 1-83.

CUTRIGHT, P. (1967) "Inequality: a cross-national analysis." Amer. Soc. Rev. 32 (August): 562-578.

DANZIGER, S. (1976) "Determinants of the level and distribution of family income in metropolitan areas, 1969." Land Economics 53 (November): 467-478.

DUNCAN, O. D., W. R. SCOTT, S. LIEBERSON, and B. D. DUNCAN (1960) Metropolis and Region. Baltimore: Johns Hopkins Univ. Press.

DURDEN, G. C. and A. V. SCHWARTZ-MILLER (1982) "Distribution of individual income in the U.S. and public sector employment." Social Sci. Q. 63 (March): 39-47.

FARBMAN, M. (1975) "The size distribution of family income in U.S. SMSA's, 1950." Rev. of Income and Wealth 21 (June): 217-237.

FOGEL, W. and D. LEWIN (1974) "Wage determination in the public sector." Industrial and Labor Relations Rev. 27 (April): 410-431.

FOOTE, N. N. and P. K. HATT (1953) "Social mobility and economic advancement." Amer. Econ. Rev. 43 (May): 364-378.

FRECH, H. E. and L. S. BURNS (1971) "Metropolitan interpersonal income inequality." Land Economics 47 (February): 104-106.

FUCHS, V. R. (1968) The Service Economy. New York: National Bureau of Economic Research.

GALLE, O. R. (1963) "Occupational composition and the metropolitan hierarchy: the inter and intra-metropolitan division of labor." Amer. J. of Sociology 69 (November): 260-269.

GAROFALO, G. and M. S. FOGARTY (1979) "Urban income distribution and the urban hierarchy-inequality hypothesis." Rev. of Economics and Statistics 61 (August): 381-388.

GREENFIELD, H. (1966) Manpower and the Growth of Producer Services. New York: Columbia Univ. Press.

HAWLEY, A. H. (1968) "Human ecology," pp. 328-337 in David Sils (ed.) Encyclopedia of the Social Sciences. New York: Macmillan.

HAWORTH, C. T., J. LONG, and D. W. RASMUSSEN (1978) "Income distribution, city size, and urban growth." Urban Studies 15 (February): 1-7.

HENLE, P. (1972) "Exploring the distribution of earned income." Monthly Labor Rev. 95 (December): 16-27.
HIRSCH, B. (1982) "Income distribution, city size, and urban growth: a reexamination." Urban Studies 19 (February): 71-74.
KUZNETS, S. (1955) "Economic growth and income inequality." Amer. Econ. Rev. 45 (March): 1-28.
LENSKI, G. E. (1966) Power and Privilege. New York: McGraw-Hill.
LINCOLN, J. R. (1978) "Community structure and industrial conflict: an analysis of strike activity in SMSAs." Amer. Soc. Rev. 43 (April): 199-220.
———and R. FRIEDLAND (1977) "Metropolitan dominance and income levels in nonmetropolitan cities." Soc. and Social Research 61 (April): 304-319.
LYDALL, H. (1968) The Structure of Earnings. Oxford: Oxford Univ. Press.
MAUME, D. S. (1983) "Metropolitan hierarchy and income distribution: a comparison of explanations." Urban Affairs Q. 18 (March): 413-429.
MINCER, J. (1974) Schooling, Experience, and Earnings. New York: National Bureau of Economic Research.
MOORE, W. (1963) Social Change. Englewood Cliffs, NJ: Prentice-Hall.
MURRAY, B. (1969) "Metropolitan interpersonal income inequality." Land Economics 47 (February): 104-106.
New York Times (1983) "New York: financial market for the world." (March 22): 12.
POULANTZAS, N. (1975) Classes in Contemporary Capitalism. London: New Left Books.
RUBINSON, R. (1976) "The world-economy and the distribution of income within states." Amer. Soc. Rev. 41 (August): 638-659.
STANBACK, T. (1979) Understanding the Service Economy. Baltimore: Johns Hopkins Univ. Press.
———P. J. BEARSE, T. J. NOYELL, and R. A. KARASEK (1983) Services: The New Economy. Totowa, NJ: Allanheld, Osmun.
STEPHENS, J. (1980) The Transition from Capitalism to Socialism. Atlantic Highlands, NJ: Humanities Press.
THOMPSON, W. (1968) A Preface to Urban Economics. Baltimore: Johns Hopkins Univ. Press.
U. S. Bureau of the Census (1983) Census of the Population: 1980, General Social and Economic Characteristics (State Editions). Washington, DC: Government Printing Office.
———(1982) Statistical Abstract of the U.S. 1982-83. Washington, DC: Government Printing Office.
———(1981) County Business Patterns, 1980. Washington, DC: Government Printing Office.
———(1973a) County and City Data Book, 1972. Washington, DC: Government Printing Office.
———(1973b) Census of the Population: 1970 Detailed Characteristics, Final Report PC(1)-D1, United States Summary. Washington, DC: Government Printing Office.
———(1972a) Census of the Population: 1970 Detailed Characteristics (State Editions). Washington, DC: Government Printing Office.
———(1972b) Census of the Population: 1970, General Social and Economic Characteristics. Washington, DC: Government Printing Office.

———(1971) County Business Patterns, 1970. Washington, DC: Government Printing Office.

WRIGHT, E. O. (1976) "Class boundaries in advanced capitalist societies." New Left Rev. 98 (July-August): 3-42.

Joel I. Nelson is Professor of Sociology at the University of Minnesota. His research interests address the relationship of work activities to income inequality. Some broader concerns pertaining to inequality are explored in his recently published Economic Inequality: Conflict Without Change *(New York: Columbia University Press, 1983).*

Jon Lorence is Assistant Professor of Sociology at the University of Houston, University Park. His research interests address the effects of changing industrial structure on occupational and economic inequality. He has coauthored numerous articles and a forthcoming book, Work, Family, and Personality: The Early Adult Years, *pertaining to the impact of work experiences on individual attainment and psychological outcomes.*

PLANNERS AND THE PUBLIC

Howell Baum, *Planners and Public Expectations* (Boston: A. Schenkman Publishing, 1983). 306 pp. $15.95 (cloth), $9.95 (paper).

Howell Baum has written a carefully documented and unquestionably provocative psychological study of the contemporary planning profession. Based on a random sample of planners in Maryland, Baum's study employed extensive interviews to investigate how planning practitioners think and feel about their work, about their status as professionals, their senses of work well or poorly done, their organizational contexts, and their efficacy more generally.

Baum's results are disturbing. Planners seem often to be an unhappy lot, overly focused on problems to the neglect of practical processes, uncertain about their professional mission, and thus in doubt about their own legitimacy as professional actors. The study seems to confirm previous research suggesting that practitioners fall into several clusters of practical types, although the proper interpretation of these types varies. What Howe and Kaufman labeled "technicians" and "politicians" (with 50% of their sample being "hybrids" of two) Baum characterizes more psychologically: There are planners claiming to be and sounding like "intellectual problem-solvers" and there are those who seem more interpersonally adept, organizationally sensitive, and politically astute. Yet what is new and provocative in this book is its tone as well as its substance.

Here is a study in the experience of organizational chaos, bureaucratic anonymity, and practical frustration. That such problems exist is hardly news, but how they are handled in the planning profession has never received the attention that it receives here. Baum tells the unhappy story—in the planners' own words, for the most part—of planners who began with visions of working to create a better society and who ended up settling for a few words of praise from their supervisor. Baum shows us vividly how that same planners who are frustrated with their own powerlessness are nevertheless often ignorant of the political and organizational settings within which they work. Here a vicious circle seems to have become a pathetic dead-end.

Baum is interested in the 'cognitive maps'' of planners. When they describe their organizations, to what do they call attention? Do they seem to have coherent images and stories that make sense of and help to explain their experiences? What is most helpful in this study is simply to have an account of the variation in planner's responses, for this raises fascinating research questions for the further study of planning professionals—to say nothing of the expected benefits this may have for the training and practice of those same professionals.

What issues, then, does Baum raise as seriously deserving attention? Note that this book reports not a study of planning practice but one of planners' self-descriptions, modes of thinking, cognitive maps, attitudes toward clients and politics, perceptions of organizational context, and so on. The study's strength is its weakness as well. No one who reads this book can help but wish to know more about the practical "cognitive maps" that planners now have. And this concern immediately raises important subsequent questions to find answers to: How are cognitive maps structured? How do they change? How do they evolve? When and how does planning education—in the classroom, in the field, in internships, in study—alter planners' cognitive maps? If the capacity of these cognitive maps was found to be relatively fixed after childhood, what would this mean for the selection of candidates for planning positions, or for planning schools, for example? But here the cart is before the horse.

Before anyone can even begin to ask such questions, a great deal more must be done to set out the notion of a cognitive map itself. Here Baum's study curiously seems to get into some of the trouble that it finds in the field. When planners are found at times to have simplistic or thin images of the organizations in which they work, it is hardly clear to the reader what might have counted as a complex or sophisticated cognitive map of the organizational environment. Certainly many of the planners to who Baum talked might have speculated (or even gossiped), for example, at length about various projects that they had worked on; but would such speculation, rich in detail as it might have been, counted as evidence of sophisticated cognitive maps, or as evidence of a fertile imagination combined perhaps with quite ordinary organizational skills?

What about the relationship between the political environment of planning and these planners' experiences and images of the world? Here again Baum's study is rich and telling, but at times only frustratingly suggestive as well. For this study is without doubt the single most compelling and sensitive study of the political and organizational alienation of contemporary planners. The work provides a feel for this problem that will give some readers a good case of empathic angst; although Baum's research is not without hope, and indeed suggestions for professional education and practice, the story is not a happy one. This, however, is all the more reason to pursue these issues and work to improve the present education practice of planning professionals.

Yet there is a problem. To be able to change planners' alienation at work, we need a coherent, systematic account of the roots—or perhaps of the reproduction—of that alienation. The roots are more (or less) important as the subsequent influences on planners' skills, images, dispositions, and cognitive maps cannot (or alternatively can) be changed. Similarly, the reproduction of that alienation is more (or less) important as current political, social, and economic influences do (or do not) alter planners' thinking, feeling, and practice. If the psychological dispositions of planners evolve and develop, then the institutional and ideological forces that frame specific problems, particular organizations, and specific regional economies will need scrutiny—for the experience and practical possibilities of planning will be affected, if not determined, by these forces as a result.

If, on the other hand, a case can be made (as Baum comes close to suggesting in places) that planners' psychological dispositions are more fixed than we might ordinarily think—only in California jokes do personalities change overnight—then there will be important lessons for the planning profession and indeed for all of the helping professions as well to learn about the character of professional practice. If school teachers, counselors, social workers, and public administrators of all sorts also provide evidence of the frustration and organizational blindness that Baum has found, does this evidence in any way weaken his argument about the need to assess the psychological traits of professional planners? Surely not. Yet the very force of the psychological findings seems to call for a complementary institutional, political, and sociological analysis of those results. This is to call for research that Baum has not set out to do, but it is work that his own provocative study makes now more compelling than ever.

Finally, Baum seems painfully aware of the methodological limitations of his own (and others') work. His many suggestions and provisional findings, then, become hypotheses for others to corroborate or weaken. His careful listening should prompt others to do interviews of still greater depth and perhaps still others to link such interviews to observations of actual practice. Linking interviews to such observation of practice not only would serve as a check on the planners' self-reports, it would make even more clear than this important study just how planners' psychological dispositions, skills, and cognitive maps systematically influence—and are influenced by—the institutional processes and politics of planning practice.

—*John Forester*
Cornell University

PUBLIC PROPERTY AND PRIVATE POWER

Hendrik Hartog, *Public Property and Private Power: The Corporation of the City of New York in American Law, 1730-1870* (Chapel Hill: University of North Carolina Press, 1983). 274 pp. $27.50 (cloth).

The question of the legitimate, rightful, or appropriate powers of municipalities has vexed American politics for over 150 years. No less than the legal debates in the 1820s, contemporary arguments over the sovereign status of municipal corporations contain a philosophical righteousness sufficient to convince any observer that the very essence of self-governance is at stake. In point of fact, cities are limited in their revenue options by state constitutional and statutory constraints, and those that have sought revenue flexibility through expansion of their proprietary functions have run aground on the relatively uncharted shoals of municipal liability under federal antitrust legislation. To the dismay of local officials, recent Supreme Court decisions such as *Lafayette v. Louisiana Power & Light* (1978) and *Community Communications v. Boulder* (1982) have reaffirmed that the actions of cities are not necessarily clothed in the sovereign immunity enjoyed by states. In the face of burgeoning costs of local services and restricted sources of revenue, it seems a bit fatalistic to cite Dillon's Rule and shrug one's shoulders in helpless dismay.

In this context, *Public Property and Private Power* is quite illuminating. In an exhaustive legal history, Hartog examines the evolution of the legal status of the municipal corporation of the city of New York. The focus of his research is the shift in the legal basis of municipal corporation rights from the holding and management of private estates (private property granted by royal charter) to statutory authorization by the state legislature. He documents legal and political processess by which, between 1730 and 1800, public action in the city of New York was transformed from a collection of private actions warranted by sets of ordinances or conditions of land conveyance to a collection of judicially determined public responsibilities fulfilled by public employees and requiring the collection of general revenues.

The catalyst of this transformation was, of course, the ascendancy of Republican political values in the eighteenth century. In Hartog's view, the municipal corporation could no longer legitimately govern with powers delegated to it under royal charter and, therefore, shifted the source of its authority to statutory authorization. This shift, he maintains, was conscious, purposeful, and voluntary, as such legislative authorizations were primarily initiated by city officials themselves. As long as the state legislature complied with city needs for specific authorizations, the municipal corporation was able to exercise as much sovereign discretion as it had under royal charter.

The shift eventuated a dramatic and irreducible legal tension between the corporation's public responsibilities and its private rights. This tension is demonstrated in the case of *Brick Presbyterian Church v. Mayor of New York* (1823), in which the city in its public role under state statute attempted to regulate the use of private property that it had granted earlier under its charter rights. The outcome of the case—that the city in its public role could legally regulate church cemeteries—reflected commonly accepted and applied judicial doctrine concerning the duality of corporation functions. The corporation's private (sovereign) rights remained intact only in those functional areas not preempted by state statute; but in functional areas addressed by statute corporation property holdings were interpreted by the courts as creating explicit public obligations.

This duality of public and private functions presented few difficulties to city authorities as long as they maintained as amiable relationship with the state legislature. But the benign symbiosis was interrupted by the judicial activism of the 1830s, an activism Hartog attributes to an emerging distrust in the ability of legislative bodies to make wise public decisions. The judicial interpretation that became thoroughly entrenched as the core doctrine of local government law by the 1840s (some 30 years before Dillon's *Treatise* was published) required that local action follow specific and unambiguous statutory language, even in areas of "traditional" functions and despite "clear legislative intent" in areas of broader grants. Judicial authority had effectively been interposed between the state legislature and the city, and state statutes served only as an impetus for judicial interpretation of local authority. By 1850, the legal status of municipal corporations was a matter of judicial definition.

The public-private distinction developed in the early nineteenth century was completely undermined in the process. Property holdings and rights of the corporation, long held as private and thus invulnerable to intervention by the state, were interpreted as held solely for public purposes to be determined by the state legislature. This eliminated the last traces of similarity in legal status (with respect to autonomy) between municipal and private corporations, and no sphere of municipal activity was immune from legislative intervention. Even enabling state legislation, whether general or specific, could not create a sphere of autonomous action; it only created a basis for judicial reinterpretation (and perhaps redefinition) of municipal legal status. Consequently, the municipal corporation could claim immunity from liability only for those actions specifically authorized by state statute, by which the state demonstrated an active interest in, and endorsed, an explicit municipal role. Municipal actions beyond those authorizations would be subject to standard forms of private liability.

Public Property and Private Power is a definitive study of the evolution of the legal status of municipal corporations in the eighteenth and nineteenth centuries. It demonstrates a continuity of judicial interpretation from the legal battles over waterlot grants in the 1830s through the recent Supreme Court cases denying to municipal corporations automatic sovereign immunity from antitrust claims. It establishes the legal and historical foundations of Dillon's Rule, and therein provides thoughtful perspective on the much-debated and still current issue of municipal sovereignty. Although it focuses on one (albeit unique) municipal corporation, its political and legal-historical perspectives are of much wider applicability.

—*James R. Alexander*
University of Pittsburgh
at Johnstown

URBAN DISPLACEMENT RESEARCH
Local, National, International

Dennis E. Gale, *Neighborhood Revitalization and the Postindustrial City: A Multinational Perspective* (Lexington, MA: Lexington Books, 1984). 183 pp. $22.00 (cloth).

John J. Palen and Bruce London (eds.) *Gentrification, Displacement, and Neighborhood Revitalization* (Albany: State University of New York Press, 1984). 271 pp. $34.50 (cloth), $12.95 (paper).

Michael H. Schill and Richard P. Nathan, *Revitalizing America's Cities: Neighborhood Reinvestment and Displacement* (Albany: State University of New York Press, 1983). 184 pp. $29.50 (cloth), $10.00 (paper).

Gentrification-caused displacement in urban neighborhood rebitalization continues to be a controversial issue in many redeveloping cities. The debate over the magnitude and impact of displacement and the choice of an appropriate public policy response remains unresolved.

This issue assumed national significance during the Carter administration, when opponents of displacement criticized federal policy as inadequate. This influenced the U.S. Department of Housing and Urban Development (HUD) to revise and increase its estimates of the magnitude of displacement, undertake a national study of displacement, and fund several local antidisplacement experimental projects. When the Reagan administration assumed office, it immediately rejected any federal role in regulating federally assisted activities leading to displacement. This policy has transformed the displacement debate into a largely localized concern.

As the three books reviewed here suggest, the Reagan administration's disavowal of federal responsibility for displacement has not made the issue disappear. For example, in *The Transformation of San Francisco,* Chester Hartman (1984) argues that the process of redevelopment, originally through urban renewal and later through gentrification, has significantly reduced San Francisco's poor and minority population and changed the city's character. He predicts,

> The future of the non-rich in San Francisco, and in other U.S. cities with similar downtown growth pressures and patterns, is also an uncertain one. It is not likely they will be shoved out of the city altogether. Rather, they will increas-

> ingly concentrate in more outlying parts of the city, in overcrowded conditions caused by a need to double up in order to afford prevailing rent and ownership costs, and forced to pay 40, 50 percent, and more of their income for housing. More and more they will become a permanent underclass supporting, through their labor and taxes, a predominantly middle- and upper-middle-class population and a city that exists largely to serve those who do not live there. [Hartman, 1984: 326].

In contrast to Hartman's account, the empirical research of others has not substantiated claims that displacement has had such a significant impact on urban neighborhoods in cities undergoing revitalization.

Princeton researchers Michael Schill and Richard Nathan studied nine neighborhoods in five cities: Boston, Cincinnati, Denver, Richmond, and Seattle. They surveyed tenant outmovers over a one-year period (1979-1980), seeking to determine the magnitude, causes, and impact of displacement in representative neighborhoods. They found that an average of 23% of their sample was displaced. They did not find that those displaced conformed to popular stereotypes of displacees as predominantly poor, minority, and elderly. They did find a strong correlation between lower income and the likelihood of tenant displacement. Most displaces moved to nearby neighborhoods. Comparing those involuntarily displaced with voluntary movers, their survey revealed that a majority of the former rated their new housing and neighborhood as either good or excellent and better than their former residence and neighborhood, although similar ratings were higher among the latter group.

Based on their findings, the authors conclude that any harm attributable to involuntary displacement is outweighed by its benefits and that cities should encourage the urban reinvestment process. They do suggest reforms that could be adopted by local government to reduce the admitted hardship to some displaces caused by involuntary displacement (see, for example, Bryant and McGee, 1983). These include tenant protection and preservation of low-cost housing (pp. 139-142).

As the authors admit, their methodology had limits. Among those that could have biased their findings were the following: (1) the choice of selected representative neighborhoods, rather than a citywide sample; (2) the snapshot study period of only one year; (3) nonresponse, especially by transients (the response rate was only 35%; and (4) the difficulty of defining involuntary displacement and its impact for opinion survey purposes.

A more mixed review is given by Frank DeGiovanni in his six-city (Atlanta, Cincinnati, Denver, Hartford, Philadelphia, and San Francisco) analysis of displacement in selected neighborhoods, which appears in Palen and London's collection. DeGiovanni notes that although cities have seen housing renovated and tax assessments in creased though reinvestment, the displacement of lower-class tenants and diminution of the lower-income rental housing supply may offset the benefits of gentrification (pp. 82-84). In another analysis DeGiovanni notes that the profile of in-mover homeowners is quite different than that of in-mover tenants in two neighborhoods in Atlanta and Philadelphia. The former were typically young, upper-income professionals conforming to the popular "yuppie" image of gentrifiers. In contrast, the latter generally had the same lower socioeconomic status as the long-term residents of those neighborhoods (DeGiovanni and Paulson, 1984). He suggests that as long as affordable rental housing remains available in gentrifying neighborhoods, there can be significant social and economic diversity. However, he could not predict whether this diversity could be sustained in the future.

Dennis Gale's empirical research did not consist of survey data. Instead, Gale studied selected census tracts in five cities (Atlanta, Cincinnati, Denver, San Francisco, and Washington, D.C.) using 1970 and 1980 census data to determine demographic shifts attributable to gentrification. Gale concluded that over this decade the net effect of gentrification was an increasing number of more affluent, better educated newcomers replacing long-term residents of a lower socioeconomic class. However, this pattern was not consistent. Moreover, Gale found little evidence of significant changes in the racial composition of these neighborhoods. Gale concluded that revitalization was generally characterized by an upward socioeconomic transition. Overall, revitalizing neighborhoods lost population. Outmigrants were replaced mostly by city residents, not suburbanites.

Palen and London's collection includes additional American case studies of Milwaukee, New Orleans, and New York. Articles by the editors, Barrett Lee, David Hodge, and Jeffrey Henig, provide informative analyses of the many methodological problems confronting researchers addressing this topic, whatever the source of their data and the time frame of their studies. Lee and Hodge analyzed 1974-1976 Annual Housing Survey data from 60 metropolitan areas to test the hypothesis that displacement disproportionately burdens the urban underclass—the elderly, low-income, black, and female-headed households. Henig explored the impact of displacement on the elderly in nine cities, based on data from the R. L. Polk *Profiles of Change* during the mid-late 1970s.

The Palen and London collection provides an international perspective. Noting the similarities in the international pattern of urban revitalization and gentrification, the editors have included essays on these issues in Australia, Canada, Great Britain, and Western Europe. Case studies of such cities as London, Melbourne, and Vancouver provide comparative examples. The authors of these case studies all conclude that the process and impact of gentrification-caused displacement may be affected by the degree of governmental intervention.

Gale also presents a comparative multinational perspective. His own research includes studies of Amsterdam, London, Paris, and Stockholm. He notes similarities in the "strong social class implications of revitalization" (p. 135). However, he indicates that in Western Europe three factors have combined to reduce displacement: (1) the varying central city housing stock; (2) the absence of extensive slums and deteriorating housing; and (3) the more elaborate network of public intervention in the housing market (p. 149).

Gale points out that the gentrification phenomenon must be understood in the context of the restructuring of the economy of the postindustrial city. He cautions planners against targeting inordinate amounts of government assistance to provide subsidized housing in the central city. Instead, he suggests that economic development, employment training, and income maintenance for the population most vulnerable to displacement may be better long-term strategies (p. 165). Nevertheless, Gale does propose a displacement mitigation strategy for local government consisting of four elements: (1) a housing information system; (2) efforts to disperse middle-class demand for older urban housing; (3) displacement retardant mechanisms (property tax relief and tenant protection; and (4) a displacement relief fund (pp. 93-105).

Whether displacement is of such a magnitude as to justify governmental intervention in the housing market and the extent of such intervention often depends on the ideological perspective of the researcher. Palen and London include two essays on the ideology and class significance of gentrification and the importance of these factors in social science research on this subject. The class significance of the gentrification-displacement phenomenon is critical to all of the research contained in these volumes. The central question is whether urban revitalization signals middle- and upper-income domination of the central city or, alternatively, that diverse mixed class neighborhoods are an attainable goal. Palen and London conclude by cautioning (p. 265),

> In the study of phenomena such as gentrification, our best effort can only be directed toward understanding who decides what these policies will be and who does, and does not, benefit from the policies implemented. Inevitably, where class interests become so salient, ideology enters into the analysis and the achievement of true understanding of the causal processes involved becomes no mean task.

It is noteworthy that researchers such as Gale, Nathan, and Schill suggest a variety of policies and programs that local government might institute to reduce involuntary displacement. These recommendations are made despite their findings that widespread involuntary displacement resulting in serious hardship cannot be documented. This view supports the position that government can act to promote an integrated (socially, racially, and economically) version of revitalization without having to prove the necessity of instituting such policy based on researchers' prior proof of massive involuntary displacement. This is especially important in light of the long-term nature of the gentrification process, in which dramatic short-term residential turnover patterns in revitalizing areas are rare. In fact, as several authors mention, some American cities have acted to prevent or reduce displacement, usually in response to serious political conflict over current and potential displacement of lower-income groups.

As many distressed American central cities consciously compete to attract the middle-class resettlement of older declining neighborhoods, social scientists should continue to study not only the impact of the dynamics of neighborhood change and public policies affecting gentrification but also the process and context in which gentrification-caused displacement is debated and researched and the outcomes. As Palen and London suggest, this may be the most valuable contribution of social scientists.

—*W. Dennis Keating*
Cleveland State University

REFERENCES

BRYANT, D. C. and H. W. McGEE (1983) "Gentrification and the law: combatting urban displacement." Washington Univ. J. of Urban and Contemporary Law 25: 43-144.

DeGIOVANNI, R. R. and N. A. PAULSON (1984) "Household diversity in revitalizing neighborhoods." Urban Affairs Q. 29 (December): 211-232.

HARTMAN, C. (1984) The Transformation of San Francisco. Totowa, NJ: Rowman & Allanheld.

New From Sage!

URBAN ETHNICITY IN THE UNITED STATES

New Immigrants and Old Minorities

edited by LIONEL MALDONADO,
University of Wisconsin, Kenosha
& JOAN MOORE,
University of Wisconsin—Milwaukee

Hundreds of thousands of non-Europeans have settled in the United States since immigration laws changed in the mid-1960s. The contributors to this collection point out that neither urban specialists nor the general public have fully recognized the effect of this immigration on the American city. How do the newcomers differ from the older monorities? Are metropolitan areas more divided as a result of this influx? How have different sectors—education, health, criminal justice, and so on—responded to the more diverse ethnicity of the inner cities? The authors provide detailed answers to these and many more questions about the new immigrants.

This collection contains two parts. Part I gives basic historical and demographic analyses: a review of past efforts to reform the immigration system, a profile of the post-1965 immigrants, a case study of immigration issues in Los Angeles, and a critical assessment of existing data and research on new immigants. Part II examines specific institutional responses to current problems: race, color, and language diversity in the schools; ethnic divisions of the urban labor market; political economy of ethnic crime; and new demands on the social welfare and mental health system.

Complete with an extensive, up-to-date bibliography, **Urban Ethnicity in the United States** is a useful reference work for researchers, practitioners, and policymakers in urban and minority affairs, education, health and social services, and other fields affected by recent immigration.

CONTENTS: Preface S. GREER / Introduction L. MALDONALDO & J. MOORE // **I. Historical, Demographic, and Ecological Considerations** // 1. Immigration Reform and Immigration History: Why Simpson-Mazzoli Did Not Pass M. CONK / 2. Post-1965 Immigrants: Demographic and Socioeconomic Profile M.G. WONG / 3. Immigration Issues in Urban Ecology: The Case of Los Angeles P. GARCIA / 4. Improving the Data: A Research Strategy for New Immigrants J. HERNANDEZ // **II. Institutional Contexts and Responses** // 5. Race, Color, and Language: Changing Schools in Urban America R.R. FERNANDEZ & W. VELEZ / 6. Urban Labor Markets and Ethnicity: Segments and Shelters Reexamined M. FREEDMAN / 7. Political Economy and the Social Control of Ethnic Crime E.R. MILLER & L.H. KLEINMAN / 8. Ethnicity and Social Welfare in American Cities: A Historical View R.S. MAGILL / 9. Ethnicity, Mental Health, and the Urban Delivery System W.T. LIU & E.S.H. YU / 10. Rainbow's End: From the Old to the New Urban Ethnic Politics S.P. ERIE / References

Urban Affairs Annual Reviews, Volume 29
1985 (June) / 304 pages / $29.95 (h) / $14.95 (p)

SAGE PUBLICATIONS, INC.
275 South Beverly Drive,
Beverly Hills, California 90212

SAGE PUBLICATIONS LTD
28 Banner Street,
London EC1Y 8QE, England

SAGE PUBLICATIONS INDIA PVT LTD
M-32 Market, Greater Kailash I, New Delhi 110 048, India

mposium:
e Local Impacts
Economic Change

est Editors:
san E. Clarke
tevens Redburn
rry Buss

urban affairs
quarterly

volume 21, number 2 / december 1985

SAGE PUBLICATIONS

urban affairs quarterly

SAGE Publications / *Beverly Hills* / *London* / *New Delhi*

urban affairs quarterly

volume 21, number 2 / december 1985

contents

Symposium:
The Local Impacts of Economic Change
Edited by: SUSAN E. CLARKE
University of Colorado, Boulder
F. STEVENS REDBURN
U.S. Department of Housing and Urban Development
TERRY BUSS
Youngstown State University

The Local Impacts of Economic Change
SUSAN E. CLARKE
F. STEVENS REDBURN
TERRY BUSS **139**

Urban Dependencies: *New Forms of Use and Exchange in U.S. Cities*
HARVEY MOLOTCH
JOHN R. LOGAN **143**

Communities in Crisis: *The Social and Political Effects of Steel Closures in France, West Germany, and the United Kingdom*
RAY HUDSON
DAVID SADLER **171**

Economic Restructuring and the Rise of Urban Social Movements
SUSAN S. FAINSTEIN
NORMAN I. FAINSTEIN **187**

Nine Fallacies of Local Economic Change
ANDREW KIRBY **207**

Other Articles

Swedish Housing in the Postwar Period
RICHARD P. APPELBAUM **221**

The Impact of Metropolitan School Desegregation on Public Opinion: *A Longitudinal Analysis*
JEFFREY A. RAFFEL **245**

Whose Neighborhood? *The Role of Established Residents in Historic Preservation Areas*
TIMOTHY MAHER
AIN HAAS
BETTY LEVINE
JOHN LIELL **267**

Book Review Essay

State of the Art in Urban Research: 1923
FREDERICK M. WIRT **282**

MANUSCRIPTS should be submitted to the editors in care of The Editors, **URBAN AFFAIRS QUARTERLY**, Center for Metropolitan Studies, University of Missouri, 8001 Natural Bridge Rd., St Louis, MO 63121. Include *five* (5) copies of the manuscript. Full-length manuscripts should not exceed 25 pages total and research notes should not exceed 10 pages total (*including* footnotes, references, and tables or figures). All text, footnotes, and references should be typewritten with one-inch margins and double-spaced. All references to the author's previous work should be omitted in the text. Footnotes and bibliographic citations should follow the current **UAQ** style. Copies of the style sheets may be obtained from the editors or the publisher. A brief biographical paragraph describing each author's current affiliation, research interests, and recent publications should be submitted, and an abstract of approximately 100 words should accompany each copy of the manuscript.

Manuscripts will not be returned to authors. Please keep copies for your own needs. The editors assume that manuscripts are for the exclusive consideration of **UAQ** and have not simultaneously been submitted elsewhere.

BOOKS FOR REVIEW should be sent to Professor Bryan D. Jones, Book Review Editor, **URBAN AFFAIRS QUARTERLY**, Department of Political Science, Wayne State University, Detroit, Michigan 48202. Potential contributors of book review essays are encouraged to correspond with the book review editor before submitting manuscripts.

The Editor and Publisher are grateful to the Center for Urban Affairs and Policy Research, Northwestern University, for providing facilities and ancillary services for URBAN AFFAIRS QUARTERLY.

URBAN AFFAIRS QUARTERLY is published four times annually—in September, December, March, and June—by Sage Publications, Inc., 275 South Beverly Drive, Beverly Hills, CA 90212.

Subscriptions: Regular institutional rate $63.00 per year. Individuals may subscribe at a one-year rate of $25.00. Add $6.00 for subscriptions outside the United States. Orders from the U.K., Europe, the Middle East, and Africa should be sent to London address (below). Orders from India should be sent to the New Delhi address (below). Noninstitutional orders **must** be paid by personal check.

Second class postage paid at Beverly Hills, California. ISSN 0042-0816

This journal is abstracted or indexed in **Sage Urban Studies Abstracts, Human Resources Abstracts, Educational Administration Abstracts, Sociological Abstracts, Abstracts for Social Workers, ABC POL SCI, Sociology of Education Abstracts, Urban Affairs Abstracts, Sage Public Administration Abstracts, International Political Science Abstracts, Ethnic Studies Bibliography, Public Affairs Information Service, Ekistic Index, Current Contents, Social Science Citation Index,** and **United States Political Science Documents,** and is available on microfilm from University Microfilms, Ann Arbor, Michigan.

Back Issues: Information about availability and prices of back issues may be obtained from the publisher's order department (address below). Single-issue orders for 5 or more copies will receive a special adoption discount. Contact the order department for details. Write to London office for sterling prices.

Inquiries: Address all correspondence and permissions requests to SAGE PUBLICATIONS, Inc., 275 South Beverly Drive, Beverly Hills, California 90212. Inquiries and subscriptions from the U.K., Europe, the Middle East, and Africa should be sent to SAGE PUBLICATIONS Ltd, 28 Banner Street, London EC1Y 8QE, England. From India, write to SAGE PUBLICATIONS INDIA Pvt. Ltd, P.O. Box 4215, New Delhi 110 048 India. Other orders should be sent to the Beverly Hills office.

Advertising: Current rates and specifications may be obtained by writing to the Advertising Manager at the Beverly Hills office (address above).

Claims: Claims for undelivered copies must be made no later than three months following month of publication. The publisher will supply missing copies when losses have been sustained in transit and when the reserve stock will permit.

Change of Address: Six weeks' advance notice must be given when notifying of change of address. Please send old address label along with the new address to insure proper identification. Please specify name of journal. POSTMASTER: Send change of address to: Urban Affairs Quarterly, c/o 275 South Beverly Drive, Beverly Hills, CA 90212.

SYMPOSIUM
The Local Impacts of Economic Change

SUSAN E. CLARKE
University of Colorado, Boulder

F. STEVENS REDBURN
Office of Policy, Development and Research, HUD

TERRY BUSS
Youngstown State University

In the last decade or so, cities have been affected by a set of powerful international economic forces: the growth of a new class of corporate and financial institutions largely independent of either local or national government regulation; a drastic shift in the international division of labor, both among industrial nations and between them and previously nonindustrial societies; and a deeper interpenetration of national economies through foreign investment and heightened trade. These powerful forces have combined to dramatically alter the circumstances of cities and urban regions that grew up during the preceding industrial era.

We have much to learn about the present and eventual consequences of these international economic changes for places that thrived in previous decades. Already, however, we can see that there will be winners and losers: Some areas have employment and income losses in some sectors that are being at least offset by gains in other sectors, whereas other areas appear to be, or are becoming, economically redundant.

In both transitional and declining areas, international economic change produces simultaneous pressures to recapitalize industries that use cities, to preserve or to liquidate existing capital investments in cities, and to protect the personal and community interests in cities as places to

---

AUTHORS' NOTE: *The Colorado Center for Public Policy Research at the University of Colorado, Boulder supported the development of this symposium. We would like to acknowledge the help of Mary French and Ron Brunner, the Center director, in bringing out this issue.*

URBAN AFFAIRS QUARTERLY, Vol. 21 No. 2, December 1985 139-141

live. These pressures translate into political conflict and the potential for both innovation and disorder.

Despite the powerful economic currents affecting cities of the industrial era, local decision makers are not entirely helpless. The responses of both national and local governments and community leaders call for analysis, to determine both why they respond as they do and with what impacts on economic and social conditions in transitional and declining cities.

The four articles in this symposium are all addressed to the questions raised above: What is happening to established urban areas as a result of global economic changes, and how will they, or can they, respond? These analyses, frankly, are more troubled and perhaps less optimistic about the local impacts of economic change than the analyses of the authors in *Urban Affairs Quarterly*'s June 1985 symposium, "Whatever Happened to the Urban Crisis?" The distinctive insights generated by these two symposia stem from different responses to two pervasive questions regarding local economic development: a pragmatic query about what policy tools work to bring about the desired development, and a continuing concern with the limitations of the public sector's efforts to contend with market forces.

Molotch and Logan examine the changing economic hierarchy of U.S. cities as a function of two distinct sets of urban interests: "those seeking wealth through the development, sale or rent of land and buildings . . . and those whose primary interest in place is [as] a setting for daily life and production." Their use of the concepts of use value and exchange value to frame redevelopment conflicts offers a powerful means of examining the interests and issues stimulated by restructuring processes. The normative implications they draw from their analysis of the emerging urban system are equally provocative. Their argument that some strategically placed cities are able to "up the ante for growth" in the conditions they impose on capital for access to place challenges local officials to come up with development policies that benefit public as well as private interests. To the extent that these strategically placed cities drive harder, better bargains, Molotch and Logan claim they will create a ripple effect throughout the urban hierarchy, one that improves the bargaining position and investment potential of all other communities.

Hudson and Sadler's case study of several European steel communities highlights the painful adjustments to economic change experienced by those production centers lower down the emerging economic hierarchy. Their analysis reveals the difficulty of constructing effective public policies, at either a national or local level, to mitigate the economic losses borne by residents of these unlucky places. Indeed, they argue that the structural effects of such policy efforts may be to increase competition between areas for investment and jobs and to alter the political terrain in ways detrimental to the real interests of workers. Their pessimistic conclusion is that policy alternatives must take as their point of departure "the bankruptcy of past and present state intervention."

The Fainsteins' article examines the contrasting case of a major U.S. metropolitan area making the transition to a new role as a "command post for world financial capital": New York City. Their focus is on urban social movements and the political factors that influence their impacts. Noting that the collectivities generated by economic restructuring "have so far not developed the consciousness of action groups," they consider several possible explanations for this quietude in a time of economic upheaval. The response they advocate is the development of a mass political party that could provide the ideological and organizational resources that would allow territorially based local groups to link their specific concerns with larger economic issues and to articulate a coherent set of political demands. This grassroots-based national political coalition is the only option they see with the potential for redirecting the American economic system while providing the resources for redressing local concerns. The experiences of the Green Party in Germany raise some cautionary notes: The problems such grassroots-based national coalitions have with electoral stability and internal tensions, which the Fainsteins acknowledge, are momentous and debilitating. Many of the issues raised by economic restructuring processes may not be capable of resolution through electoral politics, raising the specter of new policy institutions capable of further channeling and containing grassroots discontent.

Kirby's concluding article serves as a starting point for further research. His approach, as he claims, is iconoclastic and provocative: He disputes, for example, the cautious optimism implicit in Molotch and Logan's analysis by declaring that it is a fallacy to believe that localities can structure cost-effective economic development policies. His justification for taking this "spoiler" stance is to challenge the assumptions underlying much current economic development policymaking and, in the process, to lay the groundwork for a more thoughtful policy response to the local impacts of economic change.

Changes in the international division of labor and the territorial organization of multinational corporations have altered the forms of urbanization in the United States. Like the "primate cities" of the Third World, North American cities have increasingly specialized in economic activities that provide neither a balanced employment base for local residents nor opportunities for autonomously generated growth based on the local market. We describe several emerging forms of cities—the headquarter city, innovation center, module production city, border entrepot, and retirement center. We argue that the urban future for average residents of such cities is bleak, and that efforts to change this future will require coordinated action among people in different cities and in the Third World.

URBAN DEPENDENCIES
New Forms of Use and Exchange in U.S. Cities

HARVEY MOLOTCH
University of California, Santa Barbara

JOHN R. LOGAN
State University of New York, Albany

Our goal is to suggest how, in the ongoing context of competition within and across cities for development and growth, the emerging transnational system of production is redefining the nature of these local struggles and affecting the stratification of U.S. cities and groups within them. Because of organizational changes in the larger political economy, cities' search for capital is leading to different kinds of urban roles and an urban hierarchy based on the kind of deal a place can make with outside investors. We argue that different sorts of U.S. urban areas are, as a consequence, experiencing changes in the way money is made from the manipulation of place and in the way people live. Finally, we offer a guide for more effec-

AUTHORS' NOTE: *We thank Maureen Jung for sharing her insights and sources; Steve Clayman provided valuable research assistance. Financial support was provided through a grant from the Academic Senate, University of California, Santa Barbara. This research was partly supported by the Center for Population Research of the National Institute of Child Health and Human Development, Grant 1R01HD1727201.*

URBAN AFFAIRS QUARTERLY, Vol. 21 No. 2, December 1985 143-169

tive political strategies—grounded in the nature of the urban system—that might help citizens overcome the urban futures that otherwise lie ahead.

In contrast to strains of determinism found in both ecological and neo-Marxian thinking (see Domhoff, 1986), we view the city as an arena of structured activism (Form, 1954) in which individual and group striving occurs within and gives shape to specific sets of productive relations across space (Molotch, 1967, 1976, 1979; Logan, 1978; Molotch and Logan, 1984; Logan and Molotch, forthcoming). This means for us that within each type of urban area, regardless of its hierarchical slot in the system, there are particular local political options that are available and that can affect the overall structure.

More specifically, there are two distinct sets of urban interests (and local political agendas that follow from them) in any U.S. urban area. Some people seek wealth through the development, sale, or rent of land and buildings; others' primary interest in place is as a setting for daily life and production. These two contrasting sets of purposes, often in direct conflict with one another, correspond to the Marxian description of commodities as providing for both exchange value and use value. In reference to the exchange value of urban space, this means there is a set of actors who push for local growth maximization to increase returns from real estate manipulation and other business activities specifically dependent on local growth—collectively making up the "growth machine" (Molotch, 1976). Such coalitions support policies that are often environmentally destructive, fiscally damaging, and socially regressive for urban populations (see Appelbaum et al., 1976; Appelbaum, 1978). There are other sets of actors, oriented toward use values of urban space, who make the effort, usually only sporadically and with weak consequence (Stone, 1976, 1982, 1984), to thwart at least those exchange maneuvers directly damaging their immediate life-course interests (e.g., neighborhood threats).

Drawing upon much recent scholarship in urban political economy (e.g., Gordon, 1977, 1978; Soja et al., 1983; Friedmann and Wolff, 1982; Storper and Walker, 1983; Feagin, 1985), we are able to see that competitions within places as well as across them are increasingly determined by dynamics beyond the borders not only of individual cities but of the nation-state itself. In particular, the much heralded "new international division of labor" (e.g., Cohen, 1981; Moulaert and Salinas, 1983) conditions relations within and across places. In the former spatial division of labor, people in the rich countries, under the aegis of "their own" capitalist firms, processed into finished products the raw materials imported from the poor regions. In the new order the products themselves are being made outside the rich countries; the raw material/finished product dichotomy loses its ability to distinguish what people in various countries do and, we would add, the domicile of the coordinating firm also becomes a matter of increased ambiguity. Places within all countries are being pressured toward new sorts of roles that entail specific consequences for the exchange and use value strategies of local people and institutions.

DEPENDENCY IN THE UNITED STATES

One evidence of the growing link between U.S. places and the international economic order is the substantially increased share of the U.S. economy represented by foreign trade—doubling from 3.8% of GNP to 7.8% over the 1950-1979 period (Glickman, 1983). Just as critically, there has been change in the nature of this foreign trade with direct effects on particular American cities and regions:

(1) The relative share of U.S. agricultural exports has increased rapidly, at the expense of manufactured goods exports, generating losses in the traditional manufacturing heartland. By 1983, the United States' deficit in merchandise trade was over $60 billion (Kristof, 1984).
(2) Although the U.S. has remained relatively successful in high-technology fields based on heavy investments in research and development, mass production of some high-technology products, such as circuit boards and silicone chips, has tended to move abroad.
(3) Rapid expansion of international trade has resulted in growth of the white-collar service and financial sectors of major cities, particularly New York, Los Angeles, and San Francisco. Service exports from these centers—data processing, insurance, advertising, medicine—helped provide a net annual services trade surplus of $30-40 billion in the 1979-1983 period (Kristof, 1984).

After decades in which U.S. dominance deeply affected the economies and cultures of peoples abroad, the United States is itself being subjected to penetration from outside. Foreign firms and foreign subsidiaries of U.S. firms are taking larger and larger shares of consumer markets in sectors in which U.S. producers once enjoyed a worldwide commanding lead. In an important twist in this regard, much of the so-called "foreign competition" comes from U.S. corporations operating abroad; a third of U.S. imports come about this way (Tabb, 1984: 304).

A central feature in this transnationalization process is the changing nature of firms operating in the United States, regardless of which national flag they might fly. The emerging multilocational, multinational corporations are not just larger versions of previous forms, although they do have the extraordinary political and economic potency that size alone implies (Vernon, 1975; Domhoff, 1970, 1983; Herman, 1981: 180). More important, they are *qualitatively* distinct (Hymer, 1979b; Amin, 1974). One simple implication of their multilocational character is that not all corporate administration, production, and distribution necessarily occurs in the same place, or even in the same kind of place. Various sorts of corporate activities (making a certain product, providing a specific support role) can be at different sites. Just as important, by becoming multinational in the geographical range of these operations, a firm can transcend the sovereignty levels of all units of government. Through such devices as transfer pricing, multiple sourcing, international financing, and joint ventures, firms become difficult targets for political units to tax and regulate, no matter what their levels of "relative autonomy" might otherwise imply (see Barnet and Muller, 1974; Rugman and Eden, 1985). A firm becomes increasingly difficult to trap in space because it becomes a chimera—a target that physically moves, redefines its internal relations and its external boundaries—in effect, transforming itself as the need may arise (see Hymer and Rowthorn, 1979; Friedmann and Wolff, 1982: 312).[1]

Corporations, even "ours," are thus becoming less "American," and that tendency carries profound implications for the relation between people and their place. Industrial U.S. society was created more or less as a series of parochial events; local families managed and supplied capital for industries in their regional surroundings (Navin and Sears, 1955; Davis, 1963: 89; Jung, 1985). Prosperity for industrial production in a given area implied wealth for urban rentiers and increased wages for workers (Wolfe, 1981). It has been tempting to take this connection between private and public prosperity for granted, to presume, in the U.S. context, that wealth generated for corporations inevitably trickles down to the local working class. This sort of assumption has made it easy for some important urban analysts (e.g., Peterson, 1981) to reify cities as a simple unity standing for a common public interest, and to reason that whatever brings growth to a place, on whatever basis, brings a better life to all.

Although such a thesis has always been open to doubt, the new conditions make it less plausible than ever.

LESSONS FROM THE THIRD WORLD: THE PRIMATE CITY

Multinationals' share of Gross World Product, estimated at 20% in 1971, is expected to reach 40% by 1988 (Jazairy et al., 1977, as cited in Blackbourn, 1982: 147). Just as corporate investments from rich countries do not necessarily better the lives of ordinary people in poor societies (see, e.g., Hymer, 1972, 1979a, 1979b; Portes and Walton, 1981; Frank, 1967; Chase-Dunn, 1975; Peet, 1980; Bullock and Firebaugh, 1984; Bornschier and Chase-Dunn, forthcoming), analogous impacts may lay ahead for those specific American cities (and subgroups within them) that will play similarly dependent roles in the future. The Third World "primate city" (Linsky, 1965; see also Davis and Golden, 1954; Sovani, 1964; McGee, 1967), with its concentrated control points, excessive speculation, sprawled squatter settlements, and inflated land prices (Portes and Walton, 1976: 28) may be a relevant scenario for the United States. Although the extrapolation of such prospects to the U.S. case may well be overdrawn, the exercise can heuristically use existing world urban experience to pose new ways of thinking about the futures of U.S. cities.

VARIETIES OF THE EMERGING U.S. CITY

With such a model among others in mind, we can envision five different roles that U.S. urban places are plausibly going to perform, given the interplay of transnationalization of production, internal local growth struggles, and certain secular demographic trends. These are the headquarters, the innovation center, module production and processing platform, Third World entrepot, and retirement site. These roles differ conceptually from the better-known schema of functionally integrated urban hierarchies (Duncan et al., 1960), based on our assertion of a *trans*national system, the integration of which is accomplished through active networking of goal-oriented institutions and organizations. We are not trying to create static ideal urban types or an exhaustive listing, but rather to indicate some of the ways that use and exchange values are beginning to cluster in specific kinds of places. For each urban setting, we demarcate the underlying economic organization at work and then describe how particular use and exchange value gains and losses are taking shape.

HEADQUARTERS

Among U.S. places, we count only a handful—New York, Los Angeles, and possibly San Francisco and Chicago—as thriving centers of corporate dominance (see Ross, 1982; Birch, 1979; Schmenner, 1982; Palmer and Friedland, forthcoming). Ecologists have long emphasized the crucial role of a small number of cities as the coordinating centers of national economies, but they characteristically take the "natural" efficiencies of these places as the key to their success. For the ecologists, locational advantage (e.g., centrality, transport access) causes some places to grow large through their ability to service or produce for nonlocal areas. Large size then generates a self-sufficient market for the goods that are produced, leading to an internal division of labor that creates economies of its own, further sustaining growth and development (Duncan et al., 1960; see Berry and Kasarda, 1977: 276, for a contemporary application to the sunbelt cities). Even though metropolitan areas may rise and decline, they do so in response to factors inherent in the efficiency-maximizing dynamics of population, spatial constraints, and technological advance.

In a break with such demographic reasoning, some recent rethinking interprets the great metropolis as a response to the organizational needs of the modern corporation (see, e.g., Palmer and Friedland, forthcoming). The ongoing trend toward monopolistic and oligopolistic control of product markets, for example, ipso facto feeds the administrative growth of the cities in which major corporations already are established. As firms grow larger, increasing amounts of economic activity involve transactions within them as goods and services are moved from one plant or office to another of the same corporate unit (Noyelle, 1983: 116). The market mechanism (less geographically specific) is replaced by intrafirm bureaucracies that are, again, located at the major headquarter cities. Corporate mergers also have a general tendency to build the previously existing headquarter cities, because they contain the dominant firms that acquire the less dominant ones (see Dicken, 1976; Smith, 1982; Vartabedian, 1984).

Such cities then come to provide the kind of agglomeration economies that maximize the specific productive efficiencies increasingly important to modern firms. Corporate headquarters typically carry out tasks of an "orientation" nature (Thorngren, 1970; see also Stephens and Holly, 1980: 164) in which inputs (often face to face) from certain other business and service enterprises are critical. Compared to past patterns, the production system makes use of a much larger array of specialized services needed "up-front." Accounting and law firms advise management on finance, personnel practices, licensing, and international contracting; engineering consultants and graphic design studios assist in product development and packaging; advertising agencies stimulate consumer demand; and specialized catalog and media merchandisers generate orders (see Stanback et al., 1981). Public relations firms and political consultants advise on how to manage publics and government officials whose support or acquiescence may be indispensable. The American economy's much noted shift toward "services" is actually a trend toward *producer* services that facilitate the development, manufacture, importation, and distribution of products (Noyelle, 1983: 118). The changing nature of the firm, then, dictates the nature of the contemporary headquarter metropolis, and places with the right support mix will grow.

The importance of firm organization causes us to take a closer look at exactly what sorts of benefits are being delivered by these agglomerations of "orientation" and "support" services. If these spatial arrangements increase the efficiencies of firms, the new organizationally oriented spatial theories are rather compatible, albeit updated, elaborations of the older ecological models. But an alternative is that the real specialty of these places is the *control* they facilitate over a firm's own operations and those of other firms, both locally and nonlocally (see Hymer, 1979a, 1979b; Friedmann and Wolff, 1982). The difference implied by control and efficiencies is critical. Arrangements that facilitate control can be present merely because of the advantage they provide for one group of actors in opposition to the interests of others. Neo-Marxists analyzing the labor process (e.g., Braverman, 1974; Gintis, 1976) have made a similar distinction regarding the work process; running an efficient, even profitable, firm may do little good if management cannot continue to appropriate for itself the fruits of production. This means managers may tolerate less efficiency (even lower corporate profits) rather than create work arrangements that might, for example, risk worker insurgency. This is a difference between "quantitative" and "qualitative" efficiency or between "technical efficiency" and what Gordon (1977: 31) calls "capitalist efficiency" (see also Marglin, 1974; Gordon, 1976). If it's efficiency at all, it's a kind of "crackpot efficiency" (see Mills, 1959), in which maximization of control at the expense of production means that a narrow, proximate rationality obscures collectively irrational outcomes.

One headquarter city activity of increasing importance is the manipulation of corporate financial assets, sometimes in order to merge one firm with another or (in more recent cases of "unfriendly takeovers") to prevent such mergers. Such merging and conglomeration activity may have little to do with enhancing productive efficiency (Nelson, 1959: 7; Herman, 1981: 101). Instead, a goal may be building paper profits for a given set of market investors whose stock rises with the *appearance* of growth and vitality. In other instances an acquisition is guided by the need of one firm to gain the tax credits of a failing firm. Sometimes the aim is to get control over a "cash cow" that can then be milked for still other financial maneuvers. On still other occasions a firm's managers may strive to attract a "white knight" takeover bid because such an arrangement will enhance their own employment security compared to an alternative merger possibility.

Whether or not it serves any larger efficiency, the headquarter city provides a rich array of the "producer services" that facilitate such control manipulations (e.g., "junk bond" brokerage houses). The headquarter city, then, may be attractive to capital because of its agglomerations that service this "paper entrepreneurialism" (Reich, 1983) of manipulating financial assets to establish wealth advantage. Unhinged from the underlying processes that actually produce wealth, and not easily forced to share the fruits of its manipulations with local residents, the headquarter's units can thrive in the face of marginal surrounding populations. The slums of the great cities provide, as in the Third World model, clear evidence of the phenomenon (see Marcuse, 1981; Ross and Trachte, 1983).

INNOVATION

Malecki (1980) has outlined a number of different geographic patterns of research and development (R&D). Some of these activities are directly supportive of corporate decision making, and these tend to be located adjacent to other "producer services" within the headquarter city. In still other cases, when it is important for each plant operating under a corporate wing to have its own R&D facility nearby (e.g., a raw materials testing lab), "research" activity is dispersed in the same pattern as other routine corporate functions. Finally, in instances when R&D activities can be footloose from all these concerns, they can be located where professional labor and other research-related assets (e.g., major universities) are found (see Jobert, 1975). This is the "pure" type at the top of the "product cycle" in which the special agglomeration benefits peculiar to innovation can come into play. Examples of such innovation centers are Austin, Texas, Cambridge, Massachusetts, the Silicon Valley towns of Northern California, and the Research Triangle area of North Carolina.[2]

Once again, however, these agglomerations are themselves not created through intrinsic "natural" efficiencies; they are helped along and nurtured by the local elites who have a use for them. A clear illustration is the case of the Microelectronics and Computer Technology Corporation—a newly created private firm with the mission of keeping the United States ahead of Japan in the microelectronics field. Jointly funded under government encouragement by 12 of the most important American firms in advanced technology, the new company needed a site for its $100 million plant. Fifty-seven cities submitted bids, with Austin, Texas, and various California locations (particularly San Diego) becoming the main contenders. Austin got the project, but only after locals offered a laundry list of concessions, including subsidized land, mortgage assistance for employees, and $15 million in faculty chairs at the University of Texas (Rivera, 1983; King, 1985).

Certainly as common as the higher education route (and often linked with it) is the use of military contracting as leverage for R&D-based growth strategy. What we have been calling innovation centers are, to a significant degree, war preparation centers. The Defense Department, accounting for about one-third of all R&D spending in the United States, has been, according to Reich, "the center of high-technology industrial policy in this country" (quoted in Schrage, 1984: 3). More than is the case for civilian R&D (which is, unlike the military R&D, located predominately outside of the sunbelt; Cohen, 1977: 219), the defense-related high-tech complexes depend on the war machine for their sustenance.[3] In contrast to consumer goods production, security considerations preclude going abroad, making defense development a secure, albeit wasteful, domestic industry for those areas able to attract it (Taplin, 1984: 3; Keller, 1983: 350). This "vast addiction," as George Kennan (1984: 78) has called it, causes certain growth elites to foster national and local resource allocations that encourage unproductive, inefficient industrial development in their midst. Whatever conveniences and cost savings such agglomerations may imply for the component facilities, they do not serve a larger productive efficiency for the system as a whole. But they do benefit the confluence of local and cosmopolitan interests whose political and entrepreneurial skills have brought them into existence.

MODULE PRODUCTION PLACES

Other types of places lack any special qualities that would make them peculiarly desirable as investment sites. Instead, their futures are tied to routine production tasks. They have in common a dependence on control centers elsewhere and an expendable status in the system of places. Some such emerging "module cities" (Molotch and Logan, 1984) are sites in which traditional products are being manufactured using newer technologies (e.g., robotized auto plants; see Hill, 1982; Hill and Negrey, forthcoming). Others attract a governmental bureaucratic function that has a durable future: Baltimore, for example, landed the national Social Security headquarters. Certain places, particularly those without histories of labor militance and minority unrest, have destinies tied to white-collar information processing. Omaha, Nebraska, has become the "800" telephone exchange center of the country; Sioux Falls, South Dakota, is now Citicorp's credit operations center (Sassen-Koob, 1984: 143). Other cities, for reasons more closely following the logic of central place theory, will find niches as distribution centers, but could be easily replaced by many other spots more or less equally centralized vis-à-vis the same market areas.

Some module cities, rather than being new destinations for migrating capital, are likely to be the old factory cities of the Northeast and Midwest, struggling for some sort of viable role under the new order. The restructuring of such declining places depends, in part, on the ability to provide the cheap open land ("greenfields") needed for modern production techniques. Along with the availability of low-cost and tractable labor (Storper and Walker, 1983), this is one of the factors stimulating the dispersal of factories to the periphery of the large metropolitan areas and stimulating the growth of smaller, semirural towns in the Midwest and South (Beale and Fugitt, 1978: 157-180; Sassen-Koob, 1984: 146).

The effortful strivings of elites in these old manufacturing cities to physically and socially retrofit their turf for new development sharply illustrate the requirements for module growth. The case of Detroit makes the process clear.[4] As measured by sales volumes, assets, and the number of worldwide employees controlled by the firms headquartered within it,

Detroit (in 1975) ranked second only to New York among U.S. cities in international dominance (Stephens and Holly, 1980: 176). This is due, of course, to the significance of the U.S. auto giants. But Detroit is not now and never really has been a headquarter city, despite the fact that several of the world's largest corporations have their head offices within or adjacent to it. Detroit is a center of production and the location of headquarters that guide such production, but it is not a place with particularly good support for exerting control or engaging in paper entrepreneurialism. Thus, although at the center of the "automotive realm" (Hill, 1984: 314), firms are in Detroit *despite* its deficiencies as a place for control and manipulation. This means that module cities have little capacity to expand their headquarter functions beyond what they already have.

This has not thwarted some module production centers from making quixotic efforts to use physical intervention to build themselves into headquarter cities. In Detroit's case the result was construction of the Renaissance Center—a complex of round office towers, complete with a dramatic Portman-designed, atrium-centered convention hotel. It is a design clone of installations that have succeeded easily in San Francisco and Los Angeles. But the results have been less successful in Detroit; the heavily vacant (and policed) complex sits amid acres of undeveloped rubble, economically teetering on various forms of insolvency. Detroit's maneuver to bring greenfields within its boundaries (the neighborhood clearance for General Motors' "Poletown" plant) will at least produce a modern auto factory which, however, may never create enough extra jobs or generate sufficient taxes to offset its fiscal and social costs.

The glittering physical success of other nonheadquarter cities should not be mistaken for evidence that they have permanently escaped Detroit's fate. Houston's corporate growth is essentially a recapitulation of Detroit's development; this city also appears not to be a sustainer of corporate headquarter functions (see Hill and Feagin, 1984). The implication is that as its core industries decline (Texas's oil will be depleted by the early 1990s), Houston will have to join Detroit at the unhappy rear in the queue for capital investment.

The lowest tier among the module places will be occupied by places serving as social or physical dumping grounds for production carried out elsewhere. Leaders of three hard-up inland California towns (Avenal, Adelanto, and Blythe) are courting state prison authorities, who "usually . . . don't run into this kind of reception" (Hurst, 1983), to locate a new penitentiary in their towns because of the jobs and money it would bring. One rural town in South Dakota has proposed itself as a site for disposing of low-level radioactive wastes as a strategy to develop the local economy (New York Times, 1984). Hanford, Washington, "the city that loves nukes" (Licht, 1983: 5), welcomes nuclear waste as its development strategy. As the need grows for waste sites, being a dump emerges as the residual role for places unable to perform higher functions.

ENTREPOT ACTIVITIES

American border cities play specialized entrepot roles, newly important given increased commercial activity with and higher rates of immigration from Third World regions. These U.S. cities typically have large immigrant populations and many social and organizational ties with urban areas on the other side of the border (Bloomberg and Martinez-Sandoval, 1984). Examples include Miami, with its large Cuban population; El Paso and Brownsville, Texas (60% and 70% Hispanic in 1980); and San Antonio (now the tenth largest American city, with half of its population Spanish-speaking). In various ways, San Diego and even Los Angeles (in addition to its other important roles) have entrepot city attributes, from both Hispanic and Asian labor.

Border cities attract capital because of their low-paid foreign workers, who either migrate for the day or week (border people) or take up permanent residence (Bloomberg and Martinez-Sandoval, 1984). This highly tractable and vulnerable labor force is useful in a number of economic sectors. Some of the southern border cities are major tourist centers requiring service workers at the lowest occupational rungs (busboys, dishwashers, maids, etc.). Cheap labor also makes these cities well suited for sweatshop manufacturing, particularly in those industries that do best when designers and marketing experts can have their production apparatus nearby. In the growing garment industry of Southern California about 80% of employees are undocumented immigrants from Central America. Most of these are women workers (Soja et al., 1983: 221), and about 90% of the firms employing them are in violation of major sections of the state labor code (Clark, 1983: 282). Even in the so-called high-tech field, many small U.S. firms (of which there are a good number) require low-wage assemblers. It is only the large firms carrying out routinized production activity that can easily move abroad (Musgrave, 1975: 13; Portes and Walton, 1981: 143; see also Yago et al., 1984; Soja et al., 1983: 226).

The border cities also function as trade and financial centers for importing, marketing, and distributing imported goods, including illicit materials, such as drugs and counterfeit "brand-name" products.[5] They are also export platforms; Miami is the location for Latin American regional offices of 55 U.S. multinationals (Cohen, 1977: 218). Money is laundered or otherwise dispersed in the growing Miami banking industry; fluctuating with the strength of the dollar against the peso, San Diego is a major shopping destination for Mexican nationals. Polyglot populations of "new immigrants," different in skin tone, legal status, and ideological proclivities from previous waves (i.e., the prototypical European immigrants), are tied to a wide range of industrial sectors.

RETIREMENT CENTERS

A different sort of relevant migration derives from the aging of the country's domestic population, as well as the changing pattern of that aging. People retire earlier with fewer children and with weaker ties to the children they do have (who are themselves more mobile than in the past). The consequence is increasing geographic concentration of large numbers of the elderly in places with good climates in the South and West. Elderly migration has also been part of growth in states such as Vermont and New Jersey, where retired people can find a semirural environment, often within reach of kin elsewhere in the Northeast (Biggar, 1980).

Growth strategies vary across the retirement cities; some places press for more of the same, whereas others, such as Tampa and St. Petersburg, seek to augment retirement with other types of industry (Mormino, 1983). Growth elites in Atlantic City, New Jersey, were able to alter the "moral standards" of state government to make their city a gambling resort, thereby dramatically disrupting the lives of many of the retired elderly as well as other low-income residents (Trillin, 1979; Sternlieb and Hughes, 1983).

To the extent that elderly people's towns and regions specialize only in residential uses, their futures are bound up with the individual wealth of their residents. As with suburban towns that ring American cities, the prosperity of such bedroom communities will depend on the affluence levels of those who sleep within them. Following the pattern already in place among elderly people's suburban towns (Fitzpatrick and Logan, 1985), cities of the elderly will likely have low average household incomes, poor housing, and high taxes. Whole cities are becoming dependent on pensions and social security payments to support the local economy, and will rise and fall with the future of the pensions system. To the degree that the federal government manages to make medical care and old age social service assistance a private or local government responsibility, such cities (and their respective populations) are headed for a special kind of crisis. The longer life expectancy of women will make them a large part of the dependent population, and more of these women than in the past will have been low-wage workers with inadequate pension benefits. As "prisoners of space" (Rowles, 1980) the old are especially dependent on local support networks that run the risk of being both socially and fiscally quite weak. There may lie ahead old people slum cities, disproportionately female, dependent, and without strategic recourse.

EMERGING PATTERNS OF USE AND EXCHANGE

All of the urban place roles we have described will give rise to place-specific social consequences. We now turn to a review of these implications in terms of rents, urban services, and ways of life, seeking to discover the ways in which the pursuit of exchange and use values will yield different results under each circumstance.

RENTS

Real estate entrepreneurs and their associates in headquarter cities, the innovation centers, border cities, and more affluent retirement areas will gain most, in spatial terms, from the transformation of the industrial order. In the headquarter cities, booming high-rise construction is the symptom of an enormous press on space by investors, many of whom are foreign (Ricks and Racster, 1980; Jackson, 1980; Byron, 1982). In the early 1980s, New York City construction rates were far ahead of the rest of the country, with new office construction amounting to more than $700 million annually (Sassen-Koob, 1984: 150). In Los Angeles, a city that had to invent its downtown through renewal and redevelopment programs, high-rise office space increased by over 50% in the decade after 1972 (Soja et al., 1983: 224).

In the residential market the pattern is equally clear: It is in the headquarter cities and innovation centers that cosmopolitan capital, local rentiers, and the more ordinary affluent bid up price.[6] San Francisco, Los

Angeles, and New York are among the three most costly cities in the country in which to live (Eaton, 1980; Associated Press, 1985). Other large cities with weaker headquarter economies (e.g., Philadelphia, Detroit, Baltimore) have much cheaper housing costs (with Chicago in between). The other high-cost areas are in the affluent resort regions (particularly Hawaii) and the important innovation centers (e.g., the Northern California Bay Area towns, Southern California coastal counties, and, to a lesser extent, the Boston area). Housing costs in retirement centers appear to run parallel to the surrounding areas.

For those without financial stakes in land and buildings in the developing zones, the place entrepreneurs' triumphs do not imply benefits; they mean costs. Even the high-wage earners of the headquarter cities—the "professional-managerial class" (Ehrenreich and Ehrenreich, 1979)—are somewhat penalized by the higher housing prices they must pay. For those fulfilling the less remunerative roles, the penalty is more severe; particularly in the sunbelt, where workers' wages still trail those in the industrial heartland (Perry and Watkins, 1977: 293-298; Hill and Negrey, forthcoming; see also, Silver, 1984), high housing costs imply a lower real standard of living.

TAXES AND PUBLIC SERVICES

Taxation is at least a conceivable means to tap the local economy on behalf of a region's less affluent residents, primarily by providing public services of special utility to the poor. But module production centers and most retirement areas are likely to be unable to provide such income redistribution through taxes, and regions experiencing the most robust economic development are not inclined to tax or spend at a high level or in a very progressive way. Unlike the experience of the old frostbelt cities, which in their heyday led the nation in welfare, education, and health expenditures, the contemporary boom regions eschew outlays that might compensate the poor for living in the midst of so much wealth or having to pay such high rents.

Indeed, we see in the "tax revolts" of two of the country's most advanced high-tech states (California's Proposition Thirteen and Massachusetts' Proposition Two and a Half) an effort to roll back the amounts of rent and profits that otherwise might be spent for public betterment. Real estate investors seeking higher returns have teamed up with affluent homeowners, the most privileged and resourceful of residents, to create policies that lowered their own taxes and those of business groups generally (Hogan, 1980; Lo, 1984). At least in the California case, the result has been decreased local government support for social services and creation of users' fees to make public services "pay their own way." Since public goods tend to benefit poorer people, users' fees are regressive; even public facilities are being privatized. Declines in public services are then used as further justification (however dubitable) for siphoning off even more resources to support the growth infrastructures that are so glibly portrayed as "building the tax base." The increased competition for capital, now proceeding on a worldwide scale, means that elites in all areas—even the expanding headquarter centers—have preempted any possible move toward local wealth redistribution in an avalanche of proposals for strengthening this capacity to serve capital's needs.

WAYS OF LIFE

In the most privileged areas, particularly the affluent innovation centers, local governments can be prodded by residents into demanding that developers mitigate damage to the use values of the well off. Even so, such growth almost inevitably intensifies traffic congestion, pollution, and overuse of public resources. A reaction is often a robust environmental movement that maintains surveillance and, on occasion, secures policies that control at least the pace of development (see Baldasarre and Protash, 1982).

In the case of the retirement city, the coming of large concentrations of elderly residents transforms more variegated local communities into homogenous social settings. Depending on the social class of the new residents, specific types of political and social consequences can follow. Among the nonaffluent elderly places such as Santa Monica and West Hollywood, California, for example, the result has been strong backing for rent control legislation and a "let live" attitude toward others with alternative lifestyles (e.g., gays in newly incorporated West Hollywood); common cause is made against the local landlords. In more homogeneously affluent areas, such as Sun City, Arizona, the salient feature is a rather finely graded and narrow-ranged specification of acceptable lifestyles (Fitzgerald, 1983).

Life in the headquarter cities is sharply differentiated by the economic role of each residential group. Professionals and skilled white-collar households benefit from easy access to work (often two different work sites) and a rich mix of cultural opportunities. This urbane lifestyle poses an alternative American ideal; the dour gothic imagery of knitting needle and pitchfork replaced by BMW and low-fat cuisine. Gentrification inserts a version of the good life, resembling suburbia (in its whiteness) and the innovation centers (in educational levels), into the central city. Although these changes are only a modest demographic blip in any U.S. city (Nelson, 1984), they have important ideological significance: All of the amenities (boutiques, theaters, etc.) that spin off from headquarter development help make the total package more appealing. A trendy vision of "urban rebirth" helps justify, in both headquarter cities where it might work and module places where chances are less favorable, the subsidized destruction of the working-class neighborhoods left over from the manufacturing era.

For module cities, the kinds of growth that can threaten working-class neighborhoods usually come less from boutiques than from the potential for new forms of routine business activity. Firms need large tracts of open land, either for horizontal mass manufacture (as in Poletown) or for "business parks" containing warehouse and "back office" functions. If the scale is large enough, these tracts provide relatively controlled physical environments in what otherwise may be inhospitable surroundings. Some potential sites exist in the burned-out blocks remaining from the ghetto insurrections of the 1960s, as well as parcels cleared through accidental fires or arson profiteering by heavily insured building owners. Many landlords long ago began a disinvestment process that leaves their structures with little market value. Clearance, through redevelopment funding, can be used to acquire even high-value properties that need to be eliminated.

The continuing decline of the remaining poor people's neighborhoods (whether of the headquarter or module city) may foster social adaptations appropriate to the growing economic marginality of their populations in what has been aptly termed a "peripheralization at the core" (Sassen-Koob, 1984: 140). There may develop an elaboration of reciprocity among kin and neighbors and informal exchange of goods (Stack, 1974; Portes and Walton, 1981). There may be new systems of exchange and even new sorts of formal organizations created. This is the sort of thing that social workers like to celebrate as "self-help" and visionaries as "backyard revolution" (Boyte, 1980) or "urban social movements (Castells, 1983). But it is not necessarily self-help that makes possible upward mobility or effective political action; it is more likely the adaptive necessity for sheer survival found among destitute people all over the world (see Walton, 1982: 122).

SUMMARY AND POLICY IMPLICATIONS

We have emphasized that places will be performing not just different roles, but stratified ones, with the fates of various groups within places similarly shaped by the sort of arrangement that is made to sustain the growth process. A corollary is that the future of a city can never be deduced from its own internal potential or trajectory, but rather how it is institutionally integrated into the international system through which production and rent collection are organized. Under current arrangements of both their internal organization and external integration, the world's cities are engaged in a self-defeating, cutthroat competition. Those places at the top of the hierarchy twist their agenda to attract microelectronics firms so they won't have to settle for waste dumps; those at the bottom compete for waste dumps, and on the poorest terms, because otherwise they will not get even waste dumps. The growth dynamic in this system of cities informally puts into practice the philosophy of the enterprise zone across the entire range of places—cities should compete with one another in how far they can reduce place constraints on the organization of capital.

There are alternative strategies that might better promote use values in urban communities. But these efforts are best waged not by particular cities in isolation from one another, but as part of a program that recognizes how the system of cities actually works and how its destructive tendencies can be defeated through coordinated actions across urban areas. In essence, U.S. cities must stop competing among themselves for capital and use their relatively high levels of legal autonomy to compete as a collective force against the growth machine system that has captured them all.

UPPING THE ANTE FOR GROWTH: WHERE TO BEGIN

Although all places can, in principle, change the conditions they impose on capital for access to place, certain cities are more strategically able than others to drive the hard bargain. We look to those places at the top of the hierarchy (i.e., headquarter cities, innovation centers, affluent retirement areas) as the vanguard whose actions might change the urban system. Just as the sweatshops of Asia set the world standard for how low wages can go in routine assembly, places at the top set the terms for how high capital will have to bid to operate somewhere. High places need to raise that standard. Some privileged California cities—for example, San Francisco, Santa Barbara, and Santa Monica—now sometimes require industrial developers to offset the housing demand they generate by providing subsidies for low- or middle-income housing. Affluent Nantucket, Massachusetts, taxes all real estate transactions in order to acquire property that can be preserved as open space.

Such policies create, in effect, a development tax—a tax that, if high enough, may deflect capital to other zones. As the privileged places get tougher, capital's locational options are somewhat squeezed; investors must move down the place hierarchy in search of a satisfactory site. When the price of entry is raised at any given class of places, the effect is to strengthen the bargaining position of places on the rung below. All places gain through this process, including the places at the bottom, which have to make the most deleterious deals. This is a wealth "trickle down" we can believe in. Nor does this general strategy require a bluffing attitude by localities; since so much of the growth that has come to cities in the past has not provided net benefits for the majority of residents, merely pursuing the use value interests of citizens will be enough to justify the relevant policies. Localities at all levels have been subsidizing projects that fail to deliver promised benefits, which would have been built even without the subsidies, or which backfire and actually exacerbate the problems they were designed to address (see Schmenner, 1982; Bridges, 1965; Swanstrom, 1985). The consequence of policies based in collective self-interest, particularly if begun at the top of the hierarchy, would set off a dramatic reverberation throughout the urban system.

DEALING WITH THIRD-WORLDING

There is still the dilemma of the runaway shop: How can we deal with firms' capacity to escape even national boundaries and put all productive operations abroad? How can localities enact policies on behalf of use values if they are locked in competition with communities across the world that can so easily underbid them? Protectionism, an easy enough response, may only lead to reprisals around the world as well as further immiserate Third World peoples who now depend on these "exported jobs" for their meager livelihoods.

The way out of this dilemma rests on our acceptance of the view that Third World societies, as places lowest on the hierarchy, face even more severe difficulties than U.S. localities when dealing with outside capital. To the degree to which Third World growth, under current institutional arrangements, disfigures indigenous economies and social structures, the export of U.S. jobs does nothing to increase the life chances of the masses of people. The good deals that Detroit or Akron give to corporate investors are nothing as compared to the deals offered in Seoul, Ankara, or Bopahl. Local elites, themselves created through cross-world penetration (Hymer, 1979a, 1979b), act to keep down the social costs of outside investment. U.S. foreign policy has been assiduously devoted over the last century to lowering the costs of capital investment abroad, even to the point of undermining foreign governments whose policies thwart such investment (Tanzer, 1968).

The upshot for our purposes is clear enough: Anything that can cause other governments to raise the costs of foreign investment will *per force* limit the degree of capital flight. Such limits will diminish the capacity of capital to play one U.S. locality against the other or to threaten the paychecks and social wages of U.S. workers. In other words, American workers and their union representatives should, following this analysis, support the antiimperialistic movements of the Third World—not just out of common decency but to protect their own jobs and communities. The results would likely be higher use values for people in both settings.

THE EFFICIENCY "DILEMMA"

Neoclassical theory would predict that the restriction of capital movement must inevitably decrease productive efficiency; even if there are some proximate use-value gains, the long-term consequence must be lower levels of life if firms lose their ability to autonomously optimize locational strategies. But although efficiency considerations do play some role, locational outcomes and particular forms of urban agglomeration are the result of institutionalized interests whose interplay is no more inherently connected to efficiency than it is to social justice. Intervention in the urban system on behalf of use values implies little about a loss of efficiency; strengthening the hand of citizens over the geographic conditions of production is as likely to enhance meaningful productivity as undermine it.

NOTES

1. There is a contrasting view: The large size of the multinational firm makes it increasingly visible, thus making attention to the details of its operations more feasible (see e.g., Warren, 1975). For reasons we state, size is not the critical issue.

2. Using three types of industrial sectors (aerospace, electrical, and electronics and instruments), Malecki has isolated 23 places he calls innovation centers. Using SIC codes as the basis for such a typology, he is forced into lumping together diverse sorts of activities into a single urban type; this makes it impossible to isolate the more basic research functions that are analytically so important to us (see Baron and Bielby, 1984, on the issue of sector typologies). Thus, Malecki's method leads to some anomalous results; Dayton, Miami, and Baltimore become innovation centers along with Boston, San Diego, and Phoenix.

3. Hill and Negrey (forthcoming) point out that federal expenditures generally shortchange the frostbelt region, or at least the Great Lakes States.

4. Our understanding of Detroit as a prototype of the declining industrial city owes much to the work of Richard C. Hill (1981, 1982, 1984; Hill and Feagin, 1984).

5. The counterfeit production of name-brand merchandise is now big business worldwide, estimated by the International Chamber of Commerce to constitute between 3% and 9% of total world trade (James, 1985: D-4).

6. Although often attributed to "excess" environmental regulation (Frieden, 1979; Miller, 1981; Downs, 1984), the available evidence clearly indicates that it is speculation that has been responsible for most of the housing-cost inflation that hit the economically thriving regions in the last decade (see Molotch and Kasof, 1981; Appelbaum, 1985).

REFERENCES

AMIN, S. (1974) Accumulation on a World Scale. New York: Monthly Review Press.

APPELBAUM, R. (1985) "Regulation and the Santa Barbara housing market." Report to the California Policy Center, University of California, Santa Barbara.

———(1978) Size, Growth and U.S. Cities. New York: Praeger.

———J. BIGELOW, H. KRAMER, H. MOLOTCH, and P. RELIS (1976) The Effects of Urban Growth. New York: Praeger.

Associated Press (1985) "Housing prices across the U.S." Santa Barbara News-Press (May 23): A-9.

BALDASARRE, M. and W. PROTASH (1982) "Growth controls, population growth, and community satisfaction." Amer. Soc. Rev. 47, 3: 339-346.

BARNET, R. J. and R. E. MULLER (1974) Global Reach. New York: Simon & Schuster.

BARON, J. N. and W. T. BIELBY (1984) "The organization of work in a segmented economy." Amer. Soc. Rev. 49, 4: 454-473.

BEALE, C. L. and G. FUGITT (1978) "Population trends in nonmetropolitan cities and villages in subregions of the United States." Demography 15, 4: 605-620.

BERRY, B.J.L. and J. D. KASARDA (1977) Contemporary Urban Ecology. New York: Macmillan.

BIGGAR, J. C. (1980) "Reassessing elderly sunbelt migration." Research on Aging 2: 177-190.
BIRCH, D. L. (1979) The Job Generation Process. Cambridge, MA: MIT Program on Neighborhood and Regional Change.
BLACKBOURN, A. (1982) "The impact of multinational corporations on the spatial organization of developed nations: a review," pp. 147-157 in M. Taylor and N. Thrift (eds.) The Geography of Multinationals. Cambridge: Cambridge Univ. Press.
BLOOMBERG, W. and R. MARTINEZ-SANDOVAL (1984) "This Hispanic-America urban order: a border perspective," pp. 112-132 in G. Gappert and R. Knight (eds.) Cities in the 21st Century. Beverly Hills, CA: Sage.
BORNSCHIER, V. and C. CHASE-DUNN (forthcoming) Transnational Corporations and Underdevelopment. New York: Praeger.
BOYTE, H. (1980) The Backyard Revolution: Understanding the New Citizen Movement. Philadelphia: Temple Univ. Press.
BRAVERMAN, H. (1974) Labor and Monopoly Capital. New York: Monthly Review Press.
BULLOCK, B. and G. FIREBAUGH (1984) "Richer versus poorer LDCs: do world system characteristics matter?" Presented at the annual meeting of the American Sociological Association, San Antonio.
BYRON, D. (1982) "High-priced boom molds new skyline." Los Angeles Times 25 (April): I, 1, 3, 30, 32.
CASTELLS, M. (1983) The City and the Grassroots: A Cross-Cultural Theory of Urban Social Movements. Berkeley: Univ. of California Press.
CHASE-DUNN, C. (1975) "The effects of international economic dependence on development and inequality: a cross-national study." Amer. Soc. Rev. 40: 720-738.
CLARK, D. L. (1983) "Improbable Los Angeles," pp. 268-308 in R. M. Bernard and B. R. Rice (eds.) Sunbelt Cities. Austin: Univ. of Texas Press.
COHEN, R. B. (1981) "The new international division of labor: multinational corporations and urban hierarchy," pp. 287-315 in M. Dear and A. J. Scott (eds.) Urbanization and Urban Planning in Capitalist Society. New York: Methuen.
———(1977) "Multinational corporations, international finance, and the sunbelt," pp. 211-226 in D. C. Perry and A. J. Watkins (eds.) The Rise of the Sunbelt Cities. Beverly Hills, CA: Sage.
DAVIS, K. and H. GOLDEN (1954) "Urbanization and the development of preindustrial areas." Econ. Development and Cultural Change 3: 6-24.
DAVIS, L. (1963) "Financial immobilities and finance capitalism." Explorations in Entrepreneurial History 1, 1(second series): 88-105.
DICKEN, P. (1976) "The multiplant business enterprise and geographical space: some issues in the study of external control and regional development." Regional Studies 10, 4: 401-412.
DOMHOFF, G. W. (1986) "The growth machine and the power elite: a challenge to pluralists and Marxists alike," in R. Waste (ed.) Community Power: Directions for Future Research. Beverly Hills, CA: Sage.
———(1983) Who Rules America Now? A View for the 80's. Englewood Cliffs, NJ: Prentice-Hall.

———(1970) The Higher Circles. New York: Random House.
DOWNS, A. (1984) "Blueprint for a fairer housing policy." Los Angeles Times 16 (September): IV, 5.
DUNCAN, O. D., W. R. SCOTT, S. LIEBERSON, B. DUNCAN, and H. WINSBROUGH (1960) Metropolis and Region. Baltimore: Johns Hopkins Univ. Press.
EATON, W. (1980) "Survey finds S.F. has highest housing costs in nation: L.A. in second place." Los Angeles Times 5 (June): I, 9.
EHRENREICH, B. and J. EHRENREICH (1979) "The professional managerial class," pp. 5-45 in P. Walker (ed.) Between Labor and Capital. Boston: South End Press.
FEAGIN, J. R. (1985) "The global context of metropolitan growth: Houston and the oil industry." Amer. J. of Sociology 90 (May): 1204-1230.
FITZGERALD, F. (1983) "Interlude." New Yorker 25 (August): 55-109.
FITZPATRICK, K. and J. R. LOGAN (1985) "The aging of the suburbs, 1960-80." Amer. Soc. Rev. 50 (February): 106-117.
FORM, W. (1954) "The place of social structure in the determination of land use." Social Forces 32 (May): 317-323.
FRANK, A. G. (1967) Capitalism and Underdevelopment in Latin America. New York: Monthly Review Press.
FRIEDEN, B. (1979) The Environmental Protection Hustle. Cambridge, MA: MIT Press.
FRIEDMANN, J. and G. WOLFF (1982) "World city formation: an agenda for research and action." Int. J. of Urban and Regional Research 6, 3: 309-344.
GINTIS, H. (1976) "The nature of the labor exchange and the theory of capitalist production." Rev. of Radical Pol. Economics 8, 2: 36-56.
GLICKMAN, N. J. (1983) "International trade, capital mobility, and economic growth: some implications for American cities and regions in the 1980's," pp. 205-239 in D. Hicks and N. Glickman (eds.) Transition to the 21st Century: Prospects and Policies for Economic and Urban-Regional Transformation. Greenwich, CT: JAI Press.
GORDON, D. (1978) "Capitalist development and the history of American cities," pp. 25-63 in W. K. Tabb and L. Sawers (eds.) Marxism and the Metropolis. New York: Oxford Univ. Press.
———(1977) "Class struggle and the states of American urban development," pp. 55-82 in D. Perry and A. Watkins (eds.) The Rise of the Sunbelt. Beverly Hills, CA: Sage.
———(1976) "Capitalist efficiency and socialist efficiency." Monthly Rev. 28, 3: 19-39.
HERMAN, E. S. (1981) Corporate Control, Corporate Power. New York: Cambridge Univ. Press.
HILL, R. (1984) "Economic crisis and political response in the motor city," pp. 313-339 in L. Sawers and W. Tabb (eds.) Sunbelt/Snowbelt: Urban Development and Regional Restructuring. New York: Oxford Univ. Press.
———(1982) "Transnational capitalism and the crisis of industrial cities." J. of Intergroup Relations 10, 3: 30-41.
———(1981) "Economic crisis and political response in the motor city: alternative strategies for saving Detroit." Proceedings of the International Conference on Economic Crisis and Political Response in the Auto City: Detroit and Turin. Detroit, December.
———**and J. R. FEAGIN (1984) "Detroit and Houston: two cities in global perspective."** Presented at the annual meeting of the American Sociological Association, San Antonio.

HILL, R. and C. NEGREY (forthcoming) "The politics of industrial policy in Michigan," in S. Zukin (ed.) The Politics of Industrial Policy: Lessons from the United States and France.

HOGAN, M. (1980) "Newport Beach: a storm rages over development." California Business (June): 65-68.

HURST, J. (1983) "Two small towns believe that crime pays, after all." Los Angeles Times 31 (July): I, 1.

HYMER, S. (1979a) "The multinational corporation and the law of uneven development," pp. 386-403 in G. Modelski (ed.) Transnational Corporations and World Order. San Francisco: Freeman.

———(1979b) The Multinational Corporation: A Radical Approach. Cambridge: Cambridge Univ. Press.

———(1976) The International Operations of National Firms. Cambridge, MA: MIT Press.

———(1972) "The internationalization of capital." J. of Econ. Issues 6 (March): 91-111.

———and R. ROWTHORN (1979) "Multinational corporations and international oligopoly: the non-American challenge," pp. 183-208 in S. Hymer (ed.) The Multinational Corporation: A Radical Approach. Cambridge: Cambridge Univ. Press.

JACKSON, R. (1980) "Foreign investors love New York." Real Estate Rev. 10, 3: 55-61.

JAMES, B. (1985) "Fakes are big business." Santa Barbara News-Press 3 (February): D-1, e.

JAZAIRY, I., P. KUIN, and J. SOMARIA (1977) "Transnational enterprises," pp. 355-369 in J. Tinbergen (ed.) Reshaping the International Order: A Report to the Club of Rome. New York: New American Library.

JOBERT, B. (1975) "Planning and social production of needs." Sociologie et Societes 6, 2: 35-51.

JUNG, M. (1985) "Organizational perspectives on firm formation and transformation." University of California, Santa Barbara. (unpublished)

KELLER, J. (1983) "The division of labor in electronics," pp. 346-373 in J. Nash and M. Kelley (eds.) Women, Men, and the International Division of Labor. Albany: State Univ. of New York Press.

KENNAN, G. (1984) "Two letters." New Yorker 24 (September): 55-80.

KING, W. (1985) "U of Texas facing cuts in its budget." New York Times 17 (March): 12.

KRISTOF, N. D. (1984) "New era in service exports?" New York Times (October 24): D, 1.

LICHT, J. (1983) "The nuclear waste lottery." Re:Sources 3, 2: 1-7.

LINSKY, A. S. (1965) "Some generalizations concerning primate cities." Annals of the Association of Amer. Geographers 55 (September): 506-513.

LO, C. (1984) "Mobilizing the tax revolt: the emergent alliance between homeowners and local elites," pp. 293-328 in L. Kriesberg (ed.) Social Movements, Conflict and Change. Greenwich, CT: JAI Press.

LOGAN, J. (1978) "Growth, politics and the stratification of place." Amer. J. of Sociology 84 (September): 404-416.

———and H. MOLOTCH (forthcoming) Urban Fortunes. Berkeley: Univ. of California Press.

MALECKI, E. J. (1980) "Corporate organization of R and D and the location of technological activities." Regional Studies 14: 219-234.

MARCUSE, P. (1981) "The targeted crisis: on the ideology of the urban fiscal crisis and its uses." Int. J. of Urban and Regional Research 5, 3: 330-355.
MARGLIN, S. (1977) "What do bosses do?" Rev. of Radical Pol. Economics 6, 2: 60-112.
McGEE, T. G. (1967) The Southeast Asian City: A Social Geography of the Primate Cities of Southeast Asia. London: G. Bell.
MILLER, J. (1981) "Assessing residential land price inflation." Urban Land 40, 3: 16-20.
MILLS, C. W. (1959) The Sociological Imagination. New York: Oxford Univ. Press.
MOLOTCH, H. (1979) "Capital and neighborhood in the United States." Urban Affairs Q. 14, 3: 289-312.
———(1976) "The city as a growth machine." Amer. J. of Sociology 82, 2: 309-330.
———(1967) "Toward a more human, human [sic] ecology." Land Economics 43 (June): 336-341.
———and J. KASOF (1981) "The impacts of land use constraint: environmentalism, speculation and the housing crisis." Presented at the annual meeting of the American Sociological Association, New York.
MOLOTCH, H. and J. LOGAN (1984) "Tensions in the growth machine: overcoming resistance to value-free development." Social Problems 31, 5: 483-499.
MORMINO, G. R. (1983) "Tampa: from hell hole to the good life," pp. 138-161 in R. Bernard and B. Rice (eds.) Sunbelt Cities. Austin: Univ. of Texas Press.
MOULAERT, F. and P. W. SALINAS [eds.] (1983) Regional Analysis and the New International Division of Labor. Boston: Kluwer-Nijhoff.
MUSGRAVE, P. B. (1975) Direct Investment Abroad and the Multinationals: Effects on the United States Economy. Washington, DC: Government Printing Office.
NAVIN, T. and M. V. SEARS (1955) "The rise of a market for industrial securities." Business History Rev. 29, 1: 105-138.
NELSON, K. P. (1984) "Distressed cities and migration." Presented at the annual meeting of the American Sociological Association, San Antonio.
NELSON, R. (1959) Merger Movements in American Industry: 1895-1956. Princeton, NJ: Princeton Univ. Press.
New York Times (1984) "Plan for nuclear dump divides Dakota town." (November 4): I, 76.
NOYELLE, T. J. (1983) "The implications of industry restructuring for spatial organization in the United States," pp. 113-133 in F. Moulaert and P. W. Salinas (eds.) Regional Analysis and the New International Division of Labor. Boston: Kluwer, Nijhoff.
PALMER, D. and R. FRIEDLAND (forthcoming) "Corporation, class, and city system," in E. Mizruchi and M. Schwartz (eds.) The Structural Analysis of Business. New York: Academic Press.
PEET, R. (1980) "The consciousness dimension of Fiji's integration into world capitalism." Pacific Viewpoint 21, 2: 91-115.
PERRY, D. and A. WATKINS (1977) "People, profit, and the rise of the sunbelt cities," pp. 277-306 in D. Perry and A. Watkins (eds.) The Rise of the Sunbelt Cities. Beverly Hills, CA: Sage.
PETERSON, P. E. (1981) City Limits. Chicago: Univ. of Chicago Press.
PORTES, A. and J. WALTON (1981) Labor, Class and the International System. New York Academic Press.
———(1976) Urban Latin America: The Political Condition from Above and Below. Austin: Univ. of Texas Press.

REICH, R. (1983) The Next American Frontier. New York: Penguin.
RICKS, D. and R. RACSTER (1980) "Restrictions on foreign ownership of U.S. real estate." Real Estate Rev. 10, 1: 111-115.
RIVERA, N. (1983) "High tech firm picks Austin over San Diego." Los Angeles Times 18 (May): IV, 1, 2.
ROSS, C. (1982) "Regional patterns of organizational dominance: 1955-1975." Soc. Q. 23 (Spring): 207-219.
ROSS, R. and K. TRACHTE (1983) "Global cities and global classes: the peripheralization of labor in New York City." Review 6, 3: 393-431.
ROWLES, G. D. (1980) Prisoners of Space? Exploring the Geographical Experiences of Older People. Boulder, CO: Westview.
RUGMAN, A. and L. EDEN [eds.] (1985) Multinational and Transfer Pricing. New York: St. Martin's.
SASSEN-KOOB, S. (1984) "The new labor demand in global cities," pp. 139-172 in M. P. Smith (ed.) Cities in Transition. Beverly Hills, CA: Sage.
SCHMENNER, R. W. (1982) Making Business Locational Decision. Englewood Cliffs, NJ: Prentice-Hall.
SCHRAGE, M. (1984) "Pentagon high-tech role debated." Los Angeles Times 23 (October): IV, 3, 4.
SILVER, H. (1984) "Regional shifts, deindustrialization, and metropolitan income inequality." Presented at the annual meeting of the American Sociological Association, San Antonio.
SMITH, I. (1982) "The role of acquisition in the spatial distribution of the foreign manufacturing sector in the United Kingdom," pp. 221-252 in M. Taylor and N. Thrift (eds.) The Geography of Multinationals. Cambridge: Cambridge Univ. Press.
SOJA, E., R. MORALES, and G. WOLFF (1983) "Urban restructuring: an analysis of social and spatial change in Los Angeles." Econ. Geography 59, 2: 195-230.
SOVANI, N. V. (1964) "The analysis of overurbanization." Econ. Development and Cultural Change 12, 2: 113-122.
STACK, C. (1974) All Our Kin. New York: Harper & Row.
STANBACK, T. M., Jr., P. BEARSE, T. N. NOYELLE, and R. KARASEK (1981) Services: The New Economy. Totowa, NJ: Allanheld, Osmun.
STEPHENS, J. D. and B. P. HOLLY (1980) "The changing pattern of industrial corporate control in the metropolitan United States," pp. 161-180 in S. D. Brunn and J. W. Wheeler (eds.) The American Metropolitan System: Present and Future. New York: John Wiley.
STERNLIEB, G. and J. W. HUGHES (1983) The Atlantic City Gamble. Piscataway, NJ: Center for Urban Policy Research.
STONE, C. (1984) "City politics and economic development: political economy perspectives." J. of Politics 46, 1: 286-299.
———(1982) "Social stratification, nondecision-making and the study of community power." Amer. Pol. Q. 10, 3: 275-302.
———(1976) Economic Growth and Neighborhood Discontent. Chapel Hill: Univ. of North Carolina Press.
STORPER, M. and R. WALKER (1983) "The theory of labour and the theory of location." Int. J. of Urban and Regional Research 7, 1: 1-43.
SWANSTROM T. (1985) The Crisis of Growth Politics. Philadelphia: Temple Univ. Press.

TABB, W. (1984) "The New York City fiscal crisis," pp. 298-322 in W. K. Tabb and L. Sawers (eds.) Marxism and the Metropolis. New York: Oxford Univ. Press.

TANZER, M. (1968) The Sick Society. New York: Holt, Rinehart & Winston.

TAPLIN, R. (1984) "Women in world market factories: east and west." Presented to the Society for the Study of Social Problems, San Antonio.

THORNGREN, B. (1970) "How do contact systems affect regional development?" Environment and Planning A 2, 4: 409-427,

TRILLIN, C. (1979) "Assemblage: U.S. Journal: Atlantic City, NJ." New Yorker 8 (January): 44-48.

VARTABEDIAN, R. (1984) "For California, 1983 was year of the merger." Los Angeles Times 20 (May): V, 1.

VERNON, R. (1975) "Foreward," pp. vii-xii in D. Kujawa (ed.) International Labor and the Multinational Enterprise. New York: Praeger.

WALTON, J. (1982) "The international economy and peripheral urbanization," pp. 119-136 in N. Fainstein and S. Fainstein (eds.) Urban Policy Under Capitalism. Beverly Hills, CA: Sage.

WARREN, B. (1975) "How international is capital?" pp. 135-141 in H. Radice (ed.) International Firms and Modern Imperialism. Harmondsworth: Penguin.

WOLFF, A. (1981) America'a Impasse: The Rise and Fall of the Politics of Growth. New York: Pantheon.

YAGO, G., H. KORMAN, S-Y WU, and M. SCHWARTZ (1984) "Investment and disinvestment in New York, 1960-1980." Annals, AAPSS 475 (September): 28-38.

Harvey Molotch is Professor and Chair of Sociology at the University of California, Santa Barbara. In addition to his interests in urban issues, he continues to carry out research on mass media and, most recently, on power in conversation.

John R. Logan is Associate Professor of Sociology at the State University of New York in Albany. He is coauthor, with Harvey Molotch, of Urban Fortunes ***(University of California Press, in press). In addition, he is continuing research on the patterns and politics of suburban community development in the United States.***

The historical geography of the growth of the steel industry in Western Europe led to communities that were heavily, even wholly, reliant on the jobs and wages generated by steel production. In this article we focus on some of the social and political implications for such communities of contraction in the steel industry since the mid-1970s.

COMMUNITIES IN CRISIS
The Social and Political Effects of Steel Closures in France, West Germany, and the United Kingdom

RAY HUDSON

DAVID SADLER

University of Durham

The historical geography of the growth of the steel industry in old established industrial countries, such as those of Western Europe and the United States, resulted in the development of communities heavily, if not wholly, reliant on the jobs and wages directly and indirectly generated by steel production. When the high growth rates of the 1950s and 1960s were replaced by recession in these countries in the 1970s, these communities were particularly susceptible to the effects of the changing international geography of production, the juxtaposition of the selective expansion of the newly industrializing countries, and the accelerated deindustrialization of the old heartlands that had been the birth places of industrial capitalism.

In this article we focus on some of the political and social changes associated with the contraction of the steel industry in three of the major steel producing countries of the European Community since the mid-1970s. Closure decisions have often been contested from within the communities that would be affected by them. One reason for this is that there seemed little chance of attracting alternative employment to them if jobs in steel were to go, while the intimate links between the pattern of work and the cultural history of these communities means that a way of life,

URBAN AFFAIRS QUARTERLY, Vol. 21 No. 2, December 1985 171-186

rather than just jobs, is at stake. Another reason is that in the European Community (EC), with considerable involvement in steel production by national governments and by the supranational EC, closure decisions have often been correctly seen as political rather than narrowly economic in origin. But although closures have frequently been contested, anticlosure campaigns have almost invariably been unsuccessful and there has been a close association between reductions in employment in the steel industry and the rise of unemployment in steel-closure areas. A variety of state initiatives have been devised to contain the social and political costs that localized mass unemployment brought with it, but these too have been almost entirely unsuccessful. It is these issues that are addressed in the rest of this article.

CONTESTING PLANT CLOSURES AND JOB LOSSES IN THE STEEL INDUSTRY

SOME EXAMPLES FROM FRANCE, WEST GERMANY, AND THE UNITED KINGDOM

In recent years many major steel producers within the European Community, actively encouraged and aided by both national governments and the supranational European Community, have attempted to restore competitiveness and profits, or at least stem hemorrhaging losses, by closing capacity and/or drastically cutting employment. These cuts have been concentrated in localities that, because of their historical development, depended heavily on steel production as a source of jobs and wages. The high level of state involvement has meant that the locationally concentrated collapse of employment has frequently been regarded, correctly, as the outcome of transparently "political" decisions rather than simply as the outcome of the logic of "economic" processes and market forces. The deep attachment to such places, built up through generations living, learning, and working in them, has been a prime reason why such job losses have generally been contested in a variety of ways. The most notable feature of these anticlosure campaigns has been the extent to which they have been confined to local areas, local people, and, apparently, local issues. (See Figure 1 for the locations of the towns and regions referred to in this article.)

A particularly stark example of this was the unsuccessful campaign mounted in 1979 and 1980 to save Consett steelworks in northeast En-

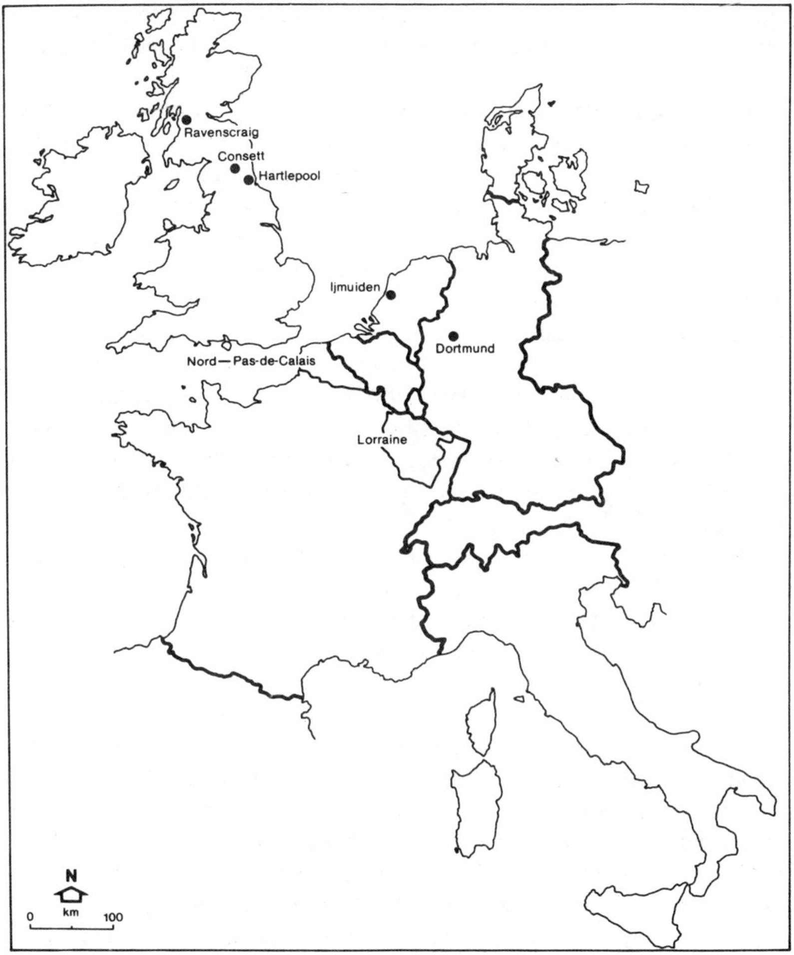

Figure 1: Selected Steel Towns and Regions in the European Community

gland. This was confined to the town of Consett itself, with steelworkers and their immediate supporters there isolated from both wider regional and national bases of support. The "Save Consett" campaign was conducted solely on the argument that it was a profitable steelworks, that its closure was "a grave commercial error" (J. Carney, cited in Hudson and Sadler, 1983a), and, by implication, that it should remain open and some other works within the British Steel Corporation (BSC) should close. For at no point in the campaign was the decisive reason for its proposed closure, BSC's plans to cut overall capacity and their relation to the political strategies of the U.K. central government, raised or contested (for a fuller analysis, see Hudson and Sadler, 1983a, 1984). Furthermore, in those cases in which there initially was a more marked degree of unity between steelworkers at national level—as in the late 1970s in France, where protests against plant closures in Lorraine and the Nord were supported by national strike action—this subsequently evaporated to leave individual plants at best fighting in isolation, at worst competing for survival. In this case, the policies of the French state, in terms of differential redundancy payments and differential allocations of resources supposedly to attract new industries to areas affected by steel closures, played an important role in fragmenting steelworkers on a plant and regional basis (for a fuller analysis, see Hudson and Sadler, 1983b). In general, then, the ways in which steelworkers in these localities identified their interests as place specific and organized to protect them ultimately involved setting themselves in competition with other groups of steelworkers in an attempt to secure some employment.

This is by no means the only manner in which closure proposals have been greeted, however. Another option has been for proposed closure decisions to trigger the formation of territorially based alliances, embracing a broader spectrum of social groups and interests than simply steelworkers and their families. Such alliances can be constructed, for example, because locally based and tied small businesses in retailing and other private service sector activities perceive the threat to their existence that is posed by the imminent precipitous decline of purchasing power that accompanies mass job loss. Once formed, the subsequent development and/or dissolution of these alliances can be central to competitive struggles to preserve particular plants. Three examples will be given of this. The first concerns opposition to steel closures in Lorraine. Partly reflecting a definite sense of regional identity, of being Lorrainese, a result of the region's history of being alternately transferred between France and Germany, regionally based business interests recognized the threat posed by steel closures and began to organize against them before the steel workers and unions. An organization, the *Avenir du Pays Haut* (APH), was created, specifically intended to protect the Lorrainese economy, and played an important role in broadening the social basis of protests against steel closures, at least until February 1979. The onset of violent protests from that date by autonomous groups of steel workers resulted in the APH increasingly distancing itself from the anticlosure movement (see Hudson and Sadler, 1983b). Continuing support for the anticlosure campaign would have involved endorsing a challenge to the state's monopoly of the legitimate use of physical force and ultimately to the class structure of French society, which the state both reflects and guarantees, and hence to the class position of its own members.

The second example relates to the successful (as of November 1984) defense of Ravenscraig steelworks in Scotland. Speculation as to its future grew in the autumn of 1982, against a background of a debate as to whether BSC could continue to operate its five major integrated production complexes. A broadly based campaign to oppose the threat of closure developed rapidly, involving not only steelworkers but also groups of workers from other industries in other parts of Scotland. Moreover, drawing on a history of nationalist sentiment in Scotland and an attachment to Scotland as a place with shared meanings that cut across class and other social divisions (for example, see Harvie, 1977; Nairn, 1977; Smith and Brown, 1983), the campaign developed to encompass a wide spectrum of social groups within Scotland. One important element in it was an influential cross-party Scottish parliamentary lobby, presented with ammunition by a report of the Parliamentary Committee on Scottish Affairs (1982) on the significance of Ravenscraig to the Scottish economy. Such was the breadth and strength of the campaign that, despite the admission that it was costing BSC £100 million per annum to keep Ravenscraig open (Parliamentary Industry and Trade Committee, 1983, paras. 219 and 225), its future was guaranteed as a steelmaking plant until 1985. Whether it will be further guaranteed remains to be seen, although there is every indication that Ravenscraig will be afforded a privileged status in future BSC capacity reductions in recognition of the strength of the campaign to keep it open. What the success of the 1982-1983 campaign demonstrates, even if it turns out to be only temporary, is that in certain conditions territorially based alliances can force a recognition of the fact that ultimately such closure decisions are political, that the right to live, learn, and work in a particular place can be defended successfully against the logic of capitalist production (for fuller details, see Sadler, 1984b).

The final example is more complicated, also involving individual plant, regionalist, and nationalist dimensions. It relates to Hoesch's decision to end steelmaking at Dortmund, in the eastern part of the Ruhr in West Germany (for the historical background to this, see Jablonowski and Offermans, 1974; Schröter and Zierold, 1977). The course of this (unsuccessful) campaign was strongly conditioned by the merger of Hoesch with the Dutch steel company, Hooghoven, in the 1960s, to form a new company, Estel. This subsequently broke up in the early 1980s. Fears as to the ending of steelmaking in Dortmund in 1980 led to the formation of a broad cross-class alliance, the *Burgerinitiative Stahlwerk*, to try to guarantee continued steel production in Dortmund, rather than this being further concentrated at Hooghoven's coastal Ijmuiden works, with Dortmund reduced to a steel-rolling plant. The broad social base of the protest movement soon dissipated in 1981, however, partly because it led to the focus of attention being switched to providing alternative employment rather than preserving steelmaking. Pressures to contest the closure proposals became much more centered on the Dortmund works and steelworkers. The separation of Hoesch and Hooghoven led to both a revival and a redirection of protest, amid an atmosphere of considerable uncertainty about the proposed restructuring of steel production in West Germany involving the major steel groups (Krupp and Thyssen). For, having severed the Dutch connection, the possibility was open to the Dortmund branch of the IG Metall Union to propose, in December 1982, nationalization of West Germany's steel industry as a means of securing Dortmund's future (and even though the union at national level was opposed to nationalization, a compromise between local and national levels was agreed upon, whereby proposed government financial aid would take the form of acquiring share capital in the steel companies). Thus, the focus of the campaign altered as it evolved. It began as a regionally based cross-class protest movement, became transformed to one with a narrower basis centered on steelworkers in Dortmund itself, and eventually proposed nationalization to preserve steelmaking at Dortmund (for further analyses, see Sadler, 1984a, 1984c) as those whose employment was threatened by closure attempted to construct a viable basis from which to oppose it. This exemplifies the shifting territorial basis on which class interests come to be defined in attempts to build a degree of unity within at least parts of the working class—a unity that is always a contingent and fragile one, likely to break down into intraclass competition for jobs based on identification with particular places.

ANTICLOSURE CAMPAIGNS IN CONTEXT

LOCALIZED MASS UNEMPLOYMENT

Central to the emergence of anticlosure protests in steel communities has been a recognition of the potentially destructive cultural, economic, and social impacts of closure. These fears have generally been shown to be realistic ones, especially in terms of local labor market conditions. For example, the end of steelmaking had a profound impact on Consett: The reason for the town's existence was the steelworks, two-thirds of the 3,500 people made redundant lived there, and many others were dependent on work in some way associated with the works. Even before Consett's 3,500 steelworkers were made redundant on closure, unemployment was at a high level, not least because of the run down of employment at the works prior to closure; in July 1980, the registered unemployment rate in the travel-to-work area (Derwentside District, comprising Consett and Stanley) was the second highest in the northern region at 14.9%. By January 1981, it had risen to 23.5%, with male unemployment around 30% in mid-1981. It subsequently remained at high levels with an overall rate of 23.8% in March 1984, and a male rate of almost 30%. The steelworks closure was not the only major one in this period, however. Several branch plants, mainly in the Stanley area, closed down or cut employment: Ransome, Hoffman, and Pollard (manufacturers of ball bearings) closed with the loss of 1250 jobs in 1981, and the other major branch plant, Eveready (making dry batteries), has reduced its workforce by about 800 since the late 1970s. The vulnerability of the "branch plant economy" was starkly revealed, and much of the employment brought to the area under the stimulus of regional policy and the recreation of labor reserves (mainly in response to the earlier rounds of pit closures, especially in the 1960s; see Regional Policy Research Unit, 1979) disappeared. From mid-1980 to mid-1981 alone, half of Derwentside's manufacturing jobs were lost and substantial losses also occurred through negative multiplier effects on the consumer service sector. The "local economy" (almost wholly externally controlled) thus suffered a substantial deindustrialization and was to be further undermined by more job losses, and the public service sector (local government, education, health, etc.) has been so constrained by central government-imposed expenditure cuts that a partial solution via employment in expansion of public services was made impossible. These expenditure restrictions plus the collapse of branch plant employment had an important effect in conditioning the way in which the 1980s "reindustrialization" strategy was conceived. It is difficult to overemphasize the gravity of the employment decline experienced in Consett—it is, at least in some respects, a "redundant space" (Anderson et al., 1983); at the same time, it is not a redundant space to those who (ultimately) have to continue to live there. For them it still has meaning as the place where they live, if no longer work.

The significance of the steel industry to particular communities can be further demonstrated by another example from northeast England: the run down of employment since the 1970s by the British Steel Corporation in Cleveland County. Employment in the steel industry in Cleveland fell from 29,000 in 1971 to 23,000 in 1978, mostly because of the ending of steelmaking at Hartlepool. Employment further fell to 18,000 by 1981, and the accelerating pace of job losses continued, with over 12,000 redundancies in the period from January 1981 to October 1983. Redundancies in steel have been of considerable significance in raising the total numbers of registered unemployed in Cleveland to over 55,000 by the start of 1984. Data on unemployment by industry of last employment indicate that by May 1982 (the last date for which such information is available) over 5,500 redundant steelworkers had failed to find fresh employment in Cleveland, and this makes no allowance for people moving from the area or dropping out of the labor force; nor does it include those who were made redundant in the steel industry, found a new job, and were subsequently made redundant again. In other words, as a bare minimum, over 10% of those unemployed in Cleveland at that date had been made redundant by the steel industry. Furthermore, long-term unemployment in the county became of far greater significance in the period after 1981, because of the problems experienced by redundant steelworkers in finding alternative employment and the virtual ending of apprenticeships, restricting job opportunities for school-leavers. Between July 1981 and January 1982, the proportion of registered unemployed in Cleveland out of work for a year or more rose from 24.6% to 42.2%. A similar picture emerges from Consett; of those made redundant in 1980, only 31% had found employment two years later.

Nor are these conditions unique to steel closure areas in northeast England. Quite the contrary: In those regions in the rest of the United Kingdom, and in other European Community countries in which there have been significant steel closures, both total and long-term unemployment rates considerably exceed generally high national levels (for example, see Hudson, Rhind et al., 1984). In general, then, steel closures in the European Community have resulted in increased unemployment, as they have done in Australia (Donaldson, 1981; Donaldson and Donaldson, 1983) and the United States (Buss and Redburn, 1983).

GOVERNMENT POLICY RESPONSES

Communities affected by substantial steel closures in the European Community are generally located in regions that are eligible for both national government and European Community regional and social policy aid, as well as aid through the European Coal and Steel Community. Nevertheless, there has often been a recognition that more is needed, partly because of the strength and vitality of some of the anticlosure campaigns. In France, for example, the government created a Special Industrial Adaption Fund (the FSAI) in September 1978 as a way of channeling more financial aid into steel closure areas. Another response has been to create new institutional arrangements to try to accelerate the growth of new jobs, often with a heavy emphasis on the formation and growth of small firms: for example, by the creation of the British Steel Corporation (Industry) subsidiary. This was seen as of particular importance as a symbol of BSC's social conscience during the massive closure program, with it operating in each major closure area (Taylor, 1982). Often, however, the responsibility for new institutions and initiatives has been thrust back onto local governments and communities as central governments disengage from an attempt to solve unemployment problems. Although they generally lack the resources and expertise to tackle problems of mass unemployment, local governments also feel a need to respond to them and on occasion claim, not entirely convincingly, that they can solve local problems via local efforts.

These points can be exemplified with respect to Consett, where the Derwentside Industrial Development Agency (DIDA) was set up in the wake of the steelworks closure to "reindustrialize" the town. The reindustrialization strategy has several components, including public sector infrastructural investment, environmental improvements, and an industrial incentives package. It is spearheaded by DIDA, a local enterprise trust which took over the earlier operations of British Steel's job creation subsidiary, BSC (Industry) Ltd. The local government authority, Derwentside District Council, is actively involved with the work of DIDA and has seconded its first industrial development officer, appointed as a response to the steelworks closure, as DIDA's chief executive. Almost all the components of the strategy were put forward before the closure as part of an attempt to show concern for the area, part of an attempt by the British state to legitimize its involvement in closing the steelworks there and in causing the consequent rise in unemployment.

The reindustrialization strategy has had some success: DIDA claimed that by March 1984 its "portfolio" of projects (those helped by DIDA and by its predecessor BSC (Industry) since 1979) had created 1,950 new jobs. About 60% of these jobs were in new small businesses; inward investment has brought relatively few jobs—only 18 projects that, as of March 1983, contributed 337 new jobs. Despite the incentives, inward investment from established firms is difficult to secure; competition between promotional agencies is fierce, and these branch operations are much scarcer and smaller in terms of jobs created than in the 1960s. Although the agency maintains that the portfolio of projects has significant growth potential in terms of future "job commitments," it is difficult to share its optimism when set against the failure to reach commitment figures in the past. It is highly unlikely that the objective set for the agency and its predecessor, BSC (Industry), in 1980 of securing 6,000 new jobs within 5 years of closure will be achieved (see also Financial Times, 1984a). It is also difficult to believe that this group of small businesses will show substantial growth; evidence from elsewhere indicates that failure is more likely (Storey, 1983). Moreover, despite the agency's hopes of developing the area as a center for high technology, this has patently not been the case: For instance, the showpiece "No. 1" industrial estate has only one firm engaged in "high-tech" operations, a small microcomputer company. This lack of success can be contrasted with the successful efforts of the Scottish Development Agency with regard to microelectronics (see Financial Times, 1984b: Scottish Development Agency, 1982, n.d.). Also, any job gains must, at the very least, be considered in the context of *continuing* job losses in the rest of the Derwentside economy. In aggregate, the strategy has *not* replaced the 3,500 job opportunities at the steelworks. At best, it is now compensating for post-1980 losses, and the effect on unemployment figures—bearing in mind the influence of MSC schemes discussed below—is negligible (see also Robinson and Sadler, 1984). Nevertheless, the wildly overoptimistic claims as to how many jobs could be created have the important effect of assuming away the unemployment problem and so giving a plausibility to the state's claims to be able to manage unemployment crises.

It is also important to point out that it would have been surprising had there been no reindustrialization of the area. Just as the dominance of the steelworks within the local labor market discouraged small firm formation in the past, so the removal of this dominant employer creates some conditions favorable to it in the early 1980s—in particular, the creation of a large labor reserve (see Hudson, 1983). Financial incentives provide a further stimulus, offering a package of incentives probably as generous as are offered anywhere in the United Kingdom (Derwentside lacks only an Enterprise Zone). Furthermore, the process and policy of reindustrialization draws strength from continuing high levels of unemployment that reduce wages, undermine unionization, and allow different work practices to be enforced. The strategy has, in fact, offered few jobs for ex-steelworkers because of the type of jobs created—it is significant that there are reported shortages of female sewing machinists in Derwentside

District—and because many of the new employers in any case seek cheaper green labor. Moreover, the policy of encouraging entrepreneurship has little relevance to those with the skills and experience gained at the works; few of Consett's new small businessmen are ex-steelworkers.

One consequence of the inability of the reindustrialization strategy to make much impact on unemployment in Consett has been to create further demands for legitimation, to which the state has responded via the increasing intervention of the Manpower Services Commission (MSC). Nationally, MSC activities are now substantial and have grown rapidly as unemployment has increased: The annual budget now approaches £ 2 billion (see Coffield, 1984; Ryan, 1984). Derwentside has shared in this growth, becoming more and more dependent on the Youth Training Scheme (YTS), which offers work experience and training for unemployed school-leavers, and the Community Programme (CP), a make-work scheme for the long-term unemployed.

Criticisms of YTS have been made both locally and nationally (Allum and Quigley, 1983). The Scheme undoubtedly puts downward pressure on wages; trainees can be exploited as free labor and training is often poor or too limited. In a place like Derwentside the key question is "training for what?" as there are so few job opportunities available after the completion of a year's "training." YTS, therefore, often represents little more than a raising of the school leaving age, an unsatisfactory transition between school and unemployment that is intended to offer an introduction to the value and meaning of the work ethic.

The Community Programme provides temporary employment for one year on projects deemed beneficial to the community. To be eligible for a CP place, it is necessary to have been registered unemployed for 6 months out of the last 9 if under age 25, or for 12 out of the last 15 if over 25. CP is now important in Derwentside: For many people it offers the only opportunity to have temporary respite from unemployment. By February 1984, there were 875 filled CP places in the district. The two main agencies running programs are the Young Men's Christian Association and the Boys Brigade, offering a range of activities from building and decorating to entertainment projects, photography, and community care. Much of the work is manual and low skill. CP is chronically underresourced, many of the places are part time, and wages are low, often hardly above benefit levels. That there are considerable numbers of applications for places on these schemes indicates the absence of alternatives in the job market and also the need for a program that is able to restore a degree of dignity and activity to unemployed people. CP is accepted as a lifeline, even though it clearly has major shortcomings, simply because it is all that is offered; at the same time, the strength of demand for CP places allows the state to point to the appropriateness and success of its policies to alleviate unemployment.

Such measures are by no means confined to Consett, as similar ones exist in other U.K. steel closure areas. Not only are they ineffective in creating the numbers of jobs needed in steel closure areas, they also represent a considerable cost to public expenditure. This is true of both those intended to create new jobs and those intended to cope with the failure to create sufficient jobs to lower unemployment to acceptable levels. Overall, the costs of creating new jobs is difficult to assess. Comprehensive data on such costs are not available for steel closure areas. Reasonable estimates of current costs of job creation in old industrial areas—which include some steel closure areas—are available for Enterprise Zones in the United Kingdom, however. The first 11 Zones were designated in 1981, and by May 1983, it was estimated that there were 8,065 jobs in them, created at a public expenditure of £16,500 each (Roger Tym and Partners, 1984). Yet clearly, even at this level of public expenditure per job, the job creation impact in relation to prevailing unemployment levels is minimal. With regard to the latter set of costs, the cost of MSC activities needs to be considered. Over the period 1984-1985, costs per place on the CP will average £4,400 and on YTS, £2,100 (Manpower Services Commission, 1984). Clearly, these represent only part of the financial costs to the U.K. national government. In other steel closure areas in the European Community similar calls are made on national government and European Community resources. Yet the actual job creation effects are minimal, and this in turn generates demand for further expenditure to contain some of the impacts of unemployment. Nevertheless, these are seen as costs that have to be met in order to maintain the appearance of official concern for steel closure areas and people in them and so contain potential challenges to state power and the existing social order; put another way, the need to avoid a crisis of legitimation requires that such costs be borne, even when they run counter to the Thatcherite political philosophy of the unbridled rule of market forces.

CONCLUDING COMMENTS

The apparent inability of state policy measures to adequately resolve the problems of unemployment facing people in steel closure areas raises some important issues. For clearly to even contain the impacts of unemployment within barely acceptable limits in such areas imposes considerable strains on public expenditure, especially when many other areas and programs are making claims for state support in a climate dominated by central government attempts to contain public expenditure. It is nevertheless clear that these financial costs directly and indirectly generated by closure fail to adequately reflect the profound threats posed to the cultural and social fabric of one-industry communities faced with the collapse of that industry, as these threaten to remove the material basis around which their cultural history and social fabric have been constructed (for example, see Hudson, Peck et al., 1984). On the other hand, there are the claims of locally based agencies, such as the Derwentside Industrial Development Agency, that they can "solve" the problems with existing powers and resources. Such claims thereby legitimate more effective competition in the place-market for new investment and jobs, people pricing themselves back into work, and the associated policy prescriptions of the supply-side economics of the New Right, as the routes by which to solve localized unemployment problems. But the point is that such solutions do not remain localized ones, but rather set in motion an intensified competition for jobs between areas and calls for parallel agencies to promote this competition, which both reflects and reproduces territorially based divisions within the working class. Localized solutions thus become generalized ones, attention is switched away from the conflicting interests of capital and labor, and the terrain on which the debate about unemployment is conducted is significantly altered. The state also significantly alters its role so that there is no longer any commitment to provide employment but merely to provide the framework within which local communities compete in the place-market for jobs.

Seen in this light, caught as they are between those tangled and conflicting pressures, the prospects for those people trapped in communities in steel closure areas do indeed look bleak. Are there solutions? If there are, they will take their point of departure from the bankruptcy of past and present state intervention in such localities; in this sense, they will be born of the politics of despair. The experiences of Consett point toward this conclusion, posing an alternative that radically redefines the nature of the "problem" and "solution." For, to the Derwentside Unemployed Group, the "problem" lies in the imposition of "solutions" from the outside—such as those of the Manpower Services Commission or of a new generation of companies seeking to exploit people in the district and those who seek to attend them. Rather, the "solution" is to be sought within the community itself, via the development of a "critical self-awareness" that may help it "formulate its own future." What in practice such an approach will yield remains to be seen. It is unlikely that it will result in significant employment creation in the conventional sense of wage-labor, and the prospect of permanent mass unemployment, with all its implications for material levels and styles of living, remains the most probable one for many communities in steel (and coal mining, and motor vehicles production, and petro-chemicals, etc.) areas in Western Europe and the United States. But to expect it do so, and to judge it in these terms, is to miss the point, for this may well revolve more around a collective conscious decision to withdraw from the place-market and redefine social life around values other than those of the market place.

Although in the long run this must involve a redefinition of the prevailing forms of cultural and political organization in such localities, it need not be a purely negative process. The recent experiences in mining communities in Great Britain during the 1984-1985 strike suggest this (see Beynon, 1985). But in any case, the point is that such an alternative can only be worked out in practice by those involved: It cannot be theorized a priori.

REFERENCES

ALLUM, C. and J. QUIGLEY (1983) "Bricks in the wall: the youth training scheme." Capital and Class 21: 5-17.

ANDERSON, J., S. DUNCAN, and R. HUDSON [eds.] (1983) Redundant Spaces? Social Change and Industrial Decline in Cities and Regions. London: Academic Press.

BEYNON, H. [ed.] (1985) Digging Deeper. London: Verso.

BUSS, T. F. and F. S. REDBURN (1983) Shutdown at Youngstown. Albany: State Univ. of New York Press.

COFFIELD, F. (1984) "Is there work after the MSC?" New Society (January 26): 128-130.

DONALDSON, M. (1981) "Steel into the '80's—the rise and fall of BHP." J. of Australian Pol. Economy 10: 37-45.

———and T. DONALDSON (1983) "The crisis in the steel industry." J. of Australian Pol. Economy 14: 33-43.

Financial Times (1984a) "Job creation fails to stem unemployment." (March 6): 7.

———(1984b) "Scotland: a painful re-birth." (March 6): 24.

HARVIE, C. (1977) Scotland and Nationalism. London: Allen & Unwin.

HUDSON, R. (1983) "Regional labour reserves and industrialization in the EEC." Area 15, 3: 223-230.

———and D. SADLER (1984) "Contesting works closure in Western Europe's old industrial regions: defending place or betraying class?" in A. J. Scott and M . Storper (eds.) Production, Work, Territory. London: Allen & Unwin.

———(1983a) "Anatomy of a disaster: the closure of Consett steelworks." Northern Econ. Rev. 6: 2-17.
———(1983b) "Region, class and the politics of steel closures in the European Community." Society and Space 1: 405-428.
HUDSON, R., F. PECK, and D. SADLER (1984) "Undermining Easington: who'll pay the price of pit closures?" Report to the Easington District Council.
HUDSON, R., D. RHIND, and H. MOUNSEY (1984) An Atlas of EEC Affairs. London: Methuen.
JABLONOWSKI, H. and J. OFFERMANS (1974) Teilkrise ohne Ende. Goiganz.
Manpower Services Commission (1984) Annual Report. Sheffield: author.
NAIRN, T. (1977) The Break-Up of Britain. London: New Left Books.
Parliamentary Committee on Scottish Affairs (1982) "The steel industry in Scotland." House of Commons Paper 22, Session 1982/83.
Parliamentary Industry and Trade Committee (1983) "The British Steel Corporation's prospects." House of Commons Paper 212, Session 1982/83.
Regional Policy Research Unit (1979) "State regional policies and uneven development: the case of North East England." Final Report RP 270 to Centre for Environmental Studies, London.
ROBINSON, F. and D. SADLER (1984) "Consett after the closure." University of Durham, Occasional Publications, 19.
Roger Tym and Partners (1984) Monitoring Enterprise Zones: Year Three Report. London: author.
RYAN, P. (1984) "The new training initiative after two years." Lloyds Bank Rev. 152: 31-45.
SADLER, D. (1984a) "The steel crisis and the Ruhrgebiet of West Germany: problem, perspective and position," pp. 149-207 in R. Hudson (ed.) Regional Development in Capitalist Societies—New Trends and Interpretations. Publication 38, Institute for Transport, Tourism, and Regional Economy. Copenhagen: Copenhagen School of Economics.
———(1984b) "Works closure at British Steel and the nature of the state." Pol. Geography Q. 3, 4: 297-311.
———(1984c) "Region, class and the restructuring of the EEC steel industry during the recession." Ph.D. thesis, University of Durham.
SCHRÖTER, L. and H. ZIEROLD (1977) "Economic development in the Ruhr: genesis of a crisis." Abteilung Raumplanung 7: 5-16.
Scottish Development Agency (1982) Report 82. Glasgow: author.
———(n.d.) Electronics in Scotland—The Leading Edge. Glasgow: author.
SMITH, P. and P. BROWN (1983) "Industrial change and Scottish nationalism since 1945," pp. 241-262 in J. Anderson et al. (eds.) Redundant Spaces in Cities and Regions. London: Academic Press.
STOREY, D. (1983) The Small Firm: An International Survey. London: Croom Helm.
TAYLOR, J. (1982) "New jobs for old: the case of British Steel Corporation (Industry) Ltd." Northern Econ. Rev. 4: 28-35.

Ray Hudson is Senior Lecturer in Geography at the University of Durham. His research interests focus on spatial uneven development in Southern and Western Eu-

rope. Current research includes work on the industrialization of rural areas in Southern Europe, and the reasons for and impacts of restructuring of the coal, chemical, steel, and textile industries in Western Europe's old industrial regions.

David Sadler is Research Fellow in Geography at the University of Durham. His research interests are centered on traditional industries and communities in decline in northeast England and Western Europe.

The rise of social movements in postwar American cities has been associated with economic reorganization and urban redevelopment. But we argue that although economic change in the cities and social migration motivated by national economic forces provided the objective conditions within which movements arose, specifically political factors were determinative. The first part of this article explores in theory the linkages between economic change and social mobilization. It concludes that urban movements must be understood within the context of both routine urban politics and national political events. Using New York City as a case, we go on to show that before and after the national black movement of the 1960s, popular urban protest was commonplace, yet was channeled and contained by the political system. Thus, in recent years, despite enormous economic reorganization and decline in the situation of the lower classes in New York, urban movements have not arisen. Rather, communal protest is isolated, institutionalized in various mechanisms for citizen participation, and results, at best, in a few concessions. The final section of the article assesses the possibilities of social action rooted in urban movements. It argues that only a national movement and political party can establish the context for powerful mobilizations at the urban level.

ECONOMIC RESTRUCTURING AND THE RISE OF URBAN SOCIAL MOVEMENTS

SUSAN S. FAINSTEIN
Rutgers University
NORMAN I. FAINSTEIN
New School for Social Research

Five years ago the United States was in the midst of a crisis characterized by economic stagnation, falling profits, and accelerating inflation. Commentators predicted that capitalists would respond by seeking to restructure the economy so as to enhance profitability. The question at that time was whether capital was sufficiently united to enforce its solution and whether popular resistance would be so destabilizing as to make this approach unworkable. For the moment, at least, "the recapitalization of capital" has proceeded on course (see Tomaskovic-Devey and Miller, 1982). Under the aegis of the Reagan administration, the aim of enlarging corporate profits has been achieved through a set of interrelated mea-

URBAN AFFAIRS QUARTERLY, Vol. 21 No. 2, December 1985 187-206

sures: (1) restructuring of state finance and expenditure to increase regressivity on both sides of the ledger; (2) direct government mobilization of capital through vastly increased defense expenditures; (3) lowering of the social wage with a consequent downward pressure on private sector wages; (4) reduction of regulatory costs to industry; and (5) restructuring of the workplace through reorganization of work, increased opposition to unions, breaking up of jobs into lower-skilled components, substitution of part-time for full-time workers at lower rates of pay and benefits, and the export of jobs to lower-wage areas within the United States and overseas. This strategy has operated simultaneously through the agency of the state and within the confines of the "private" economy.

The capitalist response to economic crisis has had obvious negative consequences for the working class. There has been a substantial redistribution of income upwards. Despite the resumption of economic growth, unemployment and underemployment continue to be extremely high. Within the urban realm current policies have produced an increase in poverty combined with a decline in the availability of affordable housing and social services. For the first time since the Great Depression, conditions are on a serious downward trend for the lower 25% of the population, but, for the moment at least, protest is minimal. This article is concerned with the form of resistance to the capitalist strategy within urban areas and the reason for its particular character. Put more broadly, it addresses the question of the link between national political mediation of economic change, urban structure and politics, and the character of urban social movements (USMs). The scheme of the article is first to examine the connections between economic change, political intervention, and urban social movements in general, then briefly to look at how these linkages played themselves out in New York City over the past 40 years. The next section evaluates the current situation in New York. The concluding discussion reflects on the possibilities of social action.

ECONOMIC FORCES AND URBAN SOCIAL MOVEMENTS

Economic change generates forces that may instigate, or at least influence, a course of collective social action. Thus, the postwar restructuring of advanced capitalist economies set in motion processes of group migration and urban redevelopment that were associated in various cities with the appearance of social movements. Although new social conditions do not automatically produce particular political forms, retrospectively we can show how they interacted with political institutions and cultural/ideological traditions to determine the configuration of urban movements at particular historical moments.

Social movements, as we use the concept, are emergent action groups that seek social transformation and depend for their success on the mobilization of social collectivities (Fainstein and Fainstein, 1974: 237ff; Castells, 1983: 291). Because their successes and failures in achieving goals directly affect their future size and capacity for further action, social movements never assume a permanent form—hence, the description "emergent." Their objective of transformation cannot be reduced merely to new programs or reforms and, by definition, always threatens entrenched interests. Accordingly, movements necessarily engender resistance and produce conflict. Movements are the products of social collectivities, which consist of members with shared statuses or social conditions. They aim to convert particular common characteristics into perceived solidarities; that is, to create an action group that recognizes common grievances, agrees on remedies, and incurs costs in achieving its program. Although social movements may resort to protests, demonstrations, boycotts, strikes, and riots, these forms of action do not in themselves define a movement. Politics may be disorderly and even violent yet not involve a social movement unless a collective actor emerges that pursues a transforming program.

Urban social movements are a type of social movement rooted in collectivities with a communal base and/or with the local state as their target of action. The communal base of such movements may derive from common locations in real space (i.e., contiguous territory) or in the organization of the built environment (e.g., public housing occupants, renters). Because groups with shared statuses are normally clustered within the urban landscape, common topography and housing tenure frequently coincide with collective class, racial, or ethnic identities. Where these identities produce cultural communities coterminal with physical communities, the specifically territorial base for joint action becomes most potent. A prime example is provided by the black power movement in the United States, in which race, class, tenantry, and ghettoization established solidarities along several dimensions simultaneously.

The local state need not be the object of urban social movements. Their activities may range from rent strikes against private landlords to efforts at self-help and autonomous communalism. But in the advanced capitalist nations with large welfare states and governmental penetration of civil society, USMs almost always collide with the local state as it acts to service, police, and redevelop urban communities.

Conflicts between the state and USMs take on three principal forms (a similar approach is developed by Castells, 1983: 321): First, communal demands for territorial self-management may give rise to USMs seeking community control, decentralization, and political participation in the operation of state agencies. Local governments and USMs may thus become involved in struggles over political power or, more generally, over the institutional arrangements that determine relative shares of power. Second, USMs frequently make demands for more or better collective consumption goods, such as schools, public housing, and health care facilities. To the extent that the local state manages or allocates such goods (whether or not it actually produces them), it again may become the adversary of USMs. Third, social movements may arise around issues of communal defense, constituting efforts to protect the physical and cultural integrity of territorial units from state penetration, whatever its form: noxious policing, siting of unwanted facilities (which may include public housing, drug-treatment clinics, and the like), highway construction, and urban renewal schemes.

In the process of combating the local state, USMs are themselves shaped by the character of political institutions (parties, pressure groups) and governmental programs. Accordingly, it is not possible to analyze USMs separately from "routine" or normal politics. Most of the time liberal democracies are capable of containing collective demands within regular channels. At particular historical moments, however, economic transformations, in conjunction with political determinants, establish the objective conditions within which urban social movements may arise. The character of these conjunctures, as they have occurred in the postwar period, can be outlined as follows.

First, changes in the division of labor, as well as in the character and location of production, altered patterns of migration and settlement. In the United States the capitalization of southern agriculture during the 1950s greatly intensified the black migration to northern cities that had begun during the war; simultaneously, whites rapidly suburbanized. By the time American cities lost their manufacturing industries in the 1960s and 1970s, they already were homes to large, lower-class, racial minority populations. These collectivities provided the base for an important urban social movement.

Second, new urban economic functions required the physical restructuring of the built environment. Throughout the advanced capitalist nations, the manufacturing city has been transformed by the service economy. Private investors have produced office towers, chic restaurants, and up-scale housing in previously working-class residential districts, and, generally, massive changes in the physiognomy of old cities. With few exceptions the state, commonly through some local administrative agency, either has been the direct agent of change (e.g., in building transportation infrastructure and in clearing land for urban renewal) or has subsidized and regulated the activities of capital. Everywhere, residents resisted urban redevelopment. On occasion, the scale of mobilization and the presence of "proactive" programs (Tilly, 1976), asserting political claims beyond just defense of neighborhood, created social movements around redevelopment issues.

Third, in some cities economic forces created housing shortages that became politicized into a housing crisis. Depending on a whole set of economic and political factors, migration and physical redevelopment together with low income and/or insufficient private housing production resulted in inadequate housing for substantial segments of the urban population. Dependence on public provision of housing increased, but public subsidy was usually insufficient to meet escalating demand. Discontent has led to rent strikes, squatting, and demonstrations that set off and became elements in social movements. (See Castells, 1983, for examples in France and Latin America, and Ceccarelli, 1982, for a discussion of Italy.)

Finally, economic transformations affected the fiscal capacities of state agencies that supported the social wage and collective consumption. Here again, many institutional factors mediated between economic conditions and governmental expenditures. Only in the United States did local economic performance so significantly determine the financial situation of a local state which, in turn, played a critical role in collective consumption. In this country—and to a lesser degree in Britain—the collapse of manufacturing economies in old cities produced local fiscal stress and sharp cutbacks in social expenditures. But instead of political mobilization and the rise of social movements, the result has so far been a disciplining of the lower classes. Thus, the strength and perhaps even the direction of the causal linkage between economic restructuring and the political implications of urban crises appear to be indeterminate. In the absence of an extant political movement or of the leadership that could create one, radicalizing objective economic conditions were seized upon by conservative political forces to reduce the political capacity of the lower classes.

Although economic restructuring changes urban objective situations and the potentials for mass action, political relations and events, both national and local, determine the rise, fall, and character of USMs. Alignments at different levels of the political system may reinforce or crosscut one another. For example, Katznelson (1981) argues that class-based urban mobilization could never overcome the structuration of American urban politics precisely because of the extreme disjuncture in the United States of a national class politics rooted in production and a local ethnic politics rooted in community. Blacks as a social group, Katznelson correctly claims, were the fundamental exception, creating a powerful national and urban social movement, perhaps the only genuine USM in recent American history. Moreover, particular sequences of national events in the United States—including the explosion of the civil rights movement, along with a series of governmental programs (ranging from those such as urban renewal that uprooted blacks to community action to those such as Model Cities that helped mobilize them) and the search by the left wing of the Democratic party for a new urban constituency—all profoundly determined the political situation in the system of cities. These national political and programmatic forces simultaneously encouraged the rise during the 1960s of USMs and of the concessionary regimes that responded to them (see the regime typology in Fainstein et al., 1983).[1] Before and after black mobilization, local politics manifested conflict and popular protest, but not urban social movements.

At any given time, different urban settings will be more or less conducive to the rise of political movements, depending on several related, specifically political factors: (1) the ability of political parties and governmental institutions to contain and channel mobilizations; (2) the relative receptivity of local regimes to action group formation and pressure (see Browning et al., 1984); (3) the unity of urban elites; and (4) the availability of alternative political ideas that can create an oppositional consciousness among a significant sector of the citizenry. When all of these factors come together, we see an urban politics of noninstitutionalized mobilizations advancing innovative ideologies (i.e., "new urban meanings"; Castells, 1983); urban social movements arise and transform what is perceived to be normal urban politics.

This last point needs to be emphasized. The presence of urban movements changes the whole character of elite response to popular demands and opposition, whether for social welfare benefits, affirmative action in employment, or neighborhood preservation. Every potential protest at these times can turn into a mass mobilization and political crisis. Government managers, elected officials, and economic leaders become jittery and begin to take notice of demands from social groups associated with disorderly politics and movements (Piven and Cloward, 1977). In this way, institutionalized politics and power within the economy are strongly although indirectly affected by the availability of popular mobilization as a political resource.

In sum, therefore, we come to three general conclusions about the connection between economic forces and urban social movements:

(1) Economic restructuring conditions the rise of USMs (and their fall), but political factors are determinative.
(2) Urban movements cannot be explained by analyses that stay at the urban level.
(3) Urban social movements are not an antinomy to routine urban politics, but must be understood as reflecting a moment in urban politics when significant conflict cannot be institutionalized or suppressed.

THE CASE OF NEW YORK CITY, 1945-1980

New York City in the postwar years exemplified each of the linkages theorized above between economic restructuring and the rise of urban social movements. It was typical of older American cities in its postwar socioeconomic transformations, although it was among the fortunate subset in which new capital investment remained high. So instead of merely declining, it was continually restructured over the entire period. It lost much of its resident white population between 1950 and 1980, when about 3.2 million whites left the city. During the same years, about 1.2 million blacks, mostly from the South, and about the same number of Hispanics replaced them. New York's economic base was just as dramatically transformed. The city experienced a decline of half a million manufacturing jobs over the 30-year period, most rapidly between 1965 and 1975; service employment expanded just as sharply, so that by 1980, total employment (3.3 million) was at virtually the same level as it had been in 1950 (Fainstein and Fainstein, 1984: Tables 1 and 2).

Primarily under the auspices of governmental programs, land use and transportation systems were reorganized (not, however, as a result of a unified strategy, or even with an explicit conception of the city's economic future). More than two dozen major urban renewal projects were completed, as were over 100 miles of highway and several huge bridges and tunnels. During the process, perhaps half a million people were displaced and many working-class neighborhoods were destroyed (Fainstein and Fainstein, 1984). The city further suffered through a perennial housing crisis, marked by low vacancy rates and high levels of abandonment, with publicly supported housing always falling far short of demand.

Finally, the accelerating decline in manufacturing combined with the national recession following the 1973 oil embargo to create a deteriorating fiscal situation. Because the city had expanded its social consumption expenditures in the previous years while maintaining high outlays for capital accumulation, it was forced ever more heavily into debt. For this reason, financial stress (shared by many other cities) evolved in New York into a world-famous fiscal crisis.

The history of the city shows that the political meaning of economic changes depends on national and local political situations, and that there is far from a direct connection between general trends in capitalist development and the appearance of social movements. The particular timing and sequence of events is especially critical, as can be seen in the politics of urban redevelopment. In large part because of the role of Robert Moses and the relatively independent agencies he controlled, massive physical development projects were implemented in New York City before 1960, almost a decade earlier than in most other places and prior to the black mobilizations and new consciousness of the 1960s. Every project produced resistance. In the case of the Cross-Bronx Expressway (Caro, 1974: 850ff.) and the Verrazano Bridge access roads in Brooklyn, residents engaged in the entire gamut of legitimate political activity. Citizens groups were formed to "save our neighborhoods"; state legislators and city council members provided support; and hundreds of demonstrators rallied time and again. There was similar communal resistance to urban renewal projects (see Davies, 1966; Lowe, 1967). Moreover, and in contrast to most cities, the victims of redevelopment were mainly white, ethnic constituencies incorporated into the city's political system. The elasticity of that system was, however, sufficient to contain and institutionalize even large-scale opposition. Party leaders took bold public stands while making private deals. Local leaders were bought off time and again. The social, business, and professional elites of the city held a united front, buttressed by an ideology equating redevelopment and highways with progress. Thus, although protest was continuous, no genuine social movement took form.

After 1958, however, a new political situation began to develop. A liberal reform movement within the Democratic party threatened the future of Robert Wagner's mayoral regime. In the following years Wagner himself became a reformer. Moreover, local Democratic party leaders, faced with serious opposition from reformers, became more committed and effective representatives of grass-roots interests, while intellectuals developed an increasingly powerful critique of traditional redevelopment and highway schemes. The result was a redirection of city policy in favor of rehabilitation, and a somewhat more cautious approach to highway construction. It was not until the mid-1960s, however, that the city was forced to abandon virtually all plans to restructure lower-income neighborhoods, for by then minority groups were fully mobilized in a multifaceted political movement. Although this movement was neither mainly precipitated by the physical redevelopment of the city nor centered about development as an issue, it effectively changed the balance of power between political leaders and citizens, as well as between capital and community.

The black urban movement in New York as in most cities was a direct product of the national civil rights movement. By the early 1960s, that movement was turning to the North and making demands for political and economic empowerment (see Piven and Cloward, 1977). In response, the Ford Foundation and the Kennedy administration established a number of antipoverty, community action agencies, including HARYOU-ACT in Harlem, Mobilization for Youth on the lower east side of Manhattan, and other "gray areas" programs (see Clark, 1965; Marris and Rein, 1967). In 1965, the Johnson Administration implemented its national community action program, and New York City its Council Against Poverty; a year later, the Model Cities program was created for impoverished urban areas. Each of these governmental programs became involved in tumultuous contests for political control, and provided a focus for large-scale black mobilizations that frequently involved violence or its threat. A second strand of the black movement in the city during the 1960s involved efforts to control police behavior through a civilian review board. In addition, the welfare rights movement among largely black clients intertwined with significant efforts to establish communal and client control over health and mental-health agencies.

But the most powerful force of all grew out of the failures of boycotts and other protest activity to achieve racial integration of the city's schools. By 1968, a black-centered movement for community control of education had shut down the school system, produced continual public mobilization and conflict, and virtually polarized the city into armed camps drawn along racial lines. The trenches of traditional urban politics were fully under assault from the one social group that could simultaneously advance demands for political and economic power, for communal autonomy, and for new forms of political representation. (See Fantini et al., 1970; Fainstein and Fainstein, 1974.)

The "concessionary" regime of Mayor John Lindsay, a Republican and Liberal party nominee, was sympathetic to black demands (although its attitude toward white, ethnic proletarians was much more negative). Liberal forces were further strengthened by the election of a black and a Hispanic to the powerful Board of Estimate, which controlled budget allocations and capital projects. In his first administration (1966-1969), Lindsay substantially increased social consumption expenditures, targeted housing and rehabilitation programs to black and Hispanic neighborhoods, encouraged community control, and succeeded, overall, in averting the disastrous level of rioting experienced in Los Angeles,

Detroit, and many other cities. His regime simultaneously facilitated black mobilization, became its target, and effectively coopted black leadership.

By 1969, however, the political situation was changing. On the local level the movement for community control had broken beyond institutional bounds and had mobilized powerful white opposition. Lindsay needed electoral support from white unionized city workers in the schools and in the uniformed services; he therefore assented to the protection of agency prerogatives from client control. Conservative forces in the state legislature enacted a school decentralization law that had the appearance of implementing community control, but in actuality put power into the hands of school officials, the teachers union, and the Catholic Church. The economic growth of the 1960s turned into the stagnation of the early 1970s. The city's financial base grew ever weaker for Lindsay's dual policies of high social consumption and capital accumulation subsidies (see Shefter, 1977; Morris, 1980). Nationally, the black movement, like the local manifestations that it spawned and that nurtured it, was caught in the contradictions of a racial program. For many reasons beyond the scope of this discussion, blacks were simply unable to fashion an interracial, working-class alliance. Instead, the black movement exacerbated white racial and ethnic consciousness, as it threatened the tenuous hold of the white working class on schools, jobs, and neighborhoods. By the time of Nixon's 1972 reelection, the national movement was dead and urban political movements had dissipated with it.

The rise of social movements in New York and elsewhere was connected with economic change in that migration concentrated minority groups in big cities and economic growth permitted expanded social expenditures and even more rapidly rising expectations. The decline of USMs cannot be connected with any particular economic impetus, as it preceded the sharp economic downturn of the 1970s. The recession of 1973-1975 and the fiscal crises of 1977-1978, however, reinforced the new conservative balance of local and national political forces that had been heralded by Nixon's 1968 election. Within New York City these forces ultimately became consolidated under the "conserving" regime of Mayor Edward Koch, creating a situation highly inimical to the formation of new progressive grass-roots movements. Koch was first brought into office in 1977 by an electoral coalition of the city's Jewish and Catholic communities. Since then, the Koch regime has governed in tandem with the financial and corporate leaders who were appointed to the bodies empowered to put the city back on sound fiscal course—the Emergency Financial Control Board and the Municipal Assistance Corporation. This new constellation of authority signaled the end of a divided elite. Although the gains of the previous period were not wholly abandoned, grass-roots forces lost the initiative in framing the urban agenda.

NEW YORK IN THE 1980s

The sharp revival of growth in New York City since 1979 has taken place within an economy in which the composition differs markedly from that of earlier periods of expansion, and it has had strikingly different consequences for low-income groups. It is interesting that employment in the front offices of manufacturing firms has steadily declined from a peak of 86,000 in 1969 to a relatively trivial 41,000 in 1983 (Ehrenhalt, 1984: 43), indicating that New York's rebound does not result directly from its being a center for corporate headquarters. Rather, the city's function as command post for world financial capital has precipitated a vast enlargement of the finance-insurance-real estate (FIRE) and business services sectors. The burgeoning of international trade, the substitution of financial controls and informational technologies for physical agglomeration of goods-producing firms, the activity of the financial and legal industries in facilitating corporate mergers, acquisitions, and deal making, the accelerating movement of funds made possible by electronic financial transfers and turned over by financial institutions have all contributed to the city's economic resurgence.

New York's role as a node for the circulation of world capital meant that even in the first stage of the current restructuring, before the capitalist strategy had produced an expansion of national output, employment in the city increased. After seven consecutive years of drastic job loss, employment began to expand in 1976 and, except for a relatively small dip during the 1981-1982 recession, continued to grow steadily each year (Ehrenhalt, 1984: 13). The great majority of the 195,000 net jobs added between 1976 and 1983 were in finance and business services; the extraordinarily steep decline in the goods-producing sector occurring simultaneously resulted in a loss of one out of every five manufacturing jobs during the same period (Ehrenhalt, 1984: 16). Thus, the overall national shift from a goods- to a service-producing economy took on an exaggerated form in New York City, which has a low share of the still growing high-tech manufacturing sector.

Functional shifts in New York's economy expressed themselves geographically, both in terms of the location of jobs within the city and in terms of the residences of employees within the expanding sectors. Ninety percent of the city's private sector net job growth between 1977 and 1983 was in Manhattan, attesting to that borough's dominance of white-collar employment (Ehrenhalt, 1984: 31). Within the metropolitan region nearly two-fifths of the more than $108 billion private sector payroll in 1983 was generated in Manhattan, and its share of the regional economy has been increasing since 1977 (Ehrenhalt, 1984: 33).

The explosive growth of jobs within the central business district (CBD), however, did not produce a corresponding gain in employment among city residents. One indicator that the benefits of expanding employment have not reached unemployed city residents is stability in the employment-to-population ratio (i.e., the number of people employed as a percentage of the total working-age population). While the number of payroll jobs in the city rose by 5% between 1977 and 1983, the number of employed residents barely changed over that time. Improvement in the unemployment rate resulted not from an increase in jobs for city residents but from a drop in the number of people seeking work (Tobier, 1984: 88). In 1983, the city's employment/population ratio stagnated at 49%, nine points below the comparable national figure (Tobier, 1984: 89). Not only did commuters acquire most of the new jobs generated by expansion of nonmanufacturing employment, they also held higher-paying jobs than city residents. Thus, in 1980, commuters from Westchester, Rockland, Putnam, and Bergen Counties working in New York City had mean annual earnings of $27,500, almost double the $13,900 figure for city residents. Nearly one-half of commuters from these counties worked in executive and professional jobs, compared to about one-fourth of city residents (Ehrenhalt, 1984: 35).

If the benefits of economic restructuring could be said to trickle down to the mass of city residents, they were felt primarily in the expansion of the tax base. Whereas in 1978 the city raised $8.12 billion of its $12.9 billion total revenues from its own sources and $9.56 of $14.2 billion in 1981 (New York City Council on Economic Education, 1982), internally raised revenues grew in 1985 to an estimated $12.96 billion of an $18.8 billion total, an increase of 36% in the last four years. The city's improved revenue position permitted it both to enhance services and to reembark on a variety of costly capital expenditure programs, with varying implications for its low-income citizens, as we will discuss below.

A further indication of expansion in the financial and service sectors, and itself a driving force in the growth of personal and corporate wealth, was a huge increase in commercial real estate development. In the five-year period of 1976-1980, only 10 office buildings, comprising a total of 3 million square feet, were constructed in the Manhattan CBD; in the succeeding five years, 47 new buildings were completed, totaling 32 million square feet, or a ten-fold increase (Armstrong and Milder, 1984). This enormous growth in commercial space, however, did not go along with a corresponding residential expansion. In fact, one explanation for the increase in commutation to the CBD was the city's housing crisis, resulting from a combination of miniscule new construction, changing household composition, gentrification, and abandonment. Whereas the city's population grew by 78,000 people between 1981 and 1984, there was a net gain of only 9,000 rental housing units (New York Times, 1985). New housing units constructed during 1981-1983 totalled 30,578, half the number built during the single postwar peak year of 1962 (Sternlieb and Listokin, 1985: Table 2). Given the attrition rate due to fire, abandonment and consolidation of small units into larger ones, this rate of new construction barely exceeded losses to the stock; hence, the low net increase.

The expansion of job opportunities for the professional and executive class that works in the growing economic sectors of the Manhattan CBD has resulted in the widely publicized gentrification of centrally located residential areas (Chall, 1984). As a consequence of limited new construction and enormous pressure on existing supply, median rents since 1950 have grown from 19% to 30% of household income, and 3 of every 10 tenants spend at least 40% of their incomes on rent (Berger, 1985).

While the young urban professionals are running hard to keep in place, the poor are rapidly losing ground. Reduced governmental assistance, shifts in the character of employment—including a drastic reduction of the city government's workforce—and lack of affordable housing have caused poverty rates and homelessness to soar. Between 1976 and 1982, the number of poor New Yorkers, as measured by the federal Census's threshhold level, increased by 37%, from 17.5% to 24% of the total population (Tobier, 1984: 36). This compares with a national increase over the same years of 27% (from 11.8% to 15%), indicating that the city's new prosperity is highly encapsulated. Although the rise in poverty during these years is partly explained by the outmigration of upwardly mobile households, much of it is attributable to a decline in income of those remaining (Tobier, 1984: 47-53). These increasingly impoverished families and individuals had to compete for housing in a more and more restricted market. During the winter of 1984-1985, more than 20,000 people a night were receiving lodging in city shelters; thousands more were being accommodated in single-room-occupancy hotels; and countless others were doubling up with family and friends.

BASES OF CONFLICT: THE CASE OF TIMES SQUARE REDEVELOPMENT

Despite the severe impacts of the current course of economic development on the poor, and especially on blacks and Puerto Ricans (see Tobier, 1984), no potent, citywide movement for housing, welfare services, educational reform, or racial mobilization has appeared. There has, however, been a considerable amount of small-scale activism around issues of land use and housing. It is in this arena that changes in the city's economic structure have become most immediately visible and where their impacts have been most direct. The recent controversy over the redevelopment of Times Square exemplifies the clash between the interests supporting commercial development and low-income residents fearful of losing their homes.

Long in gestation, pressure to redevelop this centrally located portion of Manhattan accelerated as sites suitable for office development disappeared from the East Side. Original proponents of city-sponsored redevelopment had envisioned an entertainment center. But the city's planners seized the opportunity created by dissatisfaction with the character of Times Square to propose converting the highly congested but stagnating area into a massive new office complex as part of the largest urban renewal project in the country. Under the auspices of New York State's Urban Development Corporation (UDC), which is exempt from the zoning and citizen participation requirements that restrict city-sponsored efforts, the project managers approved a plan involving 4 million square feet of office space, an additional 2.4 million square feet of wholesale mart, a 550-room hotel, and renovation of nine theaters (New York State, 1984a). Land will be acquired through the use of eminent domain; tax abatement estimated at $650 million over 15 years will subsidize development (Mollenkopf, 1984). In return, the developers have pledged approximately $60 million toward subway improvements and theater renovations. The 42nd Street site of the proposed structures is currently used by a number of small businesses. Although some of these are the sex-related industries that make Times Square a popular target for renewal, the great majority are reputable establishments that require the lower rentals available in the area.

Although affected businesses have been seeking to block the project in the courts, the strongest political opposition has come from the adjacent Clinton residential neighborhood. This district, with family incomes well below the Manhattan median, has been strongly resisting gentrification for the last decade. Efforts by landlords to vacate buildings have included extreme harassment of tenants: moving in addicts and prostitutes, using thugs to intimidate holdout tenants, as well as the more common ways of making life difficult, such as withholding heat and maintenance. The establishment of a Clinton Preservation District in 1977, requiring special approval for any alterations of land use, marked a political victory for opponents of gentrification. But residents fear that the impact of a huge new office development within a five-minute walk will finally tip the scales and drive out the remaining working-class occupants (see Fainstein, forthcoming). Nor do most of them foresee any advantages to themselves in the creation of more white-collar jobs in the area.

Mobilization against the project spawned a new community organization, the Clinton Coalition of Concern, which held rallies, published a newspaper, sent busloads of residents to public hearings, and badgered local elected political officials. The coalition, through the mediation of the Community Board (the official local mechanism for citizen input in planning matters) and the elected representatives, managed to gain some concessions from the city before final passage of the resolution approving the project. Principal among these was a grant of $25 million for preservation of low-income housing, small businesses, and neighborhood facilities. Essentially, however, militant protest was channeled through regular political institutions and, although gaining some benefits for the community, had no effect on the overall planning process or the ultimate project.

Times Square represents the classic land use controversy created when the growth of the service economy creates strong pressures for CBD expansion. As in San Francisco's South of Market Street district (see Hartman, 1984), mixed-use areas next to the CBD become identified by city planners as the logical place for further development. Because such inner-city areas frequently house a disproportionate share of unsavory uses, public sentiment tends to applaud their extirpation. When the scale of proposed development is vast, the potential for profit takes off; the more space constructed, the greater is the profit opportunity, not just for the developer but also for lenders, attorneys, real estate brokers, the construction industry, and so on. New York City, even with tax abatement, stands to gain over $400 million in new revenues in the first 15 years of the project (New York State, 1984b)—and, again, the larger the project, the greater the return. Little wonder, then, that at the Board of Estimate hearing on the resolution approving the 42nd Street project, ardent supporters testifying in favor of the measure included the governor, both United States senators, the mayor, two former mayors, and a host of developers, construction union officials, theater owners, and civic leaders. The opposition of Clinton residents and the misgivings of organizations concerned with planning and aesthetics appeared as trivial nitpicks in the face of such riches.

Times Square illustrates the way in which the government of New York City has chosen to ride the crest of economic restructuring. Although the city has begun to demand that developers mitigate the transit impacts of their enterprises by contributing to the renovation of subway stations, and thereby to the infrastructure for further expansion, it has made no effort even to analyze, much less compensate for, the housing impacts of office development. Any private-sector endeavor that adds to the city's economic base is welcomed, regardless of its effect on the employment situation or living conditions of the resident population. Zoning exists primarily as a bargaining chip rather than a limit on bulk and density. The city gives up restrictions on building size in return for amenity contributions. But these contributions, which are contained in the development area and thereby add to the attractiveness of the developer's property, are much smaller than the taxes foregone through abatements. Without the pressure of a citywide political force pressing for redistributive policies, growth has become once again the overriding objective of New York's municipal government.

The reasons for the absence of such a force are manifold. Within the country as a whole no tendency exists to put the situation of poor New Yorkers within a context of meaningful action. The absence of a national movement to structure New York's situation by providing either ideological or organizational resources means everything depends on local leadership. But within the city, leadership that ostensibly represents low-income people is highly fractionalized and personalized. The recent split between black and Hispanic leaders who had been seeking to agree on a minority candidate for mayor has reinforced the lines of division. At the same time the governing regime, which during the concessionary period of the 1960s and early 1970s incorporated minority-group communal interests, has reconstituted as a relatively unified elite with the clearcut objectives of stimulating accumulation and restoring services to middle-class neighborhoods.

THE POSSIBILITIES OF SOCIAL ACTION

The quietude of the last six years contrasts with the turbulence of the period before 1974, also a time of economic growth within the city and nation. One approach to explaining the differences would be to compare the factors that caused expansion at the two different times. It is not evident, however, that a particular growth configuration produces militant consciousness while another does not. Marx predicted that an increase in factory labor would lay the basis for working-class solidarity, and to some extent he was right. Yet expansion of government employment for many years dampened collective action until suddenly the public sector became the principal locus of new union organization. The movement of the working class out of manufacturing into either service occupations or unemployment, the increasing impoverization of a substantial proportion of the population, the feminization of poverty, the increase in the number of foreign-born all constitute changes in civil society that can be traced to economic factors and that create new possibilities for the formation of urban social movements.

The collectivities generated by economic restructuring, however, have so far not developed the consciousness of action groups. Several factors have prevented them from identifying and acting on their common interests:

(1) The massive entry of women into the labor force masked male unemployment and reduced wages by maintaining a family income. Moreover, the reduction of male blue-collar employment and increase in female white-collar work meant that an increasing proportion of the workforce was in occupational categories traditionally hard to mobilize.
(2) As has been the case throughout the century, ethnic and racial divisions have restricted working-class solidarity. New immigration, particularly the recruitment of illegal immigrants into the worst jobs, has exacerbated the difficulty of mobilizing low-income people.
(3) Conservatives have succeeded in developing a coherent ideology in which individuals are seen as the victims of clumsy and misguided governmental programs, to be saved by private-sector initiatives. Leftists have not been able to generate a counter-ideology that specifies a villain and offers a path of redemption.

As the New York case illustrates, common concern with territorial interests has offered one of the few contemporary bases for collective mobilization. Neighborhood organizations, however, suffer from all the conditions that circumscribe groups whose members are united only by common occupation of a nonsovereign territory: narrowness of issues, part-time leadership, cross-cutting cleavages, individual geographic mobility, and few financial resources. To overcome these obstacles requires an overarching ideology, as black power once was, but such a meaning system is extraordinarily difficult to formulate on a neighborhood basis.

Castells's (1983) *The City and the Grassroots* is the most elaborate of recent efforts to devise a theory giving territorially based movements a key role in progressive social transformation. He contends that "people tend to consider cities, space, and urban functions and forms as the mainspring for their feelings" (Castells, 1983: 326), an assertion open to serious challenge. But if we do accept that the emotions associated with residence and collective consumption can be channeled into mass consciousness, the problem of effective organization remains. The defining localism of urban movements, even if they are tied into nonplace-based mobilizations, limits effectiveness to discrete local issues. Without a unifying organizational structure, an alliance of disparate movements remains just that. Andre Gorz, in confronting this problem, returns to the possibilities of the radical political party, even while recognizing its inherent liabilities. He comments that the rigidities of political parties have caused "fundamental debates over the production and the transformation of society . . . [to shift] to clubs, churches, universities, associations and movements" (Gorz, 1982: 118). But Gorz recognizes that politics will always involve contradictions resulting in permanent tension. Although critical of contemporary political parties of the left, he nevertheless argues for their necessity.

Could a mass party develop within the United States that would engage the energies of social movements based in the realm of reproduction (e.g., the women's movement, the peace movement, environmentalism, urban movements)? The American left has time and again foundered on its inability to build an influential political party.

Europeans, disillusioned with the narrow rigidity of Communist parties and the cooptation of socialist ones, tend to scoff at American leftists who dream of working-class parties in this country. But, in fact, the absence of such institutions has been critical in keeping the United States as conservative as it is—in narrowing both the range of ideology and the extent of welfare-state programs. The absence of such a mass party has reinforced the containment of urban radicalism at the local level. Yet the basis of American electoral politics in relatively small territorial jurisdictions means that political organizing at the grass-roots level, even when inspired by primarily local issues, can potentially feed into broader movements. Urban social movements in themselves can do little to affect the forces that are restructuring the American economy. They can, however, contribute to a national political coalition aimed at redirecting the course of the American economy and the distribution of its benefits. For now, their capability of doing so awaits the formation of a collective consciousness that identifies their common situation and poses an alternative to a legitimating formula based on the primacy of economic accumulation.

NOTE

1. We divide the years 1950-1981 into three periods according to the character of urban political regimes. The three types of regimes are as follows: (1) directive (1950-1964), characterized by direct state intervention in the built environment and exclusion of lower-class interests from the decisional process; (2) concessionary (1965-1974), characterized by continuing state intervention, but with a simultaneous expansion of collective consumption and improved representation of lower-class interests; and (3) conserving (1975-1981), characterized by reduced state activity in both development and collective consumption, with the maintenance of some of the concessions of the previous period.

REFERENCES

ARMSTRONG, R. and N. D. MILDER (1984) "Employment in the Manhattan CBD and back-office locational decisions." City Almanac 18 (June/August): 4-18.

BERGER, J. (1985) "Failure of plan for homeless reflects city housing crisis." New York Times (February 19).

BROWNING, R., D. R. MARSHALL, and D. TABB (1984) Protest Is Not Enough. Berkeley: Univ. of California Press.

CARO, R. (1974) The Power Broker. New York: Alfred A. Knopf.

CASTELLS, M. (1983) The City and the Grassroots. Berkeley: Univ. of California Press.

CECCARELLI, P. (1982) "Politics, parties, and urban movements: Western Europe," pp. 261-276 in N. Fainstein and S. Fainstein (eds.) Urban Policy Under Capitalism. Beverly Hills, CA: Sage.

CHALL, D. E. (1984) "Neighborhood changes in New York City: are the gentry returning?" Amer. Demographics 6 (October): 19-23, 44.

CLARK, K. (1965) Dark Ghetto. New York: Harper & Row.

DAVIES, J. C. (1966) Neighborhood Groups and Urban Renewal. New York: Columbia Univ. Press.

EHRENHALT, S. (1984) "Changing configurations in the regional labor market," pp. 2-32 in New York City's Changing Role in the Regional Economy. Proceedings of the Seventeenth Annual One-Day Institute. New York: New York City Council on Economic Education.

FAINSTEIN, N. and S. FAINSTEIN (1984) "The politics of urban development: New York City since 1945." City Almanac 17 (April): 1-24.

———(1974) Urban Political Movements. Englewood Cliffs, NJ: Prentice-Hall.

FAINSTEIN, S. [ed.] (forthcoming) Special Issue of City-Almanac on Redevelopment of 42nd Street.

———et al. (1983) Restructuring the City. New York: Longman.

FANTINI, M., M. GITTELL, and R. MAGAT (1970) Community Control and the Urban School. New York: Praeger.

GORZ, A. (1982) Farewell to the Working Class. Boston: South End Press.

HARTMAN, C. (1984) The Transformation of San Francisco. Totowa, NJ: Rowan & Allenheld.

KATZNELSON, I. (1981) City Trenches. New York: Pantheon.

LOWE, J. (1967) Cities in a Race with Time. New York: Random House.

MARRIS, P. and M. REIN (1967) Dilemmas of Social Reform. New York: Atherton.
MOLLENKOPF, J. (1984) Speech at Times Square Center Conference, sponsored by the Regional Plan Association and the New York Chapter of the American Planning Association, November 14.
MORRIS, C. (1980) The Cost of Good Intentions. New York: Norton.
New York City Council on Economic Education (1982) 1983-1984 Fact Book on the New York Metropolitan Region. New York: author.
New York State Urban Development Corporation (1984a) 42nd Street Development Project, Final Environmental Impact Statement. New York: author.
———(1984b) "42nd Street development project, update." (mimeo)
PIVEN, F. and R. CLOWARD (1977) Poor People's Movements. New York: Pantheon.
SHEFTER, M. (1977) "New York City's fiscal crisis: the politics of inflation and retrenchment." Public Interest 48 (Summer): 98-127.
STERNLIEB, G. and D. LISTOKIN (1985) "Housing in New York City: matrix and microcosm." Rutgers University. (unpublished)
TILLY, C. (1976) "The major forms of collective action in Western Europe, 1500-1975." Theory and Society 3 (Fall): 365-375.
TOBIER, E. (1984) The Changing Face of Poverty: Trends in New York City's Population in Poverty, 1960-1990. New York: Community Service Society.
TOMASKOVIC-DEVEY, D. and S. M. MILLER (1982) "Recapitalization: the basic U.S. urban policy of the 1980s," pp. 23-42 in N. Fainstein and S. Fainstein (eds.) Urban Policy Under Capitalism. Beverly Hills, CA: Sage.

Susan S. Fainstein is Professor of Urban Planning and Policy Development at Rutgers-the State University of New Jersey. She and Norman Fainstein are currently studying the postwar history of New York City. They are the principle authors of Restructuring the City, *editors of* Urban Policy Under Capitalism, *and have published books and articles on planning theory, political economy, and social movements.*

Norman I. Fainstein is Professor of Urban Affairs and an Associate Dean in the Graduate School of Management at the New School for Social Research. He and Susan Fainstein have collaborated on numerous projects and are coeditors of Ethnic and Racial Studies.

This article examines current literature dealing with local economic change and concludes that there are serious confusions extant within that material. Nine specific fallacies are identified, and these are grouped into three distinct categories. In the first instance, definitional problems of time and space are dealt with, notably the assumptions that local economic initiatives are a recent phenomenon. The second group of fallacies examined includes discussion of the possibility of creating jobs, the political imperatives faced by local jurisdictions, and the extent to which local economic initiatives may benefit a specific locality. The third grouping extends the latter idea, and considers the nature of local economies within broader political and world economy contexts. The article concludes with an outline of how local economic development might be more successfully examined.

NINE FALLACIES OF LOCAL ECONOMIC CHANGE

ANDREW KIRBY
University of Colorado

This article has an iconoclastic function, which is to argue that many assumptions concerning local economic issues are outmoded and ill-directed. This is an assertive proposition, but each of the following cases will indicate a context within which parts of the wide, cross-disciplinary literature that focuses on economic regeneration are flawed. The overall intention of the article is thus to move toward a rejection of several accepted positions, and in turn to indicate where more developed arguments are required. The discussion is divided into nine subsections, each of which deals with what is identified as a fallacious argument. The emphasis is on the impacts of economic change and concomitant political responses, rather than the detailed processes of economic restructuring, which have been discussed in detail by researchers such as Doreen Massey (Massey and Meegan, 1982) and elsewhere in this issue. The list of fallacies begins with some definitional problems relating to time and space, and is then extended by examining some of the most basic inten-

AUTHOR'S NOTE: *This article was modeled on previous attempts to identify fallacies within a body of literature. I am most familiar with Glantz's (1977) work on the fallacies of natural disaster, although others exist. It is, I am sure, a fallacy that all such analyses must identify* nine *fallacies.*

URBAN AFFAIRS QUARTERLY, Vol. 21 No. 2, December 1985 207-220

tions of local economic initiatives. The article concludes with an examination of recent theoretical discussions that relate local economies to developments within the world economy, which suggests that local issues cannot be considered in isolation from wider socioeconomic and political matters.

NINE FALLACIES

THE PROBLEMS OF LOCAL ECONOMIC CHANGE ARE RECENT PHENOMENA

One of the most obvious aspects of any examination of the literature dealing with urban change, economic restructuring, and policy responses is the implicit assumption that some disequilibrium is currently in evidence, which threatens to destroy a previous period of economic harmony. Commentators such as Hart, Young, and Mason (in Young and Mason, 1983), for instance, point to the recent nature of economic downturn and concomitant policy responses in countries such as the United States, the United Kingdom, and the Federal Republic of Germany.

This interpretation may well be correct when viewed in terms of the recent past, but it does then cut us off from an analysis of events taking place perhaps 50 or even 100 years ago. Analysis of such periods is of course instructive. Returning to 1903, for example, we find the city clerk of Lawrence, Massachusetts, inviting industrialists to "remove their industrial plants" to the city, in order to take advantage of the water supply free from any taint of malaria, unsurpassed railroad facilities, reliable labor, educational advantages, and healthy and sunny homes (Keogh, 1903: 114-115). Brief historical analysis indicates that these attempts at boosterism were as unsuccessful then as they frequently are today. Therefore, this is a valuable exercise, in that it underlines the long-run nature of the problem of local economic initiatives and removes the simplistic possibility that the whole issue can be examined via contemporary analyses, with an emphasis on recent high-technological shifts. This historical dimension will be examined further below.

LOCAL ECONOMIC CHANGE IS THE SAME IN ALL PLACES

Having suggested that the time frame of analysis is important, we can also usefully continue to examine the spatial contexts of economic change and economic initiative. Most often, emphasis is given to the dimensions of *urban* change, a point developed by Molotch and Logan elsewhere in this issue. It is unsurprising that the problems faced by metropolitan centers should demand greater attention, for there the social outcomes of economic disintegration are most clearly realized. This notwithstanding, it is unfortunate that much policy debate has become centered on one specific locus of economic demise, at the expense of the deeper processes at work. In effect, the generic problem of restructuring has metamorphosized into a place-specific issue, such as that frequently identified as "the inner city problem" (Friedman, 1983).

The major problem with this kind of focus, however, is that the process of economic change and concomitant attempts to regenerate local economies are, to an important degree, shaped by place-specific conditions, to the extent that it becomes difficult to generalize across regions, and throughout the entire urban hierarchy, about what is taking place. To take one specific example, it is clear that the business climate in the United States can be taxonomized into broad regions by building in considerations such as right-to-work legislation, the cost of living, the quality of life, and labor availability. The popularity of publications such as *Places Rated Almanac* reflects the extent to which these differences between regions are also part of a more widespread perception of spatial variations in economic potential and the quality of life (Boyer and Savageau, 1985). For these reasons, there is self-evidently a major difference between locations in terms of their ability to compete for particular types of economic development; different parts of the urban landscape, urban-rural contrasts, and different regions are all important components of economic development opportunities (Malecki, 1984).

What this means in practice is that standardized economic policies for implementation at the local scale cannot reflect the diversity of local economies and opportunities. Glickman (1984), for instance, rightly criticizes future federal Enterprise Zones (EZs) as part of new urban policy development, on the grounds that they will not attract desirable job types. EZs are, however, also targeted for nonmetropolitan areas, and are less likely to be unsuccessful there. Due to the different mix of opportunities, including lower land costs and the types of labor available, it is possible to attract developments—such as high-technology parks—that are unlikely to be placed in high-density locations. As James (1984: 166) notes in relation to existing state initiatives, "few (if any) . . . programs are designed to foster high-tech activities in distressed cities." The need for greater sensitivity to local circumstances is in consequence indicated, with important implications for policy development and evaluation.

A logical outcome of this line of thought is a recognition that local economic initiatives do not take place within a social and economic vacuum, but are part of the competition between a large number of such local units. This is explored in turn below.

ECONOMIC CHANGE IS ABOUT *MAKING JOBS*

A decade ago, Harvey Molotch (1976: 320) argued that "local growth does not make jobs: it distributes jobs." As he pointed out, macroeconomic factors determine the conditions of capital accumulation, and these in turn determine the extent to which national levels of employment growth occur. In consequence, any locality is dependent upon its ability to attract its share of investment, or more simply its share of employment growth. The logic of this statement, however, still runs counter to accepted wisdom, in both research and policy fields. It remains usual to discuss the "entrepreneurial spirit" of specific places—the "merchantism of Chicago" or the "oil and space men of Houston" (Suttles, 1984: 291)—as if these individuals were able to spontaneously generate economic development. It is also counter to political wisdom, which has a fondness for small business growth: that is, the incubation of economic activities based on local ideas, local talent, and minimal capital (e.g., Leone and Struyck, 1976). Birch's study of the job generation process, undertaken at MIT, enjoyed a flurry of political popularity on both sides of the Atlantic during the early 1980s, because it seemed to underscore the effervescence of small firms (Birch, 1979; Butler, 1981; Hall, 1981); it is in the same context that we are to understand the evolution of Enterprise Zones, again in both Europe and the United States, as offering the possibility of "something for nothing" or, more specifically, some volatile economic growth for minimal outlay.

The reality, of course, is rather different. Various studies suggest that the small business sector contains many small-scale actors who *lack* entrepreneurial skills, and that significant local expansion is more usually the result of external investment (Cochrane, 1983). Birch's study was rapidly discredited because of an unsubstantiated emphasis given to small firms and incorrect use of data (James, 1984: 164-165). Furthermore, studies of EZs have consistently suggested that job generation in location A is frequently at the expense of disinvestment and plant closure in location B outside the EZ, and in consequence there is a necessity to continually increase incentives for firms that expand payrolls, rather than simply establishing themselves (Butler, 1984).

LOCAL ECONOMIC INITIATIVES AUTOMATICALLY BENEFIT THE LOCALITY

Having suggested that investment leaks backward and forward between areas, it is also logical to question the extent to which the benefits of the economic development process can be viewed as local. Implicit in the existence of subnational political initiatives is the assumption that there will be such *local* economic benefits. Superficially, this must be true. A warehouse, branch plant, or clerical department all involve jobs, taxes, and economic spinoffs—in terms of horizontal linkages, for instance. Once we delve beneath the surface, however, it becomes less clear that the benefits of such developments are always in evidence. Two broad issues present themselves. In the first instance, there is rarely any way in which a jurisdiction can ensure that its own economic activities maintain levels of investment within the jurisdiction, or even actually employ local residents. Inspection of the 1980 Census shows that there is significant job leakage across city boundaries, with approximately one-quarter of residents typically working outside the city (for analysis, see Friedland, 1982). Second, and as a corollary of this, firms will employ residents of any locality, and may often recruit highly skilled employees from entirely different regions or low-wage employees from different countries. Some types of economic development are even predicated on the assumption that regeneration will displace low-income residents and replace them by commuting labor and new, high-income residents.

LOCALITIES ARE ABLE TO NEGOTIATE THE TERMS OF LOCAL ECONOMIC INCENTIVES

Following on from discussion of the concentration of benefits within one locality, we must also ask to what extent attempts to attract investment are necessarily cost effective. Recent studies indicate a broad range of possible tools available to jurisdictions, including direct investment, the use of pension funds, revenue bond financing, tax exemptions, aid for factory expansion, and income and/or property tax waivers (see Luger, 1984). Two inferences can immediately be made here. In the first instance, localities are frequently in competition, one with another, to attract investment, and consequently the possibility of diminishing returns on the cost of "boosterism" is ever present for any one jurisdiction. Second, many corporations are attracted to localities by less publicized attributes, such as lax pollution legislation and low minimum wages. In such contexts, the locality may explicitly be attracting industrial activity that will offer low wages and pay marginal attention to the natural environment. Some industrial processes involve major negative externalities, which may ultimately prove detrimental to that environment, and to future economic expansions. There are numerous examples of communities that have embraced particular types of industrial activity, only to find that they are threatened by toxic materials (Brunn et al., 1983).

Of course, the reason that such Faustian bargains are made relates to the balance of power that exists between corporate capital on one hand and jurisdictions on the other. The political need to attract investment in situations of high unemployment and the competition identified above may push local governments into positions in which capital is able to extract what Jones and Bachelor (1984) have termed a "corporate surplus." They identify situations in which the jurisdiction is so keen to attract a particular corporation that the latter is able to demand a number of concessions that will underwrite the costs of expansion or relocation. The case from which this argument is developed is the now infamous Poletown case in Detroit, in which the construction of a new Cadillac plant in the city was predicated upon the removal of 3438 individuals and the destruction of 144 existing businesses, schools, a hospital, and 16 churches. All this was in the face of intense neighborhood opposition. The irony of this "capitulation," as Jones and Bachelor describe it, is that the promised number of jobs has not ultimately appeared (Clark and Dear, 1984). Clearly, this example is drawn from a case of extremely high unemployment, but the general issue of the cost effectiveness of local initiatives remains widely applicable (see Friedland, 1982, for an empirical elaboration, and James, 1984, for specific examples).

SOME LOCATIONS ARE ABLE TO GENERATE A COMPARATIVE ECONOMIC ADVANTAGE VIA A POLITICAL COMMITMENT TO GROWTH

The notion of a corporate surplus, as outlined above, implies that investment is attracted solely by a mix of economic and locational factors, and that the jurisdiction offering the best deal wins. This perspective has been criticized, however, within some parts of the literature, notably for the way in which it downplays the ability of a jurisdiction to offer political leadership, which is seen to be important in attracting private investment. Catanese (1984: 192), for instance, writes of "a new era of public-private partnerships, which will revive the dormant energy of the American private enterprise system, in order to create a cathexis of planning implementation." Clearly, such a view envisages a very different balance of power between corporations and jurisdictions. For example, in his book on the successes and failures of particular city managers in attempts to attract development finance, Mollenkopf (1983) places particular emphasis on the political climate within an urban area. This, he argues, is ultimately much more important in terms of attracting investment than the more traditional economic considerations (lower wage rates, right-to-work legislation) emphasized by economists (e.g., Sternleib and Hughes, 1975).

Mollenkopf's discussion of the progrowth coalition in cities such as Houston or Phoenix is interesting in that it underlines the importance of noneconomic issues in the growth process. It is also plausible that reinvestment in the sunbelt states was helped by a lack of zoning constraints and local governments—usually run by city managers—predisposed toward rapid growth (Mollenkopf, 1983: 248-250). However, as Molotch and Logan (1984) point out, the progrowth coalition in such states is being rapidly eroded as citizens intuitively recognize some of the fallacies of growth that have been identified in this article. There are numerous examples of this resistance: the Colorado Winter Olympics in 1976 (Fitzsimmons, 1985), the Peripheral Canal in California, oil drilling off Santa Barbara, and several other instances cited by Molotch and Logan (1984). These examples do not indicate that rapid expansion in sunbelt states is now at an end. What they do demonstrate is that the circulation of capital depends on the attractions of particular places *at particular moments*, and that this is a continuous process of uneven development, rather than a specific process that will automatically favor certain political-economic conditions. A progrowth coalition may be a prerequisite for economic development: It is not, however, any form of guarantee of such development.

GROWTH POLITICS ARE SOLELY ABOUT JOBS

The kinds of examples discussed by Molotch indicate that local economic affairs do have a political component, but that this political dimension is rather complex. It is often argued that local economic initiatives are predicated upon conditions of unemployment and the problems of political legitimacy that stem from disinvestment (Doherty, 1983). There are, however, several strands to this type of argument, as Piven and Friedland (1984: 408) indicate:

> Under conditions of economic slowdown, the local population makes intense demands for public employment and public services to compensate for the hardships imposed by the private market. But economic slowdown

also means the fiscal capacity of urban governments is seriously impaired. When the pie is shrinking and both popular and investor demands are rising, the potential for intense political conflict is high.

Therefore, jobs are not the only issue. Of greater importance is the fact that the argument regarding the potential for intense conflict remains undemonstrated in most cases. Despite sporadic violence throughout Europe, there is little evidence that a decade of high unemployment has resulted in a serious challenge to either the legitimacy of the state or the growth practices of local units. Similar conclusions may also be reached concerning the United States. One reason for this is the difficulty experienced by individuals in piecing together the separate components of experience in an advanced, urban society (see, for example, Castells, 1983a). Issues like rent strikes rarely spill over into protests about unemployment, and the failures of city administrations rarely produce coalitions among the many groups harmed by fiscal stress. This is particularly true in the United States, where the "city trenches" effectively separate community politics from those of the workplace (Katznelson, 1981). As the examples above also indicate, one community may be unmoved by the economic needs of its neighbors, and will be prepared to resist the growth machine with cries of "not in our backyard."

The net result of this fragmented popular activity is that politicians have the choice *not* to make jobs central to the political rhetoric of local administrations (James, 1984). More important within the political arena are the communitywide benefits that derive from economic activity, such as property taxes and, even more important, sales taxes. The latter provide for public services and support municipal employees. For these reasons, jurisdictions will invest both time and public money in their attempts to attract investments, although these may involve low-skill, low-wage jobs, such as those on offer in shopping malls. As Herr (1982) indicates, attempts to lure retailing activities away from downtown sites out to suburban jurisdictions have less to do with aggregate job totals and far more to do with the millions of dollars in taxes that are involved.

LOCAL ECONOMIC AFFAIRS CAN BE EXAMINED INDEPENDENTLY OF THE NATIONAL STATE

The discussion of local political directions cannot be undertaken without an understanding of the relationships between different levels of government. It is usual, of course, to point to the roles played by different levels of government in the creation of policy packages (see *inter alia*

House, 1983), and some commentators have sought to explain such relationships in a political context: We may note, for example, Mollenkopf's (1983) thesis on the role of national political parties in encouraging types of local economic development via federal aid, which he identifies as a bid to attract urban electoral support. Such interpretations, although valid, ignore the more basic relations that exist between the components of any administrative hierarchy.

Clearly, past programs such as the Great Society and Model Cities in the United States, the Inner Cities legislation in the United Kingdom, the Stadtbaufordungsgesetz in West Germany, and their equivalents elsewhere reemphasized a division of powers between levels of government that left the highest tiers of authority in charge of economic development and focused local attention on issues of consumption and reproduction (Kirby, 1982). This division of labor, however, has changed during the last decade, with the growth of local economic initiatives addressed here; but this is only the most visible of the changes that have taken place in terms of intergovernmental responsibilities. National emphasis swung away from neighborhood revitalization toward Urban Development Action Grants and Comprehensive Employment Training (itself since scrapped). Major changes have also taken place in the extent to which social programs are underwritten at the federal level, with the result that many local programs are underfinanced, and poverty is rising among marginalized groups—such as women—with great rapidity (Marston, 1985).

An understanding of this apparent shift lies deeper than the political level. A fluctuating relationship between state and local state is based on the position of the former in the world economy, the rising rates of unemployment and falling rates of accumulation in most advanced economies during the 1970s, and the rising levels of local state spending. What we have witnessed in countries such as the United States and the United Kingdom is an attempt to recapitalize the national economy, to reduce support for many local programs, to limit social expenditure, often by taking direct control of other local programs, and to encourage local political machines to take responsibility for economic development, as well as social welfare, within their jurisdictions. In this way, we see a dramatic change in the nature of relations between the state and the local state. Social expenditure is being reduced and voluntarism is promoted in its place. Where this is resisted, as with the metropolitan counties in Great Britain, the offending political units are demolished. The role of local government—traditional in recent decades—of providing welfare goods is being undermined by the removal of national funds, and most significantly, local unemployment is being treated at the local scale. This makes the problem of job generation harder to deal with, for, as we have seen, economic initiatives have to respond to pressures other than unemployment; it does, however, fragment the national economic demise and makes concerted opposition to national policies unusual, a point emphasized by the geographical fragmentation and ultimate collapse of the recent year-long miners' strike in Great Britain.

Only in exceptional cases, therefore, does it make any sense to examine local affairs in isolation from broader political and organizational structures, as in the small number of attempts to develop freestanding socialist economic experiments in Great Britain after World War I (the Little Moscows) or in contemporary Italy (Red Bologna). These are, to reiterate, isolated examples (Bassett, n.d.).

LOCAL ECONOMIC AFFAIRS CAN BE EXAMINED INDEPENDENTLY OF THE WORLD ECONOMY

A shift to analysis of national political and economic issues points to the fact that we cannot attempt to understand the complexities of local economic affairs *in situ*. Above it has been argued that there exist communalities of economic change across many types of local jurisdiction, and that these have brought forth similar responses for many decades. In addition, it has been argued that current diagnoses are only to be understood in the context of some explicit model of state-local state relations. I have also pointed to the manner in which job or tax generation in location A is tied into patterns of investment and disinvestment at many other locations.

This draws us inextricably toward a view of local economic affairs that is anchored to the big picture of national and international actions (Thrift, 1985). This is no easy task, because it becomes tempting to formulate a "total history" of the sort favored by Braudel (1984), a large canvas upon which the sum of human relations is painted. Such an approach has its merits, but it would in this instance take us away from some central issues. As argued above, it is clear that some important changes are taking place in the form and nature of the local state, a metamorphosis that is likely to have important implications for social interrelationships and political practice (Castells, 1983b). What we need is some theoretical framework that will allow us to examine local economic developments, while also integrating these into broader notions of change. The old tools—such as the labor market—mean little in an era of transnational capital and discontinuous economic activity (Clark, 1981). What is required is a historical approach that indicates the way in which specific *space economies* were created (Massey, 1984). Such local economies have developed particular economic practices and, in consequence, certain social and political relations, which in turn have had an impact on the processes of reinvestment and economic restructuring.

Of course, space economies did not develop in isolation, and each economic unit fit into regional, national, and international markets. The sum of the various factors within particular space economies has ultimately determined the manner in which contemporary responses to restructuring and fiscal stress have emerged. We have begun to flesh out this analytical blueprint, using the example of the textile industry in specific locations in New England, beginning with the establishment of the factory system in the midnineteenth century and continuing up to the contemporary situation of high-tech developments (Marston and Kirby, 1984). It is clear that this kind of integrated approach—drawing on historical, geographical, social, and political data, in addition to economic information—can generate a sophisticated analysis of local economic change, an analysis that necessarily avoids the kinds of fallacious reasoning that have been identified in this article.

CONCLUSIONS

The purpose of this article has been to strip away some of the debris that has accumulated around the topic of local economic development. In their haste to focus on contemporary problems and current solutions—many of them related to high technology—some researchers have lost sight of the central issues involved in this question (see Coates, 1982). To recap, it has been argued here that local economic change cannot be understood solely in terms of local affairs, or solely in terms of economic questions. What we see as a contemporary problem of restructuring and policy development is really only the tip of the political-economic iceberg. Beneath this one issue—albeit highly complex—are to be found a large number of other issues, some political, some economic, some local, many national or international. The situation in which a particular community finds itself is closely bound up with broad shifts of investment, its own economic and social evolution, and the changing contexts of government at many scales.

One response to this apparent complexity is intellectual paralysis, an inertia that cannot deal with broad topics that extend across time and space. The alternative to this is a realization that everyday life cannot be artificially compartmentalized; to attempt such a convenience is both anti-intellectual and, more important, against the interests of coherent policymaking.

REFERENCES

BASSETT, K. (n.d.) "Political responses to the restructuring of the local state." University of Bristol. (mimeo)

BIRCH, D. L. (1979) "The job generation process." Massachusetts Institute of Technology. (mimeo)

BOYER, R. and D. SAVAGEAU (1985) Places Rated Almanac. New York: Rand McNally.

BRAUDEL, F. (1984) Perspective of the World. New York: Harper & Row.

BRUNN, S. D., R. ZEIGLER, and J. H. JOHNSON (1983) Technological Hazards. Washington, DC: Association of American Geographers.

BUTLER, S. (1984) "Free zones in the inner city," pp. 141-156 in R. Bingham and J. P. Blair (eds.) Urban Economic Development. Beverly Hills, CA: Sage.

———(1981) "Supply side in the inner city enterprise zones in America." Built Environment 7, 1: 42-49.

CASTELLS, M. (1983a) The City and the Grassroots. Berkeley: Univ. of California Press.

———(1983b) "Crisis, planning and the quality of life." Society and Space 1, 1: 3-22.

CATANESE, A. J. (1984) The Politics of Planning and Development. Beverly Hills CA: Sage.

CLARK, G. L. (1981) "The employment relation and spatial division of labor." Annals of the Association of Amer. Geographers 71, 3: 412-424.

———and M. DEAR (1984) State Apparatus. Boston: Allen & Unwin.

COATES, J. F. (1982) "New technologies and their urban impact," pp. 177-194 in G. Gappert and R. V. Knight (eds.) Cities in the 21st Century. Beverly Hills, CA: Sage.

COCHRANE A. (1983) "Local economic policies: trying to drain an ocean with a teaspoon," pp. 285-311 in J. Anderson et al. (eds.) Redundant Spaces in Cities and Regions. London: Academic Press.

DOHERTY, J. (1983) "Racial conflict, industrial change and social control in post-war Britain," pp. 201-240 in J. Anderson et al. (eds.) Redundant Spaces in Cities and Regions. London: Academic Press.

FITZSIMMONS, A. R. (1985) "A geography of growth along the Colorado Front Range." Master's thesis, University of Colorado.

FRIEDLAND, R. (1982) Power and Crisis in the City. London: Macmillan.

FRIEDMAN, A. (1983) "Social relations at work and the generation of inner city decay," pp. 51-66 in J. Anderson et al. (eds.) Redundant Spaces in Cities and Regions. London: Academic Press.

GLANTZ, M. (1977) "Nine fallacies of natural disaster." Climatic Change 1, 1: 69-84.

GLICKMAN, N. (1984) "Economic policies and the cities: in search of Reagan's real urban policies," J. of the Amer. Planning Association 50, 4: 471-478.

HALL, P. G. (1981) "Enterprise zones: British origins, American adaptation." Built Environment 7, 1: 5-12.

HERR, M. (1982) "Metropolitan political fragmentation and political conflict in the location of commercial facilities," pp. 28-44 in K. R. Cox and R. J. Johnston (eds.) Conflict, Politics and the Urban Scene. London: Longman.

HOUSE, J. W. (1983) United States Public Policy. Oxford: Clarendon Press.

JAMES, F. J. (1984) "Urban economic development: a zero-sum game?" pp. 157-174 in R. Bingham and J. P. Blair (eds.) Urban Economic Development. Beverly Hills, CA: Sage.

JONES, B. D. and L. W. BACHELOR (1984) "Local policy discretion and the corporate surplus," pp. 245-268 in R. Bingham and J. P. Blair (eds.) Urban Economic Development. Beverly Hills, CA: Sage.

KATZNELSON, I. (1981) City Trenches. New York: Pantheon.

KEOGH, J. (1903) Semi-Centennial History of Lawrence. Lawrence, MA: Bailey & Rushforth.

KIRBY, A. M. (1982) "The external relations of the local state," pp. 88-106 in K. R. Cox and R. J. Johnston (eds.) Conflict, Politics and the Urban Scene. London: Longman.

LEONE, R. A. and R. STRUYCK (1976) "The incubator hypothesis." Urban Studies 13, 4: 325-331.

LUGER, M. (1984) "Does North Carolina's high-tech development program work?" J. of the Amer. Planners Association 50, 3: 280-289.

MALECKI, E. (1984) "High technology and local economic development." J. of the Amer. Planning Association 50, 3: 262-269.

MARSTON, S. A. (1985) "The feminization of poverty." Professional Geographer.

———and A. M. KIRBY (1984) "A reconstruction of the space economy concept." Presented at the Regional Science Association, Denver.

MASSEY, D. (1984) Spatial Division of Labour. London: Macmillan.

———and R. MEEGAN (1982) The Anatomy of Job Loss. London: Methuen.

MOLLENKOPF, J. (1983) The Contested City. Princeton, NJ: Princeton Univ. Press.

MOLOTCH, H. (1976) "The city as a growth machine: towards a political economy of place." Amer. J. of Sociology 82, 2: 309-331.

———and J. LOGAN (1984) "Tensions in the growth machine: overcoming resistance to value-free development." Social Problems 31, 5: 483-499.

PIVEN, F. F. and R. FRIEDLAND (1984) "Public choice and private power: a theory of fiscal crisis," pp. 392-415 in A. M. Kirby et al. (eds.) Public Service Provision and Urban Development. New York: St. Martin's.

STERNLEIB, G. and J. HUGHES (1975) Post-Industrial America. New Brunswick, NJ: Rutgers Center for Urban Policy Research.

SUTTLES, G. D. (1984) "The cumulative texture of local urban culture." Amer. Soc. Rev. 90, 2: 283-304.

THRIFT, N. (1985) "Taking the rest of the world seriously?" Environment and Planning A, 17: 7-24.

YOUNG, K. and C. MASON (1983) Urban Economic Development. London: Macmillan

Andrew Kirby is Assistant Professor in the Department of Geography and holds an appointment within the Institute of Behavioral Science, University of Colorado,

Boulder. His recent publications include The Human Geography of Contemporary Britain *(Macmillan, 1984),* Public Provision and Urban Development *(St. Martin's, 1984), both of which are coedited, and the* Politics of Location *(Methuen, 1982). Professor Kirby is a member of the editorial board of* Cities *and review editor of* Political Geography Quarterly.

This article examines Swedish housing policy during the postwar period. It looks at the extent to which Social Democratic housing goals have been met, and some reasons for the successes and failures of Swedish housing programs. Of particular interest is the effort to steer housing production toward nonmarket alternatives, by means of "socialist market" mechanisms. Some of the problems created by this hybrid approach are identified and current efforts to resolve them are discussed.

SWEDISH HOUSING IN THE POSTWAR PERIOD

RICHARD P. APPELBAUM
University of California, Santa Barbara

In 1965, amid much fanfare, Sweden embarked on a ten-year program to bring affordable housing within reach of its 8 million people. By 1975, more then one million units had been constructed, greatly overreaching original targets, with average annual increases of 20%-25% over previous construction rates (Nesslein, 1982: 241). With housing defined as a public right, construction was directed toward the public-owned and cooperative sectors. In 1970, for example, 43% of all construction was undertaken by nonprofit municipal housing companies, with an additional 16% done by cooperatives. Owner-occupied homes accounted for 28% of the total, with private rental housing amounting to only 13%. A complex system of subsidies and housing allowances assured that no person need spend more than 20% of his or her income on housing. By the mid-1970s it appeared that supply had been brought into balance with demand, and that Sweden had achieved its goal of providing adequate and affordable shelter to its population.

In the following pages we will examine the means and extent to which the "Swedish miracle" was achieved. Sweden's approach is of particular interest in that national policy sought to foment nonmarket alternatives alongside traditional (albeit highly regulated) ones. It was the expectation of Swedish policymakers that such alternatives would, over time, prove more attractive than owner-occupied homes and private rentals. These alternative housing forms were to be achieved by means of inducements

URBAN AFFAIRS QUARTERLY, Vol. 21 No. 2, December 1985 221-244

or steering mechanisms that redirected private investment toward non-profit forms of tenure. As we shall see, these mechanisms included interest subsidies, land use planning, and controls on prices and rents—all within the context of a vastly expanded public commitment to the housing sector.

Yet the Swedish zeal for a middle way has not been without its problems. In attempting to socialize housing within a market economy, Sweden was able to achieve a great many of its objectives; yet there have always been difficulties not far beneath the surface. In particular, the economic and ideological appeal of home ownership has continued to remain strong as the Swedish population has become increasingly middle class. As a result, some of the gains achieved over the past two decades now appear to be threatened.

THE THIRD STREAM: NONMARKET ALTERNATIVES TO PRIVATE HOMES AND RENTALS

The roots of Sweden's current housing policy originated immediately after World War II, when the ruling Social Democratic party began to think of housing in terms of what subsequently has been referred to as the "socialist market."[1] By the end of World War II, partly as a consequence of rapid urbanization, the people of Sweden were among the most poorly housed in Europe, particularly in the rapidly growing metropolitan areas of Gothenburg, Malmo, and Stockholm. Of the 2.1 million dwellings, 38% were owner-occupied, with most of the rest involving various forms of tenancy—mainly private rentals (35%) or rentals based on employer-employee relationships (10%). Only 2% were rentals in public housing, and 5% cooperatives (Lundqvist, 1981: 1). It was in this context that the Social Democrats sought to encourage the provision of nonmarket housing, while at the same time "reeducating" the public to the virtues of more communal tenure forms in contrast to the privatizing tendencies of the conventional suburban home. In power almost continuously since 1932 (the exception was the 6-year period 1976-1982), they have had an unparalleled opportunity to do so.

In 1945, the Royal Commission on Housing and Redevelopment, which had been in existence since 1933, issued its report calling for a comprehensive national housing policy. Under the Commission's program all risks were to be socialized; speculation would be eliminated.

The program became the guidepost for three decades of Swedish housing policy. Its objectives are summarized by Headey (1978: 74), as follows:[2]

> (1) To eliminate the housing shortage by means of a Fifteen-Year Programme (1946-1960). The output of new housing was to be stabilized at a level that would be sufficient to meet the increase in the number of households and also meet the need for improving housing standards and urban redevelopment.
>
> (2) To raise space standards by increasing the production of dwellings containing at least two or three rooms and a kitchen. The use of one-room flats as family housing was condemned.
>
> (3) To raise equipment standards in new housing and to improve older dwellings. Standards for rural housing were to be brought up to the same level as for urban housing.
>
> (4) To keep down rent levels, partly through government action, so that spacious, modern, family dwellings would be within reach of average wage earners. It was considered that an average industrial worker should pay no more that 20% of his wage for a fully modern flat consisting of two rooms and kitchen.
>
> (5) To encourage public financing of housebuilding.
>
> (6) To invigorate local authorities in their housing activities.
>
> (7) To discourage speculative building by offering favorable loan terms to individuals, housing associations and local authorities.

Before examining in some detail exactly how these objectives were to be achieved, it may be useful to briefly comment on the political context of Swedish housing policy.[3] The "organizing of Swedish society" (Headey, 1978: 60) into politically active interest groups was largely completed during the decade following World War II. These groups, which can be classified as supporting either the Social Democrats or the bourgeois parties (as they are called in Sweden), play a central role in Swedish politics. On controversial issues they are represented on the Royal Commissions, which generate national policy as well as build consensus. Interest groups are thus frequently and formally consulted, and in exchange play important roles in eventual policy implementation.

In the housing sphere those groups generally supporting the Social Democrats' programs include the construction, trade, and white-collar unions; the League of Municipalities; the large cooperative associations; the National Association of Swedish Public Housing Enterprises (SABO); and the National Tenants' Union. The "pro-bourgeois" interest groups include the university graduate and higher civil servants' unions; farmers' organizations; employers and industrialists' federations; private builders; landlord and homeowner associations; and the banks. The very success of the Social Democrats' housing program has served to build the strength and membership of those groups that supported it. General public opinion, at least until recently, has also strongly favored the Social Democrats' approach: Before they became relatively affluent, most Swedes supported programs that promised cheaper public and cooperative housing, housing allowances, and other forms of subsidy (Headey, 1978: 64).

The stage was set for the present approach during the beginning of World War II, when housing construction all but ceased. In the face of rapid urbanization, public demand soon outstripped supply in the larger cities. In response to the perceived failure of the private market, the Social Democratic government became heavily involved in housing production, subsidizing over 90% of wartime construction during the period 1942-1945. Building targets were met each year (Headey, 1978: 72). The increased state intervention clearly favored nonprofit builders and working-class consumers at the expense of developers, private investors, landlords, and potential homeowners. It was made possible partly because of the national consensus generated by the war, but also because of the Social Democrats' decisive electoral victory of 1941, when they obtained a clear majority for the first time since winning power in 1932. When the war ended the Social Democrats could therefore point to past successes, relying on the administrative legacy of greatly enhanced wartime planning. It is against this backdrop that the vision of the 1945 Royal Commission must be assessed.

The Social Democrats by no means had free rein to promote a thorough-going socialist housing program. During most of the 44-year period 1932-1976, they were forced into coalition governments (legislative majorities were held only from 1941 to 1951 and from 1967 to 1973). As Headey (1978: 59) summarizes the Social Democrats' position, "retention of power hinges on 5% of voters and seats, so that public opinion and the parties and interest groups which represent centrist opinion have to be carefully cultivated. Compromise is a political necessity not just a national characteristic." Yet at the same time, the importance of almost half a century of Social Democratic governance should not be underestimated: The party became strong and disciplined, both nationally and locally (where it held power as well), while administrators and bureaucrats could become reasonably confident that the government's housing programs were relatively permanent.

COOPERATIVE HOUSING IN SWEDEN

The cooperative movement was Sweden's first major alternative to private rental housing, with its origins preceding the Social Democratic government by about two decades.[4] The principal cooperative organization—the National Association of Tenants' Savings and Building Societies (HSB)—was founded in 1923-1924 on the initiative of the National Tenants' Association, at a time when wages were falling and rents rising.[5] HSB developed a two-tier structure—a regional savings society, which also provided technical assistance, and local tenant-owner associations, which the national organization aggressively sought to create. By offering depositors who eventually purchased coop units preferential interest rates, HSB was able to raise substantial amounts of capital to greatly increase the amount of cooperative construction under its sponsorship. The Association was (and is) run democratically, with elected boards based in the local projects. HSB thus combined building and savings, cooperative ownership and mutual assistance. It grew rapidly during the 1930s, becoming a nationwide movement. As its capital base grew, HSB was able to acquire suppliers' firms and manufacturing facilities, and engage in bulk purchases. At the present time, HSB estimates its total membership at almost 350,000.[6]

A second cooperative association, Svenska Riksbyggen, was founded in the 1940s, at a time when 40% of the members of the building trades were out of work. Riksbyggen's membership base was in the trade unions, and it was originally intended to revitalize the home construction industry by building public housing units as well as cooperatives. Smaller than HSB, it presently manages some 180,000 dwelling units. Together, HSB and Riksbyggen account for two-thirds of all cooperatives and approximately one out of every ten dwelling units in Sweden (Lundevall, 1976: 38).

The cooperative movement in Sweden was highly self-conscious about its goals, seeking no less than the transformation of housing tenure in the country. It sought to provide quality housing at prices working people could easily afford, removing housing from the inflationary effects of the marketplace. The cooperative form of tenure itself—a hybrid between tenancy and private ownership—was appealing in that it promised security while presumably discouraging "privatization." Until 1969, resale controls prevented units from being resold at market prices, thereby guaranteeing price stability as well. It was anticipated that once cooperatives had acquired a significant segment of the market, private rents would be forced down in competition.

PUBLIC UTILITY HOUSING

While cooperatives were therefore a part of the socialist vision of housing as a "social right, rather than a private good,"[7] the cooperative movement came to occupy the conservative position within the Social Democratic approach to housing. The more radical position, favored by the socialists, was to deny private ownership forms altogether, in the form of a greatly expanded "public utility housing" sector. Under this approach, private landlords would eventually be displaced by more public forms of ownership. This was to be achieved through the massive construction of flats by nonprofit municipal housing companies, financed by the central government, and facilitated by significantly enhanced local empowerment.

The Housing Provision and Building Acts of 1947 allocated to the municipalities responsibility for solving the housing shortage, along with the right to decide how all land within the municipal boundaries was to be used (Svensson, 1976: 5-13). This "planning monopoly" made possible extensive land banking, long-range planning, and the construction of public housing units on municipally owned land. Municipalities were given the rights of expropriation and first refusal on land, and later (in 1973) were given the right to expropriate existing rental housing that failed to comply with building standards (Jussil, 1975: 176-177).[8] The national government viewed its role as providing enabling legislation and financing; the localities had the responsibility for planning and construction.

By 1980, there were some 250 municipal housing corporations throughout Sweden, which produced two-thirds of all rental construction during the previous decade. One-quarter of all dwelling units were owned by these companies—amounting to half of all rentals. Within the cities, close to three-quarters of all new housing construction occurred on municipally owned lands. Tenancy in public housing extended well into the middle class; indeed, an objective of the massive public housing construction that occurred during the period 1965-1974 was to "declass" this form of tenure. As with the cooperative movement, the long-term strategy underlying public housing was to increase the market share to the point where public housing became price-leading. Because such units were provided on a nonprofit basis, this in turn would make housing generally available at lower prices (Lundqvist, 1981: 1).

Thus, Swedish postwar housing policy, particularly during the period 1965-1974, sought through heavy governmental subsidy and strong local planning to steer new construction away from the private sector and toward the public rentals and quasi-private cooperative ownership preferred by the Social Democrats (Jussil, 1975). By 1980, 20% of all housing units were owned by municipal housing companies, and 15% were in cooperatives. At the same time, the share of private rentals had declined to only 20% of the market, with owner-occupied homes making up the balance (about 40%; Swedish Institute, 1980: 2-3).

Table 1 summarizes recent trends for the multifamily housing stock.[9] We see that almost two-thirds of all units built in 1945 were private rentals, whereas approximately one-fourth were in cooperatives and one out of eleven in public enterprises. Cooperative housing construction peaked in 1960 at 38%, and subsequently has fluctuated around postwar levels. Private enterprise construction had declined to only 12% by 1979, whereas public enterprise construction increased to 68% in 1975 and declined somewhat thereafter. As a consequence, the multifamily housing stock went from 80% private rentals in 1945 to 38% in 1975. Cooperatives at that time accounted for almost a fourth of the multifamily housing stock.

THE "SWEDISH MIRACLE"

The accomplishments of the Social Democrats in achieving their housing objectives during the period 1965-1974 were, by any standards, substantial. By allocating an annual average of 6.7% of GNP to housing[10] a total of 1,005,600 units were constructed (Headey, 1978: 48). The ten-year program witnessed:

(1) *The large-scale construction of housing of a quality unimaginable two decades earlier*: In 1945, only 21% of all dwelling units in Sweden had a bath or shower, 36% had an inside toilet, and 46% had central heating. These figures had improved only marginally by 1955. By 1974, however, fully 93% of all households enjoyed central heating, shower or bath, inside toilet, refrigerator, stove, and other modern amenities (Headey, 1978: 50-51). Slum areas have been eliminated, although one study estimates that "some 8000 people have no decent home" (Wiktorin, 1982: 248).[11] Although historically Swedish housing had been small and crowded by American standards, this situation had also improved considerably by the 1970s, with a shift in construction to larger two- and three-bedroom units.

Most significantly, working-class people enjoyed these amenities to the same extent as those in the middle class. In 1974, for example, 97% of

TABLE 1
Multifamily Housing in Sweden: Newly Completed Units and Existing Stock by Ownership Type, 1945-1979

	Newly Completed Units						Existing Stock*				
	1945	1960	1965	1970	1975	1979	1945	1960	1965	1970	1975
Private Enterprises	65%	21%	20%	19%	12%	12%	80%	55%	49%	41%	38%
Housing Cooperatives	26	38	27	22	20	27	11	22	24	24	24
Municipal and Public Utility Enterprises	9	41	53	59	68	61	9	23	27	34	38
Total:	100%	100%	100%	100%	100%	100%	100%	100%	100%	100%	100%

SOURCE: Svenska Riksbyggen (1980: 4, 6).
*1979 not available.

salary earners lived in "modern" dwellings with a full range of amenities; the figure for wage earners was 92% (Headey, 1978: 51-52). In fact, one of the principal achievements of Swedish housing policy was to provide for all Swedes the housing opportunities available in most countries only to the middle class. Headey (1978: 50, 52-53) has summarized this accomplishment:

> In most countries—as in Sweden in the past—lower income groups are constrained to live as tenants of either private landlords or public authorities in relatively poor, run-down neighborhoods. In modern Sweden, by contrast, working class people, like middle class people, have an effective choice of living in cooperative as well as tenant housing and also of being owner-occupiers. . . . The significance of this extension of opportunity should not be minimized. In most countries working class people are not able to choose whether to live in town, close to work and entertainment, or to join the green wave living in simulated countryside. The Swedish worker is relatively fortunate in being able to house his family according to preference rather than according to the tyranny of what economists, accustomed to analyzing "free" rather than socialized markets, term "effective demand."

There is some evidence that the lowest-income people are not as well-housed as middle- and working-class Swedes. Immigrants, for example, are more likely to live in overcrowded conditions: One study in 1976 found that one-quarter of Finnish workers and almost one-half of immigrants from southern Europe were living two or more to a room (excluding kitchens and living rooms). The same study concludes, however, that "people with unsatisfactory housing conditions . . . [are] very marginal in proportion to the whole population," tending to be low-income and low-status, but otherwise heterogeneous in terms of ethnicity, household size, and social record (Wiktorin, 1982: 248-250).

(2) *The creation of planned suburban communities*: For ideological as well as economic reasons, a great deal of housing construction consisted of large apartment complexes, particularly in the major metropolitan suburbs. In the Stockholm area, for example, close to four out of every five people lived in apartments by 1970 (Daun, 1979: 1), and nationwide the figure is currently almost half.

Suburban housing, particularly those public housing projects built during the late 1950s and early 1960s, were often characterized by the alienating high-rise functionalist architecture often associated with Swedish public housing. Yet much recent construction has been in row houses and small flats, in well-planned suburban communities built around service and commercial centers, and integrated with highly efficient mass transit systems. The visitor to the Swedish suburbs is struck by their "new towns" atmosphere—cluster development, large amounts of open space, children's play areas, centrally located shops, and a range of amenities seldom found in their U.S. counterparts.[12]

(3) *The elimination of private landlords as a significant force in the determination of rents*: When the postwar system of rent controls was lifted in Sweden in 1975,[13] with the decontrolling of 350,000 private rental units in the larger urban areas (Nesslein, 1982: 237), the groundwork had already been laid for the operation of the "socialist market" in rent setting. A series of national laws, beginning with the Rent Act of 1968, established key safeguards for tenants, including mandatory collective bargaining between tenants' and landlords' organizations. Every year representatives of the large nonprofit municipal housing companies negotiate rent levels with representatives of the National Tenants' Association. Under law, public sector rents then serve as guidelines for rents in the private sector. Rents are determined on the basis of "utilization value" only—equal rent for dwellings of equal quality.

Although under rent control rents reflected initial production expenses (with adjustments for rising costs), utilization value rent setting is designed to ensure that newer, more costly units in a locality are not priced above older units of comparable quality (Nesslein, 1982: 237). Under this "fair rent structure," neither location nor capital costs are supposed to influence rents: Only the size of a unit, its amenities, and its overall maintenance level are to be considered. This has resulted in a system that "leads to rent agreements that are independent of the property owner's actual costs" (Ronmark, 1981: 11). In practice, this means that the large public and private rental companies must practice "rent pooling," whereby rents in their newer, high-cost units are subsidized by rents in older, lower-cost ones.[14]

Because of these "fair rent" provisions in Swedish housing laws, tenants are protected against large rent increases, a major source of involuntary displacement. Tenants enjoy other protections as well, particularly safeguards against arbitrary eviction. Swedish law also protects against eviction through "luxury renewal"—the upgrading of property so that it becomes too expensive for its present tenants. It is, in fact, very difficult for landlords to evict tenants who pay their rent on time. Disputes over lease conditions and violations, as well as rent levels, are handled by local rent tribunals, and, on appeal, by the National Housing Court. Landlords who fail to maintain their units adequately are subject to stringent controls. Under the 1973 Housing Renewal Act, local rent tribunals can force landlords to bring their units up to acceptable standards. The 1977 Housing Management Act empowers the rent tribunals to temporarily suspend landlords from management duties until necessary repairs have been done; in extreme cases, the right of landlords to mortgage their property can be suspended for up to five years (Lundqvist, 1981: 26).

(4) *The creation of a system of housing allowances, reaching almost 40% of all households (Nesslein, 1982: 236), that guarantees that no household need pay an excessive percentage of its income on housing*: Allowances are based on income, number of children, age, and housing expenditure. They extend to households in all three forms of tenure, reaching 26% of home owners, 33% of cooperative owner-tenants, and 42% of tenants in public and private rental housing (Lundqvist, 1981: 20).[15] Support levels were at one time pegged at one-fifth of household income, although the inflation of recent years has made such a goal increasingly remote. Although as recently as 1974 families with children spent an estimated 16% of their income on rents, there is evidence that the figure for all households may now be considerably higher, possibly approaching 25%.[16] For all households receiving allowances, approximately one-third of housing expenditures are covered (Lundqvist, 1981: 20). For a typical working-class family paying roughly one-quarter of its

income for rent (approximately $200 per month), allowances would cover 54% of rent payments (Swedish Institute, 1980: 3). Unlike the United States' Section 8 program, housing supports thus extend well into the middle class, so that recipients are not stigmatized.

(5) *Municipal land-banking of almost all remaining developable land in the major urban areas*: Public lands are then used for the construction of public nonprofit housing units, leased to developers or sold outright under stringent controls, with the consequence that three-quarters of all construction done in the municipalities (excluding urban renewal) has been done on municipal holdings (Heimburger, 1976: 31). Furthermore, under the so-called "land condition," state loan subsidies for the construction of rental units are made only for projects built on land obtained from municipalities (Svensson, 1976: 31-32). Because, as we will see below, such subsidies are in fact sizable, this affords the localities further leverage over speculation and land use generally.

Swedish municipalities, along with responsibility for assuring the provision of adequate housing, have been granted extremely strong land use planning powers in order to do so. National legislation empowers localities to set construction, design, and equipment standards for all housing, regulating its type, location, and timing (Nesslein, 1982: 238). Under the "planning monopoly," all development must reflect annual and rolling five-year municipal plans. As previously noted, localities have rights of expropriation and first refusal (Svensson, 1976: 14-32; Jussil, 1975: 176), with compensation laws designed to discourage speculation. They are also in a position to get land procurement loans and lease-hold loans on highly favorable terms (Jussil, 1975; Swedish Institute, 1980: 3).

(6) *The elimination of shelter poverty*: In Sweden, where the average blue-collar worker earns $12,000 a year, an unsubsidized four-bedroom unit rents for about $245 a month (all utilities included). A comparable cooperative costs $40 less (estimated from Lundqvist, 1981: Tables 5 and 6; Svenska Riksbyggen, 1980: 8). According to Headey (1978: 86),

> There is now a housing surplus rather than a shortage and almost everybody lives in a good quality dwelling in a pleasant neighborhood. The government could reasonably claim that it had achieved its stated aim that "The whole population should be provided with sound, spacious, well planned and appropriately equipped dwellings of good quality at reasonable costs."

Nonetheless, new problems have emerged, and housing controversies are as fierce as ever in Sweden. Before examining some of these difficulties, however, let us first look at the mechanisms by which the Swedish government has steered housing investment in the direction dictated by the "socialist market."

STEERING MECHANISMS

The Swedish government has used two principal means to achieve its housing objectives: legislation empowering localities to solve their own housing problems, and the financial mechanisms necessary to do so. I have mentioned some of the former: the planning monopoly and land condition, rights of preemption and expropriation, and strong powers of code enforcement that at the same time prevent luxury renewal. There are also provisions in the tax code to discourage speculation. Since 1968, the capital gains tax has been strengthened, with a rate of 75% for short-term gains, net of a small deductible (see Svensson, 1976: 28-29). The chief financial mechanisms have included housing allowances, loans to municipalities for land banking, and a system of interest subsidies designed to promote more public forms of ownership. Interest subsidies, in fact, constitute the main steering mechanisms by which the Swedish government is able to direct the marketplace toward socially desired objectives.

The financing of construction is based on large government subsidies to private borrowers (see Lundqvist, 1981: 17). Of the total cost of land and development, 70% is financed through long-term (40-year) private "primary loans" at slightly below-market rates.[17] A variable part of the remaining 30% is financed by "state housing loans"—the portion being larger for preferred types of tenure. Thus, nonprofit municipal public housing corporations receive the entire 30% in state loans; cooperatives receive 29%; owner-occupied houses, 25%; and private rentals, 22%. This in effect means that no monies need be advanced for the construction of public housing, while cooperatives require only 1% of the total cost; detached homes, 5%; and private rentals, 8%.

This preferred investment hierarchy is reinforced by a parallel system of loan subsidies. New housing in Sweden has a "guaranteed mortgage interest rate" on the entire loan, set initially at extremely low levels, with government subsidies covering all interest payments in excess of the guaranteed rate. For cooperatives and rental units, the guaranteed rate in 1981 was 3% for the first year of the loan, rising at 0.25% per year thereafter until reaching the market rate. For owner-occupied homes, the initial rate was 5.5%, rising considerably more steeply at 0.5% per year. Together, these financial mechanisms have worked well historically to discourage the production of single-family homes vis-à-vis other forms of tenure,[18] and to encourage the production of public rentals instead of private ones.

The steering effects of interest subsidies were originally to be secured by a tax system that neutralized any economic bias in favor of single-family housing. Although homeowners in Sweden were allowed to deduct the unsubsidized portion of interest paid on mortgage loans from taxable income as if it were a business expense, such an expense was to be set against the hypothetical income that would result from actually renting the property out—income that was then taxed at 2% (Headey, 1978: 86-87).[19] When nonsubsidized interest rates were also at 2%, taxes more or less offset the interest deductions (Headey, 1978: 87; Lundqvist, 1981: 21), and homeowners received no tax benefit by virtue of their tenure. As we will see below, this is no longer the case.

SOME RECENT PROBLEMS

By the mid-1970s, Sweden had pronounced its housing problems essentially solved. With the completion of the "one million" program, supply had in theory been brought into balance with demand. The minimum standard of two bedrooms for a four-person family was widely achieved. Speculation had largely disappeared because of a "balanced" market, the removal of most developable urban land from the marketplace, and the replacement of market rental pricing by a system of rent negotiations. The termination of the postwar system of rent controls as unnecessary in a "balanced market" was a direct result of these achievements.

The past five years, however, have revealed some fundamental problems.[20] Increasingly affluent Swedes have begun to demand (and receive) detached suburban homes, despite more than forty years of socialist "education" promoting the virtues of public housing and cooperatives. Whereas surveys in the 1950s indicated that only 30%-40% of the population preferred to live in detached homes, the figure is now 80%-90% (Daun, 1979: 2, 6). Today, 72% of all newly constructed units are single-family homes, a dramatic reversal from ten years ago (Table 2). Only one-fifth of all units are in public rentals. Vacancy rates in high rises, especially in the suburban areas, rose in the early 1970s, although in some areas shortages are again being felt.[21] In some projects middle-class Swedish tenants have been replaced by immigrant workers, who now number one-eighth of the total population. Segregation is regarded as a potentially serious problem.

TABLE 2
New Housing Production in Sweden by Type of Housing, 1970-1979

Housing Type	1970	1975	1979
Single-Family (1-2 units)	32%	63%	72%
Multi-Family (3+ units)	68%	37%	28%
	(100%)	(100%)	(100%)

SOURCE: Svenska Riksbyggen (1980: 5).

THE RECOMMODIFICATION OF SWEDISH HOUSING?

The highly successful cooperative sector has come increasingly to resemble ordinary home ownership. Coop members now have total control over the use and resale of their units. This control was greatly reinforced with the removal of resale price controls on cooperative units in 1969. Prior to that time, Swedish law conferred control over equity appreciation onto the directing boards of the major cooperative organizations, who generally limited price increases to the initial down payment, augmented for any improvements plus some compensation for the rate of inflation. In 1969, however, HSB dropped its resale price controls. A variety of reasons were given: the existence of a black market for coop units in the face of housing shortages, the difficulty of enforcement, the unfair advantage conferred on owners of private homes.[22] The political climate in general was one of harsh criticism of the Social Democratic housing programs on the part of the nonsocialist media and parties, reinforced by housing shortages in the major urban areas (Headey, 1978: 83-86). The Social Democrats received their lowest popular vote since 1932 in the municipal election campaign of 1966 (42.2%). Decontrol of rents and coop unit prices were part of the general restructuring of the government's housing policies that followed.

Presently, coop members are free to sell their shares on the open market. There are pressures to make legal what already exists in fact—private ownership of cooperative units, or the condominium form of ownership.[23] As a result of these developments, there are strong pressures to convert rental units to cooperatives, especially in Stockholm, where a housing shortage is again being felt. Although such conversions are at present a marginal problem in Sweden, where they do occur they are highly profitable, both because (as in this country) the combined value of coop units greatly exceeds the value of the building as a rental and because under Swedish financing cooperatives qualify for favorable terms on government rehabilitation loans.[24] Conversions, which tend to be favored by private landlords and tenants who benefit by acquiring their unit, are strongly opposed by the National Tenants' Association and the National Association of Swedish Public Housing Enterprises (SABO), which view conversion as a retreat from the "socialist market" and a threat to their political power base.[25] They fear that the most desirable rental housing will be sold off, lost to the inflationary market stream. Because of "rent pooling," rents in all the remaining apartments could then go up, if the units that were converted were the older, less costly ones (Lundqvist, 1981: 28). The central cities, where much of the desirable rental housing is located, would then become gentrified, with resulting displacement and economic segregation. Tenants in the remaining rental housing would be left with the stigma that attaches to public housing in the United States.

The major cooperative associations have taken somewhat different positions on the conversion issue. Although HSB stands to benefit from the management contracts it would gain, it has close historical ties with the National Tenants' Association, and therefore has shown no interest in converting public housing to cooperatives. Riksbyggen, closely affiliated with organized labor, favors conversions, but under new cooperative forms that would end speculation. Under its spring 1981 "housing rights" program, for example, a vacated unit would be resold to the association, which would then sell it to another member. This would be equivalent to reestablishing equity controls on cooperative shares. Another Riksbyggen program (the Stockholm Model) envisions the formation of cooperative tenant management association boards in public housing, which would subcontract managerial responsibility from the companies (who would be represented on the boards). This would produce a "quasi-conversion," one that realizes the goal of cooperative management while leaving the unit legally in the public domain.

The nonsocialist governing coalition of 1976-1982 favored a return to market allocations in housing. A 1981 governmental committee, for example, charged with responsibility for developing legal options for condominium ownership, recommended "making possible a quite considerable change from tenancy to cooperatives," involving the conversion of as much as 40% of public rentals (cited in Lundqvist, 1981: 28). Needless to say, this would represent a dramatic reversal of close to four decades of Swedish housing policy. With the return of the socialists to power in September 1982, however, there has been a return to the original ideals of the cooperative movement, in the form of resale restrictions such as those envisioned in Riksbyggen's housing rights program. It is highly unlikely that the Social Democrats will permit significant amounts of cooperative conversion so long as they remain in power.

The reasons for recent trends away from the ideals of the "socialist market" are many and widely debated. They have partly to do with the very success of the Social Democrats in producing an affluent middle-class society that views homeownership with increasing favor. In the rental sector, the reasons also reflect dissatisfaction with bureaucracy and inflexibility in public housing management, in which enormous municipal companies are seen as unresponsive to the needs of tenants. The once-radical tenants' movement is now a mass organization of some 600,000 tenants that functions primarily to negotiate rental agreements among tens of thousands of units.

SOME "QUALITATIVE" ISSUES

These difficulties are widely acknowledged, and some tentative steps have been taken to confront what were once referred to as the "qualitative" issues of Swedish housing (Headey, 1978: 93). Foremost among these are changes in the management of public rental units that would give tenants a considerably greater role to play (Lundqvist, 1981: 29-35). These changes range from slightly expanded managerial responsibility to codetermination, or joint tenant-management decision making. Experiments with the latter have begun in public housing corporations outside of Stockholm (Nackahem) and Gothenburg (Alebyggen), where tenant committees help determine the budget for maintenance and are able to rebate savings to residents.

A somewhat more far-reaching approach, "selective tenancy," was launched by the National Association of Swedish Public Housing Enterprises (SABO) in May 1981. Under this concept, the large citywide corporations set up mini-companies in each housing complex, where tenants have access to the full budgeting process. Tenants are then able to choose how to spend the money allocated to their complex; setting, for example, higher or lower standards of service (with corresponding increases or decreases in rents). A major purpose of these programs is to promote the ideal of economic democracy among tenants, decentralizing at least one aspect—management—of tenant-landlord relations.[26] At present they are limited in scope, voluntary for the housing companies, and, according to Swedish tenant leaders, have not yet sparked the imagination of most tenants.

Other qualitative issues include equipping dwellings with services to benefit families in which both parents work, and adapting dwellings to the special requirements of singles, divorcees, and old people living alone (Headey, 1978: 94).[27] Finally, a large part of recent Swedish research on housing has focused on the issue of energy efficiency. This is vital, both because of Sweden's long and harsh winter climate and because of the escalating costs of imported energy.

PREFERENCES FOR PRIVATE OWNERSHIP

The principal problem, as viewed by the Social Democrats, remains the move toward more private forms of ownership. This is attributed to several factors. There is unquestionably an increased preference for owner-occupied housing, particularly in the suburbs. Although the demand for apartments remains strong in the larger cities, the high-rise public housing flats in the suburbs often combine the geographic and social isolation of suburban living with all of the disadvantages of small apartments (Kemeny, 1978: 318). The costs of apartment living are also high relative to other forms of tenure. Because of the Swedish system of rent pooling, rents on older units (with lower financing costs) are the same as rents on new units of comparable quality: As we have seen, the former subsidize the latter. Given the relative newness of the Swedish public housing stock, the high costs of recent construction have served to raise average costs, although the costs on newer units have been somewhat lowered. It will be some time before rent averaging brings overall costs down (Kenemy, 1978: 318).

These disadvantages of rental housing are reinforced by tax laws that increasingly work to the advantage of homeowners. Of the three forms of housing, owner-occupancy is in theory the most expensive, once maintenance, heating, and utilities are taken into account. One study, for example, estimated that in 1978 an average homeowner spent $255 per month, compared with $245 for tenants and $205 for cooperatives (Lundqvist, 1981: 15). When the homeowner's tax deductions were taken into account, however, the cost of homeowning dropped to $195, the least expensive of the three forms. The study concluded that an "average homeowner could get almost one-fourth of his total housing expenditure covered by the increase in disposable income caused by the right to deduct his deficits on housing from his taxable income" (Lundqvist, 1981: 22). As Swedes have become increasingly affluent, even the middle class now confronts high marginal tax brackets. Homeowners' interest deductions are thus extremely attractive.

With the recent rise in housing costs and interest rates, homeowners' tax deductions have become the most rapidly growing form of government housing expenditure. In 1975, tax deductions for owner-occupants amounted to 33% of all governmental subsidies for the existing housing stock; by 1978, the figure had grown to 42% (Table 3). One recent estimate has found expenditures on tax deductions to be as high as 53% of the current housing total (International Union of Tenants, 1982: 1-2). During the three-year period, tax expenditures relative to homeownership grew more than twice as fast as those on housing allowances and interest subsidies combined—122% versus 55%. This has placed a severe strain on Swedish fiscal resources.

Although the nonsocialist government had encouraged these trends, the new socialist coalition remains committed to the old vision of equal cost for equal quality, regardless of tenure. In June 1981, Sverker Gustavsson, director of the National Swedish Institute for Building Research, outlined to me a three-part program the Social Democrats have sought to implement since their return to power in 1982. First, a systematic across-the-board attempt to eliminate what crowding remains, thereby addressing one of the chief objections to much of the public housing built during the 1960s. Second, greater tenant participation in management, building on the tentative experiments presently under way. Finally, a restructuring of the subsidy program, with the goal that no household should pay more than one-fifth of its income on housing.

How the Social Democrats can afford such a program is another matter. It is highly unlikely that the costly but popular tax breaks for homeownership can be altogether abolished, for example. On the other hand, the Social Democratic victory, although small, was decisive: They received 45.5% of the popular vote and 166 seats (out of 349) in Parliament, compared with 45.1% and 163 seats for the three other parties combined.[28] The new government is confronted with an international economic recession, enormous public expenditures (two-thirds of the GNP), and large budget deficits. The Swedish economy, like that of most other Western nations, has been stagnant, with declining investment and output. Rising import costs have led to sizable balance-of-payment deficits, with the resulting need to borrow abroad at high interest rates. Unemployment is close to 4%—high by Swedish standards. It is within this context that the Social Democrats confront the difficult task of resolving Sweden's present housing problems.

TABLE 3
Governmental Subsidies to Existing Housing Stock in Sweden, 1975-1978

	MILLIONS OF DOLLARS*				PERCENT			
Form of Subsidy	1975	1976	1977	1978	1975	1976	1977	1978
Housing Allowances	$ 720	$900	$960	$1,060	44.5%	44.1%	38.7%	36.8%
Mortgage Interest Subsidies	360	440	560	620	22.2	21.6	22.6	21.5
Tax Deductions for Owner-Occupants	540	700	960	$1,200	33.3	34.3	38.7	41.7
Total:	$1,620	$2,040	$2,480	$2,880	100.0%	100.0%	100.0%	100.0%

SOURCE: Lundqvist (1981: Table 7).
*Estimated at 5 Swedish Kroner to the dollar.

CONCLUSIONS

Sweden has made unprecedented strides in achieving the goal of providing adequate and affordable shelter to the vast majority of its population. It has done so largely within the framework of a market economy: developing an attractive alternative of nonmarket housing alongside owner-occupied homes and private rentals. The methods used have been various; but all can be characterized as steering investment and production toward social objectives, while heavily regulating the remaining private rentals. The success of Sweden's programs can be attributed to a strong central government unified under a single (socialist) party for much of the past half century, an institutional framework that permitted a high degree of central planning, and, undoubtedly, the existence of a relatively small and homogeneous population with a strong commitment to achieving widely shared national goals.

Yet we have seen that many of the gains achieved during the 1960s and 1970s now appear to be threatened. Newly affluent Swedes are demanding detached, privately owned homes in the suburbs. Vacancies exist in some urban apartment complexes, whereas scarcities exist in others. In some locales rental housing is increasingly becoming segregated residences for immigrant workers. Cooperative housing—always an uneasy hybrid between the socialized public sector and private ownership—appears to be tilting in the latter direction, with the relaxation of resale price controls. There are strong pressures to permit the conversion of public rental housing to cooperative ownership, which could mean a return to market allocation in the rental sector.

Why this turn away from the "socialist market?" Although both affluence and dissatisfaction with bureaucratic inflexibility are frequently cited as the principal reasons, I believe that a major part of the explanation lies in the very compromises that permitted the "Swedish miracle" in the first place: the attempt to steer a middle ground between a socialized housing sector and a market economy. Sweden chose not to seek direct government financing of housing, nor did it attempt to eliminate all of the advantages of private ownership. Rather, it was hoped that through the creation of a massive public rental housing sector, supply and demand could be brought into balance and the marketplace itself socialized. Although this strategy worked very well for awhile, its inherent weaknesses have become evident during the current economic cycle. High interest rates have made government interest subsidies very costly. At the same time, the failure to decisively eliminate home tax deductions has created an increasingly attractive tax shelter, both because high interest payments mean higher deductions and because Swedish tax brackets are high. As a result, home tax deductions consume a growing portion of Swedish housing expenditures, while homeownership has become the most economically advantageous form of tenure.

In Sweden politics is compromise, and compromise made Sweden's substantial housing gains possible. It remains to be seen if the Social Democrats can surmount the present difficulties and remain true to their original vision of treating housing as a social right rather than a private good. The socialist market may yet turn out to be a contradiction in reality as well as a contradiction in terms.

NOTES

1. In Headey's (1978: 44) terms, "'socialist' because it was intended to operate in accordance with governmentally imposed policy objectives and priorities, 'market' because competition among builders providing different types of housing (multifamily apartment blocks, single-family houses, etc.) for different types of owner and tenant was not wholly abolished."

2. Headey bases his summary on Greve (1971: 63).

3. The following discussion is based on Headey (1978: 57-97).

4. Another alternative—what is termed "self-help" construction in the United States (in Sweden it is called "small house building")—originated during the same period. It involves do-it-yourself construction on a cooperative and nonprofit basis, under the direction of a public agency (Smahusavdelningen), which arranges for everything except labor. Some 12,000 units were provided in the Stockholm area during the period 1927-1976,

targeted at working-class households (Witt-Stromer, 1977). Another form is the "collective" house, dating to 1935 and the architectural school of Sven Markelius. Collective houses were large apartments with common kitchens and public space. This form, once seen as a major solution to the housing problem, has never amounted to more than a small number of units (Vestbro, 1979).

5. Lundevall (1976: 3-4) notes that wages fell 30% during the period 1920-1923, whereas rents rose 20%. HSB was not the first cooperative association in Sweden, but its influence in creating a national cooperative movement was decisive.

6. Members pay annual dues to the local organization and, in some cases, are required to deposit funds with the savings association as well. In exchange, they receive a place in the queue for units and the right to "codetermination" in the affairs of the local and national organizations, on the one-person-one-vote principle. Membership is open to anyone who chooses to join. See HSB (1975) for a detailed discussion of HSB's history and operations, punctuated with numerous photographs and coop design renditions. For a more general collection of articles on the Swedish coop movement, see HPP (1976).

7. Phrase of Sverker Gustavsson, Director of the National Swedish Institute for Building Research, in personal interview, June 1981.

8. Compensation is at market value, although since 1972, in certain cases of rapid land inflation, it corresponds to market value ten years prior to the taking, under the theory that the increased value is due to community-initiated improvements and amenities (Heimburger, 1976: 28-29).

9. Single-family housing tends overwhelmingly to be privately owned, although there has been a slight trend toward cooperative and public ownership in this sector as well. In 1976, for example, 94% of single-family homes were classified as privately owned, with 5% publicly owned and 1% in cooperatives. By 1979, the figures were 87%, 8%, and 5%, respectively (HPP, 1980: 13).

10. Investment levels reached a high of 7.4% of the GNP in 1966-1970, and have averaged 6.8% since the early 1950s. The United States has invested approximately 4.6% (Headey, 1978: 179; Nesslein, 1982: 239).

11. This study goes on to note that slum "tendencies" still remain: "In almost every municipality there exist at least a few badly maintained houses, more or less exclusively occupied by alcoholics, criminals and other social outcasts." Such houses are not geographically concentrated, however (Wiktorin, 1982: 248).

12. For a comparison of Swedish and American suburbs, see Popenoe (1977).

13. Rent and price controls were enacted in 1942, with rent controls being gradually phased out in smaller towns and urban areas throughout the postwar period. Rent control remained in effect in the major urban areas until 1975, however.

14. This is because the age of the unit is not supposed to be a factor in determining rents, apart from differences in quality that might be associated with age. Thus, a new unit with high capital expenses under law must charge the same rent as an old unit with low expenses, providing both are of equal quality. There is, of course, some divergence in practice from this ideal model of fair rent setting, although rents are far less variable in Sweden (when quality is controlled) than in most other countries. One study found that in a random sample of 83 public housing companies, two-thirds charged within 8% of the median rent for all units. The same study found, however, that the age of units does continue to play a significant role in determining rents (see Turner, 1981).

15. For families with children, the percentage reached by allowances is quite high. Of renters with three or more children, for example, 78% receive allowances (Lundqvist, 1981: 20).

16. Headey (1978: 57) estimated 15.6% in 1974, prior to the general price inflation of recent years. The International Union of Tenants (IUT) reports that Swedish tenants now pay 27% of their income, on the average, although it is not clear whether this figure takes into account government housing allowances (IUT, 1982: 1-2). The cooperative society Riksbyggen provides a similar estimate, noting that poorer families pay higher percentages than wealthier ones; these estimates, however, are based on assumptions about "typical" expenditures rather than actual surveys. The role of housing allowances is unclear in this case as well (Svenska Riksbyggen, 1980: 9).

17. First mortgages are provided by the Urban Mortgage Bank (established in 1909); second mortgages by the Sweden Housing Loan Bank (established in 1929). These are specially chartered commercial banks with guaranteed funds provided by the state; their loans are thus risk-free (Headey, 1978: 66).

18. Lundqvist (1981: 18) demonstrates that recent (1980-1981) changes in the subsidy system have increased the bias in favor of tenancy and cooperatives.

19. The imputed rent is a percentage of the house's assessed value, determined on a five-year assessment cycle. This system should be contrasted with that in the United States, under which interest and property taxes can also be deducted from income, while there is no requirement to offset imputed rental value against such expenses.

20. For a recent study that attributes all Swedish housing successes to postwar affluence and all the problems to "serious resource misallocation" and "housing market disequilibrium" resulting from excessive governmental intervention, see Nesslein (1982). This study suffers, however, from a highly selective interpretation of secondary materials.

21. There were 26,628 vacant units in January 1974, of which almost four-fifths were in public housing (Headey, 1978: 90). In September 1974, the vacancy rate throughout metropolitan Stockholm was 7.2%; metropolitan Gothenburg, 10.0%; and metropolitan Malmo, 7.8% (Nesslein, 1982: 241). Since that time, however, the surplusses have declined and vacancy rates are considerably lower (Stockholm, for example, was estimated to have a vacancy rate of only 1.6% in 1978; see Nesslein, 1982: 242).

22. Interviews in June 1981 with Rolf Trodin, director of Planning, HSB, and Olle Lindstrom, deputy managing director, Riksbyggen. According to Lindstrom, his studies found that 95% of all Riksbyggen sales in the early 1970s followed prices recommended by the Coop Board. He thus viewed the relaxation of controls as having little effect on prices in most cases, at least where the market was relatively balanced between supply and demand.

23. Presently one cannot legally own a flat in an apartment building in Sweden.

24. Partly because of this latter reason, however, and partly for administrative reasons, coop conversions in Sweden attempt to sell a majority of units to existing tenants.

25. The National Tenants' Association has recently criticized conversions as part of the "wild speculation in housing" (Kjellberg and Burns, 1981).

26. The key aspect, of course, remains rent setting, which is achieved through a highly bureaucratized system of tenant-management negotiations that closely resembles organized labor wage negotiations. Although the average tenant has a voice in this process, it is a very small one.

27. Facilities for the handicapped have long been a part of Swedish housing policy (see Beckman, 1976).

28. This means that the Social Democrats can govern without the necessity of forming a coalition government with the Swedish Communist party, which kept 20 seats (with 5.6% of the vote). The remaining 3.7% of the popular vote went to a small "Christian" party and the new Green party, neither of which received the 4% necessary to gain a seat in Parliament (see Leijonhufvud, 1982).

REFERENCES

BECKMAN, M. (1976) Building for Everyone: The Disabled and the Built Environment in Sweden. Information to the United Nations Conference on Human Settlements HABITAT. Stockholm: Ministry of Housing and Physical Planning.

DAUN, A. (1979) "Why do Swedish suburbs look the way they do?" Human Environment in Sweden 9 (February).

GREVE, J. (1971) Voluntary Housing in Scandinavia. Birmingham: Centre for Urban and Regional Studies.

HEADEY, B. (1978) Housing Policy in the Developed Economy. London: Croom Helm.

HEIMBURGER, P. (1976) Land Policy in Sweden: Information to the United Nations Conference on Human Settlements HABITAT. Stockholm: Ministry of Housing and Physical Planning.

HPP [Ministry of Housing and Physical Planning] (1980) Housing, Building, and Planning in Sweden: Information to 41st Session of the ECE Committee on Housing, Building, and Planning. Stockholm: author.

———(1976) Swedish Experiences of Self-Building, Co-Operation, Consumer Research, Participation: Information to the United Nations Conference on Human Settlements HABITAT. Stockholm: author.

HSB [National Association of Tenants' Savings and Building Societies] (1975) HSB's Riksforbund, HSB Sweden. Stockholm: author.

International Union of Tenants [IUT] (1982) "The Scandinavian states support ownership." Int. Information 4 (Fall): 1-2.

JUSSIL, S. (1975) "Steering mechanisms," pp. 174-179 in H. Heineman (ed.) New Towns and Old. Stockholm: Swedish Institute.

KEMENY, J. (1978) "Urban home-ownership in Sweden." Urban Studies 15: 313-320.

KJELLBERG, C. and T. BURNS (1981) "Hyrestratter blir bostadstratter i Goteborg." Preliminary report to Stockholm University.

LEIJONHUFVUD, S. (1982) "Election year '82: new exits from the middle road." Pol. Life in Sweden 15 (December).

LUNDEVALL, O. (1976) Swedish Experience of Co-Operative Housing: Information to the United Nations Conference on Human Settlement HABITAT. Stockholm: Ministry of Housing and Physical Planning.

LUNDQVIST, L. J. (1981) Housing Tenures in Sweden. Gavle: National Swedish Institute for Building Research.

NESSLEIN, T. S. (1982) "The Swedish housing model: an assessment." Urban Studies 19: 235-246.

POPENOE, D. (1977) The Suburban Environment: Sweden and the United States. Chicago: Univ. of Chicago Press.

RONMARK, K. (1981) "Housing management." Swedish monograph to the Economic Commission for Europe Committee on Housing, Building, and Planning, United Nations.

Swedish Institute (1980) Fact Sheet on Sweden. Stockholm: author.

Svenska Riksbyggen (1980) Facts on Swedish Housing. Stockholm: author.

SVENSSON, R. (1976) Swedish Land Policy in Practical Application. Stockholm: Swedish Council for Building Research.

TURNER, B. (1981) "Fair rents in Sweden—market adapted prices or . . . ?" Presented at the Swedish Institute for Building Research National Housing Conference, June.

VESTBRO, D. U. (1979) "Collective housing units in Sweden." Current Sweden (a publication of the Swedish Institute, Stockholm).
WIKTORIN, M. (1982) "Housing policy and disadvantaged groups in Sweden." Int. J. of Urban and Regional Research 6, 2: 246-255.
WITT-STROMER, H. (1977) "Owner-building of smallhouse-areas and the owners participating in administration and use of those areas." Report, Smahusavdelningen, Stockholm.

Richard P. Appelbaum is Associate Professor of Sociology at the University of California, Santa Barbara. He is the author of two books on the impacts of urban growth, and his recent monograph on the impact of governmental regulations on California housing prices was published by the California Policy Seminar. His articles on housing have appeared in Urban Affairs Quarterly, *the* Journal of Applied Behavioral Sciences, *and* The Nation.

Little research systematically examining changes in public opinion as a consequence of the implementation of a school desegregation plan involving busing has been reported. Four surveys were conducted to measure the impact of the implementation of a court-ordered metropolitan desegregation plan on a community (New Castle County, Delaware) over seven years. Results indicate that the general population remained opposed to busing after desegregation, that busing resulted in a primarily temporary decline in public school evaluations, and that feelings that blacks were receiving equal treatment in the public schools increased over time. Although white suburban opposition to busing lessened somewhat in magnitude and intensity, city and black opposition increased. Overall, those closest to the public schools were the most likely to react relatively positively to the change.

THE IMPACT OF METROPOLITAN SCHOOL DESEGREGATION ON PUBLIC OPINION
A Longitudinal Analysis

JEFFREY A. RAFFEL
University of Delaware

Despite the central place of busing to achieve school desegregation in American education and politics, little is known about the attitudinal consequences that result from its implementation. Although it is acknowledged that attitudes can play a major role in determining the success of school desegregation implementation (Henderson et al., 1981; Gatlin et al., 1978; Willie and Greenblatt, 1981; Monti, 1977; Rossell, 1978) and that "the overwhelming majority of whites oppose busing no matter how they are asked about it" (Sears et al., 1979: 371), little research has systematically examined public opinion as a consequence of the implementation of a school desegregation plan involving busing. Researchers have, instead, focused on school achievement and white flight as two consequences of desegregation. To quote Rossell (1978: 134-135),

AUTHOR'S NOTE: *The Delaware Post Secondary Education Commission, Wilmington News Journal Company, Greater Wilmington Development Council, and Brandywine, Red*

URBAN AFFAIRS QUARTERLY, Vol. 21 No. 2, December 1985 245-265

> Unfortunately, there are few studies that systematically examine the community processes associated with desegregation as critical intervening variables that might influence outcomes, or as significant outcomes in and of themselves . . . school desegregation is a policy whose goal is not simply behavioral compliance, but a change in attitude of the most fundamental kind—how one feels about one's self, one's identity, one's place in society, and the value of other individuals, their identity, and their place in society.

CRITERIA FOR USEFUL RESEARCH

A brief review of the literature on school desegregation implementation and its impact on public opinion in communities is helpful in understanding what data we would want to examine and what theoretical constructs could help us to better understand public opinion change in the school desegregation process.

Cardell Jacobson (1978) has succinctly raised the most compelling questions about school desegregation and public opinion:

> What effect does a court ruling which orders a city to desegregate its schools have on the attitudes and feelings of residents of the city? Are attitudes about racial issues hardened or eased? Is there increased resistance or resigned acceptance?

Jacobson argues that different theoretical approaches would lead one to predict different answers. The *proximity-resistance* argument would be based on the differentiation people make between the principle of desegregation, which they tend to support, and the means of busing, which has little white and modest black support. Thus, as busing becomes more proximate or real, the resistance to it would increase.

Alternatively, Jacobson argues that the attitude-conformity literature would lead one to expect that as behavior had to change, attitudes would

---

Clay Consolidated, Christina, and Colonial School Districts supported various parts of this research. Without their generous support, this article would not have been possible. Barry Morstain, David Ermann, Robert Warren, Nancy Colmer, Don Berry, and Dianne Monteith provided me with valuable assistance along the way. Finally, the College of Urban Affairs and Public Policy and the University of Delaware provided me with the time and resources to undertake and complete this work. I greatly appreciate the financial and conceptual support from all these sources.

change. Rossell (1978) describes this process in greater detail, in essence arguing that cognitive dissonance theory would suggest that as behaviors had to change, people would alter their attitudes to maintain balance and thus would become more positive. Jacobson calls this argument the *social-adjustment* argument.

The proximity-resistance argument is similar to the antibusing argument that the reality of busing is what is objectionable and negative public opinion about busing reflects that reality. The social-adjustment argument has been cited by busing proponents. Both the U.S. Civil Rights Commission (Serow and Solomon, 1979) and the National Conference of Christians and Jews (Louis Harris and Associates, 1978) have cited evidence that those most familiar with and involved in busing are more supportive. Gary Orfield (1978) has argued that information plays a critical role in acceptance. Similarly, Serow and Solomon (1979) argue that as parents of those most involved in school desegregation will have better information about success, then fears will be reduced and they will become more supportive. Does familiarity breed contempt? Or is to know busing, to love or at least tolerate it?

Jacobson's framework, however, leaves us with the following conceptual and methodological problems.

Attitude Objects: First, it is not clear what attitude object should change as a result of desegregation. Would one expect feelings about the principle of desegregation, the policy of busing, or the specific desegregation plan to change? Would one's attitudes toward the public schools be altered? Racial views? The saliency of busing? Simply put, a number of significant attitudes related to the implementation of a school desegregation plan may change as a result, and we know little about which may change in what direction.

Attitude Holders: Second, it is not clear what kinds of people should change their attitudes as a result of school desegregation. Jacobson (1978) argues that if the proximity-resistance theory holds, those facing the reality (public school parents) should be most upset. If the social-adjustment argument holds, public school parents should become more positive because their children will be involved, and nonpublic school parents should become the most negative. Raising this question leads to questions about additional groups. How will nonparents, those without children in the public or nonpublic schools, react? Can we take into account people moving across groups, partly because of the desegregation process itself: for example, whites switching children from public to nonpublic school? Will blacks react differently than whites?

Timeframe of Attitude Change: Third, the school desegregation process is a lengthy and dynamic one. The measurement of change must take place over a period sufficient to allow for long-term effects (Schweitzer and Griffore, 1981). Initial reactions may be different from reactions three years after desegregation begins. Also, the measurement of attitudes must include predesegregation measures sufficiently before the fact to minimize anticipatory socialization and population loss due to white flight. Will attitudes show steady declines or upsurges, temporary aberrations, or little change over time?

A third view of the impact of school desegregation on public opinion is based on McConahay and Hawley's (1977: 50-51) proposition that busing is a symbolic issue, like prohibition, in which "the debate is really over whose values will dominate public life and whose group will receive the concomitant public respect" not self-interest. When it comes to symbolic issues, "since they have little direct experience or reliable knowledge to guide them, [people] draw upon their values" to vote or respond to pollsters. Building on McConahay and Hawley's argument, we can speculate that although predesegregation attitudes may be based on the symbolic meaning of busing, in a community implementing a busing plan postdesegregation views may be greatly influenced by one's direct experiences. This symbolic/reality view suggests that simple predictions about the impact of busing on attitudes are unwise, because reactions will be a function of the degree and nature of one's involvement and the actual circumstances of the implementation. In other words, attitudes on various objects will be a function of the type of holder and the time of measurement.

The Data Required: These issues and questions help us to define methodological requirements of a study of attitude change in communities undergoing school desegregation. The study would be longitudinal and include attitude measurement before, during, and some time after a desegregation plan was implemented. It would include attitude items beyond one or two dimensions of attitudes toward desegregation, to allow for the analysis of different patterns of change across different attitudes. And it would include a sufficiently large sample to allow analysis of significant population subgroups, especially nonparents and nonpublic school parents, and blacks and whites.

Unfortunately, almost all studies of communities undergoing school desegregation to date are too limited in attitude object, subgroup, and/or timeframe. They tend to focus on whites only, to measure only attitudes toward integration and busing, to be one-shot rather than longitudinal, or to only examine change over short periods (Jacobson, 1978; Serow and Solomon, 1979; Slawski, 1976; Abney, 1976; Thoerny, 1979). The two most methodologically sound studies also have major limitations. Although McConahay and Hawley's (1978) work in Louisville-Jefferson County is comprehensive, attitude measurement did not begin until after desegregation was implemented. Ross's work in Boston (Estabrook, 1980), although the most methodologically sound, analyzes middle-class attitudes only, is limited to a two-year period, and, of course, is focused on a city wracked by conflict over this issue.

THE WILMINGTON, DELAWARE, METROPOLITAN CASE

In New Castle County, Delaware, we had the unique opportunity to conduct surveys of public attitudes toward desegregation and public education before and after a metropolitan busing was ordered by the federal court. These surveys meet the criteria established above and therefore provide a substantial data base to examine the interaction of school desegregation and public opinion.

In July 1978, the Wilmington School District was merged with ten suburban school districts to form the New Castle County School District (Green et al., 1982; Raffel, 1980a; Wolters, 1984). In September 1978, the nearly 100 schools of the new district were desegregated. To accomplish this, over 20,000 of the district's 65,000 pupils were bused across the old city-suburban school district lines. Under the desegregation plan, city children were bused into suburban schools for nine years and suburban children were bused into the city for three consecutive grades. Kindergarten was excluded from the plan.

Busing began peacefully, without significant protest, in part because the major antibusing group that had formed, the Positive Action Committee, had used the ballot rather than the bullhorn to voice its strong objection. The major problem during the first year of school desegregation was a five-week teachers' strike resulting from a failure to level up teacher salaries and benefits across the new district to the previously highest levels in the city of Wilmington (Sills, 1982).

Although desegregation proceeded peacefully, white support was minimal and black concern for bearing too much of the burden of busing continued. A 1980 attempt to pass a school revenue referendum was a dismal failure, with 90% of an extraordinarily high voter turn-out voting against it and all it represented (Raffel, 1980b). White flight to nonpublic schools was apparent. Although the newspapers reported higher test scores, concern for public school management and administrative problems increased.

The Delaware state legislature reorganized the New Castle County School District into four new school districts in time for the opening of school in September 1981. Three districts included a substantial part of Wilmington; the fourth included what once had been a district with about half black enrollment. These districts were more analogous to the traditional Delaware school district, each independent with approximately 10,000-15,000 students, about 25%-30% minority, and seven-member school boards elected at large from seven election districts. In October of 1983 these four school districts agreed to a business development council's request to cooperate and help fund a public opinion study of the public schools.

THE RESEARCH

The complexity of the legal, political, and educational aspects of this school desegregation case were matched by the complexities of conducting these surveys. Circumstances required different funding sources, procedures, and questions across time. All suburbanites in the survey were questioned in telephone interviews. A majority of city public school parent interviews were conducted face to face because of telephone number problems. In 1979 and 1983, a child was selected randomly during each parent interview and questions were asked about this child's school experiences.

The 1977 sample was randomly drawn from a sampling frame of addresses and supplemented with a random sample of city public school parents. In 1978, the telephone survey was conducted by random digit dialing, again supplemented with a random sample of city public school parents. Those without children of school age in 1978 were not interviewed. In 1979, the survey was conducted at the end of the first school year under the desegregation order. We attempted to reinterview all previous respondents with school-age children, but found this way only feasible in the suburbs. A new sample of city public school parents was randomly selected. In February and March of 1983, we drew a general population sample randomly through the random digit dial method (supplementing this with a sample of those addresses without telephones) and added to this an additional sample of public school parents.

We can thus compare general population and subpopulation responses from 1977 predesegregation to 1983 postdesegregation. We can make comparisons of public school and non public school parents across the four surveys (see Table 1). The results analyzed below reflect the weighting of subsamples to their proportion in the general population or subpopulation. Weighted means are indicated with asterisks.[1]

RESULTS

ATTITUDES TOWARD BUSING

New Castle County residents have not changed their minds much about whether they favor or oppose "busing both black and white children between Wilmington and suburban schools to achieve school desegregation." Three-quarters (73.9%) of the desegregation-area population opposed busing in 1977 (Table 2). In 1983, almost five years after busing began, slightly more people (79.9%) were opposed to busing.[2] There was an insignificant drop in support for busing from 18.5% to 17.5%. Basically, the slight increase in opposition comes from a decrease in the percentage of respondents in the "don't know" category. In short, there is no evidence that support for busing in the general population increased after it was implemented.

The overall results, however, mask interesting subgroup changes. As indicated in Table 2, parents with children in the public schools were about as much against busing in 1983 (80.9%) as in 1977 (78.2%). Opposition to busing increased, however, among respondents with children in nonpublic school and those with no school-aged children. The percentage opposing busing increased from 78.1 to 88.6 among nonpublic school parents and from 70.4 to 78.5 among nonparents. These changes, however, result from quite different black-white and city-suburban reactions to busing.

City and suburban results are shown in the tables. Because the vast majority of city public school parents are black (86% in 1977 and 70% in 1983) and suburbanites in all subgroups are white (over 90% in both

TABLE 1
Sample Sizes by Year

	1977	1978	1979	1983
Public School Parents				
Total	617	498	515	620
Suburban	300	303	315	500
City	317	195	200	100
Non-Public School Parents				
Total	76	75	90	106
Suburban	66	69	90	93
City	10	6	0	13
Non-Parents				
Total	208	0	0	297
Suburban	152	0	0	232
City	56	0	0	65
TOTAL	901	573	605	1023

years), results by race tend to be the same as results by location. Exceptions are noted.

Suburban opposition to busing has remained relatively constant, decreasing by only 2% between 1977 and 1983. City opposition to busing, however, increased greatly. The percentage of respondents in the city opposed to busing jumped from 33.6% in 1977 to 59.4% in 1983.

As Table 2 indicates, opposition to busing decreased, albeit slightly, in all suburban subgroups. The sharpest decline was among suburban public school parents, where the opposition dropped from 90.6% to 83.7%. The lowest decline was among nonparents. All city subgroups, however, show an increase in opposition. Opposition among city public school parents has increased to a majority from 41.4% in 1977. Those without children living in the city are now twice as likely to be opposed to busing as in 1977; the few nonpublic school parents in the city show far greater opposition.

Black public school parents and nonparents in the city and suburbs show increased opposition to busing. Although the number of responses are small, opposition to busing is now twice as great among black suburban public school parents as in 1977, and the increase is almost as great among black city nonparents. Whites in the city in all parental status groups also are now more opposed to busing.

TABLE 2
Percentage Opposing Busing by Year

	1977	1983
General Population		
Total	73.9%*(901)	79.9%* (1023)
Suburban	86.8%*(518)	84.5%*(845)
City	33.6%*(383)	59.9%*(178)**
Public School Parents		
Total	80.9%*(617)	78.2% (620)
Suburban	90.6% (300)	83.7% (520)
City	41.4% (317)	50.0% (100)
Non-Public School Parents		
Total	78.1%*(76)	88.6% (106)
Suburban	94.0% (66)	89.2% (93)
City	20.0% (10)	84.7% (13)**
Non-Parents		
Total	70.4%*(208)	78.5% (297)
Suburban	84.5% (152)	83.7% (232)
City	31.5% (56)	60.0% (65)**

NOTE: Answers given in response to the following question: "In general, do you strongly favor, favor, oppose, or strongly oppose busing both black and white children between Wilmington and suburban schools to achieve school desegregation?" Respondents "strongly opposed" and "opposed" are combined; "don't knows" are included in the totals.
*Means weighted. $^{**}p \leqslant .05$.

The responses to a direct question on the saliency of school desegregation indicate a sharp overall decline in the perceive saliency of the school desegregation issue from 1977 to 1983 (Table 3). Again, however, suburbanites feel desegregation has declined in importance, but city respondents were at least as concerned in 1983 as they were in 1977. Whereas the percentage of suburban respondents stating that the school desegregation issue was "very important" declined from 62.3% to 35.4%, the city percentage increased from 30.2% to 40.4%.

Similarly, analyses of the percentage of white suburbanites strongly opposed to busing indicates declines of 5% to 10% in all three parental subgroups from 1977 to 1983. Strong black and city opposition increased at similar rates. That is, not only has the degree of opposition changed differently in the city and suburbs, so has the strength of these feelings.

TABLE 3
Percentage Reporting that the School Desegregation Issue Is "Very Important" by Year

	1977	1983
General Population		
Total	54.5%*(901)	36.3%*(1023)**
Suburban	62.3%*(518)	35.4%*(845)**
City	30.2%*(383)	40.4%*(178)
Public School Parents		
Total	74.3%*(617)	35.9% (620)**
Suburban	80.4% (300)	33.8% (520)**
City	48.9% (317)	46.5% (100)
Non-Public School Parents		
Total	64.5%*(76)	42.5% (106)**
Suburban	71.2% (66)	43.0% (93)**
City	40.0% (10)	38.5% (13)
Non-Parents		
Total	45.2%*(208)	35.0% (297)
Suburban	53.0% (152)	34.1% (232)**
City	23.7% (56)	38.5% (65)

NOTE: Answers given in response to the following question: "We would like to know how important the school desegregation issue is to you. Is it not important, somewhat important, or very important to you?" "Don't knows" are included in the totals.
*Means weighted. **$p \leqslant .05$.

Analysis of the 1978 and 1979 surveys indicates no major discontinuities in the pattern of change reported above. For example, the percentage of suburban public school parents strongly opposed to busing held steady in 1977 and 1978 (65.4% and 66.0% respectively), dipped in 1979 to 57.2%, and dropped further to 53.4% in 1983. Similarly, although city opposition fluctuated from 1977 to 1978 (15.6% and 11.3%, respectively), it steadily increased in 1979 (18.2%) and 1983 (23.0%).

Longitudinal results from the Wilmington metropolitan desegregation area thus indicate that the introduction of busing in New Castle County led suburbanites and whites to soften their opposition a small amount and city residents and blacks to harden their opposition significantly. These changes are reflected in both attitudes toward busing and the saliency of busing. Among suburbanites, the closer one is to public schools, the greater is the decline in saliency of and opposition to busing. Public school parent opposition has decreased the most, parents of children in nonpublic school second, and nonparents least. Among city residents, public school parents have not reduced their opposition or strength of feelings, and those without school-age children appear to have increased their opposition.

EVALUATIONS OF THE PUBLIC SCHOOLS

In 1977, prior to the implementation of the school desegregation plan, 56.8% of the public rated the public schools as "good" or "excellent" as opposed to "fair" or "poor" or "don't know" (Table 4). A majority (52%) of nonparents agreed. Parents of children in nonpublic schools were more negative about the public schools (39%). Public school parents were quite positive; 71.7% of the public school parents rated the public schools at these levels in 1977. This high percentage, however, masked a large difference between the evaluations of city and suburban respondents. For example, over three-quarters (78.9%) of the suburban parents whose children went to one of the ten suburban school districts rated the schools as good or excellent; less than half (45.7%) of the city parents, whose children went to the Wilmington School District, agreed.

In the 1983 survey, 42.9% of the general population sample evaluated schools in their public school district as "good" or "excellent." Public school parents were about twice as likely to rate the public schools as good or excellent as those without children in public schools. Whereas 62.4% of the public school parents rated the schools highly, 31.2% of nonpublic school parents and 36.0% of nonparents agreed. Within the public school parents category, slightly more suburban than city parents rated the public schools highly.

Comparing the 1983 to the 1977 evaluations, it is clear that confidence in the public schools declined.[3] The overall decline of 56.8% to 42.9%, however, varies by parental status. Public school parents rating the schools as good or excellent dropped approximately ten percentage points from 1977 to 1983. Suburban public school parents viewed their public school district less positively in 1983; city public school parents were somewhat more favorable in 1983 than in 1977. Desegregation seems to have given city parents, who are primarily black, greater confidence in the public schools. Suburban public school confidence has declined.

TABLE 4
Percentage Rating the Public Schools as "Good" or "Excellent" by Year

	1977	1983
General Population		
Total	56.8%*(901)	42.9%* (1023)**
Suburban	65.5%*(518)	44.1%*(845) **
City	29.6%*(383)	37.7%*(178)
Public School Parents		
Total	71.7%*(617)	62.4% (620) **
Suburban	78.9% (300)	63.1% (520) **
City	45.7% (317)	58.6% (100)
Non-Public School Parents		
Total	39.0%*(76)	31.2% (106)
Suburban	46.9% (66)	31.2% (93)
City	10.0% (10)	30.8% (13)
Non-Parents		
Total	52.0%*(208)	36.0% (297) **
Suburban	61.3% (152)	37.5% (232) **
City	26.0% (56)	30.8% (65)

NOTE: Answers given in response to the following question: "We'd like to know what you think of the public schools in your school district. Are they poor, fair, good, or excellent?" Respondents rating the school "good" or "excellent" are combined; "don't knows" are included in the totals.
*Means weighted. **$p \leq .05$.

The largest percentage decrease in these evaluations, however, is found among nonparents. Whereas about half (52.0%) rated the public schools as good or excellent in 1977, only about one-third (36.0%) did so in 1983. Parents of children in nonpublic school were unlikely to view the public schools as good or excellent in 1977, and they were still unlikely to rate them highly in 1983. In general, in both the city and suburbs those closest to the public schools reacted relatively more positively to busing as reflected in these school district ratings.

To some degree, comparing evaluations of public schools in 1977 with those made in 1983 hides the pattern of change over time. Unfortunately, we did not interview nonparents in 1978 or 1979, so general sample comparisons across these years cannot be made. However, an analysis of parent views indicates a clear pattern.

Over 70% of public school parents rated the schools as good or excellent in the two years prior to desegregation. In 1979, at the end of the first school year of desegregation, less than half (43.6%) evaluated the schools so highly. By 1983, however, the percentage had returned to over 60%, 87% of their earlier level. Although the ratings begin at a lower base, the pattern of nonpublic school parent responses is quite similar. The percentage of Wilmington public school parents rating the schools as good or excellent, however, has steadily increased from 1977 through 1979 to 1983.

In short, although previous confidence levels have not yet been reached for all types of parents, a return to normalcy appears close at hand. The tremendous drop in evaluations that followed the onset of desegregation has been substantially overcome. School desegregation, with its resulting school district reorganization, pupil assignment plan with busing, and teachers' strike, brought an immediate and substantial decrease in the level of citizen confidence in the public schools. With the division of the county district into four school systems and the immediate trauma of desegregation over, this large drop has now been reversed and confidence levels are approaching predesegregation levels. There appears to be a return to positive views about the public schools, especially (as before) among public school parents.[4]

ATTITUDES CONCERNING DESEGREGATION EFFECTS

The results of the surveys conducted in New Castle County from 1977 to 1983 indicate a widespread increase in agreement that black students are receiving equal opportunity in the public schools (Table 5). In 1977, two-thirds (65.1%) of suburbanites and one-quarter (27.8%) of the city respondents agreed with the following statement: "Black students are getting equal educational opportunities in the Wilmington Schools." In 1983, 85.3% of the suburban sample and 68.4% of the city sample agreed with the statement that blacks were receiving equal opportunities in their school district. Although suburbanites may have felt positive before about their school district's treatment of blacks, the city increase in agreement reflects quite a positive change in attitudes. Parents of public school children in the suburbs and the city remained the most positive before and after school desegregation.

TABLE 5
Percentage Perceiving Blacks as Receiving Equal Educational Opportunity by Year

	1977	1983
General Population		
Total	59.7%*(901)	82.1%* (1023)**
Suburban	65.1%*(518)	85.3%*(845) **
City	27.8%*(383)	68.4%*(178) **
Public School Parents		
Total	63.1%*(617)	86.8% (620) **
Suburban	66.7% (300)	89.2% (520) **
City	48.7% (317)	74.0% (100) **
Non-Public School Parents		
Total	54.7%*(76)	82.1% (106) **
Suburban	72.7% (66)	83.9% (93)
City	40.0% (10)	69.2% (13)
Non-Parents		
Total	58.7%*(208)	79.8% (297) **
Suburban	61.2% (152)	83.6% (232) **
City	23.6% (56)	63.6% (65) **

NOTE: Answers given in response to the following question: "Please tell me if you strongly agree, agree, disagree, or strongly disagree (with this statement). Black students are getting equal educational opportunities (1977: in the Wilmington schools/1983: in your public school district)." Respondents answering "strongly agree" or "agree" are combined; "don't knows" are included in the totals.
*Means weighted. **$p \leq .05$.

Whereas in 1977 a majority (56.4%) of the city respondents thought that school desegregation would improve education for black students, only one-third held this positive view of desegregation in 1983. Feeling in the suburbs held relatively steady on this. About one-third were positive about the impact of desegregation on black student education before and after school desegregation was implemented.

Although suburban respondents have become somewhat more negative about the effect of school desegregation on race relations, the 1983 survey results indicate that optimistic city views of this relation have been halved. In 1977, almost half (48.9%) of the city respondents thought school desegregation would reduce racial prejudice. In 1983, less than one-quarter (24.2%) believed that improved race relations had resulted from school desegregation.[5]

On both these measures of school desegregation impact, public school parents, whether city or suburban residents, have reported the least increase in skepticism. For example, while 25.9% of 1977 suburban public school parents thought desegregation would reduce racial prejudice, 22.0% in 1983 thought desegregation had improved race relations. Among nonpublic school parents and nonparents, the percentage of positive feelings on this dimension dropped to about half of the 1977 level.

A strong relation between parental status and views about the impact of school desegregation is most evident in the results concerning discipline. As Table 6 indicates, suburbanites have become slightly less and city residents slightly more concerned about the impact of school desegregation on discipline problems. On the other hand, this concern is now of greatest import to those without children in the public schools. In the city the percentage of public school parents seeing a desegregation-discipline problem decreased substantially, while nonpublic school and nonparent concern rose substantially. In the suburbs public school parent concern dropped, while the other groups show a steady concern.[6]

In short, the residents of metropolitan Wilmington do feel that desegregation, built on a metropolitan busing plan, has increased the equality of educational opportunity for black students. Even two-thirds of the city respondents agree. But suburban views about the likely negative results of busing, so evident in 1977, have not changed substantially, and city respondents seem relatively disillusioned with desegregation. Public school parents are the most positive subgroup on all measures.

CONCLUSIONS AND IMPLICATIONS

The implementation of the metropolitan school desegregation order in New Castle County, Delaware, did not lead to greater support for the policy of busing to achieve school desegregation. Although suburban views toward busing became slightly less negative, city opposition increased. Ironically, those whose children were supposed to benefit most directly from the policy, city black parents, increased their opposition. In a policy area fraught with dilemmas and contradictions, we have a major irony.

The initial loss of confidence in the public schools resulting from busing, however, was not permanent. Although evaluations of the public

TABLE 6
Percentage Perceiving Desegregation as Worsening Discipline Problems by Year

	1977	1983
General Population		
Total	63.9%*(901)	63.7%*(1023)
Suburban	69.1%*(518)	65.3%*(845)
City	47.6%*(383)	56.8%*(178)
Public School Parents		
Total	68.4%*(617)	53.1% (620)**
Suburban	72.6% (300)	55.9% (520)**
City	51.7% (317)	38.1% (100)
Non-Public School Parents		
Total	67.2%*(76)	80.2% (106)
Suburban	77.3% (66)	82.8% (93)
City	30.0% (10)	61.5% (13)
Non-Parents		
Total	61.7%*(208)	64.9% (297)
Suburban	66.9% (152)	65.4% (232)
City	47.2% (56)	63.1% (65)

NOTE: Answers given in response to the following questions: "Please tell me whether you strongly agree, agree, disagree, or strongly disagree. Desegregation will lead to an increase in discipline problems in the schools." (1977) "Please tell me if you think desegregation has made each of the following better, worse, or if they have stayed the same . . . Discipline." (1983) Respondents answering "strongly agree" or "agree" in 1977 are combined; "don't knows" are included in the totals.
*Means weighted. **$p \leq .05$.

schools have not fully returned to predesegregation levels, they appear to be increasing. The public appears to differentiate, to some extent, busing views from school district evaluations. Although more people view blacks' educational opportunity as equal to whites', the suburban New Castle County public has not changed its mind much about the presumed effects of desegregation from its views prior to implementation on other dimensions. City respondents are also much more positive about equality of educational opportunity but more disillusioned about other effects of desegregation. It is those without children in public school, however, who show the least positive attitudinal change in both the suburbs and city. In fact, a second irony holds: In general, those least involved in the school desegregation process appear to have reacted the most negatively to it.

This pattern of attitude change suggests the limited utility of cognitive dissonance theory to explain a community's reaction to school desegregation. The opposition of suburbanites sending their children to desegregated public schools was reduced only slightly, at the same level as those who had no school-aged children or had (or put) children in nonpublic school. Perhaps the coercion involved in the busing order minimized dissonance and therefore little attitude change resulted (Cohen, 1964: 84-88). Alternatively, the salience of busing was lower among suburbanites in 1983 than in 1977. Perhaps dissonance resulted in this reduced salience. That is, suburbanites did not increase their liking for busing but, rather, decreased its importance as an issue to minimize dissonance (Cohen, 1964: 73). Suburban residents were already accepting school desegregation; they opposed busing, to them meaning the forced movement of suburban students to city schools. Thus, although southern resistance to desegregation may have waned after implementation, today the white (and to some extent black) public differentiates the object of their attitudes—desegregation remains acceptable, but busing remains objectionable.

The percentage of city parents opposed to busing increased from 1977 to 1983, although the salience of busing to them increased. It is hard to explain this change with the same cognitive dissonance explanation used to explain suburban change.

The proximity-resistance explanation, that the reality of the implementation of a desegregation plan would cause public school parents to be most upset, does not seem to hold. First, although city parents increased their concerns after implementation, suburban parents did not. Second, those without children in public school in both the city and suburbs were more likely to increase or maintain their concern about busing over time. Those with children in the public school were relatively more positive about the impact of busing.

Explaining the results reported in this article requires an explanation tied to the role of symbolism and reality over time. In 1977, busing was a symbolic issue. Suburbanites, almost all white, saw a variety of negative effects of a metropolitan busing plan; city dwellers, mostly black, were more likely to see an issue of great racial and symbolic significance to their advancement. The reality of the implementation of the plan altered some symbolically based views. For example, under the reality of the plan, city children were to be bused to the suburbs for nine years and suburban children to the city for three years. To many city blacks (and whites), this was a symbolic and substantive loss.[7] To many suburban whites, this made busing more palatable. Furthermore, those whose children were involved found that after a difficult start, desegregated schools became school again and the smaller school districts were more like their predesegregation counterparts. Those without children in public schools apparently are still reacting to the symbolism of busing. Thus, city respondents without children in public school have become more upset and their counterparts in the suburbs have maintained their opposition. Those with greater experience with the realities of the situation have moderated their views (Serow and Solomon, 1979).[8]

NOTES

1. To determine the 1977 general population and parental status subtotals, 1970 and 1980 census data and 1977 school district data were used in the weighting procedure. The 1983 results were weighted to reflect the proportions of subpopulations found in the 1983 general population of 526. Weighted means are indicated on the appropriate tables with asterisks. Alternative weighting procedures were utilized (e.g., using 1983 proportions to weight the 1977 results) but did not affect the conclusions reported herein. Note that these are samples of households, not individuals.

2. Differences between 1977 and 1983 percentages that are statistically significant are noted on Tables 2 through 6 in the second or 1983 column by a double asterisk. Differences that are not statistically significant but are significant in the context of this article are discussed in the text, usually as slight changes.

3. The Gallup Poll indicates that nationally ratings dipped and then recovered between 1977 and 1982. In 1977, 37% of the national sample gave their local public schools an A or B grade; in 1978, the percentage was 36; in 1979, the percentage dropped to 34; but in 1982, it increased back to 37%. A small part of the drop and return in Delaware may thus have been part of a national trend.

4. There are other strong indications of a return to normalcy. In 1979, parents were asked if they thought the schools were running normally "now," would be "soon," whether it would take a "few years" for them to return to normal, or whether the schools would "never" return. Few public school parents thought that the schools were now operating normally or would soon. In 1983 more than half (54%) of the public school parents thought the schools to now be or would soon be running smoothly.

5. Two items measuring symbolic white racism were included in the 1977 and 1983 surveys. On one there was a very small reduction in racism. Eight percent fewer of suburbanites agreed with the statement that "Over the past few years the government has paid too much attention to blacks and other minorities" in 1983 than 1977. On the second item the reduction was statistically insignificant; public school parents showed a greater decline.

6. If suburban parents switching their children from public to nonpublic schools tend to be more negative about busing and public schools, their movement to the nonpublic school parent subgroup would increase the measured negativism in this group and decrease it in the public school parent group. This possibility and other complex, multivariate reasons for results reported herein are now under analysis.

7. Black disillusionment with school desegregation in Delaware between 1977 and 1983 may in part reflect national trends in black attitudes toward desegregation. Louis Harris and Associates (1978) did report a drop in black support for busing to achieve school desegregation from 50% to 43% from 1963 to 1978. The percentage of black respondents favoring school integration held steady, however (70% in 1963, 71% in 1978). The percentage of blacks favoring busing in Harris's national sample in 1978 was almost identical to the percentage in Wilmington favoring busing in 1977.

8. Public school enrollment decreases among whites and blacks appear to be related to the time periods of symbolic loss. The school districts in the New Castle County desegregation area lost 20,000 white students (from a 1973 base of 68,215) in the five years of desegregation planning (1973-1977). In the five prior years (1968-1972) white enrollment was stable. In the first five years of implementation (1978-1982) white enrollment declined by 13,000 students. Black public school enrollment, which held steady at about 16,000 students between 1970 and 1977, declined slightly (8.7%) through the years of desegregation implementation. In short, white upset was related to large enrollment declines prior to and just after busing began, whereas modest black declines occurred after busing was initiated.

Although a substantial part of these changes were due to demographic, economic, and other forces, nonpublic school enrollment trends support the view that desegregation also played a role. White nonpublic school enrollment increased from 1974 to 1981, whereas black nonpublic school enrollment increased in the early 1970s, dropped as desegregation approached, and has climbed after the predesegregation high.

Despite the loss of half of the white enrollment from 1968 to 1982, white enrollment stability in New Castle County was far higher than in city school districts and metropolitan districts that were not under desegregation orders in southern and border states and about the same as in metropolitan areas under court order (Orfield, 1983). From 1968 to 1980, New Castle County had a decline of 11.6% in its white percentage of total public school enrollment compared to a mere 2.1% decline in cities, 8.3% in metropolitan areas under court order, and 17% in metropolitan areas not under order. Thus, despite the great symbolic outpouring of dislike for busing in New Castle County, white loss, heaviest before and not after desegregation began, was relatively modest, and black loss, which occurred after busing began, was almost nonsignificant.

REFERENCES

ABNEY, G. (1976) "Legislating morality: attitude change and desegregation in Mississippi." Urban Education 11 (October): 333-338.

COHEN, A. (1964) Attitude Change and Social Influence. New York: Basic Books.

ESTABROOK, L. S. (1980) "The effect of desegregation on parents' evaluation of schools." Ph.D. dissertation, Boston University.

GATLIN, D. S., M. W. GILES, and E. F. CATALDO (1978) "Policy support within a target group: the case of school desegregation." Amer. Pol. Sci. Rev. 72 (September): 985-995.

GREEN, R. et al. (1982) "Metropolitan school desegregation in New Castle County, Delaware." Final report to the Rockefeller Foundation, October.

HENDERSON, R. D., M. VON EULER, and J. M. SCHNEIDER (1981) "Remedies for segregation: some lessons from research." Educ. Evaluation and Policy Analysis 3 (July/August): 67-76.

JACOBSON, C. (1978) "Desegregation rulings and public attitude changes: white resistance or resignation?" Amer. J. of Sociology 3 (November): 698-705.

Louis Harris and Associates, Inc. (1978) "A study of attitudes toward racial and religious minorities and toward women." (November)

McCONAHAY, J. B. and W. D. HAWLEY (1978) Reactions to Busing in Louisville: Summary of Adult Opinions in 1976 and 1977. Working Paper. Durham, NC: Duke University, Institute for Policy Analysis.

———(1977) Is It the Busing or the Blacks? Working Paper. Durham, NC: Duke University, Institute for Policy Analysis.

MONTI, D. J. (1977) "Examining the desegregation process." Integrateducation 15 (November/December): 41-46.

ORFIELD, G. (1983) Public School Desegregation in the United States, 1968-1980. Washington, DC: Joint Center for Political Studies.

RAFFEL, J. A. (1980a) The Politics of School Desegregation: The Metropolitan Remedy in Delaware. Philadelphia: Temple Univ. Press.

———(1980b) "The voters grade the metropolitan desegregation plan in Delaware." Integrateducation 18 (January-August): 64-71.

ROSSELL, C. H. (1978) "School desegregation and community social change." Law and Contemporary Problems 42 (Summer): 133-183.

SCHWEITZER, H. and J. GRIFFORE (1981) "A longitudinal study of attitudes of students and parents coincident with court-ordered school desegregation." Urban Rev. 13 (Summer): 111-119.

SEARS, O., P. HENSLER, and L. K. SPEER (1979) "Whites' opposition to 'busing': self-interest or symbolic politics?" Amer. Pol. Sci. Rev. 73 (June): 369-384.

SEROW, R. C. and D. SOLOMON (1979) "Parents' attitudes toward desegregation: the proximity hypothesis." Phi Delta Kappan 60 (June): 753-754.

SILLS, J. H., Jr. (1982) "Equalizing teacher salaries: racial and policy implications in a new metropolitan public school district." Urban Education 17 (October): 351-374.

SLAWSKI, E. J. (1976) "Pontiac parents: for busing or integration?" Education and Urban Society 8 (August): 477-499.

THOERNY, A. R. (1979) Report of Survey of Parents of School Age Children. Memphis: Memphis State University, Institute of Governmental Studies and Research.

WILLIE, C. V. and S. L. GREENBLATT (1981) Community Politics and Educational Change. New York: Longman.

WOLTERS, R. (1984) The Burden of Brown: Thirty Years of School Desegregation. Knoxville: Univ. of Tennessee Press.

Jeffrey A. Raffel, Professor, College of Urban Affairs and Public Policy, is the Director of the Masters in Public Administration Program at the University of Delaware. His book, The Politics of School Desegregation: The Metropolitan Case in Delaware, *was published by Temple University Press in 1980, and his articles have appeared in* Phi Delta Kappan, Harvard Education Review, *and* Urban Education.

This report considers who is involved in urban revitalization, why some neighborhoods are more quickly revived than others, and whether participation by longtime residents in renovation of historic areas is feasible. Surveys of two preservation districts in Indianapolis revealed that recent in-migrants are in a stronger position than longtime residents to influence the revitalization process. Although incumbent homeowners are willing to join restoration activity, they often lack information and money, are less self-conscious as preservationists, and are less organized to shape the process in their own interest.

WHOSE NEIGHBORHOOD?
The Role of Established Residents in Historic Preservation Areas

TIMOTHY MAHER

AIN HAAS

BETTY LEVINE

JOHN LIELL

Indiana University at Indianapolis

City officials and the mass media have welcomed the movement to restore inner-city commercial and residential areas as a sign of urban renaissance and neighborhood revitalization. Community organizers and social scientists have focused on the return of the "gentry" and displacement of the poor as a part of this process (Gale, 1976, 1977; National Urban Coalition, 1978; Laska and Spain, 1979; London, 1980). At the core of most discussions of improvements in central cities is an assumption that such revitalization involves, even requires, luring the affluent back to areas abandoned to the poor long ago. Must redevelopment take the form of gentrification, the wholesale displacement of disadvantaged

AUTHORS' NOTE: *An earlier draft of this article was presented at the annual meetings of the North Central Sociological Association in Detroit, May 1982. The research reported here was funded by the Department of Metropolitan Development of the City of Indianapolis and by the Indiana Historic Landmarks Foundation.*

URBAN AFFAIRS QUARTERLY, Vol. 21 No. 2, December 1985 267-281

residents by more affluent ones? Or can it take the form of incumbent upgrading, a rejuvenation that involves the improvement of the physical structures by the existing inhabitants?

Scholarly literature on incumbent upgrading is almost nonexistent, with a rare exception such as Clay (1980). The mass media also overlook this form of redevelopment and focus almost exclusively on gentrification. Even when academicians and reporters lament the occurrence or possibility of displacement of the poor, the publicity about this trend—in the absence of serious discussion of an alternative to gentrification—at best generates perfunctory sympathy for the uprooted, and at worst stimulates speculative buying of low-income housing units for a profitable conversion to higher-income units. The dearth of publicity about incumbent upgrading does not necessarily signify its absence, as such activity can go on quietly. Conversely, the fanfare over gentrification may not measure its true extent as much as it reflects speculators' marketing of properties in certain districts through promotion of a new image for such areas as havens for affluent investors and homebuyers.

We suggest that the phenomenon under investigation here be labeled with a neutral term that describes the type of change without presupposing anything about the types of people involved in the process. Urban ecologists such as McKenzie (1936), for example, have used the term "succession" to refer to the changing dominance pattern within a habitat, with no explicit suggestion that the transition is triggered by the actions of any particular category of people. Revitalization, redevelopment, and renaissance are other terms that might be more serviceable, as they are less generic and more common in contemporary use for describing the process of restored faith and reinvestment in deteriorated areas.

Whatever the terminology, descriptions and explanations of central city revitalization that focus on gentrification and ignore incumbent upgrading create an illusion of severely limited options and obscure the broad range of possible forms of renewal. In this article we try to avoid the assumption that population replacement is the only possible mode of redevelopment, as we examine two central city neighborhoods that have recently experienced the reversal of a long period of decay. The object is to identify some of the characteristics of individual homeowners and whole neighborhoods that are conducive to restoration, as well as to assess the roles of longtime residents and newcomers in the process.

THE NEIGHBORHOODS UNDER STUDY

This article examines two adjacent areas in Indianapolis, Chatham-Arch and the Old Northside, which lie about one mile northeast of the heart of downtown. Mainly wood frame houses, the original structures in both districts date from 1870-1910. The Old Northside homes were initially more fashionable, but began to decay when the city's elite moved to new mansions further north after World War I. Low-income tenants became predominant in both neighborhoods. By 1970, the core census tracts of Chatham-Arch and the Old Northside were virtually identical in terms of "social vulnerability," ranking in the 100th and 99th percentiles of all Marion County tracts on a scale composed of such measures as the rates of poverty, unemployment, substandard housing, and tuberculosis (Maloney, 1973).

After a long period of housing decay, abandonment, and demolition, signs of a reversal first appeared in the Old Northside around 1974 (Indianapolis Historic Preservation Commission, 1979: 16). It was not until 1978 that the same could be said of Chatham-Arch. Revitalization of both neighborhoods is now widely anticipated.

RESEARCH METHODS

We contacted all households in single-family homes and doubles in each area, along with random samples of apartment units. Following a mailing of explanatory letters from the city planning department, door-to-door interviewers carrying official photo identification cards sought personal interviews, 30-45 minutes long, with an adult in each household. A total of 302 Old Northside residents took part in the survey during the summer of 1979, with a refusal rate of only 3%. In Chatham-Arch, 203 residents gave interviews during the winter of 1979-1980, with a similarly low refusal rate of about 5%. We will focus on the subset of households owning or contracting to buy their homes.[1] Because renters are generally not responsible for decisions about repairs and maintenance, we excluded them from the analysis.

To gauge inclination toward restoration, we used a variety of items. These were used in both neighborhoods, unless otherwise noted:

Y_1: Rating of poor maintenance of houses in the area as a serious problem/ somewhat of a problem/ not a problem or something never thought of.

Y_2: Mentioning physical improvements in answer to an open-ended item about what could be done to make area a better place to live.
Y_3: Interest in low-cost home improvement loan.
Y_4: Mentioning historic preservation in answer to an open-ended item about what kind of neighborhood one hopes to see in a few years.
Y_5: Favoring historic preservation in answer to an open-ended item about one's attitude toward it.
Y_6: Membership in a preservation-oriented community organization.
Y_7: Display of a Victorian doorknob logo (Old Northside).
Y_8: Absence of externally visible housing defects (Chatham-Arch).[2]
Y_9: Interest in learning about governmental programs to assist residents in fixing up houses in the area (Chatham-Arch).
Y_{10}: Participation in a recent clean-up campaign (Chatham-Arch).
Y_{11}: Number of major repairs or redecoration projects, costing at least $50, undertaken in last two years (Chatham-Arch).
Y_{12}: Total cost of such repairs and redecorations (Chatham-Arch).

We also measured residents' resources, backgrounds, and outlooks, with items described below. In cases of attitudinal measures, we did not always have data referring directly to the head of the household, but we assume that the respondent's views were representative of the opinions of the person(s) responsible for decisions about the upkeep of the house. In assessing the relationships between involvement in restoration and various attributes of residents, we applied tests of statistical significance, using the conventional .05 level.[3]

PERSONAL ATTRIBUTES AND INVOLVEMENT IN RESTORATION

The literature on poverty contains some explanations for urban blight in terms of the traits of individual slum residents. One could extend these to account for the appearance of restoration or continued absence thereof. We do not suggest that these theories are equally plausible, but think they are all worth testing, as formulators of policies regarding restoration in slums may apply any or all of them.

Lack of money is the most obvious explanation for the poor quality of housing in the old neighborhoods on the fringes of downtown. Residents may simply not have enough funds to make repairs and restore their homes. Poor families pay a high proportion of their income for housing, which typically strains their ability to buy adequate food, clothing, and medical care (Schorr, 1968: 350-353). Faced with limited funds and a hard choice between fixing up their houses and obtaining other necessities, the poor may sacrifice the former for the latter.

Lack of skills may be another factor. To keep homes in good condition, owners must know how to make small repairs before the damage becomes serious, or at least know when to call a repairman. The poor tend to have unskilled jobs and are thus at a disadvantage, compared with craftsmen, engineers, and other workers whose skills may be transferable to home repair projects. Not all affluent workers have such relevant occupational skills, but they tend to be more literate and articulate. The poor, in contrast, may be less able to find and make sense of do-it-yourself instructions for tools and repair manuals, or find the right repairmen to do the job for them. Their lack of education also makes poor people naive shoppers (Caplovitz, 1961; Richards, 1969), which could hamper them in arranging and paying for appropriate, timely repairs.

Lack of ambition may also account for run-down housing. People brought up in a subculture that promotes impulsiveness and fatalism (Lewis, 1968: 9-10) may never have learned the importance of thinking ahead and keeping up their homes. Critics of the notion that such a subculture flourishes in urban slums, especially black ghettos, say it is based on nothing more than scattered bits of methodologically suspect data (Valentine, 1968) and ignores the importance of unstable and harsh environments in generating apathy (Miller et al., 1968; Rainwater, 1970, 1974: 308). The failure of many slum residents to abide by certain norms does not necessarily mean they reject conventional goals such as decent housing (Gans, 1968: 208; Irelan and Besner, 1969; Horton, 1973: 47-48), but their views on historic preservation are still in question.

The thesis that people continue to live in dilapidated houses because they cannot afford the upkeep received considerable support in our findings. Household income, measured in $2500 increments, was related to most of the measures of inclination toward restoration shown in Table 1 (Y_1 - Y_6), as well as to two measures not shown: display of the preservation logo in the Old Northside ($r = .41$) and the number of major repair or redecoration projects in Chatham-Arch ($r = .61$). Economic constraint on residential choice, a second indicator based on whether respondents cited a lack of affordable housing elsewhere in answer to an open-ended question about why they live in the neighborhood, was significantly related only to the hope for future preservation in the Old northside ($r = -.26$). Only four of the twelve measures of inclination

TABLE 1
Selected Correlations Between Residents' Attributes and Inclinations Toward Restoration

Attribute	Area	Measure of Inclinaton toward Restoration					
		Y_1	Y_2	Y_3	Y_4	Y_5	Y_6
Household Income	CA	.27*	-.17	-.03	-.00	.36*	.12
	ONS	.09	.21*	-.08	.03	.12	.56*
Economic Hardship	CA	.30	-.01	.19	.14	.20	-.03
	ONS	.12	-.09	.08	-.26*	-.06	-.11
Dropout at Head of Household	CA	-.41*	.00	-.14	-.15	-.11	-.08
	ONS	-.02	-.05	-.30*	.06	-.20*	-.33*
Low Blue-Collar Head of Household	CA	.05	-.14	.25	-.06	.00	-.06
	ONS	.11	.10	-.14	-.20*	-.06	-.18*
Female Head of Household	CA	-.22	.15	.09	-.15	-.44*	-.26
	ONS	.07	.02	-.09	-.23*	-.25*	-.36*
Single Parent in Household	CA	.03	-.08	.12	.09	.04	-.09
	ONS	.10	-.12	.20	-.29*	-.40*	-.26*
Unemployment in Household	CA	-.04	-.07	-.08	.00	-.04	.00
	ONS	.10	-.16*	.22	-.24*	-.30*	-.28*
Nonwhite Head of Household	CA	.36	-.07	-.08	.00	.17	.00
	ONS	-.01	-.04	.10	-.14	-.29*	-.44*

NOTE: CA = Chatham-Arch (N = 37); ONS = Old Northside (N = 115). Y_1 = perceived seriousness of poor maintenance of houses in area; Y_2 = recommendation of physical improvements for area; Y_3 = interest in fix-up loan; Y_4 = hope for historic preservation in area's future; Y_5 = favorable attitude toward historic preservation; Y_6 = membership in preservation organization. Missing data replaced with mean.
*Significant in expected direction, at .05 level in one-tailed test.

toward restoration (Y_3, Y_8, Y_9, Y_{12}) had no significant correlation with either of the measures of financial status.

The notion that ignorance inhibits restoration also received support. We created dummy or binary variables from questions about the education and occupation of each household member, to distinguish whether the head was a high school dropout and an unskilled worker (i.e., in one of the census group categories of operatives, laborers, domestics, and service workers). These measures were inversely related to most of the measures of inclination toward restoration shown in Table 1. In addition, having a high school dropout at the head of the household was negatively correlated with display of the preservation logo in the Old Northside ($r = -.23$). Most of these correlations remained significant even after controlling for income and economic hardship. The Chatham-Arch survey included some indicators that allow us to be more specific about what kinds of ignorance are most consequential: scales of indoor and outdoor maintenance skills, a test of knowledge about the urgency of various home repairs, and a vocabulary test over technical terms found in housing contracts.[4] The last of these stood out as having the most frequent and largest correlations with measures of inclination toward restoration, being related to Y_1 ($r = .39$), Y_5 (.33), and Y_9 (.33). This suggests that homeowners' facility with contracts and credit services, which may reflect or determine their readiness to seek home improvement loans and make arrangements with professional contractors and repairmen, is more important for restoration than personal knowledge of the urgency of different types of repairs and personal ability to fix things. Only two of the twelve measures of inclination toward restoration (Y_8, Y_{12}) had no significant correlations with any of the indicators of ignorance.

To measure attributes supposedly indicative of a subculturally derived lack of concern about housing quality, we created a series of dummy variables to distinguish households with and without each of the following: a female head, a single parent, an unemployed member, and a nonwhite head.[5] These measures had many significant negative correlations with the indicators of inclination toward restoration in Table 1. In addition, having a female head was inversely related to displaying the preservation logo in the Old Northside ($r = -.17$) and the number of major repair or redecoration projects in Chatham-Arch (–.29), and having a nonwhite head was negatively associated with defect-free housing (–.45). Some of these correlations disappeared when we controlled for indicators of poverty and ignorance, and nearly all of those that remained significant (with $Y_{4\text{-}6}$, Y_8) involved measures that gauged self-conscious commitment to historic preservation rather than interest or involvement in home improvements. In fact, there were substantial correlations with some of the latter indicators in the opposite direction than what would be predicted by the culture of poverty thesis. For example, households with single parents and unemployed members were actually more likely to be interested in a home improvement loan in the Old Northside ($r = .20$ and .22, respectively). In Chatham-Arch, those with a nonwhite head were more critical of the condition of the houses around them (.36) and reported spending more on repair and redecoration projects (.36); households with unemployment were also more likely to report such expenditures ($r = .36$), as well as participation in the neighborhood clean-up campaign (.42).

In sum, each of the three explanations for variation in inclination toward restoration received some support. The proportion of significant correlations was about the same for each, but the evidence was weakest for the thesis of learned apathy, if we take into account how many substantial correlations were in the wrong direction and how many indicators of the dependent variable were not related to any of the independent variables.

A common theme in the findings was that lower-status residents—whether delineated by financial position, informational resources, or other traits—were least inclined toward restoration on the measures that gauge a self-conscious commitment to historic preservation ($Y_{4\text{-}7}$). Differences were not so apparent on measures tapping awareness of the need to fix houses, readiness to take advantage of appropriate programs, or actual involvement in home repairs.

Homeowners of different social statuses may be differentially inclined to seek out or respond to contacts from preservation-oriented groups. Previous studies have shown that higher-status renovators moving into historic neighborhoods are mindful of and attracted by the design features, investment potential, and anticipated exclusivity of such areas (Gale, 1979; Laska and Spain, 1979). This may mean that they are predisposed to be conscious of their role as restorers and their common interests with others of their kind. Such selective in-migration could account for the preservation movement's emphasis on external appearances, including the not uncommon rush to restore the facade of the house while other, less visible parts wait. Lower-status residents, in contrast, may postpone work on frills and concentrate on making the interior more comfortable, due to a practical bent, limited resources, or fear of unwanted attention to external signs of prosperity. They would thus be less interested in linking up with other preservationists in terms of self-identification, organizational affiliation, and so on.

On the other hand, there may be something about the way the restoration process unfolds that awakens the enthusiasm of higher-status homeowners and alienates the lower-status residents with regard to self-conscious commitment to historic preservation. For instance, preservation-oriented groups and government agencies may manifest different degrees of fervor in directing their information campaigns and recruitment efforts at homebuyers of different social statuses. Contractors and repairmen may provide better service to higher-status customers. The mass media, in a search for newsworthy events, may cover the high-status "urban pioneers" who contrast most dramatically with other residents, leaving lower-status homeowners without role models of historic preservationists from their own ranks. We have no definitive data on why status-group differences are most likely to be found with measures tapping a self-conscious commitment to preservation. Yet the fact that this pattern was particularly strong in the Old Northside, where renovation had been going on several years longer than in Chatham-Arch, suggests that it is less a matter of predisposition and more likely a result of the way the restoration process is played out.

NEIGHBORHOOD FEATURES AND RESTORATION

Having investigated the personal attributes of residents in Chatham-Arch and the Old Northside, we focus now on collective assets that might differentiate areas that can be renovated quickly from those that take longer or even continue to decline. Obviously, the personal attributes that account for individual homeowners' readiness to restore their houses could account for a whole neighborhood's rapid progress, if such traits were characteristic of the neighborhood on an aggregate level. Moreover, there could be a spillover effect, whereby residents deficient in these traits could draw on their neighbors for help in arranging financing, obtaining knowledge, and getting inspiration to join the restoration activity.

In terms of personal traits found to be related to inclination toward restoration above, the Old Northside homeowners were in a somewhat better position, being significantly better educated, wealthier, and less concentrated in unskilled occupations than their counterparts in Chatham-Arch. However, homeownership by nonwhites was more common in the Old Northside (23% versus 11%). Other indicators revealed more commitment to the neighborhood and optimism in the Old Northside, with residents being more likely to see themselves as leaders who contribute to neighborhood decisions (26% versus 8% in Chatham-Arch) and much more likely to have tried to influence others to move into the area (59% versus 19%).

The pattern was similar when only longtime residents (defined in the next section) were compared, suggesting that the Old Northside initially had a population more predisposed and prepared to take part in restoration. Of course, it is possible that the massive influx of newcomers to the Old Northside displaced the most vulnerable of the prior residents, leaving behind a select group of incumbents better equipped to join in restoration than their former neighbors. The reasons for out-migration from the two areas, as perceived by the longtime homeowners, were somewhat different. The exodus from Chatham-Arch seemed predominantly due to problems that drove people out, whereas the outflow from the Old Northside seemed to be caused by a combination of opportunities that pulled people away and push factors that forced them out. So out-migrants from Chatham-Arch were apparently more vulnerable to displacement than those who left the Old Northside, which suggests that some differences in collective assets predated the renovation activity in these two areas.

The literature on urban revitalization points to such neighborhood assets as proximity to the central business district, distinctive architecture, and active community organizations as important stimuli to renovation (Gale, 1979; Goldfield, 1980; Van Til, 1980). Chatham-Arch and the Old Northside are both near downtown, but they differ in other respects, generally in ways that favor the latter. First, in terms of architecture, the Old Northside has some of the most elaborate and historic structures in the city, whereas the housing stock in Chatham-Arch is substantially smaller and less ornate. Second, community organizations have a longer history and wider base in the Old Northside, where half the owner households are affiliated with at least one of four major associations. In Chatham-Arch, the one neighborhood group includes only a fourth of the much small number of homeowners there. Finally, the importance of outside institutions should not be overlooked. A recent study of lending institutions found that money for home mortgages has flowed much more readily into the Old Northside than nearby neighborhoods such as Chatham-Arch (Indianapolis-Marion County Human Rights Commission, 1979). The presence of nearly all the local television stations and many radio stations in the "media corridor" adjacent to the Old Northside may also have been a distinct asset, in terms of generating awareness of early signs of restoration and winning support for further development along this line.

INCUMBENT UPGRADING OR GENTRIFICATION?

In our opening discussion of the nature of neighborhood revitalization, we distinguished between two paths of redevelopment that can be seen as poles of a continuum of possible results of the renewal process. In light of the findings in the intervening sections, we will now make some observations about how the personal attributes and neighborhood features in the two areas might influence the outcome of revitalization.

Because the Old Northside was quite far along in the process, the direction should have been clearly established there. Indeed, in comparing the assets of homeowners who had resided continuously in the area at least since 1974 (when signs of renovation first appeared) and those who had moved in after that date, we found that the recent arrivals were in a somewhat better position to participate in restoration and to control the area's redevelopment. They were significantly more affluent, better educated, and better placed in the occupational realm people, although their racial make-up was about the same as those of the longtime residents.

While long-term residents were slightly outnumbered in the ranks of the Old Northside homeowners at the time of the survey (47% versus 53%), they had not given up on the area. They too were concerned with deterioration and were just as likely to mention physical changes in their lists of what would make the neighborhood a better place in which to live. Still, the newcomers were significantly more likely to report trying to influence others to move into the neighborhood (75% versus 42%), to see themselves as neighborhood leaders (32% versus 18%), to be able to give a valid definition of historic preservation (98% versus 79%), to belong to a neighborhood organization (70% versus 24%), and to express a commitment to restoration by displaying the Old Northside logo (62% versus 15%). So while the established residents expressed concern about upgrading the area's housing, the newcomers were far more aware of the process and better organized to control its direction.

In Chatham-Arch, the assets of the recent in-migrants far outweighed those who were living there before 1978, when signs of restoration appeared. The latter were markedly poorer, less educated, and lower in occupational status. Although the newcomers were outnumbered by more than five to one, more of them had tried to influence others to move into the area (67% versus 10%). The newcomers were somewhat better able to define historic preservation (100% versus 74%) and more aware of the existence of the neighborhood organization (83% versus 48%), although the rates of actual membership and proportions of self-styled neighborhood leaders were not significantly different.

In sum, there was no evidence of significant personal assets among the longtime residents that promise to lead to incumbent upgrading in Chatham-Arch. The newcomers were generally in a better position to shape the revitalization process self-consciously, in their own interests. Although the neighborhood is in an early stage of revitalization, it seems likely to follow the gentrifying mode of revival. On the other hand, Chatham-Arch does not have as many of the neighborhood assets that are especially alluring to middle-class in-migrants (Meadows and Call, 1978; Gale, 1979; Laska and Spain, 1979), and this may ease the pressure of gentrification and displacement.

CONCLUSION

Restoration of decayed inner-city neighborhoods can take different forms. In this article we have presented a conceptualization of the process that avoids the bias, common in the literature, of focusing on affluent "urban pioneers," to the near exclusion of the possibility of incumbent upgrading. The neighborhoods examined in this report differ in the amount of rehabilitation completed so far, but both exhibit personal and neighborhood assets that make further restoration likely. In both districts the revitalization process seems headed toward a mixture of small-scale incumbent upgrading and large-scale gentrification. Unless there is substantial intervention by public or private organizations, few of the long-time homeowners seem likely to remain and fix up their houses.

Our results suggest that the incumbent populations in inner-city areas want to take part in the renewal process, but lack the resources to do so and may even become alienated by the way the process is played out. Both researchers and planners need to become aware of the established residents' assets, both personal and collective, and their relationship to restoration potential. Although gentrification may be a quick fix, the process of incumbent upgrading or a combination of the two modes of redevelopment may generate more benefits for the city in the long run (Gans, 1977; Laska and Spain, 1979). Neighborhood improvements that attract more affluent homebuyers may produce increases in tax revenues, but the gains could be outweighed by the costly upgrading of city services demanded by middle-class returnees to near-downtown areas. The former residents of gentrified neighborhoods do not simply disappear, but crowd into other areas, possibly accelerating the process of deterioration there and producing a net loss in the city's housing stock. Only by considering the assets of both long-term residents and recent arrivals will urban policymakers come up with a coherent agenda for neighborhood renewal—

one sensitive to short-term as well as long-term benefits, serving the needs of affluent as well as poor citizens.

NOTES

1. To approximate the actual population sizes in these areas, answers of owners living in houses subdivided into apartments were counted more heavily, which compensated for the deliberate undersampling of apartment dwellers and ensured proportional representation of resident owners of multifamily structures. This raised the number of owners from 99 to 115 in the Old Northside, but the figure in Chatham-Arch (37) was not affected.

2. There was no symbol corresponding to the Old Northside logo, as Chatham-Arch was at an earlier stage in the revitalization process and residents were less self-conscious about their role as renovators. Instead, their dwellings were inspected and rated on a scale of housing quality devised by the Health and Hospital Corporation of Marion County. This index distinguishes major defects in the walls, roof, yard, and so on, from minor ones, and counts one of the former as equivalent to two of the latter in tallying flaws.

3. Significance tests are not required, inasmuch as Chatham-Arch and the Old Northside are treated as two case studies, and we have nearly complete data from the owner households in both areas. Yet such tests can serve as a way to eliminate arbitrariness and apply a standard procedure in sorting important findings from inconsequential results. They are also useful if these two areas are taken to be representative of a larger set of neighborhoods in Indianapolis or other cities, and if our results are to be used to infer what is going on in other such areas.

4. The scale of indoor maintenance skills was formed by counting how many of the following tasks someone in the household could do: replacing the furnace filter, replacing an electrical fuse, repairing a leaky faucet, fixing a clogged kitchen drain, fixing a clogged toilet drain, and painting the interior of the house. The scale of outdoor skills included the tasks of weatherstripping an exterior door, installing new storm windows, hanging a storm door, installing a new key lock, and replacing roof shingles. Both scales had high reliability scores (Cronbach's alphas around .90), and factor analysis showed each scale item having a loading of at least .50 on the same factor in the rotated matrix resulting from the varimax method. For the test on knowledge about home repairs, respondents were presented with five situations in which a shortage of funds necessitated a choice about the relative urgency of two problems, with correct answers getting one point, undecided responses meriting half a point, and incorrect guesses getting zero. Sophistication with regard to technical vocabulary of contracts was gauged by the ability to define correctly a series of real estate terms (default, escrow account, accelerated depreciation, discount points, subsidized interest, deferred payment), which formed a satisfactory scale.

5. We considered another item measuring identification with the lower class, in the form of a preference for mostly or exclusively low-income people in the neighborhood's future, but found only one person in either area who expressed such a bias (by saying he did not want any more doctors or lawyers moving in). We attempted to construct a poverty culture scale from these variables, but no combination of items satisfied our criterion of a reliability score of at least .70.

REFERENCES

CAPLOVITZ, D. and L. LIEBERMAN (1961) The Consumer Behavior of Low Income Families. New York: Columbia University Bureau of Applied Social Research.

CLAY, P. (1980) "The rediscovery of city neighborhoods," pp. 3-16 in S. Laska and D. Spain (eds.) Back to the City. New York: Pergamon.

GALE, D. (1979) "Middle class resettlement in older urban neighborhoods." J. of the Amer. Planning Association 45 (July): 293-304.

———(1977) The Back-to-the-City Movement Revisited. Washington, DC: George Washington University, Department of Urban and Regional Planning.

———(1976) The Back-to-the-City Movement . . . Or Is It?" Washington, DC: George Washington University, Department of Urban and Regional Planning.

GANS, H. (1977) "Why exurbanites won't reurbanize themselves." New York Times (February 12): 21.

———(1968) "Culture and class in the study of poverty," pp. 201-228 in D. Moynihan (ed.) On Understanding Poverty. New York: Basic Books.

GOLDFIELD, D. (1980) "Private neighborhood redevelopment and displacement." Urban Affairs Q. 15 (June): 453-468.

HORTON, J. (1973) "Time and cool people," pp. 31-50 in L. Rainwater (ed.) Black Experience. New Brunswick, NJ: Transaction.

Indianapolis Historic Preservation Commission (1979) Old Northside Historic Area Preservation Plan. Indianapolis: author.

Indianapolis-Marion County Human Rights Commission (1979) Distribution of Residential Mortgage Loans Made in Marion County, Indiana, 1979. Indianapolis: author.

IRELAN, L. and A. BESNER (1969) "Low-income life styles," pp. 17-26 in F. Sturdivant (ed.) The Ghetto Marketplace. New York: Free Press.

LASKA, S. and D. SPAIN (1979) "Urban policy and planning in the wake of gentrification." J. of the Amer. Planning Association 45 (October): 523-531.

LEWIS, O. (1968) A Study of Slum Culture. New York: Random House.

LONDON, B. (1980) "Gentrification as urban reinvasion," pp. 72-92 in S. Laska and D. Spain (eds.) Back to the City. New York: Pergamon.

MALONEY, J. (1973) Social Vulnerability in Indianapolis. Indianapolis: Community Service Council.

McKENZIE, R. (1936) Readings in Human Ecology. Ann Arbor: Univ. of Michigan Press.

MEADOWS, G. and S. CALL (1978) "Considering housing market trends and resident attitudes in planning urban revitalization." J. of the Amer. Institute of Planners 44 (July): 295-305.

MILLER, S., F. REISSMAN, and A. SEAGULL (1968) "Poverty and self-indulgence," pp. 416-432 in L. Ferman et al. (eds.) Poverty in America. Ann Arbor: Univ. of Michigan Press.

National Urban Coalition (1978) Displacement. Washington, DC: author.

RAINWATER, L. (1974) Social Problems and Public Policy: Inequality and Justice. Chicago: Aldine.

———(1970) Behind Ghetto Walls. Chicago: Aldine.

RICHARDS, L. (1969) "Consumer practices of the poor," pp. 42-60 in F. Sturdivant (ed.) The Ghetto Marketplace. New York: Free Press.

SCHORR, A. (1968) "Slums and social insecurity," pp. 349-368 in L. Ferman et al. (eds.) Poverty in America. Ann Arbor: Univ. of Michigan Press.
VALENTINE, C. (1968) Culture and Poverty. Chicago: Univ. of Chicago Press.
VAN TIL, J. (1980) "Citizen participation in neighborhood transformation." Urban Affairs Q. 15 (June): 439-452.

Timothy Maher is Assistant Professor of Sociology at Indiana University at Indianapolis and a lifelong resident of a historic inner-city neighborhood. He combines research on urban affairs with active involvement in restoration activity and central city community organizations.

Ain Haas is Associate Professor of Sociology at Indiana University at Indianapolis and has conducted a number of surveys in the United States and Sweden. His work focuses on public views of workplace democracy and other reforms.

Betty Levine is Assistant Professor of Sociology at Indiana University at Indianapolis. She specializes in public policy and the sociology of religion. She has experience as a social worker and is a recent ex-suburban in-migrant to an area in the beginning stages of restoration.

John Liell is Professor of Sociology at Indiana University at Indianapolis. A longtime resident of the inner city, he directed Community Action Against Poverty in Indianapolis, helped plan the city's Model Cities Program, served as executive director of the Consortium for Urban Education, and has done extensive consulting work for community groups.

STATE OF THE ART IN URBAN RESEARCH: 1923

William B. Munro, *Municipal Government and Administration* (New York: Macmillan, 1923). 2 volumes.

The study of urban politics and policy, accelerated by crises and national programs in recent decades, employs several analytical paradigms. But sixty years ago there was primarily one perspective, dominated by the author reviewed here. Bestsellers, William B. Munro's two volumes in 1923 represented the culmination of several decades of urban reform and, in turn, generated widespread interest in even more work. As Charles Adrian reports in his ongoing study of this era, the years after Munro's work appeared found reform flourishing quietly, although national reform programs captured the headlines in the 1930s.

The Munro volumes generate both boredom and occasional delight, as well as incisive understanding about a world of urban governance now passed away. How did Munro and his companions perceive urban phenomena? How did that compare with today? Was all that earlier work just so much waste for our own research tasks, rather like reading manuals on the care of carriage horses? What is absent from this earlier account? What is found there that is not found today? And what is found in both the earlier and recent analyses?

WHAT WAS ABSENT?

There are some striking omissions in these landmark books: First, there was little explanation of variations in urban practices. For instance, questions such as "why do some cities do A and others B?" are not asked. Rather, the empirical emphasis was upon description of central tendencies of any given practice.

Second, few comparative local data are organized in a way to support this empirical emphasis, except by referring to the "Cleveland Plan" or

URBAN AFFAIRS QUARTERLY, Vol. 21 No. 2, December 1985 282-287

the "Buffalo Plan" and their operations. Typical of this lack of focus is the fact that there are only three tables and one graph in 1,000 pages.

Moreover, equal treatment is not given to items in any set of reform proposals. Scanning the length of paragraphs on the pros and cons of any measure would tell you Munro's preference. Incidentally, the indexing is superb, as paragraph summaries abound in the margins.

Fourth, there is no indication of how decisions are actually made in the policy world. The second volume deals entirely with administrative mechanisms and a range of public services, but nowhere is the reader told *how* decisions about structure and delivery were made. The emphasis is on formal powers and organizations, rather than on processes.

Fifth, there is almost nothing on intergovernmental relations, especially on the state role (except in public health) or federal role (except in health and vocational education) in supervising municipalities. Characteristically, a chapter on the city and the state focuses almost entirely on constitutional relationships. No web of interacting units is seen here. Rather, the city appears to be floating on its own, like that cloud city in a *Star Wars* movie.

There is also no perception of differential benefits among city groups that today we conceptualize as underlying governing structures and elections forms. Rather, the emphasis is on benefits of structures (efficiency, honesty, equity) that ostensibly *all* citizens desired and sought. For Munro, these are seen as what we came to term "public goods."

Consequently, there is no explanation of the role of status or ethnicity and their attendant group conflict in urban politics and policy. Typically, there is no chapter on urban interest groups.

Finally, as implied above, there is no separation noted between value and empirical propositions. Rather, value propositions are advanced as empirical propositions. For example, home rule is seen as positive because it increases civic education and participation; but no evidence is advanced, only an assertion of both the causation and the value preference.

WHAT WAS PRESENT THEN BUT IS NOT NOW?

If that list seems enough to reject further study of this genre of research, note some of the special qualities that are more often found in

Munro's work than in current writing: First, there is an overwhelming prescription of the right way to act or the right structure about almost anything imaginable. Want to know the proper width of a city street? The proper distance between two lamp posts? Whether to pay councilmen? How to improve fire prevention (wooden buildings were still a major hazard)? On and on, a grand list is offered on how make the city a better place to live. No summary of what we know about city governance today would attempt such prescription, and we may be the poorer for it.

Second, there is a deep knowledge of the history of urban practices from antiquity and across modern systems. There are 80 pages in Volume I before Munro gets to the American municipal scene. Thereafter, each chapter is laden with examples of past and current practices in other nations. This generates a rich sense of the commonality of certain urban problems among nations. On balance, Munro is far more cosmopolitan than those who write on American cities today.

Munro also has an unwavering optimism about the city's capacity, both to reform and to govern itself. There is an allied confidence that the city is not a harmful but a beneficial place for citizens. No Jeffersonian or rural condemnation of cities is found here. Rather, the city is seen as a source of creativity and societal health. It is reminiscent of Eric Hoffer's aphorism, decades later, that the farm and suburb are for drop-outs in the life of the society.

Furthermore, Munro shows a constant concern with constitutions and laws as factors that were not only sources of power but forces that could actually shape society. There is much in this belief of the *polis* shaping society that the Athenians would have understood. Given the legal-institutional and normative orientation of political science 60 years ago, this is understandable. There are separate chapters on city charters, the city as a municipal corporation, and cities' rights and liabilities at law. The implicit assumption is that cities don't make laws, laws make cities.

The volumes also display a vibrant appreciation of the role of party activities in local services, a reminder of a bygone day when party systems were omnipresent and not just historical leftovers. Note also the concern with political factions and cliques in world history as being a natural part of the urban scene. So this work is not antiparty, but anticorrupt party.

WHAT WAS PRESENT THEN AND IS NOW?

But from time to time there emerges in Munro's volumes explicit or assumed concepts and evaluations that do share much with the contemporary urban research:

First, there is a sense of the city as a social construct, linked to dominant social trends and economic vectors. Two chapters focus on the socioeconomic causes and consequences of urban growth. Munro raises questions about this societal link that are familiar in our time; he also raises a truly novel one: Are there physiological differences between city and country folk? (He finds none.)

Munro also shares with us an awareness of the special role of party identification. He cites its origins in the family, notes its size in the population, and sets out its function for the political system. Although he called it "habit," he demonstrates an awareness of the causes and consequences of party identification far ahead of the postwar election research. He also follows Charles Merriam in emphasizing the important functions that parties provide for society.

Furthermore, both Munro and contemporary analysts lament the inadequacies of urban service systems. Some services came off well with Munro, for example, education; early in the century, the best schools in America were in central cities. But many others were judged inadequate in quantity and quality. And like some current writers, Munro was quite clear about how this deficiency should be remedied.

Also, both identify common urban problems. Foremost was crime, but of a different kind than today; note the special problems of the drinking dive, the drug den, and the brothel. Other common then (as now) include corruption in office, congestion of traffic and housing, inefficiency and excessive spending in administration, and the need for more revenue. When Munro reached to other nations or into the past to show the continuing presence of these common problems, he generated a special sense of the urban system as a social, not just an American, phenomenon in human history.

Attendant on these problems, Munro and contemporary analysts both note the conflict between efficiency and equity in urban service delivery. Munro tried to solve the problem by urging that honest and responsive governance would provide both values. We are less sanguine about that today, but the drive for both values remains, although they are still in tension.

Finally, a continuing wonder emerges in both eras at the city's variety and complexity, but Munro is more explicit in his concern for achieving a better city. His concern was passionate, as evidenced here:

> The great city is a stupendous thing—the most intricate piece of social mechanism that the hand of man has created. Who that knows London, for example, can measure in his mind the length and the breadth, the heighth and depth of that leviathan community? . . . What a fermenting vat lies simmering and hid? Gay mansions, with supper rooms in full light. . . . Wretchedness cowers into truckle-beds or shivers hunger-stricken into its lair of straw . . . while councillors of state sit plotting, and playing their high chess game, whereof the pawns are men.
>
> The dream of a better city is one of the oldest in human history. All literature is saturated with it. . . . It has been the everlasting dream of humanity. And humanity will continue to struggle for it, to struggle toward it. And some day, somewhere, to the sons of men the dream will come true [pp. 490-491].

The kinds of questions that urban scholars today ask of the city may have improved, but the style of expression has not. Yet in both there is this "everlasting dream of humanity" about a better city, about Aristotle's belief that people came into cities to live, but stayed there to live well.

WHAT CAN WE LEARN FROM THESE PIONEERS?

This is no place here for a fuller treatment of this question, but there are still several suggestions that Munro's volumes generate:

First, whether in textbooks or more specialized studies, it would help to hear the writer's vision of the city expressed in an explicit fashion.

Second, there is more need to extend our knowledge of non-American cities in order to devise and test the theory of peripheral decision centers in modern national governments. It is not description that is needed, but thinking about the way in which the periphery is both enhanced and bounded by such forces as national currents of ideas, social movements, and values; local traditions of decision making; and developments in non-governmental areas, such as the economy and the professions.

Ultimately, there is a need to return to the normative questions that were overt in an Aristotle and a Munro, but covert in much current writing on cities. How do we devise local governance that maximizes citizen interest and involvement? How do we balance equity and efficiency in a total system of policy delivery, even if it is not possible in each part of that system? What is the proper mix of program inputs from neighborhoods or clients and from professionals?

It is possible that a renewed interest in more explicit normative questions could come from reviewing this earlier state of the art. We need not get lost in the flood of prescriptions that dominated 60 years ago. But a clearer statement of what the normative goals of inquiry are would benefit all who work in this field. How do these goals exist in tension with others, and what are the consequences of recommendations based on them? Here, the next generation of scholars could enrich urban studies in a way that moves beyond both Munro and today's scholars.

—*Frederick M. Wirt*
University of Illinois

Of Special Interest...

CITIES IN TRANSFORMATION

Class, Capital, and the State

edited by MICHAEL PETER SMITH,
Department of Political Science, Tulane University

Cities in Transformation ties the study of "the Urban Question" to development in general social theory. The authors—all significant contributors to the study of urban political economy—debate the scope of individual and local action within the structure of advanced capitalist urbanization. From both Marxian and Weberian traditions, they explore: the system-level dynamics of economic, political, and social structures; new structural patterns of domination and inequality; social consciousness; and the social movements that may or may not emerge from street-level politics.

Holistic in approach, **Cities in Transformation** reaffirms the interdisciplinary character of urban studies as a field that necessarily encompasses political science, history, sociology, economics, planning, and policy analysis.

"This excellent anthology brings us up to date on theoretical developments and empirical research within the framework of left urban political economy. While the twelve authors . . . explore many issues, a main theme unifies the essays—the utility of structuralist analysis for understanding the urban question."

—International Journal of Urban and Regional Research

CONTENTS: **I. Introduction** // 1. Urban Structure, Social Theory, and Political Power MICHAEL PETER SMITH // **II. Urban Political Economy and Social Theory** // 2. The Structuralist Critique in Urban Studies C.G. PICKVANCE / 3. Structure, Agency, and Urban Redevelopment ROBERT A. BEAUREGARD // **III. From Theory to Empirical Research** // 4. Structural Fetishism in the New Urban Theory J. ALLEN WHITT / 5. The Fiscal Crisis of the City MICHAEL D. KENNEDY / 6. Urbanization in the World-System: New Directions for Research CHRISTOPHER CHASE-DUNN // **IV. Economic Growth and the Restructuring of Cities** // 7. Urban Political Economy: Emergence, Consolidation, and Development RICHARD CHILD HILL / 8. The New Labor Demand in Global Cities SASKIA SASSEN-KOOB / 9. American Cities: The Production of Ideology MICHAEL PETER SMITH & DENNIS R. JUDD // **V. Structural Change and Social Conflict in the City** // 10. Debate on the Theory of Space: Toward an Urban Praxis M. GOTTDIENER / 11. Structuralism, Class Conflict, and Urban Reality DAVID C. PERRY / 12. Space and Society: Managing the New Historical Relationships MANUEL CASTELLS

Urban Affairs Annual Reviews, Volume 26
1984 / 288 pages / $28.00 (h) / $14.00 (p)

SAGE PUBLICATIONS, INC.
275 South Beverly Drive,
Beverly Hills, California 90212

SAGE PUBLICATIONS LTD
28 Banner Street,
London EC1Y 8QE, England

SAGE PUBLICATIONS INDIA PVT LTD
M-32 Market, Greater Kailash I, New Delhi 110 048, India

URBAN AFFAIRS *Quarterly*

volume 21, number 3 / march 1986

SAGE PUBLICATIONS

URBAN AFFAIRS *Quarterly*

SAGE Publications / *Beverly Hills* / *London* / *New Delhi*

URBAN AFFAIRS *Quarterly*

volume 21, number 3 / march 1986

contents

Editors' Note 291

Urban Response to Federal Program Flexibility:
Politics of Community Development Block Grant
KENNETH K. WONG
PAUL E. PETERSON 293

The Reagan Urban Policy and Its Impacts
HAROLD WOLMAN 311

Energy and Urban Form:
A Human Ecological Critique
VALERIE A. HAINES 337

Comment on "Energy and Urban Form"
JON VAN TIL 355

The Effect of Economic Dependence on Urban Primacy:
A Cross-National Panel Analysis
R. SCOTT FREY
THOMAS DIETZ
JANE MARTE 359

The Determinants of Gentrification in the United States:
A City-Level Analysis
BRUCE LONDON
BARRETT A. LEE
S. GREGORY LIPTON 369

Housing Constraint and Household Complexity in Metropolitan America:
Black and Spanish-Origin Minorities
LAUREN J. KRIVO
JAN E. MUTCHLER 389

Economic and Policy Implications of Hosting Sports Franchises: *Lessons from Baltimore*
ARTHUR T. JOHNSON 411

Reevaluating the Benefits and Costs of Industrial Revenue Bonds
MATTHEW R. MARLIN 435

Rejoinder to Matthew R. Marlin's "Reevaluating the Benefits and Costs of Industrial Revenue Bonds"
THOMAS A. PASCARELLA
RICHARD D. RAYMOND 443

Book Review Essay

Suburbanization, Segregation, and Politics
ROY B. FLEMMING 448

MANUSCRIPTS should be submitted to the editors in care of The Editors, **URBAN AFFAIRS QUARTERLY,** Center for Metropolitan Studies, University of Missouri, 8001 Natural Bridge Rd., St Louis, MO 63121. Include *five* (5) copies of the manuscript. Full-length manuscripts should not exceed 25 pages total and research notes should not exceed 10 pages total (*including* footnotes, references, and tables or figures). All text, footnotes, and references should be typewritten with one-inch margins and double-spaced. All references to the author's previous work should be omitted in the text. Footnotes and bibliographic citations should follow the current **UAQ** style. Copies of the style sheets may be obtained from the editors or the publisher. A brief biographical paragraph describing each author's current affiliation, research interests, and recent publications should be submitted, and an abstract of approximately 100 words should accompany each copy of the manuscript.

Manuscripts will not be returned to authors. Please keep copies for your own needs. The editors assume that manuscripts are for the exclusive consideration of **UAQ** and have not simultaneously been submitted elsewhere.

BOOKS FOR REVIEW should be sent to The Editors, **URBAN AFFAIRS QUARTERLY,** Center for Metropolitan Studies, University of Missouri, 8001 Natural Bridge Road, St. Louis, MO 63121. Potential contributors of book review essays are encouraged to correspond with Professor Susan MacManus, Book Review Editor, **URBAN AFFAIRS QUARTERLY,** Department of Political Science, Cleveland State University, Cleveland, OH 44115, before submitting manuscripts.

URBAN AFFAIRS QUARTERLY is published four times annually—in September, December, March, and June—by Sage Publications, Inc., 275 South Beverly Drive, Beverly Hills, CA 90212.

Subscriptions: Regular institutional rate $63.00 per year. Individuals may subscribe at a one-year rate of $25.00. Add $6.00 for subscriptions outside the United States. Orders from the U.K., Europe, the Middle East, and Africa should be sent to London address (below). Orders from India should be sent to the New Delhi address (below). Noninstitutional orders **must** be paid by personal check.

Second class postage paid at Beverly Hills, California. ISSN 0042-0816

This journal is abstracted or indexed in **Sage Urban Studies Abstracts, Human Resources Abstracts, Educational Administration Abstracts, Sociological Abstracts, Abstracts for Social Workers, ABC POL SCI, Sociology of Education Abstracts, Urban Affairs Abstracts, Sage Public Administration Abstracts, International Political Science Abstracts, Ethnic Studies Bibliography, Public Affairs Information Service, Ekistic Index, Current Contents, Social Science Citation Index,** and **United States Political Science Documents,** and is available on microfilm from University Microfilms, Ann Arbor, Michigan.

Back Issues: Information about availability and prices of back issues may be obtained from the publisher's order department (address below). Single-issue orders for 5 or more copies will receive a special adoption discount. Contact the order department for details. Write to London office for sterling prices.

Inquiries: Address all correspondence and permissions requests to SAGE PUBLICATIONS, Inc., 275 South Beverly Drive, Beverly Hills, California 90212. Inquiries and subscriptions from the U.K., Europe, the Middle East, and Africa should be sent to SAGE PUBLICATIONS Ltd, 28 Banner Street, London EC1Y 8QE, England. From India, write to SAGE PUBLICATIONS INDIA Pvt. Ltd, P.O. Box 4215, New Delhi 110 048 India. Other orders should be sent to the Beverly Hills office.

Claims: Claims for undelivered copies must be made no later than three months following month of publication. The publisher will supply missing copies when losses have been sustained in transit and when the reserve stock will permit.

Change of Address: Six weeks' advance notice must be given when notifying of change of address. Please send old address label along with the new address to insure proper identification. Please specify name of journal. POSTMASTER: Send change of address to: Urban Affairs Quarterly, c/o 275 South Beverly Drive, Beverly Hills, CA 90212.

FROM THE NEW EDITORS

With this issue, *Urban Affairs Quarterly* is located at a new home, the Center for Metropolitan Studies at the University of Missouri—St. Louis. Since its founding in September 1965, *UAQ* has been the leading American journal for interdisciplinary urban research. Throughout the 1960s, *UAQ* published scholarly analyses of the compelling issues defining the "urban crisis": for example, racial discrimination and segregation, urban violence, poverty, disparities in education, crime, and suburban white flight. As social, economic, and cultural priorities have changed, so has the content of the journal. In the 1980s, the ascendant issues are related to international economic interdependence and urban growth, regional competition and conflict (the Sunbelt versus the Frostbelt), the economic transformation of older cities (deindustrialization, tourism, and service sector growth), the gentrification of older neighborhoods, and new service delivery innovations (such as privatization of urban services).

In our view, our most important editorial responsibilities are to ensure that *UAQ* will continue to be responsive to the scholarly community that it serves. Urban scholars will ultimately make the decisions about what should be published in these pages so that the journal continues to reflect the evolving urban scene.

The pivotal element in this editorial process is peer review. All papers submitted to *UAQ* are sent to three referees, chosen on the basis of their demonstrated expertise in the appropriate subject matter or specialty. We make editorial decisions only when adequate peer review is in hand. We are also committed to the principle that invited articles should be the exception, not the rule.

The several associate editors and an expanded editorial board provide scholarly input from several academic disciplines—political science, sociology, planning, history, black studies, economics, law, demography, and geography. One-third of the membership of the editorial board will change each year, making room for a frequent infusion of new ideas and perspectives.

We would like to thank the previous editor, Albert Hunter, and former managing editor, Rodney Nelson, for their assistance during the transition period. Bryan Jones, the former book review editor, also has been very helpful. Our thanks also to the Center for Urban Affairs and Policy Research at Northwestern University.

A CALL FOR PAPERS

We want to take this occasion to issue a call for papers. We encourage the submission of manuscripts and papers that the authors feel can contribute significantly to a fuller and more precise understanding of urban problems and issues. Articles on a wide variety of topics, and from all disciplinary perspectives, are published by *UAQ*. Authors normally will be notified regarding publication decisions within two months of the date of submission.

URBAN RESPONSE TO FEDERAL PROGRAM FLEXIBILITY
Politics of Community Development Block Grant

KENNETH K. WONG
University of Oregon

PAUL E. PETERSON
Brookings Institution

Categorical programs, considered the backbone of "creative federalism" in the 1960s, are no longer in vogue in the 1980s. The increasing prominence of block grants in our federal grant system merits a closer look at the likely policy consequences following program consolidation. Our longitudinal study of the Community Development Block Grant in two large cities suggests that the increased level of local discretion resulted in less emphasis on the redistributive needs of low-income residents. Moreover, decisions with respect to the block grant inevitably become part of the local political process, and in these two cities, were influenced by mayoral preferences.

Categorical programs, considered the backbone of "creative federalism" in the 1960s, are no longer in vogue in the 1980s. Replacement of categoricals with block grants in the 1970s was seen by many policy-makers as an effective means to eliminate bureaucratic red tape, restrain the federal role, enhance local discretion, and encourage private-sector incentives. In addition to the consolidation of 57 categorical programs into 9 block grants, as authorized in the 1981 Omnibus Budget Reconciliation Act, the Reagan administration proposed a $47 billion "swap" of federal and state services, which would have further reduced federal direction of intergovernmental programs. If the Reagan "new

AUTHORS' NOTE: *This is a revised draft of a paper presented at the 1982 annual meeting of the Association for Public Policy Analysis and Management at Minneapolis. The revision has benefited from the comments of three anonymous referees.*

URBAN AFFAIRS QUARTERLY, Vol. 21 No. 3, March 1986 293-309

federalism" proposal were fully enacted, categorical programs' portion in the federal grant-in-aid system would drop from 79% in 1980 to a mere 34% in 1986 (Pechman, 1982).

The increasing prominence of block grants in our federal grant system merits a closer look at the likely policy consequences following program consolidation. The new flexibility has shifted many policy decisions from federal administrative agencies to local institutions. In the absence of tight federal regulations, block grant resources become increasingly subject to local economic and political interests. Our longitudinal study of one major block grant in two big cities suggests that the increased level of local discretion resulted in less emphasis on the redistributive needs of low-income residents. Moreover, decisions with respect to the block grant inevitably became part of the local political process and, in these two cities, were influenced by mayoral preferences. The mayors, with the help of their key political advisers, allocated block grant resources in such a manner as to benefit themselves politically without sacrificing the communities' long-term economic interests. Before documenting these findings on the management of the Community Development Block Grant programs in Milwaukee and Baltimore, an elaboration on our basic arguments is needed.

DEFINING URBAN FISCAL CONCERNS AND POLITICAL LEADERSHIP

Both local economic constraints and political leaders influence block grant policy decisions. In reaching these conclusions, we differ from recent studies of federal program management. In much of this literature, the emphasis is on the pluralism of the urban political system, and the city's economic constraints are largely overlooked. Political leadership is also seen as having only modest importance (one exception is Mollenkopf, 1983). According to many analysts, given the pluralistic political environment, differences must be resolved through compromise, plans must be delayed, policies must be modified to satisfy diverse participants, and allocative benefits must be secured through coalitional resources (Pressman and Wildavsky, 1973; Derthick, 1972; Browning et al., 1984). Political leaders are mere brokers who resolve the issues others place before them.

Although the pluralistic approach has been well developed and has enriched much of our understanding of the ways federal programs are carried out, it is not by itself an adequate explanation for policy decisions taken at the local level, particularly in the period of fiscal austerity that began in the mid-1970s. Although political realities may have consequences, they do so in a context in which the economic needs and fiscal interests of local communities place important limitations on the choices made. Organized demands become effective only when they do not contradict the economic interest of the community.

Local discretion under the block grant arrangement is likely to mean less attention to redistributive needs. Regardless of their internal power alignment, local communities attempt to maximize their economic prosperity. Local communities are more constrained than the federal government by the environmental context in which they operate, because they have to compete with one another in exporting their goods (Peterson, 1981). Local jurisdictions cannot regulate the flow of productive resources—labor and capital. Without economic growth, the local government faces a stable or shrinking fiscal base. Accordingly, local communities are most likely to promote the types of policies that enhance their economic well being and to avoid policies that have negative effects on the local economy.

Because of the competitive context in which local communities operate, one can usefully distinguish between "developmental" and "redistributive" policies. *Developmental* policies are those public programs that enhance the economic position of the city in its competition with other areas. These policies strengthen the local economy, enhance the local tax base, and generate additional resources. By contrast, *redistributive* policies are those programs that benefit low-income residents but, at the same time, may negatively affect the local economy by attracting the needy and discouraging entry of productive resources. One can roughly calculate whether a policy is redistributive by estimating whether those who pay for services in local taxes are those who are receiving the services. If there is no overlap at all, such as in welfare assistance to nontaxpayers, it is a case of pure redistribution. Thus, in order to preserve the city's fiscal base, local administrations are constrained to place economic development objectives ahead of any concern they might have for social equality. With ambiguous federal objectives and an emphasis on local discretion, block grants allow leaders of local communities to pursue their own (very likely developmental) goals with the monies that block grants made available. We hypothesize that the federal government's redistributive intent, as often embedded and enforced in the categorical structuring of the grant-in-aid system, will be increasingly difficult to realize under the decentralized mechanism.

Categorical grants not only restricted local flexibility, they also were carried out within an intergovernmental system in which professional identifications and expertise become valuable political resources (Nathan et al., 1977). As the move to the block grant takes place, we expect the value of these resources to diminish. Instead, we expect to find the influence of elected politicians and their political allies to be more salient. First, political leadership is required for the effective pursuit of the development goals. Often, institutions dominated by policy professionals tend toward insularity and isolation from other institutions and sources of political support (Weidner, 1967). These professionals have fewer incentives to mobilize outsiders or to relinquish standard operating procedures. In contrast, political leaders are capable of mobilizing the private sector and of soliciting support for their policies from the electorate and various community groups.

As elected leaders become involved, they turn federal programs in a developmental direction not only because they are economically beneficial to the local economy but also because they are politically beneficial to the city leadership. The benefits of a developmental policy are widely enough distributed that policymakers are not likely to suffer much criticism for their efforts. Mayor Richard Daley, for example, was remembered as the prime figure in coordinating the interests of his political machine, the professional bureaucrats, and the downtown business for Chicago's development (Gove and Masotti, 1982). Richard Lee of New Haven, an equally consummate politician, was able to turn his widely publicized achievement in urban renewal into continued electoral support (Dahl, 1961; Wolfinger, 1974). Likewise, Boston's popular mayor, John Collins, was responsible for the ambitious use of federal funds to improve the rapid transit system (McQuade, 1966). As past chairman of San Francisco's redevelopment agency, Mayor Joseph Alioto successfully put together a political coalition of labor, real estate, and corporations as the organizational basis for his urban renewal programs (Hartman, 1974; Brugmann and Sletteland, 1971).

Finally, block grants allow local leadership to employ portions of the federal resources in ways that are even more directly related to their own political needs. Studies of political machines have long explained public resource allocation in terms of partisan calculations (Banfield and Wilson, 1963). Machine bosses were characterized by their effective delivery of a wide variety of material incentives in return for their votes. While categorical program distributions are governed in part by regulations, block grants can now be used in a less restrictive manner to recruit new supporters, consolidate existing loyalties, and suppress dissidents. What once may have been the exclusive practice of the political machine can now become the general norm for many city leaders.

THE COMMUNITY DEVELOPMENT BLOCK GRANT

These analyses are substantiated in our study of the implementation of the Community Development Block Grant (CDBG) in Baltimore and Milwaukee during the first seven program years, 1975-1981. As a major pillar of the Nixon administration's "new federalism," the 1974 Community Development Block Grant consolidated seven categorical programs and allowed for extensive local discretion in federally funded community development programs. Unlike its categorical predecessors, the block grant was governed by loosely defined requirements with respect to application, evaluation, and audit procedures. For example, the 1974 program consolidation reduced grant regulations from 2,600 pages to 120 pages, the number of annual applications from 5 to 1, and the average application size from 1,400 pages to 50 pages (GAO, 1977). Local jurisdictions were not required to create specialized administrative agencies.

Although the emphasis on local discretion remained intact, the CDBG legislation also encouraged local attention to the needs of the low-income population. The original legislation represented a compromise between those senators who wanted a greater federal presence at the local level and the Nixon administration's proposals for a more restrained federal role. As a result, the 1974 law allowed for a substantial degree of local flexibility but, at the same time, required the local use of federal dollars to provide "decent housing and suitable living environment and expanding economic opportunities, principally for persons of low and moderate income" (Section 101 (c) of Title I of the 1974 Housing and Community Development Act). Indeed, among the seven areas of eligible activities were some highly redistributive services, such as the "reduction of the isolation of low income group and the promotion of neighborhood diversity." Subsequent legislative amendments in 1977 and 1978 tightened the provisions related to citizen participation from low-income neighborhoods, housing assistance plans, and the more "targeted" use of federal resources for the inner-city poor. In these Carter years of "creeping recategorization," the HUD monitoring role became more vigorous. Although these redistributive emphases have been substantially relaxed under the Reagan administration, the CDBG legislation (particularly during the 1978-1980 period) did encourage the localities to pursue certain redistributive goals.

To examine how the CDBG was being implemented, intensive research was carried out in Baltimore and Milwaukee. The two cities were selected for their differences (on contextual details of the two cities, see Wong, 1983; Peterson and Wong, 1985). While both were hard-pressed, declining central cities, Milwaukee, with its more diversified industries, had proven more capable of maintaining its economic base. Since the 1960s, Baltimore has experienced severe population loss and industrial out-migration, falling retail sales, and widespread neighborhood decay. Although the two cities have been governed under strong mayoral leadership, local political culture also differed. Whereas "machine-style" politics prevailed in Baltimore, Milwaukee inherited strong reform tradition. Because of these differences in fiscal needs, as well as local norms and practices, we were able to see how different local administrations responded to the federal block grant arrangement.

To supplement documentary sources, interviews were conducted with federal and local officials and with informed observers of the block grants in these two cities during 1981-1982. Interviews with local housing officials included top-level administrators in city hall, members of the staff responsible for the CDBG programs, and representatives of community groups. News reporters, academics, and other informed observers were also consulted. Together with documentary sources, these interviews provided us with the information that formed the basis of our analysis. Quotations in this article are taken directly from these interviews.

CITIES' FISCAL INTEREST AND BLOCK GRANT IMPLEMENTATION

Despite significant differences in political culture between Milwaukee and Baltimore, local leaders' responses toward the greater degree of flexibility in community development were strikingly similar.

Recognizing their weakened economic capacity, local political leaders focused their CDBG programs on developmental goals, even though this meant that CDBG only modestly addressed the communities' redistributive needs. Specific development strategies were found to be varied. Although both administrations concentrated a significant amount of federal resources on housing preservation, Baltimore was more anxious to revitalize its downtown and commercial base. In both cases, these policy choices proved to be electorally rewarding to leadership. In this section, we will look at how the economic needs of each of the two cities had an impact on community development strategies. The next section will focus on the extent to which political considerations had their own impact.

In the absence of tight federal guidelines, local officials saw CDBG federal allocation as another lump sum available to the city that was flexible enough to be allocated in whatever ways they preferred. In Milwaukee, community development resources were used to preserve the property-owner neighborhoods at the city's outer rings. In Baltimore, the administration had directed CDBG projects to support the city's ambitious and glamorous revitalization plan in the very heart of the city's downtown commercial area. CDBG resources were seldom used to ameliorate the housing needs of the inner-city poor, which were estimated to be as many as one-third of the renter-households in both cities.

INCREASING PROMINENCE OF DEVELOPMENTAL PROJECTS IN MILWAUKEE

The Community Development Block Grant has played a vital role in Milwaukee's revitalization strategy, the primary objective of which was to sustain property value and neighborhood stability in the city's outlying communities. Consistent with this broad community development goal, Milwaukee's neighborhoods were categorized into three distinct types, according to their economic vitality (City of Milwaukee, 1977). Geographically, the "inner core" overlapped with the inner city, while the "stable neighborhoods" were predominantly outlying areas adjacent to the suburbs. The "transitional areas" lay between these two rings. This pattern was often referred to as the "doughnut and the doughnut hole" among local officials, with the "doughnut" being the transition area, and the "hole" the inner-city slums too deteriorated to be worth preservation efforts. Needless to say, the three areas had very different economic characteristics. The further an area was from the inner city, the more stable was its property value. The outlying stable areas, consisting of 64% of the city's housing stocks, had the healthiest investment environment with high and increasing homeownership, active market sales, and rising prices. By contrast, the housing stock in the inner core had the "lowest assessed values, the lowest rate of owner occupancy, and the highest vacancy rate relative to the other areas."

To curb the deteriorating trend from proliferating beyond the inner core, elected leaders in Milwaukee decided to focus on the preservation of transition neighborhoods. Since 1979, the emphasis on housing preservation and rehabilitation has become the leading CDBG priority (City of Milwaukee, 1979). Significantly, these CDBG programs were seen as vital in the maintenance of a stable property-owner base in Milwaukee. As one official proudly pointed out, "Blighted areas have not expanded as a result of our many CDBG rehabilitation loan programs." Another administrator concurred: "Because CDBG helped to preserve the housing stock and stabilize the living environment in transitional areas, new families were more willing to buy their houses in the city." Consequently, as suggested in Table 1, CDBG resources being spent for developmental housing purposes increased steadily from 36% of the total entitlement to almost 60% over the first seven program years. By contrast, other (mostly allocational) expenditures have steadily declined. Capital improvement projects, such as sewerage and waterworks, which lacked a clear policy focus, were rated as less favorable. By 1982, capital improvement projects were receiving merely half of what they used to get in the initial program period, while the total sum allotted for "house-keeping purposes" shrank considerably.

BALTIMORE'S RENAISSANCE

Encountering economic problems more severe than those in Milwaukee, officials in Baltimore had, for some years, initiated more comprehensive community development policies to combat against any further deterioration of the city's fiscal base. Since the early 1970s, city officials have underscored both the preservation of existing housing stocks and the revitalization of those deteriorating neighborhoods in which massive demolition and relocation projects had previously been carried out. These housing policies were further reinforced by numerous joint city-business endeavors to revitalize the downtown and the central business district. Unless such a grand development scheme was undertaken, city officials were concerned that consumers would stay away from the city's downtown, and homeowners would choose to move out of the city altogether.

TABLE 1
Expenditure Pattern of CDBG Funds in Milwaukee and Baltimore, 1975-1981

	1975-76	1976-77	1977-78	1978-79	1979-80	1980-81	1981-82
MILWAUKEE							
Developmental	35.9%	41.7%	54.7%	44.8%	50.3%	54.3%	58.5%
Redistributive	0.6	0.6	0.2	6.3	2.3	5.0	3.8
Allocational	63.5	57.8	45.0	48.9	47.4	40.7	37.7
Total Percent	100.0	100.1	99.9	100.0	100.0	100.0	100.0
Total Allocation (in $million)	13.4	13.4	12.6	20.0	21.4	22.8	22.5
BALTIMORE							
Developmental	71.2	49.2	59.3	56.7	60.2	54.0	55.6
Redistributive	0.6	2.3	4.0	3.7	3.1	5.2	8.3
Allocational	28.2	48.5	36.7	39.6	36.7	40.7	36.0
Total Percent	100.0	100.0	100.0	100.0	100.0	99.9	99.9
Total Allocation (in $million)	30.6	30.9	47.4[a]	35.3[b]	49.0[c]	36.8[d]	35.7[e]

SOURCES: Milwaukee, Community Development Agency, **CDBG Program: Project Summary**, from 1975-76 to 1981-82. Baltimore, Department of Housing and Community Development, **CDBG Program: Project Summary**, from 1974-75 to 1981-82. Categorization and percentage calculations are our own. In some cases, total percentages exceed 100 or are less than 100 due to rounding off figures.

NOTE: Definitions of the three expenditure categories are found in Peterson (1981). We have been highly selective with regard to what is classified as developmental. Preventing the further spread of "slums and blighted" influences from deteriorated areas through urban renewal projects, reinforcing the quality of housing stocks in transitional areas largely through joint endeavors with loan institutions in the private sector, and encouraging further private sector involvement in downtown/commercial projects are clearly developmental activities and are so classified. On the other hand, all services delivered to the handicapped and the elderly (regardless of their income brackets), and those projects for which only low-income residents were eligible are classified as redistributive. Finally, allocational programs included those additional services that reinforce routine municipal responsibilities. These projects varied from water and sewage works, community cultural and recreational activities, instructional and library services to the maintenance of planning and administrative staffs. Although in many cases these projects reinforce developmental activities, because their purpose remains somewhat ambiguous the middle classification is more appropriate.

a. This total included $13,621,102 Urban Renewal Surplus fund and $4,735,000 anticipated "Program Income," in addition to the $29,042,000 federal CDBG allocation. The city did not provide data on the use of **only** the federal CDBG allocation from 1977 to 1981.

b. This total included $7,108,100 anticipated "Program Income" in addition to the $28.24 million federal allocation.

c. This grand total included $17,818,800 anticipated "Program Income" in addition to the $31,185,000 federal allocation.

d. This grand total included $521,000 anticipated "Program Income" and $2,463,900 "city bond" funds, in addition to the $32,579,744 federal allocation.

e. This grand total included $660,000 anticipated "Program Income" and $2.3 million "city bond" funds, in addition to the $32.58 million federal CDGB allocation.

Deeply concerned with the much weakened city fiscal base, the William Schaefer administration called for the city's "renaissance," through which Baltimore would be recognized and praised "as a vital, full-blown, modern metropolis." What was emerging was opulence alongside adversity. In a flamboyant manner, Mayor Schaefer used a combination of CDBG funds, private sources, and other federal grants and loans to engage in an extensive variety of revitalization projects in the central financial district and its surrounding areas, as well as in various designated transitional neighborhoods. The well-known Harbor Place, Convention Center, World Trade Center, the Hyatt, and the $12 million Walbrook Shopping Center were some of the projects that made up the city's "renaissance." To attract new homeowners, particularly young, professional couples, local officials promoted the Coldspring "New Town In-Town" project, which was subsidized with over $15 million in CD funds. Federal block grant resources also helped to maintain residential rehabilitation in its many decaying areas, improve the living environment in deteriorating neighborhoods, and demolish slums and blighted areas throughout the city. CDBG-funded projects were said to have brought about the revitalization of Upton, Union Square, Reservoir Hill, South Baltimore, Fells Point, Barley Circle, and a number of transitional communities throughout Baltimore. In light of these highly visible developmental activities, city officials firmly believed these projects could "bolster the city's real estate tax base as well as providing additional jobs." As shown in Table 1, these developmental activities consistently consumed well over half of Baltimore's block grant funds over time. At the same time, neighborhood revitalization has been further supported by a variety of capital improvement undertakings, which constituted a significant portion of the stable allocational expenditure.

MODEST REDISTRIBUTIVE ACTIVITIES IN THE TWO CITIES

Unlike developmental programs, redistributive concern was far from a central feature on the two cities' community development agenda. As shown in Table 1, neither city has spent more than one-tenth of its block grant resources on housing services for the poor in any single year between 1975 and 1981. While Milwaukee fluctuated in its services for the poor, Baltimore has consistently expanded its redistributive activities from less than 1% to more than 8% of its block grant budget in the seven-year period. Although both cities have steadily increased their redistributive spending, in part due to the Carter administration's "creeping recategorization," the redistributive realm remained modest throughout the years. Since the CDBG started in 1975, Milwaukee officials have only initiated one major project of a purely redistributive character, which improved the physical conditions of public housing units during 1978-1979. Most of the very few redistributive undertakings were related either to the elderly (such as providing them with transportation) or to the handicapped (mostly on accessibility to buildings). Other services were provided to certain disadvantaged groups, such as counseling service to delinquents and hot-line service for the mentally disturbed. There was also a medical check-up program for all city residents. In Baltimore, the few redistributive projects included services for the elderly, legal aid, public housing security, and a number of Model Cities-type activities. In short, despite the impact of the Carter years, our two cases suggest that only a small portion of the CD fund was used to meet housing-related needs of the aged and the low-income groups.

Despite their modest efforts in providing housing services to the needy, city officials had virtually no difficulty in complying with federal regulations, which required that 75% of the CDBG funds be spent on "low and moderate income" residents in a three-year period. Given the fact that relatively large areas of the two cities fell below the median income level, city officials enjoyed a considerable amount of discretion in targeting block grant resources to those neighborhoods in which the most critical developmental efforts were needed. CDBG-funded projects in poor areas, moreover, did not need to be redistributive. Constructing new shopping centers and improving the quality of housing stock in transitional neighborhoods provided typical examples of projects that were located in less well-off communities but were largely designed to strengthen the local tax capacity. Other undertakings, such as the pulling down of blighted structures in deteriorating neighborhoods, often improve the living environment of the affected communities but, at the same time, substantially displace poor families who can no longer afford the higher rent. These are the kinds of policy consequences that one expects to find in central cities such as Baltimore and Milwaukee. In other words, our analyses differentiated between, on one hand, those CDBG projects that were located in deteriorating neighborhoods but constituted an important component of the city's overall redevelopment strategy and, on the other, those programs that primarily delivered services to the low-income population without generating remunerative returns. In short, the use of CDBG funds in low- and moderate-income neighborhoods notwithstanding, officials in both Milwaukee and Baltimore had designed their CDBG projects in ways that were consistent with the citywide revitalization programs.

POLITICAL INFLUENCE AND THE BLOCK GRANT

The decentralized character of the block grant not only allows the local administration to focus on the city's economic concerns, it also enables political elites to exercise more complete influence over program resources. Studies of the early years of the CDBG have recognized the exercise of program control by local "generalists," the declining importance of administrative expertise in prior categorical programs, and the rising significance of electoral concerns (Nathan et al., 1977a, 1977b; Dommel et al., 1978, 1980, 1982). Our study not only confirms these findings, but further suggests that the prominent role of local political elites has continued to expand beyond the initial program years. Even more important, political power seems to have emanated from the federally endorsed local discretion over CDBG funds. Indeed, an effective exercise of political leadership is evident in the programs in the two cities. While Baltimore and Milwaukee were readily distinguished in their local norms and administrative practices, their elected leadership seemed to have accrued considerable political gains from their block grants, particularly through their active involvement in a number of highly visible, communitywide, developmental projects. In neither case did professional administrators play a predominant role in major decisions.

POLITICAL LEADERSHIP IN MILWAUKEE

Milwaukee's socialist-progressive tradition has not precluded Henry Maier from becoming a powerful mayor over his two-and-a-half-decade tenure. The mayor not only won an unprecedented electoral victory following his handling of the 1967 racial disturbances, his cautious fiscal policy has proven to be popular throughout the 1970s. Mayor Maier's influence was expanded because of the community development block grant. The administration's emphasis on housing preservation in transitional neighborhoods was said to have particularly pleased the southside residents, who backed the mayor during the unusually close race in 1980. Although there had been numerous well-publicized incidents of disagreement during the initial program period, the mayor and powerful members of the city council reportedly came to terms on most of the CDBG issues. Neighborhood preservation as the leading program priority was widely endorsed by city council members, who were anxious to maintain a healthy environment in their respective communities. To make sure that block grant policies were politically beneficial to them, influential council members actively participated in the decision-making process. Indeed, program priorities and allocative guidelines were worked out between the political elites and were found to be the most important determinants on CDBG spending (Steger, 1984).

As the block grant became more institutionalized with well-defined priorities, about the only controversy among political leaders was over financing their pet projects. Political allies and supporters of the mayor were often hired as consultants, rewarded CDBG projects, and appointed as citizen representatives to the CDBG advisory bodies. As one neighborhood worker summarized, "Neighborhood groups are seen as either pro- or anti-mayor." CDBG resources also reinforced the mayor's "patronage" base in the city administration. Administrative expense in the CDBG, although slightly lessened in recent years, remained high enough to support a staff of some 20 people as well as a disproportionately large planning body. Given that the block grant did not encourage any "island of functional power" but, instead, consolidated the mayoral influence, it was no surprise that informed observers concluded, "The biggest winner of the CDBG is the Maier administration."

POLITICAL LEADERSHIP IN BALTIMORE

Unlike Milwaukee, Baltimore has all the characteristics of a machine-like city with a tradition of patronage practices. With no exception, Mayor Schaefer was the prime figure in the community development block grant. The mayor was "entirely committed, and has an obsession with Baltimore," said an official. "He is not ruthless, but allows nothing to get in his way." The mayor was particularly concerned with the block grant because it played an essential role in his "renaissance" to revitalize the city's declining commercial and residential bases. Equally important was the fact that the Schaefer administration had so far been judged by the extent to which the mayor was able to realize his renaissance. As a result, the Schaefer administration used the community development resources to demonstrate its commitment to the revitalization plan, thereby sending a clear signal to the private sector that downtown interests were regarded as paramount. Often, millions of CD dollars were allocated to the mayor's renaissance projects without much discussion outside the mayor's inner circle and without properly informing the federal agency (Smith, 1980).

In order to mobilize community support for his renaissance, Mayor Schaefer allocated portions of the CDBG funds to coopt neighborhood groups. Community groups that supported the administration's renaissance have been getting the lion's share of the many CDBG-funded rehabilitation and Model Cities-type services. Outspoken dissenting groups were said to have disturbed the mayor, who seemed to want to avoid public controversy. These organizations received hardly any CDBG projects. For example, the Coalition of Peninsula Organizations (COPO), which represented the area south of the Inner Harbor, was not allocated any CDBG dollars for two years because its leaders had criticized the mayor's community development policies. Significantly, the mayor's tactics seemed to be working. Some previously dissenting leaders joined the administration, and others were more willing to moderate their opposition in exchange for city grants. As a result, under Schaefer's leadership, the city's renaissance came alive and neighborhood revitalization was vigorously pursued. Because of these diversified CDBG-funded, land-use policies, the mayor claimed that the city had gone through a phase in which "its residents, disheartened by the exodus to the suburbs and the racial strife of the 1960s, began to see that Baltimore had potential." "We were dying on the vine," the mayor reflected, "I had to convince my own people first that the city had a future" (Baltimore Sun, December 31, 1980). And the mayor seemed to have done it and, indeed, was rewarded by an overwhelming victory for a fourth term in 1983.

CONCLUSIONS

Our study on the community development block grant indicates that the cities' economic needs predominantly shaped program priorities, once the federal government replaced well-defined program objectives and regulations with an emphasis on local discretion and flexibility. Responding to fiscal necessity, political leadership in Milwaukee and Baltimore effectively directed block grant resources toward fiscally beneficial developmental goals, while paying modest attention to the housing needs of the poor.

The pervasiveness of economic constraints, however, cannot displace the importance of political factors. Instead, politics operates within these economically shaped limits. Specifically, the adoption of different developmental projects in Milwaukee and Baltimore is in part due to the political elites' electoral concerns. In Milwaukee, Mayor Maier and influential city council members supported the preservation policy, which focused on neighborhoods in transition, because such a development strategy was both economically and electorally sound. In Baltimore, the more comprehensive strategy that revitalized the city center was believed to be necessary to encourage further business involvement, so vital to the city's economic recovery. Undoubtedly, through their direct participation in major revitalization projects, local leaders were able to serve both the communities' economic interest and their own electoral ambitions.

Given the CDBG experiences in Milwaukee and Baltimore, it is likely that central cities in the 1980s will adopt a developmental strategy in their use of federal block grants. Redistributive needs are not likely to gain recognition under the more politicized block grant arrangement. Also, the few redistributive activities will become even more confined to the few deteriorating neighborhoods. For example, the urban leadership is unlikely to channel resources for low-income housing projects outside of these decaying areas. Given the extent of fiscal constraints, localities will be extremely reluctant to use block grant dollars to provide for citywide redistributive services. The Reagan administration's spending cuts and policy on program consolidation will only reinforce these local preferences. In short, the federal block grant approach seems likely to render an intergovernmental grant system that is less capable of promoting redistributive objectives. Finally, although developmental choices are both economically and politically attractive, limited federal resources preclude a uniform distribution of developmental programs throughout the city. Instead, local officials are expected to target their developmental undertakings in those designated transitional neighborhoods, where the more critical battle against further urban decay is being fought.

Central cities, facing enormous economic challenges since the mid-1970s, often require political leadership to bring about neighborhood stability and a revitalized local economy. Our study of the CDBG in two big cities suggests the kinds of urban responses that are likely to occur when the federal government relaxes its regulatory presence. Program flexibility, although ill-suited for redistributive purpose, seems effective in promoting community revitalization. The current federal policy emphasis on local discretion is likely to encourage an even greater degree of local innovation in dealing with each city's own specific set of social and economic problems. But given the cities' fiscal priorities and the limited pool of available resources, it is unlikely that urban leaders, at least for some time, will be capable of addressing the needs of their impoverished residents.

REFERENCES

BANFIELD, E. and J. Q. WILSON (1963) City Politics. New York: Vintage Books.

BROWNING, R. P., D. R. MARSHALL, and D. H. TABB (1984) Protest Is Not Enough. Berkeley: Univ. of California Press.

BRUGMANN, B. and G. SLETTELAND [eds.] (1971) The Ultimate Highrise. San Francisco: Bay Guardian.

City of Milwaukee, Community Development Task Force (1979) Funding Allocation Guide for Community Development Block Grant Funds. Milwaukee: Author.

City of Milwaukee, Department of City Development (1977) Toward a Comprehensive Plan: A Preservation Policy for Milwaukee. Milwaukee: Author.

DAHL, R. (1961) Who Governs? New Haven, CT: Yale Univ. Press.

DERTHICK, M. (1972) New Towns in Town: Why a Federal Program Failed. Washington, DC: Urban Institute.

DOMMEL, P. and Associates (1978) Decentralizing Community Development. Washington, DC: U.S. Department of Housing and Urban Development.

———(1980) Targeting Community Development. Washington, DC: U.S. Department of Housing and Urban Development.

———(1982) Decentralizing Urban Policy: Case Studies in Community Development. Washington, DC: Brookings Institution.

General Accounting Office (1977) The Federal Government Should but Doesn't Know the Costs of Administering Its Assistance Programs. Washington, DC: Author.

GOVE, S. and L. MASOTTI [eds.] (1982) After Daley: Chicago Politics in Transition. Urbana: Univ. of Illinois Press.

HARTMAN, C. (1974) Yerba Buena: Land Grab and Community Resistance in San Francisco. San Francisco: Glide.

McQUADE, W. (1966) "Urban renewal in Boston," pp. 259-277 in J. Q. Wilson (ed.) Urban Renewal: The Record and the Controversy. Cambridge, MA: M.I.T. Press.

MOLLENKOPF, J. (1983) The Contested City. Princeton, NJ: Princeton Univ. Press.

NATHAN, R., P. DOMMEL, S. LIEBSCHUTZ, and M. MORRIS (1977a) "Monitoring the block grant program for community development." Pol. Sci. Q. 92, 2.

NATHAN, R. and Associates (1977b) Block Grants for Community Development. Washington, DC: U.S. Department of Housing and Urban Development.

PECHMAN, J. [ed.] (1982) Setting National Priorities: The 1983 Budget. Washington, DC: Brookings Institution.

PETERSON, P. E. (1981) City Limits. Chicago: Univ. of Chicago Press.

———and K. WONG (1985) "Toward a differentiated theory of federalism: education and housing policy in the 1980s." Research in Urban Policy 1: 301-324.

PRESSMAN, J. and A. WILDAVSKY (1973) Implementation. Berkeley: Univ. of California Press.

SMITH, F. C. (1980) "A special investigative report." Baltimore Sun (July).

STEGER, M. A. (1984) "Group influence versus decision-making rules: an analysis of local CDBG allocational decisions." Urban Affairs Q. 19, 3.

WEIDNER, E. W. (1967) "Decision-making in a federal system," pp. 229-256 in A. Wildavsky (ed.) American Federalism in Perspective. Boston: Little, Brown.

WOLFINGER, R. E. (1974) The Politics of Progress. Englewood Cliffs, NJ: Prentice-Hall.

WONG, K. (1983) "Federalism and public policy implementation." Ph.D. dissertation, University of Chicago.

Kenneth K. Wong is Assistant Professor of Political Science at the University of Oregon, and received his Ph.D. from the University of Chicago. His research on the local implementation of federal housing and education programs has appeared in Research in Urban Policy.

Paul E. Peterson is a Senior Fellow and Director of Governmental Studies at the Brookings Institution. He is the author of City Limits *(Chicago, 1981) and* The Politics of School Reform, 1870-1940 *(Chicago, 1985), editor of* The New Urban Reality *(Brookings Institution, 1985), coeditor of* The New Direction in American Politics *(Brookings Institution, 1985), and is preparing (with Kenneth Wong and Barry Rabe) a monograph,* When Federalism Works.

Publisher's Note: The following information is printed in accordance with U.S. postal regulations: Statement of Ownership, Management and Circulation (required by 39 U.S.C. 3685). 1A. Title of Publication: URBAN AFFAIRS QUARTERLY. 1B. Publication No.: 00420816. 2. Date of Filing: October 1, 1985. 3. Frequency of Issue: Quarterly. 3A. No. of Issues Published Annually: 4. 3B. Annual Subscription Price: institutions, $60.00; individuals, $25.00. 4. Location of Known Office of Publication: 275 South Beverly Drive, Beverly Hills (Los Angeles), California 90212. 5. Location of the Headquarters or General Business Offices of the Publishers: 275 South Beverly Drive, Beverly Hills (Los Angeles), California 90212. 6. Names and Complete Addresses of Publisher, Editor, and Managing Editor: Publisher: Sara Miller McCune, 1102 South Oakhurst Drive, Los Angeles, California 90035; Editors: Dennis R. Judd, Dept. of Political Science, University of Missouri, St. Louis, MO 63121, Donald Phares, Center for Metropolitan Studies, University of Missouri, St. Louis, MO 63121; Managing Editor: None. 7. Owner (if owned by a corporation, its name and address must be stated and also immediately thereunder the names and addresses of stockholders owning or holding 1% or more of total amount of stock. If not owned by a corporation, the names and addresses of the individual owners must be given. If owned by a partnership or other unincorporated firm, its name and address, as well as that of each individual must be given.): Sage Publications, Inc., 275 South Beverly Drive, Beverly Hills, California 90212; Sara Miller McCune, 1102 South Oakhurst Drive, Los Angeles, California 90035; George D. McCune, 1102 South Oakhurst Drive, Los Angeles, California 90035; Estate of Marvin Sirot, Mohawk Lane, Greenwich, Connecticut 06830; Gustave Sirot, Wingate Road, Guilford, Connecticut 06340; John B. Hurford, 220 East 63rd Street, New York, New York 10021; Albert L. Zesiger Foundation, BEA Associates, Inc., One Citicorp Center, 5th Floor, 153 East 53rd Street, New York, New York 10022; Judith Zesiger, 1125 Fifth Avenue, New York, New York 10028; Morris Janowitz, 1357 E. 55th Place, Chicago, Illinois 60637. 8. Known Bondholders, Mortgagees, and Other Security Holders Owning or Holding 1% or More of Total Amount of Bonds, Mortgages or Other Securities: None. 9. For Completion by Nonprofit Organizations Authorized to Mail at Special Rates (Section 423.12, DMM only): Not Applicable.

10. Extent and Nature of Circulation	Av. No. Copies Each Issue During Preceding 12 Months	Actual No. of Copies of Single Issue Published Nearest to Filing Date
A. Total no. copies printed (net press run)	2103	2128
B. Paid circulation:		
1. Sales through dealers and carriers, street vendors and counter sales	5	3
2. Mail subscription	1512	1515
C. Total paid circulation (sum of 10B1 and 10B2)	1517	1518
D. Free distribution by mail, carrier or other means: samples, complimentary, and other free copies	65	64
E. Total distribution (sum of C and D)	1582	1582
F. Copies not distributed:		
1. Office use, left over, unaccounted, spoiled after printing	521	546
2. Return from news agents	0	0
G. Total (sum of E, F1 and 2—should equal net press run shown in A)	2103	2128

11. I certify that the statements made by me above are correct and complete. (Signed) Steven D. Synhorst, Manager, Distribution Operations.

THE REAGAN URBAN POLICY AND ITS IMPACTS

HAROLD WOLMAN
University of Salford

The intent and effectiveness of the Reagan administration's urban policies have been the focus of much debate. This article analyzes Reagan's first-term urban policies and assesses their effects. Changes in budgetary requests, authorizations, and outlays during Reagan's first term are tracked for the full spectrum of urban programs. An attempt is also made to analyze the spatial and programmatic consequences of the changes in expenditure levels. Determination of the success or failure of the Reagan administration's urban policies is largely dependent on who is asking the questions and how they are asked.

President Reagan's policy toward the nation's urban areas has marked a sharp change of direction from that of his predecessors of both parties. The president has argued that the primary federal role toward subnational areas is to assure a healthy national economy, which, in turn, will bring about healthy urban economies. That may be termed "the rising tide lifts all boats" principle. Consistent with the approach, the president's *Urban Policy Report* (1982: 4) stated that "the foundation for the Administration's urban policy is the Economic Recovery Program." The 1984 report restated this basic philosophy, observing that "a healthy economy is our most powerful tool for revitalizing our cities and improving their fiscal positions" (1984: i).

With respect to the more conventional federal programmatic approach to urban problems, the president observed in his Program for New Economic Recovery (1981: 4-10), "There is no convincing evidence that these programs have been effective in creating new jobs or capital investment or are actually needed to promote local and regional development." His 1982 *Urban Policy Report* (1982: 46) concluded that

AUTHOR'S NOTE: *Research for this article was undertaken while I was a Senior Research Associate in the Public Finance Program at the Urban Institute.*

URBAN AFFAIRS QUARTERLY, Vol. 21 No. 3, March 1986 311-335

federal urban programs, however well intentioned, generally have been "unsuccessful—sometimes particularly so." Programmatic efforts to address urban problems are properly the role of state and local governments, rather than of the federal government. The report states (1982: 46) that "The Reagan Administration intends to devolve the maximum feasible responsibility for urban matters to states and through them to their local governments."

This article's broad concern is with the spatial consequences of the administration's policy. I will begin by briefly describing the nature of the urban problems facing the Reagan administration.

URBAN PROBLEMS AND THE URBAN POLICY DEBATE

During the latter part of the 1970s, it was widely acknowledged that many of America's cities faced severe economic, fiscal, and social problems. Furthermore, a conventional wisdom developed on the nature of these problems. The problems were of two kinds: First, metropolitan-area population and employment had decentralized, leaving central cities trapped within fixed boundaries with a disproportionately high share of the needy populations and social problems (unemployment, poverty, crime, poor health), but a disproportionately low share of the tax base. In addition, central cities had a high share of minority residents, so that the problems suffered by these groups were superimposed upon—and frequently seen to be identical to—urban problems.

Second, the economic performance of many metropolitan areas, particularly in the older regions of the country, suffered relative to other areas. This decline in economic performance reflected both changes in the structure of the national economy (a relative shift from the manufacturing to the service sector) and a deterioration in the competitive advantage of the older metropolitan areas that resulted in higher costs for firms located in those areas. The consequences, particularly for metropolitan areas dependent on manufacturing, were disproportionately high rates of unemployment. Thus, of the 16 largest SMSAs (excluding Washington D.C.), the 7 in which more than 25% of all employment was in the manufacturing sector in 1980 had 1983 unemployment rates averaging 11.0% compared to an average of 7.3% for the 9 SMSAs listed that were less dependent on manufacturing.

Two basic problems are thus acknowledged: a central city fiscal and social problem and a metropolitan-area economic problem, the latter concentrated primarily in older regions of the country. The urban policy debate has focused on how to respond to these problems. Prior to the Reagan administration, two polar positions had been established. Proponents of the first position contended that efforts should be made to revitalize America's urban areas through policies designed to attract economic activity back to these areas (jobs to people). This was essentially the strategy of the Carter administration, although its centerpiece, the national Development Bank, was never enacted. Proponents of this approach generally argued that economic revitalization was also the long-term solution to central-city fiscal and social problems. Federal fiscal assistance was seen as necessary until economic revitalization occurred.

Proponents of the second position contended that trends could not be reversed, urban areas would have to adjust to different kinds and lower levels of economic activity and that federal policy should be directed to encouraging labor mobility (people to jobs). An appropriate public policy would provide interim assistance to communities undergoing economic adjustment and, more generally, address federal problems toward the needs of people, wherever they live, rather than to places. This was the set of views espoused by the Commission for a National Agenda for the 1980s. The commission saw the major policy question in terms of whether federal domestic policy should be place-oriented or people-oriented and argued in favor of a policy to aid people wherever they live rather than a policy of aiding places. In that vein it advocated (1980: 102) a national "guaranteed job program for those who can work and a guaranteed cash assistance program for both the 'working poor' and those who cannot work."

The Reagan urban policy largely ignored the framework of the previous debate, which was couched in terms of whether federal domestic policy should be directed toward moving jobs to people or people to jobs. In effect, it chose neither, although its rhetoric at times appeared to favor the less activist people-to-jobs orientation. Instead, the Reagan urban policy reflected a market approach that places greatest emphasis on national economic performance and envisioned a relatively minor and residual federal role toward urban areas.

The market approach posits that the problems of urban areas and their residents will be solved through the operations of normal market mechanisms. It assumes that both labor and capital are highly mobile. Unemployed labor in large urban areas will migrate to areas of job availability. At the same time, unemployed resources will drive down factor prices in distressed urban economies relative to other areas, thus increasing the return on capital and providing the incentive for additional capital investment and job creation. The result will be a new equilibrium, but at a lower level of population and economic activity. And all this will occur with little or no federal intervention.

The primary role of the federal government would thus be to assure a growing and well-functioning national economy. In this context, urban economic vitality would be assured and central-city fiscal problems would disappear as the central-city tax base increased. Because the administration, at least in its 1984 urban policy report (1984: 11), recognizes "that neither the general economic recovery nor the increasing capacity and willingness of state and local governments and their residents to help themselves will solve the problems of all cities," it accepts a legitimate but secondary federal role in "helping them anticipate and adjust to structural change."

The practical implications of the Reagan urban policy approach for cities are far-reaching: a reduction in federal assistance to cities; a redirection of federal aid to state rather than to local governments; a decrease in the relatively modest (compared to other countries) national government role in redistributing resources from wealthy to poor communities; a decline in federal concern with the impacts of national economic policy on cities, with the fiscal well-being of cities and with local economic development; a reliance on adjustment through markets as the means of dealing with urban economic decline and high unemployment within urban areas; and a residual federal role in providing adjustment assistance.

THE REAGAN URBAN PROPOSALS

The Reagan administration's legislative and budgetary proposals affecting programs of direct concern to cities generally reflected its articulated urban policy. In his budget revision message submitted in February 1981, shortly after he took office, the president proposed a series of program terminations and budget reductions in programs relevant to urban areas (see Appendix). In addition, the president did propose one new program for urban areas. Legislation was to be introduced to establish urban enterprise zones in well-defined poverty areas within cities. Federal tax incentives were to be provided to induce businesses to locate within these areas.

Overall, the president proposed reductions in FY 1982 federal grant outlays to states and localities (exclusive of aid to individuals) of approximately $11 billion (17.5%) compared to what outlays would have been had policies in effect at the beginning of President Reagan's term simply been projected into the future (termed a pre-Reagan baseline budget). The president's proposed reductions in programs of concern to urban areas are listed in Table 1. If subsidized housing is excluded, these reductions imply a decline of 44.0% from FY 1982 pre-Reagan baseline budget authority levels and 22.1% from FY 1982 pre-Reagan baseline outlay levels.

ACTUAL CHANGES IN URBAN POLICY

Inevitably, the Reagan administration was unable to achieve all of its proposed terminations and reductions. The most significant immediate change was the termination of the CETA public service employment program. The program of the Economic Development Administration continued, but at a substantially reduced funding level. Mass transit operating assistance and federal highway aid for urban systems were not terminated, although budget authority for mass transit was reduced by nearly one-third over current policy levels for FY 1982. However, the Surface Transportation Act of 1982, incorporating a new five cent tax on gasoline, greatly expanded funding for mass transit. Budget authority for FY 1983 was approximately $1 billion higher than in FY 1982 and erased nearly all the FY 1982 cuts.

The Local Education Agency block grant was not approved and compensatory education remained as a separate program. Other block grants—in education, health and social services—were enacted, but in a less sweeping form than the president had proposed. (See Appendix comparing proposed to actual changes.)

Most of the major reductions in programs of concern to urban areas were achieved during the president's first year, although the budgetary impacts of these reductions were cumulative, exacting additional reductions from current policy levels in FY 1983 and beyond. These cumulative reductions were mitigated somewhat by additional funding for programs enacted in response to the recession—in particular the $4.6

TABLE 1
Reagan's Proposals for Urban Programs for FY 1982 ($ in millions)

Program	Budget Authority FY 1982			Outlays FY 1982		
	Pre-Reagan Baseline, FY 1982	Proposed Reduction from Pre-Reagan Baseline	Percentage Reduction	Pre-Reagan Baseline, FY 82	Proposed Reduction from Pre-Reagan Baseline	Percentage Change
CDBG and UDAG[a]	4,750	584	12.3	4,625	12	0.3
CETA-PSE	3,955	4,644	117.4	3,771	3,566	94.6
Mass transit operating grants	1,208	103	8.5	876	96	11.0
Mass transit capital grants	3,650	950	26.0	2,800	270	9.6
Municipal wastewater treatment grants	3,610	3,610	100.0	4,220	125	3.0
Economic Development Administration[b]	1,034	769	74.4	1,023	440	43.0
Elementary and secondary education[c]	6,061	1,498	24.7	5,797	106	18.3
Health and social services[d]	9,491	2,697	28.4	9,334	2,540	27.2
Assisted housing[e]	27,123	3,536	13.0	6,894	10	0.1
Total	60,882	18,391	30.2	39,340	7,165	18.2
Toal Excluding Housing	33,759	14,855	44.0	32,446	7,155	22.1

SOURCE: **The White House, America's New Beginning: A Program for Economic Recovery** (Washington, D.C., February 18, 1981).

a. Reagan's proposals called for an integration of both the Community Development Block Grant (CDBG) and Urban Development Action Grant (UDAG) programs into a "more efficient and flexible grant mechanism."

b. Includes proposal to eliminate regional commissions.

c. Includes funding for both the proposed Local Education Block Grant and the proposed State Education Block Grant.

d. These include proposals for both the Social Service Block Grant (including both Title XX and community services) and the various health block grants. The Social Service Block Grant implied a reduction of $1.451 billion in budget authority and $1.208 billion in outlays for FY 1982 compared to Carter's FY 1982 budget. Data for the Congressional Budget Office 1982 baseline are not available.

e. Includes proposals for both a reduction in the number of assisted units and an increase in the tenant rent contribution from 25% of income to 30%.

billion Jobs Bill shaped by Congress and enacted with presidential acquiescence rather than support in early 1983. (The Jobs Bill was, despite its title, additional aid to states and localities for a wide range of federal programs.) In addition, Congress passed an expanded version of a presidentially proposed rental rehabilitation assistance program, authorizing $150 million in aid for rental rehabilitation assistance and $200 million for new rental construction, primarily for large cities, for FY 1984. However, the president's proposed urban enterprise zone legislation has yet to be enacted.

The net result of all these changes was substantial reduction in funding for urban-oriented programs. Outlays for FY 1982 federal grants-in-aid to state and local governments (excluding grants to individuals) fell by $9.5 billion from the FY 1982 pre-Reagan policy baseline (16.7%). By FY 1984, grants to state and local governments were 12.1% less than the pre-Reagan policy baseline. Budget authority and outlays fell for most programs of concern to urban areas (see Appendix and Table 2). If the subsidized housing programs are excluded,[1] FY 1982 budget authority for the set of programs listed in Table 2 fell 36.5% below its FY 1982 pre-Reagan baseline while outlays fell 23.0% below baseline levels. The declines in budget authority are slightly below those of the president's proposal of 44.0% for a similar set of programs,[2] whereas outlay reductions actually exceeded his proposed 22.1%.

CHANGES IN IMPLICIT URBAN POLICY

We turn now to an examination of changes in implicit urban policy. Implicit urban policies are policies that, although not directed primarily at urban areas, nonetheless affect them. In fact, since nearly all federal activities have some effect on urban areas, an examination of implicit urban policy really asks the question, "What is the urban impact of all federal government policies?" Such a task is clearly beyond the scope of this article. Instead, I will confine myself to a brief discussion of nonurban programs and national economic policy, two particularly salient components of implicit urban policy. In doing so, I recognize that I am ignoring several important sources of federal impact on urban areas. Indeed, it is likely that in aggregate the effects of implicit urban policy on urban areas far outweigh those of explicit urban policy.

CHANGES IN NONURBAN PROGRAMS

The discussion of President Reagan's explicit urban policy dealt nearly exclusively with programs provided to governmental units. Most of these were place-oriented policies, although the distinction between place- and people-oriented policies is operationally a fuzzy one (some of these programs—e.g., job training, community services—are designed to serve people who happen to reside in the place receiving aid).

TABLE 2
Urban Program Pre-Reagan Baselines and Actual Funding, FY 1982 ($ in millions)

	Budget Authority			Outlays		
	Pre-Reagan Baseline, FY 1982	Actual FY 1982	Percentage Change	Pre-Reagan Baseline, FY 1982	Actual	Percentage Change
CDBG	3,886.0	3,456.0	-11.1	4,656.0	4,127.7	-11.3
UDAG	662.0	439.7	-33.6	729.0	500.3	-31.4
CETA-PSE	3662.0	0	-100.0	3,868.0	139.0	-96.4
Mass transit	4,997.7	3,497.7	-30.0	4,011.0	3,868.9	-3.5
Wastewater Treatment	3,544.0	2,400.0	-32.3	4,133.0	4,300.0	4.0
EDA	610.0	198.5	-67.5	537.0	405.0	-24.6
Compensatory education	3,884.2	3,033.9	-21.9	3,403.0	3,105.0	-8.8
Social Services Block Grant	3,279.0	2,580.0	-21.3	3,266.0	2,567.0	-21.4
Community Services Block Grant	586.0	348.0	-40.1	591.8	376.0	-36.5
Subsidized housing	28,637.0	16,367.0	-42.8	6,981.0	6,860.0	-1.7
TOTAL	53,748.0	32,321.2	-66.3	32,175.8	26,248.9	-18.4
TOTAL Excluding Housing	25,111.0	15,954.2	-36.5	25,194.8	19,388.9	-23.0

SOURCE: Calculations based on unpublished Congressional Budget Office tabulations.

Nonetheless, there is another set of programs that is unambiguously people-oriented: federal programs that provide, either directly or through the states, assistance or services to individuals, regardless of where they live. Changes in benefit levels and/or eligibility occurred in a variety of these people-oriented federal programs, including AFDC, Social Security, food stamps, Medicaid, and Medicare. These changes affect urban areas in two ways. First, they affect recipients of these programs in urban areas (in many cases, recipients of these programs reside disproportionately in large urban areas). Second, to the extent that individuals lose their eligibility for federal programs or receive reduced benefits, greater demands may be placed on state and local programs, such as general assistance or public hospitals.

Another class of federal program may also affect urban areas. Changes in federal policy toward states may have a second-order impact by reducing the ability of states to provide fiscal assistance to their localities. As a result of both reductions in federal aid and the recession, state general revenues increased (Joint Economic Committee, 1983: 18) by only 6.6% between FY 1981 and FY 1982, a real decline of 1.1%, and state operating aid to large cities (over 250,000) fell by 3.4%, a real decline of 4.2%. (However, state aid expanded again as state economies began to recover from the recession; the Joint Economic Committee survey projected a 12.5% increase in state operating aid to large cities between 1982 and 1983.)

Finally, changes in defense programs and federal procurement policy will have a differential effect upon geographic areas. Defense outlays increased by 31.7% between FY 1981 and FY 1983. According to a 1980 study by Georges Vernez,[3] per capita defense outlays go disproportionately to suburbs and small and medium-sized cities and to the Pacific, Mountain, and South Atlantic regions. Large cities receive disproportionately low per capita amounts of defense expenditures (Vernez, 1980). Thus, if the additional defense outlays were distributed in the same manner as existing outlays, large cities would be relatively disadvantaged.

NATIONAL ECONOMIC POLICY

President Reagan's economic policy was based on "supply side economics," featuring substantial tax cuts not offset by corresponding reductions in government spending and, thus, high federal deficits. The Federal Reserve's monetary policy, through the fall of 1982, was very restrictive, with extremely high interest rates. The consequences of these policies were a recession (real GNP declined by 2.4% between the first quarter of 1981 and the fourth quarter of 1982, and national unemployment rates reached 10.7%) and a substantial decline in the rate of inflation from a 13.5% increase in 1980 to a 6.0% increase in 1982.

A recession affects both local government revenues and demand for its services. A simulation of state and local revenues under the counterfactual economic assumptions of a nonrecessionary[4] economy indicates that the recession cost states and localities $53.4 billion during FY 1982 and FY 1983, an amount equal to 6% of actual state and local revenues received during that period.

However, it is likely that the effect fell disproportionately on state rather than local governments, since the primary revenue bases of the former (income and sales) are more sensitive to changes in the economy than are property values, the dominant tax base for local government. Clearly, however, local governments that derive revenue from income taxes and sales suffered revenue shortfalls unless they undertook discretionary changes in tax rates.

While the recession undoubtedly reduced the own-source revenue for urban governments, the drop in inflation also reduced the rate of growth of their costs. The state-local price deflator, a measure of increases in costs states and local governments must pay for the goods and services they purchase, rose only 14.6% between 1981 and 1983, compared to 20.4% for the two prior years.

Declines in cost must be offset, however, against increases in the volume of services provided because of increases in demand. Recession-induced increases in demand occur primarily in income support and social service programs. These are functions for which local responsibility in most states is lodged predominantly at the county level, and for which the state bears the major responsibility for financing nonfederal costs. Thus, increases in demand would be reflected first through increased expenditures at the state rather than local level.

By mid-1983, the combination of looser monetary policy and stimulative fiscal policy brought about by the high deficits produced a vigorous recovery. Real GNP rose by 3.7% during 1983 and 6.8% during 1984, and the unemployment rate had fallen to 7.3% by the end of 1984. The revenue yields of most of the local governments adversely affected by the recession began to improve and recession-induced increases in demand began to slacken. Total state and local receipts increased by nearly 9% during FY 1984, compared to only 5.5% in FY 1982 and 7.4% in FY 1983.

THE IMPACT OF CHANGES IN URBAN POLICY

Changes have occurred in both explicit and implicit federal urban policies. The initial impact of these changes has fallen, in some cases, on urban governments and, in others, on urban residents. (In many cities, of course, it has fallen on both simultaneously.) The effects on urban governments are the most visible. Effects on urban governments ultimately have, in most cases, effects on urban residents through adjustments in local tax and service levels; however, rarely do local governments simply "pass through" the effects of federal changes directly to their residents.

IMPACTS ON URBAN GOVERNMENTS

The most obvious initial impact on urban governments was the reduction in federal aid. Data from the government Division of the Bureau of the Census show a 3.9% decline in total federal aid (outlays) to large cities between FY 1981 and FY 1982, and a 13.6% decline in aid to large counties during that period. Since the Census data do not distinguish between federal aid for operating purposes and federal aid for capital purposes, a survey of city governments by the U.S. Congress Joint Economic Committee (JEC) must be relied on for more detailed analysis. According to the survey, per capita federal aid for operating purposes for large cities (over 250,000) fell by 15.5% between FY 1981 and FY 1982. However, federal aid does not account for a high share of total local revenues; federal operating aid as a percentage of total current general revenues for large cities declined from 14.6% in FY 1981 to 11.6% in FY 1982.

Normally, when federal aid declines, state aid increases. However, the joint impact of the recession and federal aid cuts placed state governments under extreme fiscal pressure; according to the JEC survey, per capita state operating aid to large cities consequently fell by 3.4% in FY 1982. Overall intergovernmental aid fell from 29.9% of total current revenues to 25.6%.

Despite the reductions in intergovernmental aid, total current per capita revenue for the large cities increased by 6.1% in FY 1982.[5] While this constitutes a slight (1.7%) decline in real terms, it nonetheless indicates a substantial effort to replace lost intergovernmental aid with locally raised funds. Per capita local property tax revenues increased by 11.0%, other local tax revenues by 14.3%, and fees, user charges, and miscellaneous revenues by 12.4%.

These increases in local revenues reflect both automatic changes in tax bases and discretionary changes in tax bases and rates. These latter discretionary increases involve the political act of "raising local taxes" and are responses to reductions in intergovernmental aid and shortfalls in locally raised revenue due to the recession.

Indeed, a surprising number of local governments took the politically difficult step of raising taxes. The Urban Institute examined, through a telephone survey, the discretionary tax behavior of 26 large cities between 1980 and 1983, and found that the effective property tax rates (property tax as a percentage of market value) had increased in 11 of these cities. Local sales tax rates rose in 7 of the 16 cities with local sales taxes and income tax rates rose in 6 of the 8 cities with such a tax.[6]

As a consequence of these changes in intergovernmental aid and local revenues, total expenditures of large cities were able to increase by 5.6% between FY 1981 and FY 1982, a 2.1% decline in real terms. Current expenditures rose by 6.2%, while capital expenditures fell by 0.2%.

Many of the cuts affecting urban area governments do not pass through city government budgets, but affect county government, school districts, and other special districts. In large counties (above 300,000 in population) increases in local revenues more than made up for reductions in intergovernmental aid so that total general revenues actually increased by 9.21% (1.2% in real terms) between FY 1981 and FY 1982 and total expenditures rose by 7.8% (no change in real terms). Large county current expenditures rose by 9.4%, while capital expenditures actually declined by 5.0%.

IMPACT ON URBAN RESIDENTS

Between 1980 and 1982, U.S. real median income (prior to taxes) fell by 4.9%. During the same time period, real median income fell by 5.0% in metropolitan areas of more than one million people, and by 5.4% inside central cities of these metropolitan areas. However, during the height of the recession, from 1981 to 1982, real median income fell by 1.6% nationally compared to 3.1% for large metropolitan areas and 2.8% for the central cities of these areas. While real income dropped nationally, it is clear that large metropolitan areas and their central cities experienced a disproportionate decline.

Between 1980 and 1982, the national unemployment rate rose from 7.0% to 9.5%, or by 2.5 percentage points. During the same time period, the rate for the largest metropolitan areas rose from 6.8% to 9.5%, or

2.7 percentage points, and the rate for central cities rose from 10.6% to 13.8%, or by 3.2 percentage points.[7] Again, large metropolitan areas—and particularly their central cities—appeared to suffer disproportionately.

Finally, the number of individuals with income below the poverty level rose from 13% of the nation in 1980 to 15% in 1982, an increase of 2 percentage points. During that same period, the percentage of central-city residents in poverty rose from 17.2%, an increase of 2.7 percentage points.

Thus, on the economic performance data most readily available, it appears that central cities in particular, and large metropolitan areas to a lesser extent, worsened their positions relative to the economy of the rest of the nations during the first two years of President Reagan's term.

However, preliminary data suggest that these areas experienced a relative improvement of their position during 1983 as the national economy began to grow (real GNP increased by 3.7% in 1983 compared to a decline of 2.1% in 1982). During 1983, unemployment rates for large metropolitan areas fell to 8.6%, compared to 9.5% nationally. Real per capita income grew by 1.6% in the large metropolitan areas and by 0.2% in their central cities, while declining slightly (–0.1%) nationally, and the central-city poverty rate fell from 19.9% to 19.8%, while increasing nationally from 15% to 15.2%.

THE IMPACT ON URBAN AREAS COMPARED TO THE REST OF THE COUNTRY

Did changes in federal programs affect large urban areas more adversely than the rest of the country? To address this question, I examined the impact of federal funding reductions on the flow of federal funds to large cities compared to other areas of the country. Taking 14 of the 15 largest central cities in the United States (excluding Washington, D.C.), I examined a variety of federal programs and activities for which federal funds were reduced in FY 1983 from their pre-Reagan baselines in order to determine whether the impact of the reductions fell disproportionately on these large cities. I calculated the per capita distribution of federal funds to these large urban areas for each of these programs or activities in FY 1980[8] and compared them to per capita distributions both for the suburbs of these areas and for the nation as a whole. Areas with relatively high initial per capita distribution would obviously be disproportionately affected (i.e., suffer greater absolute per capita reductions) as a result of federal spending reductions that did not affect the relative distribution of funds among areas.

If we assume that no change occurred in the distribution of federal funds, and that the only change was a reduction in the amount that would have been distributed had benefits or program levels not been cut, it is clear that large central cities were much more seriously affected than either their suburbs or the nation as a whole. In fact, it is likely that changes in distribution brought about by the consolidation of federal categorical programs into block grants to be distributed by the states further adversely affected large cities (Wolman, 1984: 46-50). However, I have excluded from the analysis programs in which I know important changes in distribution procedures occurred.

Given the nature of the data, we can make comparisons that include public assistance payments, Medicaid, Medicare, federal highway aid, and aid to the educationally disadvantaged for only 4 of the 14 cities (New York, San Francisco, Baltimore, and Philadelphia). These 4 cities received an average of $1,830 per capita for the programs listed in Table 3, compared to $1,070 per capita for the nation as a whole. Thus, a percentage reduction in funding for this set of programs from pre-Reagan baseline levels would have reduced the flow of federal funds to these large central cities on average by approximately 1.7 times as much per capita as for the entire nation.

If the five programs for which data are unavailable for all 14 cities are excluded from the analysis (see above), per capita federal aid for the remaining programs experiencing reductions is still higher in the central cities ($900 per capita average for the 14 cities) than in the nation as a whole ($779). Federal aid is particularly low in the suburbs, averaging only $539 per capita for the suburbs of the 14 cities (see Table 4).

As urban economies and labor markets in general encompass the metropolitan area—or at least central city and the relatively close suburbs—it is relevant to ask how the entire core county would fare from funding reductions in these programs. The 11 counties for which usable data are available received a total of $1,118 per capita for these programs (including all the programs listed in Table 3), compared to $1,109 for the nation as a whole, suggesting no differential impact of large metropolitan economies. Indeed, if defense pay and contracts (for which funding was increased rather than reduced) are included, these large metropolitan economies were advantaged. The 11 large metropolitan counties received, on average, $663 per capita for defense pay and contracts, compared to $475 per capita for the nation as a whole.

TABLE 3
Average Per Capita Distribution in the United States and Four Cities, Selected Federal Programs, FY 1980 (Dollars)

Program	U.S.	Four Large Cities[a]
Food Stamps	38	75
School Lunches	10	11
EDA - Public Works Grants and Loans	1	1
EDA - Business Development Assistance	0	2
Education Aid for the Disadvantaged (Ch. 1)	11	19
Income Support - AFDC	31	89
Community Health Centers	1	6
Medicaid	64	155
Medicare (Hospital + Supplemental Insurance)	150	267
Social Security (Retirement, Disability + Survivors)	517	632
Community Development Block Grant (CDBG)	12	41
Public Housing	5	15
Urban Development Action Grant (UDAG)	3	6
Section 8 Low-Income Housing Assistance	4	8
Comprehensive Employment and Training (CETA)	25	59
Airport Development and Aid Program	3	6
Mass Transit Formula Grants (Operating Assistance)	7	31
Highway Planning and Construction	39	131
Construction Grants for Wastewater Treatment	20	102
Civil Service Retirement and Disability	65	97
Veterans' Pensions	63	81
TOTAL	1,070	1,830

SOURCE: Urban Institute calculation from U.S. Community Services Administration, "The Geographic Distribution of Federal Funds Report for Fiscal Year 1980," various states.
a. New York, San Francisco, Baltimore, and Philadelphia.

TABLE 4
Average Per Capita Distributions in the United States and Major City Areas, Selected Federal Programs, FY 1980

Program	U.S.	Fourteen Large Cities	Suburbs
Food Stamps	38	56	24
School Lunches	10	13	6
EDA - Public Works Grants and loans	1	1	0
EDA - Business Development Assistance	0	1	0
Community Health Centers	1	3	0
Social Security	517	504	384
Community Development Block Grant (CDBG)	12	27	7
Public Housing	5	8	1
Urban Development Action Grant (UDAG)	3	7	0
Section 8 Low-Income Housing Assistance	4	5	2
Comprehensive Employment and Training (CETA)	25	47	1
Airport Development and Aid Program	3	5	0
Mass Transit Formula Grants	7	23	1
Construction Grants for Wastewater Treatment	20	44	9
Civil Service Retirement and Disability	65	65	60
Veterans' Pensions	63	81	44
TOTAL	774	900	539

SOURCE: Urban Institute calculation from U.S. Community Services Administration, "The Geographic Distribution of Federal Funds Report for Fiscal Year 1980," various states.

ANALYSIS

President Reagan's urban and regional policies envisioned a dramatically altered federal role with respect to subnational areas in general and urban areas in particular. He rejected the Carter urban policy premise that federal policy should be directed toward revitalizing cities by attracting jobs to distressed cities. Instead, the president proposed a reduction in federal aid for urban areas, a consolidation of federal categorical programs into block grants, and a restructuring of intergovernmental relations that would emphasize federal relationships with state governments and state responsibility for urban problems. In this section, I will first consider the extent to which policies, as finally adopted, represent the kind of dramatic change in federal urban policy that Reagan desired. I will then examine the probable long-term consequences of his approach.

THE EXTENT OF CHANGE

First, it is clear that the contrast with President Carter's urban policy is overdrawn for the simple reason that few federal programs designed to bring about the type of place-oriented urban revitalization envisioned by the Carter urban policy were successfully enacted. The prime exception was the Urban Development Action Grant (UDAG) program, which became law in 1977. However, the Carter administration's major urban proposal—the National Development Bank—was never enacted, leaving HUD's UDAG program and Economic Development Administration's grant and loan programs as the primary federal urban economic revitalization activities. Together, the urban-oriented activity of these two programs never reached the level of $1 billion annually. Ironically, President Reagan's major positive urban proposal—the creation of urban enterprise zones—would have been, if enacted, an expansion of the Carter administration's jobs-to-people urban economic revitalization approach.

The consolidation of categorical programs into block grants had less of an impact on urban areas than might have been expected, particularly if the funding reductions that accompanied the block granting are set aside. Few programs of major importance to urban areas were consolidated into block grants, although a variety of lower priority programs (e.g., urban rat control, lead-based paint poisoning, desegregation assistance) were included. However, the major proposals affecting cities—consolidation of the Community Development Block

Grant and UDAG and the placing of Aid for Compensatory Education into a local school district block grant—were not enacted in his first term.

Judging the importance of the funding reductions revolves around the question of how large is large, and from whose perspective the question is being viewed. From the perspective of the federal government, a 30% reduction from current policy levels in federal aid for programs of direct concern to urban areas might be considered substantial and dramatic.

From the local perspective, the reduction appears much less dramatic. Local governments do not budget on a current policy basis, but on a nominal basis; they evaluate federal aid not in terms of changes from future aid they might have received had policy not changed, but in terms of changes from aid received the previous year. In addition, relatively little federal aid passes through local government general fund budgets, thus largely isolating the general fund fiscal condition from the immediate effects of federal fiscal cuts. Finally, the lag between reductions in federal budget authority and reductions in outlays—particularly for capital grant programs—suggests that local governments may not yet have felt the full impact of the cuts.

For all of these reasons, the view from local government is mixed. On one hand, the structure and amount of federal aid has undergone relatively modest change. On the other hand, the federal government's fundamental role has been altered: It is now seen as part of the problem rather than as part of the solution. During most of the previous two decades, the federal government has responded to local government fiscal difficulties during recessionary periods by providing countercyclical aid. During the 1981-1983 period (prior to the congressionally initiated Jobs Bill), the federal government not only failed to provide countercyclical aid, it contributed to the difficulties of local government by reducing existing aid!

Nonetheless, many city and county governments responded to the recession and the reduction in federal aid by increasing their own taxes. In some cases, state aid also rose. As a consequence in overall terms, real expenditure and service reductions were, in most cases, modest. Within this overall context, however, some specific programs and activities heavily supported by federal funds may have been cut substantially or even dropped when federal funds for these programs fell, with resulting hardship for recipients of these services.

In general, the impact of policy changes during the Reagan years fell more directly on city residents than on city governments, and residents of central cities were affected more adversely by the recession than were residents elsewhere. In addition, the increases in state and local taxes paid by city residents frequently exceeded federal tax reductions. Increases in state and local tax and federal Social Security taxes exceeded federal income tax reductions for median-income families in 21 of the 26 cities examined by the Urban Institute, and the increase in total tax burden generally was greater for lower-income families.

THE REAGAN LEGACY: THE LONG-TERM CONSEQUENCES

Perhaps the most significant accomplishment of the Reagan administration was its success in redefining the traditional domestic policy agenda. In the process, the prominence of urban problems, which for two decades had been near the top of that agenda, was substantially reduced. Instead, President Reagan substituted an emphasis on national economic performance and market-induced adjustment as the primary approach to urban policy. How well is this approach likely to work?

First, the administration argument that assuring a healthy and growing national economy is the most effective means of improving the well-being of cities and their residents is undoubtedly true. Thus, the unemployment rates of the 30 large metropolitan areas for which BLS provides data declined from 8.6% in 1983 to 6.4% in May, 1984, as the national economy recovered vigorously from the recession. In the absence of any sizable urban-specific programs, this improved performance of large urban economies can be attributed almost wholly to national economic growth.

However, the rising tide did not lift all boats equally. The Pittsburgh SMSA, for example, had an unemployment rate of 10.7% and Buffalo, Chicago, Cleveland, Cincinnati, St. Louis, and Seattle all had rates above 8%, well in excess of the national average. Boston, Dallas, and Washington, D.C., all had unemployment rates of less than 4%. It is quite likely that had data for central-city residents rather than metropolitan area residents been available, the spatial disparities would have been much more pronounced.

The long-term consequences of the Reagan urban policy are thus dependent on the extent to which a high-growth national economy not only improves the condition of urban areas but on the extent to which it reduces disparities between urban areas with the most serious problems and the rest of the nation. Unfortunately, national economic growth cannot necessarily be relied upon to reduce these disparities, because, as the National Academy of Sciences (1983: 10) points out,

> Growing and declining manufacturing and service sectors of the economy are often located in different places. Some of the sectors that are in decline will not be substantially revived by general economic recovery because structural changes in those sectors will permanently eliminate many jobs that previously existed.

In a very real sense, the Reagan Urban Policy thus sets up a straw man and begs, by so doing, the essential question. The fact that national economic growth is the single most important factor in improving urban economic conditions does not, as the Reagan urban policy implies, logically lead to the conclusion that urban policy is unnecessary or counterproductive. Some urban areas, and particularly their central cities, will continue to suffer problems even during national economic growth, although the problems may not be as severe as when the national economy is not growing. Why should not a spatially targeted urban policy be addressed to these problems as a complement to a national economic growth policy? The federal government is not faced with the dilemma of choosing one or the other.

The standard argument opposed to subnational development policies is that efforts to induce capital to move from areas of relatively high to relatively low productivity will result in reduced national efficiency and output. Even if this were true, it is unlikely that the reduction would be very great and, many would argue, would be a small price to pay for increased spatial equity.

However, the argument is not necessarily true. It assumes that urban economic regeneration must occur through subsidies attracting firms to areas of low productivity. It also assumes that there is a fixed supply of capital and entrepreneurs and that any increase in investment in one part of the country comes at the expense of another part with no (or negative) national impact. But most local economies have unrealized potential for indigenous growth in the form of residents who, perhaps because of local barriers, are not fully utilizing their entrepreneurial abilities and their capital. If this unrealized potential can be exploited through encouraging and assisting the emergence of local entrepreneurs (without necessarily providing subsidies to capital), the resulting increases in urban economic activity will not come at the expense of other areas and will add to net national output.

The Reagan administration has made one exception in its overall urban policy reliance on national economic performance and market mechanisms. It has proposed legislation to establish urban enterprise zones. Although the legislation has not been passed by Congress at the time of this writing, more than 20 states have enacted their own enterprise zone legislation in anticipation of congressional approval. The form of the administration's only major urban initiative is particularly ironic, as it is emphatically place-oriented ("jobs to people"), despite the rhetoric in its 1982 urban policy report.

Enterprise zones, however, are quite unlikely to be an effective positive urban policy approach. The conceptual problems with the enterprise zones have been well critiqued elsewhere (Logan, 1983; Walton, 1983; Bendick, 1983). The basic problem is that of providing incentives for location in a relatively small area within a metropolitan labor market without increasing jobs actually available within the area. Indeed, this has been the experience in the United Kingdom, where the enterprise zone concept originated. An evaluation of the U.K. enterprise zone program (Catalano, 1983: 49) states that enterprise zones

> have not resulted in a net job gain to either the local or the national economy. Although they have strongly influenced the choice of location within an area, almost all establishments and jobs could have been created anyway. Moreover, a significant proportion—about 40%—of firms moving into the zones are relocations, usually from within the same conurbation.

CONCLUSION

The Reagan urban policy, even if successful in its own terms, is unlikely to substantially narrow the existing disparities between large urban areas and the remainder of the country or, indeed, the disparities among urban areas themselves. Nor is it likely to address successfully the structural problems faced by many declining urban areas. If these are defined as "the urban problem," then the Reagan policy fails to address them. If, however, some absolute improvement in the overall economic and social well-being of urban areas and their residents is identified as "the urban problem," there is little question that national economic growth is likely to bring that about (although not every individual will benefit). The urban policy of the first term of the Reagan administration can thus be perceived as either failure or success—largely depending on who is asking the question and how it is being asked.

APPENDIX
Programs of Concern to Urban Areas

President's Proposal (1981 except where noted)	Changes Enacted	Change in Funding, FY 81-83[a] ($ = millions in Budget Authority, except where noted)
Termination of CETA-PSE program.	Program terminated (1981).	-2399 (100%)[b]
Termination of remainder of CETA and replacement with block grant to states (1982).	Termination of CETA; replacement by Job Training Partnership Act at substantially reduced funding levels.	-192 (-8.6%)[b]
Termination of the Economic Development Administration and its programs.	Programs reduced sharply, but not terminated.	-456.2 (-73.0%)
Phasing out of Mass Transit Operating Subsidies by FY 1984; substantial reduction in mass transit capital grants; no funds for new rail starts (1982).	Surface Transportation Act of 1982 imposes new 5 cent tax on gasoline, 1 cent of which is dedicated to transit. Mass transit programs are restructured into a separate capital grant and a new mass transit block grant. Budget authority levels in FY 1983 are slightly higher than those of FY 1981. Limits placed operating subsidies at approximately 80% of FY 1981 levels.	245.6 (7.2%)
Phasing out of federal aid for Urban System Highway Program by FY 1984.	Retention of program at approximately pre-Reagan levels.	-9 (-1.0%)[b]
Termination of Municipal Wastewater Treatment Program and restructuring of new program at funding levels 50% below present.	Restructuring of program; federal matching grants reduced from 75% to 55% for projects funded after Oct. 1984. Funding reduced from present levels.	FY 1980-83 -970 (-28.5%)[c]
Reduction in funding for grants-in-aid for airport construction, including phasing out of grants for largest airports.	Funds for program increase slightly; large city airports not phased out.	
Termination of urban parks program.	Program not eliminated, but funds cut drastically in FY 1981, both by the pre-Reagan budget ($45 million) and by an additional $19 million of post-Reagan recisions. The 1983 Jobs Bill restored approximately 2/3 of the total FY 1981 reductions; however, funding was reduced drastically again in FY 1984.	FY 1980-83 -25 (-38.4%)
Creation of a Local Education Agency Block Grant to include Title I ESEA compensatory education, desegregation assistance, education for the handicapped, adult education, and bilingual education. Funding levels reduced.	Block grant not created. Various programs remain categorical programs with the exception of desegregation assistance, which becomes part of the elementary and secondary education block grant. Funding levels reduced for various programs through FY 1981 recisions and FY 1982 cuts.	FY 1980-83 Compensatory Ed. -15.3 (-0.4%) Vocational Ed. -82.9 (-9.1%) Bilingual Aid -28.9 (-17.3%) Impact Aid -28.4 (-34.5%) Handicapped Ed. 150.4 (14.3%)
Creation of a state education block grant consolidating 35 categorical programs.	Block grant created (Ch. 2). Includes several programs previously allocated directly to local school districts. New program sends funds to states, which determine how funds are allocated to school districts. Local districts may use funds as they see fit. Substantial funding reduction achieved through recisions in FY 1981 and further reductions in FY 1982.	FY 1980-83 -240.6 (-27.2%)
Consolidation of 25 health categorical programs into a Health Services Block Grant and a Preventive Health Block Grant with reduced funding levels.	Consolidation of 21 health programs into four block grants to states: Primary Care, Maternal and Child Health, Preventive Health and Health Services, and Alcohol, Drug Abuse, and Mental Health. Programs consolidated included community health centers, community mental health centers, Home Health Services, rodent control, alcoholism project grants, and lead paint poisoning. All of these programs had previously largely bypassed the states and been funded directly to local governments or providers with little state involvement. FY 1982 funding for new blocks 16.4% less than FY 1981 total for consolidated programs.	-155.6 (-9.6%)
Creation of a social service block grant including the Title XX social service program	Creation of separate block grants for social services (essentially the	Social Service Block Grant

(continued)

APPENDIX (Continued)

President's Proposal (1981 except where noted)	Changes Enacted	Change in Funding, FY 81-83[a] ($ = millions in Budget Authority, except where noted)
and the programs of the Community Services Administration (1981).	previous Title XX program) and for community services. Funding levels reduced compared to previous programs.	-316 (-10.6%)
Elimination of Community Services Block Grant (FY 1985).	Jobs Bill provides an additional $225 million for Social Services Block Grant for FY 1983, an amount which is retained for FY 1984.	Community Services Block Grant (-30.4%)
Consolidation of the Community Development Block Grant program and UDAG program into a single program at reduced funding levels; consolidation of CDBG and General Revenue Sharing program (1983).	CDBG and UDAG retained as separate programs with modest reductions in funding. CDBG funding increased by $1 billion for FY 1983 (higher than pre-Reagan levels) as a result of 1983 Jobs Bill; however, the additional funding was not retained in FY 1984. CDBG funds for entitlement (large) cities reduced from 75% to 70% of total.	CDBG: 762 (20.6%) UDAG: -235 (-34.8%)
Termination of housing rehabilitation loan program; replacement with a new rental rehabilitation grant program (1983).	Terminated in FY 1982; however, a new rental rehabilitation program funded at $150 million annually was enacted, at the president's request, in late 1983.	-130.0 (FY 1980-83) (-100%)
Reduction in budget authority for subsidized housing to levels approximated, 13% below that planned for FY 1982; increase in tenants' contribution from 25% of income to 30% of income.	Greater reductions than proposed for FY 1982 budget authority; increase in tenants' contribution as proposed. Funds for new Section 8 and public housing units cut drastically.	-23,624.0 (-80.2%) Change in housing units reserved from available budget authority: Section 8 (new) -59,861 (-81.0%) Section 8 (existing) -18,143 (-21.3%) Public Housing -34,370 (-94.5%)
Enactment of housing voucher program at level sufficient to fund 80,000 units. Conversion of Section 8 into voucher; elimination of all new construction.	Housing voucher demonstration program enacted (1983). Voucher funds provided for 15,000 units.	Program to begin in FY 1984
Enactment of rental rehabilitation assistance program providing aid to cities for housing rehabilitation (1983).	Rental rehabilitation assistance grants to be provided on formula basis to cities. Funds to be used for housing rehabilitation in low-income neighborhoods only. Enacted new rental construction program providing funds to city governments with severe housing shortages. Funds provided on discretionary basis. Funds for both rehabilitation and construction to be provided on a 50% matching basis. Section 8 new construction program terminated.	Program to begin in FY 1984 Program to begin in FY 1984
General Revenue Sharing renewed and maintained at current level (1983) in nominal terms.	General Revenue Sharing renewed and maintained at current level in nominal terms.	0
Jobs Bill: Under pressure from Congress, president proposes $4.3 billion recession relief legislation (1983).	$4.6 billion in additional funding for various existing programs, including $1 billion for CDBG, $225 million for Social Services Block Grant, and $100 million for EDA public works.	
Urban Enterprise Zones: incentives to attract business to identified distressed neighborhoods in each of 75 cities. Incentives would include 10% tax credit per employee plus additional credit for employees who are poor and/or live in the zone, and elimination of capital gains tax on property in zone.	Not enacted.	

SOURCES: Office of Management and Budget (1982, 1983, 1984), U.S. Conference of Mayors (1981-1984).

a. When substantial recisions brought about by Reagan occurred in FY 1981 funding, FY 1980 funding levels are used.

b. Outlays.

c. Reductions from originally passed pre-Reagan FY 1981 budget (i.e., reductions for which Reagan administration is responsible) amount to $870 million, or 26.4%.

d. Changes from originally passed pre-Reagan FY 1981 budget amount to an increase of $20 million, or 100%.

NOTES

1. The subsidized housing programs are excluded because of the substantial time lag between changes in budget authority and changes in outlays. Massive funding changes occurred in subsidized housing programs, but these changes were obscured because changes in housing budget authority are translated into changes in housing outlays over a 25-40-year time period. Budget authority for housing fell from a pre-Reagan baseline figure of $28.6 billion for FY 1982 to $16.4 billion for that year. The immediate effect on housing outlays for FY 1982, however, was negligible.

2. There are slight differences between the programs listed in Tables 3 and 4, the most important of which is the inclusion of the President's Health Block Grant proposal in Table 3.

3. Using 1976 outlay data, Vernez calculated that the economies of large central cities (over 300,000) received 19% more federal public assistance and income support outlays and 48% more health outlays than would have been the case had these outlays been distributed on a per capita basis. See Vernez (1980).

4. The assumptions of the counterfactual used are specified as alternative number 2 in Sawhill and Stone (1984: 86).

5. Local tax revenue collected by all local governments rose by 12.2% during FY 1982 and by an additional 7.6% in FY 1983, both well in excess of inflation (Bureau of the Census, 1983).

6. This information comes from the Urban Institute.

7. The unemployment data are derived from BLS Employment and Earnings, which provide data for 30 of the nation's 34 largest metropolitan areas, and from BLS Geographic Profiles of Employment, which provides data for 11 large central cities.

8. FY 1980 ran from October 1979 through September 1980. It is, in effect, two years rather than one year prior to when most of President Reagan's reductions took effect. However, FY 1980 is the last year for which geographic distribution of federal funds to substate area data are available.

REFERENCES

BENDICK, M. (1983) "Federal tax incentives, federal expenditures, and inner city economic revitalization." Presented to the Committee on Ways and Means, U.S. House of Representatives, November 17.

Bureau of the Census, U.S. Department of Commerce (1983) Quarterly Summary of Federal, State and Local Tax Revenue. Washington, DC: Government Printing Office.

CATALANO, A. (1983) A Review of U.K. Enterprise Zones. CES Paper 17. London: CES Ltd.

GLICKMAN, N. (1980) The Urban Impact of Federal Politics. Baltimore: Johns Hopkins Univ. Press.

GOLD, S. (1983) State and Local Fiscal Relations in the Early 1980s. Washington, DC: Urban Institute.

HANSON, R. (1983) Rethinking Urban Policy. Washington, DC: National Academy Press.

Joint Economic Committee of the United States Congress (1983) Trends in the Fiscal Condition of Cities: 1981-1983. Washington, DC: Government Printing Office.

LOGAN, J. (1983) "The disappearance of communities from national urban policy." Urban Affairs Q. 19 (September): 75-90.

NATHAN, R., F. DOOLITTLE, and Associates (1983) The Consequences of Cuts. Princeton, NJ: Woodrow Wilson School of Public and International Affairs.

Office of Management and Budget (1982) Budget of the United States Government, Fiscal Year 1983. Washington, DC: Government Printing Office.

———(1983) Budget of the United States Government, Fiscal Year 1984. Washington, DC: Government Printing Office.

———(1984) Budget of the United States Government, Fiscal Year 1985. Washington, DC: Government Printing Office.

Panel of Policies and Prospects for Metropolitan and Nonmetropolitan America, President's Commission for a National Agenda for the 1980s (1980) Urban America in the 1980s: Perspectives and Prospects. Washington, DC: Government Printing Office.

PETERSON, G. (1983) Economic Analysis of the Effects of Business Cycles on the Economy of Cities. Washington, DC: Urban Institute.

———(1984) "Federalism and the states," pp. 213-260 in J. Palmer and I. Sawhill (eds.) The Reagan Record. Washington, DC: Urban Institute.

President of the United States (1984) Program for a New Economic Recovery. Washington, DC: Government Printing Office.

SAWHILL, I. and C. STONE (1984) "The economy," pp. 69-105 in J. Palmer and I. Sawhill (eds.) The Reagan Record. Washington, DC: Urban Institute.

United States Conference of Mayors (1981-1984) The Federal Budget and the Cities.

U.S. Department of Housing and Urban Development (1982) The President's National Urban Policy Report, 1982. Washington, DC: Government Printing Office.

———(1984) The President's National Urban Policy Report, 1984. Washington, DC: Government Printing Office.

VAUGHAN, R. (1977) The Urban Impacts of Federal Policies (Vol. 2). Santa Monica, CA: Rand Corporation.

VERNEZ, G. (1980) "Overview of the spatial dimensions of the federal budget," pp. 67-102 in N. Glickman (ed.) The Urban Impacts of Federal Policies. Baltimore: Johns Hopkins Univ. Press.

WALTON, J. (1982) "Cities, jobs, and politics." Urban Affairs Q. 18 (September): 5-7.

Harold L. Wolman is currently Visiting Professor of Politics at Bedford College, University of Salford in London. He has recently served as a Senior Research Associate in the Public Finance Program at the Urban Institute. His primary research interests include housing policy and the budgetary process as it relates to urban programs.

ENERGY AND URBAN FORM
A Human Ecological Critique

VALERIE A. HAINES
University of North Carolina at Chapel Hill

Studies of the relationship between urban form and energy use have used scenarios to examine the relative energy efficiency of three spatial configurations of urban systems: centralization, multinucleation, and sprawl. Their results have been contradictory. This article develops a human ecological critique of these studies by examining the events included in each scenario. The results suggest that these contradictions are more apparent than real: Multinucleation is the most energy-efficient urban form. They also suggest that energy may now be a relatively weak determinant of urban form.

In the last decade we have witnessed a growing concern for the so-called energy crisis. In the urban context, this concern has centered on whether energy constraints will retard or reverse contemporary redistribution trends. These trends have been studied in detail by human ecologists (see Kasarda, 1978, 1980; Wardwell and Gilchrist, 1980; Hawley, 1981; Zelinsky and Sly, 1981). Unfortunately, like other sociologists, human ecologists have paid little attention to the energy question. This has led Duncan (1978: 1) to conclude, "A scientist investigating the relationships energy and society can expect little help from the literature of sociology published in the last 20 years."[1]

Duncan's conclusion does point to a major gap in the sociological literature. At the same time, it is misleading because it ignores the importance of human ecological theory and research for investigations of the relationship between energy and urban form. Planners have investigated this relationship by constructing scenarios to examine the relative energy efficiency of alternative spatial configurations of urban systems. These scenarios are valid only if their component forecasts are

AUTHOR'S NOTE: *I would like to thank John D. Kasarda and Peter V. Marsden for their comments on earlier drafts of this article.*

URBAN AFFAIRS QUARTERLY, Vol. 21 No. 3, March 1986 337-353

correct. Human ecological studies of population and employment redistribution patterns suggest that, for some scenarios, this is not the case. In this article I use these data to develop a human ecological critique of studies in the relationship between energy and urban form.

Most of these studies begin by assuming that energy constraints are a powerful determinant of urban form. In this article their importance is an empirical question and not an a priori assumption. The precipitating event, the Arab oil embargo of late 1973 and early 1974, constitutes a "natural" experimental intervention, and if energy factors are important determinants of urban form, then pre- and post-embargo settlement patterns should differ.

In this analysis only central city to suburban and metropolitan to nonmetropolitan redistribution patterns are considered. Following Zelinsky and Sly (1981), these patterns are investigated in terms of the following residential categories: central city and ring (which together define metropolitan) and nonmetropolitan. The time period studied is from 1970 to 1980; data for subsequent years are not available.

HUMAN ECOLOGY AND ENERGY PLANNING

In the planning literature two interrelated yet distinct sets of strategies have been proposed to generate an energy-efficient urban form: transportation strategies and land use strategies. Transportation strategies are designed to reduce energy consumption through direct intervention in the transportation sector. They are reactive strategies to reduce the energy costs associated with existing spatial structures. Land use strategies are also directed toward energy consumption in the transportation sector. Their locus of intervention differs, however. Their proponents argue that by altering the spatial form of cities it may be possible, in the long run, to decrease travel demands and, hence, to reduce transportation energy consumption.

In developing these strategies, planners have focused on the transportation sector for three reasons. First, this sector relies primarily on nonrenewable forms of energy. In 1977, the transportation sector consumed approximately 25% of the total energy budget of the United States and, of this, 95% was petroleum (Byrne, 1979). All of the major scenarios describing alternative energy futures predict a growing imbalance between long-run nonrenewable energy supplies and projected demands (see Landsberg, 1974; Stobaugh and Yerglin, 1979; Ross and Williams, 1981). This imbalance is most problematic for end-use sectors such as transportation. Second, as planners have become more concerned with conservation, they have directed more attention to end-use sectors, where either the probability of implementing conservation measures is greatest or the greatest reductions in energy availability would be experienced in the event of a chronic and severe energy shortage. The transportation sector meets both of these criteria. Third, transportation is a major determinant of urban spatial structure (Cornehls, 1977; Alonso, 1978; Van Til, 1982).

This linking of transportation and urban spatial structure is also characteristic of the human ecological approach. The principal explanatory variables in this approach are transportation and communication technologies. According to human ecologist Amos Hawley (1950, 1981), an understanding of modern urban phenomena and, specifically, of the locational choices of households and firms, presupposes an understanding of the reduction of the friction of space brought about by new means of transportation and communication.

Like their planning counterparts, human ecologists stress the causal relationship between mode of transportation and urban spatial structure (Berry and Kasarda, 1977; Hawley, 1981). Not surprisingly, both groups have focused their attention on the automobile, the most recent transportation innovation for overcoming the friction of space. The energy costs of this technological means of expanding local territorial systems have been ignored in most human ecological research. This research has focused instead on its implications for contemporary redistribution patterns. As will be shown, these studies of contemporary redistribution patterns can make an important contribution to the investigation of the relationship between energy and urban form.

THE RELATIONSHIP BETWEEN ENERGY AND URBAN FORM

Table 1 summarizes the conclusions on the relative energy efficiency of alternative spatial configurations of urban systems of a series of studies. The headings of the columns indicate the alternatives compared in each study. These alternatives were reconceptualized here to fit the three-fold classification of urban spatial patterns that dominates the planning literature: centralization, multinucleation, and sprawl. Under the CS Framework, only centralization and sprawl are considered. The

CMS Framework compares the centralization, multinucleation, and sprawl alternatives.

Table 1 shows that the results of these studies are contradictory. Studies using the CS Framework conclude that centralization is the most energy-efficient urban form, but those using the CMS Framework favor multinucleation. In the planning literature, these contradictory findings are often dismissed as a by-product of the state of the art of energy planning. Burby and Bell's (1978: xv) conclusion that "we do not know enough about how we can best become an energy efficient nation" is a case in point. My analysis of the scenarios included in these studies suggests a different explanation: The contradictions are more apparent than real.

All of the studies in Table 1 use scenarios as their principal data source. Like other correlative forecasting techniques, scenarios are dependent upon the information generated by extrapolative and speculative forecasting techniques. Scenarios are used primarily to synthesize this information to provide descriptions of future conditions and future events (Jantsch, 1967; Gershuny, 1976).

Scenarios allow a comprehensive view of alternative futures and the costs and benefits of operationalizing the decisions necessary for their attainment. They are characterized by two limitations that are particularly relevant to my critique. There is no rationale (1) for choosing the optimum number of scenarios to be evaluated or (2) for choosing the events to be included in each scenario. Users are free, therefore, to consider only the centralization and sprawl alternatives and to exclude important influences on urban form, such as transfer payments, major sectoral changes in industry, and the development of total energy systems. Except to point to this limitation, my analysis does not address these influences. Its scope is restricted to the events planners have included in their scenarios.

Each of the three scenarios (sprawl, centralization, and multinucleation) includes four primary events: (1) predominant housing structure, (2) principal mode of transportation to work, (3) employment distribution, and (4) population distribution. Where these scenarios differ is in their extrapolative and speculative forecasts for each event. The contents of these forecasts for each scenario are summarized in Table 2, which also shows whether these forecasts are supported by current census and human ecological data.

The energy efficiency of the alternative settlement patterns is determined by combining the trends in household energy consumption and transportation energy consumption. Household energy consump-

TABLE 1
Conclusions of Land Use Studies Concerning the Most Energy-Efficient Urban Form

Study	CS-Framework	CMS-Framework
Bacon, 1973	centralization	
Franklin, 1974	centralization	
Real Estate Research Corp, 1974	centralization	
Council on Envirn Quality, 1975	centralization	
Hoben, 1975	centralization	
Nadler, 1975	centralization	
Kydes et al., 1976		multinucleation
Slayton, 1976		multinucleation
Cornehls, 1977	centralization	
Burby and Bell, 1978		multinucleation
Carroll, 1978	centralization	
Edwards, 1978		multinucleation
Roberts, 1978	centralization	
Romanos, 1978		multinucleation
Soot and Sen, 1979		multinucleation
Windsor, 1979		multinucleation
Small, 1980		multinucleation
Van Til, 1980, 1982		multinucleation
Keyes, 1981		multinucleation

NOTE: The CS framework identifies studies that compare the centralization and sprawl configurations. The CMS framework compares centralization, multinucleation, and sprawl.

tion is predicted by Event 1: Single-family dwellings are more energy intensive than multiple-family dwellings. Transportation energy consumption is predicted by Event 2—public transportation is more energy efficient than automobiles—and by Event 5—distance to work. Event 5 is derived by combining Event 3 and Event 4. If either the employment distribution forecast (Event 3) or the population distribution forecast

TABLE 2
Primary Events of Land Use Scenarios

Scenario	Event	Forecast	Supported by Data
Sprawl	1	single family dwellings	+
	2	automobile	+
	3	reconcentration	–
	4	deconcentration	+
Centralization	1	multiple family dwellings	+
	2	public transit	–
	3	reconcentration	–
	4	reconcentration	–
Multinucleation	1	single family dwellings	+
	2	automobile	+
	3	deconcentration	+
	4	deconcentration	+

NOTE: Event 1 = predominant housing structure; Event 2 = principal mode of transportation to work; Event 3 = employment distribution; Event 4 = population distribution. + refers to forecasts that are supported by current census and human ecological data; — refers to those forecasts that are not supported by these data.

(Event 4) is incorrect, then the forecast for Event 5 is also incorrect. Table 2 shows that this is the case for both the sprawl and centralization scenarios.

THE CS FRAMEWORK

Under the CS Framework, sprawl is energy-intensive because it combines single-family dwellings with commuting by automobile over the long distances that result from population deconcentration and employment reconcentration. Centralization is energy efficient because it combines the energy efficiency of multiple-family dwellings with (1) the greater use of mass transit that follows from increases in gasoline prices and (2) the short distances to work that result from the clustering of residences (population reconcentration) and jobs (employment reconcentration).

As Table 2 shows, both scenarios are open to question. The forecasts for Event 1 (predominant housing structure) are correct in both the sprawl and centralization scenarios. Multiple-family dwellings are more energy efficient than single-family dwellings (Sweet, 1974; Keyes and Petersen, 1977; Grier, 1978). The relative household energy inefficiency of ring and nonmetropolitan residential categories may be overstated, however, for three reasons. First, although multiple-family dwellings are most common in central-city locations, data from the Annual Housing Survey show that, even there, they account for less than 50% of available housing units.[2] Their actual percentages range between 48.2% in 1974 to 49.9% in 1978. Second, from 1974 to 1980, more new single-family dwellings were built in rings than in central cities; however, the same holds for new multiple-family dwellings.[3] Third, the percentages of dwellings with energy-efficient structures (e.g., storm windows, storm doors, and attic or roof insulation) are consistently greater in non-central-city locations.[4]

The forecasts for transportation energy consumption under the sprawl and centralization scenarios can also be questioned. As Table 2 shows, current census and human ecological data do not support the forecast for Event 2 (principal mode of transportation to work) in the centralization scenario. Planners generally agree that a shift from private to public modes of transportation would result in significant reductions in energy consumption in the transportation sector (see Goss and McGowen, 1972; Goldstein and Moses, 1975; Dewees, 1976). Where they disagree is on the feasibility of this conservation strategy.

In their attempts to assess its feasibility, planners have relied primarily on retrospective studies of the responses of individuals and households to energy shortages and rising gasoline prices. Gasoline prices have not substantially altered automobile travel patterns in the direction of greater use of mass transit to reduce either the number or the distance of work trips (Gilbert and Dajani, 1974; Myers, 1975; Becker et al., 1976; Peskin and Schofer, 1977; Keyes, 1981). There is some evidence to suggest that rising fuel prices have resulted in a reduction in the number of nonwork trips (Myers, 1975; Corsi and Harvey, 1977). Since it is the length of the work trip that is generally held to be the primary determinant of transportation energy consumption (Soot and Sen, 1979), these reductions have not resulted in major overall decreases in per capita energy consumption.

The principal response to increasing gasoline prices has been to shift to smaller, more energy-efficient cars rather than to reduce the number of automobile miles driven. During the period between 1945 and 1977, the number of automobiles, trucks, and buses in the United States increased from 29.5 million to 128.6 million, an increase of 336%

(Downs, 1979). Downs argues that because multiple car ownership was an important factor in the accelerating rate of increase, increases in per capita automobile ownership occurred in spite of the energy crisis and increases in the price of both gasoline and cars.

Findings like these have led planners to question much of the conventional wisdom that underlies current energy-sensitive transportation policies. As Lave (1978: 297) states, "many of our most cherished beliefs about transportation and energy simply are not true." Of particular relevance is his conclusion that public transit cannot attract people out of cars. Census survey data for SMSAs show that energy shortages have not produced a greater use of public transit. Twenty-one SMSAs surveyed in 1970 and again in 1975 showed a 3.4% decline in the use of mass transit as a major mode of travel to work. For 20 different SMSAs surveyed in 1970 and 1976, 19% of the workers used public transportation in 1976, a decrease of 5.6% from 1970. Of all the SMSAs surveyed, only Honolulu showed an increase in public transit use.[5]

Energy efficiency is only one of the criteria used in choosing one mode of transportation over another. To date, other criteria, including time, comfort, dependability and convenience, have favored the automobile (Dewees, 1976; Dendrinos, 1979; Henley et al., 1981). Dendrinos (1979) suggests that where time remains the principal selection criterion, it is unlikely that higher gasoline prices associated with energy shortages will result in reduced gasoline consumption.

The studies reviewed here suggest that the relationship between energy prices and energy consumption for the transportation sector may be nonlinear. It seems plausible that once gasoline prices reach a certain value relative to income, energy efficiency may become a more powerful determinant of both work and nonwork travel patterns and, hence, of urban spatial structure.[6] The implication of income as an important determinant of the effectiveness of transportation strategies is particularly relevant in the nonmetropolitan context. Kasarda (1980) suggests that since the costs of living are generally lower in nonmetropolitan areas, metropolitan to nonmetropolitan migrants may have higher real incomes. *Where necessary*, therefore, they can afford to pay the energy costs of commuting. The inclusion of the qualifier, "where necessary," reflects the fact that both people and jobs are moving away from metropolitan areas, a fact ignored under the CS Framework.

Planners who accept the popular conception of sprawl as undesirable, uncontrolled, and haphazard growth at the urban periphery (Popenoe, 1979) focus exclusively on the population dimension of the population: opportunity ratio. As a result, they fail to incorporate human ecological data on employment redistribution patterns in their scenarios. These data document the ongoing process of employment relocation to both rings and nonmetropolitan areas (see Beale, 1975; Muller, 1976; Berry and Kasarda, 1977; Kasarda, 1978, 1980, 1982a, 1982b; Hawley, 1981; Fugitt and Beale, 1984).[7] The forecasts of the sprawl scenario for Events 3 (employment distribution) and 5 (distance to work) are therefore incorrect.

These forecasts are also incorrect in the centralization scenario. Here the reconcentration forecasts for Event 4 (population distribution) are also problematic. Population reconcentration has not occurred in the post-energy-crisis years surveyed here (Kasarda, 1980; Long and DeAre, 1982; Long, 1983). Instead, Long and DeAre (1980) have documented an accelerating rate of deconcentration to nonmetropolitan areas for the time period of 1974 to 1978. Using the 1970 SMSA definition, they found that the nonmetropolitan growth rate was 1.99 times as great as the metropolitan growth rate before the energy crisis (1970-1974) and 2.25 times as great after the energy crisis (1974-1978). The growth rate differential widened when the 1974 and 1980 SMSA definitions were used, thus confirming that the energy crisis has not retarded or reversed population deconcentration.[8]

THE CMS FRAMEWORK

If both population and employment tend to "sprawl," as the human ecological data suggest, then the future population: opportunity balance is most closely approximated by the multinucleation scenario. To the extent that existing studies of the relationship between energy and urban form include human ecological data on Events 3 (employment distribution) and 4 (population distribution), their predictions support the position that multinucleation is more energy efficient than other spatial configurations of urban functions. Given the low probability of a shift from private to public modes of transportation, distance traveled is the most logical locus of intervention for policies designed to reduce transportation energy consumption. By decreasing the spatial separation of urban functions, multinucleation allows the efficient use of transportation energy that conventional wisdom associates with centralization.

Multinucleation is an energy-efficient urban form for two major reasons. Its spatial configuration allows clustering of land uses to reduce trip length for both nonwork and work trips without producing congestion. Commercial, educational, and recreational activities are becoming more widely available in ring and nonmetropolitan areas (Muller, 1976; Romanos, 1978; Kasarda, 1980; Fugitt and Beale, 1984). Where they are available, households are willing to satisfy their nonwork needs close to home (Edwards, 1978).

For work trips, the relevant clusters are residence-employment clusters. In 1975, 60.9% of ring workers lived in rings; 99.6% of nonmetropolitan residents worked in nonmetropolitan areas. For all residential categories, within-category commuting distances and times were lower than their between-category counterparts, exactly what the clustering hypothesis predicts.[9] More recent data also support this hypothesis. Thus, for example, Morrison and Abrahamse's (1982) analysis of the commuting distances of metropolitan to nonmetropolitan migrants showed that most workers end up closer to their jobs. Their commuting distances do not differ from those of the nonmigrant workers; only a small fraction become long-distance commuters.

The second reason for the greater efficiency of the multinucleated urban form is that, when analyzed from a functional rather than a spatial perspective, it involves the development of relatively dominant regional employment centers in the urban hierarchy (Romanos, 1978; Greene, 1980). The development of such centers both reflects and contributes to the change in the functional role of central cities in the urban hierarchy. As these changes continue, they may contribute to other changes that would further reduce the energy intensiveness of the multinucleated pattern. Thus, for example, their development may (1) produce the regular commuting patterns necessary for the introduction of regional public transportation systems (Ward and Paulhaus, 1974; Schneider and Noguchi, 1977; Greene, 1980), (2) create the conditions in which trucks are the most energy-efficient mode of freight transport,[10] and (3) maximize the implementation potential of telecommuting.

Recent studies by both human ecologists (e.g., Berry and Kasarda, 1977; Hawley, 1981) and urban planners (e.g., Slayton, 1972; Harberson, 1974; Gray et al., 1977) suggest that telecommuting will bring about further decentralization of business firms. For some occupations, telecommuting can also reduce transportation energy consumption directly by eliminating the separation of jobs and homes. These efficiency gains would hold across all spatial configurations. The impact of telecommuting would be greatest, however, in the multinucleated form in which both the direct and indirect effects hold.

CONCLUSION

Multinucleation is the planning equivalent of the human ecological concepts of a multinodal, multiconnected social system and a polycentric ecological field. This energy-based labeling of multinucleation as the most probable future urban form defines a significant point of convergence between planners and human ecologists. This spatial configuration also describes the most probable impact of telecommuting on the form and development of urban systems (Gray et al., 1977; Kasarda, 1980). These multiple points of convergence suggest an interesting case of structural isomorphism: The relative energy efficiency of multinucleation holds for both of the redistribution patterns considered here, suburbanization (Edwards, 1978; Romanos, 1978) and nonmetropolitan growth (Gray et al., 1978; Van Til, 1982).

This convergence around multinucleation can be interpreted in two ways. Pronucleation planners argue that large-scale recentralization of population and employment is unlikely. For them, energy costs are an important determinant of urban form, and these costs favor multinucleation. Human ecologists agree that energy factors are unlikely to retard or reverse contemporary redistribution patterns. The human ecological critique developed here suggests the possibility that they are unlikely to do so, however, because energy is now a relatively weak determinant of urban spatial structure. The hypothesis tested predicts that if energy factors are powerful determinants of urban form, then pre-and postembargo settlement patterns should differ. They do not. The evidence presented here suggests instead that the energy efficiency of multinucleation may be a fortuitous consequence of the location choices of households and firms.

This conclusion applies only to the 1970s, however. Each of the qualifications introduced in this article suggests that, in a situation of chronic scarcity, energy may become a more powerful determinant of urban form. On its future role, my position converges with pronucleation planning. My critique remains relevant even in this context, however, because it specifies a relationship between contemporary and future urban forms that differs from the dominant position in pronucleation planning. Van Til's (1982) analysis of the spatial implications of living with energy shortfall illustrates this position.

Two assumptions inform Van Til's position on the future role of energy: (1) Energy shortfall is likely; therefore, (2) energy will become an important determinant of both the dispersion (land use) and mobility (transportation) dimensions of urban scale. Under these assumptions, urban scale will not continue to increase; spatial change will be drastic.

Van Til's analysis also makes an assumption about contemporary settlement patterns: "The direction of spatial development in the U.S. experience has been steadily toward population deconcentration and spread" (Van Til, 1982: 79). This depiction of current settlement patterns is the conventional description of sprawl that the human ecological data show is incorrect. The movement toward multinucleation has already begun. Even if energy becomes a more important determinant of urban form in the future, spatial change will not be drastic. Instead of generating a fundamentally different urban form, energy constraints will intensify contemporary redistribution patterns. Emphasizing this continuity may facilitate the implementation of energy-sensitive policies because, as Van Til stresses, Americans are less likely to resist policy innovations that are not perceived as disruptive to their way of life.

NOTES

1. A survey of three major sociology journals—*American Journal of Sociology, American Sociological Review*, and *Social Forces*—suggests that Duncan's conclusion still holds. Zelinsky and Sly's (1981) application of the ecological complex to the study of the relationship between population redistribution and personal energy consumption for the 1960s is a major exception to this trend.

2. The data are from the *Annual Housing Surveys* of 1973, 1974, 1975, 1976, 1977, 1978, 1979, and 1980.

3. The data on new construction are from the *Annual Housing Surveys* of 1974, 1975, 1976, 1977, 1978, 1979, and 1980.

4. The data on energy efficient structures are for single-family dwellings. They are from the *Annual Housing Surveys* of 1974, 1975, 1976, 1977, 1978, and 1979.

5. The data on the 1970 to 1975 change in commuter use of public transit are from the U.S. Bureau of the Census, *Current Population Reports*, Series P-23, No. 68, Table 2. The 21 SMSAs surveyed were Paterson, NJ, Philadelphia, Chicago, San Francisco-Oakland, San Bernardino, Hartford, Rochester, NY, Columbus, OH, Cincinnati, Milwaukee, Kansas City, Atlanta, Miami, New Orleans, San Antonio, Portland, San Diego, Springfield, MA, Madison, Newport News-Hampton, and Colorado Springs. The data for the 1970 to 1976 change are from the U.S. Bureau of the Census, *Current Population Reports*, Series P-23, No. 72, Table E. The 20 SMSAs surveyed were New York, Baltimore, Cleveland, St. Louis, Buffalo, Indianapolis, Omaha, Providence, Birmingham, Denver, Honolulu, Houston, Louisville, Seattle-Everett, Allentown, PA, Grand Rapids, Las Vegas, Oklahoma City, Raleigh, and Sacramento.

6. There is some evidence for this suggestion in the planning literature. More recent investigations of the income-price relationship have shown that, at the level of individual

households, medium- and lower-income households are likely to respond more rapidly to energy price changes because the impact of these increases on their real incomes is felt sooner (Romanos, 1978). This differential response time has led some critics of higher gasoline prices to conclude that policies to curb consumption by increasing fuel costs will concentrate a disproportionately large share of the negative consequences of energy shortages in those subpopulations who not only consume less energy already but also spend a greater proportion of their income on energy (Burby and Bell, 1978; Grier, 1978; Julias, 1978).

7. Space limitations preclude the presentation of these data. They are discussed in these articles. Data on employment deconcentration to ring communities are available in the series of articles by John D. Kasarda. Data on employment deconcentration to nonmetropolitan areas are available in Fugitt and Beale, 1980.

8. Data on population distribution trends for 1970 to 1980 for the central city, ring, and nonmetropolitan residential categories are available in the U.S. Bureau of the Census, *Current Population Reports*, Series P-20 No.s 262, 273, 285, 305, 320, 331 and 353.

9. These data are from the U.S. Bureau of the Census, *Current Population Reports*, Series P-23, No. 72.

10. Modes of freight transport can be ranked on overall energy efficiency (from high to low) as follows: pipeline, railroad, waterway, truck and airplane. When extrapolating from this ranking, however, it is important to note that a mode of transport that shows a relatively low efficiency overall may be relatively energy efficient under some circumstances. Harberson (1974) has shown that, when compared with railways, trucks are more efficient for short hauls and very low volumes.

REFERENCES

ALONSO, W. (1978) "Metropolis without growth." Public Interest 53: 68-86.

BACON, E. N. (1973) "Energy and land use." Urban Land 73: 13-16.

BEALE, C. L. (1975) The Revival of Population Growth in Nonmetropolitan America. Washington, DC: U.S. Department of Agriculture, Economic Development Division, Economic Research Service.

BECKER, B. W., D. J. BROWN, and P. B. SCHARY (1976) "Behavior of car owners during the gasoline shortage." Traffic Q. 30: 469-483.

BERRY, B. J. and J. D. KASARDA (1977) Contemporary Human Ecology. New York: Macmillan.

BURBY, R. J. and A. F. BELL [eds.] (1978) Energy and the Community. Cambridge, MA: Ballinger.

BYRNE, R. M. (1979) "The impact of energy costs and supply prospects on land development practices." Urban Land 38: 6-12.

CARROLL, I. O. (1978) "Calculating community energy demands," pp. 39-46 in R. J. Burby and A. F. Bell (eds.) Energy and the Community. Cambridge, MA: Ballinger.

CORNEHLS, J. (1977) "The automobile society: urban design and environment." Traffic Q. 31: 571-590.

CORSI, T. M. and M. E. HARVEY (1977) "Travel behavior under increases in gasoline prices." Traffic Q. 31: 605-624.

Council on Environmental Quality (1975) "The costs of sprawl in the USA." Ekistics 239: 266-272.
DENDRINOS, D. S. (1979) "Energy costs, the transport network, and urban form." Environment and Planning A 11: 655-664.
DEWEES, D. N. (1976) "Travel cost, transit and control of urban motoring." Public Policy 24: 59-79.
DOWNS, A. (1979) "The automobile population explosion." Traffic Q. 33: 342-367.
DUNCAN, O. D. (1978) "Sociologists should reconsider nuclear energy." Social Forces 57: 1-22.
EDWARDS, J. L. (1978) "The effect of land use on transportation energy consumption," pp. 47-59 in R. J. Burby and A. F. Bell (eds.) Energy and the Community. Cambridge, MA: Ballinger.
FRANKLIN, H. M. (1974) "Will the new consciousness of energy and the environment create an imploding metropolis?" Amer. Institute of Architects J. 62: 28-36.
FUGITT, G. L. and C. L. BEALE (1984) Changes in Population, Employment and Industrial Composition in Nonmetropolitan America. Working Paper 84-20. Madison: University of Wisconsin, Center for Demography and Ecology.
GERHSUNY, J. (1976) "The choice of scenarios." Futures 8: 496-508.
GILBERT, G. D. and J. S. DAJANI (1974) "Energy, urban form and transportation policy." Transportation Research 8: 267-276.
GOLDSTEIN, G. S. and L. N. MOSES (1975) "Transport controls, travel costs, and urban spatial structure." Public Policy 23: 355-380.
GOSS, W. P. and J. G. McGOWAN (1972) "Transportation and energy—a future confrontation." Transportation 1: 265-289.
GRAY, P., J. M. NILLES, and D. A. LOPEZ (1977) "Communications for transportation: implications for traffic engineering." Transportation Engineering 47: 19-24.
GRAY, P. J., M. NILLES, and D. A. LOPEZ (1977) "Communications for transportation: implications for traffic engineering." Transportation Engineering 47: 19-24.
GREENE, D. L. (1980) "Urban subcenters: recent trends in urban spatial structure." Growth and Change 11: 29-40.
GRIER, E. S. (1978) "Energy consumption in American households," pp. 3-13 in R. J. Burby and A. F. Bell (eds.) Energy and the Community. Cambridge, MA: Ballinger.
HARBERSON, R. W. (1974) "Some transport policy implications of energy shortages." Land Economics 50: 387-396.
HAWLEY, A. H. (1950) Human Ecology: A Theory of Community Structure. New York: Ronald Press.
———(1981) Urban Society: An Ecological Approach. New York: John Wiley.
HENLEY, D. H., I. P. LEVEN, J. J. LOUVIERE, and R. J. MEYER (1981) "Changes in perceived travel cost and time for the work trip during a period of increasing gasoline costs." Transportation 10: 23-34.
HOBEN, J. E. (1975) "The costs of sprawl." HUD Challenge 6: 24-26.
JANTSCH, E. (1967) Technological Forecasting in Perspective. Paris: OECD.
JULIAS, S. D. (1978) "Conserve or consume: how households and neighborhoods vary," pp. 15-18 in R. J. Burby and A. F. Bell (eds.) Energy and the Community. Cambridge, MA: Ballinger.
KASARDA, J. D. (1978) "Urbanization, community and the metropolitan problem," pp. 27-57 in D. Street and Associates (eds.) Handbook of Contemporary Urban Life. San Francisco: Jossey-Bass.

———(1980) "The implications of contemporary redistribution trends for national urban policy." Social Sci. Q. 61: 373-400.

———(1982a) "Adapting policy to new urban realities." Presented at the University of Chicago Conference on the Future of our City.

———(1982b) "Urban industrial transformation and minority opportunity." Presented to the Office of Policy Development and Research, U.S. Department of Housing and Urban Development.

KEYES, D. L. (1981) "The influence of energy on future patterns of urban development," pp. 309-325 in A. P. Solomon (ed.) The Prospective City. Cambridge: MIT Press.

———and G. E. PETERSON (1977) Metropolitan Development and Energy Consumption. Washington, DC: Government Printing Office.

KYDES, A. D., J. B. SANBORN, and T. O. CARROLL (1976) Regional Land Use and Energy Modeling. Upton, NY: Brookhaven National Laboratory, Department of Applied Science.

LANDSBERG, H. H. (1979) Energy: The Next Twenty Years: Report by a Study Group Sponsored by the Ford Foundation and Administered by RFF. Cambridge, MA: Ballinger.

LAVE, C. A. (1978) "Transportation and energy: some current myths." Policy Analysis 4: 297-315.

LONG, L. H. (1983) Population Redistribution in the U.S.: Issues for the 1980s. Population Trends and Public Policy No. 3. Washington, DC: Population Reference Bureau.

———and D. DEARE (1980) Migration to Nonmetropolitan Areas: Appraising the Trend and Reasons for Moving. Washington, DC: Government Printing Office.

———(1982) "Repopulating the countryside: A 1980 census trend." Science 217: 1111-1116.

MORRISON, P. A. and A. ABRAHAMSE (1982) Is Population Decentralization Lengthening Commuting Distances? A Rand Note. Santa Monica, CA: Rand Corporation.

MULLER, P. O. (1976) The Outer City: Geographical Consequences of the Urbanization of the Suburbs. Resource Paper 75-2. Washington, DC: Association of American Geographers.

MYERS, S. (1975) "Don't count on higher fuel prices to halt urban sprawl." Amer. Institute of Architects J. 63: 35-36.

NADLER, P. S. (1975) "New chance for cities: high cost energy will tip the scales in favor of cities over suburbs and exurbs." Real Estate Rev. 4: 24-28.

PESKIN, R. L. and J. L. SCHOFER (1977) The Impacts of Urban Transportation and Land-Use Policies on Transportation Energy Consumption. Washington, DC: U.S. Department of Transportation, Office of Research.

POPENOE, D. (1979) "Urban sprawl: some neglected sociological considerations." Sociology and Social Research 63: 255-268.

Real Estate Research Corporation (1974) The Costs of Sprawl: Environmental and Economic Costs of Alternative Residential Development Patterns at the Urban Fringe. Washington, DC: Government Printing Office.

ROBERTS, J. S. (1978) "Energy conservation and land use: prospects and procedures," pp. 33-38 in R. J. Burby and A. F. Bell (eds.) Energy and the Community. Cambridge, MA: Ballinger.

ROMANOS, M. C. (1978) "Energy-price effects on metropolitan spatial structure and form." Environment and Planning A 10: 93-104.

ROSS, M. H. and R. H. WILLIAMS (1981) Our Energy: Regaining Control. New York: McGraw Hill.

SCHNEIDER, J. B. and T. NOGUCHI (1977) Transit's Role in the Creation of the Polycentric City: An Initial Assessment. Research Report 77-6. Urban Transportation Program Departments of Civil Engineering and Urban Planning. Seattle: University of Washington.

SLAYTON, W. L. (1976) "Tomorrow's city will look like a collection of small towns." Planning 42: 14-16.

SMALL, K. A. (1980) "Energy scarcity and urban development patterns." Int. Regional Sci. Rev. 5: 97-117.

SOOT, S. and A. SEN (1979) "Metropolitan work-trip energy consumption patterns." Traffic Q. 33: 275-279.

STOBAUGH, R. and D. YERGIN (1979) Energy Futures. Report of the Energy Project at the Harvard Business School. New York: Random House.

SWEET, A. L. (1974) "Effects of residential building type on energy consumption." Building Research 74 (April/June): 18-24.

U.S. Bureau of the Census (1974) Mobility of the Population of the United States: March 1970 to March 1973. Current Population Reports, Series P-20, 262. Washington, DC: Government Printing Office.

———(1974) Mobility of the Population of the United States: March 1970 to March 1974. Current Population Reports, Series P-20, 273. Washington, DC: Government Printing Office.

———(1975) Mobility of the Population of the United States: March 1970 to March 1975. Current Population Reports, Series P-20, 285. Washington, DC: Government Printing Office.

———(1977) Geographical Mobility: March 1975 to March 1976. Current Population Reports, Series P-20, 305. Washington, DC: Government Printing Office.

———(1978a) Geographical Mobility: March 1975 to March 1977. Current Population Reports, Series P-20, 320. Washington, DC: Government Printing Office.

———(1978b) Geographical Mobility: March 1975 to March 1978. Current Population Reports, Series P-20, 331. Washington, DC: Government Printing Office.

———(1978c) Selected Characteristics of Travel to Work in 21 Metropolitan Areas: 1975. Current Population Reports, Series P-23, 68. Washington, DC: Government Printing Office.

———(1978d) Selected Characteristics of Travel to Work in 20 Metropolitan Areas: 1976. Current Population Reports, Series P-23, 72. Washington, DC: Government Printing Office.

———(1980) Geographical Mobility: March 1975 to March 1979. Current Population Reports, Series P-20, 353. Washington, DC: Government Printing Office.

———(1981) Geographical Mobility: March 1975 to March 1980. Current Population Reports, Series P-20, 368. Washington, DC: Government Printing Office.

U.S. Department of Commerce, Bureau of the Census (1975) Annual Housing Survey: 1973. Washington, DC: Government Printing Office.

———(1976) Annual Housing Survey: 1974. Washington, DC: Government Printing Office.

———(1977) Annual Housing Survey: 1975. Washington, DC: Government Printing Office.

———(1978) Annual Housing Survey: 1976. Washington, DC: Government Printing Office.

———(1979) Annual Housing Survey: 1977. Washington, DC: Government Printing Office.
———(1980) Annual Housing Survey: 1978. Washington, DC: Government Printing Office.
———(1981) Annual Housing Survey: 1979. Washington, DC: Government Printing Office.
———(1982) Annual Housing Survey: 1980. Washington, DC: Government Printing Office.
VAN TIL, J. (1980) "A new type of city for an energy short world." Futurist 14: 64-70.
———(1982) Living With Energy Shortfall. A Future for American Towns and Cities. Boulder, CO: Westview.
WARD, J. D. and N. C. PAULHAUS, Jr. (1974) Suburbanization and Its Implications for Urban Transportation Systems. Department of Transportation Report TST-74-8. Washington, DC: Government Printing Office.
WARDWELL, J. M. and C. J. GILCHRIST (1980) "The distribution of population and energy in nonmetropolitan areas: Confluence and divergence." Social Sci. Q. 61: 567-580.
WINDSOR, D. (1979) "A critique of *The Costs of Sprawl.*" J. of the Amer. Institute of Planners 45: 279-292.
ZELINSKY, W. and D. F. SLY (1981) U.S. Population Redistribution and Personal Energy Use. Final Report Submitted to the National Science Foundation. Washington, DC: Government Printing Office.

Valerie A. Haines is a doctoral candidate in the Sociology Department at the University of North Carolina at Chapel Hill. Her interests include social theory, human ecology and urban sociology.

COMMENT ON "ENERGY AND URBAN FORM"

JON VAN TIL
Rutgers University Camden College

Valerie Haines makes an important contribution to our understanding of the relations between energy and urban form in her article. By systematically examining a series of projections after the passage of some years, she illuminates both the risks and the benefits of seeking to understand the future.

Haines seeks to construct a "natural experiment" by seeing if the energy upheavals of the 1970s did, indeed, lead to any changes in spatial and settlement patterns in the United States. Such changes, she properly notes, were anticipated as possibilities by many authors who sought to comprehend the emerging form of spatial patterns.

Social scientists conventionally have been content to focus their studies on what has happened, rather than on what might or will happen. However, understanding what will happen (insofar as that is comprehensible) is at least as important an intellectual and practical task as knowing what has already happened. Therefore, forecasting and futuring have become increasingly prevalent and respectable activities in a wide range of social sciences.

Haines examines the work of 19 such social scientists who sought to predict spatial futures from energy patterns in the late 1970s and early 1980s. She notes that each of these studies employed scenario development as the principal methodology, which is subject to problems of arbitrariness in the selection of the number of scenarios and the choice of events contained within scenarios. Therefore, the testing of scenario-based studies after the fact becomes an important task for social scientists.

Haines finds that the scenario-based studies led to two different sets of projections: one toward recentralization as a reversal of sprawl, the other toward the development of "multinucleation." She asserts that

URBAN AFFAIRS QUARTERLY, Vol. 21 No. 3, March 1986 355-358

recent trends demonstrate the superiority of the second type of projection, but not for the reasons asserted by these scenarists. Rather, multinucleation is occurring despite the failure of energy patterns to emerge as a significant force. It occurs because of ecological laws governing the location choices of households and firms.

What Haines is asserting, then, is that the scenarists who developed energy-driven models of spatial change predicting multinucleation are guilty of what William Dunn (1981) has described as "errors of the third type." They have arrived at the "right answer" while not posing the "right question."

My own work is seen by Haines to demonstrate the errors of these multinucleational scenarists. By failing to recognize that the new future is already aborning, I am seen to have committed the error of positing, as a current reality and future possibility, the continuing spread of sprawl. I have reached the "right" answer, Haines implies, but for the wrong reason. The proper question to ask is not "Will we move toward a multinucleated future in the event of energy shortfall?" but is, rather, "How rapidly will energy shortfall increase the current movement toward multinucleation?"

Thus, the central question in Haines's work involves the disagreement between two schools of urbanists as to the present direction of urban form. On one hand stand the discoverers of multinucleation, led by John Kasarda.[1] On the other stand the observers of spread and sprawl, led by Brian Berry.[2] Haines claims that the Kasarda group is more closely in touch with reality, but she does not explain their advantage. She only reviews several of their studies and identifies them as representing a "human ecological" rather than a "planning" approach.

The question of the validity of the differing sets of findings is obviously important, and would be worth a series of dispassionate studies by persons not closely identified with either camp. Perhaps a special issue of this journal could be devoted to the controversy, with efforts made to assess the evidence on each side while examining carefully for emerging trends. Meanwhile, the question remains of our national adaptability to the potential of energy shortfall. Here I would gladly modify my own previously stated position. I would continue to state that multinucleation is the proper remedy for energy shortfall. I would modify my earlier position that spread would yield to multinucleation in the face of shortfall. Now I would say, having read Haines, that the pace of multinucleation can be expected to be further enhanced by any increased awareness of shortfall, while urban scale will surely contract in such an event.

I conclude with an observation about the role of futures studies in contemporary urban sociology. On the whole, I am impressed with the contribution made by the 19 scholars whose work forms the data base for Haines's study. Their work addresses important questions about the changing face of American society. Although few of their scenarios can be seen to have "come true," that is not the point of the futures studies enterprise.[3] Rather, what is sought is a way of showing, "This is what might come to pass, if a combination of existing trends and specific events occur. Let us learn from this potentiality and find ways to discover what responses we would want to make to it, before it becomes a reality. Let us be clear as to what we want, and how it relates to what might come to pass. Then let us try to assure the achievement of the best future that we can."

Writing from my Philadelphia home, two miles from the site of the MOVE conflagration, one week after the shootout and fire, it seems important to note once again the need for the best possible futures planning. It is simply a fact of life that worst-case scenarios can become realities in urban society. Helping to assure that this is understood is a vital scholarly responsibility.

NOTES

1. For references to this work, see Haines's article (this issue).
2. See, for example, Berry (1980).
3. For an extraordinarily useful periodical on the best of futures studies, see *Future Survey: A Monthly Abstract of Books, Articles, and Reports concerning Forecasts, Trends, and Ideas about the Future*. Bethesda, MD: World Future Society.

REFERENCES

BERRY, B. (1980) "Urbanization and counterurbanization in the United States." Annals of the Amer. Academy of Pol. and Social Sci. 451 (September): 13-21.

DUNN, W. N. (1981) Public Policy Analysis: An Introduction. Englewood Cliffs, NJ: Prentice-Hall.

Jon Van Til is Associate Professor and Chairman of the Department of Urban Studies and Community Development at Rutgers University's Camden College. He is the author of Living with Energy Shortfall: A Future for American Towns and Cities *(Westview Press, 1982), and is a board member of the Urban Affairs Association.*

THE EFFECT OF ECONOMIC DEPENDENCE ON URBAN PRIMACY
A Cross-National Panel Analysis

R. SCOTT FREY
Kansas State University

THOMAS DIETZ
George Mason University

JANE MARTE
George Washington University

Dependency theorists have become increasingly interested in examining the effects of international economic dependence on such measures of national development as economic growth, income inequality, and overurbanization. Yet limited systematic research exists examining the effect of economic dependence on urban primacy. Panel regression analysis was used to examine the effects of economic dependence and several control variables on urban primacy for a sample of 53 nations. That is, circa 1970 primacy (based on Davis's 4-city index of first-city primacy) was regressed on circa 1955 measures of urban primacy, economic dependence (investment dependence or export dependence on raw materials), gross national product per capita, land area size, and population growth between 1950 and 1970. Results of the analyses indicated that both measures of economic dependence had positive—albeit nonsignificant—effects on urban primacy.

Dependency theorists maintain that international economic dependence (understood in terms of trade, aid, or investment) hampers the internal development of those countries occupying subordinate positions in the world economic system (e.g., Baran, 1957; Emmanuel, 1972; Frank, 1972; Wallerstein, 1974; Amin, 1976; Chase-Dunn and Rubinson, 1977; Cardosa and Faletto, 1979; Frank, 1979). Economic dependence is seen as retarding economic growth and producing income

URBAN AFFAIRS QUARTERLY, Vol. 21 No. 3, March 1986 359-368

inequality by reducing a nation's capacity to control its resources, accumulate capital, invest in productive and diverse economic enterprises, and pursue a program of balanced economic growth (see Chase-Dunn, 1975: 722-724; Rubinson, 1976: 643-644; Frank, 1979). Findings of crossnational research indicate that international economic dependence does have negative effects on aggregate economic growth (Chase-Dunn, 1975; Rubinson, 1977; Bornschier et al., 1978; Bornschier, 1980; Stokes and Jaffe, 1982) and income equality (Chase-Dunn, 1975; Rubinson, 1976; Bornschier et al., 1978; Bornschier and Ballmer-Cao, 1979; Evans and Timberlake, 1980; Stack and Zimmerman, 1982).

Interest in the link between economic dependence and national development has not been restricted to the study of economic development. Attention has increasingly been directed to the examination of the effect of economic dependence on urbanization (e.g., Berry and Kasarda, 1977: 386-400; Roberts, 1979; Sokolovsky et al., 1980; Walters et al., 1980; Ettlinger, 1981; Chase-Dunn, 1982a). Dependency theorists argue that overurbanization ("urbanization without industrialization;" Higgins, 1967) and urban primacy (upward deviation from a log-normal city-size distribution; Zipf, 1941) are a direct result of overspecialization in the export of raw materials and the unbalanced and capital-intensive character of foreign investments (see Berry and Kasarda, 1977: 386-400; Roberts, 1979: 47-49, 106-107; Kentor, 1981: 202-204; Chase-Dunn, 1982a: 3-4). Crossnational research suggests support for the hypothesized effects of economic dependence on urbanization, for both overurbanization (Timberlake, 1979; Lunday, 1980; Kentor, 1981) and urban primacy (Linsky, 1969; Mehta, 1969; McGreevy, 1971; Vapnarsky, 1975; Timberlake, 1979; Chase-Dunn, 1982b) are reported to vary as a direct function of economic dependence.

Urban primacy, unlike economic growth, income inequality, and overurbanization, has not been subjected to systematic study, since extant research is characterized by one or more of the following shortcomings: use of cross-sectional designs (Linsky, 1969; Mehta, 1969), reliance on bivariate statistical techniques (Linsky, 1969; Mehta, 1969; McGreevy, 1971; Vapnarsky, 1975), and use of small and unrepresentative samples (McGreevy, 1971; Vapnarksy, 1975; Timberlake, 1979; Chase-Dunn, 1982b). We remedied these deficiencies by using panel regression analysis to examine the effects of lagged measures of primacy, economic dependence, and three control variables on 1970 (circa) urban primacy for a sample of 53 nations.

DATA AND METHOD

SAMPLE

Nations for which data on all variables could be attained were included in the analysis. The sample consists of 53 countries and includes both developed and developing countries. Unlike previous research examining the effects of economic dependence on various measures of development (e.g., Chase-Dunn, 1975; Timberlake, 1979; Kentor, 1981), we included both developed and developing countries in order to enhance the generalizability of findings.

DEPENDENT VARIABLE

Population size data (circa 1950 and 1970) for the largest four cities were used to construct a measure of primacy. The measure of primacy used was Davis's (1969: 242-246) 4-city index of first-city primacy: the ratio of the population of the largest city to the summed populations of the next three largest cities. Although this ratio and variations of it have been used by previous researchers (Berry, 1961; Ginsburg, 1961: 36; Mehta, 1969; Timberlake, 1979), it has been criticized for confusing "cases in which the two largest cities are very primate with cases in which the distribution is not primate" (Chase-Dunn, 1982a: 6-7; see also Walters et al., 1980: 11). This is a legitimate criticism of the 4-city index, but the fact remains that the pattern of urban primacy facing many countries is one in which the largest city is many times larger than other cities in the city-system. As a result, we confined our analysis to the 4-city index.

INDEPENDENT VARIABLES

Two measures of economic dependence were used: investment dependence per capita and export dependence on raw materials. Investment dependence is Chase-Dunn's (1975: 728) measure of economic dependence: the ratio of mean annual value of dollar profits earned by foreign countries on investments during the years 1950-1955 to 1950 population. Export dependence on raw materials is Ginsburg's (1961: 106) measure of percentage of total exports identified as raw materials in 1955. Researchers examining the effect of economic dependence on urban primacy have used either investment dependence (Timberlake, 1979) or variations of the export dependence measure (Linsky, 1969; Mehta, 1969; McGreevy, 1971). This is the first time that both measures have been used in the same analysis and provided the opportunity for assessing the robustness of the effect of economic dependence on urban primacy.

CONTROL VARIABLES

Three variables were included in the analyses as controls: population growth during the period from 1950 to 1970, land area size in 1955, and gross national product per capita (GNP/capita) in 1955. These variables were included because previous research indicates that they covary with urban primacy. Based on the findings of previous research, it was expected that population growth would have a positive effect on primacy (Linsky, 1969), land area size would have a negative effect on primacy (Mehta, 1969), and GNP/capita would have a negative effect on primacy (Linsky, 1969; Mehta, 1969; Timberlake, 1979).

METHOD OF ANALYSIS

Panel regression analysis was used to estimate the effect of each measure of economic dependence on urban primacy. That is, ordinary least-squares regression was used to estimate parameters of the following equation, which summarizes the hypothesized effects of variables on urban primacy:

$$Y_t = a + b_1 Y_{t-1} + b_2 X_2 + b_3 X_3 - b_4 X_4 - b_5 X_5 + e$$

where

Y_t = urban primacy, 1970;

a = intercept;

b = coefficient to be estimated;

Y_{t-1} = urban primacy, 1950;

X_2 = economic dependence (investment dependence/capita, $\bar{X}$ 1950-1955, or export dependence, 1955);

X_3 = population growth, 1950-1970;

X_4 = land area size, 1955;

X_5 = GNP/capita, 1955;

e = residual term.

TABLE 1

Results of Panel Regression of Urban Primacy on Lagged Primacy, Investment Dependence, Population Growth, Land Area Size, and GNP/Capita (N = 53)

	Primacy, 1970[a]		
Regressor Variable	Unstandardized Coefficient (b)	Standard Error	Standardized Coefficient (B)
Primacy, 1950[b]	.726**	.166	.526
Investment dependence, $\bar{X}$ 1950-55[c]	.816	.999	.112
Population growth, 1950-70[d]	-.602	1.011	-.094
Area, 1955[e]	.001	.028	.007
GNP/capita, 1955[f]	-.089	.058	-.252
Intercept	135.774*	74.562	
R^2	.355		
$\bar{R}^2$	.286		

NOTE: An analysis based on 35 nations with GNP/capita of $405 and less was conducted. Results of this analysis were not substantially different from results reported above for the full sample. The variance-decomposition measure suggested by Belsley et al. (1980: 85-191, esp. 156-159) was used to assess the impact of multicollinearity. In no case did collinearity appear to degrade estimates.

$*p \leqslant .10$; $**p \leqslant .05$.

a. Sources: Yates (1973), **Statesmen Yearbook** (1973-1975), Kurian (1978), **World Book Encyclopedia** (1978), and Banks and Overstreet (1981).

b. Sources: **Statesmen Yearbook** (1951, 1955, 1958), Davis (1969: 163-233), and Jones (1975: 353).

c. Source: International Monetary Fund (1956-1958).

d. Sources: population, 1950 (Davis, 1969: 66-67, 73; International Bank for Reconstruction and Development, 1980); population, 1970 (Newspaper Enterprise Association, 1974; International Bank for Reconstruction and Development, 1980).

e. Sources: El-Shakhs (1972: 33-35) and Newspaper Enterprise Association (1974).

f. Source: Ginsburg (1961: 18).

TABLE 2
Results of Panel Regression of Urban Primacy on Lagged Primacy, Export Dependence on Raw Materials, Population Growth, Land Area Size, and GNP/Capita (N = 53)

	Primacy, 1970		
Regressor Variable	Unstandardized Coefficient (b)	Standard Error	Standardized Coefficient (B)
Primacy, 1950	.706*	.167	.512
Export dependence on raw materials, 1955	.907	.983	.150
Population growth, 1950-70	-.694	1.031	-.108
Area, 1955	-.006	.027	-.030
GNP/capita, 1955	-.057	.056	-.161
Intercept	70.720	84.425	
R^2	.357		
$\bar{R}^2$	.289		

NOTE: See notes to Table 1 for sources of data. Data source for Export Dependence on Raw Materials, 1955, is Ginsbury (1961: 106).

RESULTS

Sources of data and results of the analyses are presented in Tables 1 and 2. Table 1 contains results of the investment dependence analysis and Table 2 contains results of the export dependence analysis.

INVESTMENT DEPENDENCE

Results indicate that with the exception of populaton growth (b = -.602; B = -.094) and land area size (b = .001; B = .007), all variables had the expected net impacts on primacy: The lagged dependent variable had a positive effect (b = .726; B = .526), investment dependence had a positive effect (b = .816; B = .112), and GNP/capita had a negative effect (b = -.089; B = -.252). However, only the lagged dependent variable had a significant effect on primacy. Since the net effect of investment dependence is neither exceptionally strong nor statistically significant at conventional levels, there is only weak support for the thesis that investment dependence affects urban primacy.

EXPORT DEPENDENCE ON RAW MATERIALS

Results are generally consistent with those of the investment dependence analysis. Population growth had an unexpected negative effect on primacy (b = -.694; B = -.108), whereas the remaining four variables had the expected net effects on primacy: The lagged dependent variable had a positive effect (b = .706; B = .512), export dependence had a positive effect (b = .907; B = .150), area had a negative effect (b = -.006; B = -.030), and GNP/capita had a negative effect (b = -.057; B = -.161). Although four of the five regressor variables had the hypothesized net effects on primacy, only the coefficient for the lagged dependent variable reached statistical significance. Such results indicate only partial support for the argument that export dependence affects urban primacy.

SUMMARY AND CONCLUSIONS

The argument that urban primacy varies across nations as a direct function of economic dependence has received increased attention from proponents of the dependency perspective. Incorporating corrections for shortcomings of previous research, we presented results of two tests of the dependency thesis. Results of the analyses indicated that the net effects of investment dependence and export dependence on primacy were small and nonsignificant. These results, however, do not lead us to reject the argument, for the results of both investment dependence and export dependence were in the predicted direction. Additional research, based on the full range of available measures of dependence and primacy, is needed before the dependency conception of urban primacy can be considered adequately tested.

REFERENCES

AMIN, S. (197) Unequal Development: An Essay on the Social Formations of Peripheral Capitalism. New York: Monthly Review Press.

BANKS, A. S. and W. OVERSTREET [eds.] (1981) Political Handbook of the World: 1981. New York: McGraw-Hill.

BARAN, P. (1957) The Political Economy of Growth. New York: Monthly Review Press.

BELSLEY, D. A., E. KUH, and R. E. WELSH (1980) Regression Diagnostics. New York: John Wiley.
BERRY, B.J.L. (1961) "City size distributions and economic development." Econ. Development and Cultural Change 9: 573-588.
———and J. D. KASARDA (1977) Contemporary Urban Ecology. New York: Macmillan.
BORNSCHIER, V. (1980) "Multinational corporations and economic growth: a cross-national test of the decapitalization thesis." J. of Development Economics 7: 191-210.
———and T. BALLMER-CAO (1979) "Income inequality: a cross-national study of the relationship between mnc-penetration, dimensions of the power structure and income distribution." Amer. Soc. Rev. 44: 487-506.
BORNSCHIER, V., C. CHASE-DUNN, and R. RUBINSON (1978) "Cross-national evidence of the effects of foreign investment and aid on economic growth and inequality: a survey of findings and a reanalysis." Amer. J. of Sociology 84: 651-683.
CARDOSA, F. H. and E. FALETTO (1979) Dependency and Development in Latin America. Berkeley: Univ. of California Press.
CHASE-DUNN, C. (1975) "The effects of international economic dependence on development and inequality: a cross-national study." Amer. Soc. Rev. 40: 720-738.
———(1982a) "World division of labor and the development of city-systems: a longitudinal cross-national study." Comparative Research 9: 3-9.
———(1982b) "Latin American cities in the world-system." Presented at the Seminar on Structural Development and Social Problems of the Latin American City, Working Group on Latin American Urbanization, Tepotzlan.
DAVIS, K. (1969) World Urbanization, 1950-1970 (Vol. 1). Berkeley: University of California, Institute of International Studies.
EL-SHAKHS, S. (1972) "Development, primacy, and systems of cities." J. of Developing Areas 7: 11-35.
EMMANUEL, A. (1972) Unequal Exchange. New York: Monthly Review Press.
ETTLINGER, N. (1981) "Dependency and urban growth: a critical review and reformulation of the concepts of primacy and rank-size." Environment and Planning A 13: 1389-1400.
EVANS, P. and M. TIMBERLAKE (1980) "Dependence, inequality and growth in less developed countries." Amer. Soc. Rev. 45: 531-552.
FRANK, A. G. (1972) "The development of underdevelopment," pp. 3-17 in J. D. Cockcroft et al. Dependence and Underdevelopment. New York: Anchor.
———(1979) Dependence Accumulation and Underdevelopment. New York: Monthly Review Press.
GINSBURG, N. (1961) Atlas of Economic Development. Chicago: Univ. of Chicago Press.
HIGGINS, B. (1967) "Urbanization, industrialization, and economic development," pp. 117-155 in G. H. Beyer (ed.) The Urban Explosion in Latin America. Ithaca, NY: Cornell Univ. Press.
International Bank for Reconstruction and Development (1980) World Tables 1980. Baltimore: Johns Hopkins Univ. Press.
International Monetary Fund (1956-58) Balance of Payments Yearbook (Vols. 7-9). Washington, DC: Author.
JONES, R. [ed.] (1975) Essays on World Urbanization. London: George Philip.

KENTOR, J. (1981) "Structural determinants of peripheral urbanization: the effects of international dependence." Amer. Soc. Rev. 46: 201-211.

KURIAN, G. T. (1978) Encyclopedia of the Third World. New York: Facts on File.

LINSKY, A. S. (1969) "Some generalizations concerning primate cities," pp. 285-294 in G. W. Breese (ed.) The City in Newly Developing Countries. Englewood Cliffs, NJ: Prentice-Hall.

LUNDAY, J. (1980) "Dependency and urbanization: an analysis of dependence effects on over-urbanization." Johns Hopkins University. (unpublished)

McGREEVY, W. P. (1971) "A statistical analysis of primacy and lognormality in the size distribution of Latin American cities, 1750-1960," pp. 116-129 in R. M. Morse et al. (eds.) The Urban Development of Latin America, 1750-1920. Stanford, CA: Stanford Univ. Press.

MEHTA, S. K. (1969) "Some demographic and economic correlates of primate cities: a case for reevaluation," pp. 295-308 in G. W. Breese (ed.) The City in Newly Developing Countries. Englewood Cliffs, NJ: Prentice-Hall.

Newspaper Enterprise Association (1974) The World Almanac and Book of Facts. New York: Doubleday.

ROBERTS, B. (1979) Cities of Peasants: The Political Economy of Urbanization in the Third World. Beverly Hills, CA: Sage.

RUBINSON, R. (1976) "The world economy and the distribution of income within states." Amer. Soc. Rev. 41: 638-659.

———(1977) "Dependence, government revenue and economic growth, 1955-1970." Studies in Comparative Int. Development 12: 3-28.

SOKOLOVSKY, J., J. KENTOR, P. WALTERS, P. ARREGUI, and C. CHASE-DUNN (1980) "Economic networks, political boundaries and city systems in the capitalist world-economy." Presented at the annual meeting of the American Political Science Association, Washington, DC.

STACK, S. and D. ZIMMERMAN (1982) The effect of world economy on income inequality: a reassessment." Soc. Q. 23: 345-358.

Statesmen Yearbook (1951ff) New York: St. Martin's.

STOKES, R. and D. JAFFE (1982) "Another look at the export of raw materials and economic growth." Amer. Soc. Rev. 47: 402-407.

TIMBERLAKE, M. F. (1979) "Economic dependence, internal urban and labor force structure, and problems of development: a quantitative, cross-national study." Ph.D. dissertation, Brown University.

VAPNARSKY, C. A. (1975) "The Argentine system of cities: primacy and rank-size rule," pp. 369-389 in J. E. Hardoy (ed.) Urbanization in Latin America: Approaches and Issues. Garden City, NY: Anchor/Doubleday.

WALLERSTEIN, I. (1974) The Modern World-System: Capitalist Agriculture and the Origins of the European World Economy in the Sixteenth Century. New York: Academic Press.

WALTERS, P., J. KENTOR, P. ARREGUI, C. CHASE-DUNN, and J. SOKOLOVSKY (1980) "Conceptualization of the urbanization process in the core and the periphery." Presented at the annual meeting of the Society for the Study of Social Problems, New York.

World Book Encyclopedia (1978) Chicago: World Book-Childcraft International.

YATES, N. [ed.] (1973) The International Yearbook and Statesmen's Who's Who. London: Burke's Peerage.

ZIPF, G. K. (1941) National Unity and Disunity. Bloomington, IN: Principia Press.

R. Scott Frey is Assistant Professor of Sociology at Kansas State University. His current research interests include methods of public policy analysis, patterns of Third World urbanization, and the relationship between economic dependence and technological risk in Third World nations.

Thomas Dietz is Assistant Professor of Sociology at George Mason University. His research interests center on the use of scientific information in the policy process and the cross-national determinants of population and environmental policy.

Jane Marte is a Ph.D. candidate in the Department of Sociology at George Washington University. She is interested in Third World revolutions.

THE DETERMINANTS OF GENTRIFICATION IN THE UNITED STATES
A City-Level Analysis

BRUCE LONDON
Florida Atlantic University

BARRETT A. LEE
Vanderbilt University

S. GREGORY LIPTON
University of Virginia

The literature on gentrification has yielded a number of competing explanations of the phenomenon. These include demographic, ecological, sociocultural, and political-economic interpretations. By linking the results of a survey of the presence and significance of gentrification with data from 48 of the 51 cities in the Permanent Community Sample, we are able to assess why some cities are candidates for gentrification while others are not and to determine the relative usefulness of the competing explanations listed above. We find some support for aspects of each interpretation.

Gentrification is the widespread emergence of middle- and upper middle-class enclaves in formerly deteriorated, inner-city neighborhoods. This phenomenon represents a marked reversal of the usual pattern of urban neighborhood change. As such, it has become a major focus of theoretical and practical concern.

However, the newness of the phenomenon—most renovation has taken place since 1975—means that the causes and consequences of the gentrification process remain poorly understood. Although there is a burgeoning literataure on the topic (see Palen and London, 1984), the vast majority of this work is based on the observation of one or a few cases. The analysis of gentrification must be taken beyond the case study

URBAN AFFAIRS QUARTERLY, Vol. 21 No. 3, March 1986 369-387

level if we hope to develop a thorough understanding of the phenomenon and its policy implications.

To date, only a handful of studies of gentrification or displacement have examined the phenomenon in samples of cities (see Black, 1975, 1980; Clay, 1979; Gale, 1984; Henig, 1980; Lee and Hodge, 1984; Lee et al., 1985; Lipton, 1977; Spain, 1980, 1981). Of these, most tend to simply document the extent of gentrification and describe some of its correlates at the neighborhood level rather than determining what characteristics of cities (rather than neighborhoods) make them likely candidates for gentrification. One exception is Lipton's (1977) attempt "to explain why some cities enjoyed urban-core revival." Using 1970 data on the 20 largest cities in the U.S., Lipton conducted correlation and regression analyses of the relationships among five factors (level of administrative activity, manufacturing activity, commuting distance to the fringe, migration of the poor to the city, and race) and measures of the presence of strong residential cores (number and percentage of core tracts with median family income and median educational attainment greater than that for the SMSA). In general, he found that cities with centers dominated by white-collar employment and with long commuting distances to the suburbs had strong high-status cores.

Although this study was influential as an early effort to both document "central-city revival" and provide a causal analysis of that trend for a sample of cities, it can be criticized in a number of ways. First, as gentrification occurs in cities of all sizes, an analysis limited to the nation's 20 largest cities may prove misleading. Second, most gentrification has taken place since 1970; by using 1970 data, Lipton's study may be missing the most important portion of the trend. Third, his cross-sectional dependent variables measure the presence of a high-status urban core, but this "strong core" may be due to factors other than gentrification or revival (i.e., perhaps many of these tracts have always been high in status). Fourth, the use of tracts as units may obscure the "patchwork" quality of gentrification, which could be under way on some blocks within a tract while deterioration dominates the remainder (Lee and Mergenhagen, 1984). Finally, Lipton's causal analysis reflects a reasoned choice of five factors that may influence revival, but this study was published prior to the appearance of the bulk of the literature on gentrification. A review of that literature yields both a wider array of potential causal variables and a greater ability to specify explanations of gentrification drawn from alternative theoretical perspectives (see London, 1980).

These observations suggest the need for a current study of gentrification that (1) is theoretically informed, (2) is based on a substantial number of cities of varying size, (3) employs an appropriate comparative measure of gentrification, and (4) is causally oriented—that is, tries to explain why some cities are likely candidates for gentrification whereas others are not.

One possible strategy for conducting such a study would be to survey knowledgeable informants in a sample of cities regarding the presence or absence and, if present, the significance of gentrification in their cities. This is the approach adopted in the present research. We will discuss, in turn, the existing literature on the causes of gentrification, hypotheses generated by that literature, our survey and sample, and the development of measures of gentrification for each city in our sample.

EXPLAINING GENTRIFICATION

The literature on gentrification incorporates a number of theoretically divergent, ad hoc explanations of the phenomenon. These include demographic, ecological, sociocultural, and political-economic interpretations (London, 1980; London and Palen, 1984).

DEMOGRAPHIC EXPLANATIONS

Both demographic and ecological explanations tend to emphasize the variables in the "ecological complex": population, social (or sustenance) organization, environment, and technology (Duncan, 1959). The demographic version suggests that certain recent changes in both population composition and basic demographic processes have, in the aggregate, contributed to gentrification, itself a form of migration. The "coming of age" of the baby boom generation is one such factor (Bourne, 1978; Cades, n.d.; Clay, 1979; Kern, 1977). The unprecedented number of young adults is placing tremendous demands on the housing supply; these demands are being met, in part, by the "recycling" of inner-city neighborhoods.

Several other demographic factors are believed to be important. For example, the rising age at first marriage, improved contraceptive devices, declining fertility rates, later birth of the first child, increasing entry of both single and married women into the labor force, and the rising number of dual wage-earner families all presumably contribute to gentrification. Taken together, they may represent a decline of the sort of "familism" that played such an important part in the post-war flight to the suburbs (Bourne, 1978; Cades, n.d.; Kern, 1977). In other words, the relatively affluent, young, childless couple, not having to worry about the quality of inner-city schools and the shortage of playgrounds, is likely to choose to live in the city, close to places of work and recreation. To the extent that aggregate demographic changes are producing more family units of this type than ever before, we have another partial explanation of gentrification in the 1970s and 1980s.

ECOLOGICAL EXPLANATIONS.

Approaches recently developed to test an ecological explanation of migration and population redistribution (Frisbie and Poston, 1975, 1978; Sly, 1972; Sly and Tayman, 1977) might be profitably applied to the study of gentrification. Building on the work of Gibbs and Martin (1959), ecological research has found that variations in the "sustenance organization" (i.e., the number, mixture, and salience of various primary, secondary, and tertiary sustenance activities) are strongly related to patterns of population change. It may well be that cities whose sustenance organizations are disproportionately high in white-collar activity and free from the residential disamenities associated with manufacturing and other noxious industrial land uses are those most likely to experience gentrification.

Recent trends toward the decentralization of industry and the increasingly "corporate" nature of the nation's major cities lend added significance to these ecological speculations.

SOCIOCULTURAL EXPLANATIONS

The central assumption of the sociocultural point of view is that no ecological phenomenon, including gentrification, can be fully understood if the focus of explanation is solely on structural phenomena to the exclusion of those learned, cultural values that often motivate individual behavior. Firey's (1945) classic study of "sentiment and symbolism as ecological variables" illustrates the salience of "culture" in determining locational choices and land use patterns (see also Bailey and Mulcahy, 1972; Sjoberg, 1965; Willhelm, 1962).

A wide variety of specific "causes" of gentrification fall under the general sociocultural rubric. Some of these emphasize changing values, attitudes, and lifestyles as factors contributing to the new migration of middle- and upper middle-class people to the inner city. This sort of analysis challenges the conventional wisdom regarding the pervasiveness of an antiurban value system in America (Allen, 1980). It has long been argued that some sort of "rural ideal" (Warner, 1962) motivates our location choices. We flock to the surburbs as a compromise between the rural lifestyle we seek and the need to be near employment and services in the city. It is possible, however, that greater *proportions* of our population than ever are becoming "pro-urban": They consciously choose to live in cities precisely because of the cultural, recreational, and other amenities that cities have to offer. Such changes in values or lifestyle preferences may be reciprocally related to the demographic changes stressed above and may thus contribute to the trend toward gentrification.

If value changes are indeed under way, they may become cumulative. People often do what is in vogue. If enough urban pioneers define the inner city as an appropriate place to live and then proceed to demonstrate its viability, others could follow their lead. The result is "inner-city chic" and, ultimately, rapid rates of gentrification.

Another variation on the sociocultural approach focuses on the persistence of dominant American values rather than on changing values. Fusch (1978), for example, relates gentrification to a number of the core cultural values identified by Williams (1970): economic success, individuality, and so on. The restoration of a home in an inner-city (often historic) area may be a new way to express self-identity and symbolize material success. The search for new means to realize these long-standing goals may itself, however, be an expression of such cultural phenomena as the Bicentennial (with its rediscovery of the American past), the historic preservation movement, and the waves of nostalgia sweeping the nation. Regardless of whether we are dealing with core values, value changes, or value conflicts, sociocultural factors must be taken into consideration for a full understanding of gentrification.

POLITICAL-ECONOMIC EXPLANATIONS

Political-economic analyses of gentrification are clearly divided into traditional and Marxist approaches. The former tends to emphasize competition, supply and demand, market efficiency, the impersonality of the liberal state, and related concepts, whereas the latter is concerned with intergroup power relationships and the uneven costs and benefits of neighborhood change.

As an example of a traditional approach, Cades (n.d.) explains "urban residential reconstruction" at least partly in terms of conventional economic theory and the political and legal changes of the late 1950s and early 1960s. In an analysis that assumes the centrality of market forces, he sees the decreasing availability of suburban land, rampant inflation in suburban housing costs, rising transportation costs, the relatively low cost of slum "shells," and antidiscrimination and school desegregation laws interacting to encourage gentrification.

Marxist approaches rely less on the "invisible hand" of political and economic forces in their analysis of gentrification. Smith (1979), for example, suggests that "American gentrification has been actively planned and publicly funded." Emphasis is placed on the role of economic interests and political power in guiding neighborhood change. The questions of "who decides?" "who benefits?" and "who pays?" are directly addressed. The implication is that powerful interest groups follow a policy of neglect of the inner city until such time as they become aware that policy changes could yield tremendous profits. Then, policies change accordingly, with little regard for those powerless inner-city residents who will be displaced from their homes. All this is legitimated by reference to "the public interest" and predictions of the end of "the urban crisis."

The image of the city as a growth machine guided by land-based interest groups is potentially appropriate here (Molotch, 1976). A loose coalition of realtors, business leaders, developers, government officials, and financial institutions plays a significant role in the development and underdevelopment of a city's space. Smith suggests that such interest groups actually "developed areas as slums" in the 1950s by their refusal to lend money for productive investment. Reversals of such "redlining" policies are increasingly common today as powerful "clients," aware of the profit to be made in inner cities, are persuading lending institutions to finance rehabilitation projects in areas formerly considered too risky. These efforts are often accompanied by the sort of advertising "boosterism" (Molotch, 1976) that is designed to encourage the return of the middle class to the city.

An additional political-economic insight applicable to the analysis of gentrification is Gordon's (1978) discussion of the relationship between the stages of capital accumulation and urban form. He argues that the commercial, industrial, and corporate stages of capital accumulation are each conducive to different distributions of people and functions in space. Industrial accumulation, in particular, encouraged the polarization of cities and suburbs by race and class. The corporate city, on the other hand, is characterized by the decentralization of industry and the dispersal of working-class residential areas on the one hand, and a proliferation of corporate headquarters and employment opportunities in the tertiary sector on the other. Remembering the earlier reference to the correlation between central-city revival and administrative activity (Lipton, 1977), we would suggest that "the stage of capital accumulation" is another possible factor contributing to gentrification.

HYPOTHESES

These alternative explanations of gentrification each contain readily testable hypotheses regarding the determinants of gentrification in the United States in the 1970s and 1980s. For example, the demographic approach suggests that, for a sample of cities, gentrification should be positively associated with the size of the baby boom cohort and negatively associated with the degree of "familism." The ecological or sustenance organization approach suggests that gentrification is related negatively to the extent of manufacturing activity and positively to size of the white-collar or professional labor force.

The sociocultural approach implies that, as urban amenities are apparently a major force that attracts the gentry to cities, there should be a positive relationship between gentrification and the amount of cultural activities that a city has to offer. A second version of this approach implies that communities that consciously place a high value on preservation and renovation activities will be likely candidates for gentrification. If the "local culture" supports such activities, individuals may be encouraged to share these prourban values.

The traditional version of the political-economic approach emphasizes the supply of, and demand for, housing as key determinants. In effect, it argues that population increase has stimulated demand for housing. This is, therefore, an essentially demographic approach that may be subsumed under the "baby boom hypothesis" cited above. The Marxist version of this approach, however, does point to unique hypotheses. Specifically, its focus on the profit-making activities of powerful interest groups in the "corporate city" suggests that gentrification should be positively associated with both a strong corporate presence and the presence of local actors who possess the ability to intervene in the real estate market in a manner that would lend momentum to the process of gentrification.

DATA AND METHODS

DEPENDENT VARIABLES

As noted above, we have gathered data on gentrification by surveying knowledgeable informants in a nationwide sample of cities. Included in our sample are 48 of the 51 cities in the Permanent Community Sample (PCS) developed by Clark and his colleagues (see, for example, Clark, 1968). Three cities (Bloomington, MN; Euclid, OH; and Warren, MI) have been excluded from the usual PCS sample because they are newly developed suburbs and, as such, are not a legitimate part of the "population at risk" of gentrification. Our initial goal was to link our measures of gentrification to this already existing, widely used, and exceedingly rich data set.

With this in mind, we devised a gentrification questionnaire[1] and mailed it to over 150 sociology, political science, and urban studies departments in colleges and universities in the 48 cities in July 1983. Departmental chairpersons were requested—if they could not provide the information themselves—to pass the questionnaire on to a colleague familiar with the phenomenon. A follow-up mailing was sent to nonrespondents in September 1983. The total response rate was 68.4%. One to five responses were received for each city except Cambridge and Malden. Information on the latter two was gathered through telephone interviews.

The responses to this questionnaire enabled us to create two measures of gentrification. The first (G1) is a simple measure of the presence or absence of gentrification, scored as follows: 0 = no identifiable gentrification; 1 = one residential area clearly identified; 2 = two areas identified; 3 = three or more areas identified. The second measure (G2) is an attempt to tap the level of significance of gentrification in each city. Respondents were asked to indicate the extent to which (1) media attention has been directed toward gentrification, (2) the potential negative consequences of gentrification have been publicly discussed by citizens' (or other) groups, (3) local government has directed attention to the phenomenon, and (4) local business people have encouraged the process. This measure ranges from 0 to 8 and is calculated as follows: (1) media coverage—2 = major series or consistent coverage, 1 = occasional coverage, , 0 = little coverage; (2) citizen discussion—2 = frequently, 1 = occasionally, 0 = infrequently; (3) local government attention—2 = considerable, 1 = moderate, 0 = minimal; and (4) business involvement—2 = considerable, 1 = moderate, 0 = minimal. These measures of the extent and significance of gentrification are highly correlated ($G1 \times G2 = .90$).

In cases in which more than one questionnaire was received for a given city, a single score for the city was determined by simply summing the scores of each respondent and dividing by the number of respondents. Interrater agreement was very high. It was rare for respondents to vary by more than one category in their perceptions of the significance of the various groups (media, business, etc.) for the process. Also, contradictory responses regarding the presence of gentrification were received in only 3 cases. Follow-ups determined that these respondents were confusing gentrification with either incumbent upgrading or publicly funded programs such as block grants.

Responses indicate that 19 cities in the sample have experienced no gentrification, 7 cities have only one gentrified neighborhood, 7 cities have two, and 15 cities have three or more.[2] Similarly, gentrification was considered insignificant in 20 cities, while 13 cities had significance scores between one and four, and 15 cities had significance scores in excess of four.

INDEPENDENT VARIABLES

Indicators were developed using 1970 census data to measure four of the underlying concepts implied by the hypotheses listed above. (It is important to note the time lag built into our analysis. Gentrification is a process that began in the 1970s. Our goal is to determine what conditions early in the decade were conducive to gentrification over the course of the decade and into the 1980s.) Size of the baby boom population is simply a measure of the proportion of each city's population falling between the ages of 15 and 24 in 1970. This cohort would mature to become the young home buyers of the 1970-1980 decade. Note that this variable has been logged to normalize its distribution. Our other demographic variable follows the precedent set by social area analysis (Shevky and Bell, 1955; Bell, 1955), measuring familism in terms of the proportion of each city's population falling between the ages of 0 and 5. The ecological concepts of industrial land use and white-collar presence are measured by the percentage of the labor force employed, respectively, in manufacturing industries and in professional, technical, and kindred occupations.

Our cultural activities index was suggested by previous measures of the cultural activities of communities. Studies by Allen (1969, 1973), for example, suggest that cultural facilities (or middle-class leisure-time activities) help "to make a community attractive to young middle-class people with urbane interests" (i.e., our urban gentry) (1973: 67). The presence of cultural centers, art galleries, museums, symphonies, film societies, theater groups, and so on should attract the "prourban" individual. Our measure of such cultural activities is the number of entries each city had in *The Official Museum Directory* (American Association of Museums, 1982) per 100,000 people. Entries were not restricted to museums alone, but included art galleries, botanical gardens, zoos, planetariums, and a wide variety of other cultural amenities.

Our other sociocultural indicator, historic preservation effort, is a measure of the number of residential historic districts in each city (per 100,000 people) listed in the National Register of Historic Places as of September 30, 1982. This may be interpreted as reflecting the local value placed upon preservation and related renovation activities. A strong community commitment to such efforts should be conducive to gentrification. Both sociocultural measures were logged to normalize their distribution.

Finally, political-economic concepts were measured in two ways. First, we developed an indicator of corporate presence derived from the *Fortune 500* index of industrial and service corporations in the United States. We calculated, separately, the number of headquarters of the top 500 industrial corporations in 1970 and 1982 and the top 500 service corporations in 1982 located in each of our 51 cities (data on "the service 500" were not available in 1970). These measures were standardized (Z scores) and summed to provide a measure of overall corporate presence throughout the decade.

Our second political-economic indicator, the realtor ratio, is a measure of the number of real estate establishments in the county[3] encompassing each city in 1974 divided by the population of the city. The realtor ratio measures the presence and potential influence of a key component of the "growth machine" coalition. Realtors are a prototypical example of a land-based interest group that stands to make substantial gains by "boosting" the gentrification process. We argue that low realtor ratios should be associated with high rates of gentrification.

This is the case because the realtor ratio is analogous to Hawley's (1963) MPO (managers, proprietors, and officials) ratio. Both are measures of the concentration of power of the groups under consideration. In Hawley's terms, the greater the concentration of interest groups, the greater their ability to mobilize personnel and resources toward desired ends. Therefore, the fewer the number of real estate establishments per capita, the greater the concentration of realtor power and, as a result, the greater the potential ability of realtors to cooperate in the promotion of gentrification by manipulating the market (rather than merely responding to the market).

METHODS

Our hypotheses will be tested in two stages. We will first examine the simple bivariate correlations between each of our independent and dependent variables (see Table 1). We will then attempt to assess the relationship between each independent and dependent variable while holding constant the influence of all other independent variables and, in so doing, test the relative efficacy of each of the alternative explanations of gentrification. In order to accomplish this, we will regress our measures of gentrification simultaneously on our measures of the demographic, ecological, sociocultural and political-economic "explanations."

Note that this procedure yields regression equations containing eight independent variables for a sample of 48 cities. Since a common rule of thumb in studies of this sort is to limit the analysis to roughly one independent variable for every ten cases, we will first inspect the full equations and then generate more parsimonious equations by deleting any variables that are insignificant in the preliminary analysis. If both the full and parsimonious equations yield similar results, we can be more confident of their validity. Also, as analyses using aggregate data frequently suffer from high correlations among the independent variables, we must take steps to assure that our regression coefficients are not affected. These steps will be discussed below.

FINDINGS

The last two columns of Table 1 indicate that all of our hypotheses are supported—in sign if not in magnitude—at the zero-order level. Both

TABLE 1
Correlation Matrix with Means and Standard Deviations

	(1)	(2)	(3)	(4)	(5)	(6)	(7)	(8)	(9)	(10)
DEMOGRAPHIC										
1. Baby Boom Cohort[a]	1.00	-.06	-.33	.52	.33	.51	-.16	.05	.23	.26
2. Familism		1.00	.39	-.52	-.07	-.26	-.38	-.15	-.15	-.25
ECOLOGICAL										
3. % Employed in Manufacturing			1.00	-.40	-.24	-.62	-.08	-.09	-.38	-.41
4. % Professional				1.00	.27	.56	.32	.18	.04	.16
SOCIOCULTURAL										
5. Historic Preservation Effort[a]					1.00	.44	-.09	.38	.42	.43
6. Cultural Activities Index[a]						1.00	-.08	.12	.34	.39
POLITICAL ECONOMIC										
7. Realtor Ratio							1.00	.21	-.33	-.29
8. Corporate Presence								1.00	.30	.33
9. Presence of Gentrification									1.00	.90
10. Significance of Gentrification										1.00
Mean	-1.71	7.88	25.16	.16	1.39	3.10	6.69	.00	1.38	2.54
Standard Deviation	.15	1.37	9.97	.06	1.43	.93	14.69	1.65	1.30	2.57

SOURCES: 1-4, U.S. Bureau of the Census (1973); 5, U.S. Department of the Interior (1979, 1980, 1981, 1982, 1983); 6, Association of American Museums (1982); 7, U.S. Bureau of the Census (1976); 8, Fortune (1971a, 1971b, 1983a, 1983b); 9-10, author's survey.

measures of gentrification are positively correlated with the size of the baby boom cohort and proportion professional, and negatively with the age 0-5 cohort and percentage employed in manufacturing. Gentrification is also positively correlated with both sociocultural measures and the corporate presence measure, and it is negatively correlated with the realtor ratio.

It is the multiple regression analysis in Table 2, however, that should prove most revealing as a means of assessing the usefulness of each of the alternative explanations. A comparison of the zero-order coefficients in Table 1 with the standardized coefficients in Table 2 shows that, in general, the relationships observed at the zero-order level remain quite stable after the introduction of multiple controls. In fact, the single most telling implication derived from Table 2 is that, by and large, hypotheses derived from each explanation—and, therefore, each of the explanations themselves—are supported by the data analysis. With the exception of proportion professional, the signs for all coefficients are in the predicted direction and, reading across equations, all independent variables except baby boom cohort, proportion professional, and the cultural activities index are statistically significant (or closely approach significance) in one or both of the full equations (eqs. 1 and 3). It appears that gentrification is likely to be both present and significant in cities with relatively low levels of familism (a demographic factor) and of manufacturing employment (an ecological factor), high historic preservation effort (a sociocultural factor), and both a strong corporate presence and high concentration of realtor power (political-economic factors). Furthermore, these same results are derived from the more parsimonious equations (eqs. 2 and 4) from which we have deleted the baby boom, professional, and cultural activities indicators. Observe, too, that the deletion of these three variables minimizes problems of multicollinearity, for they are the only variables in the correlation matrix with coefficients greater than $\pm$ .50.

DISCUSSION

This pattern of results has important theoretical and practical implications. As the reader will recall, one of the goals of our research was to test the relative usefulness of four competing explanations of gentrification. Even a cursory reading of the literature makes clear that different researchers have focused on certain determinants of gentri-

TABLE 2
Multiple Regression of Presence and Significance of Gentrification on Demographic, Ecological, Sociocultural, and Political-Economic Variables

	Presence of Gentrification		Significance of Gentrification	
	(1)	(2)	(3)	(4)
DEMOGRAPHIC				
Baby Boom Cohort[a]	.61 (.07)		.60 (.03)	
Familism	-.23 (-.24)*	-.15 (-.16)	-.55 (-.29)*	-.49 (-.26)*
ECOLOGICAL				
% Empl. in Manufacturing	-.04 (-.30)*	-.04 (-.29)**	-.07 (-.27)*	-.07 (-.28)**
% Professional	-4.86 (-.24)		-3.98 (-.10)	
SOCIOCULTURAL				
Historic Preservation Effort[a]	.20 (.22)*	.18 (.20)*	.35 (.20)	.35 (.19)*
Cultural Activities Index[a]	.04 (.03)		.08 (.03)	
POLITICAL-ECONOMIC				
Realtor Ratio	-.03 (-.39)**	-.04 (-.45)**	-.07 (-.43)**	-.08 (-.45)**
Corporate Presence	.21 (.27)**	.21 (.27)**	.45 (.29)**	.44 (.29)**
Constant	5.808	3.522	10.037	8.219
R^2	.474	.451	.491	.487
Adjusted R^2	.366	.385	.386	.426

NOTE: N = 48; standard coefficients in parentheses.
a. Logged to normalize distribution.
*B at least 1.5 times its standard error; **B at least 2 times its standard error.

fication, usually to the exclusion of other possible "causes." This is easy enough to understand: We all have our "favorite approaches" to the study of urban phenomena; we all adhere to one or another theoretical perspective. So, as a result, some of us do demographic studies, others do political-economic analyses, and so on.

The problem is that this sort of theoretical partisanship tends to produce myopic analyses. When we separate ourselves into ecologists, demographers, socioculturalists, and political-economists, we inevitably produce small increments to knowledge, but any given piece of research does not yield a full understanding of the phenomenon under investigation. And this is precisely what has happened to date in the study of gentrification.

This observation is confirmed by the results of our data analysis. We have found that hypotheses derived from each explanation are supported in our data analysis. Although the political-economic explanation receives the strongest empirical support (i.e., both political-economic indicators are strongly significant in all equations, their beta coefficients are as high as, or higher than, those of other variables, etc.), none of the other explanations can be dismissed. It appears that all of the theorists who studied gentrification have had a valid insight (or two, or three), but that no one has been completely right or completely wrong because no one has ventured beyond the boundaries of their chosen theoretical perspective. Our results underscore the need for a more eclectic approach to the study of gentrification.

One such approach has been suggested by London (1980). He has noted that an analysis of gentrification as a social movement is not well developed in the literature, but that it holds great potential for providing a "synthesis" of the multiple causes of the phenomenon. Our basic finding that a combination of variables derived from four widely divergent perspectives remain significant predictors of gentrification may be interpreted as tentative support for this point of view.

The social movement perspective emphasizes the encouragement of ideologies of "prourbanism" and urban revival, ideologies that are realized by preserving historic old homes in the inner city (a sociocultural aspect). These ideologies are fostered by realtors, lenders, and other elites with land-based interests (the political-economic approach) in order to motivate the behavior of the recently increasing numbers of young, affluent, childless households (the demographic factor) that inhabit the corporate, postindustrial city (an ecological component).

Such an approach holds great promise for yielding a more comprehensive understanding of gentrification. It suggests that all perspectives are necessary to understand the process, but none, by itself, is sufficient. In so doing, it both applauds and criticizes the literature on gentrification. The praise is for the valid insights produced by each theoretical perspective; the disapproval is directed at the refusal to actively pursue the insights generated by alternative points of view. As such, the social movements explanation of gentrification is an intriguing possibility that is implicit in—albeit clearly not "proved" by—our results, and that merits further consideration.

NOTES

1. Our questionnaire included the following definition of gentrification:

> Gentrification is a type of neighborhood change taking place within many inner city areas (within two or three miles of the central business district). It is characterized by middle class people moving into poor or working class residential areas, renovating the homes, and eventually coming to equal or outnumber the original residents. The result is often a dramatic change in the overall socio-economic status of the inhabitants and in the physical appearance of the area. It is important to emphasize that this change is brought about through predominantly, but not necessarily exclusively, private market activity. In other words, it is not a public program like urban renewal, but public sector actions may influence its progress.

2. The following cities were found to have three or more areas of gentrification (their scores on the "significance of gentrification" measure are in parentheses): Albany (6.67), Atlanta (4.50), Birmingham (4.00), Boston (8.00), Buffalo (5.17), Charlotte (6.00), Fort Worth (5.00), Indianapolis (4.67), Milwaukee (3.00), Minneapolis (3.50), St. Louis (5.00), St. Paul (5.50), St. Petersburg (5.00), San Francisco (6.50), and Seattle (7.50).

3. County data on real estate establishments were obtained from the census publication, *County Business Patterns*. For precedent on the use of counties as units of analysis in testing growth machine hypotheses, see Lyon et al. (1981). These authors argue that the economic interests of progrowth elites transcend municipal boundaries. Furthermore, realtor data are not available for cities.

REFERENCES

ALLEN, I. L. (1968) "Community size, population composition, and cultural activity in the smaller community." Rural Sociology 33: 328-338.

———(1973) "Mass society and small towns: middle-class cultural activity in Iowa towns," pp. 67-90 in W. Erbe (ed.) Urbanization, Migration and Social Change: Iowa Enters the 1970s. Iowa City: Iowa Urban Community Research Center.

———(1980) "The ideology of dense neighborhood redevelopment: cultural diversity and transcendent community experience." Urban Affairs Q. 15: 409-428.

Association of American Museums (1982) The Official Museum Directory. Skokie, IL: National Register.

BAILEY, K. D. and P. MULCAHY (1972) "Sociocultural versus neoclassical ecology: a contribution to the problem of scope in sociology." Soc. Q. 13: 37-41.

BELL, W. (1955) "Economic, family, and ethnic status: an empirical test." Amer. Soc. Rev. 20: 45-52.

BLACK, J. T. (1975) "Private market housing renovation in central cities: a ULI survey." Urban Land 34: 3-9.

———(1980) "Private market housing renovation in central cities: a ULI survey," pp. 3-12 in S. B. Laska and D. Spain (eds.) Back to the City. New York: Pergamon Press.
BOURNE, L. S. (1978) Perspectives on the Inner City: Its Changing Character, Reasons for Decline and Revival. Research Paper 94. Toronto: Center for Urban and Community Studies, University of Toronto.
CADES, S. (n.d.) "Rebuilding the urban residential core: the end of an American anomaly." Department of Sociology, Washington College.
CLARK, T. N. (1968) "Community structure, decision-making, budget expenditures, and urban renewal in 51 American communities." Amer. Soc. Rev. 33: 576-593.
CLAY, P. L. (1979) Neighborhood Renewal: Middle-Class Resettlement and Incumbent Upgrading in American Neighborhoods. Lexington, MA: Lexington Books.
FIREY, W. (1945) "Sentiment and symbolism as ecological variables." Amer. Soc. Rev. 10: 140-148.
Fortune (1971a) May: 172-204.
———(1971b) June: 100-125.
———(1983a) May 2: 226-247.
———(1983b) June 13: 152-175.
FRISBIE, W. P. and D. L. POSTON (1975) "Components of sustenance organization and non-metropolitan population change: a human ecological investigation." Amer. Soc. Rev. 40: 773-784.
———(1978) "Sustenance differentiation and population redistribution." Social Forces 57: 42-56.
FUSCH, R. (1978) "Historic preservation and gentrification: a search for order in the urban core." Presented at the annual meeting of the Association of American Geographers, New Orleans.
GALE, D. E. (1984) Neighborhood Revitalization and the Postindustrial City: A Multinational Perspective. Lexington, MA: Lexington Books.
GIBBS, J. P. and W. T. MARTIN (1959) "Toward a theoretical system of human ecology." Pacific Soc. Rev. 2: 29-36.
GORDON, D. M. (1978) "Capitalist development and the history of American cities," pp. 25-63 in W. K. Tabb and L. Sawers (eds.) Marxism and the Metropolis. New York: Oxford Univ. Press.
HAWLEY, A. H. (1963) "Community power and urban renewal success." Amer. J. of Sociology 68: 422-431.
HENIG, J. R. (1980) "Gentrification and displacement within cities: a comparative analysis." Social Sci. Q. 61: 638-652.
HICKS, A., R. FRIEDLAND, and E. JOHNSON (1978) "Class power and state policy: the case of large business corporations, labor unions and governmental redistribution in the American states." Amer. Soc. Rev. 43: 302-315.
KERN, C. R. (1977) "High income neighborhoods in the city: will the new demography guarantee their future?" Presented at the annual meeting of the Regional Science Association, Philadelphia.
LEE, B. A. and D. C. HODGE (1984) "Social differentials in metropolitan residential displacement," pp. 140-169 in J. J. Palen and B. London (eds.) Gentrification, Displacement and Neighborhood Revitalization. Albany: State Univ. of New York Press.
LEE, B. A. and P. M. MERGENHAGEN (1984) "Is revitalization detectable? Evidence from five Nashville neighborhoods." Urban Affairs Q. 19: 511-538.

LEE, B. A., D. SPAIN, and D. J. UMBERSON (1985) "Neighborhood revitalization and racial change: the case of Washington, D.C." Demography 22 (November).

LIPTON, S. G. (1977) "Evidence of central-city revival." J. of the Amer. Institute of Planners 45: 136-147.

LONDON, B. (1980) "Gentrification as urban reinvasion: some preliminary definitional and theoretical considerations," pp. 77-92 in S. B. Laska and D. Spain (eds.) Back to the City. New York: Pergamon Press.

———and J. J. PALEN (1984) "Introduction: some theoretical and practical issues regarding inner-city revitalization," pp. 1-26 in J. J. Palen and B. London (eds.) Gentrification, Displacement and Neighborhood Revitalization. Albany: State Univ. of New York Press.

LYON, L., L. G. FELICE, M. R. PERRYMAN, and E. S. PARKER (1981) "Community power and population increase: an empirical test of the growth machine model." Amer. J. of Sociology 86: 1387-1400.

MOLOTCH, H. (1976) "The city as a growth machine: toward a political economy of place." Amer. J. of Sociology 82: 309-332.

PALEN, J. J. and B. LONDON [eds.] (1984) Gentrification, Displacement and Neighborhood Revitalization. Albany: State Univ. of New York Press.

SHEVKY, E. and W. BELL (1955) Social Area Analysis: Theory, Illustrative Application, and Computational Procedures. Stanford, CA: Stanford Univ. Press.

SJOBERG, G. (1965) "Theory and research in urban sociology," pp. 157-190 in P. M. Hauser and L. F. Schnore (eds.) The Study of Urbanization. New York: John Wiley.

SLY, D. F. (1972) "Migration and the ecological complex." Amer. Soc. Rev. 37: 615-628.

———and J. TAYMAN (1977) "Ecological approach to migration re-examined." Amer. Soc. Rev. 42: 783-795.

SMITH, N. (1979) "Gentrification and capital: theory, practice, and ideology in Society Hill." Antipode 11.

SPAIN, D. (1980) "Black-to-white successions in central city housing: limited evidence of urban revitalization." Urban Affairs Q. 15: 381-396.

———(1981) "A gentrification scorecard." Amer. Demographics 3: 14-19.

TABB, W. K. and L. SAWERS [eds.] (1978) Marxism and Metropolis. New York: Oxford Univ. Press.

U.S. Bureau of the Census (1973) Census of Population, 1970. Characteristics of the Population, Vol. 1: Parts for Selected States. Washington, DC: Government Printing Office.

———(1976) County Business Patterns, 1974. Parts for Selected States. Washington, DC: Government Printing Office.

U.S. Department of the Interior (1979) National Register of Historic Places: Annual Listing of Historic Properties. Federal Register, Vol. 44, No. 26, Part II (February 6): 7415-7649.

———(1980) National Register of Historic Places: Annual Listing of Historic Properties. Federal Register, Vol. 45, No. 54, Part II (March 18): 17446-17519.

———(1981) National Register of Historic Places: Annual Listing of Historic Properties. Federal Register, Vol. 46, No. 22, Part II (February 3): 10622-10679.

———(1982) National Register of Historic Places: Annual Listing of Historic Properties. Federal Register, Vol. 47, No. 22, Part III (February 2): 4932-4968.

———(1983) National Register of Historic Places: Annual Listing of Historic Properties. Federal Register, Vol. 48, No. 41, Part II (March 1): 8626-8679.

WARNER, S. B., Jr. (1962) Streetcar Suburbs: The Process of Growth in Boston, 1870-1900. Cambridge, MA: Harvard-MIT Press.
WILLHELM, S. M. (1962) Urban Zoning and Land-Use Theory. New York: Free Press.
WILLIAMS, R. M., Jr. (1970) American Society: A Sociological Interpretation. New York: Knopf.

Bruce London is Associate Professor in the Department of Sociology and Social Psychology at Florida Atlantic University. His book, Gentrification, Displacement, and Neighborhood Revitalization *(with J. John Palen), was recently published by the State University of New York Press.*

Barrett A. Lee is a member of the sociology faculty at Vanderbilt University. In addition to a continuing interest in gentrification, he is currently conducting research on neighborhood racial change, resident associations, and community attachment.

S. Gregory Lipton is Associate Professor in the Urban and Environmental Planning Program at the University of Virginia and administers Virginia's evening planning program in Falls Church. He is currently investigating the impacts of federal neighborhood conservation programs.

HOUSING CONSTRAINT AND HOUSEHOLD COMPLEXITY IN METROPOLITAN AMERICA
Black and Spanish-Origin Minorities

LAURA J. KRIVO
Ohio State University

JAN E. MUTCHLER
Pennsylvania State University

The extent to which minority group members live in nuclear family households may be mediated by factors other than choice. Using data from the 1970 Census, we test the relationship between certain aspects of housing constraint/availability and household complexity for the black and Spanish-origin populations in SMSAs in the United States. In particular, we examine the effects of residential segregation, income, new housing, and housing vacancy on a measure of the tendency for adults to live in households in which they are nonnuclear members while controlling for other relevant variables. The results support our hypotheses for both the black and Spanish-origin groups, suggesting that factors determining the availability of housing do have implications for the household structure of these populations.

Sociologists have long recognized the importance of economic factors in shaping social phenomena. Both short- and long-term fluctuations in the economy have been shown to affect patterns in marriage, child-bearing, labor force participation, and a host of other outcomes. Indeed, the economic vacillations of the past decade serve as stern reminders of how severely a national economic crisis is reflected in the lives of individuals and families.

AUTHORS' NOTE: *We would like to thank W. Parker Frisbie, Robert Kaufman, and Dudley Poston for their comments and suggestions on this article. We also thank Thomas Van Valey for making a portion of the indices used in the analysis available to us.*

URBAN AFFAIRS QUARTERLY, Vol. 21 No. 3, March 1986 389-409

The housing industry is traditionally considered one of the most sensitive indicators of economic strain. Patterns of the past decade illustrate this responsiveness. Following the residential construction boom of the early 1970s, new housing starts plummeted in 1974 and failed to reach the 1972-1973 levels again by the end of the decade. Other housing shifts paralleled this overall decline as rental units became more scarce and the average sales price of both new and existing single-family homes experienced more than a two-fold increase between 1970 and 1978 (U.S. Bureau of the Census, 1980). Of course, these aggregate trends mask substantial regional and local variation in availability and price of housing. Changes in the construction and cost of housing have created an acute housing affordability problem for large portions of households (Frieden et al., 1977; Mayer, 1977). In light of fluctuating interest rates and high unemployment, the state of the local housing market is a serious matter for families and individuals alike. Above and beyond individual ability to pay, market factors may severely constrain the housing options available to the householder through either a shortage of housing or a shortage of affordable housing.[1]

How do families and individuals cope with the housing squeeze in their own communities? Existing perspectives on household formation have little to offer in helping answer this question. Traditionally, researchers have taken a normative approach to the family life cycle in which each stage in the cycle is related to a specific household structure (Glick, 1957, 1977). Deviations from this expected life course pattern over time have been explained by changes in the norms and laws relating to the family. It has also been suggested that variations in family and household patterns among racial and ethnic groups are influenced by cultural differences in the value and function of the family. Another perspective conceptualizes the household as a coping device used to minimize the hardship of poverty through consolidating economic resources. In particular, household structure is examined as an economic as opposed to a cultural phenomenon among minority groups (Angel and Tienda, 1982; Tienda and Angel, 1982).

Yet all of these existing perspectives ignore the impact that housing constraints should have on household formation. Numerous historical examples suggest that housing shortages or booms usually prompt adaptations in household composition. Michael et al. (1980) speculate that the growth in new housing during the 1950s may have played a role in determining household composition by prompting an increase in single-person households. We would expect that a tight and expensive housing market would prompt a concentration rather than a diffusion of households. No relationship has been demonstrated empirically between constriction of the housing market and changing household structure.

Our approach incorporates this relationship between housing and households into the study of household formation. We argue that above and beyond the exigencies of life cycle, culture, and individual economic resources, the state of the housing market will influence the degree to which families and individuals find it possible to maintain separate versus combined (or extended) residences. This approach may be particularly germane in the case of socially and economically disadvantaged populations, who suffer inordinately from the housing squeeze. In particular, our focus on Spanish-origin and black households is based on the contention that these groups may respond to different levels and types of housing constraints than do majority households. A clearer specification of the avenues through which housing availability might affect differential household composition is therefore of particular importance both for the explanation of minority household structure and for an understanding of the social implications of societywide housing shortages and shifts as we are witnessing in the 1980s.

THE RELATIONSHIP BETWEEN HOUSING CONSTRAINT AND HOUSEHOLD COMPLEXITY

When an individual or family cannot find or afford a housing unit, some form of strain or adaptation to the situation must result. Many households suffer from economic strain by continuing to pay sizable portions of their income for housing. However, households may also turn to family, friends, or the state for aid. It is well known that families are a source of financial and emotional support in such circumstances (Angel and Tienda, 1982; Kennedy and Stokes, 1982). One study found, for example, that economic aid from family members was a significant source of assistance in paying the high cost of housing. Kinship networks also furnish housing along with other forms of economic and noneconomic assistance to new migrants (Keefe, 1980; Tienda, 1980).

Limitations in the type and location of available housing create difficulties in finding a suitable dwelling unit in which to live beyond those difficulties created by a household's lack of economic resources. As housing costs increase and housing construction remains low, the difficulties that families face in maintaining a home become heightened.

One means of adapting to such problems is for economically disadvantaged families to double up in single households in which financial burdens are shared. The findings of Angel and Tienda (1982) support this argument, showing that the addition of family members to a household appears to be a response to economic strain. But these authors do not examine the part played by housing availability in this process of extended household formation.

The existence of relative housing shortages during recessions may have a particularly significant effect on social groups that already face widespread constraints in the housing market. For example, blacks suffer from persistent differential treatment from whites when looking for housing. Discrimination and steering severely limit the housing choices available to black households (Foley, 1973; Pearce, 1979; Pol et al., 1982). In addition, the black housing market is disproportionately affected by housing displacement: Housing units in which blacks live are much more likely to be demolished, condemned, or destroyed than those occupied by whites (Dahmann, 1982).

The high levels of black/white residential segregation that exist in metropolitan areas across the United States (Taeuber and Taeuber, 1965; Van Valey et al., 1977) reflect the fact that the neighborhoods in which black families and individuals may buy or rent housing are severely restricted. Although direct evidence on the treatment of Spanish-origin households in the housing market is scarce (e.g., Krivo, 1982), this group also has experienced moderate levels of residential segregation from Anglos in U.S. urban areas (Grebler et al., 1970; Lopez, 1981; Massey, 1979).

Clearly a population that is residentially concentrated within certain areas of the city has, in effect, a more limited supply of obtainable housing. Wilson (1979: 108) summarizes the outcome of this situation:

> The main effect of discrimination on the residential behavior of blacks is the restriction on the range of residential packages that blacks may choose from. However, it is clear that *low*-income black households are most affected by the economic costs of living in segregated neighborhoods. These households are placed at a serious disadvantage when the supply of housing in black neighborhoods is limited because they cannot outbid higher-income households for available decent housing.

Therefore, minorities may be unable to rent or buy adequate and/or affordable housing even within their own segregated neighborhoods.

This limitation may promote an increase in the doubling up of families and adult individuals as a means of adaptation.

However, factors besides residential segregation also constrain the housing choices of minority groups. Both the level of vacancies and the amount of new housing reflect the general availability of housing in an area. Obviously, when the availability of housing is low in a metropolitan area, less housing is open for residents to rent or buy. New housing also affects the extent of white movement that may "make way" for a minority's expansion into new neighborhoods (Hawley, 1950; Marshall and Stahura, 1979). In other words, with new housing to move into, more affluent households might be more likely to vacate their present units and thereby make older and hence probably cheaper units available (White, 1971).

More subtle forces constraining housing availability cannot be directly measured, but may be indicated by characteristics of the area. For instance, the percentage of minority households that are home-owners might be an important proxy for the relative tightness of minority housing markets, as purchasing a home appears to be the most formidable obstacle that minorities face in the housing market. For a variety of reasons, including discrimination (see, for example, Foley, 1973; Pearce, 1979), it is far more difficult for minority households to become homeowners than it is for majority white households. This is demonstrated by the fact that black households must have a considerably higher income than comparable whites to purchase a home (Henretta, 1979; Jackman and Jackman, 1980; Wilson, 1979). Furthermore, blacks and whites report similar preferences in housing (Farley et al., 1978; Pettigrew, 1973), yet minorities are much less likely than whites to be homeowners independent of income (Foley, 1973; Pearce, 1979). The fact that blacks require more income than whites to purchase a home demonstrates that market constraints other than those due to household resources must affect blacks. Thus, in areas in which fewer minority households own their homes, it is likely that they are facing greater housing market constraints.

The presence of a relatively large minority population may also increase the likelihood of a higher level of household complexity through its effect on discrimination in the area. The percentage of minority households in a given locality tends to increase inequality and/or discrimination as the majority group attempts to limit the competition posed by a greater relative size (Blalock, 1967; Brown and Fuguitt, 1972; Frisbie and Neidert, 1977). Therefore, this percentage could indirectly affect greater minority household complexity through its impact on housing discrimination and other forms of housing constraint. Finally, ability to pay for housing is of obvious importance in determining the type of housing a group can afford. In areas in which minority income is low, there will be pressure to relieve economic strain by moving in with family or friends, or by adding adults to the household (Angel and Tienda, 1982; Tienda and Angel, 1982).

Given the various economic and structural constraints imposed on minority groups in their search for housing, households may be motivated to adjust their composition accordingly. Consequently, we hypothesize that minority household complexity varies positively with measures of residential constriction. Specifically, in an area in which the supply of housing available to a minority group is more limited and minority incomes are relatively low, household adaptations may be expected. These adaptations would take the form of both an increase in the doubling up of families into single households and an increase in the addition and retention of single adults, such as adult children or aged parents, in the home of relatives. Our expectation is that areas having higher levels of residential segregation, lower vacancy rates, less new housing, lower levels of homeownership, a greater percentage of minorities, and lower per capita minority incomes will be characterized by higher degrees of household complexity (more doubling up) among minority group households when other relevant factors are controlled.

Clearly, factors other than housing availability operate in determining household complexity. For instance, a high dependency ratio of aged adults to total adults may produce a high level of complexity, through the joining of households that frequently occurs with old age. A high percentage of single-headed family households might also increase the tendency for doubling up (Burch, 1979). In addition to economic contributions, extra adults who help with household chores and child care may ease the strain of domestic work and thereby allow the head to reallocate time into work outside the home. Therefore, when there is a large concentration of single-headed households, a higher level of household complexity would be expected.

Additionally, the region in which a metropolitan area is located may have an effect on household complexity beyond that captured by the structural, economic, and demographic factors measured here. For blacks, the South has been characterized by greater discrimination than other regions. The constraints placed on black households in the South may therefore have affected an increase in the doubling up of households as an adaptation to the local situation. Region may also be important for the Spanish-origin group, as the distinct Spanish-origin subpopulations are regionally segregated. Of particular importance for this study is the fact that Mexican Americans, who are most concentrated in the Southwest, are often considered to be highly familistic. This would mean that Mexican Americans may have more complex households than other populations. Thus, it is important to distinguish this group from the Puerto Ricans, who are almost exclusively located in the Northeast. Including a variable for region in the analysis permits a crude control for these distinctions.

Finally, for the Spanish-origin population only, the relative proportion of the population that is foreign-born should have an important impact on household complexity. In particular, recent immigrants tend to rely on friends and relatives already in the host country for economic and social support. Such support might include a sharing of place of residence. The relatively large number of foreign-born persons of Spanish origin living in the United States may, therefore, significantly increase the household complexity of this population. Another reason to control for the percentage of the Spanish-origin population that is foreign-born is the high correlation of Hispanic/white residential segregation and the relative size of the foreign-stock Spanish-origin population (Massey, 1979).[2] These variables are included as controls in our analysis, following the expectation that a higher percentage of aged, location in certain regions of the country, and a high percentage of single-headed households will be accompanied by higher levels of minority household complexity. A relatively larger Spanish-origin population that is foreign-born is also expected to be associated with a higher level of Spanish-origin household complexity.

DATA AND METHODS

Separate cross-sectional regression analyses are performed to test the hypotheses developed above for both black and Spanish-origin populations.[3] In each case, SMSAs are included when at least 1% of their total 1970 population was composed of the minority group being examined.[4] The analysis of the black population includes 206 (or 86%) of all SMSAs, and the analysis of the Spanish-origin population includes 132 (or 56%) of the 1970 SMSAs. All independent variables were obtained or computed from U.S. Census data for 1970 (U.S. Bureau of the Census, 1972a, 1972b). A description of these variables and a list of their sources are presented in Table 1.

The operationalization of household complexity is somewhat less straightforward. As Burch (1980) points out, there has been a great deal of variability in the indices used to measure complexity. Clearly, household size alone is not sufficient, largely reflecting the number of children in a population. Given the general definition of complexity as "the presence of one or more adults in the household other than a marital pair of the same generation" (Burch, 1980: 25), we have chosen to use the number of nonnuclear adults in households as an indicator of complexity. Furthermore, given the ambiguous classification of nonfamily members of a household as "lodgers, partners, or resident employees," we have chosen the most conservative path of including only nonnuclear family members over the age of 18, such as brothers and sisters, parents, in-laws, other relatives, and adult children, in our measure of complexity.

The exclusion of all nonfamily members means that we are actually measuring doubling up in the family and not a more general level of overall household complexity. However, this choice is preferable to the alternative inclusion of lodgers in the measure, as lodgers are probably motivated by very different factors than other nonrelatives, such as friends or partners, in choosing to live with individuals outside their own nuclear family. Thus, their inclusion would make the interpretation of effects ambiguous.

All adult children are included because an important part of our argument implies that adult children might either stay at home or move in with their parents or other relatives because they are unable to find or afford their own housing units. However, there is a group of adult children who are still in school and completely dependent upon their parents and whom it would be preferable to exclude. But there is no way to determine which children are in this position at any age. Consequently, the inclusion of all adult children seems conceptually more satisfying than the elimination of all adult children from the measure.[5] Finally, the use of adults only is preferable to including individuals of all ages, as nonnuclear children are normally part of a household for reasons other than housing constraints, be they individual factors or larger factors affecting their parents.

This measure of complexity could be termed the "prevalence" of nonnuclearity among minority adults, and is computed as follows:

TABLE 1
Definition and Sources of Independent Variables

Variable	Definition	Source
Residential Segregation	Index of Dissimilarity	Census of Population, 1970[a]
Vacancy Rate	Percent of all housing vacant	Census of Housing, 1970, Table 8
New Housing	Percent of 1970 housing built after 1960	Census of Housing, 1970, Table 43
Home Ownership	Percent of all minority-headed housing units owned by their residents	Census of Housing, 1970, Tables 8 and 69
Income	Standardized yearly per capita income of all black or Spanish-origin persons[b]	Census of Population, 1970, Tables 94 and 100
Percent Minority	Percent of the population which is black or percent which is Spanish-origin	Census of Population, 1970, Tables 23 and 96
Age Structure	Percent of total black or Spanish-origin adult[c] population which is age 65 and over	Census of Population, 1970, Tables 23 and 96
Percent Foreign Born-Spanish origin only	Percent of total Spanish-origin population which is foreign born	Census of Population, 1970, 6th count summary tapes
Percent Single Headed Households	Percent of all family households headed by a currently unmarried individual	Census of Population, 1970, 6th count summary tapes
Region	Dummy variables for location in the South, Southwest, or Northeast. Reference category is the remaining states	Major Census regions

a. These indices were computed by T. Van Valey at Western Michigan University.
b. Although our interest is in households, per capita income is used so that the relationship being tested is not predetermined. Higher median household income could easily be the outcome of a greater tendency for areas with more doubled-up households to have greater average numbers of earners per household. As the consumer price index is available for only a small number of SMSAs, per capita income is standardized by a price relative index in order to adjust for differences in the cost of living across SMSAs. The price index that we use is the ratio of an SMSA's median gross monthly rent to the median of all the SMSAs' median gross monthly rents. To standardize income values, the population's yearly per capita income is divided by this price index.
c. Adults include all persons over age 18.

$$Y = \frac{\text{nonnuclear minority adults living in relative's households}}{\text{all minority adult household members}}$$

Y thus represents the percentage of adults living with relatives in households in which they are not themselves members of the nuclear family of the head, or who are adult children of the head. This index was computed from the sixth count summary tapes of the 1970 Census of Population.

An examination of the values of the complexity measure for the black and Spanish-origin samples shows that the levels of household complexity for both groups are higher than for Anglos, although Spanish-origin households are somewhat less complex than black households. An average of 18.3% of black and 15.9% of Spanish-origin adults live in family households of which they are not nuclear members, whereas only 13.0% of Anglos do so. Because the distribution of this variable is highly skewed, we use as our dependent variable in the regression analysis the natural log of the complexity measure.

Two independent variable transformations were necessary as well. For the black sample, the net relationship of percentage minority and percentage vacant housing with household complexity was found to be curvilinear. As almost all cases fall along the first section of the curve, before the turnpoint of a curvilinear equation specified as a parabola, a log transformation appropriately specifies these relationships. The interpretations of the logged dependent and independent variables are straightforward. With a logarithmic dependent variable, the coefficients for the independent variables can be interpreted such that a one-unit change in X results in a (b × 100)% change in the level of unlogged Y. In the cases in which the independent variables are also logged to adjust for curvilinearity, the coefficients for these variables can be interpreted as a 1% change in the level of unlogged X resulting in a b% change in the level of unlogged Y. We turn now to a discussion of our results.

RESULTS

Zero-order correlations among all of the variables in the analysis along with the means and standard deviations are presented in Table 2 for both the black and Spanish-origin samples.[6] Several strong correlations between independent and dependent variables emerge at this point. Percentage minority, percentage aged, percentage single-headed, and region (the Southwest for the Spanish-origin population and South for blacks) all exhibit high to moderate correlations with complexity at the zero-order level for both the Spanish-origin and black samples. However, intercorrelations among some of the independent variables for blacks represent a marked contrast to those for the Spanish-origin group in direction and magnitude of effect. For instance, percentage minority is negatively related to residential segregation in the Spanish-origin sample, but positively related to segregation in the black sample. Similarly, both percentage owner-occupied and percentage of adults over 65 are negatively related to segregtion in the Spanish-origin sample, but are positive and near zero in the black sample. This suggests that the relationship between housing and household complexity might differ between the two groups. As we discuss below, similar differences are evident in the multivariate case as well, and so a discussion of their implications will be addressed at that point.

The outcome of a regression for the black population of the log of household complexity on our measures of housing constriction and the controls discussed above is included in Table 3. Control variables are entered first (Columns 1 and 2) followed by the structural constraint variables (Columns 3 and 4). These results indicate that both the control variables and the full model, which adds the structural constraint variables, are quite successful in explaining inter-SMSA variation in black household complexity. The addition of the structural constraint variables significantly increases the amount of variance explained.

The control variables alone (Columns 1 and 2)—age structure, percentage of single-headed households, and region—account for 55% of the variation in the log of the percentage of nonnuclear adults. Also, all three control variables are significant, with the percentage of single-headed having the largest single effect. Clearly, these control variables are important factors in explaining black household complexity. This conclusion is reinforced by examining the full model, in which the structural constraint variables are added (Columns 3 and 4). The inclusion of the structural constraint variables reduces the effects of the three controls, but significance is retained in each case. Even more importantly, the amount of variance in black household complexity explained by the model escalates to 73%, approximately a one-third increase from the amount explained by the control variables alone.

In the full model, three of the six variables measuring structural constraint are significant at the .01 level. Among these variables, percentage minority is the most important predictor of complexity. The

TABLE 2

Zero-Order Correlations Between Log of Percentage of Nonnuclear Adults in Minority Population and Predictor Variables: SMSAs, 1970

A. The Black Population

N = 206	Log of Percent Non-nuclear Adults	Segre-gation	Log of Percent Minority	Percent of Adults Over 65	Per Capita Income	Log of Vacancy Rate	Percent New Housing	Percent Owner Occupied	Percent Single Headed	South
Segregation	.18									
Log of Percent Minority	.71	.20								
Percent of Adults over 65	.39	.01	.22							
Per Capita Income	-.18	-.02	-.37	.09						
Log of Vacancy Rate	.08	-.12	.29	.31	-.36					
Percent New Housing	.04	-.12	.27	-.12	-.65	.44				
Percent Owner Occupied	.21	.05	.16	.38	-.07	.42	.15			
Percent Single Headed	.59	.26	.34	.14	-.18	-.13	-.13	-.14		
Region: South	.51	-.06	.61	.40	-.35	.59	.39	.27	.16	
Mean	2.88	71.31	2.03	11.02	1794.96	1.66	27.41	45.40	24.48	.40
Standard Deviation	.23	11.71	.93	4.16	266.38	.39	9.38	11.85	3.51	.49

B. The Spanish-Origin Population

N = 132	Log of Percent Non-nuclear Adults	Segre-gation	Percent Minority	Percent of Adults Over 65	Per Capita Income	Vacancy Rate	Percent New Housing	Percent Owner Occupied	Percent Foreign Born	Percent Single Headed	South-west	North-east
Segregation	.06											
Percent Minority	.47	-.47										
Percent of Adults over 65	.44	-.38	.46									
Per Capita Income	-.22	-.26	-.11	.30								
Vacancy Rate	.04	-.38	.29	.26	.11							
Percent New Housing	-.20	-.48	.05	.11	-.02	.27						
Percent Owner Occupied	.24	-.41	.29	.46	.26	.39	.23					
Percent Foreign Born	.07	-.23	.05	.28	.21	-.08	.26	-.11				
Percent Single Headed	.58	.18	.44	.12	-.46	-.10	-.26	-.26	-.13			
Region: Southwest	.36	-.39	.58	.42	-.20	.48	.25	.35	-.13	.31		
Northeast	.05	.51	-.17	-.27	-.23	-.37	-.39	-.68	-.04	.47	-.30	
Mean	2.72	39.93	8.79	6.02	2058.07	5.96	28.80	48.51	13.23	11.43	.34	.15
Standard Deviation	.31	12.41	14.41	2.81	421.67	2.64	9.58	14.93	9.87	4.74	.48	.36

TABLE 3
Regression of Log of Percentage of Nonnuclear Adults in Black Population on Measures of Housing Constraint and Selected Control Variables, SMSAs 1970

Independent Variables	Control Model b (1)	Control Model B (2)	Full Model b (3)	Full Model B (4)
Percent of Adults over 65	.00990** (.00287)	.1787	.00820** (.00260)	.1480
Percent Single Headed	.03312** (.00315)	.5048	.02517** (.00297)	.3836
Region: South	.16829** (.02436)	.3591	.09367** (.02810)	.1999
Per Capita Income			.00006 (.00005)	.0668
Log of Percent Minority			.12033** (.01279)	.4867
Log of Vacancy Rate			-.13258** (.03124)	-.2257
Percent New Housing			.00016 (.00137)	.0065
Residential Segregation			-.00065 (.00079)	-.0330
Percent Owner Occupied			.00343** (.00085)	.1765
Constant	1.89532		1.89615	
R^2	.549		.730	
Adjusted R^2	.542		.717	
N	206		206	
Standard Error of Estimate	.156		.122	

NOTE: Standard errors are presented in parentheses below unstandardized coefficients.
*$p \leq .05$ for a one-tailed t-test; **$p \leq .01$ for a one-tailed t-test.

vacancy rate also has a strong effect in the predicted direction. So although demographic controls have a strong influence on the tendency for black adults to double up, housing constraints such as fewer housing vacancies also affect the level of household complexity net of demographic variables.

Only the percentage of housing that is owner-occupied has a significant effect in the opposite direction of that predicted. We proposed that high levels of homeownership would reflect a more open housing market for minorities, which would lead to lower levels of complexity. However, a greater degree of homeownership is found to be related to a higher level of black household complexity. It may be that, given higher levels of complexity and therefore more adults per household, average household income may rise sufficiently to permit relatively more housing purchases. It may also be that, in areas with relatively more owners, there is a greater abundance of detached single-family dwellings and, therefore, relatively greater numbers of large units with room for additional household members.

The results of the regression for the Spanish-origin population are presented in Table 4. Again, the controls are added first (Columns 1 and 2), followed by the structural constraint variables (Columns 3 and 4). In this sample, the percentage foreign-born among this minority population is also included as a control variable, as this variable does not reflect a constraint of the market. The explained variance for the control model is somewhat lower than that for the black sample, but it is still sizable; 49% of the intermetropolitan variation in Spanish-origin household complexity is explained by the four control variables. Again, percentage single-headed is the most important predictor in the control variable model. The percentage foreign-born is not significant, and Spanish-origin household complexity is not significantly different in SMSAs in the Southwest than in metropolitan areas outside of the Southwest or Northeast.

Turning to the full model (Columns 3 and 4), we see that household complexity is significantly increased by adding the structural constraint variables. The addition of the structural constraint variables increases the amount of variance in Spanish-origin household complexity explained from 49% in the control model to 62% in the full model.

Including the structural constraint variables changes the effects of the control variables somewhat. The percentage foreign-born is now significant in the expected direction, but regional differences are completely insignificant. Also, the effects of age structure and percentage single-headed are weaker yet still highly significant. Of greater substantive interest here, however, is the fact that four of the six structural constraint variables are significant in this model. The percentage owner-occupied is the strongest predictor (although it is positive as in the black sample). Residential segregation, percentage new

TABLE 4
Regressions of Log of Percentage of Nonnuclear Adults in Spanish-Origin Population on Measures of Housing Constraint and Selected Control Variables, SMSAs 1970

Independent Variables	Control Model b (1)	Control Model B (2)	Full Model b (3)	Full Model B (4)
Percent of Adults over 65	.03405** (.00871)	.3043	.02104* (.00930)	.1880
Percent Single Headed	.04113** (.00579)	.6200	.03176** (.00628)	.4788
Percent Foreign Born	.00178 (.00223)	.0558	.00780** (.00223)	.2447
Region: Southwest	.00017 (.05578)	.0003	.04285 (.05839)	.0648
Northeast	-.13485* (.07697)	-.1543	-.01093 (.08242)	-.0125
Per Capita Income			-.00010* (.00006)	-.1328
Percent Minority			.00251 (.00196)	.1149
Vacancy Rate			-.00222 (.00820)	-.0187
Percent New Housing			-.00549* (.00242)	-.1670
Residential Segregation			.00586** (.00219)	.2314
Percent Owner Occupied			.00868** (.00189)	.4118
Constant	2.04257		1.81311	
R^2	.485		.624	
Adjusted R^2	.465		.589	
N	132		132	
Standard Error of Estimate	.230		.202	

NOTE: Standard errors are presented in parentheses below unstandardized coefficients.
*p ⩽ .05 for a one-tailed test; **p ⩽ .01 for a one-tailed test.

housing, and per capita income also have strong effects on Spanish-origin household complexity, and these effects are all in the expected direction. The importance of these indicators of structural constraint in explaining variation in Spanish-origin household complexity lends support to our argument that constraints in the housing market play a role in determining household complexity.

DISCUSSION AND CONCLUSION

The availability of affordable, decent housing continues to be an important social issue. Although minorities and the poor have always struggled with this problem, the economic crises of the past few years have greatly expanded its scope. Even more advantaged groups are now having to cope with an increasingly unaffordable housing market.

We have considered adaptations in household structure as one mechanism available to cope with these housing constraints. Although we acknowledge the influence of cultural and life-cycle factors, economic and housing constriction may additionally affect household structure. For families and individuals to survive and to get the most out of their housing expenditures, additional adults or families may be added to the household. Our empirical findings support this proposition to a large extent, in a test among Hispanic and black minorities.

Although the results reported for both the black and Spanish-origin populations provide support for our structural argument, differences between the two populations in the relationships found between the structural constraint variables and household complexity are also notable. We find that the percentage minority and the vacancy rate are both significant predictors of household complexity for the black population, but not for the Spanish-origin population. In contrast, per capita income, percentage new housing, and residential segregation have significant effects on Spanish-origin but not black household complexity. These differences suggest that, although generally housing constraints do influence household complexity, the means by which this process takes place vary between these two minority groups.

Why might the avenues through which housing constraint influences household complexity differ between the black and Spanish-origin populations? One plausible reason is that blacks face a greater degree of discrimination in their access to many positions in society, including residential location.[7] In the housing market, this means that individual and household resources are less important determinants of one's housing choice and hence of one's household living arrangement. It is also possible that this means blacks are more discriminated against in purchasing homes. This latter point is particularly relevant in assessing the effect of housing vacancy as a measure of housing constraint because vacancy is far more tightly tied to the rental than the homeowner's market (U.S. Bureau of the Census, 1983).

This line of argument would explain several of the differences between the black and Spanish-origin populations in the effects of the structural constraints found here. The percentage black has long been considered to have an important influence on discrimination, with larger minority populations facing greater discrimination as the majority group attempts to limit competition (Blalock, 1967; Brown and Fuguitt, 1972; Frisbie and Neidert, 1977). It is for this reason that we argued that the percentage minority indirectly measures discrimination in the housing market. If direct discrimination is a more prevalent means of limiting housing availability for the black than for the Spanish-origin population, this could explain why the percentage minority variable has a significant effect on black but not on Spanish-origin household complexity.

The greater prevalence of direct discrimination against blacks could also mean (as noted above) that income has a much weaker influence on housing choice, thereby explaining the significance of per capita income as a structural constraint variable in the Spanish-origin but not the black analysis. Also the possibility that there is greater discrimination against blacks in purchasing homes could explain the significance of the vacancy rate variable in the black but not the Spanish-origin equation, as the rental market is more tightly connected to the vacancy rate. It could also explain the significance of percentage of new housing in the Spanish-origin but not the black analysis.

One last structural constraint variable shows a different effect for the black and Spanish-origin populations—residential segregation. This may occur because it seems reasonable that the meaning of residential segregation is different at very high than at low to moderate levels of segregation. An increase in segregation from low or moderate levels might indicate far greater increases in housing constraint than do increases in segregation from very high levels. If such is the case, this would explain why residential segregation has a significant effect for the Spanish-origin population but not for the black population; the

Spanish-origin population tends to experience moderate levels of residential segregation, whereas the black population uniformly experiences very high residential segregation (as shown in Table 2).

In sum, both conceptual and empirical support is found for a structural approach to household complexity among Spanish-origin and black minorities, although the means by which housing structure affects household formation are different for the black than for the Spanish-origin population. Although cultural and individual resource explanations cannot be ignored, they too often become catch-alls for intergroup differences. Our findings suggest that structural factors that are related to minority status play important roles in determining at least one phenomenon for which cultural and individual explanations are often advanced—household structure.

Our findings also suggest important avenues for future research examining how the processes of housing constraint differ between the black and Spanish-origin minorities. It is crucial to test whether the speculations outlined above are valid. Do blacks actually confront more discrimination in the housing market than Spanish-origin households? Is this why black household formation seems to respond to very different structural constraints? Or are other explanations needed? In addition, it would be useful to determine whether other groups, including the white majority, also alter their levels of household complexity in response to structural housing constraints. Last, it would be of interest to assess whether more open housing markets result in household diffusion, thereby increasing the prevalence of single-person households, as Michael et al. (1980) suggested.

NOTES

1. In this article we conceptualize housing constraint as including both actual and relative components. That is, an area may suffer from an actual housing shortage, making it difficult or impossible to locate housing as occurred during the Depression. More likely at the present time, costs may be so high or growth so rapid that affordability and suitability are the key issues. These are examples of housing constraint that may especially affect minority group members by pricing them out of the market.

2. The issue of nativity is not a problem for blacks in the U.S., of which only 1.1% are foreign-born (U.S. Census, 1972a; U.S. Summary, Table 68).

3. Standard census definitions are used to identify the Spanish-origin population. In 1970, this group included persons of Puerto Rican birth or parentage in New York, New

Jersey, and Pennsylvania. It includes persons of Spanish language and persons not of Spanish language but of Spanish surname in the five Southwestern states (i.e., Arizona, California, Colorado, New Mexico, and Texas). Finally, it includes persons of Spanish language in the remaining states.

4. Although it is theoretically possible that a large SMSA would have a significant number of either black or Spanish-origin households living in it while that minority group constituted less than 1% of the total population in the SMSA (with a population of 1 million, for example, 5000 black households would constitute only .50% of the total population), using either 1.0% or 100 households as the minimum criterion for inclusion in the analysis results in the same samples.

5. We recognize, however, that some concern may arise over the inclusion of adult children in this measure. We therefore performed an identical analysis that excluded adult children from the numerator. The results were largely comparable to those reported later in this article, providing additional support for our structural argument.

6. The means and standard deviations in unlogged form are presented below for those variables entered in the equation as logged values. Only the percentage of nonnuclear adults is logged in the Spanish-origin equation. Its mean, in unlogged form, is 15.90, with a standard deviation of 4.30. Three variables are logged in the black equation. Their means and standard deviations, in unlogged form, are as follows: percentage of nonnuclear adults ($\overline{X}$ = 18.31, s = 3.78), percentage black ($\overline{X}$ = 11.17, s = 9.20), and vacancy rate ($\overline{X}$ = 5.68, s = 2.44).

7. We initially suspected that another possible source of the different results obtained for the black and Spanish-origin equations might be that separate sets of SMSAs are represented in these equations. Regional and other systematic differences between the samples of SMSAs could have been responsible for the effects noted. However, when the black and Spanish-origin equations are estimated using a sample of 109 SMSAs common to the analysis for both groups, we find that the results are comparable to those reported here.

REFERENCES

ANGEL, R. and M. TIENDA (1982) "Determinants of extended household structure: cultural pattern or economic need?" Amer. J. of Sociology 87 (May): 1360-1383.

BLALOCK, H. M. (1967) Toward a Theory of Minority Group Relations. New York: John Wiley.

BROWN, D. L. and G. FUGUITT (1972) "Percent nonwhite and racial disparity in nonmetropolitan cities in the South." Social Sci. Q. 53 (December): 573-582.

BURCH, T. K. (1979) "Household and family demography: a bibliographic essay." Population Index 45 (April): 173-195.

———(1980) "The index of overall headship: a simple measure of household complexity standardized for age and sex." Demography 17 (February): 25-37.

DAHMANN, D. C. (1982) Housing Opportunities for Black and White Households: Three Decades of Change in the Supply of Housing. Special Demographic Analysis CDS-80-6, U.S. Bureau of the Census. Washington, DC: Government Printing Office.

FARLEY, R., H. SCHUMAN, S. BIANCHI, D. COLASANTO, and S. HATCHETT (1978) " 'Chocolate city, vanilla suburbs': will the trend toward racially separate communities continue?" Social Sci. Research 7 (December): 319-344.
FOLEY, D. L. (1973) "Institutional and contextual factors affecting the housing choices of minority residents," pp. 85-147 in A. Hawley and V. P. Rock (eds.) Segregation in Residential Areas. Washington, DC: National Academy of Sciences.
FRIEDEN, B. J., A. P. SOLOMON, D. L. BIRCH, and J. PITKIN (1977) The Nation's Housing: 1975 to 1985. Cambridge, MA: MIT-Harvard Joint Center for Urban Studies.
FRISBIE, W. P. and L. NEIDERT (1977) "Inequality and the relative size of minority populations: a comparative analysis." Amer. J. of Sociology 82 (March): 1007-1030.
GLICK, P. C. (1957) American Families. New York: John Wiley.
———(1977) "Updating the life cycle of the family." J. of Marriage and the Family 39 (February): 5-13.
GREBLER, L., J. W. MOORE, and R. C. GUZMAN (1970) The Mexican-American People: The Nation's Second Largest Minority. New York: Free Press.
HAWLEY, A. (1950) Human Ecology. New York: Ronald Press.
HENRETTA, J. C. (1979) "Race differences in middle class lifestyle: the role of home ownership." Social Sci. Research 8 (March): 63-78.
JACKMAN, M. R. and R. W. JACKMAN (1980) "Racial inequalities in home ownership." Social Forces 58 (June): 1221-1234.
KEEFE, S. E. (1980) "Acculturation and the extended family among urban Mexican Americans," pp. 85-111 in A. Padilla (ed.) Acculturation: Theory, Models, and Some New Findings. Boulder, CO: Westview.
KENNEDY, L. and D. W. STOKES (1982) "Extended family support and the high cost of housing." J. of Marriage and the Family 44 (May): 311-318.
KRIVO, L. J. (1982) "Housing price inequalities: a comparison of Anglos, Blacks, and Spanish-origin populations." Urban Affairs Q. 17 (June): 445-462.
LOPEZ, M. M. (1981) "Patterns of interethnic residential segregation in the urban Southwest, 1960 and 1970." Social Sci. Q. 62 (March): 50-63.
MARSHALL, H. and J. STAHURA (1979) "Black and white population growth in American suburbs: transition or parallel development?" Social Forces 58 (September): 305-328.
MASSEY, D. S. (1979) "Residential segregation of Spanish Americans in United States urbanized areas." Demography 16 (November): 553-563.
MAYER, N. (1977) Homeownership: The Changing Relationship of Costs and Incomes, and Possible Federal Roles. Washington, DC: Congressional Budget Office.
MICHAEL, R. T., V. R. FUCHS, and S. R. SCOTT (1980) "Changes in the propensity to live alone: 1950-1976." Demography 17 (February): 39-56.
PEARCE, D. M. (1979) "Gatekeepers and homeseekers: institutional patterns in racial steering." Social Problems 26 (February): 325-342.
PETTIGREW, T. F. (1973) "Attitudes on race and housing: a social psychological view," pp. 21-84 in A. Hawley and V. Rock (eds.) Segregation in Residential Areas. Washington, DC: National Academy of Sciences.
POL, L. G., R. F. GUY, and A. J. BUSH (1982) "Discrimination in the home lending market: a macro perspective." Social Sci. Q. 63 (December): 716-728.
TAUBER, K. E. and A. F. TAUBER (1965) Negroes in Cities. Chicago: Aldine.
TIENDA, M. (1980) "Familism and structural assimilation of Mexican immigrants in the United States." Int. Migration Rev. 14 (Fall): 383-408.

———and R. ANGEL (1982) "Headship and household composition among Blacks, Hispanics, and other Whites." Social Forces 61 (December): 508-531.

U.S. Bureau of the Census (1972a) Census of Population and Housing, 1970: General Population Characteristics. Washington, DC: Government Printing Office.

———(1972b) Census of Population and Housing, 1970: General Housing Characteristics. Washington, DC: Government Printing Office.

———(1980) Statistical Abstracts of the United States: 1980. Washington, DC: Government Printing Office.

———(1983) Census of Housing, 1980: General Housing Characteristics. Washington, DC: Government Printing Office.

VAN VALEY, T. L., W. C. ROOF, and J. E. WILCOX (1977) "Trends in residential segregation: 1960-1970." Amer. J. of Sociology 83: 826-844.

WHITE, H. C. (1971) "Multipliers, vacancy chains, and filtering in housing." J. of the Amer. Institute of Planners 37 (March): 88-94.

WILSON, F. D. (1979) Residential Consumption, Economic Opportunity, and Race. New York: Academic Press.

Lauren Krivo is Assistant Professor of Sociology at Ohio State University. Her research interests include the study of inequalities in housing markets in the United States, Black and Spanish-origin household composition, and the causes of geographic variation in labor market outcomes.

Jan Mutchler is Assistant Professor of Sociology at Pennsylvania State University. Her research interests include family and household demography, with a special emphasis on minorities and demographic and structural approaches to the study of underemployment.

ECONOMIC AND POLICY IMPLICATIONS OF HOSTING SPORTS FRANCHISES
Lessons from Baltimore

ARTHUR T. JOHNSON
University of Maryland,
Baltimore County

The acquisition and/or retention of professional sports franchises is a significant element in the economic development plans for many cities. With few exceptions, sports franchise owners demand public subsidies under the threat of relocating their teams during lease negotiations. Despite these escalating demands and apparent franchise instability, many cities continue to pursue sports franchises. This article, using Baltimore as a case study, seeks to determine whether a sports team is "worth it," and provides a discussion of the types of public policy issues local officials confront as they negotiate with franchise owners. The analysis concludes that if team owners continue to abuse their monopoly advantage at the bargaining table, cities will have no choice but to seek legislative or judicial means of altering that balance of power.

The acquisition and/or retention of professional sports franchises is a significant element in the economic development plans of many large cities. Nearly 50 American cities host professional sports teams in baseball, basketball, football, and hockey. With few exceptions, these franchises receive public subsidies in some form, usually below market rents for their use of publicly owned stadiums and arenas or tax breaks for privately owned sports facilities. Since 1980, nearly half of these cities have been confronted with demands for increased subsidies, such as stadium improvements, lower rent, and tax breaks. Almost without exception, removal of the franchise from the host community was an implied, if not explicit, threat underlying negotiations.

AUTHOR'S NOTE: *This article was originally distributed as a working paper by the Maryland Institute for Policy Analysis and Research at the University of Maryland Baltimore County.*

URBAN AFFAIRS QUARTERLY, Vol. 21 No. 3, March 1986 411-433

Despite escalating demands and apparent franchise instability (Johnson, 1983: Tables 1-3) many cities (e.g., Buffalo, Birmingham, Phoenix, Nashville, Jacksonville) continue to pursue sports franchises. Those who favor the presence of a sports team in their city and accept the concomitant public costs cite the expected economic benefits (additional jobs, tax revenue, and increased business activity) derived from the team's presence, as well as improved civic pride among citizens and increased prestige for the city, as justifying the subsidies. Critics, however, contend that only already wealthy team owners benefit from such subsidies and question the extent of predicted economic benefits in light of the size of the necessary subsidies. Much of the debate centers on indirect economic benefits and intangible social goods, both of which are difficult, if not impossible, to measure. In fact, civic boosters tend to inflate their value while critics and muckrakers tend to underestimate or discount entirely their value (Johnson, 1982).

Benjamin Okner (1974: 346), whose analysis remains the most informative, was forced to conclude that "it is impossible to generalize about whether the local subsidy of a sports facility is 'worth it' to any particular community." The impossibility of such a task is due as much to measurement problems as to the difficulty of obtaining the necessary data, parts of which are protected by law (e.g., tax returns), much of which is not a matter of public record, and some of which simply will not be released.[1] For this reason, as well as the fact that each city's lease arrangements differ from those of other cities, comparisons are difficult to make. Still, there is value in analyzing one city's experience for local policymakers as well as for those interested in attempting to generalize about the relationship between a professional sports franchise and its host community.[2]

The first part of this article, using Baltimore as a case study, seeks to determine whether or not hosting a professional sports franchise is "worth it." It does so by comparing the public revenues derived directly from a sports franchise with those public expenditures made in support of the sports franchise. Assuming that the intangible and indirect benefits of hosting a sports team exceed its intangible and indirect costs,[3] we may conclude that a sports franchise is "worth it" when public revenues directly attributable to a sports team equal or exceed its direct public costs.[4]

The second part of the article, again relying on the Baltimore experience, explores specific aspects of the negotiation process that occurs between franchise owners and municipal officials. This makes explicit the types of public policy issues local officials confront as they negotiate with franchise owners, and will provide a clearer understanding of why the issue of sports franchise relocation has become a national public policy issue that Congress has been requested to resolve.

BALTIMORE SPORTS: 1953-1984

Baltimore became a modern-era sports town in 1953 with the arrival of the National Football League's Colts, who previously had been a financial failure in Dallas. In 1954, the financially strapped and inept Browns moved from St. Louis to play baseball in Baltimore.[5] That same year Memorial Stadium, the city's outdoor sports facility, was completed. Three decades old, the stadium has been dubbed the worst in the NFL, and the Orioles have described their offices as the worst or next to the worst in baseball.

By the late 1950s, the Colts had built a winning team and played to sell-out crowds until the late 1970s. In 1983, with a losing team and the front office in apparent disarray, Colt attendance averaged 37,441 per game, the lowest in the NFL. Ironically, the team might have been the most profitable in the NFL due to the lowest team salary and a generous lease.

The Orioles also built a winning team and could boast of the best won-lost percentage (.569) from 1957 to 1984 of any baseball team. Yet until 1979, the Orioles struggled each year to attract 1,000,000 fans. Despite drawing 1,613,031 spectators in 1982, the team reportedly lost between $500,000 and $1 million. In 1983, the team broke the 2 million attendance mark for the first time in its history, won the World Series, and turned a profit of approximately $3 million.

Chicago-based Robert Irsay owns the Colts and Washingtonian Edward Bennet Williams owns the Orioles. The fact that neither has local interests in Baltimore led to fears, often fueled by the owners themselves, that they might relocate their teams. After Williams bought the Orioles in 1979, many speculated that he would take the Orioles to Washington or its suburbs. Irsay, since 1976, openly shopped his team in Los Angeles, Indianapolis, Phoenix, Memphis, and Jacksonville, among other cities. During February and March of 1984, he reportedly was a handshake (Phoenix) and a signature (Indianapolis) away from relocating to another city. Irsay's actions brought him ridicule and derision in the local press, from state legislators, and especially from the public.

During the final week in March, the city, the state, and corporate leaders offered Irsay a multimillion dollar package to counter Indianapolis's offer. If he remained in Baltimore, the Colts owner would have received a $15 million loan at 6.5% interest for ten years (local business leaders pledged to raise more than $500,000 annually needed to meet the prime rate of 11%), a guarantee by business leaders of an average of 43,000 tickets sold for each home game, and $4.4 million in cash by selling the Colts' training facility to Baltimore County in return for a guarantee that he could lease it back at $1 a year. In return, public officials asked for a six-year lease, which would have brought another $7.5 million in stadium improvements, including sky boxes. In total, nearly $12 million in local and state funds were offered to Irsay.

At the same time, legislation granting the city eminent domain power over professional sports franchises was speeding through the state legislature. On the snowy night of March 28, the Colts' property was packed into nine Mayflower moving vans (donated free of charge by the Indianapolis-based company) and shipped to Indianapolis. The next day, the state enacted the eminent domain legislation and the city began its legal efforts to return the Colts to Baltimore.

Lease negotiations with both teams have been difficult since the mid-1970s. The Oriole lease for 1975 was renegotiated to help ease the financial problems of the team owners. The Colts demanded a lease based on dollar parity with the Orioles. Colt ownership argued that the teams should pay the same dollar amounts. Such an agreement was reached in 1977 and was made retroactive to 1975. It was to extend for three two-year periods to 1983.

The decline in Colt popularity, matched by a growth in Oriole fan appeal, resulted in an increase in rent for the Orioles, as rent was based on a percentage of gross ticket receipts. Refusing to sign the lease extension for 1980-1981, Irsay argued that it was not fair for the Colts to pay the same rent for 8 games that the Orioles paid for nearly 81 games. He demanded that parity be achieved by using the same rental formula rather than dollar amounts. This finally was agreed to, and a three-year lease was signed in June 1981.

For the 1982 season, the Orioles and the city of Baltimore signed a one-year precedent-breaking lease, which was renewed for the 1983 season. The lease called for the city to share team profits equally with the Orioles, once profits exceeded amusement and admission tax revenues.[6]

The amusement and admission tax is a locally imposed tax collected by the state. The tax is equal to 10% of the ticket price. The rent due the city can be expressed as

$$R = A + 1/2\,(P-A)$$

where R = rent
A = amusement and admission tax revenues
P = profits.

When there are no profits to share the city will receive its tax revenues.

This formula continues as the foundation of a three-year lease signed in June 1984. However, armed with the knowledge of what the city and state offered Irsay, Williams was able to define in the lease as team revenues nearly $2 million of a newly awarded concessions contract, most parking revenues, and all scoreboard advertising revenues. Revenues from each of these sources previously had gone directly to the city. In addition, the city agreed to $1.6 million in stadium improvements. In the meantime, those seeking the return of professional football are pressuring city officials to support the construction of a new stadium. With this background, we now attempt to determine whether professional football and baseball in Baltimore are worth it.

BALTIMORE'S SPORTS REVENUES AND EXPENDITURES

Table 1 identifies public expenditures by the city of Baltimore in support of the Colts and Orioles from 1977 to 1983. The major costs within stadium expenditures are those of personnel and "contractual services," which include utilities. The city supplies ground crews for football games and supplements the Orioles' ground crew. The city also supplies clean-up crews after the games, washroom attendants, first-aid attendants, complaint clerks, electricians, plumbers, and all necessary emergency and maintenance employees for each home game. Additionally, employees are needed on a daily basis to maintain and manage the stadium. Personnel costs, including fringe benefits, rose steadily from $547,487 in 1977 to $757,989 in 1983. Similarly, contractual services (including utilities) increased annually from $315,556 in 1979 to $788,039 in 1983.

TABLE 1
Baltimore City Public Expenditures Attributable to Professional Baseball and Football

Activity	1977[a]	1978	1979[b]	1980	1981[c]	1982[d]	1983[b]
A. Memorial Stadium	948,372	1,111,020	1,304,567	1,300,036	1,467,894	1,516,020	1,617,256
B. Police	364,923	395,450	498,244	522,032	441,681	567,017[e]	714,334[e]
C. Capital Expenditures[g]	--	--	--	556	211,484	169,139	16,212
D. Debt Service	--	--	--	--	--	--	--
Total Expenditures	1,313,295	1,506,470	1,802,811	1,822,624	2,121,059	2,252,176	2,347,951
Total Attendance	1,643,035[f]	1,456,917	2,018,900	2,130,646	1,360,899	1,720,677	2,549,569

SOURCES: City of Baltimore Accounting Operations Detail Register, and Fiscal Division, City of Baltimore Police Department.

a. All figures are based on calendar year and, therefore, include full baseball and football seasons. Encumbrances are excluded.
b. Includes baseball playoffs and World Series.
c. Baseball strike.
d. Football strike, four home games played.
e. Estimated.
f. Includes seven regular season football games and one playoff game.
g. City General Funds only. Maryland has committed $1 million annually since 1979 to capital improvements at Memorial Stadium.

The major item of expense beyond those of the stadium is for police services. Police officers assigned to sports events at the stadium for security and crowd control purposes are paid on an overtime basis.[7] Forty such officers are assigned to baseball games and, beginning in 1981, 80 officers were assigned to football games. Prior to 1981, 60 officers were paid by the city and 20 were paid by the Colts. Thirty to 40 officers are assigned to traffic-control duty for baseball games, depending upon attendance. A major portion of this expense is absorbed by assigning personnel to traffic control duty as a portion of their normal working shifts. This also is done for proximal post security, the deployment of officers on special posts near the stadium for crime suppression purposes.

The bulk of capital expenditures for stadium improvements has come from the state government. Since the mid-1970s, the city has budgeted $300,000 annually for capital expenditures, but actually has expended much less than that amount from its general funds.[8]

In sum, total city expenditures to support the Colts and Orioles have escalated annually. Whereas police costs are related to the number of games played and attendance trends, stadium costs are not. Total expenditures are affected more by city employee salary increases and inflation than by the number of games played or attendance figures.

Table 2 reports the revenues derived by the city as a direct result of hosting professional baseball and football franchises from 1977 to 1983. Four revenue sources are identified; (1) rental payments by the franchises, (2) revenues from tangential activities such as concession sales, parking fees, and commissions from scoreboard advertising, (3) other payments related to the use of the stadium, and (4) the admissions and amusement tax. The players' strikes of 1981 and 1982, the unique 1982-1983 Oriole lease, and irregular Colt rental payments make year-to-year comparisons difficult. Nevertheless, some observations can be made.

First, baseball accounts for the bulk of city sports revenues. This is true by virtue of the fact that the Orioles play 81 home games compared with 8 Colt home games in a full season.

Second, under traditional lease arrangements, whereby the city receives a percentage of gross ticket receipts, rental revenues are sensitive to attendance fluctuations. This is not necessarily the case under the terms of the 1982-1983 Oriole lease. As Oriole rental payments are determined by the franchise's financial position at the year's end as well as by the admissions tax collected, the city may not receive a dollar

TABLE 2

Total Revenue Generated for Baltimore Attributable to Professional Baseball and Football

Revenue Source	1977[a]	1978	1979[b]	1980	1981[c]	1982[d]	1983[b]
A. Team Rent	323,154	128,078[e]	835,001	623,975[e]	737,424	150,179	830,927[e]
B. Concessions, Parking & Scoreboard Advertising	106,382	105,664	461,009	403,577	402,369	287,296	453,030
C. Other Stadium Revenue	8,131	9,198	10,454	9,757	117,457	8,517	22,144
D. Admissions Tax From Baseball	390,000	384,000	928,000	751,000	516,000	854,041	1,513,433
E. Admissions Tax From Football	483,000[h]	437,000	367,000	428,000	439,000	178,100	479,241[f]
Total Revenue	1,310,667	1,063,940	2,601,464	2,216,309	2,212,250	1,478,133	3,298,775
Total Attendance	1,643,035[g]	1,456,917	2,018,900	2,130,646	1,360,899	1,720,677	2,549,569

SOURCES: Baltimore Accounting Operations Detail Register and independent anonymous sources (for admissions tax information).

NOTE: For key to notes a-d, see Table 1.

e. Includes Colts' rent due this year, but paid in succeeding year.

f. Estimated by author.

g. Includes seven regular season football games and one playoff game.

in rent even if attendance increases over the previous year's total (as happened in 1982). Even an extremely large attendance increase (as in 1983) will not ensure a significant rental payment. Alternatively, a large team profit (perhaps the result of a lucrative cable television contract) can result in a significant rental payment without an increase in attendance.

A third observation is that concession sales, parking fees, and charges for scoreboard advertising are significant revenue sources. With the exception of scoreboard advertising, these revenue sources also are sensitive to attendance fluctuations (assuming constant prices and a stable number of parking spaces). The more fans there are, the more cars will be parked and concessions sold.

Finally, it is evident from Table 2 that the admissions tax is the most important revenue producer for the city. It is sensitive to attendance as well as ticket prices. Its sensitivity to ticket prices is evidenced by 1979 and 1983 revenue figures. In those years, the Orioles qualified for postseason play. Playoff and World Series tickets cost three to five times the amount of regular season tickets (1983 American League Play-Off tickets cost $15 and $20; World Series tickets cost $25 and $30), and most games sell out. During the regular season, due to the selection of different priced seats and the availability of lower-priced seats at most games, rental revenue is more sensitive to total attendance than to ticket price (assuming ticket price has no effect on attendance).

In sum, city revenues from professional baseball and football, unlike city expenditures in support of those sports, are dependent upon attendance and, to a lesser degree, ticket price. Baseball is a more significant revenue producer than football. Qualifying for postseason play in baseball can produce a significant increase in city revenues, mainly due to the admissions tax. The city assumed much more of a risk than did the Orioles in signing the 1982-1983 and 1984 leases. This is so because a bad year guarantees loss of rental revenues, whereas even a great year does not guarantee rental income equal to that of previous years. Rental income for 1983, for example, failed to equal 1980 rental and concession income and barely exceeded that of 1979.

Table 3 compares annual sports derived revenues with sports expenditures. Baltimore has been able to generate revenues in excess of expenditures in three of seven years. In such years, there is little doubt that municipal investment in sports teams is worth it. Obviously, such excess revenues are not guaranteed. Significant amounts of public dollars can be lost, as happened in 1982. It is at such times that the valuation of intangible and indirect benefits and costs is crucial to answering the question of whether public investment in sports is worth it.

If one estimates the values of intangible and indirect benefits at a much higher level than like costs (which appears to be reasonable in most cases), it is clear from the Baltimore data that sports teams are worth it even when direct revenues do not exceed expenditures. In the case of Baltimore, with the exception of 1982, losses were relatively small, and in all likelihood were made up by sales tax revenues generated by the teams and their fans and other secondary economic activity associated with teams.

IS BALTIMORE REPRESENTATIVE?

This should not be taken as a definitive answer, however. It is significant that Baltimore expends no money for debt service. Cities that have built new sports facilities or have financed major stadium renovation projects with borrowed funds incur significant annual debt service payments. Okner (1974: 341) found that the relationship between recentness of construction and operating loss is attributable directly to amortization of principal and interest on outstanding debt.

Baltimore officials chose to avoid debt service payments by granting more favorable lease conditions to the Colts and Orioles for use of its older stadium in lieu of building a new one. According to the former director of recreation and parks (Tawney, 1977: 2) "not building a new stadium but granting the teams more favorable leases is a far more inexpensive method of maintaining strong major league franchises."

Many assert that lease concessions are the result of blackmail by team owners threatening to relocate. The Baltimore experience demonstrates that, although fear of losing one's team is a factor in lease negotiations, concessions can be a premeditated public policy. If one accepts the possibility that lease concessions can equal what might be paid in debt service, the case of Baltimore suggests that sports teams can be worth it.

This conclusion is bolstered by those sports facilities that claim operating surpluses. For example, New Jersey's Meadowlands sports complex, with its four sports teams (five in 1985) and race track, produced operating revenue surpluses of $10 million in 1981 and $3.4

TABLE 3

Baltimore City Revenue Versus Expenditures Attributable to Colts and Orioles

	1977[a]	1978	1979[b]	1980	1981[c]	1982[d]	1983[b]
A. Total Expenditures	1,313,295	1,506,470	1,802,811	1,822,624	2,121,059	2,252,176[e]	2,347,951[e]
B. Total Revenue	1,310,667	1,063,940	2,601,464	2,216,309	2,212,250	1,478,133	3,298,775[f]
Expenditures > Revenues	2,628	442,530	--	--	--	774,043	--
Revenues > Expenditures	--	--	798,653	393,685	91,191	--	950,824

SOURCES: Tables 1 and 2
NOTE: For key to notes a-d, see Table 1.
e. Includes estimated police expenditures.
f. Includes estimated admissions tax revenues from football.

million in 1982 (New York Times, 1983: 40). The Oakland Coliseum, Los Angeles Coliseum, and Houston Astrodome are other examples of stadium operations that reportedly do not incur deficits. Each, like pre-1984 Baltimore, normally have had more than one major tenant.

Flaherty (1982: 446-447), however, has warned that

> many things are not always what they appear to be. For example, ask a public stadium operator what the financial condition of his stadium is and he may give you a figure and call it a surplus. Rarely does this figure include the annual payments on a bad debt. Thus a stadium with a so called surplus may end up making the city 1-2 million dollars poorer.

Specific examples of stadium-bonded indebtedness and consequent deficits are reported regularly. New York City is paying more than $1.4 million annually in debt service for its renovation of Yankee Stadium and from 1976 to 1980 received an annual average rental payment of only $281,200 from the Yankees (Vitullo-Martin, 1978: 13; New York Times, 1980: 1); New Orleans annually expends nearly $11 million on debt service and $13 million for operating costs in support of the Superdome, incurring an annual deficit of approximately $5 million (Connick, 1976: 490); the District of Columbia could not acquire sufficient revenue from R.F.K. Stadium to make annual interest payments, redeem any bonds, or retire the stadium debt by its due date (Select Committee, 1977: 166); and, after it joined the National Hockey League, Buffalo was forced to absorb annual deficits, the bulk of which were attributed to bonded indebtedness, of $248,000 in 1971, $828,688 in 1972, and $653,000 in 1973 for its Memorial Auditorium (Weekly Bond Buyer, 1974: 11).

Local officials have sought to protect their taxpayer-constituents from increased tax burdens by attracting private support (e.g., Indianapolis, Pittsburgh), exploiting federal programs, especially Industrial Revenue Bonds and Economic Development Administration programs (e.g., Buffalo, Hartford), spreading the burden among their state's taxpaying population (e.g., Louisiana, New York, New Jersey), or imposing special taxes on others, such as hotel-motel guests (e.g., Houston, Indianapolis). Several of those cities planning domed stadiums foresee a combination of such strategies (e.g., Phoenix, Tampa, Tulsa; see Attner, 1984: C3; Kurtz, 1984: A3, Hautzer, 1984: 1).

Baltimore is representative. Sports teams can be worth it if a sports facility can boast more than one major tenant (or is multipurpose) and if negotiated concessions and/or bonded indebtedness do not exceed a certain point. The Baltimore case (pre-1984) described above meets those conditions. The question of worth becomes more debatable when only one tenant exists and concessions and/or debt service have become excessive. Post-1983 Baltimore appears to be representative of that situation. In such instances, the worth of hosting sports teams can only be determined by the valuation of their net intangible and indirect benefits.

POLICY DILEMMAS

No generalization from a single case can be accepted as valid until tested further. However, based on Baltimore's experience, several observations that are relevant to other sports communities can be made. Each of these is suggestive of policy dilemmas little recognized in the literature.

INDIRECT AND INTANGIBLE BENEFITS

First, the case is supportive of Okner's (1974) conclusions that the answer to the question of a sports franchise's worth to a community is arguable and hinges on the valuation of indirect and intangible benefits and costs. Whereas team owners enter lease negotiations with their financial position as a primary interest, local officials have broader considerations. They are aware that sports fans and the general public have developed psychological commitments and emotional attachments to a team. Indeed, local officials and team owners encourage such community identity. The Buffalo Bills football team, for example, was the centerpiece for the city's "Talking Proud" civic campaign.

The recognition by local officials of a sports team's intangible value should not be criticized. Municipalities invest in many activities that have no direct payoff, but presumably are of intangible value. Concert halls, theaters, museums, and even zoos are good examples. The "psychological health" of a city is just as important as its fiscal condition. Thus, investment in cultural and recreational activities is a common and expected practice of municipal government.

Baltimore supports several cultural and recreational activities (e.g., two art museums, a zoo, a symphony orchestra, a children's museum, and a science center) that cost the city more than its net sports investment. These activities may reach fewer citizens, have a class or racial bias in spectatorship, or provide fewer indirect benefits. This is not to resurrect the arts-sports debate, but to note that, from a public policy perspective, it is valid to justify investment in sports in terms of intangible benefits and a city's "psychological health."

Furthermore, local officials understand that the net costs of a franchise represent a small fraction of the city's budget. Baltimore's budget in 1982, when the sports deficit was $774,000, (see Table 3) was $1.6 billion. A net loss of even a million dollars has a negligible impact on taxpayers of a large city (Baade and Chessen, 1984). The public, for the most part, ignores or remains insensitive to the economic aspects of the team's relationship to the city.

Given these facts, the actual dollars involved in lease negotiations will be of much greater importance to a team owner than to public officials, who also are attempting to calculate intangible net benefits. We should not be surprised, therefore, to find owners driving harder bargains and public officials making lease concessions to retain a team and its intangible benefits.

Ironically, this is demonstrated by the experiences of cities that have lost teams, such as New York, Baltimore, Los Angeles, and Oakland. In no case were the mayors of those cities unwilling to meet owner demands for increased public expenditures. In fact, in the Baltimore case, the package offered to Irsay to keep him in Baltimore was of greater dollar value than that offered by Indianapolis (Canzian, 1984: 1). Team owners in each of these cities were determined to relocate for personal reasons or to realize a larger profit through other means (e.g., a larger cable television market attracted Davis; the promise of sell-outs in a new stadium attracted Irsay and Jets owner Hess; a lucrative real estate deal attracted Rams owner Rosenbloom).

Thus, the importance of indirect and intangible benefits and costs is not only that they make it difficult to determine accurately and objectively a sports team's net value to a city, they also are important for the dilemma that local officials confront when they negotiate with team owners. On one hand, they will be criticized if they agree to lease conditions that lead to deficits; on the other, if they stand firm they will be criticized for creating ill will with team owners and forcing the team to leave the city.

STADIUM RENOVATION AND NEW CONSTRUCTION

Second, the Baltimore experience is illustrative of another policy dilemma that leaders of fiscally stressed sports cities face with regard to constructing a new sports facility. The Baltimore case also may be predictive of the likely future of cities presently possessing modern sports facilities.

Pressures are mounting in Baltimore to construct a new stadium as a result of the Colts' departure and Williams's reluctance to sign a long-term lease. The city's policy of granting lease concessions in lieu of a new stadium implies that at some point revenues will not be sufficient to cover stadium operating costs, forcing the city to seek other revenue sources and ways of reducing or avoiding stadium expenditures.[9]

It is logical that a point must be reached at which it no longer will be acceptable to either the city or the team to pursue additional lease concessions. From the city's perspective, more favorable rental terms will prove to be too costly or will not be possible (if no rental payments are made, what else can be done, unless you make payments to the team?). From the team's perspective, there will be a point at which it does not believe more favorable lease conditions will be worth the cost of being in an inadequate stadium. Baltimore arguably reached this point in 1984.

When such a point is reached by the city or team, the issue of a new stadium cannot be avoided. If a city's economy is dependent on attracting dollars from external markets (i.e., tourists, conventions, corporate relocations) as is Baltimore's, it must develop and maintain a seductive and dynamic image in those markets. Modern sports facilities, especially those that are domed, are perceived by many to be important components in municipal image building (Yacik, 1982: 52; Attner, 1984: 63; Kurtz, 1984: A3). However, the expenditure by a fiscally stressed city of millions of dollars for a sports stadium, that many will view as a subsidy for wealthy team owners, is certain to be opposed by taxpayers groups, representatives of the poor, and community activists. This is the dilemma with which officials in Baltimore, Cleveland, Detroit, and New York struggled in 1984.

Once the decision to build a new facility is inevitable, team and city officials must negotiate, apart from lease arrangements, the stadium site. Frequently, this will pit center-city interests against those of suburban neighbors. Fierce sports wars have been fought between city and suburban forces in Boston, New York, Buffalo, and Detroit.

City officials fear losing the intangible and indirect benefits produced by a team when it relocates to a suburban site. Rosentraub and Nunn (1978), however, in a study of stadiums in Irvine and Arlington, Texas, concluded that such benefits are not captured by the suburban community and do spill over into the center city. At the same time, the center city is relieved of the costs attendant to hosting sports teams.

Therefore, it might be a wise strategy for city officials to encourage suburban stadiums, if Rosentraub and Nunn's conclusions are valid for other communities. There are tradeoffs, however. First is the danger that the city will no longer be identified with the team. For example, the NFL's New York Giants are now referred to simply as the "Giants" since they are located in suburban New Jersey. Teams may adopt a regional or state name, forsaking the city, as did the New England Patriots, California Angels, and New Jersey Nets. If another city is nearby it may benefit more than the former host community. The Baltimore Bullets are now known as the Washington Bullets, even though they are located in Maryland. As it is impossible to measure the value of community identity, it is difficult to assess the potential cost of a move to the suburbs.

A second consideration for municipal officials must be the potential for alternative uses of the existing stadium or the land the stadium occupies. If no alternatives are available or if the stadium must be maintained for another team, the loss of a team to the suburbs will not be acceptable. On the other hand, if viable alternatives exist for the use of the stadium or its land, relocation may not hurt the city.

These same issues will confront cities that currently possess modern stadiums 20 to 40 years from now, when the bulk of baseball and football franchises' leases expire.[10] Today's new stadiums are tomorrow's outmoded and ill-regarded facilities. For example, the Houston Astrodome, the prototype of today's domed stadiums, has been the object of $45 million (the original cost of the dome) worth of capital improvements before it has reached the age of 20 years. The Baltimore experience, therefore, is not only illustrative of policy issues regarding stadium renovation and construction that presently confront several cities, but also may be predictive of dilemmas that other cities will face in the early years of the twenty-first century.

PUBLIC-PRIVATE INTEREST CONFLICT

Finally, Baltimore's experience demonstrates the interest conflicts that exist with regard to the sports franchise relocation issue. The interests of communities in maintaining their teams are pitted against the private property rights of sports franchise owners.

Team owners enjoy their financial success due to receipt of antitrust exemptions (especially the right to pool broadcast rights to their games by virtue of Public Law 87-331), exploitation of the public's good will, and the granting of sizable public subsidies. The decision to host a sports team, as we have seen, requires a significant and continuing investment of public funds, often in facilities with limited alternative uses.

Critics contend that the acceptance of subsidies and other forms of public support creates an obligation on the part of team owners to remain in their host communities. In response to the Oakland and Baltimore cases, they are seeking legislation that will restrict team movement.

The sports leagues and owners oppose such action. The leagues have sought legislation to grant them the right to control team movement, which they lost in the Raiders case (*Los Angeles Memorial Coliseum Commission* v. *NFL*, 726 F.2d 1397). The owners invoke the principles of private ownership, and argue that they should be able to operate their businesses as they see fit and pursue profit maximization.

Although restrictive legislation would solve the franchise relocation problem, it would be poor public policy.[11] Advocates are seeking to translate the moral obligations of some into the legal obligations of all team owners. Advocates draw an analogy to the plant relocation issue, but it is a superficial one that does not support their position. Manufacturing plants and other large economic entities with the right to relocate have a greater economic impact upon a community because they employ on a full-time basis more local residents (who cannot or do not wish to move with the firm, unlike athletes, who accept movement as part of their career) and operate on a year-round basis. The 95th and 96th Congresses chose not to enact legislation designed to respond to the economic and social impacts of plant closings and relocations. Supporters of restrictive legislation, therefore, must demonstrate how sports operations differ from other business ventures and why only sports franchise owners' rights are to be restricted to achieve community protection.

The crux of the problem is the unequal balance of power between team and city officials at the negotiating table. This is a result of the monopoly situation of the leagues and individual owners, combined with an excess demand for teams relative to their supply. Absent resolution of these conditions, and without legislative relief, a city must seek its own means of protecting its treasury while retaining its teams. The fact that cities, including Baltimore, do show a profit from their stadium operations indicates it is possible to earn revenue from a sports team and that restrictive legislation is overreaction to specific cases of owners abusing their powers or failed negotiating strategies of cities.

Although team owners and city officials have conflicting interests, it is important to acknowledge the fact that when a team does well financially it is likely the city will do well also. The two have a mutual interest in the team's on-the-field and off-the-field performance. This especially is true when a lease provides the city with a percentage of a team's gate receipts (and concessions and parking receipts), as most do.

The 1982-1983 Oriole lease dramatically symbolized the concept of partnership between a city and its team. In presenting the lease to the Board of Estimates for its approval, the former director of recreation and parks (Tawney, 1982) stated,

> the contract is designed so that if the Orioles do well at the gate and in other revenue areas such as radio, television, and cable television the city will also do well . . . it helps the club have a more sound fiscal status in times of difficulty.

He also described it as

> a marketing tool to demonstrate to the fans of the City and the metro-area that the baseball team needs strong support to remain competitive in the American League . . . convince baseball fans that their admission price and concession goods expenditures represent a very large contribution to *the City of Baltimore's revenue proceeds* [Tawney, 1982; italics added].

Use of the partnership concept to describe the relationship between a city and team is not meant to deny legitimate financial interests of the team owner but, rather, to stress that there also exist legitimate financial interests of the municipality. Just as the owner invests and risks his or her money, the city invests and risks public dollars in the team. It is not unreasonable to suggest that, like the owner of a franchise, a city should be compensated for the risk it undertakes when it invests in a team. It is unreasonable for a team to demand guaranteed profits, as the city certainly has no guarantee that it will realize a return on its investment. The realization of a payoff for the city on its investment is dependent on the team drawing a sufficient number of fans. This is affected by a team's on-the-field performance as well as management decisions and behavior.[12] The city has no control over either of these factors.

It will be argued by some that reliance on a partnership notion is naive, especially as team owners enjoy an advantage in power at the bargaining table.[13] However, if that advantage is exploited to force the city to make financial concessions that are economically unwise, resistance, conflict, and resentment are sure to follow. It is certain that a point will be reached at which the city will have no choice but to seek to alter the basis for the team's advantage. It will be less expensive and potentially more profitable for the city to seek legislative or judicial solutions than to continue to increase its sports subsidies.

This, in fact, is occurring. In addition to the restrictive legislative proposals already discussed, Oakland and Baltimore are in state and federal courts attempting to apply eminent domain laws to the teams that abandoned them. If either the legislative or judicial efforts succeed, the advantage in the relationship will shift to the city. If this occurs, a sports team may expect no better treatment from a city than it has given to it. Thus, it may be in the long-term financial interests of the franchise to acknowledge its moral obligations to deal fairly with its partner and to refrain from abusing its monopolist's power in its relationship with a municipality, in which case the appeal to the notion of partnership is not naive.

SUMMARY

Public subsidies of sports franchises are not unique. Horton (1979: 112-113), for example, observes that

> discussion of municipal economic development options usually involves variations on the common theme of targeting specific benefits to individual businesses. . . . Today the major issues concern how, not

whether, local government should engage in economic development policies.

The team-city relationship and public policy decisions that affect that relationship are of great public interest due to the high visibility and popularity of professional sports.

This analysis has found that public investment in sports can be worth it. For this to be the case, it is essential that more than one tenant makes use of a city's sports facilities, lease concessions be reasonable, and the size of debt service be limited. Often the valuation of intangible and indirect benefits and costs will determine the question of worth. Thus, the condemnation of sports subsidies whenever the ledger sheet shows that expenditures exceed revenues is overly simplistic.

The article has identified policy dilemmas that stem from the existence of intangible benefits flowing from a team's presence and sports subsidies. The legislative and judicial efforts to restrict the movement rights of sports franchise owners will continue as long as cities perceive owners as abusing their power advantage in negotiations with local officials. For this reason, it is in the interest of both parties that franchise owners recognize the value of public support in the coproduction of professional sports events, and behave as responsible partners in what has become a quasi-public industry.

NOTES

1. Okner (1974: 334) observed, "Even though these are public facilities for which one should be able to obtain information easily, most of the cities either do not keep separate accounting records for their stadiums and arenas or are extremely reluctant to release such information. It is impossible to know the extent to which such reluctance is the result of not having the information or an attempt to keep it out of the public spotlight."

2. See Miller (1984: 260-264), for a discussion of the problems of comparison in the social sciences and the utility of single-case analysis.

3. Most probably would accept this assumption. Johnson (1982) and Okner (1974) are two of the few who even discuss intangible costs.

4. Not included in this analysis are revenues derived from sales tax on sports purchases (by the team and consumers), income tax on wages earned by employees of the franchise and others affected by it, real estate tax foregone on the land a publicly owned sports facility occupies, and the value of depreciation of a facility.

5. This article focuses only on the Colts and Orioles. A professional basketball team moved from Baltimore to the Washington suburb of Landover, Maryland, in 1974.

Attempts to field a major league hockey team failed in 1975. A minor league hockey team presently plays in the city-owned civic center, as does a professional indoor soccer team. The soccer team sells out nearly each of its games.

6. Team revenue included ticket receipts from home and away games, spring training receipts, radio and television income, scorecard advertising income, concession novelty sales income, yearbook and scorecard income, and admission tax revenues. All royalty income and profits from the sale of players' contracts are excluded from operating revenue. The team's federal tax payments are excluded from operating expenditures.

7. It is less expensive and administratively simpler to arrange for overtime duty on game days than to alter normal patrol assignments each game day. Presumably, if officers were taken from their beats for stadium duty, the costs of crime in those areas would offset overtime savings.

8. The $300,000 traditionally has come from a state grant for open space and the city's apportionment from transfer taxes. As the transfer tax receipts are virtually automatic, it is arguable that they should be viewed as state funds. For the purpose of this article, they will be so viewed. The capital expenditures in Table 1 reflect the initial years of a five-year plan for $720,000 in city funds to be committed to stadium improvements. For FY 1984 the city budgeted $150,000 instead of its $300,000 annual appropriation. This was a reflection of the city's fiscal difficulties as well as the expected use of state bond money.

9. In February 1984, the city awarded a six-year concessions contract. The city is to receive 44.2% commission on annual gross sales (expected to be at least $10 million). Relevant to the concerns of this article, the concessionaire agreed to pay $2 million in advance to obtain the contract, spend $2 million for capital improvements on stadium facilities and $100,000 on the press boxes, and provide $90,000 for scholarships to local universities. The 1984 Orioles' lease defines as team revenues the $1.5 million of the $2 million advance and the city's 44.2% commission on gross sales.

10. Of 19 major league baseball franchises that use publicly owned stadiums, 11 have their leases expire sometime after the year 2000. Similarly, the leases of a majority of National Football League franchises expire in the twenty-first century.

11. For a more complete analysis of this legislation and alternative policy options, see Johnson (1983, 1985).

12. Many commentators in Baltimore, for example, believe Irsay attempted to create a justification (poor fan support) for franchise relocation by fielding a poor team and behaving in a way to alienate the public. Similar speculation occurred in Minneapolis with regard to Calvin Griffith.

13. Those who suggest that the idea of partnership is of little value in dealing with this issue must explain away the behavior of owners such as Dan Rooney, Jerold Hoffberger, John Fetzer, and Ruly Carpenter, who have not operated from purely profit motives. See Brower (1976) and Markham and Teplitz (1981: 25-31).

REFERENCES

ATTNER, P. (1984) "For many cities, there's no place like a dome." Washington Post (June 8): c3.

BAADE, R. and J. CHESSEN (1984) "The sports tax." Presented at the meetings of the Eastern Economic Association, New York.

BROWER, J. (1976) "Professional sports team ownership: fun, profit and ideology of the power elite." J. of Sport and Social Issues 1, 6: 16-51.

CANZIAN, E. (1984) "Md.'s offer to Irsay revealed as most lucrative." Baltimore Sun (April 1): 1.

CONNICK, W. (1976) "Statement," pp. 489-507 in U.S. Congress, House Select Committee on Professional Sports, Inquiry into Professional Sports, Part 1. Hearings, Ninety-Fourth Congress, Second Session. Washington, DC: Government Printing Office.

FLAHERTY, C. (1982) "Statement," pp. 446-453 in U.S. Congress, Committee on the Judiciary, U.S. Senate, Professional Sports Antitrust Immunity. Hearings, Ninety-Seventh Congress, Second Session. Washington, DC: Government Printing Office.

HAUTZER, A. (1984) "Nation experiences boom in costly sports facilities." Weekly Bond Buyer (May 6): 1.

HORTON, R. (1979) "Economic development," pp. 112-133 in R. Horton and C. Brechter (eds.) Setting Municipal Priorities. Montclair, NJ: Allanheld, Osum.

JOHNSON, A. (1982) "The uneasy partnership—cities and professional sports: public policy considerations." Presented at the annual meeting of the North American Society for the Sociology of Sports, Toronto.

———(1983) "Municipal administration and the sports franchise relocation issue." Public Administration Rev. 43 (November/December): 519-528.

———(1985) "The professional sports franchise relocation issue," in J. Frey and A. Johnson (eds.) Government and Sports: Public Policy Issues. Totowa, NJ: Rowman & Allanheld.

KURTZ, H. (1984) "Cities building new stadiums to lure major teams, money." Washington Post (January): A3.

MARKHAM, J. W. and P. TEPLITZ (1981) Baseball Economics and Public Policy. Lexington, MA: D.C. Heath.

MILLER, T. (1984) Public Sector Performance. Baltimore: Johns Hopkins Univ. Press.

New York Times (1980) "Yankee Stadium pays the city a bit more in fees but problem remains." (August 25): 1.

———(1983) "Meadowlands revenues dropped sharply in '82." (April 17): 40.

OKNER, B. (1974) "Subsidies of stadiums and arenas," pp. 325-347 in R. Noll (ed.) Government and the Sports Business. Washington, DC: Brookings Institution.

ROSENTRAUB, M. and S. NUNN (1978) "Suburban city investment in professional sports: estimating the fiscal returns of the Dallas Cowboys and Texas Rangers to investor communities." Amer. Behavioral Scientist (January/February): 393-414.

Select Committee on Professional Sports, U.S. House of Representatives (1977) *Final Report*. Inquiry into Professional Sports. Washington, DC: Government Printing Office.

TAWNEY, D. (1977) "Memo to Baltimore City Board of Estimates." (March 3).

———(1982) "Memo to Baltimore City Board of Estimates." (April 22).

VITULLO-MARTIN, J. (1978) "Yankee Stadium: a good principle badly implemented." Fiscal Observer (October 12): 13-14.

Weekly Bond Buyer (1974) "Memorial Auditorium in Buffalo suffers continuing losses." (October 7): 11.

Arthur T. Johnson is Associate Professor of Political Science at the University of Maryland, Baltimore County. He is coeditor (with James H. Frey) of Government and Sports: Public Policy Issues *(Rowman & Allanheld).*

REEVALUATING THE BENEFITS AND COSTS OF INDUSTRIAL REVENUE BONDS

MATTHEW R. MARLIN
Old Dominion University

In a recent article in this journal it was argued that the costs of Industrial Revenue Bonds exceed their benefits and the program, therefore, should be abolished. This note reevaluates the benefits and costs as presented in that article. It is concluded that the costs enumerated in the previous study were overstated whereas the benefits were understated. Among the social costs discussed, only transaction costs and distributional consequences are found to be valid. Absent from the previous study's benefit considerations was the increased capital formation resulting from low-interest Industrial Revenue Bonds.

In a recent article in this journal, Pascarella and Raymond (1982) analyzed the use of Industrial Revenue Bonds (IRBs) and concluded that costs exceed benefits and therefore the program should be terminated. Much of their cost/benefit analysis was based on the presumption that IRBs influence firms to locate in less than optimal locations where the true social costs of production exceed the subsidized production costs faced by the firm. The Pascarella and Raymond study found two closely related costs to society that result from such subsidization. First, "If the subsidies are successful they will induce firms to market goods that are worth less to the public than they cost to produce" (1982: 76). Second, subsidized production of the good in a high-cost, nonoptimal location will increase supplies, lower prices, and force firms located in low-cost, optimal regions to cease production. "The subsidy will therefore succeed in shifting some production activity from low-cost to high-cost scales" (1982: 76).

The purpose of this note is to determine to what extent IRBs have succeeded in shifting production from low- to high-cost locations and, hence, to what extent the costs enumerated by Pascarella and Raymond

URBAN AFFAIRS QUARTERLY, Vol. 21 No. 3, March 1986 435-441

accompany the use of IRBs. The other costs associated with the program, noted in a number of studies (Kaufman, 1981), will be briefly mentioned. The potential benefits of IRB financing also will be briefly addressed and some conclusions regarding the desirability of continued IRB financing will be offered.

COSTS OF IRB FINANCING

To the extent that IRBs induce location at inefficient sites, an examination of their use would reveal a significant percentage of these bonds being received by "footloose" firms. These are firms that do not require proximity to nonmobile markets or resources, and therefore are free to locate in any region. Alternatively, IRBs used to finance market or resource-oriented businesses and the IRBs used by the local firms would indicate no loss in locational efficiency due to the IRB subsidy. The former businesses would be optimally located adjacent to population centers or necessary resources, and local businesses orginally established without the subsidy must be assumed to be in efficient locations.

Table 1 disaggregates the use of IRBs in the Norfolk-Virginia Beach SMSA by the local or nonlocal status of receiving firms and by the location orientation of their industry.[1] Local firms included businesses already established in the SMSA that used IRBs to expand local operations or to move to a new site within the SMSA. New businesses financed with IRBs (primary development partnerships) are included in the local category. Nonlocal bond recipients were all multistate, national, or international corporations with headquarters outside the SMSA that used IRBs to initiate local operations.

The local users of IRBs shown in the first rows of parts A and B of Table 1 were originally established in the SMSA without the use of location subsidies, and therefore it is assumed that these 427 bond recipients were located in low-cost, optimal locations. Operations initiated in the SMSA by nonlocal firms (row 2) were predominantly market-oriented businesses such as restaurants, hotels, retail franchises, wholesalers, nursing homes, and such. Optimal location for these businesses requires proximity to the markets served. All else the same, it appears that these IRB-financed projects were not induced by the subsidy to locate at high-cost sites. The same holds true for the port- and

TABLE 1
Location and Orientation of IRB-Using Firms, 1973-1982

A) By Number of Issues

	Orientation				
	Market	Port	Other Resource	Foot-Loose	Total
Local Firms	325	44	15	42	427
Non-local Firms	67	1	5	19	92
Total	393	45	20	61	519

B) By Dollar Volume ($ Millions)

	Orientation				
	Market	Port	Other Resource	Foot-Loose	Total
Local Firms	$310.7	$85.3	$12.0	$37.2	$445.2
Non-local Firms	94.1	1.5	12.9	36.0	144.5
Total	$404.8	$86.8	$24.9	$73.2	$589.7

NOTE: Five IRBs valued at $2.2 million could not be classified because of insufficient information.

resource-oriented operations financed with IRBs: The subsidy apparently has not induced high-cost location choices for these firms.[2]

The one sector indicated in Table 1 that presents the possibility of inefficiency through subsidized location at an otherwise unprofitable location involves the 19 footloose operations of nonlocal corporations valued at $36 million. These projects included 4 warehouse/assembly facilities, a publishing house, a photo processor, and 13 manufacturing facilities. Assuming that the IRB subsidy was the determining location factor in these instances, the conclusion to be drawn is that only about 4% of the IRB issues and 6% of the dollar volume may have involved real economic costs stemming from inefficient location patterns.

Because the evidence indicates that few IRB-receiving firms were even potentially induced to locate in inefficient, high-cost locations, neither of the first two "real" costs theorized by Pascarella and Raymond actually coincide with the use of IRBs. Instead, the evidence supports the Congressional Budget Office (1981: 48) conclusion that IRBs have little or no impact on the location decisions of their recipients.

Four other costs of IRBs were enumerated in the Pascarella-Raymond study: overinvestment in capital, distortions in the municipal bond market, lost federal tax revenues, and administrative costs. The first of these was considered to be a real economic cost in the analysis, and implies that the subsidization of capital leads to its being substituted for other inputs and therefore leads to a misallocation of resources. However, the CBO (1981: 54) stated that increasing capital investment may have been a congressional objective of the IRB program. This being the case, "misallocations" biased toward more capital spending would represent the attainment of a policy objective and would therefore constitute a benefit, not a cost.

The second "cost" of IRBs is based on the presumption that increased volumes of IRBs add to the overall supply of tax-exempt bonds, push their prices down and their yields up. The lower price of IRB-financed private capital is therefore offset by a higher price for more traditional state and local public capital. The result will be a reallocation of capital from the public to the private sector. Although numerous studies have documented this occurrence (Hendershott and Koch, 1977; Kane, 1981), it is still debatable whether or not such a "distortion" represents a cost or benefit to the economy as a whole. From a "supply-side" or laissez-faire perspective, such cost shifting from the private to the public sector will lead to better economic performance and increased growth (Hailstones, 1982: 109).

The third cost cited by Pascarella and Raymond, lost federal revenues, has also received a significant amount of attention in the literature (Galper and Toder, 1981; Kormendi and Nagel, 1981) but whether this is truly a cost to society is again open to debate. The total output of the economy would suffer from these revenue losses only if the federal government were to use the revenues in a manner that would generate more benefits than increased private capital formation. The estimation of alternative benefits goes beyond the scope of this study, but again it can be argued that proponents of private sector development would perceive the shift of resources from the public to the private sector as benefit rather than a cost.

The final cost discussed by Pascarella and Raymond has received little attention, but it has had a significant impact on the distribution of IRB users. The high legal and administrative costs associated with issuing IRBs (technically municipal bonds) necessitate that the bond be for at least $150,000 in order to be overall less costly than conventional taxable financing.[3] The size distribution of IRBs in the Norfolk-Virginia Beach SMSA is presented in Table 2. It can be seen that the administrative costs of IRBs have biased their use away from smaller projects (and, hence, smaller firms). In addition, the administration costs do have an impact on overall economic efficiency because they represent increased transaction costs on investment projects.

In summary, the "costs" of IRBs presented by Pascarella and Raymond and others are for the most part either nonexistent or of dubious nature. Because IRBs apparently have little or no effect on location decisions, they result in no spatially inefficient distribution of capital. Increased private capital formation arising from the diversion of resources from the public to the private sector may in fact be a benefit rather than a cost. The only clear inefficiency resulting from the use of IRBs is the high administrative costs that bias their use away from small firms and increase the cost of investment transactions.

BENEFITS

The CBO perceived three potential objectives of IRBs: to assist small business to procure financing, to direct capital to depressed regions, and to stimulate investment in general. As discussed above, high administrative costs make the first objective unattainable for IRBs. Because IRBs do not significantly influence firm location, the second objective is also unattainable. The Pascarella-Raymond study tested for the achievement of this objective only. Not surprisingly, they found no positive correlation between regional unemployment and IRB use. Instead, it should have been expected that areas of low unemployment were growing areas with more opportunities to avail themselves of industrial subsidies. In the absence of policies restricting the geographic distribution of IRBs, a negative correlation between bond use and unemployment (found in two cases) should have been anticipated (Pascarella and Raymond, 1982: 79-80).

Apparently, the only CBO objective that has been achieved through the use of IRBs is an increase in the overall level of investment made possible by the reduction in interest rates charged for private capital formation. The efficiency of IRBs vis-à-vis other policy instruments, such as accelerated depreciation or the investment tax credit, is an issue that requires further research. However, the omission of increased

TABLE 2
Size Distribution of IRBs by Dollar Volume, 1973-1982

Dollar Range ($ thousands)	Number of IRBs	Total Dollar Volume ($ millions)
$ 0 -150[a]	32	$ 4.0
$ 150-250	78	$ 16.8
$ 250-500	144	$ 55.4
$ 500-1,000	133	$102.2
$1,000-5,000	111	$254.1
$5,000-10,000	7	$ 58.0
$0ver $10,000[b]	6	$101.4

a. Includes one IRB FOR $597,000 redistributed to 14 separate firms.
b. These projects were allowed under the exemptions to the Tax and Revenue Expenditure Control Act of 1968.

investment from the Pascarella-Raymond benefit calculations obviously distorts the overall evaluation of the relative costs and benefits of IRBs.

CONCLUSIONS

The purpose of this study was to reevaluate the benefits and costs of IRBs, especially as they were presented by Pascarella and Raymond. It was shown that the only obvious cost associated with IRBs involves the distributional and transaction effects associated with the high administrative costs of issuing them. Location inefficiencies were shown to be nonexistent, and the diversion of resources from the public to the private sector can as easily be classified as a benefit as it can a cost.

Weighed against the costs are the benefits of increased private capital formation. Although this study has not produced empirical estimates of benefits and costs for purposes of comparison, it has presented a number of arguments that must be considered when evaluating the desirability of maintaining or eliminating the use of IRBs. In particular, it has demonstrated the Pascarella-Raymond conclusion that costs exceed benefits is based on an incorrect assumption about location influence and an incomplete evaluation of other benefits and costs.

NOTES

1. The Norfolk-Virginia Beach SMSA is composed of five independent cities in southeast Virginia with a 1982 population of about 815,000.

2. Port-oriented projects were those involving the region's ship repair industry, shipping, dredging, and other port-related activity. Resource-orientation included oceanfront resort hotels and food processing operations that require proximity to the agricultural inputs produced in the region.

3. $150,000 was considered to be the effective minimum in the SMSA as of 1983. In the past it has been lower, but increased rules and regulations governing the issue of IRBs as well as inflation have pushed the minimum up significantly during the past few years.

REFERENCES

Congressional Budget Office (1981) Small Issue Industrial Revenue Bonds. Washington, DC: Government Printing Office.

GALPER, H. and E. TODER (1981) "Modeling revenue and allocation effects of the use of tax-exempt bonds for private purposes," pp. 85-116 in G. Kaufman (ed.) Efficiency in the Municipal Bond Market: The Use of Tax Financing for Private Purposes. Greenwich, CT: JAI Press.

HAILSTONES, T. J. (1982) A Guide to Supply-Side Economics. Richmond, VA: Robert F. Dame, Inc.

HENDERSHOTT, P. H. and T. KOCH (1977) An Empirical Analysis of the Market for Tax-Exempt Securities. New York: New York University Monograph Series in Finance and Economics.

KANE, E. J. (1981) "Tax exemption, economic efficiency, and relative interest rates," pp. 1-12 in G. Kaufman (ed.) Efficiency in the Municipal Bond Market: The Use of Tax-Exempt Financing for Private Purposes. Greenwich, CT: JAI Press.

KORMENDI, R. C. and T. NAGLE (1981) "The interest rate and the tax revenue effects of mortgage revenue bonds," pp. 117-148 in G. Kaufman (ed.) Efficiency in the Municipal Bond Market: The Use of Tax-Exempt Financing for Private Purposes. Greenwich, CT: JAI Press.

PASCARELLA, T. A. and R. D. RAYMOND (1982) "Buying bonds for business: an evaluation of the industrial revenue bond program." Urban Affairs Q. 18 (September): 73-89.

Matthew R. Marlin is Assistant Professor of Economics at Old Dominion University. His research interests are in the area of urban and regional economics and tax-exempt bond markets. He has published articles in professional journals dealing with various aspects of public subsidies and regional economic development.

REJOINDER TO MATTHEW R. MARLIN'S "REEVALUATING THE BENEFITS AND COSTS OF INDUSTRIAL REVENUE BONDS"

THOMAS A. PASCARELLA
Hiram College
RICHARD D. RAYMOND
Kent State University

Matthew Marlin's analysis does not support his position. Our earlier research of industrial revenue bonds is correct and we continue to argue that the IRB program creates economic inefficiencies, increases the federal deficit, and serves no apparent public purpose. The elimination of the program is in the best interest of the nation.

Matthew Marlin contends that we have failed adequately to support the conclusion that the federal government should "eliminate the IRB program with all of its associated costs and inequities" (Pascarella and Raymond 1982: 84). He purports to demonstrate empirically that IRBs generate minimal locational inefficiencies and further argues that both the increased capital formation generated by IRBs and their "adverse" effect upon the municipal bond market should be classified as benefits of the program. We will attempt to show that Marlin's empirical analysis does not support his conclusion. Due to space limitations, we will not comment in detail upon Marlin's contention that increased capital formation and a redirection of investment from the public to the private sector are beneficial effects of IRBs. We will argue, however, that these effects should not be used to provide primary justification for the IRB program, even if they are regarded as beneficial.

Marlin presents data showing that over 85% of the IRB financing in the Norfolk-Virginia Beach area went to firms that were "market-,"

URBAN AFFAIRS QUARTERLY, Vol. 21 No. 3, March 1986 443-447

"port-," or "other resource-" oriented. Since "Optimal location for these businesses requires proximity to" markets, ports, and other resources, Marlin concludes that "the subsidy apparently has not induced high-cost location for these firms" (Marlin, this issue). If the only markets, ports, and "other resources" available to these firms were located in the Norfolk area, this argument would be correct.[1] But this is clearly not the case for a great many of the firms and activities involved. For instance, Norfolk is certainly not the only area possessing the port facilities necessary for shipping and ship repair. An effective location subsidy would operate by stimulating an uneconomic or inefficient expansion of such activities in some areas at the expense of other potential sites.[2] This is also true for "market-" and "other resource-" oriented activities. The figures presented by Marlin thus convey no information about the extent of the locational inefficiencies generated by IRBs.

The nature of the legislation and its administration admittedly make it appear unlikely that IRBs cause systematic or intended changes in location. IRBs are currently available in all 50 states (Rivlin, 1983: 305). However, locational inefficiencies may result from differences in state and local administration of the IRB legislation. To the best of our knowledge, no empirical work relating to the magnitude of these inefficiencies has been completed.

We agree with Marlin when he argues that IRBs are unlikely to have any impact upon the location decisions of "nonlocal firms . . . such as restaurants, hotels, retail franchises, wholesalers, nursing homes" (Marlin, this issue). These firms are driven in their behavior by demographic data, traffic patterns, and other retail-oriented criteria. In such cases, since the IRB program is not effective in influencing the private entrepreneur, it generates no public benefits. Benefits accrue exclusively to the private firm in the form of reduced financing charges. These observations lead us to oppose IRBs because they serve no apparent public purpose. We are puzzled when the same observations lead Marlin to support IRBs.

A potential source of inefficiency that has received little attention is suggested by the Marlin data. Approximately 75% of IRB financing in the Norfolk area went to local firms "to expand local operations or to move to a new site within the SMSA" (Marlin, this issue). The IRB legislation is structured so that local firms in general must either expand or move in order to qualify for a subsidy. This may stimulate an overexpansion of local firms. It may also give rise to a game of musical chairs played by firms attempting to qualify for IRB subsidies. For instance, a firm renting office space may be able to cut its costs by purchasing and renovating new space with IRB financing. This type of activity entails real costs in addition to the legal and administrative expenses involved. Once again, the magnitude of this type of inefficiency has not been established, but anecdotal evidence indicates that it does exist.

Our position with respect to any increased capital formation that may be generated by IRBs is quite simple: We do not feel that it is legitimate to defend the IRB program by placing primary reliance upon the existence of "benefits" that may be generated more effectively and efficiently with alternative policies. Previous discussions of this point are quite brief (Congressional Budget Office, 1981: 44-45, 54-56; Musgrave and Musgrave, 1984: 703; Pascarella and Raymond, 1982: 75). The fact that this issue has not been considered at great length does not mean that "the efficiency of IRBs (in increasing capital formation) vis-à-vis other policy instruments . . . requires further research" (Marlin, this issue). Medical journals contain few articles demonstrating that chain saws should not be used in surgery. Similarly, few authors have felt it necessary to dwell at length on the obvious inferiority of IRBs as a tool to increase capital formation. A repetition of the textbook case for the greater economic efficiency, barring externalities, of general as opposed to specific subsidies would accomplish little.

A similar objection applies to Marlin's suggestion that higher interest rates on municipal bonds should be considered a benefit of the IRB program. If Congress wishes to reduce the allocation of resources to the state and local public sector, there are policies that will accomplish this much more efficiently than IRBs: for example, elimination of the tax-exempt status on state and local bond interest or a direct reduction in federal grants to states and localities. In fact, the use of IRBs to reduce the size of the state and local public sector coupled with the continuation of federal grants to subnational jurisdictions and tax exemptions on municipal bond interest would imply a profound confusion on the part of Congress.[3]

The scenario that has unfolded around IRB legislation may not be completely atypical. Congress initially passed legislation in an attempt to achieve certain vaguely defined goals. It has become apparent that the achievement of these goals has not been furthered significantly by this legislation. In the process, however, some strong vested interests have been created. These interests understandably resist any attempts to eliminate the legislation. To defend their position, the proponents of the law produce a large, and perhaps questionable, list of the "accidental" benefits generated by the program—even an ill wind blows some good.

The response of Congress emanates from a combination of confusion and political expediency. Instead of repealing the ineffective law (and possibly making changes to recapture any "accidental" benefits lost thereby), Congress works hard to convert their chain saw into a scalpel. Their efforts do not inspire confidence.

We continue to feel that there is ample evidence to support our initial position: IRBs should be either eliminated or, if this is impossible, emasculated and targeted.

NOTES

1. Even under these extreme circumstances, the IRB subsidy would generate inefficiencies by stimulating an overexpansion of the eligible activities.

2. This is the example used by Musgrave (1969: 804) to demonstrate the inefficiencies that may be generated when locational choices are dictated by distributional considerations. The fact that the case considered by Musgrave (the construction of a shipyard in West Virginia rather than in Norfolk) was obviously exaggerated, does not affect the validity of the basic point involved.

3. Marlin's position relating to lost federal revenues is difficult to follow. His argument seems to imply that IRBs cause a shift of resources equal in value to the lost federal revenues from the public sector to private capital formation. Under existing circumstances, however, the direct impact of the increased tax revenues resulting from the abolition of IRBs would serve primarily, or exclusively, to reduce the federal budget deficit. A thorough analysis of the potential resource shift would require an investigation of IRBs within the context of a complete macroeconomic model. The allocation of public resources between current expenditures and capital formation would also have to be considered. The results of such an analysis are not readily apparent.

REFERENCES

Congressional Budget Office (1981) Small Issue Industrial Revenue Bonds. Washington, DC: Government Printing Office.

MUSGRAVE, R. A. (1969) "Cost benefit analysis and the theory of public finance." J. of Econ. Literature 3 (September): 797-806.

———and P. B. MUSGRAVE (1984) Public Finance in Theory and Practice. New York: McGraw-Hill.

PASCARELLA, T. A. and R. D. RAYMOND (1982) "Buying bonds for business: an evaluation of the industrial revenue bond program." Urban Affairs Q. 18 (September): 73-89.

RIVLIN, A. M. (1983) "CBO's position on tax-exempt financing for private activities." Municipal Finance J. 4, 4: 303-313.

Thomas A. Pascarella is Assistant Professor of Economics and Management at Hiram College. He has extensive government experience in Ohio and in the Chicago area as Director of Planning for several agencies and as Assistant City Manager.

Richard D. Raymond is Professor of Economics at Kent State University. His research interests are in the areas of urban economics and the economics of education.

BOOK REVIEW ESSAY

SUBURBANIZATION, SEGREGATION, AND POLITICS

Henry C. Binford, *The First Suburbs: Residential Communities on the Boston Periphery, 1815-1860* (Chicago: University of Chicago Press, 1985). 304 pp. $25.00 (cloth).

Arnold R. Hirsch, *Making the Second Ghetto: Race and Housing in Chicago, 1940-1960* (Cambridge: Cambridge University Press, 1983). 362 pp. $24.95 (cloth).

Matthew Edel, Elliott D. Sclar, and Daniel Luria, *Shaky Palaces: Homeownership and Social Mobility in Boston's Suburbanization* (New York: Columbia University Press, 1984). 459 pp. $40.00 (cloth), $18.00 (paper).

Richard P. Taub, D. Garth Taylor, and Jan D. Dunham, *Paths of Neighborhood Change: Race and Crime in Urban America* (Chicago: University of Chicago Press, 1984). 264 pp. $25.00 (cloth).

The classic ecological model of city growth and neighborhood succession developed in Chicago is over 50 years old. Yet with its emphasis on how a few impersonal forces such as transportation and social and economic competition for urban space first establish, then continuously alter, urban spatial structures, this perspective retains its vitality in thinking about the arrangements of people and activities in cities. It has weaknesses, of course. Its conception of growth as rippling outward from the city's core in concentric waves to affect land uses and population patterns, even with sectoral revisions, is inadequate for a metropolitan era, when suburbanization is not tightly tied to central cities and polycentrism more often is the norm than the exception. Indeed, the history of civic boosterism and local autonomy in America raises questions about the passivity of suburban communities even half a century ago. Moreover, the Chicago school slighted the role of government and other institutions and downplayed politics and

URBAN AFFAIRS QUARTERLY, Vol. 21 No. 3, March 1986 448-454

conflict. Urban structures often were portrayed as evolving from "natural" processes that might be complicated or perhaps temporarily contained by such factors but not fundamentally disrupted.

Both directly and indirectly the four books reviewed here address these concerns. Binford's history of antebellum Cambridge and Somerville sets out to correct the notion that Boston gave birth to its suburbs and that transportation was the midwife as exemplified by its streetcar suburbs later in the nineteenth century. Edel and his colleagues, on the other hand, accept the basic outlines of the ecological model, particularly the filtering of housing, but give it a Marxian spin by arguing that Boston's suburbanization grew out of a "compromise" between capital and labor in the late 1890s that trapped workers in an illusion of mobility. In Chicago, Hirsch emphasizes how white violence and public and private institutions drew the metes and bounds of its second ghetto between 1940 and 1960. Taub and his associates, although not ignoring institutional actors in their study of Chicago neighborhoods, concentrate their theoretical interests on the dynamics of "tipping" and on investment decisions by homeowners in racially changing neighborhoods or those with high crime rates.

SUBURBANIZATION IN BOSTON

Binford's well-crafted narrative, which is amply documented, shows how Cambridge and Somerville evolved into residentially-oriented, commuter-based, politically independent communities that in effect were precursors of modern suburbs some time before the advent of streetcar suburbs. During the early decades of the nineteenth century, he makes clear, suburbanites played a strong hand in building their own communities. They did not try to create local autarkies free from all outside influences but, rather, fostered ties with Boston that were beneficial to them and on their own terms. The book's early chapters convincingly show how local elites and entrepreneurs, more so than Bostonians, exploited the locational advantages of being on Boston's fringe by initiating and promoting public improvements such as bridges and roads, often with the aid and assistance of public monies or legislation, a measure of their clout with the state. They also cut a template for future real estate speculators to follow by developing large parcels of land they owned along the transportation routes or near facilities they had promoted. At times Binford glosses over the financial details of these ventures, but it is evident these early suburbanites were not pawns for Beacon Hill interests.

This community building process was neither democratic nor egalitarian because it was localized. Early leaders were members of a cohesive, multifunctional, patrician elite that nevertheless ultimately broke down into a more pluralist configuration. Suburbanization similarly modified the social mix of residents, the nature and scope of local government, and the citizens' role in suburban governance; all of which can be interpreted, at some risk of doing Binford's analysis a disservice, as moving the communities in a *gesellschaft*-like direction. Binford does a nice job of showing how these changes led residents to define their vision of a suburban community and what, as well as who, it should include.

These events look like mere perturbations in the workings of Boston's suburbanization, as portrayed by Edel, Sclar, and Luria, who pick up the story in 1890 and follow it through to 1970. Drawing on the ecological model's depiction of growth as setting off chains of housing moves, ordered by wealth or class, they contend that housing assets are devalued to make them affordable to the next group because demand for the housing at its old price declines. This process of devaluation means that all but the wealthy must continually scramble to keep their places on a downward-moving escalator. Devaluation is further aided by governmental actions that upset housing markets, provide the infrastructure for suburbanization, and perpetuate the balkanization of local governments, leading to tax and service inequities. With these conditions in mind, Edel and his colleagues argue that moving to the suburbs results in few gains, if any, in upward mobility for nonupper-class members while causing their demobilization as a force for social change.

In *Shaky Palaces* the authors bit off more than they could digest in one volume. Confronted with a task that focuses on housing values and social mobility over 80 years of history in as many suburban communities, Edel and his colleagues have written a sprawling, disjointed book that too often asserts more than it can prove. In particular, the chapters on devaluation fail to build an iron-clad case for the "up the down escalator" metaphor. For example, Chapter 3 shows that, except during the Depression, housing values in real terms followed *upward* trends in Brookline and Somerville, although their rates of increase differed. Chapter 4 looks at the entire metropolitan area with mixed results. A gradient model in accord with the ecological model showed a strong relationship between suburban housing value and distance from Boston's core and location in particular sectors. Yet median family income and ethnicity, used as surrogates for class, were weakly associated with these factors, unlike the classic model, which undermines confidence that housing value changes varied systematically with suburban affluence.

Gains in housing appreciation are also compared with other forms of investment in Chapter 4. Overall, housing value increases kept pace with inflation between 1950 and 1970, but Edel et al. go on to argue that, if compared to the performance of other investments that the better off presumably make, the less well off at best broke even on their housing purchases. This may be unfair and reflect an inequitable income distribution, but it is not the argument presented earlier. Moreover, as the authors admit, such comparisons face several problems because of housing's uniqueness as both an investment and a commodity. Still, the point remains that widespread, inevitable devaluation is not established in these chapters.

The "entrapment" argument rests on data from a sample of Bostonians who moved to the suburbs for the period 1890 to 1910, a study of more recent Somerville residents, and an analysis of college attendance patterns. One aspect of the entrapment argument is that housing purchases retard intergenerational social mobility. The data for the 1890-1910 sample support this hypothesis. Yet why can it be expected that this relationship has persisted to the present in light of changing methods of financing and government policies as well as widespread homeownership? The Somerville study found that length of residential tenure, a substitute for homeownership status, was statistically insignificant yet negatively related to intergenerational mobility. But how typical is Somerville of Boston's other suburbs? Finally, socioeconomic status was found to affect access to prestigious colleges, but there is nothing here on mobility across generations.

The strongest chapter centers on the role of developers in channeling urban growth. Even here the examples are too limited to divulge much in the way of details as to who won, who lost, and why in the process of converting suburban land to urban uses. The concluding chapters suffer from an eagerness to elevate the discussion above such matters, although the political economy of suburban growth might have been best revealed in this way—to paint in broad strokes the outlines of the social forces that led to capital's "compromise" to open up the suburbs to labor in order to forestall more radical changes during a time of worker militancy. These are disappointing chapters. The basic facts are not wrong, but they are laced together through abstruse interpretations into an argument that is never fully explained; moreover, it is difficult to accept, given Binford's description of growth on Boston's fringe 50 years earlier.

RACIAL SEGREGATION IN CHICAGO

The classic ecological model drew on conditions in Chicago as they existed prior to World War II for its generalizations about urban patterns and processes. In his excellent history of how Chicago's second ghetto emerged after 1940, Hirsch underscores government's mounting importance in reinforcing housing segregation in the city. White violence, which etched the boundaries around the first ghetto and the Black Belt, kept much of its force in marking the second's borders, but postwar governmental involvement in housing markets altered the dynamics of neighborhood succession.

Stripping Hirsch's analysis to its essentials, white reactions to Chicago's growing black population divided along class and ethnic lines. Chicago's major institutions and its middle and upper classes exploited their access to local and state governments to multiply public powers over land use and housing, which they then used to change or maintain the racial balance of areas where they had investments or residences. Postwar etiquette, if not attitudes, about race relations changed, however, and private concerns had to be cloaked in public interest terms emphasizing integration. Educated and prosperous whites, Hirsch argues, were more adept at this than working-class ethnics. His case studies of the Lake Meadows slum clearance project and of the University of Chicago's role in managing the racial balance of the Hyde Park-Kenwood communities illustrate this argument and shed new light on the depths of the participants' racial concerns through his access to original documents, correspondence, internal memoranda, and other material.

Whereas the city's major institutions, businesses, and middle to upper classes learned to use planning to control or reverse the succession process, working-class ethnics relied on violence and protest. Housing riots and, later, battles with blacks over the use of public facilities erupted as previously white areas were invaded or as succession took place. Hirsch's analyses of the major incidents, especially their social organization and political focus, as well as the Chicago Commission on Human Relations' efforts to suppress newspaper coverage of them, are nicely done. Equally informative is his case study of how these incidents and fear of their reoccurrence, along with mayoral transitions, the need to relocate residents displaced from slum clearance projects such as Lake Meadows, and the city council's usurpation of site selection decisions all combined to transform the Chicago Housing Authority from an agency with modest integration goals into a bureaucracy that rebuilt and reanchored the Black Belt with massive high-rise public housing projects.

Hirsch takes a broad historical perspective compared to Taub, Taylor, and Dunham, who focus on individual decision making from a rational, public choice perspective in their study of neighborhood succession and housing deterioration. Their sophisticated investigation uses a variety of data and rests on a nearly balanced sample of eight neighborhoods differing in their crime rates, racial stability, and property value trends. The chapters on homeowner investment decisions, tipping, and reactions to crime and neighborhood change represent significant contributions to, and modifications of, the classic ecological model warranting the attention of urban scholars. The following comments only skim the surface of these chapters.

Deterioration of a neighborhood's housing stock and whether white neighborhoods become all black ones once some proportion of black residents is exceeded are both collective outcomes of many individual decisions. In analyzing homeowner decisions to maintain or improve their housing, Taub and his associates empirically validate a "threshold" model in which an individual's willingness to invest depends on what proportion of his or her neighbors are fixing or upgrading their own houses. As a social diffusion process, as long as the distribution of thresholds is such that there are a few "pioneers" with very low thresholds who pay little heed to their neighbors' reluctance to invest and the neighborhood is not saturated with "conservatives" with extremely high thresholds, the proportion of individuals making housing investments cumulates, triggering others at successively higher levels in a snowball-like fashion, until the area's maximum level of investment is reached. Controlling for marital/family status, income, and age of housing, Taub et al. find that both black and white residents had higher thresholds in racially mixed or "racially encoded" areas and that crime was an indirect factor that depressed residents' expectations regarding the market for their houses.

In their analysis of racial tipping, which builds on Schelling's "bounded-neighborhood model," they argue that the significance of racial attitudes and tolerance has been overstated. Instead, they conclude that expectations of racial turnover are influenced primarily by residents' perceptions of the "structural position" of their neighborhood or the amount of competition for housing and the ratio of black-white housing demand. Thus, in highly competitive markets, they find residents have low expectations of tipping, but as markets get weaker these expectations rise and become increasingly sensitive to the black-white demand ratio. A neighborhood's structural position strongly influences residents' market evaluations, and if the fear of crime, not actual victimization, is high, then investment decisions will be negatively affected and expectations of tipping mount, all of which sets the stage for deterioration and neighborhood change.

CONCLUSIONS

A common theme runs through these books. Ecological processes do not dictate the structural arrangements of cities. The location and movement of people reflect the actions taken by often autonomous entities with the ability to control access to urban space. Antebellum suburbs, turn-of-the-century developers, and twentieth-century bureaucracies and institutions, the authors explain, guided or redirected these processes. Even Taub and his associates, despite their emphasis on how individual decisions collectively affect neighborhood deterioration and succession, stress the critical role of neighborhood institutions as "pioneers" in kicking off housing investments and the importance of organizations outside neighborhoods that label, "racially encode," or otherwise influence their structural positions in urban housing markets. Individual choice is highly contextual in their analysis, and the influence of neighborhood residents should not be exaggerated.

The number and kinds of institutional actors, their varying degrees of latitude, and the underlying orderliness of the consequences of their acts, suggesting some means of coordination whether through markets or politics, pose daunting analytical challenges. Edel and his colleagues floundered at this point as they tried to sum up Boston's suburbanization as the outcome of labor's struggle with capital. Nonetheless, it is clear from these books that how public and private organizations shape urban spatial patterns and manage population changes and other ecological factors remains high on the research agenda.

—*Roy B. Flemming*
Wayne State University

CITIES IN STRESS

A New Look at the Urban Crisis

edited by M. GOTTDIENER,
University of California, Riverside

This collection of readings addresses the question: What has happened to the urban crisis? The contributors reexamine our understanding of the relation between city crisis and recovery through detailed case studies of the adjustment process of urban regimes to the social and fiscal strains of the 1970s. In a separate section, the implications of these case studies and of the historical record of recent city restructuring are used to evaluate urban theory itself, and to modify current theoretical arguments about city development.

Each paper is introduced by the editor's evaluation of previous work in the field, and the volume concludes with a summary assessment of its relevance to the evolving debate between Marxian urban theory and its conventional rivals.

CONTENTS: Introduction M. GOTTDIENER // **I. Historical Perspectives** // 1. The Sense of Crisis: A Historian's Point of View E.H. MONKKONEN / 2. Where Has the Urban Crisis Gone: How Boston and Other Large Cities Have Stemmed Economic Decline A. GANZ // **II. Case Studies** // 3. Local Control of Fiscal Stress J. MATZER, Jr. / 4. Urban Populism, Fiscal Crisis, and the New Political Economy T. SWANSTROM / 5. Local Government and Fiscal Stress: An Exploration Into Spending and Public Employment Decisions R. STEIN, E. SINCLAIR & M. NEIMAN / 6. Electoral Coalitions, Minority Mayors, and the Contradictions in the Municipal Policy Agenda D.R. JUDD // **III. Theoretical Perspectives** // 7. Structural Theories and Urban Fiscal Stress I.S. RUBIN & H.J. RUBIN / 8. Finance Capital and the City A.M. SBRAGIA / 9. Collective Responses to the Urban Crisis: Ideology and Mobilization J.R. HENIG / 10. The Crisis of Local Government in Great Britain: An Interpretation C.G. PICKVANCE / 11. Retrospect and Prospect in Urban Crisis Theory M. GOTTDIENER

Urban Affairs Annual Review, Volume 30
1986 (February) / 320 pages (tent.) / $29.95 (c) / $14.95 (p)

SAGE PUBLICATIONS, INC.
275 South Beverly Drive,
Beverly Hills, California 90212

SAGE PUBLICATIONS LTD
28 Banner Street,
London EC1Y 8QE, England

SAGE PUBLICATIONS INDIA PVT LTD
M-32 Market, Greater Kailash I, New Delhi 110 048, India

URBAN AFFAIRS *Quarterly*

volume 21, number 4 / june 1986

SAGE PUBLICATIONS

URBAN AFFAIRS *Quarterly*

SAGE Publications / *Beverly Hills* / *Newbury Park* / *London* / *New Delhi*

URBAN AFFAIRS *Quarterly*

volume 21, number 4 / june 1986

contents

Acknowledgments 459

Markets and Redevelopment: *The Case of Neighborhood Housing Service*
RICHARD C. HULA 461

The Dispersal of Subsidized Housing in Chicago: *An Index for Comparisons*
ELIZABETH WARREN 484

Ecological and Political-Economic Analyses of Migration to a Primate City: *Bangkok, Thailand ca. 1970*
BRUCE LONDON 501

Homelessness in the Postindustrial City: *Views from London and Philadelphia*
CAROLYN TEICH ADAMS 527

Informal Social Ties and Political Activity in the Metropolis
AVERY M. GUEST
R. S. OROPESA 550

Attachments in the Nested Community: *Evidence from a Case Study*
JEFFREY S. SLOVAK 575

Research Notes

Officer Orientations Toward the Community: *The Impact of Police Bureaucracy*
MICHAEL STEINMAN 598

Constituency of the Antigrowth Movement: *A Comparison of the Growth Orientations of Urban Status Groups*
DON E. ALBRECHT
GORDON BULTENA
ERIC HOIBERG 607

Book Review Essay

The Corporate Center Strategy: *The State in Central Cities*
JOE R. FEAGIN 617

Index 629

SAGE PUBLICATIONS / *Beverly Hills Newbury Park London New Delhi*

MANUSCRIPTS should be submitted to the editors in care of The Editors, **URBAN AFFAIRS QUARTERLY**, Center for Metropolitan Studies, University of Missouri, 8001 Natural Bridge Rd., St Louis, MO 63121. Include *five* (5) copies of the manuscript. Full-length manuscripts should not exceed 25 pages total and research notes should not exceed 10 pages total (*including* footnotes, references, and tables or figures). All text, footnotes, and references should be typewritten with one-inch margins and double-spaced. All references to the author's previous work should be omitted in the text. Footnotes and bibliographic citations should follow the current **UAQ** style. Copies of the style sheets may be obtained from the editors or the publisher. A brief biographical paragraph describing each author's current affiliation, research interests, and recent publications should be submitted, and an abstract of approximately 100 words should accompany each copy of the manuscript.

Manuscripts will not be returned to authors. Please keep copies for your own needs. The editors assume that manuscripts are for the exclusive consideration of **UAQ** and have not simultaneously been submitted elsewhere.

BOOKS FOR REVIEW should be sent to The Editors, **URBAN AFFAIRS QUARTERLY**, Center for Metropolitan Studies, University of Missouri, 8001 Natural Bridge Road, St. Louis, MO 63121. Potential contributors of book review essays are encouraged to correspond with Professor Susan MacManus, Book Review Editor, **URBAN AFFAIRS QUARTERLY**, Department of Political Science, Cleveland State University, Cleveland, OH 44115, before submitting manuscripts.

URBAN AFFAIRS QUARTERLY is published four times annually—in September, December, March, and June—by Sage Publications, Inc., 275 South Beverly Drive, Beverly Hills, CA 90212.

Subscriptions: Regular institutional rate $63.00 per year. Individuals may subscribe at a one-year rate of $25.00. Add $6.00 for subscriptions outside the United States. Orders from the U.K., Europe, the Middle East, and Africa should be sent to London address (below). Orders from India should be sent to the New Delhi address (below). Noninstitutional orders **must** be paid by personal check.

Second class postage paid at Thousand Oaks, California. ISSN 0042-0816

This journal is abstracted or indexed in **Sage Urban Studies Abstracts, Human Resources Abstracts, Educational Administration Abstracts, Sociological Abstracts, Abstracts for Social Workers, ABC POL SCI, Sociology of Education Abstracts, Urban Affairs Abstracts, Sage Public Administration Abstracts, International Political Science Abstracts, Ethnic Studies Bibliography, Public Affairs Information Service, Ekistic Index, Current Contents, Social Science Citation Index,** and **United States Political Science Documents,** and is available on microfilm from University Microfilms, Ann Arbor, Michigan.

Back Issues: Information about availability and prices of back issues may be obtained from the publisher's order department (address below). Single-issue orders for 5 or more copies will receive a special adoption discount. Contact the order department for details. Write to London office for sterling prices.

Inquiries: Address all correspondence and permissions requests to SAGE PUBLICATIONS, Inc., 275 South Beverly Drive, Beverly Hills, California 90212. Inquiries and subscriptions from the U.K., Europe, the Middle East, and Africa should be sent to SAGE PUBLICATIONS Ltd, 28 Banner Street, London EC1Y 8QE, England. From India, write to SAGE PUBLICATIONS INDIA Pvt. Ltd, P.O. Box 4215, New Delhi 110 048 India. Other orders should be sent to the Beverly Hills office.

Advertising: Current rates and specifications may be obtained by writing to the Advertising Manager at the Beverly Hills office (address above).

Claims: Claims for undelivered copies must be made no later than three months following month of publication. The publisher will supply missing copies when losses have been sustained in transit and when the reserve stock will permit.

Change of Address: Six weeks' advance notice must be given when notifying of change of address. Please send old address label along with the new address to insure proper identification. Please specify name of journal. POSTMASTER: Send change of address to: Urban Affairs Quarterly, c/o 275 South Beverly Drive, Beverly Hills, CA 90212.

ACKNOWLEDGMENTS

The editors of *Urban Affairs Quarterly* would like to express their sincere appreciation to the following persons who have served as manuscript referees during the past year.

Roger S. Ahlbrandt, Jr.
William D. Angel
Richard P. Applebaum
William Barnes
Terry L. Baumer
Robert Beauregard
Howard S. Becker
Efraim Ben-Zadok
Henry C. Binford
Robert L. Bish
John P. Blair
Donald Bogue
Calvin P. Bradford
Jeffrey L. Brudney
Christopher Chase-Dunn
Yong Cho
Beverly Cigler
Terry N. Clark
Susan E. Clarke
Leonard A. Cole
Robert Crain
Matthew Crenson
Marilyn Dantico
James N. Danziger
Jeffrey L. Davidson
Ronald M. Denowitz
Donald Dillman
Thomas J. DiLorenzo
Paul DiMaggio
G. William Domhoff
Paul R. Dommel
David Dowall
Peter K. Eisinger
Stephen Elkin
William W. Erbe
Steven Erie
Norman Fainstein
Susan S. Fainstein
Reynolds Farley
Sylvia Fava
Joseph R. Feagin
Lorna Ferguson
Claude Fischer
Roger Friedland
Ester Fuchs
Joseph Galaskiewicz
Dennis Gale
Herbert Gans
Gary Gappert
Barry J. Garner
Norman Glickman
John M. Goering
Calvin Goldscheider
Avery M. Guest
Donald Haider
John S. Hall
Chester Hartman
Richard Hay
Peggy Heilig
Jeffrey R. Henig
Rodney E. Hero
Garry W. Hesser
Richard Child Hill
Charles Hoch
Glen Holt
James R. Hudson
Richard Hula
Albert Hunter
Byran Jackson
Edward T. Jennings
Bryan D. Jones
Albert K. Karnig
Ira Katznelson
James G. Kelly
Michael D. Kennedy
Larry L. Kiser
Nancy Kleniewski
Carol W. Kohfeld
Lauren J. Krivo
Robert W. Lake
Paul Lavrakas
Barrett A. Lee
Victor LeVine
Stanley Lieberson
Roland J. Liebert
Charles Lindblom
Lyn Lofland
John R. Logan
Bruce London
Larry H. Long
Vincent Marando
Ann Markusen
Julia Marlowe
Louis Masotti
Richard C. Maurer
Bruce D. McDowell
William Michelson
Robert Mier
Carl Milofsky
Kenneth R. Mladenka
John H. Mollenkopf
Harvey Molotch
Daniel J. Monti, Jr.
Lawrence J. Mosqueda
Alvin H. Mushkatel
Richard P. Nathan
Martin L. Needleman
Max Neiman
David J. Olson
Gary Orfield
Charles Orlebeke
Elinor Ostrom
J. John Palen
Roger Parks
Thomas A. Pascarella
Diana M. Pearce
Stephen L. Percy
David C. Perry
Paul E. Peterson

ERRATUM

Please note that the opening page of the article entitled, "Housing Constraint and Household Complexity in Metropolitan America: Black and Spanish-Origin Minorities," which appeared in the March 1986 issue of *Urban Affairs Quarterly*, Volume 21, Number 3, pages 389-409, contained an error in the first author's name. The correct spelling of her name is:

LAUREN J. KRIVO

MARKETS AND REDEVELOPMENT
The Case of Neighborhood Housing Service

RICHARD C. HULA
University of Maryland

This article explores the impact of the Neighborhood Housing Service (NHS) in three urban neighborhoods. Specific elements of the local housing markets examined include the home improvement loan rate, the conventional mortgage loan rate, and housing price. The analysis questions the favorable image of the program, finding only limited evidence of a positive program impact. The article concludes by noting some limitations to market-based programs such as NHS.

The decision of the Reagan administration to target urban redevelopment programs for significant cutbacks has not been implemented without controversy. However, political debate over urban policy extends beyond budgetary issues. Indeed, one could argue that urban policy is suffering from an intellectual crisis which is as significant for program development as current budgetary limitations. Many scholars, practitioners, and citizens who were caught up in the image of a "war on poverty" in the 1960s and 1970s fail to see significant benefits from the numerous social and economic programs implemented during the last two decades. Poverty, substandard housing, large-scale structural unemployment—all conditions of the urban crisis—remain common features of the nation's cities. Indeed, as one reads texts on policy analysis or public administration, it is striking to note how often past redevelopment efforts are used as examples of government incompe-

AUTHOR'S NOTE: *Portions of this article were presented at the 1984 meetings of the Midwest Political Science Association. The research has been supported by a grant from the Division of Community Resources, University of Maryland. Computer support has been provided by the University of Maryland Computer Science Center.*

URBAN AFFAIRS QUARTERLY, Vol. 21 No. 4, June 1986 461-483

tence.[1] It is hardly surprising, therefore, that a widespread interest in alternative redevelopment strategies exists. An increasingly popular notion is that market forces rather than government planning can be used efficiently to bring about a revitalization of American cities.

A good deal of public policy claims to use the forces of the market to implement social goals. However, the assumptions which underlie specific programs may be quite different. One class of policy seeks to reduce the importance of nonmarket actors, usually government, so as to free market forces. Much of the current effort to reduce regulation is based on the premise that a market operates most efficiently with a minimum of external intervention. An alternative view argues for the utility of limited political intervention to create a well-working market system. The Neighborhood Housing Service (NHS) is an example of such a program. The Neighborhood Housing Service begins on the premise that some urban distress is a function of underinvestment on the part of private sector lending institutions. To some extent this view is consistent with the position of numerous community organizations and activists that a lack of private sector investment has had negative consequences for their neighborhoods. However, the explanations for this limited investment, as well as proposed remedies, are quite different. Community activists see underinvestment as explicit discrimination against urban neighborhoods and certain classes of people, usually racial minorities. In contrast, NHS programs argue that lenders are not originating "bankable" loans in some credit-poor communities due to ignorance that such loans could be made. The policy implications of these two positions are significant. Rejecting community-based demands for some form of credit allocation, NHS seeks to redirect investment by increasing the level of market information in credit-poor neighborhoods. Specifically, local NHS corporations attempt to bring together credit consumers and lenders willing to originate loans to qualified residents in a target community. In addition, a high-risk revolving loan fund is maintained to meet the credit needs of neighborhood residents who cannot qualify for conventional credit. State-chartered, nonprofit NHS corporations receive local government support through increased capital investment and code enforcement in the target neighborhood and federal support in the form of technical assistance from the National Reinvestment Corporation.[2]

The NHS program has widespread appeal. By 1981, the National Reinvestment Corporation reported that at least one program was operating in 103 American cities. The appeal of a low-cost, nonbureaucratic noncoercive strategy for urban redevelopment is obvious. Moreover, there is a widespread perception that NHS works. In an evaluation of NHS programs Philip Clay (1981: 78) concludes,

> Extensive changes have occurred in a sample of NHS neighborhoods in terms of lending activities, code inspections, and reinvestment activities for physical improvements. This does not mean that no problems remain after as many as seven years of reinvestment activity, but they do suggest that for a minimal investment the federal government has helped local neighborhoods begin a process that has given neighborhoods new confidence in their resources.
>
> Thus, a program that is locally defined, locally run, inexpensive, and nonbureaucratic in nature has made significant progress toward generating neighborhood reinvestment.

Although a great number of observers are enthusiastic about NHS, caution is in order. Previous evaluation efforts have had significant empirical and conceptual limitations. Theoretical assumptions embedded in the programs are seldom made explicit, and never tested. In addition, data used in evaluations are often impressionistic, with little effort made to introduce explicit controls or reference group data.[3]

EVALUATING THE NEIGHBORHOOD HOUSING SERVICE

The Neighborhood Housing Service rests on two critical assumptions. The first stresses the importance of home improvement credit in the process of neighborhood development and decline. While there is a good deal of debate over the ability of credit-granting institutions to direct investment independent of market pressures, most observers agree that the availability of such credit is a valid indicator of neighborhood health (National Commission on Neighborhoods, 1979). The positive effects of home improvement credit are seen as both direct and indirect. Having funds for needed maintenance and repair is an example of a direct neighborhood benefit. Somewhat less direct but of equal importance is the positive link between credit availability and the viability of the neighborhood housing market. Maintaining (or increasing) the quality of the housing stock is thought to increase consumer demand for neighborhood housing. Relatively high levels of consumer demand for housing in turn generates a willingness on the part of lending institutions to provide conventional mortgages to finance home sales. Such credit instruments tend to make housing transactions less expensive and easier to arrange. A second NHS program assumption argues that a given market allocation of home credit may vary significantly from the optimal distribution predicted by neoclassical economic theory. This variation is seen as a function of a lack of market information, which in a competitive market is assumed to be perfect. As one increases communication between credit consumers and suppliers, the market should move closer to the predicted optimal distribution of credit. Three concrete hypotheses can be derived from this argument:

(1) Lenders have some flexibility in how they allocate credit in local housing markets. In at least some neighborhoods which receive relatively little credit, there is a greater potential for safe investment than lenders generally assume.
(2) An increase in one type of home credit will generate an increase in other forms of credit.
(3) Increased levels of credit will have a positive effect on the overall quality of the neighborhood.

These hypotheses may be taken as a framework in which one can measure the effectiveness of specific NHS programs. This article will test each of these hypotheses in three NHS sites, one in Dallas and two in Baltimore. To test hypothesis one, the magnitude of home improvement lending by local savings institutions in each target neighborhood will be compared to lending rates in similar non-NHS neighborhoods. If the NHS program is successful, the rate of home improvement lending in the NHS target should be higher than in comparison neighborhoods. Home improvement loans are most appropriate for testing this hypothesis, since home improvement is the primary focus of the program. To test whether there is a spillover effect on various types of credit (hypothesis two), rates of conventional mortgage originations in NHS target neighborhoods will be compared with rates in similar neighborhoods without NHS programs. Finally, to test whether NHS has had a more general positive effect on the housing market, the price of housing in each of the target communities will be examined to see whether the program is associated with any measurable shift (hypothesis three). For this analysis price is taken as a measure of consumer demand. If NHS is able to stabilize or even renew a neighborhood, increased consumer demand should be reflected in increased housing prices.

THE NHS PROGRAMS

Planning for the Dallas Love Field and Baltimore Patterson Park NHS took place in 1973, with actual operations beginning in 1974. In 1978, the geographic boundaries of the Patterson Park NHS were expanded and the Govans NHS established. None of these neighborhoods was seriously blighted, since it was assumed that private sector investment could not be attracted to such areas. An effort was also made to select target communities with relatively high levels of homeownership. While the three areas chosen were by no means the poorest city neighborhoods, the median income of each fell well below the metropolitan median. In addition, there was a consensus that each of the neighborhoods had been experiencing a pattern of decline which, if not reversed, would lead to significant deterioration. This impression was supported in the Love Field area by a house-to-house survey which revealed numerous code violations. Of the 1729 units examined, code violations were noted in 1343. Although many of the violations were minor, a number of homeowners found themselves facing major home renovations (Geisel, 1977). As code enforcement increased in each target community, demand for improvement capital seemed to increase. From 1974 to 1978, the Dallas NHS originated 44 loans with a value of $168,410 from its high-risk revolving loan fund. Between 1975 and 1981, the two Baltimore programs originated 406 loans valued at $2,875,095 from their revolving accounts. While there seems to be a consensus among major actors in the program that private sector lending institutions were also more active in the target communities, initial efforts to measure this impact proved futile. Lenders were unwilling to provide information on loans made to the target communities.[4] Systematic data on the investment patterns of private sector lenders did not become available until 1977 with the implementation of the Home Mortgage Disclosure Act (HMDA). HMDA required every deposit-accepting lending institution with over $10 million in assets to make a public disclosure of the geographic distribution of various types of home credit loans originated or purchased during the calendar year.[5]

Hypothesis one predicts home improvement loan rates will be higher in NHS target communities than in similar neighborhoods without such programs. Table 1 compares these rates in each NHS target neighborhood with that of two reference groups.[6] The first is the mean lending rate for the 20 census tracts in each county with median income closest to that of each target neighborhood. The second is the mean lending rate

TABLE 1
Home Improvement Loan Rates for NHS Targets, Reference Tracts, and Average County Tracts, 1976-1980

	1976	1977	1978	1979	1980	Total
Love Field [2]						
Number of loans:						
Target	12	23	15			50
Reference [3]	7	9	17			30
Average	7	17	21			45
Value of Loans:						
Target	$49	$100	$81			$230
Reference	21	36	87			144
Average	63	99	150			295
Govans [4]						
Number of Loans:						
Target	17	17	24	21	13	91
Reference [5]	9	14	16	14	13	66
Average	7	13	14	18	12	63
Value of Loans:						
Target	$43	$52	$72	$62	$69	$297
Reference	23	43	48	55	54	223
Average	21	43	51	54	54	223
Patterson Park						
Number of Loans:						
Target	2	3	2	3	3	12
Reference	7	9	12	10	10	49
Average	7	13	14	18	12	63
Value of Loans:						
Target	$5	$9	$7	$10	$10	$41
Reference	18	27	37	33	39	153
Average	21	43	51	54	54	223

1. Lending data have been aggregated from Home Mortgage Disclosure Statements obtained from individual lending institutions. Data reported by 1970 census tract.
2. Dallas loan rate reported as loans per 1000 units of housing. Based on estimated units in tract in 1976. SOURCE: North Texas Council of Governments.
3. Dallas reference defined as mean loan rate for loan rates calculated in 20 census tracts with median income closest to the NHS tract. Based on 1976 estimate of tract income. SOURCE: National Data Planning Corporation.
4. Baltimore loan rates reported as loans per 100 units of housing. Based on number of units in tract in 1970. SOURCE: U.S. Census, 1970.
5. Baltimore reference defined as mean loan rate for loan rates calculated for 20 tracts with income closest to NHS tracts. Based on 1970 tract income. SOURCE: U.S. Census, 1970.

for all county census tracts. The reference tracts serve to "control" two important market variables, average income, and total number of housing units.[7] Although it is clear that each of these variables is strongly correlated to total demand for credit in a given neighborhood, one may question whether a set of tracts selected solely on the criteria of income can adequately serve as a control for the evaluation of NHS programs.

Certainly in any formal sense, the answer is that they cannot, since a wide range of potentially important market variables are not controlled. However, the set of comparisons presented in Table 1 can be defended on two grounds.

First, a large empirical literature has shown the overwhelming importance of income and number of units as predictors of private sector investment across neighborhoods (Pol et al., 1982; Hula, 1984). Equally important is the lack of consensus as to other appropriate market controls. For example, the final report of the National Commission on Neighborhoods (1979) concludes that there is little hard evidence to support the validity of a variety of traditional indicators of market safety such as age and location of housing stock. A second and somewhat more compelling justification for the comparison presented in Table 1 is the process used by NHS to identify target neighborhoods. NHS begins with income criteria. They seek to target low- and moderate-income (but not poverty) neighborhoods with the greatest potential for private redevelopment. Thus, one would certainly expect a difference between NHS neighborhoods and reference tracts of similar income. Indeed, these differences might well lead one to expect higher lending rates in the target areas on the basis of the selection process alone. For example, in Dallas specific criteria used in the selection process included widespread homeownership, a small elderly population, and a housing stock in relatively good repair (Geisel, 1977: 13).[8]

Table 1 presents a somewhat equivocal view of the impact of the NHS programs. Both Love Field and Govans receive significantly more home improvement credit than neighborhoods of similar income. Indeed, these investment rates are higher than the county averages for several years. Patterson Park does not fit this pattern, however. Even though the program has been in place since 1974, the investment rate remains far below tracts with similar income. Generally, Patterson Park receives only 40% to 60% of the level of investment directed to similar income areas. There is a further problem in interpreting these data as evidence that NHS had a positive impact in the target neighborhoods. In Govans, where data are available before and after the implementation of the program, one sees a relatively high investment rate before as well as after the program was established. Thus, some of the reported success of NHS programs may be the result of selecting neighborhoods which were in fact already receiving relatively high levels of investment.

Perhaps more important than short-run home improvement loan rates is whether NHS had any measurable positive impact on the overall neighborhood housing market. Two possible effects have been proposed. First was an increase in home improvement capital associated with an increase in the use of conventional mortgages to finance the sale of housing units in the neighborhoods? To examine the utilization of conventional credit, Table 2 reports rates for each of the NHS target communities. Data for census tracts with similar income and county averages are again presented in Table 2. These data provide no evidence that the rate of conventional mortgage lending is any higher in the target communities relative to areas with similar income. Only in Love Field is the conventional lending rate near the mean for similar income tracts.

The third evaluation hypothesis centers on housing prices. While an increase in housing values is usually not defined as a major goal of the program, it is reasonable to suggest that if a neighborhood revitalization project is successful, housing prices are likely to increase as consumers come to define the neighborhood as more desirable. Geisel (1977) reports that a number of realtors active in Love Field claimed that housing prices increased sharply as the program was implemented. To explore this possibility, a time series of the average selling price of housing units in each community was collected.[9] Each data point is an average monthly price. For Love Field, these data were collected for the period 1971 to 1979.[10] Similar data for Patterson Park and Govans were collected for the period 1970 to 1980. Figure 1, Figure 2, and Figure 3 provide an overview of these data. By comparing Figure 1, Figure 2, and Figure 3, several significant differences between the Baltimore and Dallas series can be seen. Perhaps most obvious is the fact that prices in the Dallas NHS target area are significantly higher than those in the Baltimore target neighborhoods. Second, there is an obvious linear positive trend in price in both Baltimore neighborhoods which seems to be absent in Dallas. Finally, as one moves across the price distribution for the two Baltimore neighborhoods, the magnitude of variance within each series appears to change. Such a shift does not appear to occur in the Dallas series.

There have been a number of suggestions as to how one should evaluate the possible impact of a discrete event on a time series. Comparing regression coefficients before and after the event is often proposed. However, this approach has been widely criticized on both methodological and substantive grounds. A critical assumption of ordinary least squares (OLS) is that the data have an underlying structure. Unfortunately, essentially random processes can, over discrete time periods, present the appearance of pattern or structure. Stochastic process models developed by Box and Jenkins (1976) are an interesting alternative to

TABLE 2

Conventional Mortgage Loan Rates for NHS Targets, Reference Tracts, and Average County Tracts, 1976-1977[1]

	1976	1977	1978	1979	1980	Total
Love Field[2]						
Number of Loans:						
Target[3]	3	14	15			31
Reference	9	12	14			34
Average	20	30	27			77
Value of Loans:						
Target	$60	$355	$450			$845
Reference	237	455	536			1228
Average	899	144	1343			3682
Govans[4]						
Number of Loans:						
Target	7	7	4	8	7	32
Reference	8	11	11	12	10	52
Average	11	18	19	15	12	75
Value of Loans:						
Target	$123	$108	$61	$161	$146	$600
Reference	141	235	267	328	291	1262
Average	359	623	761	642	544	2917
Patterson Park						
Number of Loans:	3	5	3	6	4	22
Reference	5	8	8	8	8	37
Average	11	18	19	15	12	75
Value of Loans:						
Target	$28	$71	$53	$111	$79	$342
Reference	62	129	133	187	176	687
Average	347	623	761	642	599	2917

1. Lending data have been aggregated from Home Mortage Disclosure Statements obtained from individual lending institutions. Data reported by 1970 census tract.
2. Dallas loan rate reported as loans per 1000 units of housing. Based on estimated units in tract in 1976. SOURCE: North Texas Council of Governments.
3. Dallas reference defined as mean loan rate for loan rates calculated in 20 census tracts with income closest to the NHS tract. Based on 1976 estimate of tract income. SOURCE: National Data Planning Corporation.
4. Baltimore loan rates reported as loans per 1000 units of housing. Based on number of units in tract in 1970. SOURCE: U.S. Census, 1970.
5. Baltimore reference defined as mean loan rate for loan rates calculated for 20 tracts with income closest to NHS tracts. Based on 1970 estimate of tract income. SOURCE: U.S. Census, 1970.

classical regression techniques. Box-Jenkins modeling procedures rest on an alternative assumption that a time series can be described as a function of random shocks and past values of an otherwise random series. Such models can be conceptualized as a series of filters which operate on a white noise (random) process in such a way as to generate the observed empirical series. There are three types of filters: autoregressive (AR), integrated (I), and moving average (MA). Thus, the common

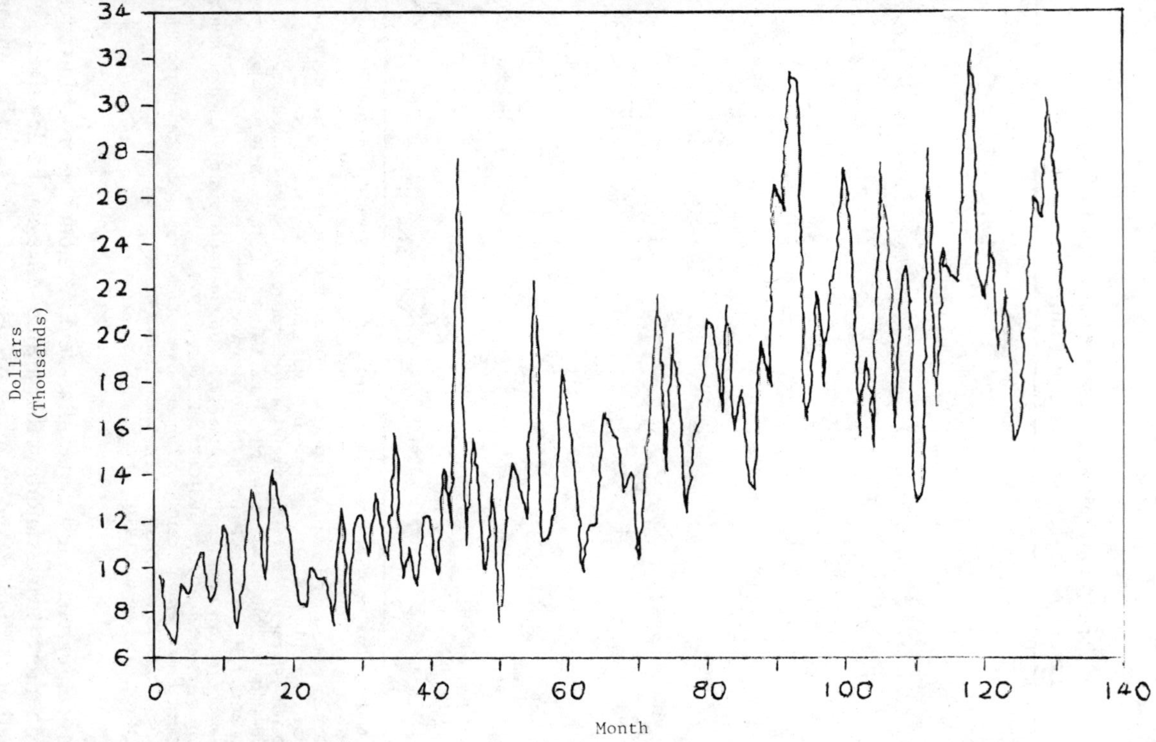

Figure 1: Govans Housing Costs, 1970-1980

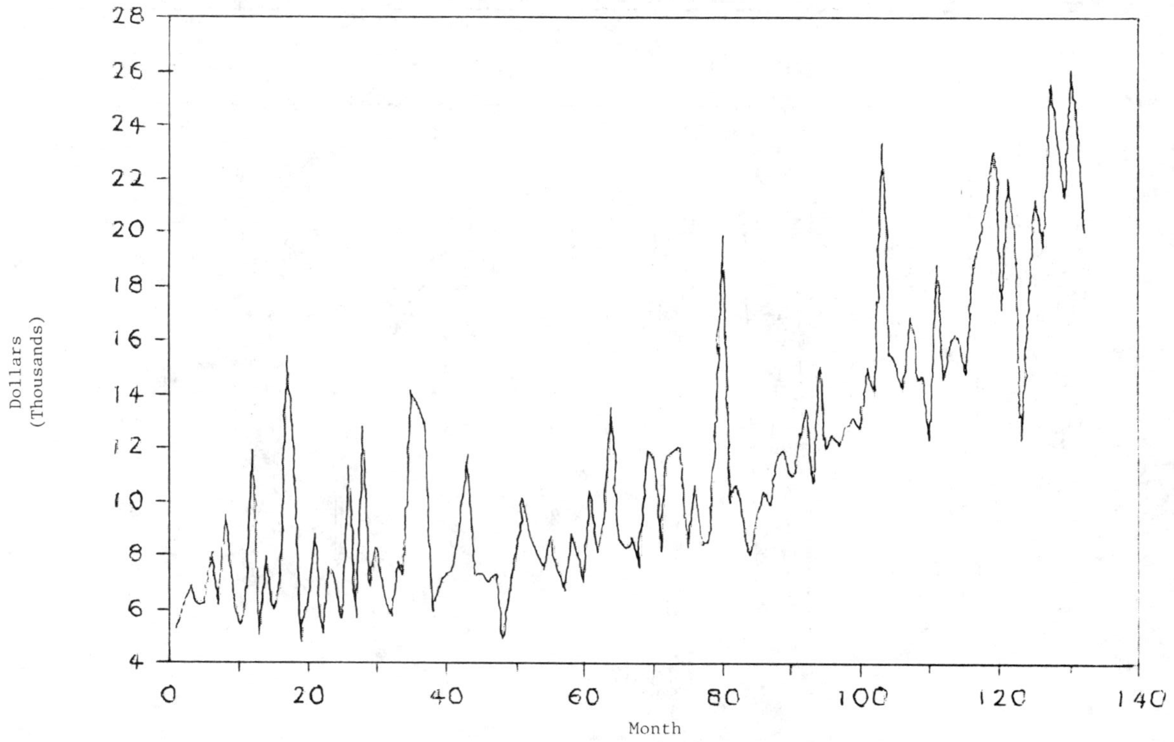

Figure 2: Patterson Park Housing Costs, 1970-1980

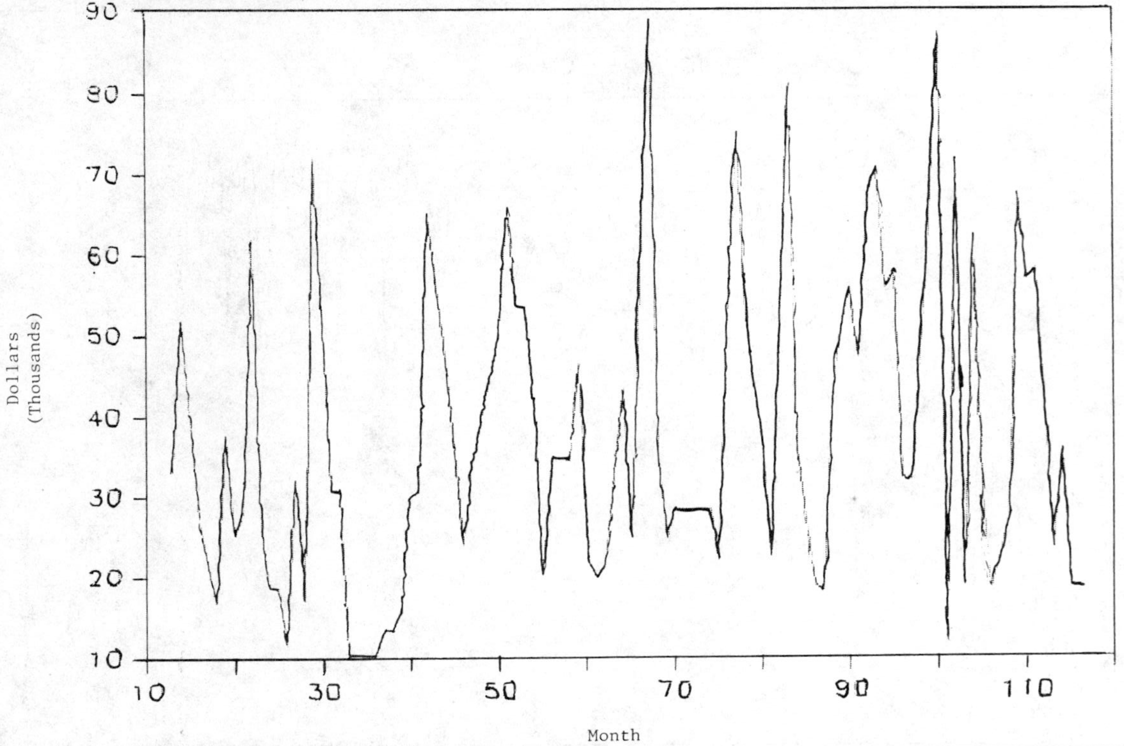

Figure 3: Love Field Housing Costs, 1971-1980

designation of such models is ARIMA models. Specific ARIMA models are described as (p, d, q) with p equal to the lag of the autoregressive parameter, d the order of differencing, and q the lag of the moving average parameter. Each filter represents a different assumption about the relationship between an observed value in a series and past values and random shocks.

Model specification is not driven so much by theoretical considerations as by how well a proposed model describes a given data set. Using general procedures outlined by McCain and McCleary (1974) and McCleary and Hay (1980), models were estimated for the monthly housing price data for each NHS neighborhood. The Dallas price series was fitted to a (0, 0, 2) model. Since the second-order moving average parameter was only marginally significant, its inclusion in the model is somewhat problematic. However, substantive conclusions based on further intervention analysis are not affected if this parameter is deleted from the model. In addition to the two moving-order parameters, a mean parameter is also statistically significant in the Dallas data. The Baltimore series required somewhat more complex models. Even before models could be estimated, each series was subjected to a natural log transformation to ensure homogeneous variance. Each series was fitted to a (0, 1, 1) ARIMA model. For the Patterson Park data, a series mean parameter was also statistically significant. Models and parameter estimates are reported in Table 3.

Once appropriate stochastic process models have been identified, it is possible to introduce an intervention term to assess the effect of some discrete event on the time series. This expanded model takes the general form

$$Y_t = N_t + F(I_t) \quad [1]$$

In this assessment model Nt represents the stochastic behavior of the time series. $F(I_t)$ is a transfer function representing the impact of some external intervention. The specific form of the intervention term is a function of the actual intervention effect. Since the primary interest of this analysis is permanent change in the target community, the possibility of a temporary shift in housing price will not be explored. However, two forms of permanent change will be considered. The first is an abrupt change in price; the second, a more gradual shift.

The simplest effect is that of an abrupt and permanent change. Estimates of such changes can be derived from the parameter associated with a zero-order transfer function of the form

TABLE 3
Overview of Box-Jenkins Models for Housing Price in NHS Target Communities

LOVE FIELD[2]

ARIMA Model: $Y_t = \Theta_o + (1-\Theta_1 B - \Theta_2 B^2)$

$\Theta_o = 375^*$

$\Theta_1 = -.36^*$

$\Theta_2 = .34^*$

Zero Order Transfer Model: $Y_t = \Theta_o + a_t(1-\Theta_1 B - \Theta_2 B^2) + \omega_o$

$\Theta_o = 309^*$

$\Theta_1 = -.32^*$

$\Theta_2 = -.28^*$

$\omega_o = 102^*$

First Order Transfer Model: $Y_t = \Theta_o + a_t(1-\Theta_1 B - \Theta_2 B^2) + \frac{\omega_o}{1-\delta_1 B}$

$\Theta_o = 330^*$

$\Theta_1 = -.33^*$

$\Theta_2 = -.30^*$

$\omega_o = 8.5$

6 = .92

GOVANS[2]

ARIMA Model: $\ln Y_t = \frac{(1-\Theta_1 B)}{(1-B)} a_t$

$\Theta_1 = .84^*$

Zero Order Transfer Model: $\ln Y_t = \frac{(1-\Theta_1 B)}{(1-B\_} a_t + \omega_\Theta I_t$

$\Theta_1 = .84^*$

$\omega_o = .004$

TABLE 3 Continued

First Order Transfer Model: $\ln Y_t = \frac{(1-\Theta_1 B)}{(1-B)} a_t + \frac{\omega_0}{1-\delta_1 B}$

$\Theta_1 = .84*$

$\omega = -.04$

$6 = -.57$

Patterson Park

ARIMA Model: $\ln Y_t = \Theta_0 + \frac{(1-\Theta_1 B)}{(1-B)} a_t$

$\Theta_0 = .009*$

$\Theta_1 = .90*$

Zero Order Transfer Model: $\ln Y_t = \Theta_0 + \frac{(1-\Theta_1 B)}{(1-B)} a_t + \omega_0 I_t$

$\Theta_0 = .01*$

$\Theta_1 = .92*$

$\omega_0 = -.12$

First Order Transfer Model: $\ln Y_t = \Theta_0 + \frac{(1-\Theta_1 B)}{(1-B)} a_t + \frac{\omega_0}{1-\delta_1 B}$

$\Theta_0 = .01*$

$\Theta_1 = .92*$

$\omega_0 = .17$

$6_1 = -.40$

1. * Indicates .05 significance.
2. Love Field data reported in units of $100. Some missing data estimated. See text for discussion.
3. Raw Govens and Patterson Park data in units of dollars. Models reported here based on natural log transformed data. See text for discussion.

$$Y_t = N_t + \omega_0 I_t \qquad [2]$$

where I = 0 prior to the intervention, and
I = 1 after the intervention.

Table 3 presents parameter estimates for the zero-order transfer function added to each ARIMA model. Only the coefficients estimated for Love Field are statistically significant. However, the Dallas model suggests that the impact of the program was dramatic indeed. Parameter estimates in Table 3 suggest that Love Field housing prices increased 38% following the implementation of NHS.[11] There are two important qualifications to be made to these findings. First, it is possible that some of the observed shift data could be an artifact of limitations of the price data. A relatively small number of high-price sales could distort the series, inflating actual increases in housing price.[12] Second, although the model parameters presented in Table 3 provide an improved statistical representation of the price series, there remains substantial unexplained variance. A visual inspection of the Dallas series reveals an upward trend in housing price after the intervention, but clearly not all monthly prices in the postintervention period are 20% to 40% greater than those preceding the intervention.

To assess whether the effect of NHS programs might be better described as a more gradual increase in prices, a first-order transformation can be added to the model. This intervention model takes the form

$$y_t = N_t + \frac{\omega_0}{1 - \delta_1 B} \qquad [3]$$

where I = 0 prior to the intervention, and
I = 1 after the intervention.

In the first-order transfer function, the ω_0 parameter is an estimate of the magnitude of change in the series. The δ_1 parameter is an indicator of the speed at which the intervention affects the series. The closer this parameter is to zero, the more rapidly the change takes place. Where the parameter is equal to zero, the intervention term reduces to a zero-order transfer function. Table 3 reports that parameter estimates for the first-order transfer functions are not statistically significant.

IMPLICATIONS

The evaluation of the NHS raises interesting issues at a number of levels. First, consider policymakers interested in local-level strategies to promote neighborhood stabilization, or even redevelopment. The data reported provide, at best, modest support for the many positive claims which have been made for the NHS program. The results of only two of nine tests (three hypotheses tested with data from three local programs) support the efficacy of NHS efforts. This includes one program which reported a higher home improvement loan rate than similar neighborhoods, and another program which appears to have experienced a shift upward in housing prices. A second program reporting a home improvement loan rate above that of similar communities is not taken as evidence supporting NHS, since the relatively high loan rates existed before the program was implemented. In the third NHS neighborhood the home improvement loan rate was significantly below those of areas with similar income. No NHS neighborhood had an above-average conventional loan rate, and a price increase was observed in neither Baltimore target community.

There are, of course, important validity threats to even these modest positive findings. Evidence that one neighborhood had a relatively high home improvement rate even before the program was implemented raises the possibility that some of the positive effects claimed for NHS are actually artifacts of the selection criteria used in the program. Perhaps the NHS selection criteria identify neighborhoods likely to undergo spontaneous revitalization. In addition, there is concern, common to all case studies, that these programs were in some way unique. Although Baltimore and Dallas represent very different settings for the operation of an NHS program, it is not possible to claim that such variation makes for a representative sample. Certainly there is no statistical justification for generalizing these results.

It is important, however, that the empirical evidence supporting the claims made for NHS not be totally discounted. As is often the case in evaluating the effect of social policy, the magnitude of a measured effect is often of less interest than the fact that an effect can be measured at all. This is particularly true for a program like NHS, which can be affected by an extraordinary range of factors over which it has no control at all. To impose too-rigorous criteria in evaluation may introduce an overly conservative bias in policy development (Aaron, 1979; McAdams, 1984). As Susan Hanson (1983) has noted, "There is a growing suspicion that the more sophisticated our tools for analysis and evaluation, the less likely we are to find successful programs." Even at a conceptual level NHS is not expected to "work" in all credit-poor neighborhoods. Neighborhood Housing Service accepts and operates within a general market perspective which holds that many credit-poor neighborhoods do not deserve greater investment. Although NHS explicitly attempts to target its programs to neighborhoods which are thought to have a high potential for attracting private investment, significant selection error (and thus program failure) seems quite likely. However, such failures do not mean that a program like NHS, placed into an appropriate neighborhood, may not have the positive effects claimed by its many supporters.

Even if one is willing to see in this analysis some evidence that NHS does work, substantive implications of the analysis ought to caution policymakers from an overly enthusiastic embrace of NHS. Consider the lack of any measurable effect on the conventional mortgage market. Although there is certainly debate on the validity of conventional credit as an indicator of the economic health of a neighborhood, most observers agree that there is at least an association between neighborhood stability and the widespread use of conventional mortgage instruments. This association is undoubtedly a function of a number of factors, including perceived financial benefits to both buyers and sellers, availability of funds, and the "approval" of local lenders of individual investment in the neighborhood. Thus, it is possible that a lack of expanding conventional credit resources may reduce potential neighborhood redevelopment. A second practical issue raised by these data concerns the increase in housing values associated with the NHS program. While it is certainly possible to argue that such an increase represents a measure of success, it should not be forgotten that such a "success" may well generate significant burdens on current community residents. Indeed, if the increase in housing value is large, and this analysis suggests that in some cases it may be, gentrification may occur. This is most likely for rental units, but may also affect owner-occupied units. Such pressures could take the form of increased taxes or demands for housing repair. The policymaker must consider the effect of NHS not simply on the physical condition of the neighborhood, but also on neighborhood residents.

The evaluation of NHS is particularly relevant to a debate as to how best to conceptualize the substantial empirical association between race, geographic location, and private sector investment (Hula, 1984; Pol et al., 1982). Is it an artifact of the market process? The result of market imperfections? Or is it an integral part of the market itself? NHS asserts it is possible to affect the flow of home credit through the manipulation of market information. The data presented in this article give only limited support to the proposition that such intervention can be successful with respect to home improvement capital. Of course, any evidence of investment shifts contradict expectations derived from neoclassical economic theory that lending rates are relatively fixed by the operation of the market and are unlikely to shift in the absence of either subsidy payments to lenders or direct public sector coercion to increase investment within target neighborhoods. Note that even if one accepts the tentative conclusion that NHS programs were able to increase home improvement loan rates, the broader, and in some sense more fundamental, goals of NHS seem not to have been met. There is almost no evidence of the positive spillover effects predicted by the Neighborhood Reinvestment Corporation. Thus, the ability of NHS to generate or maintain neighborhood revitalization remains quite problematic. At a minimum, the analysis suggests that markets are much more complex and linkages within them less straightforward than market programs like NHS assume. It seems likely, however, that the limits to market intervention are not simply a function of market complexity. This challenges the fundamental assumption of NHS that nonoptimal allocation of credit is a function of market imperfections. Thurow (1975: 55) notes,

> An observer of the economic game should be extremely reluctant to label anything that has existed for long periods of time a "market imperfection." If the phenomenon has survived, the chances are high that it is an integral part of the game and not a market imperfection. Or at least, this possibility should be seriously investigated and each of the deviant observations should be examined to see if they can be explained in some consistent manner that does not rely on ex post and ad hoc market imperfections.

Thurow's position is supported by the analysis reported above. Although there may have been some shift in loan rates, there was little evidence of predicted "economic take-off" in the target neighborhoods. Once again it should be stressed that this failure is particularly striking given the careful selection process of NHS which seeks to identify communities thought most likely to generate substantial economic demand for private sector credit.

The view that the market process itself generates discriminatory investment patterns across urban neighborhoods carries with it direct implications for both scholars and policymakers. Scholars are challenged to bring some conceptual order to the maze of empirical analysis of home credit through the development of more complete models of the political economy of urban neighborhoods. With respect to credit, a number of linkages within the market system demand further explication. For example, at the micro-level more needs to be known about the decision process of those actually involved in the loan review process. Much more also needs to be understood of the macro-level linkage between conventional private sector credit and neighborhood decline, stabilization, and revitalization. The policymaker is faced with a prospect of designing programs that will likely involve a more direct manipulation of credit markets than is possible with NHS. It is particularly noteworthy that such policy conclusions run counter to a number of political preferences held by the current federal administration. Although market solutions to public problems have widespread political appeal, their promise may turn out to be much less than popular wisdom would suggest.

NOTES

1. Perhaps the most notable example is Pressman and Wildavsky's (1973) study of the Economic Development Administration programs in Oakland. In this widely read case study, two self-professed "sympathetic" observers of the EDA goals argue that by the nature of the enterprise there was practically no chance that the EDA effort could succeed.

2. For a discussion of the structure and strategy of the Neighborhood Housing Service, see Clay (1981).

3. The most comprehensive evaluation of NHS has been reported by Clay (1981). For other discussions of NHS, see Ahlbrandt and Cunningham (1979) and Ahlbrandt and Brophy (1975).

4. A survey undertaken by the University of Texas at Arlington suggested that the major source of renovation capital in Love Field was private savings, thus casting some doubt on the claim that significant private sector investment was in fact taking place. The survey reports that 62% of the neighborhood renovations were financed by personal savings, 19% by private lenders, and 8% by the NHS high-risk revolving loan fund (Geisel, 1977).

5. One of the critical limitations to HMDA was the failure on the part of Congress to require any centralized collection of these data. For example, the HMDA data used in this article had to be collected from individual commercial banks and savings and loan associations.

6. Alternative geographic models for Patterson Park might be used. These models differ with respect to the census tracts used to approximate the boundaries of the NHS area. The first model includes all of the current Patterson Park NHS. However, portions of several tracts included in the model are not in the NHS area. A second model is more restricted, and does not include several of the "split tracts" used in the first model. Obviously, this latter model does not include the entire target area. The boundaries used in the second model better approximate the original target boundaries. To reduce error introduced by the split tracts, the more restricted model will be reported in this analysis. Since this decision has the effect of restricting the analysis to those areas which have been in the NHS area for the longest period of time, it should maximize the likelihood of observing a measurable impact. It should be noted, however, that unreported analysis of the larger geographic model was consistent with that based on the more restricted model.

7. There is, of course, some debate over the appropriate set of units which ought to be used in calculating a lending rate. In the analysis reported in Tables 1 and 2, measures of total investment have been divided by total number of housing units. The Baltimore data were taken from the 1970 U.S. Census. The Dallas data were 1976 estimates provided by National Data Planning Corporation. An alternative set of lending rates was calculated for each city using total number of single-family owner-occupied units. Data for both cities were obtained from the 1970 U.S. Census. Although the numerical values of specific rates changed, the relative rankings of the various neighborhoods did not. Total units are reported because more recent data were available for Dallas.

8. The effect of this selection process is best seen in Dallas, for which more detailed housing data are available. Comparing the NHS target community to census tracts of similar mean income, one sees that houses in the NHS target area were more expensive, had more rooms, and had greater square footage than houses in the control tracts. Only in the case of age did the target area seem to compare negatively with the control tracts. The picture is less clear for the Baltimore neighborhoods due to a lack of data on the control tracts. However, 1970 census data show that the average value housing in the target neighborhoods was similar to that in the control tracts. In addition, population stability, as measured by proportion of persons living in the same house for five years, was similar in the target and control neighborhoods. In Love Field and Govans, the proportion of minorities was higher than the average in the control tracts. Obviously, the impact of the program might have been affected by racial discrimination. Note, however, that the program assumes that the association of race and lending is an artifact of market variables other than overt discrimination.

9. Data on housing sales in Dallas were obtained from SREA Market Data Center. Data for Patterson Park and Govans were obtained from Lusk Real Estate Reporting Service.

10. There were some rather serious limitations to the Love Field data. These included missing data and extreme cases. During several months of the series no sales were reported. For these months an estimated value was placed into the series. This value was calculated as a mean of the reported price of the month before and the month after the month with no reported sales. In the series reported in Figure 3, three extreme values (sales of over $100,000) have also been replaced with such estimates. These extreme cases have been dropped because its seems highly likely that they are in error. Unfortunately, it is not possible to verify reported data provided by SREA Market Data Center. It should be noted that unreported analysis suggests that the substantive conclusions of the article are not dependent on either set of estimates. For example, although the form of the ARIMA

model fitted to the Dallas data changes somewhat if the extreme cases are left in the series, substantive conclusions derived from the intervention analysis are unchanged.

11. Because of the size of the estimated effect, each ARIMA model was estimated again using only preintervention data. The results are consistent with those presented in Table 3. A similar intervention analysis computed for a monthly price series for all of Dallas County did not indicate any significant shift. This provides further confidence that the shift described in the Love Field data in Table 3 is not an artifact of changes in the entire Dallas County housing market.

12. Note that the SREA Data Market Center, which provided the Dallas housing price data, is a data-gathering service of the American Society of Real Estate Appraisers. Since appraisers are more likely to be involved in the sale of higher-priced properties, SREA data may overstate the value of all Love Field properties.

REFERENCES

AARON, H. J. (1978) Politics and the Professors: The Great Society in Perspective. Washington, DC: Brookings Institution.

AHLBRANDT, R. and P. BROPHY (1975) Neighborhood Revitalization. Lexington, MA: Lexington Books.

AHLBRANDT, R. S. and J. CUNNINGHAM (1979) A New Policy for Neighborhood Preservation. New York: Praeger.

BOX, G.E.P. and G. M. JENKINS (1976) Time Series Analysis: Forecasting and Control. San Francisco: Holden-Day.

CLAY, P. L. (1981) Neighborhood Partnership in Action: An Assessment of the Neighborhood Housing Services Program and Other Selected Programs of Neighborhood Reinvestment. Washington, DC: Neighborhood Reinvestment Corporation.

GEISEL, P. H. (1977) The Northpark/Love Field Experience: An Analysis of the Neighborhood Housing Service in Dallas. Dallas: Institute for Urban Studies, University of Texas at Arlington.

HANSON, S. A. (1983) "Public policy analysis: some recent developments and current problems," in A. Finifter (ed.) Political Science: The State of the Discipline. Washington, DC: American Political Science Association.

HULA, R. C. (1984) "The allocation of home credit: market versus nonmarket factors." J. of Urban Affairs 6, 2: 151-165.

McADAMS, J. (1984) "The anti-policy analysts." Policy Studies J. 13, 1: 91-101.

McCAIN, L. and R. D. McCLEARY (1979) "The statistical analysis of the simple interrupted time series quasi-experiment," pp. 233-294 in T. Cook and D. T. Campbell (eds.) Quasi-Experimentation: Design and Analysis for Field Settings. Chicago: Rand McNally.

McCLEARY, R. D. and R. A. HAY (1980) Applied Time Analysis for the Social Sciences. Beverly Hills, CA: Sage.

National Commission on Neighborhoods (1979) People Building Neighborhoods. Final Report to the President and the Congress of the United States. Washington, DC: Government Printing Office.

POL, L. G., R. F. GUY, and A. J. BUSH (1982) "Discrimination in the home lending market: a macro perspective." Social Sci. Q. 63 (December): 716-728.

PRESSMAN, J. and A. WILDAVSKY (1973) Implementation. Berkeley: Univ. of California Press.

THUROW, L. G. (1975) Generating Inequality: Mechanisms of Distribution in the U.S. Economy. New York: Basic Books.

Richard C. Hula is Associate Professor of Family and Community Development at the University of Maryland, College Park. His present research interests focus on efforts to use private sector markets in the implementation of public policy. He has published this and related topics in Urban Affairs Quarterly, Social Science Quarterly, Journal of Public Policy, Journal of Urban Affairs, *and* Journal of Policy Studies.

THE DISPERSAL OF SUBSIDIZED HOUSING IN CHICAGO
An Index for Comparisons

ELIZABETH WARREN
Loyola University of Chicago

This article shows how the Index of Dissimilarity can be used to develop a measure of the dispersal of subsidized housing in American cities. The Index is applied to data for Chicago: Similar data can be generated in other cities, and comparisons can be made among cities and metropolitan areas as to the degree of dispersal achieved over the three census years 1960, 1970, and 1980. This information should be useful to public officials who administer housing programs as well as to scholars, for it provides a means to assess the degree to which the policy of "deconcentration" of subsidized housing, pursued as national policy for more than a decade, was achieved.

INTRODUCTION

Federal housing policy from the late 1960s until the early 1980s set in motion some bold new concepts for providing subsidized housing to low- and moderate-income people. One such concept was to provide broader housing choices to low-income households, such choices to include the availability of subsidized housing for the poor in middle- and upper-income neighborhoods and in racially mixed neighborhoods. The means to this end was to disperse assisted housing away from the inner city and into white neighborhoods of city and suburb. This idea was born in the aftermath of the urban riots of the 1960s. It gained strength in civil rights legislation, housing laws, and federal court decisions. While civil rights legislation stressed "fair housing," prohibiting racial discrimination in the sale or rental of housing, the housing laws, particularly those of 1968 and 1974, stressed the future placement of subsidized housing outside the inner city and away from the massive public housing projects that often became "vertical ghettos" for poor blacks.

URBAN AFFAIRS QUARTERLY, Vol. 21 No. 4, June 1986 484-500

Sufficient time has elapsed since the beginnings of the policy of dispersal that its outcome thus far can be evaluated. It is appropriate to ask whether, and to what degree, a measure of deconcentration actually did occur in cities across the country. Government studies state that the Section 8 Existing housing program[1] was a successful vehicle for this policy (Drury et al., 1978; Wallace et al., 1981), but there is no comprehensive assessment of the dispersal of all government-subsidized low-income housing. What is needed is a universal measuring tool so that we can plot a city's experience over time, or compare several cities according to the degree of dispersal achieved by the several low-income housing programs during the lifetime of the policy.

This article shows how the technique called the Index of Dissimilarity, first employed by Karl and Alma Taeuber (1965) in their study of residential segregation in cities, can be used to evaluate the dispersal of subsidized housing. Findings are presented from an analysis of the location of subsidized housing in the city of Chicago in the three census years 1960, 1970, and 1980. A separate analysis provides findings for the six-county suburban region around Chicago.

The Chicago region is a good example to use for this analysis because it is one city where strong pressures to "deconcentrate" were brought to bear by the federal district court (*Gautreaux v. Chicago Housing Authority,* 1969), the U.S. Department of Housing and Urban Development (HUD), and interest groups. These pressures aroused considerable resistance at the local level, of course, but it was hard to stand in the way of the courts, HUD, and the local public interest groups. Still today, therefore, Chicago is under a recent court order in the 15-year-old litigation (*Gautreaux v. Landrieu,* 1981) to assist 7,100 households who are Chicago Housing Authority (CHA) tenants or on the CHA waiting list and are eligible for public housing, to move away from the inner city to outlying neighborhoods of the city and suburbs. Not until this goal has been achieved will requirements of the court order be satisfied.

THE METHOD OF ANALYSIS

The Index of Dissimilarity is an expression of a difference between ratios of two discrete variables. For those who analyze segregation in cities, the variables were nonwhite and white. For this study, the variables are subsidized housing and nonsubsidized housing. The Taeubers used the census block for their analysis of residential segregation. They made the theoretical assumption that if there were no racial segregation in a city, every city block would have exactly the same percentage of a minority race as did the city as a whole. So if the whole city were 10% black, this percentage should be reflected in the population of each census block, according to the theory.

This study uses the census tract as the basis for analysis. The Index computes the difference between the norm (which is the percentage of the whole city's housing units that are subsidized) and the actual distribution. The census block is too small a unit of measurement for the relatively small number of subsidized housing units in Chicago. Census tracts are larger, many having 2,000 to 3,000 housing units in them, some more than that. They provide a more realistic base for the test proposed here.

SOURCES OF DATA

Data gathering for this analysis involved obtaining all subsidized housing projects according to number of units and their location according to census tracts in Chicago and the six-county region. Four subsidized housing programs were used in 1980: public housing, Section 221(d)(3), Section 236, and Section 8 housing. In 1970, only two of those programs were in existence: public housing and the moderate-income housing program called Section 221(d)(3). In 1960, only public housing provided shelter for some low-income households.

The two moderate-income housing programs, Sections 221(d)(3) and 236, are included because they represent a subsidy for what are sometimes called the "working poor" that public housing could not provide given the income ceilings for tenants of public housing. The two below-market interest rate (BMIR) programs provided not-for-profit corporations and developers with federal guarantees of low interest rates on loans for construction or rehabilitation of rental apartments. The savings realized by the low interest rates were passed on to the tenants in lower rents than prevailed in the market. For a time, these programs—or, rather, the housing built or rehabbed under them—appeared to be successful, but several factors intervened to make them impractical, and both programs were discontinued in the late 1970s. The high inflation of that decade made the required rents too high for many previously eligible tenants. As a result, by the early 1980s some of the BMIR buildings were converted to Section 8 rental assistance. Many that were not converted had tenants who were enabled to stay in their apartments by virtue of other special "deep" subsidies[2] provided by the government just for their circumstances. Moreover, in Chicago at least, a number of moderate-income developments defaulted. When HUD obtained title to these buildings, it adopted a policy of selling them with Section 8 rental assistance. Often this was 100% Section 8 assistance.

Figures for the moderate-income housing program units are included in this study because, in many cases, low-income people live in them. It is impossible to separate the low-income from the moderate-income households now residing in these buildings, and it is also not possible to distinguish elderly from family tenants. In order to deal with this problem, indices are presented for each housing program separately, as well as together. While this does not solve the problem of the lack of elderly-family distinctions and the mixing of income groups, it does permit the removal of those effects from the data by providing for the separate consideration of each program.

Assistance in gathering data was obtained from the Chicago Departments of Planning and Housing, the Chicago Housing Authority, HUD, and thirteen housing agencies in the six-county region. It was possible to determine the census tract location of every housing development, with the number of its units, and all Section 8 certificates in Chicago. However, it was not possible to determine by census tract the certificates in the suburban region outside Chicago; therefore, tables presenting the suburban data unfortunately must exclude the Section 8 Existing program.

The two variables for this study are designated S for subsidized housing and NS for nonsubsidized housing. There are more than 800 tracts in Chicago and more than 1,100 in the suburban region. The procedures for calculating the Index are those described by the Taeubers (1965: 237-238).[3]

THE FINDINGS

CHICAGO

The analysis of data for three census years shows the degree of dispersal of subsidized housing that occurred in Chicago (Table 1). The

TABLE 1
Index of Dissimilarity in Distribution of Subsidized Housing in Chicago, 1960, 1970, 1980

Year	Total Occupied Units	Total Subsidized Units	Percent Subsidized	Index (D)[a]
1960	1,157,409	18,257	1.6	98.40
1970	1,137,854	47,147[b]	4.1	88.37
1980	1,093,407	73,621	6.7	77.82

a. The formula used for the Index of Dissimilarity is

$$D = \text{The sum of } (S_i/S - NS_i/NS) \times 100$$

Where S_i is the sum of subsidized housing units in tract i where the percentage of subsidized to total units is greater than the citywide percentage in the given census year;

S is the total number of subsidized units in the city;

NS_i is the sum of nonsubsidized housing units in tract i where the percentage of subsidized to total units is greater than the citywide percentage;

NS is the total number of nonsubsidized units in the city.

b. The Section 23 leasing program consisted of a total of 2,419 units in 1970 (**CHA Annual Report**). Unfortunately, these could not be included in the analysis because their distribution by census tract was not recorded at that time.

findings represent a statement of the distance from equality, or evenness of the distribution, of subsidized housing that existed in each census year separately. The import of the Index is its value in a given year. The differences between years should be understood as differences from equality in each year and a measure of the percentage of units that would have to be dispersed out of the total subsidized housing stock existing at that time to achieve perfect equality.[4]

Two caveats are important here. Housing cannot be picked up and relocated; thus, the measure is not directly indicative of a desired policy objective. Moreover, achievement of the norm of perfectly equal distribution of subsidized housing in all census tracts is impossible and not practical as a policy matter. All we can get from the measure is an understanding of the distance from equality that the present distribution represents.

One further point must be made. The Section 8 Existing program allows people to receive rental assistance wherever they live or choose to live. It has been the policy of the CHA and other housing authorities in the region to distribute the certificates widely, in accordance with the policies of the 1970s. While tenants can take their certificates anywhere in the Chicago region (thanks to an arrangement among governmental units to make them "portable"), the appropriate housing authorities promise to pay a percentage of the rent of those units; they are leased and are here treated as subsidized. Over the past five years of this exchange program, 395 families (or about 80 per year) have moved from one jurisdiction to another in the six-county region, "carrying" their certificates with them (Leadership Council for Metropolitan Open Communities, October 1984: 4).

The figures in Table 1 are based on subsidized housing data for the three census years which include only public housing in 1960, public housing and Section 221(d)(3) in 1970, and four programs—public housing, Section 221(d)(3), Section 236, and Section 8 New, Substantially Rehabilitated, and Existing housing, and Section 202/8—in 1980. (The latter is usually considered as part of Section 8.) The Section 8 New and Rehab programs include some developments in which 100% of the units are subsidized and others in which a lower percentage is subsidized. This analysis includes only those units that are subsidized in such buildings.

An Index of Dissimilarity equaling 100 would represent complete concentration of subsidized housing in a certain number of census tracts, with a predominance of tracts having no assisted housing at all. An Index of 0 would be obtained if every tract had the citywide average, or, for 1980, 6.7% of its housing units subsidized.

In 1960, the total number of subsidized housing units in the city and the number of subsidized units in tracts where the percentage was above the citywide percentage were identical. Thus, there were no tracts having some subsidized housing where the citywide percentage was not exceeded. The Index of 98.4 reflects this fact.

By 1970, the Index was lower (88.37), reflecting a slight reduction in concentration of subsidized housing. The introduction of the Section 221(d)(3) moderate-income housing is only partially responsible for this reduction. A separate analysis was performed on the public housing distribution in 1970 to determine whether the moderate-income program was the primary factor in lowering the Index. The 1970 public housing Index is 91.64, suggesting that some movement toward dispersing public housing was underway. It is not clear why this would be the case, although it can be noted that the CHA built a number of housing units for the elderly in the 1960s and these, in some cases, were sited in white neighborhoods away from the inner city.

By 1980, with four housing programs in the analysis, the Index dropped to 77.82. An explanation of this apparent decrease in concentrations of subsidized housing should be sought.

The impact of the Section 8 Existing program is evident in Table 2, in which subsidized housing for low-income people is distinguished from that for moderate-income people and is categorized according to type of program and elderly-family distinctions. Although there were fewer units subsidized under the Existing program than in the public housing or Section 8 New and Rehab programs, they were far more widely distributed into 521 of Chicago's 869 census tracts. Public housing is distributed in only 116 tracts, while Section 8 New and Rehab housing is found in 69 tracts.

The range of the Index varies from 85 to 95 for all programs except the Section 8 Existing program. The Index for public housing and Section 8 New and Rehab units shows that the addition of Section 8 has had an effect on the level of concentration of housing for low-income people during the 1970s. However, the reduction is not great. The Index for public housing alone in 1970 was 91; the D for the two combined programs in 1980 was 85.

The Index for public housing alone in 1980 is the same as for 1970: 91. This is noteworthy because it confirms the fact that the Chicago Housing Authority made little progress in carrying out the court order, and indeed made little progress in adding more public housing, especially for families, to its inventory.

Moderate-income housing had an Index of 87 in 1980. The two programs under this heading were never required by the court to be dispersed; even so, they had a slightly lower D than the Section 8 New and Rehab programs. This can be attributed to the fact that Section 8 units numbered less than half of the moderate-income units in 1980.

The data on Section 8 New and Rehab units give the appearance of concentration. In fact, however, the programs in 1980 had only a relatively small number of units in a small number of census tracts. The average number of units of Section 8 per census tract was 129. Public housing, by contrast, had an average number of 344 units per tract. The latter figure does not tell of the thousands of public housing units in a few inner-city tracts. One should expect that the Index for all low-income housing will decline when and if additional new or rehabilitated subsidized housing is added to the inventory in Chicago.

Housing for the elderly is generally believed to be more acceptable to white middle-income or upper-income neighborhoods than is housing

TABLE 2
Distribution of Subsidized Housing by Program in Chicago in 1980

	Total Subsidized Units	Percent Subsidized[a]	No. Census Tracts	Index (D)
All Public Housing, Sec. 8 New, Rehab	48,915	4.47	160	85.68
Elderly[b]	14,524	1.32	78	87.29
Family	34,391	3.14	126	91.49
Public Hsg.	40,014	3.6	116	91.30
Elderly	9,404	.8	46[c]	93.82
Family	30,610	2.8	89[c]	95.98
Sec.8 New, Rehab	8,901	.8	69	89.87
Elderly[b]	5,120	.5	40[c]	92.77
Family	3,781	.3	49[c]	93.16
Sec. 8 Existing	5,555	.5	521	53.46
Elderly	2,653	.2	354[c]	58.53
Family	2,902	.3	400[c]	60.14
Moderate Income Housing	19,151	1.75	120	87.41

a. Percentages are based on 1,093,407 occupied housing units in Chicago in 1980, according to census report. When year-round housing units are used (1,173,755 units), Indices (D) are marginally lower, varying from .07 to 1.8 points lower than Indices given above.
b. Includes Section 202/8.
c. Figures do not total figure for all tracts because numerous tracts have both elderly and family subsidized housing.

for families. A review was made of the racial and income characteristics of tracts with elderly and family public and Section 8 housing, not including the Existing program. In census tracts with fewer than 30% black residents and with incomes higher than the citywide median for households in 1980, there were 1,237 elderly units but only 252 family units. This indicates that elderly housing is indeed found more frequently than family subsidized housing in such neighborhoods. However, it is also true that the preponderance of elderly housing is in lower-income tracts.

Viewing the subsidized housing programs in Chicago as a whole, the Section 8 Existing program stands out as by far the best vehicle for distributing housing assistance geographically. If dispersal were the first priority in housing policy, the Existing program and its counterpart, the housing allowance program, would be the recommended means of accomplishing the goal. Of course, dispersal is not the first priority in housing policy; the issue today is to make housing assistance available to a large and growing needy population in our cities.

THE SUBURBAN REGION

The 1970s saw a sixfold increase in the numbers of subsidized housing units in the suburban area around Chicago. Since the growth of these numbers coincides with the decade in which the policy of dispersal was emphasized, a comparison with Chicago is appropriate.

The four subsidized housing programs used in the following analysis are the same as those used for the Chicago analysis except for the Section 8 Existing program, which is excluded because its distribution by census tract is not available. The findings in Tables 3 and 4 should be examined with a view to the probable lower Index, which the inclusion of the certificate program could be expected to produce. There were 5,836 certificates in the six-county suburban region in 1980, slightly more than were present in Chicago in the same year.

Table 3 presents the findings for four housing programs in the suburban region. The Index of 80.78 is close to the Chicago Index for four programs that included Section 8 Existing units (79.60). The suburban figures illustrate that dispersal was set in motion on a much smaller base of concentrated public housing in 1970 than was the case in Chicago. Public housing was located primarily in the satellite cities of Waukegan, Elgin, Joliet, and in several low-income suburbs within Cook County. Some moderate-income housing developed in the 1960s formed the suburban inventory of 5,235 units in 1970. By 1980, the number of suburban subsidized units (which included two programs not part of this analysis, Section 235 single-family houses and municipal housing assistance programs administered by five suburban towns) totaled 29,463.

TABLE 3
Suburban Six-County Area Distribution of Subsidized Housing, Four Programs 1980

	Occupied Housing	Subsidized Housing	Percent Subsidized	No. Census Tracts	Index
Public Hsg., Mod. Inc., Sec. 8 New, Rehab Hsg.	1,393,317	19,527	1.4	121	80.78

Table 4 presents the distribution of the four housing programs taken separately. When Section 8 and public housing are combined, the Index of Dissimilarity is lower (83.91) than that for each of the two programs taken separately. Since small numbers of units in a relatively few census tracts are characteristic of subsidized housing in the suburbs, one can expect that lower Indices will appear if and when more assisted housing is added to the inventory. As of 1980, all of the low-income housing amounted to less than 1% of the occupied housing units in the six-county suburban area.

The differences with the Chicago distribution can be seen best in terms of the average number of units per tract. Public housing and Section 8 housing in the suburbs (11,679 units) are distributed in 98 census tracts for an average of 119 units per tract. In Chicago, more than 48,000 units are distributed in 160 tracts for an average of 305 units per tract.

The housing for low-income people, public housing and Section 8, have a slightly lower Index (83) than is found in Chicago (85), which has a much larger number of such housing units. Since the average number of units per tract in the suburbs (in tracts where there is subsidized housing) is 119, but in the city it is 305, it is clear that the subsidized housing in the suburbs is not heavily concentrated; the relatively few units are just not widely distributed.

The analyses of subsidized housing in Chicago and in the suburban region show that more progress toward dispersal has taken place in the suburban area than in Chicago, but that both the city and its suburbs show movement in that direction. Needless to say, the weight of decades of concentrating public housing in a few inner-city census tracts in Chicago will always show the city to have higher Indices of Dissimilarity than the suburbs and to be slower to exhibit decreases in those concentrations.

TABLE 4
Distribution of Public Housing, Section 8 New, Rehab in Suburban Six-County Area, 1980

	Subsidized Housing	Percent Subsidized[a]	No. Census Tracts	Index (D)
All Public Hsg., Sec.8 New, Rehab	11,679	.83	98	83.91
Elderly	7,574	.54	63	89.71
Family	4,105	.29	52	90.80
Public Housing	5,034	.36	40	94.42
Elderly	3,215	.23	25	95.94
Family	1,819	.13	20	97.58
Sec. 8 New, Rehab	6,645	.47	59	89.0
Elderly	4,359	.31	39	93.44
Family	2,286	.16	32	93.16
Moderate Income Housing	7,848	.56	40	92.59

a. Percentages based on total occupied housing figure in region outside Chicago of 1,393,317 according to 1980 census report.

BROADER HOUSING CHOICES?

A larger philosophical issue was posed by the idealism of the 1960s and 1970s than "deconcentration" alone. That issue concerned the desirability of providing broader housing choices to low-income people, particularly racial minorities. This philosophy was rooted in the civil rights movement, and sought to advance not only racial integration but mixed-income neighborhoods in cities by means of providing low-income housing in a dispersed pattern. A review of the economic level and racial make-up of the census tracts where subsidized housing was located in 1970 and 1980 in Chicago can provide some insight into the question whether low-income housing assistance was gradually becoming available in integrated neighborhoods with higher than average incomes. It also affords an approach to the impact of dispersal policy from a different angle, and thereby provides a means to assess the reliability of the Index of Dissimilarity.

NEIGHBORHOOD INCOMES AND SUBSIDIZED HOUSING

There was a significant change between 1970 and 1980 in the number of census tracts in Chicago with subsidized housing, from 127 to 577 (Table 5). As noted before, the Section 8 Existing program accounts for much of the change. Among the 577 tracts with subsidized housing in 1980, the number of subsidized units varies substantially from two or three Section 8 certificates to several hundred or even thousands of subsidized units. Of the 430 census tracts with less than the citywide percentage subsidized in 1980, 357 have only Section 8 Existing certificate holders, with no other housing program represented in the tract totals.

The number of census tracts with subsidized housing and higher median incomes than the citywide median increased from 13 in 1970 to 248 in 1980. Many of the tracts in 1980 did not have as much as the citywide average of subsidized housing (228), but this represents considerable movement from the situation in 1970 (6 such tracts). Among tracts with more than the citywide percentage of subsidized housing, the movement was from 7 in 1970 to 20 in 1980, a modest increase. Among the census tracts with incomes lower than the citywide median, there were 28 in 1970 that had less than the citywide percentage of subsidized housing, but 202 such tracts in 1980. Finally, among the poorer census tracts there were 86 that had more than the citywide percentage of subsidized housing in 1970, and 121 such tracts in 1980.

These findings show that, today, lower densities of subsidized housing occur much more frequently than higher densities in census tracts with median incomes higher than the citywide median. However, the lower densities mean that there is not much assisted housing in those tracts. This conclusion is consistent with the high Indices of Dissimilarity reported earlier.

DISPERSAL AND RACIAL MAKE-UP

The *Gautreaux* decision based its geographic distribution scheme for subsidized housing on a 30% black population figure as a break-point

TABLE 5
Subsidized Housing in Census Tracts According to Median Household Income in Chicago, 1970 and 1980

Chicago Median Income[a] in Tracts	Census Tracts With Subsidized Housing: Less than city-wide percentage		More than city-wide percentage		Totals	
	1970	1980	1970	1980	1970	1980
Tracts with higher than city median	6	228	7	20	13	248
Tracts with lower than city median	28	202	86	121	114	323
Totals	34	430	93	141	127	571[b]

a. Based on 1970 median income of families and unrelated individuals ($7,983) and on 1980 median household income for Chicago ($15,301).
b. In six tracts income figures were not given by the census in 1980. The total number of tracts with some subsidized housing in 1980 was 577.

for determining racially impacted areas where further production of public housing and Section 8 developments should be limited. The 30% criterion is used here to determine the degree to which housing assistance was made available in integrated or predominantly white census tracts between 1970 and 1980 (Table 6).

Significant change in housing siting policies in Chicago occurred between 1970 and 1980, although the Section 8 Existing program appears to have been relied on for much dispersal. The number of census tracts with integrated or predominantly white populations where assisted housing was located grew from 40 to 275. Dispersal of subsidized housing among white or integrated tracts can be seen in the change from 13 tracts in 1970 to 233 in 1980. It is also true that tracts with more than 30% black population and various amounts of assisted housing grew apace, from 87 to 302. Important to this picture is that Chicago's black population grew substantially in the 1970s and distributed itself widely. Focusing on the tracts with less than the citywide percentage of assisted housing, a marked increase is seen, from 34 such tracts in 1970 to 433 in 1980. By comparison, the tracts with higher than the citywide percentages of subsidized housing increased from 93 to 144. This

TABLE 6
Subsidized Housing in Census Tracts According to Percentage Black Population in Chicago, 1970 and 1980

	Census Tracts with Subsidized Housing					
	Less than city-wide percentage		More than city-wide percentage		Totals	
	1970	1980	1970	1980	1970	1980
Tracts with 30% or more black pop.	21	200	66	102	87	302
Tracts with fewer than 30% black pop.	13	233	27	42	40	275
Totals	34	433	93	144	127	577

indicates a significant slowing of the growth of assisted housing in inner-city black neighborhoods. In other words, the enunciated policy appears to have been implemented to a degree.

CONCLUSION

The Index of Dissimilarity found what has been generally known about subsidized housing in Chicago: It tends to be heavily concentrated with only the beginnings of dispersal evident by 1980. However, when all housing programs are taken together and compared over three census years, the Index gives a fair representation of a trend toward increasing dispersal.

In the expansive suburban area, there are relatively few assisted units. They appear by the Index to be concentrated, but this measure needs interpretation: The high numbers for D represent the relatively few census tracts into which the housing is distributed.

The analysis of census tracts in Chicago relating median incomes and racial characteristics to dispersal in 1970 and 1980 convey the same message: Small numbers of assisted units do appear in census tracts with median incomes higher than the city median and with predominantly white populations. Heavier concentrations of assisted housing are found in black census tracts with lower than the city's median income.

While the socioeconomic data do not give us exhaustive proof that the Index of Dissimilarity is reliable, they do support the Index figures and serve to amplify the information given by the Indices. Moreover, the income and racial data give us no evidence that the Index figures are incorrect.

The findings of this study in the Chicago region show the usefulness of the Index of Dissimilarity as a tool for measuring the dispersal of all low-income government-subsidized housing in American urban areas. It has the advantage of universality in its coverage of the geographic distribution of low-income housing in an urban area, and provides a method of evaluating changes in that distribution over time. To the extent that data are available, they allow us to measure the achievement of the policy of dispersal, and also to look more closely at individual programs and at elderly-family distributions. They provide a means to compare urban areas on this policy issue, and will allow generalizations to be made about the degree of success of the policy across the urban areas.

NOTES

1. The Section 8 Existing program allows a low-income household to obtain rental assistance from the federal government in existing housing that has been approved by the government as meeting health and safety standards. The program allows a low-income household to choose its own housing rather than being required to move into a building constructed for low-income people.

2. The "deep" subsidies are special rental assistance programs for tenants in buildings constructed under the moderate-income housing programs, Section 221(d)(3) and Section 236. Tenants were given the additional subsidies when rents increased with inflation and they were no longer able to pay them.

3. The standard formulation for the Index of Dissimilarity is presented by the Taeubers (1965) on page 236 of *Negroes in Cities.* It is $D = 1/2$ (sum of absolute values of $N_i/N - W_i/W$). The Taeubers explain why it is appropriate to use the formula employed here in their discussion of their method on page 237. The issue is to distinguish the differences that are positive from those that are negative or zero (1965: 236).

4. Some scholarly critiques of the Index of Dissimilarity were published in 1977 and 1978. These concerned the appropriateness of the Index for segregation analysis and the possible misuses of it. A dialogue between Christopher Winship and a group of Denver scholars—Falk, Cortese, and Cohen—concludes that the Index (D) is distorted by the

proportion of minority in a city. They agree that this distortion "prohibits the comparison of: (1) a city over time; and (2) cities where the proportion of the minority is different (Cohen et al., Cortese et al.)" (Falk et al., 1978: 713). Falk et al. cite Duncan and Duncan as having pointed out that "it is doubtful whether a meaningful comparison can be made of the degrees of segregation of two cities with greatly different q's" (Falk et al., 1978: 714), referring to the proportion of the minority in those cities. However, the Denver scholars believe that scholars should not stop using the Index of Dissimilarity because it has value as "a description of the percent of minority that needs to be moved to achieve evenness within a city" (Falk et al., 1978: 715).

Winship, however, thinks the Index should not be used at all to measure segregation among cities because it does not satisfy the exchange principle and "is equally sensitive to all exchanges that lower the Index" (Winship, 1978: 718).

Scholars have continued to use the Index of Dissimilarity to measure segregation, however.

REFERENCES

Chicago Housing Authority (1970, 1980) Annual Report. Chicago: Author.

———(n.d.) "Records of public housing developments and lists of Section 8 Existing program certificates according to census tracts in Chicago." (mimeo)

City of Chicago Department of Housing (1980) "Records and lists of Section 221(d)(3), Section 236, and Section 8 developments." (mimeo)

DRURY, M., O. LEE, M. SPRINGER, and L. YAP (1978) Lower Income Housing Program. Washington, DC: Government Printing Office.

FALK, R. F., C. F. CORTESE, and J. COHEN (1978) "Utilizing standardized indices of residential segregation: comment on Winship." Social Forces 57 (December): 713-716.

Gautreaux v. Chicago Housing Authority (1969) 296 F. Supp. 907.

Gautreaux v. Landrieu (1981) No. 66 C 1459 and 66 C 1460. Consent Decree.

Illinois Housing Development Authority (1980) "Records and lists of Section 236 and Section 8 developments." (mimeo)

Leadership Council for Metropolitan Open Communities (1984) Recent Developments in Housing (April and October). Quarterly reports.

TAEUBER, K. and A. TAEUBER (1965) Negroes in Cities: Residential Segregation and Neighborhood Change. Chicago: Aldine.

U.S. Department of Commerce, Bureau of the Census (1960, 1970, 1980) Census of Population and Housing. Washington, DC: Government Printing Office.

U.S. Department of Housing and Urban Development (1981) "Multi-family insured and direct loan information system, project status and control report." August 15. (mimeo)

WALLACE, J., S. BLOOM, W. HOLSHOUSER, S. MANSFIELD, and D. WEINBERG (1981) Participation and Benefits in the Urban Section 8 Program. Cambridge, MA: Abt Associates.

WINSHIP, C. (1977) "A reevaluation of indexes of residential segregation." Social Forces 55 (June): 1058-1065.

———(1978) "The desirability of using the Index of Dissimilarity or any adjustment of it for measuring segregation: reply to Falk, Cortese, and Cohen." Social Forces 57 (December): 717-720.

Elizabeth Warren is Assistant Professor of Political Science at Loyola University of Chicago. She has published monographs on housing and neighborhoods in the Urban Insights Series of Loyola University's Center for Urban Policy.

ECOLOGICAL AND POLITICAL-ECONOMIC ANALYSES OF MIGRATION TO A PRIMATE CITY
Bangkok, Thailand ca. 1970

BRUCE LONDON
Florida Atlantic University

Knowledge about internal migration to primate cities in Third World nations is limited. This article will analyze the determinants of migration to Bangkok, Thailand, ca. 1970, by focusing on the characteristics of province of origin. Theoretical issues are also addressed through the determinants analysis: The literature on primate city migration reflects a clear debate between ecological and political-economic explanations. Both explanations are defined and operationalized and their relative efficacy as predictors of migration to Bangkok is tested.

Migration to primate cities in Third World nations is a topic of considerable theoretical and practical significance. The extremely rapid growth of big cities in Third World nations has been well documented (see Davis, 1965; Population Division, 1969; Hay, 1977; Preston, 1979) as have the problems that such rapid growth poses for both city and nation (see Hauser, 1963; Sovani, 1964; Kammerschen, 1969; Turner, 1969; Beier, 1976).

This growth is known to be a function of both natural population increase within cities and net in-migration to cities, but there is considerable disagreement regarding the relative import of these two factors. Overviews of the situation tend to suggest that about one-half to two-thirds of the growth is due to natural increase within the cities themselves, and that one-third to one-half of the growth is due to rural-urban migration (Hay, 1977: 76; Beier, 1976: 4; Preston, 1979: 198; see Davis, 1965). Migration thus makes a significant contribution to a serious situation. And if it is true that "knowledge about internal migration in

URBAN AFFAIRS QUARTERLY, Vol. 21 No. 4, June 1986 501-526

most countries of the world is very sketchy" (Hawley, 1981: 293), then we are faced with a serious gap in an important area of knowledge.

This article will attempt to address this problem by analyzing the determinants of migration to one primate city, Bangkok, Thailand, during one period of time, the 1960-1970 intercensal decade. It is clear that internal migration contributed substantially to the growth of Bangkok during this time period. For example, less than one-third of the heads of households in the metropolis in the 1960s were born there (Prachuabmoh and Tirasawat, 1974). Sternstein (1976) cites a 100% increase in the net number of in-migrants to Bangkok from 1960 to 1970, and he notes that the number of migrants from each province to Bangkok increased during the decade. Also, between 1965 and 1970, net in-migration to Bangkok averaged 34,000 per year. Estimates based on registration data show that natural increase accounted for 60%-67% of the total population growth in Bangkok between 1961 and 1967, and, since migration accounts for the balance, it "constitutes a very significant contribution to total growth" (Goldstein, 1972: 18; see also Goldstein, 1969: 111).

A considerable literature on internal migration in Thailand based on census, registration, and survey data already exists (see Goldstein, 1969, 1972, 1973; Goldstein and Pitaktepsombati, 1974; International Labor Office, 1965; Ng, 1969; Prachuabmoh and Tirasawat, 1974; Sternstein, 1971, 1974, 1976; Textor, 1961). A portion of this literature focuses explicitly on migration to Bangkok (Goldstein, 1969, 1972, 1973; Goldstein and Pitaktepsombati, 1974; Prachuabmoh and Tirasawat, 1974; Sternstein, 1971, 1974, 1976). Almost all of this literature, however, is strictly descriptive—focusing on the volume, streams, direction, duration, distance, or intra- and interregional patterns of migration. There is virtually no analysis aimed at testing theories of internal migration, even at the level of a bivariate correlation analysis. This article is fundamentally different in both goals and method. The focus of attention will be placed on the demographic and economic characteristics of the province of origin of migrants—a topic that has generally been neglected in the migration literature (Elizaga, 1972)—in an attempt to develop estimates of the determinants of migration from peripheral provinces to Bangkok. In other words, multiple regression techniques will be applied to an analysis of Thai provinces in 1960 and 1970. Predictors will be developed, based on literature in the theory of migration, that will permit the estimation of the determinants of primate city migration.

A second goal of this article—concomitant with the determinants analysis—is theoretical. The literature on primate city migration (i.e., rural-urban migration) reflects a clear debate between human ecological and political-economic explanations. Sets of variables defining each theory will be operationalized, and their relative efficacy as predictors of migration to Bangkok will be tested empirically using Thai census and related data.

ECOLOGICAL THEORY: RURAL PUSH AND URBAN PULL

Historically, ecological explanations have dominated the sociological literature on rural-urban migration in Third World nations. Hawley's (1981: 285-300) work is representative of this approach. It stresses the notion of increasing numbers of people "available for redistribution." As demographic transitions occur, rising rates of natural increase yield precipitous population growth in rural areas. Population growth outstrips job opportunities and a labor surplus emerges in agriculture. As the supply of available space for cultivation diminishes, displacements from the land increase, and urbanward migration frequently occurs as a response to both rural population pressure and perceived economic opportunities in the city.

Ecological theorists do not oversimplify the role of demographic and economic variables as determinants of migration. Indeed, several other factors are seen to have important influences upon demographic and economic trends. These other independent variables include the level of agricultural technology, the level of transportation technology, and the friction of distance (see Hawley, 1950: 324-347; Hawley, 1981: 265-289). Improvements in agricultural technology tend to contribute to the redundancy of farm labor. They are, therefore, a contributing factor to the process of overpopulation and a stimulant to out-migration.

The relationship between migration and transportation technology is a bit more complex. On one hand, migration is facilitated by improvements in interregional transportation systems. Since migration rates tend to be inversely related to distance between points of origin and destination, the development of road, rail, air, and other communications networks can mediate the friction of distance by improving accessibility. On the other hand, the development of intraregional transportation facilities tends to discourage out-migration by increasing the area in which an individual may seek employment without changing residence (Hawley, 1950: 337).

In sum, ecological theory emphasizes the interplay of demographic, environmental, and technological factors with the classical economic principles of individual choice and competitive-market supply and demand (see Firey, 1945, for a discussion of the economic implications of classical ecological theory). Considerable attention has recently been directed to the ecological analysis of various types of population redistribution in the United States (see Sly, 1972; Frisbie and Poston, 1975, 1978; Sly and Tayman, 1977). In addition, one study conducts an ecological analysis of migration for Taiwan, a rapidly industrializing nation (Wilber, 1982). (To my knowledge, the theory has yet to be tested in a Third World nation.)

Basically, this literature is rooted in the classical ecological writings of Hawley (1950), Duncan (1959), Schnore (1958), and Gibbs and Martin (1959). Especially important is Duncan's (1959) concept of the "ecological complex" (also see Duncan and Schnore, 1959). This term refers to the specification of ecology's universe of inquiry in terms of the reciprocal relationships among four variables: population, (social) organization, environment, and technology (i.e., POET). Note that all of these variables are either implicit or explicit in Hawley's ecological theory.

Typically, organization is taken as the ecologist's dependent variable, and population, environment, and technology are interpreted as independent factors which explain the variance in some aspect of social organization. This ordering of variables, however, is not universal. Duncan, for example, "takes the position that variables subsumed under any of the rubrics can be treated as dependent. Following this lead, Schnore (1958: also see Duncan and Schnore, 1959) argued that many problems are best approached by treating organization as an independent variable" (Sly, 1972: 615). In fact, the ecological analysis of migration does just this by treating population change or migration (P) as a dependent variable and one or a combination of the other rubrics (O, E, T) as an independent variable.

Significantly, however, none of these researchers makes an explicit attempt to specify the relationship between other characteristics of a population and migration (i.e., P → P). In other words, each variable in the ecological complex is obviously multifaceted: There are many different environments, forms of social organization, and so on. If we fail to consider the possible impact of one dimension of a given rubric upon other dimensions of the same rubric, the inclusiveness and explanatory potential of the complex will be diminished. This is especially the case with respect to any attempt to develop an ecological explanation of migration, because one of the primary causes of migration is overpopulation (Hawley, 1950: 328-329), population pressure, or the presence of excess numbers of people in a given locale (Hawley, 1981: 287)—that is, P → P. And overpopulation, in turn, can only be meaningfully defined in relationship to sustenance organization as "the ratio of numbers to jobs available" (Hawley, 1950: 329). A comprehensive ecological analysis of migration should, therefore, include measures of all variables in the ecological complex among its independent variables (POET → migration).

POLITICAL-ECONOMIC THEORY: THE PENETRATION OF CAPITALISM

A political-economic explanation of rural-urban migration can be traced back at least to Marx's (1967: 455) discussion in Volume I of *Capital* of the forces which contributed to "the migration of agricultural laborers into the factory districts" in fifteenth- and sixteenth-centuries Great Britain. He emphasized the manner in which the evolution of the capitalist mode of production in agriculture encouraged the implementation of laws and policies which expropriated the agricultural population from the land and, thus, created a mobile proletariat available for urban labor (see, esp., 1967: 717-733).

> The spoilation of the church's property, the fraudulent alienation of the State domains, the robbery of the common lands, the usurpation of feudal clan property and its transformation into modern private property under circumstances of reckless terrorism, were just so many idyllic methods of primitive accumulation. They conquered the field for capitalist agriculture, made the soil part and parcel of capital, and created for the town industries the necessary supply of a "free" and outlawed proletariat [Marx, 1967: 732-733].

In other words, the spread or penetration of capitalism was a profound structural change. It revolutionized the conditions of production and set in motion a variety of dislocation forces which stimulated rural-urban migration. (For Lenin's comparable views on this issue, see Lenin, 1960: 556-580.)

More recent writings have focused on concepts homologous to "the penetration of capitalism" in the analysis of contemporary rural-urban migration in Third World nations. For example, a number of writers try to develop "systemic" or "structural" theories of migration that are explicitly based on causal principles standing in sharp contrast to the individualism or voluntarism implicit in more traditional ecological and microeconomic views. McGee's (1978: 211) "structural model" of rural-urban mobility and Portes's (1978) analysis of the structural determinants of migration stress the important role of processes operating at international and national levels. "By far the most important process is the penetration of capitalism into the pre-capitalist system of production" (McGee, 1978: 211). Similarly, according to Portes (1978: 8), "The penetration of capitalist techniques of production into areas of traditional production" displaces labor (see also the work of Amin, 1974; Burawoy, 1976; and McGee, 1978).

Crosscutting all of these political-economic views is the idea that primate city migration is not simply caused by a push from rural poverty and a pull to perceived urban opportunity. Nor is it a result of strictly individual responses to population pressure. The primate city is not the passive recipient of excess rural population due to forces (i.e., rural population pressure, poverty, and unemployment) beyond its control and causation. In sharp contrast, the notion of capitalist penetration suggests that forces emanating from the center, linked to the class-based pursuit of political and economic interests, put rural push (and urban pull) factors in operation. Thus, in this view the primate city would not be seen as a passive victim of forces beyond its ken, but as an active participant in contributing to the very conditions in the periphery which lead to its overpopulation via migration.

The discussions of Pearse (1971), Douglass (1983), and Roberts (1974) are especially useful for developing testable hypotheses regarding the penetration of capitalism. They help to specify the nature of the "exogenous forces" or "impulses arriving at the periphery from the center" (Pearse, 1971: 70) that stimulate internal migration. According to Pearse (1971), the basic processes are "market incorporation" and "institutional incorporation" of the rural periphery within the sphere of metropolitan influence. As Douglass (1983: 47) puts it, "The commercialization of the economy and the emergence of the centralized bureaucratic state, as primary sources of the incorporative drive, have been perpetrators of patterns of uneven social and spatial development to which migration is one of many responses." This view clearly recognizes the role of elites, economic interests, and the state in making decisions and implementing policies that influence the periphery.

THE COMMERCIALIZATION OF AGRARIAN PRODUCTION

"The most important driving force" in the process of incorporation is "the market complex" (Pearse, 1971: 71). The market penetration of rural areas leads to the juxtaposition of precapitalist forms of social and economic relationships with capitalist forms. Such changes in the "agrarian structure" (Roberts, 1978: 89ff.) as the expansion of capitalist agriculture and production for export rather than subsistence have a number of important implications for migration and urban growth. Roberts (1978: 90) suggests that the expansion of capitalist agriculture "can take the form of small farms worked mainly by the family, with the aid of high levels of mechanization and of seasonal labor, or of large-scale agrobusinesses [sic] which may export part or all of their product." Thus, as market opportunities expand, countervailing effects on migration are produced. On the one hand, some farms "increase their requirements for a cheap temporary labor force," contributing to the retention of at least some farm employees on the land (Roberts, 1978: 90-93). On the other hand, areas of capitalist farming characterized by an uneven distribution of the land (or a high degree of land concentration/large holdings), a high level of agricultural mechanization, and a focus on production for export tend to contribute to the redundancy of farm labor. As a result, such areas "'expel' more people than do areas of peasant farming" (Roberts, 1978: 90).

ECONOMIC DIVERSIFICATION AND THE DETERIORATION OF AGRARIAN CLASS RELATIONSHIPS

Another link between market penetration and rural-metropolitan migration is provided by an analysis of the closely related phenomena of "the deterioration of agrarian class relationships" (Douglass, 1983: 49) and "rural economic diversification" (Roberts, 1978: 96-98). Both terms refer to increases in social class and occupation differentiation, and the subsequent changes in patterns of interclass relationships that result from the integration of formerly isolated villages into an expanding national economy. Integral to these processes is the recent appearance of new classes/occupational groups that simply did not exist in significant numbers before market penetration. These include a new, capitalist, tertiary elite composed of craftsmen and other small-scale producers, small traders, rural entrepreneurs, commercial farmers, absentee landowners, traders, moneylenders, and government officials. According to Roberts (1978: 96), "the presence of this process [of rural economic diversification] is one of the most crucial variables affecting the patterns of internal migration. The most successful rural entrepreneurs are those most likely to leave . . . since their activities . . . will have generated the capital and skills to make migration feasible."

While the groups listed above are indicative of the increasing diversification of the rural economy, they are not the only "new classes" to emerge with market penetration. Douglass (1983: 48-49), in particular, refers to the juxtaposition of

> strata facing distinct and often antagonistic "life chances." . . . Primary indicators of this class stratification are tenancy and landlessness. . . . Social stratification has in recent years been followed by a deterioration of agrarian class relationships. Patrons . . . have been able to demand more from and give less in return to their clients from lower strata. . . . For those at the lower end of the social structure—the landless and marginal peasants dependent upon wage labor employment—the deterioration of agrarian class relations accompanied by the filling in of land frontiers has been a major factor behind the more recent turn of migration away from rural-rural movements and toward the metropolis.

In other words, the development of capitalist production generates two "selective" streams of rural out-migration: (1) migration of the poorest strata, and (2) migration of some of the most successful rural entrepreneurs.

PRESENCE OF CENTRALIZED BUREAUCRACIES

A final aspect of the theory of the incorporative drive deals with the institutional incorporation that accompanies market penetration. This form of incorporation is measured by the increasing presence of centralized bureaucracies in rural areas (Douglass, 1983: 48). To the extent that these "central command systems of the state" help to perpetuate patterns of uneven social and spatial development, they also encourage migration (Douglass, 1983).

> The drive towards incorporation brings to . . . rural localities a set of formally organized institutions . . . which are characterized by national standardization, conformity to urban cultural norms and development aims. . . . [I]nstitutional incorporation contains a coherent aim-content and is to some extent an instrument deliberately used by the state to fit out the "lagging" peripheral subcultures for their prescribed roles in the national economy and society [Pearse, 1971: 75].

For example, centralized education facilitates the integration of rural migrants in urban areas, while acculturation processes, in general, break down barriers between town and countryside. Ultimately, institutional incorporation facilitates both the social control of the periphery by the center and the movement of people and ideas between center and periphery (Pearse, 1971: 76).

In sum, a political-economic analysis of migration to primate cities should take into consideration all of the key concepts integral to the notions of "the penetration of capitalism" and "incorporative drive": market penetration and commercialization, economic diversification, deterioration of agrarian class relationships, and the presence of centralized bureaucracies.

DATA AND METHOD

The basic strategy of this article will involve (1) the operationalization of concepts derived from both ecological and political-economic theories of primate city migration using Thai census and related data gathered between 1960 and 1970; (2) the separate regression of measures of migration on, first, the ecological variables and, second, the political-economic variables; and (3) the regression of measures of migration on both sets of independent variables simultaneously in an attempt to assess the relative efficacy of the competing theories.

DEPENDENT VARIABLES

Thai data (NSO, 1972) permit the development of two distinct measures of gross migration out of a given province to Bangkok. First, "long-term migration" is a measure of the proportion of people living in the Bangkok metropolis as of the census date, April 1, 1970, who were born in each of Thailand's other 69 provinces. Second, "recent migration" measures the proportion of people from each province living in Bangkok as of the census who migrated to Bangkok after April 1, 1965.

Goldstein (1972: 14) notes that "both sets of data have all the defects inherent in these types of migration statistics, compounded by the problems associated with census taking in a developing country." In particular, it is important to note that these are not measures of net migration. They in no way account for counterstreams of migrants from Bangkok to each province or for that portion of the migrant population that came to Bangkok but returned to their place of origin (or went elsewhere) prior to the enumeration date. Nor, in the case of recent migration, does the measure account for the possibility of repeated migration by an individual between Bangkok and province of origin during the five-year interval. As a result, these measures underestimate the total amount of migration to the primate city.

Despite these flaws, the data are useful. Goldstein (1972: 14), for example, suggests that "although they give no definitive answers to the role of migration in urban growth, they clearly point to the importance of migration to urbanization." Sternstein (1971: 41) further notes that Thai census data on migration "are considered representative of the general character of migrants and as broadly indicative of the direction of movement though the magnitude is greatly understated." They may therefore be considered conservative estimates of the gross volumes of migration prior to 1970 and between 1965 and 1970.

ECOLOGICAL INDEPENDENT VARIABLES

The ecological theory outlined above suggests a number of working hypotheses regarding the relationship between the ecological complex and primate city migration. It predicts a positive relationship between out-migration and the following variables: overpopulation (P), decline of available space for agriculture (E), labor surplus (O), simple sustenance organization (O), and level of agricultural technology (T). Negative relationships are expected between out-migration and intraprovincial transportation development (T) and distance (E).

My simplest measure of overpopulation or population pressure is provincial density (i.e., total provincial population/area). But, remembering that overpopulation implies the ratio of numbers to jobs available, I also measure provincial unemployment levels (UNEMP). This is usually conceptualized as an aspect of sustenance organization related to labor surplus. I use measures of density and unemployment taken directly from the 1960 Thai census in my analysis of long-term migration. Estimates of density and unemployment in 1965 are used in the regression equations for recent migration. Note that I am careful to regress migration data gathered in 1970 on ecological data gathered in either 1960 or 1965. Ecological theory clearly views migration as a response to demographic and economic conditions. A lagged response is thus implicit in the theory, and I try to capture that temporal relationship in the analysis.

My environmental measure of decline of available space for agriculture (CLOSURE) is taken from Ramsson's (1977) analysis of closing frontiers. Essentially, Ramsson calculated the growth rate from 1937 to 1973 in the ratio of farm land to total land for each province. He then developed projections based on this growth rate of the number of years it would take for the ratio of farmland to total land to equal unity. Low projections indicate a high degree of farm frontier closure. This variable was recoded for ease of interpretability. For purposes of analysis, high values on this variable now indicate a high degree of closure or a lack of available space for farming.

The work of Frisbie and Poston (1978) employed various measures of the division of labor as indicators of level of complexity of sustenance organization. I will follow their lead, but with one important qualification. Like them, I use a standard measure of the degree of division of labor (DIVLAB):

$$\text{DIVLAB} = 1 - \frac{(\Sigma \mid X - \bar{X} \mid)/2}{\Sigma X}$$

where X = number of people in the province employed in each industry—that is, agriculture, mining, manufacturing, and so on. (For a discussion of various possible measures of DIVLAB, including the one employed here, see Gibbs and Poston, 1975). Unlike them, I focus on out-migration from provinces rather than net migration into counties. Thus, where they predict a positive relationship between DIVLAB and migration, I predict the inverse. In other words, since they find that a complex division of labor is associated with high rates of in-migration, I expect on the basis of ecological theory to find that a simple division of labor is associated with high rates of out-migration. Once again, my equation for long-term migration includes a measure of DIVLAB in

1960; my equation for recent migration includes an estimate of DIVLAB in 1965. These variables were logged to normalize their distributions.

The measure of provincial level of agricultural technology (AGTECH) is based on data published in the Thai census of agriculture conducted in 1963 (NSO, 1963). It is an index constructed by standardizing and summing provincial scores on percentage of farms using irrigation systems, mechanical devices, electric motors, tractors, sprayers, and chemical fertilizers. This index corresponds to the factor structure found in a preliminary factor analysis of these variables. As noted above, ecological theory predicts a positive relationship between AGTECH and out-migration because more sophisticated levels of technology should help to create a labor surplus.

The measure of intraprovincial transportation development (TRANTECH) used here is also an index based on standardized, summed scores for each province on measures of vehicles per capita in 1960 and 1970, percentages of the total civilian labor force employed in transportation and communications occupations in 1960 and 1970, and miles of asphalt roads in 1970. Ecological theory predicts that high levels of these factors will reduce the pressure for out-migration by improving accessibility of provincial opportunities. Therefore, a negative relationship between TRANTECH and out-migration is expected.

Finally, distance (DIST) is simply a measure of the linear distance between each provincial capital and the Bangkok metropolis. Since the friction of distance should retard movement, a negative relationship is expected between DIST and out-migration.

POLITICAL-ECONOMIC INDEPENDENT VARIABLES

The political-economic theory also suggests certain working hypotheses. In general, primate city migration should be a function of all of the major aspects of incorporation. Market penetration or the commercialization of agriculture is a complex phenomenon that will be measured in three ways: (1) a measure of the percentage of all farms in the largest size categories (greater than 60 rai) (LARGHOLD) is derived from the 1963 Census of Agriculture. This is an indicator of large-scale agribusiness and/or a high degree of land concentration. It is expected to be positively associated with out-migration. (2) Since large farms tend to be export-oriented, and since the channeling of economic surplus to the center is a major expectation derived from political-economic theories of center-periphery relations (see Walton, 1975), a dummy variable (RICETIN) was created to distinguish provinces which send surpluses of rice and tin to Bangkok (scored 1) from those that do not (scored 0). I chose rice and tin because these are two of the major commodities produced in Thailand for sale in the world market and because southern provinces do not produce a surplus of rice, but they are the only producers of tin in the nation. Thus, the combined measure of RICETIN enables the development of a comprehensive, nationwide indicator of provinces in which primary production is highly commercialized. These provinces are expected to exhibit high out-migration rates. Unpublished data on provinces which ship surplus rice to Bangkok were generously provided by Dennis M. Conley (see Conley and Heady, 1981). Information on tin production by locality in 1970 is published in the *Statistical Yearbook, Thailand* (NSO, 1972: 240). Finally, (3) level of agricultural technology (AGTECH, as operationalized above) may be conceptualized by political-economic theory as an indicator of the commercialization of agrarian production. As noted earlier, the expansion of capitalist agriculture can take the form of small family farms that use high levels of mechanization as a survival strategy (Roberts, 1978: 90). It can also take the form of large holdings that use extensive technological inputs as a labor-saving device. While the former should reduce out-migration, the latter should encourage it. Thus, where ecological theory predicts a positive relationship between AGTECH and migration, political-economic theory would predict a weak positive or, possibly, negative relationship.

Economic diversification is a second major dimension of the theory of incorporative drive. This will be operationalized in two ways. First, since the emergence of new classes of rural entrepreneurs—that is, a sort of new tertiary elite—is integral to the process of diversification, a measure of provincial change in proportions of the labor force engaged in wholesaling, retailing, and financial services (TERELITE) is developed from 1960 and 1970 census data. It is crucial to note that TERELITE is a measure of positional change (Duncan et al., 1961: 162-163) that is computed by subtracting the standardized (Z) score on a variable at time 1 from its standardized score at time 2. This measure is used for a number of reasons. Political-economic theory emphasizes the processual nature of the incorporative drive: Over time, forces emanating from the primate city begin to alter the agrarian structure. The central process is an increase in social class and occupational differentiation. Since my goal is, therefore, to understand a process of change, I should focus whenever possible on the changes revealed by my areal data in time series (Duncan et al., 1961: 160). My interest is not in the presence of tertiary elites in a province at a given point in time, but in the relative increase or decrease in proportions of this occupational group over time. Measures of absolute or proportional change are not appropriate, however, because "it is easier for a change of a given magnitude to occur when the initial observation is small than when it is large" (Duncan et al., 1961: 163). Consequently, I use the measure of positional change because the standardization procedure takes initial level into account. Finally, since the most successful rural entrepreneurs are those most likely to leave a province (Roberts, 1978: 96), political-economic theory expects a relative loss of tertiary elites to be indicative of a major out-migration stream (i.e., theory predicts a negative relationship between TERELITE and primate city migration).

A second measure captures a different dimension of economic diversification—the general degree of differentiation at one point in time rather than the specific change in proportion of a given occupational category. This is the measure of division of labor (DIVLAB) introduced above. Significantly, ecological theory and political-economic theory yield different predictions concerning the relationship between DIVLAB and out-migration. As we have seen, ecological theory predicts a negative association because people are expected to emigrate from provinces with a low DIVLAB score. Political-economic theory, on the other hand, views a cross-sectional measure of the degree of division of labor as an indication of a province's level of economic diversification (i.e., the presence of secondary and tertiary economic activity is implicit in a high DIVLAB score). And the more diverse an area, the more potential migrants (i.e., people with "urban" skills) it possesses (Roberts, 1978: 96).

Closely related to economic diversification is the process of deteriorating agrarian class relationships. Three different aspects of this phenomenon will be measured. The first indicator of deteriorating class relationships is increasing farm tenancy (TENANT). The measure of tenancy used here is a positional change score of provincial tenancy ratios for 1947 and 1973 (Ramsson, 1977). A disproportionate increase in tenancy should indicate either an increase in the number of former owners who have lost their farms or an increase in the number of farms rented to tenants for profit by large landowners or commercial farmers. In either case, it is a function of market penetration that both alters traditional, peasant agrarian structures and sets in motion the forces that encourage the out-migration of people in positions of economic subordination. This process of economic disenfranchisement is also captured by my measure of unemployment rates (UNEMP, see above). Political-economic theory predicts positive associations between primate city migration and both TENANT and UNEMP.

Finally, a positional change score derived from 1960 to 1970 census data that measures relative change in provincial proportions of farm employees (FARMEMP) attempts to measure another aspect of "increasing social stratification" (Douglass, 1983). In the most general case, market penetration usually implies labor redundancy, frequent loss of small holdings, and, as a result, out-migration. However, increasing numbers of farm employees will not be associated with out-migration if wage labor employment is available in a province. As a result of these countervailing tendencies, political-economic theory would predict a weak relationship, positive or negative, between changing proportions of farm employees and primate-city migration.

A final political-economic variable measures institutional incorporation or the presence of centralized bureaucracies. This is a positional change score, based on 1960 and 1970 census data, of the proportion of provincial labor force engaged in the provision of government services (GOVSERV). A positive association is expected between increases in this proportion and out-migration.

Three variables—UNEMP, DIVLAB, and AGTECH—have been conceptualized as *both* ecological and political-economic variables. This should not be particularly surprising. Clearly, no ecologist ignores "the market" and no political-economist ignores certain "ecological pressures." Granted, most ecologists see the market as guided by impersonal competitive forces, voluntarism, and individual choice, while political-economists emphasize the role of interest groups and power in the determination of market processes. Granted, too, that the uniqueness of each theory lies in an emphasis (perhaps overemphasis) on what the other neglects. As Roberts (1978: 101) puts it, "This emphasis on socio-structural factors in migration is not intended to be a substitute for an analysis of the spatial and economic variables that also determine migration . . . . Such an analysis is, however, insufficient to provide an understanding of migration under the rural conditions of most underdeveloped countries." The ultimate implication of all of this overlap and ostensible conceptual confusion may well be that a more balanced analysis of the causes of migration should stress both the variables that each theory shares and the variables that each theory neglects. Therefore, an analysis of each set of variables separately and one of both sets combined follows.

FINDINGS

Table 1 presents a correlation matrix for all variables analyzed. Table 2 presents the results of the regression of two different measures of primate city in-migration on (1) a set of ecological variables (columns 1 and 4), (2) a set of political-economic variables (columns 2 and 5), and (3) a combined set that includes all variables (columns 3 and 6).[1]

ECOLOGICAL VARIABLES ONLY

Considerable support for an ecological explanation of primate city migration is evident in Table 2. Closure, distance, unemployment, and transportation technology (the latter in equation 1 only) are significantly related to measures of migration, and signs for significant variables are all in the predicted direction. In addition, the model explains 45.9% and 35.5% of the variance in long-term and recent migration, respectively.[2] Note also that variables representing each rubric (P, O, E, T) are significant, and that the same general pattern of significance and approximate strength of relationships are found for both measures of migration.

POLITICAL-ECONOMIC VARIABLES ONLY

The political-economic explanation of migration also receives considerable support. Coefficients for LARGHOLD, TERELITE, GOVSERV, and TENANT are both significant and in the predicted direction for both measures of migration. DIVLAB is significantly related to long-term migration but not to recent migration. Both DIVLAB coefficients are positive, however, and this fact, in conjunction with the fact that DIVLAB is significant in a political-economic equation but not in an ecological equation, lends support to a political-economic conceptualization of the meaning of DIVLAB rather than an ecological conceptualization. In addition, the finding of no relationship between FARMEMP and migration, net of the effects of the other

TABLE 1

Zero-Order Correlations, Means, and Standard Deviations (1965 estimates above diagonal)

		1	2	3	4	5	6	7	8	9	10	11	12	13
1.	CLOSURE	-	-.13			+.44	-.38							
2.	DENSITY	-.10	-	-.44	.28	.44	.49	.43	.17	-.10	.37	-.13	.28	.11
3.	DIST	-.24	-.45	-		-.25	-.42							
4.	TRANTECH	-.36	.26	-.13	-	.62	.79							
5.	UNEMP	-.46	.43	-.26	.63	-	.67	.41	.10	-.16	.18	.08	.15	.18
6.	DIVLAB	-.40	.48	-.40	.79	.78	-	.43	.26	-.01	.29	-.04	.48	-.04
7.	AGTECH	-.09	.42	-.44	.25	.47	.44	-						
8.	LARGHOLD	.39	.17	-.41	.29	.15	.25	.27	-					
9.	TERELITE	-.30	-.13	.24	.21	-.17	.03	-.16	-.14	-				
10.	GOVSERV	-.23	.36	-.07	.26	.22	.30	.19	.00	.32	-			
11.	TENANT	.05	-.12	-.00	-.12	.11	-.04	.14	.04	-.34	-.04	-		
12.	FARMEMP	-.14	.30	-.26	.28	.22	.48	.25	.09	.13	.23	-.20	-	
13.	RICETIN	.28	.10	-.17	.01	.13	-.06	.02	.48	-.24	-.17	.06	-.26	-
	Mean	8.7	72.6	361.5	-.00	1.3	-1.3	.33	-3.3	.00	.00	.00	.00	.58
	St. Dev.	3.2	72.1	238.2	4.3	.66	.36	5.1	1.4	.56	.81	.72	.53	.50
	Mean (1965 estimate)		81.5			.89	-1.3							
	St. Dev.		77.0			.39	.34							

TABLE 2

Multiple Regression of Measures of Primate City Migration on Ecological and Political-Economic Variables (reported coefficients are beta weights)

	Long-Term Migration			Recent Migration		
	Ecological Analysis (1)	Political-Economic Analysis (2)	Combined Analysis (3)	Ecological Analysis (4)	Political-Economic Analysis (5)	Combined Analysis (6)
CLOSURE (E)	.224**		.011	.233*		.045
DENSITY (P)	.181		.202*	.194		.219**
DIST (E)	-.312*		-.323*	-.298*		-.309*
TRANTECH (T)	-.331*		-.188	-.282		-.204
UNEMP (O)	.426*	.021	.153	.327*	.081	.175
DIVLAB (O)	.242	.257**	.211	.230	.168	.181
AGTECH (T)	-.053	.019	-.143	-.078	-.025	-.184**
RICETIN		.039	-.042		.023	-.058
LARGHOLD		.185**	.173		.249**	.225**
TERELITE		-.477*	-.297*		-.398*	-.221**
GOVSERV		.308*	.227*		.275*	.193**
TENANT		.247*	.302*		.194**	.258*
FARMEMP		.006	-.067		-.052	-.123
Multiple R	.717	.769	.852	.649	.676	.776
R^2	.515	.592	.727	.422	.456	.602
Adjusted R^2	.459	.530	.663	.355	.373	.508
Increment to R^2:						
Ecol + PolEc			.204*			.153*
PolEc + Ecol			.133*			.135*

*$p \leq .05$; **$p \leq .10$.

political-economic variables, is also consistent with the political-economic model as outlined above. Only RICETIN, AGTECH, and UNEMP have no effect on migration when the other political-economic variables are controlled. Interestingly, the significant relationship found between UNEMP and migration in the ecological equation disappears in the political-economic equation. This suggests that part of the initial correlation may have been spurious due to shared variance with the political-economic variables. Finally, the political-economic model explains slightly more total variance in both long-term (53%) and recent (37.3%) migration than does the ecological model.

COMBINED ANALYSIS

It has been demonstrated that both sets of variables (ecological versus political-economic) separately explain significant and roughly equivalent portions of the variance in long-term and recent migration out of Thai provinces to Bangkok. Columns 3 and 6 in Table 2 present the results of an equation which includes both sets of variables simultaneously. Remember that the present conceptualization cites some overlap between the theories. That is, there are four uniquely ecological variables and six uniquely political-economic variables, but there are also three variables "shared" by both theories (UNEMP, DIVLAB, AGTECH). Thus, the combined equation may be interpreted as (1) a control for the effect of the uniquely political-economic variables on the ecological model, or (2) a control for the effect of the uniquely ecological variables on the political-economic model.

Some basic patterns are immediately evident. First, the increments to adjusted R^2 are substantial and significant regardless of which set of variables is considered controls. The full equations explain 66.3% and 50.8% of the variance in long-term and recent migration, respectively. And although the coefficients for many variables have decreased in magnitude and some specific patterns of significance have changed (i.e., CLOSURE, TRANTECH, and UNEMP become insignificant while AGTECH becomes significant [in equation 6]), for both equations two uniquely ecological variables remain significant (DENSITY and DIST), one shared variable is significant in one equation (AGTECH), and four political-economic variables remain significant in both equations (LARGHOLD, TERELITE, GOVSERV, and TENANT).

To reiterate the most crucial general points: For each dependent variable, a combined equation represents a significant improvement in explanatory power over either set of variables taken alone; and as patterns of significance for individual coefficients and increments to adjusted R^2 also indicate, neither set "washes out" the importance of the other.

Additional specific points of relevance may be noted by focusing on the controlling procedures. For example, if we view the political-economic variables as controls, we find that the effects of CLOSURE, TRANTECH, and UNEMP are reduced to insignificance. Apparently, their initial effects were due to their correlations with the political-economic variables. On the other hand, the coefficients for DENSITY and DIST increase in the combined equation. This suggests that these variables do not, in general, share overlapping portions of the explained variance in migration with the political-economic variables: The variance they account for is unique. In fact, the political-economic variables actually suppressed some of the importance of these two ecological factors and, with controls, their significance is clarified.

On the other hand, if we view the unique ecological factors as controls, we find that measures of both market penetration (LARGHOLD, TERELITE, and TENANT) and institutional incorporation (GOVSERV) remain significant. Although coefficients are reduced slightly for LARGHOLD and substantially for TERELITE and GOVSERV, they are actually increased for TENANT, the single best indicator of the deterioration of agrarian class relationships (Douglass, 1983).

Also noteworthy is the appearance of a significant negative relationship between AGTECH and recent migration. A negative relationship was predicted by political-economic theory, but this relationship is significant only when both sets of unique variables are included as controls. In other words, some combination of ecological and political-economic variables suppresses the effect of AGTECH on migration, and its direct effect is only revealed when all other factors are controlled.

DISCUSSION

Overall, these analyses suggest that primate city migration is primarily a function of density, distance, market penetration, and institutional incorporation. Substantive findings imply that two major streams of migration exist. One stream, indicated by findings on density, large holdings, and tenancy, is a probable result of displacements from agriculture due to economic expansion and concomitant lack of peripheral job opportunities. The other stream, indicated by the finding for tertiary elites, is a result of the frequently mentioned selectivity process that draws people possessing "urban" skills to the metropolis.

Theoretical findings require careful consideration. For example, the argument could be made that, on balance, the reported results suggest that the political-economic theory is superior to the ecological theory in explanatory power. Political-economic theory does explain more variance in migration. Also, in those cases in which the two theories predict opposite results (i.e., DIVLAB and AGTECH), findings support the political-economic predictions. Finally, in the combined equations, the effects of several initially significant ecological variables wash out, but this is not the case for political-economic variables.

On the other hand, two crucial ecological variables increase in importance in the combined equations and ecological factors do add a significant increment to adjusted R^2 over and above the political-economic variables. Clearly, an ecological analysis may well be insufficient, but it is certainly not irrelevant.

In fact, a number of observations can be made to suggest the fundamental, albeit rarely perceived, theoretical complementarity of ecological and political-economic points of view. In a sense, proponents of the two arguments talk about the same phenomena but with different vocabularies. To be specific, the theory of the incorporative drive may be interpreted as a political-economic contribution to the traditionally ecological literature on city-hinterland relationships.

Urban ecological theory has long been concerned with the influence of the metropolis on its hinterland. This research tradition dates back at least to the work of Gras (1922), and has been augmented by the efforts of McKenzie (1933), Bogue (1949), Hawley (1959), Vance and Smith (1954), and Duncan et al. (1960). In this view, the metropolis is defined in terms of its functions. Its main purpose is to exert an organizing influence upon the economic and social structures of the communities in its hinterland (Vance and Smith, 1954: 114). A spatial division of labor exists between metropolis and hinterland (or zone of influence) characterized simultaneously by metropolitan dominance and functional interdependence between differentiated parts. As Gras (1922: 186) puts it, "A metropolitan economy is the organization of producers and consumers mutually dependent for goods and services, wherein their wants are supplied by a system of exchange concentrated in the large city, which is the focus of local trade and the center through which normal economic relations are established and maintained." Ultimately, the metropolitan organization and centralization is the most efficient means of providing a large quantity, high quality, and wide variety of goods and services to the maximum number of people possible (Gras, 1922).

This ecological interpretation of city-hinterland relationships is closely related to the geographical concepts of central place theory and location theory, and these, in turn, are based on principles of classical economics. The principles of minimum cost and median location within the context of an impersonal, self-regulating market govern the process of metropolitanization and define the efficiency of the metropolis as an organization. Metropolitanization is, therefore, a type of "ecological expansion" (Hawley, 1950; Kasarda, 1972), through which a multiregional territory is brought under a single organization, integrated and administered from the urban center (Hawley, 1971: 310-311).

Ostensibly, the political-economic theory of the function of cities stands in sharp contrast to the ecological theory. The political-economic view suggests that the city within the capitalist world economy is governed by the laws of capital accumulation. The specific goal of cities is to increase productivity and stem the tendency for rates of profit to fall by creating conditions favorable to production; that is, spatially concentrating the means of production in order to reduce the time and cost of the circulation of capital (see Harvey, 1973; Lojkine, 1976; Castells, 1977; Walton, 1976).

The latter is little more than a Marxist restatement of central place theory: Central location within a capitalist economic system is a means of encouraging efficient production by minimizing cost and maximizing profit. The incorporative drive to expand markets and bring more and more territory under central control is, to a point, synonymous with ecological expansion. It is simply another term to describe the development of an organizational relationship between a dominant city and a subordinate hinterland.

One crucial factor does, however, distinguish ecological theory from political-economic. The former clearly emphasizes community-level stratification resulting from the spatial division of labor: One community is dominant, others are subordinate. The latter, however, emphasizes a group level of stratification that eschews the operation of impersonal mechanisms and "invisible hands" in defining the organizational relationships between a city and its hinterland. Instead, political-economic theory explicitly incorporates the notions of class conflict and class interests in its analysis. Ecological processes of population growth and technological change may set the parameters within which class and market interests must operate, but it is the pursuit of those interests that directly determines which of many possible outcomes will result. In the case of primate city migration, for example, population pressure and an uneven spatial distribution of economic opportunities may set the stage for migration, but the actual patterns of migration will also be shaped by the policies and decisions of entrepreneurs, bureaucrats, and the state.

The conclusion thus appears to be, not that one theory may be judged superior to the other, but that the two are complimentary. Any analysis of primate city migration must take both ecological and political-economic factors into account precisely because both contribute unique and essential influences to the process.

NOTES

1. When independent variables (IVs) show substantial correlations with each other, multiple regression coefficients may be misleading. Since any other IVs have been partialled from the relationship of each IV with Y, if any two IVs have redundant associations with Y, neither may show a significant unique effect. This can be so even when the set of IVs together is quite important (Cohen and Cohen, 1975: 115-117). As in most analyses of data on geographic areas or political entities, many of my IVs are moderately correlated. This is true both within each theoretically based set and between sets. Thus, in interpreting results, one must keep in mind that the IVs used here lay claim to overlapping portions of the Y variance. The situation is complicated when some IVs have lower reliability than others. In the present case, one can reasonably argue that the measures of most political-economic variables are less reliable than the measures of most ecological variables (e.g., DENSITY, DIST, UNEMP). This unreliability in the political-economic variables is likely to result in an exaggeration of the partialled effects of the remaining IVs (Cohen and Cohen, 1975: 372).

2. Adjusted R^2 is reported here (rather than R^2) because R^2 tends to be inflated by the combination of a small sample size and a large number of independent variables. To avoid this positive bias, the adjusted R^2 presents a more conservative estimate of the variance explained by adjusting for the number of cases and independent variables in the equation (see Nie et al., 1975: 358; Cohen and Cohen, 1975: 106-107). R^2 is reported in Table 2.

REFERENCES

AMIN, S. (1974) "Introduction," pp. 65-124 in S. Amin (ed.) Modern Migrations in Western Africa. London: Oxford Univ. Press.

BEIER, G. J. (1976) Can Third World Cities Cope? Population Bulletin 31. Washington, DC: Population Reference Bureau.
BOGUE, D. (1949) The Structure of the Metropolitan Community. Ann Arbor: Univ. of Michigan Press.
BURAWOY, M. (1976) "The functions and reproduction of migrant labor: comparative material from Southern Africa and the United States." Amer. J. of Sociology 81: 1050-1087.
CASTELLS, M. (1977) The Urban Question. London: Edward Arnold.
COHEN, J. and P. COHEN (1975) Applied Multiple Regression/ Correlation Analysis for the Behavioral Sciences. New York: John Wiley.
CONLEY, D. M. and E. O. HEADY (1981) "The interregional impacts of improved truck transportation on farm income from rice in Thailand." J. of Developing Areas 15: 549-560.
DAVIS, K. (1965) "The urbanization of the human population." Scientific Amer. 231: 40-53.
DOUGLASS, M. (1983) "The incorporative drive: central plains migrants in the Bangkok metropolis." Comparative Urban Research 10, 1: 46-67.
DUNCAN, O. D. (1959) "Human ecology and population studies," pp. 678-716 in P. M. Hauser and O. D. Duncan (eds.) The Study of Population. Chicago: Univ. of Chicago Press.
———and L. F. SCHNORE (1959) "Cultural, behavioral, and ecological perspectives on the study of social organization." Amer. J. of Sociology 65: 132-146.
DUNCAN, O. D., R. P. CUZZORT, and B. DUNCAN (1961) Statistical Geography. New York: Free Press.
DUNCAN, O. D., W. R. SCOTT, S. LIEBERSON, B. DUNCAN, and H. H. WINSBOROUGH (1960) Metropolis and Region. Baltimore: Johns Hopkins Univ. Press.
ELIZAGA, J. C. (1972) "Internal migration: an overview." Int. Migration Rev. 6: 121-146.
FIREY, W. (1945) "Sentiment and symbolism as ecological variables." Amer. Soc. Rev. 10: 140-148.
FRISBIE, W. P. and D. L. POSTON (1975) "Components of sustenance organization and non-metropolitan population change: a human ecological investigation." Amer. Soc. Rev. 40: 773-784.
———(1978) "Sustenance differentiation and population redistribution." Social Forces 57: 42-56.
GIBBS, J. P. and W. T. MARTIN (1959) "Toward a theoretical system of human ecology." Pacific Soc. Rev. 2: 29-36.
GIBBS, J. P. and D. L. POSTON (1975) "The division of labor: conceptualization and related measures." Social Forces 53: 468-476.
GOLDSTEIN, S. (1969) "Urban growth in Thailand, 1947-1967." J. of Social Sciences, Faculty of Pol. Sci., Chulalongkorn University 6: 100-118.
———(1972) The Demography of Bangkok: A Case Study of Differentials Between Big City and Rural Populations. Research Report 7. Institute of Population Studies, Chulalongkorn University.
———(1973) "Interrelations between migration and fertility in Thailand." Demography 10: 225-241.
———and P. PITAKTEPSOMBATI (1974) Migration and Urban Gowth in Thailand. Paper 14. Institute of Population Studies, Chulalongkorn University.

GRAS, N.S.B. (1922) An Introduction to Economic History. New York: Harper & Row.
HARVEY, D. (1973) Social Justice and the City. Baltimore: Johns Hopkins Univ. Press.
HAUSER, P. M. (1963) "The social, economic, and technological problems of rapid urbanization," pp. 199-217 in B. F. Hoselitz and W. E. Moore (eds.) Industrialization and Society. Paris: UNESCO.
HAWLEY, A. H. (1950) Human Ecology: A Theory of Community Structure. New York: Ronald Press.
———(1971) Urban Society: An Ecological Approach. New York: Ronald Press.
———(1981) Urban Society: An Ecological Approach. New York: John Wiley.
HAY, R., Jr. (1977) "Patterns of urbanization and socio-economic development in the Third World: an overview," pp. 71-101 in J. Abu-Lughod and R. Hay, Jr. (eds.) Third World Urbanization. Chicago: Maaroufa Press.
International Labour Office (1965) Report to the Government of Thailand on Internal Migration. Geneva: Author.
KAMMERSCHEN, D. (1969) "Further analysis of overurbanization." Econ. Development and Cultural Change 17: 235-253.
KASARDA, J. D. (1972) "The theory of ecological expansion: an empirical test." Social Forces 51: 165-175.
LENIN, V. I. (1960) Collected Works, Vol. 3: The Development of Capitalism in Russia. Moscow: Foreign Languages Publishing House.
LOJKINE, J. (1976) "Contribution to a Marxist theory of capitalist urbanization," pp. 119-146 in C. G. Pickvance (ed.) Urban Sociology: Critical Essays. London: Tavistock.
MARX, K. (1967) Capital, Vol. 1: A Critical Analysis of Capitalist Production. New York: International Publishers.
McGEE, T. G. (1978) "Rural-urban mobility in South and Southeast Asia: different formulations, different answers," pp. 199-244 in W. H. McNeill and R. S. Adams (eds.) Human Migration: Patterns and Policies. Bloomington: Indiana Univ. Press.
McKENZIE, R. D. (1933) The Metropolitan Community. New York: McGraw-Hill.
NG, R. (1969) "Recent internal population movement in Thailand." Annals of the Association of Amer. Geographers 59: 710-730.
NIE, H. H., C. H. HULL, J. G. JENKINS, K. STEINBRENNER, and D. H. BENT (1975) Statistical Package for the Social Sciences. New York: McGraw-Hill.
National Statistical Office (1963) Census of Agriculture. Bangkok: Author.
———(1972a) Population and Housing Census. Bangkok: Author.
———(1972b) Statistical Yearbook, Thailand. Bangkok: Author.
PEARSE, A. (1971) "Metropolis and peasant: the expansion of the urban-industrial complex and the changing rural structure," pp. 69-80 in T. Shanin (ed.) Peasants and Peasant Societies. Baltimore: Penguin.
Population Division, United Nations Bureau of Social Affairs (1969) "World urbanization trends, 1920-1960," pp. 21-53 in G. Breese (ed.) The City in Newly Developing Countries. Englewood Cliffs, NJ: Prentice-Hall.
PORTES, A. (1978) "Migration and underdevelopment." Politics and Society 8: 1-48.
PRACHUABMOH, V. and P. TIRASAWAT (1974) Internal Migration in Thailand. Paper 7. Institute of Population Studies, Chulalongkorn University.
PRESTON, S. H. (1979) "Urban growth in developing countries: a demographic reappraisal." Population and Development Rev. 5: 195-215.
RAMSSON, R. E. (1977) "Closing frontiers, farmland tenancy, and their relation: a case study of Thailand, 1937-1973." Ph.D. dissertation, University of Illinois at Urbana-Champaign.

ROBERTS, B. (1978) Cities of Peasants: The Political Economy of Urbanization in the Third World. Beverly Hills, CA: Sage.

SCHNORE, L. F. (1958) "Social morphology and human ecology." Amer. J. of Sociology 63: 620-634.

SLY, D. F. (1972) "Migration and the ecological complex." Amer. Soc. Rev. 37: 615-628.

———and J. TAYMAN (1977) "Ecological approach to migration re-examined." Amer. Soc. Rev. 42: 783-795.

SOVANI, N. V. (1964) "An analysis of over-urbanization." Econ. Development and Cultural Change 12: 113-122.

STERNSTEIN, L. (1971) "A first study of migration in the greater Bangkok metropolitan area." Pacific Viewpoint 12: 41-67.

———(1974) "Migration to and from Bangkok." Annals of the Association of Amer. Geographers 64: 138-147.

———(1976) "Migration and development in Thailand." Geographical Rev. 66: 401-419.

TEXTOR, R. B. (1961) From Peasant to Pedicab Driver. New Haven, CT: Yale Univ. Press.

TURNER, J. C. (1969) "Uncontrolled urban settlement problems and policies," pp. 507-534 in G. Breese (ed.) The City in Newly Developing Countries. Englewood Cliffs, NJ: Prentice-Hall.

VANCE, R. B. and S. SMITH (SUTKER) (1954) "Metropolitan dominance and integration," pp. 114-134 in R. B. Vance and N. J. Demerath (eds.) The Urban South. Chapel Hill: Univ. of North Carolina Press.

WALTON, J. (1975) "Internal colonialism: problems of definition and measurement," pp. 29-50 in W. A. Cornelius and F. M. Trueblood (eds.) Urbanization and Inequality. Beverly Hills, CA: Sage.

———(1976) "Political economy of world urban systems: directions for comparative research," pp. 301-313 in J. Walton and L. H. Masotti (eds.) The City in Comparative Perspective. New York: Sage-Halstead.

WILBUR, G. L. (1982) "Sustenance organization and migration in Taiwan." Presented at the annual meeting of the Population Association of America.

Bruce London is Associate Professor of Sociology at Florida Atlantic University. His research interests focus on urban sociology in general and Third World urbanization in particular. His book entitled Gentrification, Displacement, and Neighborhood Revitalization *(with J. Palen) was published by State University of New York Press in 1984. Other articles on Thailand have recently appeared in* Social Forces *and* Sociological Quarterly.

HOMELESSNESS IN THE POSTINDUSTRIAL CITY
Views from London and Philadelphia

CAROLYN TEICH ADAMS
Temple University

While the twin problems of homelessness and squatting are usually associated with the cities of the Third World, this article examines them in the context of Western postindustrial metropolises. It argues that the growing numbers of homeless and squatters in the United States and Europe reflect not simply the current economic situation, but rather the longer-term changes in economic and demographic structure that have accompanied the transition of such cities from industrial to postindustrial centers. A critical factor contributing to the problem has been shrinkage in the private rental sector, which must be given priority by housing policymakers.

The massive unemployment and cutbacks in government programs in the early 1980s produced a highly publicized increase in the number of "street people" in America's largest cities—a problem that remains with us at mid-decade. During the winter months each year the news media focus on the plight of destitute men and women who spend their nights on sidewalk gratings and in cardboard boxes. In cities across the United States, municipal governments, churches, and other charitable agencies have established emergency shelters to house and feed the homeless. But while the haunting images of these unfortunate people have captured the attention of the media and their audiences, a serious longer-term problem in urban housing markets has been neglected.

That problem is the maladjustment of inner-city housing markets to the new economic and demographic realities of aging urban areas, and it is occurring not only in the United States but in Western Europe as well.

AUTHOR'S NOTE: *I would like to acknowledge Keith Hoggart of King's College, University of London, for his helpful criticisms and suggestions.*

URBAN AFFAIRS QUARTERLY, Vol. 21 No. 4, June 1986 527-549

The term "maladjustment" is more accurate than "shortage" because in many places the number of existing units is theoretically large enough to house the urban population. Yet many households cannot find housing that is both affordable and suitable for their needs. At the same time, large numbers of housing units stand vacant, awaiting demolition or renovation. The presence of empty housing in cities where large numbers of families and individuals need shelter is an invitation to squatting, and that is precisely what has taken place.

In some of northern Europe's largest cities the squatting movement is now a decade old and thriving, its three centers being London, Amsterdam, and West Berlin. These three cities have not only seen scores of housing units seized while they were unoccupied, but they also have well-organized associations to assist squatter families, to publicize the plight of the homeless, and to lobby for better housing programs. While it is not so widespread in the United States, squatting has been reported in New York, Philadelphia, Newark, and San Francisco. The National People's Action, a coalition of neighborhood associations, churches, and unions, sponsored "reclaim America" conferences in five American cities in 1982, at which they held workshops to instruct neighborhood activists on the tactics of successful squatting.

Squatting and homelessness are phenomena which we associate with the cities of the Third World, where resources are too limited to supply decent shelter for everyone, while at the same time meeting other basic needs. But recent experiences in Western Europe and North America show that even some of the most affluent cities of the world contain homeless people who are desperate enough to break the law by seizing empty housing, and then to resist eviction by legal authorities.

How do we explain the failure of urban housing markets to supply enough decent, affordable housing for low-income residents? In Third World cities the generally accepted answer is the extraordinarily rapid growth of urban populations in recent decades, placing intolerable burdens on urban housing stocks. But that explanation cannot account for the incidence of homelessness in postindustrial cities, many of which have lost population in the last two decades. Why, then, with population pressure substantially relieved, do post industrial cities still have difficulty providing housing that meets minimum standards at a price that is affordable by low-income households?

My purpose in this article is to address that question, using recent experiences in both the United States and Great Britain to explore the problem itself and the responses by local government. Having done so, I will briefly consider some directions for local housing policy in the United States.

My argument is that too often policymakers see homelessness exclusively as a demand problem; in other words, they attribute homelessness to people's inability to pay for housing. That explanation is partially correct, but it is too simple an analysis. Homelessness cannot be understood purely as a product of inadequate incomes, or indeed of any combination of personal characteristics of homeless people including alcoholism, drug abuse, or family breakups. Equally important is the supply side of the equation—that is, the lack of appropriately sized and affordable units. It is the dramatic shrinkage in the supply of low-cost housing, more than a sudden and steep decline in people's ability to pay for housing, that accounts for the increasing incidence of homelessness in postindustrial cities. Rather than being a product of economic recessions or government cutbacks, homelessness is the result of long-term structural changes in postindustrial environments.

WHO ARE THE HOMELESS?

Local governments' responses to homelessness have been strongly influenced by traditional views of the kind of person who ends up on the street. There is considerable sociological literature on the homeless, most of it portraying them as older male derelicts, unattached to any family or community, usually alcoholics or drug abusers—in short, skid row residents (Bahr, 1970). This stereotype of the homeless individual as a socially marginal vagrant was reinforced by the recent appearance in many large cities of chronically mentally ill persons who had been released from public institutions to wander the streets. Recent accounts of homelessness in America, including an exhaustive federal report of May 1984 (U.S. Department of HUD, 1984), attribute the problem chiefly to personal crises in the lives of homeless individuals—evictions, family breakups, illnesses, or addictions—and depict the condition as a transient one, to be addressed by emergency services.[1]

Necessary as they are to meet an immediate need, emergency shelters and soup kitchens are not the answer to the problem of homelessness. The people for whom emergency services are designed, the street people, represent only a tiny fraction of the homeless. A far larger proportion is made up of the so-called new homeless, persons who have lost their housing and are simply unable to find any affordable alternatives. The new homeless are often younger than the traditional skid row population, more are female, and even families are now counted among them. "At no time since the Great Depression have the homeless poor represented so broad a cross-section of American society as they do today" (Hombs and Snyder, 1982).

Current estimates of the total number of homeless persons in American cities range from 300,000 to 3 million, depending on the source (U.S. Department of HUD, 1984). The welfare cuts imposed since 1980 have surely exacerbated the problem, as did the recession of the early 1980s. But they did not create it. Long before these events, urban housing markets began losing their capacity to filter low-cost housing downward to the poor. That filtering process, which was reasonably effective in supplying low-rent housing to the immigrants of earlier periods, no longer works in the postindustrial city. Why not? The answer is related to economic changes common to most aging industrial cities.

CAUSES OF THE PROBLEM

Homelessness in the big cities of Europe and America is a product of their transition from industrial centers to postindustrial service cities. The economic and demographic shifts which have marked that transition have distorted the filtering mechanism which historically allocated housing units to various socioeconomic groups according to their ability to pay. At the low end of the housing chain, many of the older units that might otherwise have served the new homeless have disappeared from the housing stock. Over time their value diminished to the point that it became economically feasible to buy, demolish, and replace them with other uses.

What forces have led to this maladjustment in urban housing markets? First, there is the dramatic transformation of urban economies from a manufacturing to a service base. The factors driving that change are too well documented to require any elaboration here. What is important for our purposes is the change in the allocation of urban space which has accompanied the economic shift. The service city, specializing in communication and information and increasingly embedded in the international economy, requires a different physical plant than was required by manufacturing centers. Urban redevelopment programs have led to the demolition of low-rent housing and its replacement by higher-order uses: offices, retail complexes, and luxury high-rise apartments. As central city employment has shifted toward the services, especially finance, distribution, educational, and professional services, white-collar workers have moved into what were formerly blue-collar neighborhoods, buying and renovating houses. This gentrification of whole districts has further eroded the supply of low-cost housing. In the process of this transformation substantial numbers of older units have been withdrawn from the market to be held vacant while they await demolition or renovation. One shelter provider in Philadelphia put it succinctly: "We turn away single-parent families every day who are being 'relocated' so that Philadelphia can be 'redeveloped.' We find ourselves asking for whom the city is being redeveloped" (U.S. Congress, 1982).

The second big contributor to maladjustment in the housing market is the changing demography of inner cities. At the same time that cheaper units have disappeared from the market, a rising share of the cities' population is now composed of new household types: childless couples, elderly people living alone, young singles living independently of their families, and the single-parent families resulting from rising divorce rates. These smaller urban households typically have limited incomes and need modestly priced shelter.

The key to the problem of homelessness in America's inner cities lies in the deterioration of the private rental sector. As one-person and female-headed households have become more numerous in the cities, they have also come to dominate the rental stock. From 1970 to 1980, the proportion of all rental units in the central cities of the United States that were occupied by traditional two-parent families declined dramatically, from 47% to 29%, apparently because inflation and federal tax policies made homeownership irresistable to those who could afford it (U.S. Bureau of the Census, 1982). At the same time, the proportion of the central city rental stock occupied by female-headed households rose from 16% to 23%, and the proportion occupied by singles rose from 23% to 40%. The median income of central city renters dropped during the 1970s from 60% of the income of homeowners in 1970 to only 50% in 1980 (U.S. Bureau of the Census, 1982). Clearly, these shifts suggest that a kind of "creaming" has taken place in which the more affluent households have left the urban rental sector while the less affluent have remained dependent on rented accommodations (U.S. Comptroller General, 1979; Gonder and Gordon, 1979; Sternlieb and Hughes, 1981).

Meanwhile, a substantial number of rented units were being removed from the stock through decay and eventual demolition. The significance of this loss is apparent from Table 1, which compares the number of rental units destroyed with those constructed in the central cities of 60 metropolitan areas during the mid-1970s, along with similar information for 10 specific cities. The total number of rental units demolished over a 3-year period in all 60 cities was one and a half times greater than the number constructed, suggesting a nationwide contraction of the urban rental market. But since national figures do not adequately

TABLE 1
Changes Over a 3-Year Period in the Rental Housing Stock of Selected Central Cities

	Old Units Removed		New Units Built	
	Number	Median gross rent	Number	Median gross rent
ALL 60 CITIES	322,700		203,300	
SPECIFIC CITIES:				
Boston (1974-77)	6,300	$141	2,600	$212
Chicago (1975-78)	33,700	145	4,300	253
Cleveland (1976-79)	6,900	124	500	185
Detroit (1974-77)	13,600	109	2,800	131
New York (1976-79)	92,400	160	27,800	258
Newark (1974-77)	7,200	141	1,200	213
Philadelphia (1975-78)	8,900	115	3,000	302
St. Louis (1976-79)	7,900	103	400	130
San Francisco (1975-78)	5,900	82	2,600	281
Washington,D.C.(1974-77)	6,100	126	1,500	294

SOURCES: U.S. Bureau of the Census (1978, 1979, 1980, 1981, 1982, 1983).
NOTE: The information presented in this table comes from the Annual Housing Survey conducted by the U.S. Census Bureau, which surveys one-third of its total sample of 60 SMSAs each year, so that the complete cycle takes three years. Thus, the figures above represent three different 3-year periods: For some cities it was 1974-1977; for others it was 1975-1978; while for still others it was 1976-1979.

portray the impact of this trend on particular cities, the table also includes information on 10 cities that were among the hardest hit by this national housing trend. Of the 41 cities that sustained net losses in their rental stock over this period, the largest losses occurred in the aging industrial centers of the Northeast and Midwest. As the table shows, the ratio of losses to gains was as high as 14 to 1 in Cleveland, 8 to 1 in Chicago, and 6 to 1 in Newark. Predictably, the new units were renting at prices significantly higher than the units that had been removed.

Admittedly, the 1970s brought an increase in the number of rental units created through conversion of nonresidential properties and subdivision of large residential units into smaller ones. In fact this "nonnew" construction actually exceeded new construction in the period of 1973-1978 (Downs, 1983). But it did not prevent vacancy rates in the urban rental sector from dropping well below the 5% that is usually considered the minimum needed to maintain mobility in the housing market.

The consequence of these massive losses is an urban housing shortage in the United States that is far worse than most of us recognize. Table 2 shows the substantial gap that existed in 1980 between the number of units needed by the lowest-income renters and the number of affordable units available to them. Nor is government housing assistance the answer; in 1980, only about 16% of renters in poverty were living in subsidized units (Dolbeare, 1985). A 1984 survey of 66 American cities reported an average waiting period of 20 months for rental housing assistance. The available supply of modestly priced rental housing fell so far short of the demand that 61% of the cities had closed their waiting lists to households seeking assistance. Even when rent subsidies were available, the survey found that over 25% of the recipients could not use them because of the shortage of units (U.S. Conference of Mayors, 1984).

To sum up, the plight of America's "new homeless" is not merely a function of the economic dislocations occurring during the early 1980s. Poverty is hardly a new phenomenon in American cities. What is new is the gradual disappearance of the lowest rung of the housing ladder, as postwar manufacturing centers have been recycled into postindustrial service cities. To a great extent our inner-city housing crisis can be explained by structural changes that are common to virtually all postindustrial cities.

A comparison of our recent experience with that of Western European cities reveals that homelessness has reached critical levels there too.

TABLE 2
Low-Income Renter Households, Compared with Affordable* Rental Units, U.S., 1980

	Income Levels		
	Under $5,000	$5,000- $6,999	$7,000- $9,999
Number of households	6,346	2,882	3,862
Number of affordable units available	2,703	2,351	5,526
Difference between need and supply	-3,643	-531	+1,664

SOURCE: Dolbeare (1985).
*"Affordable" defined as costing no more than 25% of household income.

London is one of the best examples. In London, more than in any other city in Europe, housing has been at the top of the political agenda for the last several decades, with elections won or lost on housing issues. London's squatter movement is older, larger and better organized than any other city's. Furthermore, the London case is useful in illuminating the relationships between government housing programs and homelessness. Britain provides more public housing per capita than any other Western government, and yet this elaborate and well-financed public housing system has not prevented homelessness in the British capital.

THE LONDON CASE

The story of London's population shifts over the last three decades will be familiar to anyone who knows the trends in the old industrial cities of the Northeastern and Midwestern United States. Like Boston and Chicago, Greater London has lost population since the 1950s at an accelerating rate. The most dramatic shrinkage has occurred in inner London, which by 1981 had lost one-quarter of its 1961 population.

So steady was the decline in population in the 1960s and early 1970s that housing planners for Greater London declared confidently in 1978 that "the housing situation has been tranformed over the last decade. Previously there were thousands more families than there were homes available for them. . . . But that picture has changed. . . . The housing shortage, at least in absolute terms, has almost disappeared" (GLC, 1978: 2). The trouble with that optimistic prediction was that it focused too narrowly on absolute declines in population rather than on the changing composition of London's population, especially the shift to smaller households.[2]

Many of these smaller households live involuntarily in shared housing arrangements, while constantly seeking their own quarters. A survey taken in 1978, the same year that planners pronounced the problem solved, estimated that London contained a total of 45,000 "concealed" family households made up of either single parents or married couples, plus an additional 303,000 "concealed" one-person households. Even if only one-quarter of these households really needed separate living quarters, that would constitute a pent-up demand for 87,000 housing units (Lansley et al., 1981: 10). As in the United States, a large proportion of the new smaller households—particularly the elderly and single-parent families—find themselves at the low end of the economic ladder, and therefore able to afford only low-cost rental units of moderate to small size. Consider, for example, that nearly one in four women in London heads a household. Their housing difficulties are closely tied to the fact that half the women working full-time in London in the early 1980s were earning less than $175 per week (only 15% of London's male workers earned that little) (GLC, 1982).

In virtually every important respect, London's postwar economic history parallels that of America's older manufacturing centers. Between 1961 and 1976, about 600,000 manufacturing jobs disappeared from London, so that now manufacturing is an even less important part of London's economy than it is for Britain as a whole (GLC, 1980). Meanwhile, as manufacturing jobs were lost, service jobs multiplied rapidly in London, mainly for office workers. The extraordinary office-building boom that began in the 1950s has never abated, despite the government's attempts between 1965 and 1974 to try to steer new office construction away from London's congested center.

London's status as a global city has also meant increasing competition for housing space from hotels and other types of accommodations for business visitors and tourists, company-owned executive apartments, housing for foreign diplomats, and the restaurants, shops, and cultural attractions which cater to visitors. The conflict over the Covent

Garden renewal project in the early 1970s is just one highly visible example of the way in which commercial expansion in London has displaced low-income residents.

Beginning in the mid-1960s, the influx of the professional class was most pronounced in districts containing nineteenth-century Georgian and Victorian houses, built originally for the middle classes but later handed down to less well-to-do tenants (for example, parts of the boroughs of Camden, Islington, Hammersmith, and Lambeth). Since then the gentrification of inner London has proceeded rapidly, withdrawing significant amounts of the city's older housing from the market (Hamnett and Williams, 1980).

In addition to promoting urban renewal projects which have demolished a good many low-rent units, government in Britain has contributed to the rise in urban homelessness by regulatory policies which have systematically discouraged investment in private rental properties, chiefly rent control and rules constraining landlords from removing sitting tenants from their properties. These measures were designed, of course, to protect tenants in private rentals, who constitute the least well-off of all London residents. (Both homeowners and tenants of public housing in Britain have higher average incomes than private renters.) But the well-documented impact of these policies has been to discourage investment in rental housing and to encourage owners of rental housing to sell to owner-occupiers or to convert to nonresidential uses (Milner-Holland Committee, 1965; Greve, 1965; Nevitt, 1965; Stafford, 1978; Whitehead et al., 1985). One of the most popular forms of conversion has been to short-term rentals offered to visitors at weekly rates—a type of housing that falls outside the regulations applied to long-term rental property. One estimate in 1977 put the total number of such short-term rentals in London at 100,000 (Eversley, 1977). Table 3 shows that from the early 1960s to the late 1970s, the private rental sector in London shrank by half, victim of both government policies which discouraged investors and macroeconomic trends that were reshaping London as a postindustrial service city.

But what about London's vast stock of public housing? Can we not assume that public housing has substituted for private rental housing, absorbing the displaced private tenants into municipal units? Table 3 shows that at the same time that private landlords have been discouraged in London, government building programs have created a huge stock of public housing. Stimulated by the acute postwar housing shortage, the campaign to build government housing was undertaken

TABLE 3
Tenure Pattern of Households in Greater London, 1961-1978

	1961	1971	1978
Privately-rented	42.4%	34.1%	21.5%
Public housing	18.2	24.9	31.0
Owner-occupied	36.3	40.3	45.0

SOURCE: Office of Population Censuses and Survey (1961, 1976, 1978).

most vigorously in inner London, which had the oldest housing in the London region, along with the largest concentrations of low-income families. Not surprisingly, many of the deteriorating properties slated for removal after the war were in the private rental sector. As they were torn down, public housing gradually replaced these private units, until some inner boroughs became almost entirely publicly owned. London's postwar experience is particularly instructive because it shows that even a massive commitment to public housing does not necessarily prevent homelessness.

One reason is that, unlike American public housing, British public housing has not catered exclusively or even primarily to the lowest-income group. The tendency of local housing authorities to favor the not-so-poor does not result from a simple desire to screen out "undesirables" (although such practices by project managers have occasionally been observed). In many cases it is a by-product of the guidelines that local authorities follow in allocating their units. Many low-income Londoners, especially the very old and the very young, are single and childless and thus receive few points under the allocation schemes established by London's 32 boroughs. (As the smallest units of local government, the boroughs have responsibility for building and maintaining public housing.) Even more important are the boroughs' residency requirements. To qualify for public housing in most boroughs, applicants must prove five years' residency in London and one or two years' residency in the particular borough taking the application. This requirement automatically excludes recent immigrants, many of whom are among the city's poor. Moreover, London's system of maintaining 32 separate waiting lists for public housing in the separate boroughs hampers geographic mobility in the housing market. Homeless people are reluctant to move across the city to rent a vacant apartment if by doing so they sacrifice the time in residence already accumulated in their present location. The result is that single persons, childless couples, and recent immigrants are among the least eligible for public housing. Not surprisingly, these groups are disproportionately represented among London's homeless.

Yet they are given low priority in the city's shelter programs, too. The landmark legislation passed by Britain's national government in 1977, which placed full responsibility for Britain's homeless persons on local housing authorities, specified particular population groups with "priority need" for housing: families with children, victims of disasters, the elderly, disabled, and pregnant and battered women. Whether or not the 1977 legislation actually made any difference in the numbers of people who applied to be recognized as "homeless" or in the willingness of local authorities to accept responsibility for the homeless is a subject of debate (SHAC, 1981). Figure 1 shows that between 1971 and 1979 there was a fourfold increase in the number of households accepted by London's boroughs as being genuinely "homeless," and therefore deserving of publicly provided accommodations. With the exception of the temporary downturn in the years 1975-1977, the trend was steadily upward during the 1970s. Again, we must remember that these acceptance figures do not indicate how many people claiming to be homeless were turned away by local authorities. For the year 1978-1979, for example, we know that only a little over a third of the households who applied for help in Greater London were actually given accommodations (CIPFA, 1979). Those most likely to be rejected were single persons and childless couples, for whom authorities are legally obliged to provide only "advice and assistance." As one commentator has observed, "To get yourself accepted as 'homeless' you must have children, determination and luck" (Donnison, 1971).

It appears that British authorities, like their American counterparts, tend to classify the single homeless as rootless derelicts who have in some sense chosen to detach themselves from society. And yet the British government's own research has shown that many of London's single homeless come from skilled, semiskilled, and even professional backgrounds (DOE, 1982). This profile has been confirmed by private surveys which show that fully two-thirds of London's homeless actually hold paid employment, mostly in manual labor (Housing Advice Switchboard, 1982; Self Help Housing Research Library, 1984). Like

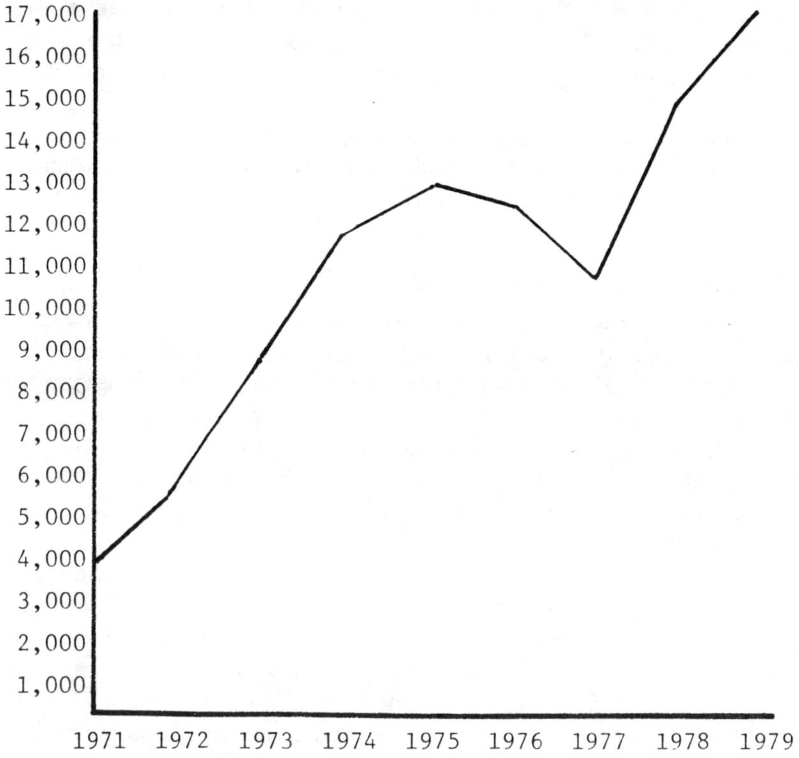

SOURCE: Lansley et al. (1981: 23).

Figure 1: Acceptance of Homeless Households by London Boroughs, 1971-1979

many childless couples, single persons find themselves homeless not so much because they are penniless as because they must rely on the shrinking stock of private rental housing in London. That may explain why singles and childless couples became increasingly active in London's squatter movement in the late 1970s.

SQUATTING AS A RESPONSE TO HOMELESSNESS

A sign of the increasing intractability of the problem and of the desperation felt by local governments in dealing with homelessness is the growing tolerance for illegal squatting. This tolerance is surprising when one considers that the act of squatting represents an assault on a fundamental value of Western liberal government—the defense of property against unlawful seizure. As a British government report put it,

> To the extent that squatters are attempting to buck the system, they clearly call into question the traditional democratic basis of current procedures, founded on the rule of law and its ordered administration [DOE, 1975].

Yet from the very first skirmishes with squatters in the late 1960s, British authorities have used eviction only as a last resort, preferring instead to tighten security on vacant properties, to cut off gas and electricity to squatted properties, and even to render empty units unlivable by ripping up floor boards, knocking out windows, pulling out basins, tubs, and toilets (a practice that squatters label "municipal vandalism"). Alternatively, squatters could be encouraged to move by banning them from the waiting list for public housing or other local housing assistance programs until they vacated the premises.

Yet as the 1970s wore on, the numbers of squatters rose, despite attempts to discourage them. A London Boroughs Association survey published at mid-decade put the number of squatters in London's municipally owned housing at 20,000, with another 5,000 in buildings owned by the regional authority, the Greater London Council (LBA, 1975). And as homelessness figures climbed in the city, housing officials appeared more and more resigned to squatting as one way of relieving the pressure.

In part the squatters' success is attributable to the tactics adopted by the activists who began organizing London's homeless to occupy vacant housing. First, whenever possible the squatters were to be working-class families rather than singles. The London activists knew they were more likely to gain favorable publicity for obviously respectable, hard-working families who "deserved" decent housing.

Second, the squatters preferred to occupy public housing units owned and managed by the local governments instead of seizing privately owned properties. The local authorities, they reasoned, would be less likely than private owners to press for immediate eviction, especially if public sympathy ran in favor of the squatters. Moreover, the local authorities would think twice about an eviction, knowing that they would probably acquire responsibility for rehousing the families made homeless once again.

So successful were the organized squatters in demonstrating their need for housing and gaining public sympathy that individual borough governments began to negotiate with squatter organizations. Typically, in exchange for permission to occupy certain specified vacant buildings owned by the borough, the squatter organization accepted responsibility for the squat. That is, the organization agreed to screen the tenants, to assist them in moving in, to manage the apartments, and to see that the squatters vacated the premises when the borough moved to reclaim the building.

The early squatter organizations demonstrated a degree of discipline over their members that inspired confidence, and so the practice of "licensing" squatters spread across the city. It was not long before a citywide organization, the Family Squatting Advisory Service, was founded to coordinate the activities of the burgeoning squatter movement. Thus, in a few short years the movement had gained *de facto* legitimacy in London. By the mid-1970s about 40% of all squats in London were authorized (DOE, 1975). Some London boroughs even found ways to assist squatters in private properties. In 1975, for example, one borough council bought a group of squatted houses from the private owners, in order to bring their illegal occupants under the umbrella of the borough's licensing system (Pettitt, 1980). The national government began encouraging local officials to make concessions to squatters:

> Local authorities should consider the possibility of licensing responsible groups who apply to occupy empty property which cannot be brought into use in any other way, and who otherwise might feel driven to unlawful squatting [DOE, 1975].

In addition to licensing, some boroughs in London granted squatters the same exemption from local property taxes that was generally given to charitable organizations. A measure of how desperate the situation had become was the decision in 1977 by the Conservative majority in the Greater London Council (GLC) to offer legitimate tenancies to all squatters illegally occupying its dwellings, provided only that they register. This amnesty meant that over 7,000 squatters were either licensed to stay where they were or rehoused in other GLC units. The steady drop since 1975 in the construction of new public housing in London, combined with the delays in renovation of old properties, has meant that borough governments have fewer and fewer alternatives to offer to the homeless. They are forced to tolerate squatting.

THE PHILADELPHIA CASE

For much the same reason, squatting has become increasingly common in American cities as low-rent housing disappears. Philadelphia's squatter movement represents a model that has influenced other American cities. Like London, Philadelphia lost population in the 1960s and 1970s, while at the same time experiencing a dramatic reduction in the size of its average household, from 3.16 in 1960 to 2.66 in 1980. With a population that was becoming progressively older, poorer, and composed of more "nontraditional" households, Philadelphia also suffered a gradual deterioration of its rental market in the 1960s and 1970s. Between 1970 and 1979, the city lost 17,400 dwellings through demolition, most of it occurring in low-income neighborhoods (PCPC, 1980). By 1981, a survey of available rental opportunities in Philadelphia showed that available rentals were almost nonexistent in most low-income sections of the city, and only 11% of the units available throughout the city were affordable to low-income households (defined as households of two or more persons earning up to $8,000 per year) (HADV, 1981). The city's stock of public housing had fallen into an advanced stage of deterioration: Fully 10% of the 23,000 units stood vacant while 14,000 people were listed on the city's waiting list for public housing. Rehabilitation of empty units has moved slowly because of operating deficits and declining federal subsidies.

Philadelphia's homeless population, now numbering between 10,000 and 13,000, reflects the expansion of the problem far beyond skid row. Only 10% to 15% of the city's homeless are on the streets because of chronic mental illness, and only 10% are chronic substance abusers. The vast majority are economically disadvantaged. Almost a third are now families, most of them headed by women (PHMC, 1985).

As in London, squatters were first attracted to vacant units that were government owned rather than privately owned. The chief target was the stock of housing that had been acquired by HUD as a result of mortgage foreclosures in its inner-city homeownership program. While HUD had been able to dispose rather quickly of the better units, those in the worst repair and the most blighted neighborhoods were simply boarded up and left empty for years at a time.

In spring 1977 a community organizer working in one of the poorest sections of the city founded the North Philadelphia Block Development Corporation and began placing homeless families in vacant HUD-owned houses. The group screened applicants in order to exclude alcoholics, drug addicts, and others who were considered to be poor risks as homeowners. All of the group's squatters were required by the organizer to sign leases agreeing to maintain the newly acquired properties at minimum legal standards. In return, these "walk-in homesteaders" had the support of an organization which had evoked a great deal of public sympathy and support, much of it from neighbors who saw the spreading abandonment as a threat to their own properties. By the end of 1977, the organization had placed 200 families in HUD-owned houses. After this initial thrust, squatting subsided for a time, but was revived in 1979, this time with support from the Philadelphia branch of ACORN, a national network of grass-roots community organizers. ACORN focused its campaign on the city's Gift Property Program, through which homesteaders acquired vacant properties for free, in exchange for an agreement to rehabilitate them. This homesteading program had a poor record of matching abandoned houses owned by the city with the hundreds of families on its waiting list. ACORN succeeded in mobilizing several dozen families in the summer of 1979 to begin moving into city-owned properties while simultaneously pressuring the city council to expand and rationalize the Gift Property Program.

As in London, government authorities in Philadelphia responded with ambivalence to squatting. Despite HUD Secretary Patricia Harris's labeling of the squatters as "no better than shoplifters," HUD appeared willing for a short time in 1977 to negotiate with them. Even the U.S. Housing Commissioner speculated openly that the Philadelphia squatter movement might become a model for a national attack on urban abandonment (Naedele, 1977). A HUD memorandum of July 1977 set forth an agreement whereby HUD would offer legalized, rent-paying tenancies to all of the squatters occupying HUD properties in exchange for a moratorium on further squats. But the agreement soon collapsed, and after several months of sit-ins in HUD's regional office, demonstrations in Washington, and more takeovers, HUD began a campaign to evict all illegal occupants from its houses. This federal stance has remained unchanged to the present, although it has been enforced only intermittently, usually in response to stepped-up squatter activity.

Unlike the federal government, city officials have taken a distinctly conciliatory position, recognizing that they do not have the resources to provide alternative housing for the squatters. With over 14,000 people on the waiting list for the city's public housing in 1977, local officials had no choice but to give tacit approval to the squatters' actions.

It took considerably longer, however, to convince the city that its homesteading program should be used as a major vehicle for sheltering poor, homeless people. As in other cities, Philadelphia's homesteading program had favored middle-income families who were seen as more likely to accomplish the desired rehabilitation of the gift properties. ACORN and other community organizers used well-publicized waves of squatting to pressure city officials into redefining the homesteading effort to make low-income households eligible to acquire properties, and to grant homesteaders a longer time period to bring the properties into compliance with standards. Further, they urged the city to expand the pool of available properties to include privately owned tax delinquent houses as well as government-owned units.

Finally, in May 1982, Philadelphia's city council passed legislation creating a mechanism for deeding abandoned tax delinquent properties over to resident squatters, provided they agree to make any repairs needed to bring the houses up to minimum code standards. In effect, the policy legalized squatting in the hope that squatters would invest enough of their own labor and capital to bring abandoned properties back into the housing stock and onto the property tax rolls. The following year the city-owned gas works reached its first agreement with a local squatter organization to provide fuel services to 300 units illegally occupied by the organization's members.

Some of the successes of Philadelphia squatters were communicated to organizers in other cities through their ACORN affiliates. Squatters and community organizers from Philadelphia visited other cities to explain how it had been done, and by 1982 there were more than 200 ACORN squatters in 13 cities (Borgos, 1986).

HOMELESSNESS AND HOUSING POLICY

The astonishing tolerance shown by public authorities toward squatters in many of Europe's urban centers and more recently in American cities indicates just how serious is the disequilibrium in the housing markets of postindustrial societies. The disappearance of large numbers of low-rent units has occurred at the same time that demographic trends were generating more demand for such units by nontraditional households in the inner city. During this time the main goal of urban renewal has been to eliminate blight and to bolster local tax bases, rather than to provide low-cost housing. Governmental concern about housing supply has focused heavily on the production of homes for the middle-class nuclear family, on the assumption that the filtering mechanism would automatically operate to improve conditions for the worst off in the housing market. But urban housing markets are more compartmentalized than the filtering model would suggest. Movement from the shrinking rental sector into the owner-occupied sector is impossible for many households in a period of high interest rates. And homesteading as an alternate route to homeownership is workable on a large scale only to the extent that it can be combined with susidies for renovating properties.

Faced with the likelihood of continuing demand from renters, especially low-income renters, local housing officials in the United States must give more attention to this sector and must do so with declining levels of federal support. Several courses of action should be pursued simultaneously. First, the stock of urban public housing must be given top priority by both local and national government. If allowed to deteriorate much further, this resource will be irrevocably lost, putting thousands more low-income renters onto the streets of our major cities. Interestingly, public housing may offer one of the few realistic opportunities to enlist the labor of low-income residents in improving their own surroundings, because it would require no capital outlays whatsoever. Tenants could be trained to perform repairs and maintenance and then supplied with the tools and materials needed to do painting, insulation, minor plumbing, and similar tasks in their own buildings. Tenants who assume these responsibilities might be given adjustments in their monthly rents, but presumably the cost to the housing authority would be far lower than the cost of having the repair work done by either full-time city employees or outside contractors. Tenant-managed maintenance and repair programs would be particularly desirable for scattered-site public housing, where the distance between units adds immeasurably to the cost of making repairs.

Second, the rehabilitation programs sponsored by cities should give greater emphasis to preserving single-room occupancy hotels and converting large houses to multiunit dwellings. Some British cities have experimented with converting old houses to "cluster flats," which combine individual bedrooms with shared kitchens, bathrooms, and living areas in order to accommodate single people, both young and old. Such downsizing is not usually advocated by housing and redevelopment officials because it is thought to decrease the value of the converted property and the surrounding area. The conversion of single-family housing to apartments or to single-room occupancy structures is generally seen by neighbors as an undesirable trend. Moreover, federal programs such as Section 8 rental assistance and Section 312 loans have typically excluded single-room occupancy housing as eligible for subsidies. But the changing composition of inner-city populations inevitably calls for more such housing, and the dearth of private investment in low-rent housing means that some responsibility for supplying it must fall to public authorities (Lincoln, 1983; Green, 1982; Paul, 1981).

Third, officials should consider expanding homesteading programs to turn properties over to prospective landlords. This is a controversial suggestion because it involves deeding abandoned tax delinquent properties to private individuals, not for their own shelter but for use as profit-making enterprises. Precedents already exist, however, in the "shopsteading" programs which some cities have established. In these schemes, entrepreneurs who are willing to renovate and open retail shops in abandoned buildings are given the deeds for a nominal sum, and then assisted with low-interest loans. Needless to say, even such inducements could not attract entrepreneurs to areas so blighted that they cannot support retail activity, so the best candidates are isolated cases of abandonment in otherwise-solid areas. Similarly, for an apartment-steading program, the best prospects would be abandoned structures in reasonably stable neighborhoods that would be large enough for the prospective buyer to live in one unit while renting out the rest to tenants. But even absentee landlords should be considered for the program, if they are otherwise qualified. Such an arrangement admittedly runs counter to the rule of most homesteading programs, which require the individual receiving the deed to occupy the house for 3 to 5 years. But considering the urgent need for rental housing in our inner cities, such stipulations must be reassessed.

Finally, especially because federal funds for housing can be expected to continue to decline over the next few years, local planners should give greater emphasis to using the Section 8 rental assistance program to keep existing rental units on the market. When the rental assistance program was inaugurated in the mid-1970s it had two major elements: one which encouraged new construction (or substantial rehabilitation) by guaranteeing developers that they would have steady paying tenants for their new units, and the other which assisted tenants to find and pay for apartments in already existing units. The Reagan administration has moved to limit Section 8 subsidies to existing units only, largely on the basis of cost; it is simply cheaper to subsidize tenants in existing units than in brand new ones. As one of the few federal tools still at their disposal, the existing-use program should be employed strategically by local planners to help stem the deterioration of the rental markets in low-income neighborhoods. In the past HUD has actively discouraged cities from placing subsidized tenants in such neighborhoods, fearing that it reinforced racial and economic segregation in the city. But if rental assistance is to be useful in helping marginal landlords to survive, then cities must use it in precisely those areas.

NOTES

1. One critic of the 1984 federal report on homelessness observed that researchers based their view of homelessness as a transient state on their interviews with shelter operators who reported rapid turnover rates of shelter beds. But the researchers neglected to consider that many shelters impose limits on the amount of time an individual can stay in the shelter (Kim Hopper's testimony in U.S. Department of HUD, 1984: 50-51).

2. While in Britain nationally about one-fifth of all households are one-person households, in London the proportion rose from 25% in 1971 to about 28% in 1980. In some parts of London, the proportion is higher still: 41% in the borough of Westminster and 36% in the borough of Camden, for example (GLC, 1980). The "borough" is the equivalent of the American municipality. Greater London encompasses 32 boroughs as well as a regional government, the Greater London Council, covering the entire metropolitan area.

REFERENCES

BAHR, H. [ed.] (1970) Disaffiliated Man: Essays and Bibliography on Skid Row, Vagrancy, and Outsiders. Toronto: Univ. of Toronto Press.

BAXTER, E. and K. HOPPER (1981) Private Lives/Public Spaces: Homeless Adults on the Streets of New York City. New York: Community Services Society.

BORGOS, S. (1986) "Low income homeownership and the ACORN squatters campaign," in Rachel Bratt et al. (eds.) Critical Perspectives on Housing. Philadelphia: Temple Univ. Press.

Chartered Institute of Public Finance and Accountacy (1979) Homelessness Statistics: Actuals, 1978-79. London: CIPFA.

Department of Environment (1975) Consultative Document: Squatting. London: Her Majesty's Stationers Office, August.

———(1977) Better Use of Vacant and Underoccupied Property, Circular 76/77. London: Her Majesty's Stationers Office, July.

———(1982) The Single Homeless. London: Her Majesty's Stationers Office, March.
DOLBEARE, C. (1985) Federal Housing Assistance: Who Needs It? Who Gets It? Washington, DC: National League of Cities.
DONNISON, D. (1971) "No more reports." New Society (May 27): 921-922.
DOWNS, A. (1983) Rental Housing in the 1980s. Washington, DC: Brookings Institution.
EVERSLEY, D. (1977) The ganglion of tourism." London J. 3, 4: 186-211.
GONDER, J. and S. GORDON (1979) Housing Needs of Non-Traditional Households: An Information Bulletin of the Community and Economic Development Task Force of the Urban Consortium. Washington, DC: Department of Housing and Urban Development, Office of Policy Development and Research.
Greater London Council (1978) A New Housing Policy for London: Author.
———(1979) GLC House Condition Survey. London: Author.
———(1980) Social Review of Greater London. London: Author.
———(1982) Economic Status of Women in London. London: Author.
GREEN, C. (1982) Housing Single, Low-Income Individuals. New York: Setting Municipal Priorities Project.
GREVE, J. (1965) Private Landlords in England, Occasional Papers in Social Administration, Number 16. London: Bell Publishers.
———D. PAGE, and S. GREVE (1971) Homelessness in London. London: Chatto & Windus.
HAMNETT, C. and P. WILLIAMS (1980) "Social change in London: a study of gentrification." Urban Affairs Q. 15, 4: 469-487.
HOMBS, M. E. and M. SNYDER [eds.] (1982) Homelessness in America. Washington, DC: Community for Creative Non-Violence.
Housing Advice Switchboard (1982) London's Neglected Homeless. London: Housing Advice Switchboard (March).
Housing Association of the Delaware Valley (1981) Philadelphia's Rental Market: Affordability and Availability. Philadelphia: HADV (May).
KINGHAN, M. (1977) Squatters in London. London: Shelter.
LANSLEY, S., G. RANDALL, and N. RAYNSFORD (1981) The London Report: Prospects and Policies for Housing. London: SHAC (April).
LINCOLN, S. (1983) "Single-room residential hotels must be preserved as low-income housing alternative." J. of Housing (July): 383-386.
London Boroughs Association (1975) Observations on Department of Environment Consultative Document: Squatting. London: LBA (September).
Milner Holland Committee (1965) Report of the Committee on Housing in Greater London, Cmnd. 2605. London: Her Majesty's Stationery Office.
NAEDELE, W. (1977) "Squatters could lead to national policy." Philadelphia Bull. (June 20).
NEVITT, A. A. (1965) Housing, Taxation, and Subsidies. London: Nelson.
Office of Population Censuses and Survey (1961, 1971) Census Reports. London: OPCS.
———(1978) National Housing and Dwelling Survey. London: OPCS.
PAUL, B. (1981) Rehabilitating Residential Hotels. Washington, DC: National Trust for Historic Preservation.
PETTITT, A. (1980) "Outwitting a private landlord in London's east end," in N. Wates (ed.) Squatting: The Real Story. London: Bay Leaf Books.

Philadelphia City Planning Commission (1980) Dwelling Units Demolished City-Wide 1970-1979. Philadelphia: PCPC.

Philadelphia Health Management Corporation (1985) Homelessness in Philadelphia: People, Needs, Services. Philadelphia: PHMC (November).

Self Help Housing Research Library (1984) Squatters: Myths and Realities. London: SHHRL (December).

SHAC (1981) Homelessness: Prospects for the 1980s, Proceedings of a One-Day Conference. London: London Housing Aid Center (May).

STAFFORD, D. C. (1978) The Economics of Housing Policy. London: Croom Helm.

STERNLIEB, G. and J. HUGHES (1981) The Future of Rental Housing. New Brunswick, NJ: Rutgers University Center for Urban Policy Research.

U.S. Bureau of the Census (1978, 1979, 1980, 1981, 1982, 1983) Current Housing Reports, Series H-170. Washington, DC: Government Printing Office.

———(1982) Current Housing Reports, Series H-150-80. Washington, DC: Government Printing Office.

U.S. Comptroller General (1979) Rental Housing: A National Problem That Needs Immediate Action. Washington, DC: General Accounting Office (November 8).

U.S. Conference of Mayors (1984) Housing Needs and Conditions in America's Cities: A Survey of the Nation's Principal Cities. Washington, DC.

U.S. Congress, Banking, Finance and Urban Affairs Committee, Subcommittee on Housing and Community Development (1982) Hearings: Homelessness in America. Washington, DC (December 15).

U.S. Department of Housing and Urban Development, Office of Policy Development and Research (1984) A Report to the Secretary on the Homeless and Emergency Shelters. Washington, DC.

WHITEHEAD, C.M.E., M. HARLOE, and A. BOVAIRDS (1985) "Prospects and strategies for housing in the private rental sector." J. of Social Policy 14, 2: 151-174.

Carolyn Teich Adams is Associate Professor of Urban Studies at Temple University. Her research and teaching interest in urban public policy has focused mainly on housing, land use, and development issues in the cities of Western Europe and the United States, and is reflected in several books and papers, including the award-winning Comparative Public Policy: The Politics of Social Choice in Europe and America *(2nd edition, St. Martin's Press, 1983).*

INFORMAL SOCIAL TIES AND POLITICAL ACTIVITY IN THE METROPOLIS

AVERY M. GUEST
R. S. OROPESA
University of Washington

This article focuses on the question of whether localized friendship patterns in the metropolis have much relationship with individual propensity to take action on localized political issues. Scholars of the classical Chicago School claim a close relationship between the two, whereas more contemporary theorists argue that social ties should have little relationship to political activity; rather, rational investments in community such as home ownerships and child rearing should be the clearly dominant correlates of political activity. Overall, our results do not strongly support either perspective. We suggest and find support for a balance perspective: specifically, that the probability of localized political activity is maximized when the individual has significant friendship ties with both the local and extra-local communities. The overall importance of balanced ties does not vary across types of communities, but we find evidence that highly localized friendships do have varying import in communities with strong, as opposed to weak, community organizational structures.

The influence of urbanization and industrialization on intimate friendship ties is a classic sociological issue. Theorists from Tonnies (1957) to Wirth (1938) have described the disintegration of intimate social ties and their replacement with more impersonal, secondary affiliations. Contemporary research has led to some revisions of this perspective. It appears that urbanization is associated with changes in the nature of

---

AUTHORS' NOTE: *This article has been supported by a grant from NICHD, Community Attachment to Metropolitan Neighborhood and Community Area. Jerald Herting provided useful comments on a previous version of this article. We are grateful to Judith Fiedler for her supervision of the interviewing process and to Gayle Coryell, Mary Beth Dahl, Barrett A. Lee, Barbara Metch, and Lynn Staeheli for their careful processing of the data. Sylvania Danielson was helpful in preparation of the manuscript.*

URBAN AFFAIRS QUARTERLY, Vol. 21 No. 4, June 1986 550-574

intimate ties rather than declines in their number (Fischer, 1976, 1982). Moreover, studies continue to suggest the consequences of friendship ties in urban populations for behaviors ranging from voting decisions to finding jobs (Berelson et al., 1954; Granovetter, 1973).

Stimulated in part by these classical concerns, other studies concentrate on intimacy within various parts or local areas of the metropolis. Here, the major concern is whether developments in high speed transportation (e.g., automobile-oriented freeways) and indirect electronic communications have led to a spatial dispersal of intimate ties, producing what Wellman and Leighton (1979) describe as a "community liberated." Some believe strongly in this trend, which leads Fischer (1976: 120) to characterize the contemporary neighborhood as "fundamentally a secondary impersonal group." Other sociologists, however, claim that the decline in localized friendship ties may be overemphasized, even though some features of neighborhood life such as jobs and services are increasingly dispersed spatially (Hunter, 1975).

Unable to directly resolve the temporal issue in this article, we focus on an important auxiliary problem, the contemporary relevance of localized friendships for understanding other aspects of social behavior. To the degree that localized intimate ties retain at least some importance and have some consequences, we may view them as an important feature of community life in the contemporary metropolis. In this analysis, the relationship of localized friendship ties to political activity in defense of territorial interests is especially emphasized.

We test two major hypotheses that directly relate the geographical dispersion of friendships to localized political activity. One viewpoint, which we identify as the *classical Chicago School approach*, is that localized friendship ties are an important stimulus to political action. The other perspective (called the *balance perspective*) is that localized friendships in themselves are not sufficient to encourage political activity. Rather, social ties outside the community, to the larger metropolitan society, must also be considered as important influences in political activity. While our general results support the second set of arguments, we also find that localized friendships are more important in some social contexts than in others.

This analysis is based on interviews in 1978-1979 with 1642 residents of the Seattle, WA, metropolitan region. Approximately 80 individuals in each of 20 different local areas, scattered throughout the central city and surrounding densely settled suburban ring, were interviewed. Consequently, it is possible to analyze general patterns across the communities and also to conduct a contextual analysis in which variations in the role of friendship ties may be investigated across the 20 different local areas. Most of the analysis explains and tests theories that attempt to account for the general relationship of localized friendship ties to political activity. In the final part of the article, we specify how the social context of the community influences the relative importance of local, as opposed to extra-local, ties in encouraging activism.

THEORETICAL-EMPIRICAL BACKGROUND

Concern with the relationship of friendship types to other behaviors in subparts of the metropolis may be traced back to what we call the *primordial view,* embodied in the writings between World Wars I and II of University of Chicago sociologists. Specifically, Robert Park (1925) argued that some parts of the metropolis recreate the complex, intimate social ties which presumably exist in more traditional, villagelike communities. Particularly in areas of residential stability, populations are bound together by these ties so that individuals experience an emotional attachment to one another and their communities. Residents are so integrated into localized social networks that they spontaneously, almost reflexively, participate in political activity to protect localized interests. Moreover, given the extreme importance of localized ties, community residents are highly motivated to maintain them by supporting the needs of local friends. Consistent with this viewpoint, Park (1925: 113) was moved to describe ward politicians in Chicago as "professional neighbors."

Until the mid-1960s, this primordial viewpoint was heavily emphasized in studies of the social bases of bossism and the political organizations found in big cities, especially Chicago (Banfield and Wilson, 1963: 115-117; Gosnell, 1935; Whyte, 1943: 210-252). From this research came the argument that individuals actively support political machines as a consequence of both general informal social ties to other residents of the community and specific affectual ties to political leaders.

In contrast to the primordial perspective, an alternate *interests viewpoint* has emerged. It has developed as a consequence of many recent studies of political activity in local areas which have concluded that various localized investments or interests are important determinants of ("rational") localized political behavior (Cox, 1982; Cox and

McCarthy, 1980). Presumably, advances in transportation and communication reduce the necessary dependence of neighborhood residents on the immediate community for social ties, creating what is sometimes described as a "community of limited liability" (Greer, 1962). In this new type of community, individuals are believed to "rationally" calculate ends which may be obtained by residence in specific territories; political activity is seen as a logical way to achieve desirable goals for the territory. Among the most important investments is home ownership, which encourages residents to be politically active as a means of protecting and enhancing their property. Also, parents may have an interest in the locale because it is a site for the socialization of their children.

Relatively recent studies of political activity and party affiliation within the general society show that friendship ties are frequently important determinants of behavior (Berelson et al., 1954; Smith and Zipp, 1983; Zipp and Smith, 1979). In some cases, friendship ties even outperform traditional social and demographic predictors (presumably tapping interests) as predictors of political behavior (Burstein, 1976). Moreover, an extensive theoretical-empirical literature has developed which argues that social networks, involving both friendships and organizational memberships, are crucial prerequisites for collective political activity (Gamson, 1975; Tilly, 1974; Oberschall, 1973).

On the whole, however, the interests perspective seems to have gained ascendancy at the expense of the primordial view as an explanation of political activity in local areas. For instance, after studying neighborhood-oriented political behavior in Columbus, Ohio, Cox portrays local areas as devoid of intimacy. Neighborhoods are inhabited by "a highly privatized household whose relations to specific others are ones of indifference" (Cox, 1982: 124). Crenson (1983: 300) takes a slightly different position after studying localized political activity in Baltimore. He argues that "communitarian social ties persist even in cities; community has not been lost, only underestimated." However, he believes, "these communitarian social ties are largely unrelated to the public service efforts of neighborhood residents." Even in Chicago, recent studies find little connection between informal localized social ties and membership in local organizations or political activity (Guterbock, 1980; Hunter, 1974). Given these findings, it seems unlikely that localized friendships in themselves will exert a strong positive influence on political activity in most areas of the metropolis.

While it is tempting to proclaim no role for friendships in localized political activity, another perspective is suggested by those who emphasize the contemporary relationship of local areas and their residents to the larger metropolitan society. Agreeing with some criticisms of the classical Chicago school position, Hunter and Suttles (1972: 45) argue that "our folk and sociological representations of the urban community are especially likely to underestimate the role of external organizations and populations in the definition and solidarity of residential groups." By this, they mean that the actions of such societal institutions as big government, corporations, and the media may have pronounced effects on the land use patterns and ways of life in local areas. In fact, even localized groups of neighbors and more formally organized community clubs may expend many of their energies in lobbying and negotiation with such metropolitan agencies as municipal government. From this perspective, then, the local community and its residents are linked into a larger communications network, involving both outside individuals and institutions. As sources of information, these outside ties may be crucial in understanding the ways in which the community deals with its problems.

Specifically, extra-local friendship ties may be crucial for developing an appreciation of which institutions affect the fate of the local community. They may also be important for identifying potential decision makers who may be "lobbied" on issues of concern to local areas. Finally, extra-local ties may be an important source of basic news about events affecting the community, and thus serve as a basis upon which informed lobbying takes place. From the perspective of this study, then, extra-local friendships may be an important source of information about the community, and thus a crucial prerequisite for localized political activity.

One unfortunate implication of this argument is that *only* extra-local ties will be important in stimulating local political activity. While concentrated extra-local ties may have certain stimulating effects, they may also lead by themselves to a feeling of apathy toward the community and its problems. Furthermore, if apathetic, individuals with only extra-local ties may have little *willingness* to gather information which might serve as a basis of political activity.

While there are limits to the role of extra-local friendship ties, we believe, nevertheless, that they may be important in conjunction with local ties. This leads us to what we call the balance perspective, from which comes the argument that a relatively equal division of local and extra-local social ties is crucial to development of political activity. The extra-local ties would have some of the stimulating effects we have suggested, but social ties and interest in the local community through some nearby friendships are also necessary to make the extra-local effects fully operative.

The balance perspective poses some contrast to those who have argued that residents of most communities are *either* locals *or* cosmopolitans (Dye, 1963; Merton, 1957). According to this view, individuals either have ties and interests in the locality or are oriented outside the community. From this perspective (but not from the balance view) "locals" are believed to be most active politically within the community. While evidence is not abundantly available to resolve this conceptual difference, our perspective is supported empirically by some work. For instance, Stamm and Weiss (1984) report that individuals with orientations to both their local communities of residence and also the larger outside community are most likely to be interested in all kinds of newspaper content. This is true regardless of whether comparisons focus on individuals identifying primarily with their residential communities, with outside communities, or with neither.

Some parallel ideas about the importance of balanced social ties are found in the work of Warren and Warren (1975, 1977), who view the aggregate political activity of neighborhoods as a consequence of both internal and external social ties. They believe that communities with primarily internal social ties engage little in outside political activity. In contrast to this article, Warren and Warren study only aggregate patterns, while we are more interested in how individuals respond to friendship patterns. Furthermore, Warren and Warren focus on the importance of all social ties, while we are more concerned with the role of friendships.

While lacking the data to test directly his argument, there are conceptual overlaps between our approach and that of Granovetter (1973). Emphasizing the social importance of "weak ties," Granovetter argues that individuals who only interact among a small circle of friends (in which the individuals primarily know one another) have a relatively provincial outlook. They are immune to the larger social currents and trends of the society and, consequently, have difficulties in obtaining "goods" which require a diverse range of contacts.

In developing his perspective, Granovetter also suggests that individuals with strong ties within a small social network may not be active politically because they are excluded from diverse communications networks which will inform them about various societal issues, upon which they might act. In contrast, individuals with weak ties (i.e., contacts linking into diverse social networks) may be more likely to act politically due to their diverse sources of communications. Clearly, the existence in the metropolis of both localized and nonlocalized social ties is not necessarily indicative of weak as opposed to strong ties, in Granovetter's strict conception of the term. But it seems likely that individuals with both types of ties would more likely be involved with diverse social networks, certainly more so than individuals who have ties only within, and perhaps also in comparison with those having ties only outside the local community.

Although lacking empirical data on actual "weak ties," Granovetter has used his thesis to suggest why Gans (1962) found that residents of Boston's West End were ineffective in mobilizing against urban renewal activity. He contended that the West End population was characterized by tightly organized, localized social networks, and thus lacked the outside ties and information to become effective opponents of renewal. In contrast, Gans attributed the political apathy of the West End to basic attitudes toward the political system which characterize working-class cultures in the United States.

Before turning to the data, it is useful to summarize the three possible arguments about the relationship of localized friendships to political activity. Scholars who advance the interests perspective believe that friendships, regardless of location, will have little relationship to political activity, while social and economic investments will dominate as predictors. Others who advocate the primordial (Chicago School) position argue that localized friendships should be strong positive predictors of localized political activity. Finally, those who maintain the balance view claim that a relatively equal division of local and extra-local friendships may be crucial.

THE SEATTLE STUDY

The 20 different geographic areas in this study, which we describe as "local areas," are equally divided between the political city of Seattle and the densely settled surrounding suburban ring in King County. Identified elsewhere (Guest and Oropesa, 1984), they all have names which are commonly recognized on maps of the metropolitan area, by local quasi-official planning-administrative districts and by the communications media.

Using household directories, a stratified random sample of residences was drawn within each area. A quota of 80 completed interviews was established, and generally filled. Details of sample selection and response rate are presented in Guest and Lee (1983a).

Many of the items in the interview, including the major ones in this article, refer to the local areas as we defined them above. To clarify the reference point, maps of the territories were presented to respondents. As expected, there was not a perfect overlap between the local areas as we defined them and the "parts" of the metropolis with which the respondents identified (in response to other questions from us). However, the degree of overlap was respectable (Guest and Lee, 1983a).

We focus on reponses to the question, "Have you taken any of the following actions in response to problems affecting the area marked on the map?" Interviewees then indicated whether they had ever "personally written a letter to an official or agency," "personally met with or telephoned an official or agency," "consulted a lawyer," "attended a public meeting," "met informally with neighbors to work on solving problems," "participated in a march or demonstration," or "worked through a club or organization to which you belong."

In Table 1, we show the percentages of all respondents who reported various forms of localized activism. Responses range from over 40% who have attended a public meeting or met informally with neighbors to slightly more than 4% who have participated in a march or demonstration. The respondents (of the 1642) averaged 1.83 acts out of a possible 7 maximum. In addition, the items typically show strong intercorrelations; a matrix of gammas among the dichotomized responses showed an average association of .725, with the range between .590 and .814.

While the items are all intercorrelated, we have decided to separate them conceptually into two sets: largely individual or privatized acts and largely collective acts, involving cooperation with others. The first three acts in Table 1 are defined as more *individual* in orientation, and the others are described as more *collective.* While this classification is not perfect, the intercorrelations among various acts within type were generally higher than across type. Furthermore, the specific items within each type related in similar patterns to various other variables.

Friendships are measured in relation to the territories as we defined them. Respondents were asked, "What proportion of your close adult friends live in the area outlined on the map?" and then patterns were

TABLE 1
Percentages of Respondents Who Have Ever Taken Political Action

1.	Personally written a letter to an official or agency (WRTLET)	22.7
2.	Personally met with or telephoned an official or agency (TELFON)	37.0
3.	Consulted a lawyer (LAWYER)	10.2
4.	Attended a public meeting (PUBLIC)	41.4
5.	Met informally with neighbors to work on solving problems (NEGHBR)	41.7
6.	Participated in a march or demonstration (MARCH)	4.2
7.	Worked through a club or organization to which you belong (CLUBWK)	25.8
		Total N = 1642

Exact question: "Have you taken any of the following actions in response to problems affecting the area marked on the map?"

NOTE: Percentages include one missing case, except for item 4, which includes two missing cases.

recorded in five closed-ended categories. We also collected information on the total amount of social contact with friends (regardless of location), but variations have little influence on the relationship between localization of friendships and political action.

BASIC PATTERNS

Table 2 shows the percentages of respondents who have participated in various specific types of localized political activity given various

TABLE 2
Percentages of Respondents Reporting Political Activity and Information Sources by Location of Friends

Type of Action	Friends in Local Area: All of Them	Nearly All	Half	Just a Few	None of Them
1. WRTLET	19.2	22.0	28.7	23.9	16.4
2. TELFON	28.9	37.1	42.3	37.8	31.8
3. LAWYER	5.8	13.7	12.7	10.5	5.1
4. PUBLIC	42.3	47.3	52.4	41.2	28.0
5. NEGHBR	34.6	42.9	54.4	44.0	27.4
6. MARCH	1.9	8.3	4.6	4.0	2.4
7. CLUBWK	21.2	32.7	33.9	25.7	14.9
8. Any Individual Act	38.5	44.9	54.4	45.0	35.7
9. Any Collective Act	53.8	64.4	72.3	59.5	40.5
Type of Information					
10. Neighbors	63.5	77.1	80.5	71.8	49.7
11. Community Groups	26.8	38.0	42.3	33.9	29.2
12. Extra-local Groups	30.8	39.5	53.7	40.9	33.6
13. Church	34.6	32.7	32.2	22.6	10.4
14. Mass Media	92.3	92.2	93.2	88.2	80.4
N	52	205	307	696	336

NOTE: Variables 1 through 7 are identified in Table 1. Variable 8 indicates participation in 1, 2, or 3. Variable 9 indicates participation in 4, 5, 6, or 7.

concentrations of local and extra-local friendship ties. We have also presented the same information for having participated in *any* individual and *any* collective acts. The number of observations in the subsequent tables is 1596, those for which information was available on all the independent and dependent variables.

Regardless of variable, the data show a curvilinear pattern, providing strong support for the balance hypothesis. Equal numbers of local and extra-local friendships are most strongly associated with political activity. Individuals with both types of ties but an imbalance in one direction or the other show less activism. The least active are those with ties almost completely concentrated at *either* the local *or* extra-local level.

At the same time, the relationship of friendships to political activism depends mildly on whether we focus on individual or collective acts. For individual acts, the differences in political activism between those with extreme concentration of local or extra-local ties are quite small. For collective acts, those with the most concentrated local ties are more likely to be active than those with concentrated extra-local ties. This seems reasonable, since localized friendships are more likely to make a "claim" on one's time when physical cooperation with others is involved. Still, the general curvilinear relationships are found for both individual and collective acts.

FRIENDSHIPS VERSUS INTERESTS

From the perspective of those believing in the interests view, two major negative claims might be made about our results. First, the effects of friendships on political activity may be unimportant, relative to the variables emphasized by the interests argument. Second, the effects of the friendships variable may be spurious, due to the interrelations with the interest variables.

To summarize the importance of friendship patterns, we have conducted a multiple classification analysis (MCA), a form of dummy variable regression analysis (Andrews et al., 1973), for the summary indicators of individual and collective political activity. This technique is especially appropriate in situations in which curvilinearity exists in the data. In MCA, eta is a particularly useful statistic, for it is considered a summary measure of the strength of the relationship between the *sets* of friendship and political activity variables. Table 3 presents the results for individual acts, while Table 4 shows the same information for collective acts. In the first column of each table, readers will find the values of eta and the deviations of each friendship category from the grand mean, when no other variables in the analysis are statistically controlled. The deviations, when added to the grand means, show the same degree of political activity for various categories of friendship, as

TABLE 3
Multiple Classification Analysis to Predict Percentage Engaging in Any Individual Political Acts

Variable	Statistical Control (1) None	(2) Investments	(3) Information	N
Friends in Local Area				
All of them	- 6.2	- 1.4	- 3.1	52
Nearly all	0.3	0.6	- 1.5	205
Half	9.8	8.4	4.4	307
Just a few	0.4	- 0.4	0.2	696
None of them	- 8.9	- 7.0	- 3.0	336
Eta or Beta	.121	.099	.050	
Home Ownership				
Renter	-15.8	-12.8		389
Owner,$0-$59,999	- 0.7	- 1.2		480
Owner,$60,000-$79,999	7.1	5.9		553
Owner,over $80,000	14.6	13.2		174
Eta or Beta	.203	.170		
Life Cycle				
Under 45, no kids	-12.4	- 7.0		366
Oldest child under 6	- 0.3	- 0.6		248
Child 6 to 17	6.8	3.3		441
Over 45, no kids	2.9	2.4		541
Eta or Beta	.144	.080		
Information Source				
Neighbors: no	-16.5		-11.3	491
yes	7.3		5.0	1105
Eta or Beta	.221		.152	
Community groups: no	- 6.6		- 4.4	1039
yes	12.3		8.2	557
Eta or Beta	.181		.121	
Extra-local: no	- 9.8		- 7.2	936
yes	13.9		10.2	660
Eta or Beta	.234		.172	
Church: no	- 2.8		- 0.5	1210
yes	8.8		1.7	386
Eta or Beta	.099		.019	
Mass Media: no	-10.7		- 4.9	189
yes	1.4		0.7	1407
Eta or Beta	.079		.036	
Grand Mean	44.6	44.6	44.6	1596
Multiple R-squared (adjusted)		.052	.101	

TABLE 4
Multiple Classification Analysis to Predict Percentage Engaging in Any Collective Political Acts

	Statistical Control			
Variable	(1) None	(2) Investments	(3) Information	N
Friends in Local Area				
All of them	- 4.5	2.7	- 1.2	52
Nearly all	6.0	6.5	2.9	205
Half	13.9	11.5	7.0	307
Just a few	10.9	- 1.0	0.9	696
None of them	-17.9	-14.7	- 9.9	336
Eta or Beta	.213	.178	.114	
Home Ownership				
Renter	-26.8	-21.6		389
Owner,$0-$59,999	- 0.5	- 1.5		480
Owner,$60,000-$79,999	13.9	11.9		553
Owner,over $80,000	16.9	14.8		174
Eta or Beta	.335	.278		
Life Cycle				
Under 45, no kids	-22.1	-12.8		366
Oldest child under 6	- 0.1	- 0.4		248
Child 6 to 17	11.0	5.0		441
Over 45, no kids	5.9	4.8		541
Eta or Beta	.254	.146		
Information Source				
Neighbors: no	-24.2		-16.6	491
yes	10.7		7.4	1105
Eta or Beta	.327		.225	
Community groups: no	-11.0		- 8.1	1039
yes	20.6		15.1	557
Eta or Beta	.306		.225	
Extra-local: no	-10.1		- 5.7	936
yes	14.3		8.1	660
Eta or Beta	.244		.139	
Church: no	- 5.2		-2.1	1210
yes	16.2		6.7	386
Eta or Beta	.186		.077	
Mass Media: no	- 9.2		-0.2	189
yes	1.2		0.0	1407
Eta or Beta	.068		.001	
Grand Mean	58.4	58.4	58.4	1596
Multiple R-squared (adjusted)		.162	.210	

indicated in Table 2 (see rows 8 and 9 of this table). Most important to our concern, the values of eta indicate that the set of friendship variables is more powerful for explaining collective acts, those requiring cooperation with others.

To determine the relative importance of friendships, we have also presented similar MCA regressions in Tables 3 and 4 for two measures of community investment, emphasized by the interest perspective, the degree to which one has economic investment in the community (value of home) and the degree of social investment (stage in the family childbearing cycle). Categories have been established to provide meaningful substantive divisions, and also a relatively equal distribution of cases. The results in the first columns of the two tables are presented again with no statistical control for the importance of other variables.

The etas in Tables 3 and 4 show that the value of home is much more strongly related to the various types of political action than the friendships variable. Increased investment in home is related positively to the probability of political action. Furthermore, the life-cycle variable is related slightly more strongly to the dependent variables then the friendship measure. However, most of the life-cycle differences occur between the young, pre-child-rearing stage and all others. It is also noteworthy that these variables, as the friendship set, are more useful for predicting collective than individual acts.

Given the greater predictive importance of the interest variables, it is possible that the relationship of friendships and political activity is spurious, that individuals with an equal balance of friendships are most active politically because they have the greatest social and economic investments in the community. To determine this, we have indicated in the second column of Tables 3 and 4 the relationship between the localization of friendships and political activity when the effects of the home ownership and life-cycle variables are statistically controlled. The coefficients in the second column for the categories of each variable set indicate the deviations from the grand mean when these controls are introduced. The analogous statistic to eta in the multivariate case is beta, presented below the deviations.

The betas indicate that the overall effects of each variable set, including friendship, are reduced slightly when the other variables are controlled. The greatest reduction occurs for the life-cycle variable. Most of the zero-order differences in political activity by friendship category remain strong. Clearly, the previously reported relationship of friendships to political activity, involving a balanced relationship, must be attributable to variables other than those emphasized by the interests perspective. Further control for differences in metropolitan-level statuses, such as educational attainment and family income, had little role in altering any of these conclusions.

Overall, the data support the conclusion that friendships are important for localized political activity, either in comparison to the influence of interest variables or when the role of the interests variables has been controlled statistically. Reliance on interests as an explanation of localized political activity is valid, but this viewpoint hardly provides a complete understanding.

INFORMATION FLOWS

We have still not answered the question of why individuals with an equal balance of friendships are most likely to act on localized political issues. Our discussion above of the balance hypothesis suggested that the relationship might arise, at least partially, from access to information. Individuals with a spatial dispersion of friendships would be exposed to more informational sources than others; at the same time, some localized social ties would provide a basis for obtaining information and sustaining interest in the fate of the community. We now turn to these questions: first, determining whether individuals with balanced friendships have more informational sources about issues, and then ascertaining whether these informational sources seem to be intervening explanations of the relationships between friendships and political activity.

In our survey, we inquired whether respondents had ever obtained information about local problems from a list of specific sources. We have combined some of these specific institutions to indicate general sources: mass media (newspaper, TV, and radio), church, neighbors, community organization or center, and extra-local governmental institution (councilman, library, or police). Unfortunately, we were not able to differentiate the mass media and churches in terms of their locality. Furthermore, we were not able to link directly the information with specific political issues or acts.

Table 2 indicates that three informational sources show the same curvilinear relationship with friendships as we identified for political activities. Reliance on neighbors, community organizations/centers, and extra-local institutions occur most frequently for those with friendships equally balanced between local and extra-local areas. The probability of using those information sources declines as friendships become more exclusively oriented in one direction.

The differences between those with balanced friendships on one hand and more concentrated friendships on the other seem most pronounced for extra-local governmental sources. For these three informational sources, the curvilinear relationship is least pronounced for use of neighbors as a source. Individuals with highly localized friendships are somewhat more likely to rely on neighbors than those with highly extra-local friendships, but those with balanced friendships still depend the most on neighbors.

The propensities to rely on the media and churches do not show the clear curvilinear patterns with friendship localization. Consistent with previous results, individuals possessing an equal balance of local and extra-local friendships are among those most likely to use these institutions as informational sources. However, individuals with highly concentrated local friendships are also among the most likely to cite these sources. Undoubtedly, many respondents obtain their information from localized media or churches, but the reason for this pattern is not clear.[1]

The curvilinear relationships of the three information sources—neighbors, community organizations/centers, and extra-local institutions—would be important possible explanations for the relationship between friendships and political activity only if they were strong predictors themselves. Using MCA, we have indicated in the first column of Tables 3 and 4 the relationship between use of these information sources and political activity, without statistical controls for any other variables. Regardless of whether eta or the deviations are inspected, the tables indicate that each of these variables is a relatively strong correlate of whether individuals have taken individual or collective political acts.

At the same time, Tables 3 and 4 also indicate that use of the media and churches as information sources have somewhat weaker relationships with the propensity to act politically than use of neighbors, community organizations, or extra-local institutions. Thus, these variables are unlikely to be important in explaining away the relationships between friendships and political activity.

INTRODUCING CONTROLS

A reasonable hypothesis is that the relationship between location of friendships and political activity is primarily due to differential use of informational sources, especially by those with an equal balance of local and extra-local friendships. To evaluate this possibility, we have included the friendship and informational variables together in MCA. The results are reported in the third column of Tables 3 and 4. To the degree that informational sources "explain" the relationship between the localization of friendships and political activity, we should find that the eta and deviations for the friendship variable become close to 0.

The tables show that controls for the information sources clearly reduce the beta value of friendships, compared with the eta value. Furthermore, the deviations become less pronounced. For instance, take the difference between persons with all friends in the community and those with half. Focusing on individual acts, we find that the difference in percentage active decreases from 18.0 to 7.5. For collective acts, the difference declines from 18.4% to 8.2%.

Unfortunately, MCA does not have a well-developed set of statistical tests to determine whether relationships among variables could occur by chance.[2] Thus, we cannot easily determine whether the residual relationship between the friendships variable and political act is statistically significant. One way of approaching this question is to focus on the question of whether the friendship variable adds a statistically significant prediction to variance in political activity, beyond that explained alone by the informational variables. When only the information sources are included as predictors of individual acts, the adjusted multiple R-squared is .101, the same as when the friendships variable is also included as a predictor. When only the information sources are included as predictors of collective acts, the adjusted multiple R-squared is .200, .010 less than when the localization of friendships is also included as a predictor. In the second case, the standard test for the differences in R-squared attributed to the inclusion of additional variables showed that the friendship variable added a statistically significant amount of variance at the .05 level, two-tailed F-test.

In summary, the data for all communities primarily support what we have called the balance hypothesis, in that individuals with a relatively equal division of friendships between the local and extra-local areas are most likely to take political action. Individuals with highly concentrated friendships, either in or outside the local area, are much less active. The only support for the primordial hypothesis is our finding that highly localized friendships are more important than concentrated extra-local friendships in predicting collective acts, presumably requiring coordination among local residents.

Somewhat surprisingly, the low activity of persons with concentrated local friends seems primarily related to their low levels of information about political issues and events in the community. Compared with other community residents, individuals with highly localized friends are even poorly informed by neighbors about local issues. In the modern metropolis, nevertheless, this finding should not be totally unexpected. Typically, local areas lack the complex and deep ties of intimacy which would lead to rapid diffusion of information and, presumably, high politization for those with highly localized friendships.

INTERCOMMUNITY VARIATIONS

Nevertheless, some of the arguments raised from the primordial perspective may be saved. In the modern metropolis, local areas clearly differ in the degree to which social ties exist among residents, and also in the degree to which community associations inform and organize local residents (Greer and Orleans, 1962; Guest and Lee, 1983c; Guest and Oropesa, 1984). In many local areas, community associations maintain strong ongoing formal structures; they serve as permanent "minutemen" to alert community residents to issues which require mass citizen lobbying. Greer and Orleans (1962) refer to these organizations as the "parapolitical structure," because they rarely have official political recognition but serve as a primary means by which residential areas provide input into the larger metropolitan society. In previous analysis of the same data set, Guest and Oropesa (1984) found that areas in the metropolis with strong community clubs are believed to be effectively represented, while dependence on groups of neighbors or public officials for political representation was less related to perceived efficacy.

The presence of instrumental community associations would especially influence individuals with localized friends to engage in collective acts for three reasons. First, individuals with localized friendships are more likely than other residents to belong to localized voluntary associations (Axelrod, 1956; Hunter, 1974). As a result, where these associations are strong, localized friends will especially have the information and social ties to motivate participation in collective acts. Second, politically involved residents communicate the need for activism with their friends (Smith and Zipp, 1983; Zipp and Smith, 1979). Due to their integration into social networks, individuals with localized friendships are highly likely to be influenced by others arguing for collective action. In this sense, individuals with highly localized friends may be mobilized because they are part of a two-step flow of communication, involving the transmission of ideas from opinion leaders to the rest of the population (Weimann, 1982).

Granovetter (1979) suggests another possibility which is consistent with our hypothesis. He argues that collective action is often based on threshold effects. That is, any population may have a wide distribution in the propensity of individuals to engage in collective behavior. Once collective behavior begins, individuals with normally low propensities for involvement will join because others with higher propensities (the instigators) are engaged. While Granovetter provides no systematic discussion of what factors (besides the individual propensities) will induce individuals to engage in collective behavior, we believe that localized friendships may be an important latent factor. Once communities are engaged in collective behavior, strong feelings of social solidarity with the community may induce individuals with localized friendships to join in.

Our sample permits a test of these ideas. Since the respondents are distributed over 20 local areas, we can investigate the relationship of friendship localization to political activity *within* each of the communities. Then, variations in this pattern may be related to differences in community characteristics. To conduct this test, we have divided the 20 communities into three roughly equal groups by their reported levels of dependence on what Greer and Orleans (1962) call the parapolitical structure—community protective associations. In our survey we asked respondents, "Who usually represents you when there is a major problem affecting this area?" Among the possible choices were "community club or neighborhood improvement associations." An analysis of these and other responses is reported elsewhere (Guest and Oropesa, 1984). In reporting the patterns in Table 5, we have combined the two categories for the most localized friendships, due to the relatively small sample sizes.

Table 5 shows the separate probability of individual and collective acts by friendship localization within each of the three types of communities. Inspection of the data shows general support for the hypothesis in regard to collective acts but less support in relationship to individual acts.

Turning first to collective acts, we find the same curvilinear relationship between the localization of friendships and activity for all

TABLE 5

Percentages of Respondents Reporting Localized Political Activity by Community Type and Location of Friends

	Degree of Parapolitical Structure		
I. Individual Acts	strong	intermediate	weak
Proportion of local friends			
all; nearly all	47.8	43.4	39.6
	(90)	(76)	(91)
half	51.6	52.1	58.3
	(93)	(94)	(120)
just a few	43.3	43.1	48.2
	(231)	(216)	(249)
none of them	32.6	37.5	38.2
	(138)	(96)	(102)
all respondents	42.8	43.8	47.2
	(552)	(482)	(562)
II. Collective Acts			
Proportion of Local Friends			
all; nearly all	74.4	59.2	52.7
	(90)	(76)	(91)
half	81.7	71.3	65.8
	(93)	(94)	(120)
just a few	67.5	52.8	57.8
	(231)	(216)	(249)
none of them	41.3	39.6	40.2
	(138)	(96)	(102)
all respondents	64.5	54.8	55.5
	(552)	(482)	(562)

NOTE: Strong parapolitical structure was indicated by at least 45% of the community reporting that they were represented by the community club/neighborhood improvement associations. The highest percentage was 81.5. Intermediate strength included a range of 34.6% to 39%. Weak strength involved percentages of 15 to 30.1. While the categories are not equal in interval, they do capture the major groupings of communities.

three types of communities. Individuals with an equal balance of friendships are most likely to act. The probability of activity declines as friendships become more geographically concentrated. In other words, the patterns for each type of community are similar to those identified for the total sample.[3]

At the same time, the relationship appears to be influenced by the dependence of the community on protective associations. For individuals with highly localized friendships, the probability of collective acts declines regularly with the degree of community organization. At the other extreme, for individuals with highly extra-local friendships, the probability of collective acts varies little with degree of community organization. Thus, in strongly organized communities, individuals with highly localized friendships have a strikingly greater probability of engaging in collective acts than individuals with overwhelmingly extra-local friendships. However, in less organized communities, the differences in these probabilities are somewhat smaller. Furthermore, those with a balance of friendships or only a few friends in the local area are also generally most likely to act in the organized communities, but the differences are less than for individuals with highly localized friendships and greater than for individuals with exclusively extra-local ties.

Turning to individual acts, we find the same curvilinear relationship between friendship localization and political activity for each of the three types of communities. However, there is less evidence of systematic differences by type of community, at least consistent with our hypothesis. Individuals with highly localized friendships are most likely to be active in the organized communities, but the differences are less pronounced than those reported for collective acts. In general, all the other categories of friendship show an *increasing* propensity for political activity as the community becomes less strongly organized. The greatest differences in political activity between those with highly localized and exclusively extra-local friendships do occur in the most organized communities, but the differences are less noticeable than for collective acts.

In the best of all worlds, it would be gratifying if the relationship between friendships and political activity varied in a statistically significant way with degree of community organization. However, standard analysis of variance tests failed to turn up statistically significant interactions for either part of Table 5. While this is disappointing, it is perhaps explainable by the fact that the general relationship between friendships and political activity is the same for all types of community (thus, a strong statistical interaction is unlikely). We have argued primarily that the degree of relationship between friendships and acts should differ by type of community, and the data generally support our hypothesis, especially for collective acts.

SUMMARY AND DISCUSSION

These results do not permit a facile interpretation of the importance of friendship ties in localized parts of the metropolis. Inconsistent with the Chicago School's primordial interpretation of community attachment, localized friendship ties do not necessarily have much relationship to political activity concerning the surrounding community. At the same time, our results suggest that political activity at the local level must be understood as more than just a product of rationalized interests.

Friendships do matter. What appears to be crucial at the local level is a mix of friendships so that individuals have ties with both community and extra-community friends. This mix appears to be especially important because these types of individuals are also more privy than other community residents to information sources which would serve as a basis of political action. In our opinion, these results indicate the complex interaction of community and extra-community worlds. Local ties apparently stimulate an interest in and concern about the community but are not in themselves a sufficient basis for individuals to act politically. When individuals with local ties are also exposed to the events and issues of the larger world, they are most strongly motivated to act. Overall, then, our results suggest the degree to which growing ties of the local community to the larger "mass society" are not necessarily inimical to community attachment and involvement.

At the same time, this study indicates that relatively localized friendships will be disproportionately important predictors of political activity when community organization facilitates internal communication. Where instrumental associations provide an organizing political base for the community, localized friendships are especially important, particularly when we focus on acts requiring cooperation with others. Where these associations are not available to politicize the community, local ties are especially likely to be ineffective in stimulating activism.

While these results allow us to save some aspects of the Chicago School argument, we also believe that they lead us beyond its perspective that communities draw only from their *gemeinschaft* social solidarity to defend their interests. Consistent with the Chicago School perspective, highly localized friendships are an important stimulus to political activity in communities with high rates of informal social interaction. At the same time, we have found that the relatively secularized instrumental association provides a basis upon which "primordial" sentiments lead to action in the community.

Finally, we would caution that our results about the relationship of localized friendships and political activity must be interpreted cautiously. Our findings that highly localized friendships have no overall positive relationship with political activity should not be generalized to argue that localized friendships have no positive correlations with other attitudes and behaviors in relationship to the local community. Indeed, there is abundant evidence to suggest that localized friendships are well correlated with such attributes of individuals as their sentiments toward the locality (Guest and Lee, 1983b) and membership in voluntary associations (Axelrod, 1956). What seems important to us is the demonstration that social ties have somewhat unusual relationships to the propensity of individuals to engage in one important form of political activity.

NOTES

1. Our data permit us to separate media information into two types: from newspapers and from TV-radio. The pattern for newspapers follows that found for most of the information sources, as individuals with an equal balance of ties show the greatest use of it. The use of TV-radio is highly concentrated among individuals with strongly localized friendships.

2. Tests of significance for variables and equations are not emphasized in this analysis because they have not been standardized for use in MCA (Andrews et al., 1973). This problem is particularly serious for determining the statistical significance of variables when their effects have been adjusted or controlled for interrelationships with other variables. The problem is less serious when attempting to assess the statistical significance of bivariate relationships, without controls for other variables. Standard one-way analysis of variance tests showed that all the independent variances in Tables 3 and 4 were statistically significant predictors at the .05 level of the dependent variables, using standard two-tailed F-tests. The explained variances for each multivariate equation in Tables 3 and 4 are statistically significant at conventionally high levels, such as the .05, two-tailed F-test.

3. As pointed out by one reviewer of this article, an alternate line of theorizing is that membership in local voluntary associations cause individuals to develop balanced friendships—that is, a mix of local and extra-local ties. Thus, the relationship between the localization of friendships and political activity would really reflect membership in community associations. However, our data viewed overall do not really support this argument. Consistent with the alternate perspective, those with balanced friendships were most likely to belong to organizations within the local area which were listed as "community club or neighborhood improvement association," or "other political or action-oriented organization." Among organizational members, there was little relationship between friendship location and political activity, as most had undertaken political acts, regardless of friendship patterns. Among the majority of the sample not belonging to these groups, the relationship between the location of friends and political activity was even stronger than in the total sample.

REFERENCES

ANDREWS, F. M., J. N. MORGAN, J. A. SONQUIST, and L. KLEIN (1973) Multiple Classification Analysis. Ann Arbor: Institute for Social Research, University of Michigan.

AXELROD, M. (1956) "Urban structure and social participation." Amer. Soc. Rev. 21 (February): 14-18.

BANFIELD, E. C. and J. Q. WILSON (1963) City Politics. Cambridge, MA: Harvard Univ. Press.

BERELSON, B. R., P. LAZARSFELD, and W. McPHEE (1954) Voting. Chicago: Univ. of Chicago Press.

BURSTEIN, P. (1976) "Social networks and voting: some Israeli data." Social Forces 54 (June): 833-847.

COX, K. R. (1982) "Housing tenure and neighborhood activism." Urban Affairs Q. 18 (September): 107-129.

———and J. McCARTHY (1980) Neighborhood Activism: Contexts, Interests, and Communication. Columbus: Center for Real Estate Education and Research, Ohio State University.

CRENSON, M. A. (1983) Neighborhood Politics. Cambridge, MA: Harvard Univ. Press.

———(1978) "Social networks and political processes in urban neighborhoods." Amer. J. of Pol. Sci. 22 (August): 578-594.

DYE, T. (1963) "The local-cosmopolitan dimension and the study of urban politics." Social Forces 41 (March): 239-246.

FISCHER, C. S. (1982) To Dwell Among Friends. Chicago: Univ. of Chicago Press.

———(1976) The Urban Experience. New York: Harcourt Brace Jovanovich.

GAMSON, W. (1975) The Strategy of Social Protest. Homewood, IL: Dorsey Press.

GANS, H. (1962) The Urban Villagers. New York: Free Press.

GOSNELL, H. (1935) The Negro Politician. Chicago: Univ. of Chicago Press.

GRANOVETTER, M. S. (1978) "Threshold models of collective behavior." Amer. J. of Sociology 83 (May): 1420-1443.

———(1973) "The strength of weak ties." Amer. J. of Sociology 78 (March): 1360-1380.

GREER, S. (1962) The Emerging City: Myth and Realty. New York: Free Press.

———and P. ORLEANS (1962) "The mass society and the parapolitical structure." Amer. Soc. Rev. 27 (October): 634-646.

GUEST, A. M. and B. A. LEE (1983a) "Consensus on locality names within the metropolis." Sociology and Social Research 67 (July): 374-391.

———(1983b) "Sentiment and evaluation as ecological variables." Soc. Perspectives 26 (April): 159-184.

———(1983c) "The social organization of local areas." Urban Affairs Q. 19 (December): 217-240.

GUEST, A. M. and R. S. OROPESA (1984) "Problem-solving strategies of local areas in the metropolis." Amer. Soc. Rev. 49 (December): 828-840.

GUTERBROCK, T. M. (1980) Machine Politics in Transition. Chicago: Univ. of Chicago Press.

HUNTER, A. J. (1975) "The loss of community: an empirical test through replication." Amer. Soc. Rev. 40 (October): 537-552.

———(1974) Symbolic Communities: The Persistence and Change of Chicago Local Communities. Chicago: Univ. of Chicago Press.

———and G. D. SUTTLES (1972) "The expanding community of limited liability," pp. 44-81 in G. D. Suttles (ed.) The Social Construction of Communities. Chicago: Univ. of Chicago Press.

MERTON, R. K. (1957) Social Theory and Social Structure. New York: Free Press.

OBERSCHALL, A. (1973) Social Conflict and Social Movements. Englewood Cliffs, NJ: Prentice-Hall.

PARK, R. E. (1925) "The city: suggestions for the investigation of human behavior in the urban environment," pp. 1-46 in R. E. Park et al. (eds.) The City. Chicago: Univ. of Chicago Press.

SMITH, J. and J. F. ZIPP (1983) "The party official next door: some consequences of friendship for political involvement." J. of Politics 45 (November): 958-978.

STAMM, K. R. and R. J. WEIS (1984) "Community orientations and news interest: a functional analysis." Seattle: University of Washington School of Communications. (unpublished)

TILLY, C. (1974) "Do communities act?" pp. 209-240 in M. P. Effrat (ed.) The Community: Approaches and Applications. New York: Free Press.

WARREN, D. I. and R. B. WARREN (1975) "Six kinds of neighborhoods." Psychology Today 9 (June): 74-80.

WARREN, R. B. and D. I. WARREN (1977) The Neighborhood Organizer's Handbook. Notre Dame, IN: Univ. of Notre Dame Press.

WEIMANN, G. (1982) "The 2-step flow of communication." Amer. Soc. Rev. 47 (December): 764-773.

WELLMAN, B. and B. LEIGHTON (1979) "Networks, neighborhoods, and communities: approaches to the study of the community question." Urban Affairs Q. 14 (March): 363-390.

WHYTE, W. F. (1943) Street Corner Society: The Social Structure of an Italian Slum. Chicago: Univ. of Chicago Press.

WIRTH, L. (1938) "Urbanism as a way of life." Amer. J. of Sociology 44 (July): 3-24.

ZIPP, J. F. and J. SMITH (1979) "The structure of electoral political participation." Amer. J. of Sociology 85 (July): 167-177.

Avery M. Guest is Professor of Sociology, University of Washington. The article in this issue continues past research on the nature of social attachment to local areas in the metropolis. Guest is currently studying U.S. occupational mobility in the late 1800s.

R. S. Oropesa is a Ph.D. candidate in sociology at the University of Washington. His current research focuses on the social bases of neighborhood mobilization, and on the importance of ethnicity and generation in explaining U.S. occupational mobility in the late 1800s.

ATTACHMENTS IN THE NESTED COMMUNITY
Evidence from a Case Study

JEFFREY S. SLOVAK
Rutgers University—Newark

Studies of emotional attachments to local communities in America have not generally included the conceptualization of the nested community offered by Albert Hunter and Gerald Suttles. Thus, most have not addressed the differential degree to which city dwellers forge attachments to different levels of community, or the social processes behind those emotional links. This article attempts to speak to those issues. It is based on surveys conducted in a high-rise apartment development in downtown Newark, New Jersey, a site selected strategically to yield respondents living in a "defended neighborhood" sited at the symbolic heart of a larger "community of limited liability." Using correlation and multiple regression analyses, the article examines the sources of respondents' attachments to each of those levels of the nested community. In the former, attachment is found to be in part a positive function of immersion in local interactional networks (as in other studies) but in larger part a positive reaction to perceived safety in the neighborhood's environs. In the latter, attachment is found to be both a positive carryover of more local attachments and a negative reaction to the conditions of contemporary urban life. Further analysis demonstrates the empirical distinctiveness of these attachments and the processes giving rise to them. The article concludes with a discussion of the implications of these findings for future research on emotional links to nested communities.

Classical urban theorists saw the city as destroyer of tradition and engine of liberation (Wirth, 1938; Simmel, 1905; Smith, 1979). They portrayed the city dweller as one engaged in a broad range of narrow, segmented roles and relationships, and detached from local networks of intense interaction and support. The city was a "world of strangers" (Lofland, 1973) with few sentimental attachments to one another or the larger community. Despite its intuitive appeal, however, contemporary research has shown this picture to be overdrawn. Ethnographies (Gans, 1962; Suttles, 1968) have uncovered community among people and in settings where it was unexpected, and broader surveys (Kasarda and Janowitz 1974; Hunter, 1974, 1975; Fischer, 1982) have generalized that

URBAN AFFAIRS QUARTERLY, Vol. 21 No. 4, June 1986 575-597

beyond inner-city and ethnic neighborhoods. While varying in intensity across persons, attachment to community persists in the contemporary city.

With its empirical "rediscovery," scholars began to refine the concept of community itself. Albert Hunter and Gerald Suttles (1972) made a significant contribution here by formulating from their own and others' (Janowitz, 1967; Greer, 1972) research the notion of the nested community: a four-level structure composed of face-block, defended neighborhood, community of limited liability, and expanded community of limited liability, with every urbanite simultaneously a member of all four. Hailed as a major conceptual advance in the field (Olson, 1982), the nested community has begun to prove its conceptual worth in recent research (Slovak, 1984; Guest and Lee, 1983).

Most extant studies of attachment to community do not specify the nested level of it which they address, so most speak only indirectly to variations in the attachment process across levels. Nonetheless, if the different levels of community are rooted in different social institutions designed to fulfill different life needs, as Hunter and Suttles suggest, then the social bases for attachment to them should vary as well. The aim of this article is to shed some light on this issue of differential attachments. It reports on research conducted in a case study setting, a high-rise apartment building in Newark, New Jersey. By virtue of its design and the services for residents it encompasses, the building approximates a vertical neighborhood in its own right. In this research, it is so treated; the four-level nested community is reduced to a dichotomy, the building is considered a combined face-block/defended neighborhood, and the larger city stands for the two limited liability communities. By proceeding thusly, the analysis allows us to (1) replicate parts of earlier studies (Foley, 1952; Hunter, 1975; Kasarda and Janowitz, 1974) of attachments to the immediate community in a research context not typically examined in such work, (2) identify the degree to which attachments to different levels of community are generated by different variables and hence different social processes, and (3) offer, based on those results, a preliminary model of the overall process of attachment in the nested community.

SETTING, METHODS, AND DATA QUALITY

Hallmark House is a 429-unit, 25-story apartment building in downtown Newark, New Jersey. Built in 1966, the building was planned as a small residential neighborhood, with its first floor devoted to shops and services—a dry cleaner, a beauty salon, a self-service laundry, offices for an attorney and a physician, and a confectionary/restaurant—which draw the bulk of their clientele from residents. The roof, accessible only to residents, holds a common recreation space and a sun deck, both of which offer impressive views of the surrounding region.

Site design and security precautions further reinforce the impression of Hallmark House as a small vertical neighborhood. The building and its grounds fully occupy a small city block in Newark. While exit from the building is possible from three or four places, entry and access to the elevators and, thus, to the residential apartments are limited to the main entrance. This is protected by a buzzer-intercom system and a watchman, and visitors are also visible to a switchboard operator. Hallmark House is not fully self-contained, but protective technology and building design have made it a more controlled setting than most conventional neighborhoods.

Few residents come to Hallmark House to forge community; rather, the primary draw is undoubtedly the combination of reasonable rent and convenient access to the outside world it offers. Hallmark House is a building for persons of lower-middle/middle-class status. Monthly rents for its units (as of 1981) were quite reasonable, ranging from about $300 for studios to $600 for two-bedroom apartments, the largest in the building. With regard to convenience, the building has an optimal location. City Hall, Newark's police headquarters and municipal courts, a federal office building, and the main post office are less than one block from Hallmark House; the downtown shopping district is three blocks distant; the city's major corporations are three to six blocks distant; and various cultural and educational institutions are little farther away. Residents are linked to all these by foot, taxi, or buses which stop at the corner of the Hallmark site. Roughly six blocks from the building lies Newark's Penn Station, offering rail links to New York City (fifteen minutes distant) and other points throughout the Northeast. Less than fifteen minutes away by car lies Newark International Airport and the world.

From all this, the Hallmark House residents would seem a propitious group of subjects for a study of attachments to different levels of the nested community. Others (Lofland, 1973; Merry, 1981) have noted the importance of a sufficient set of amenities and a sufficient degree of access control in a community before its members will forge networks of interaction and common sentiment; Hallmark House has both. At the same time, the building offers access to the outside world and to most of the major amenities and institutions Newark has to offer. The residents of Hallmark House stand squarely at the intersection of the immediate communities of the face-block and defended neighborhood and the larger communities of limited liability.

While observations and informal interviews were conducted for this study, its primary data are derived from the responses of a sample of residents to a self-administered questionnaire disseminated in early 1982. Lack of research resources precluded any more than one mailing of questionnaires to a sample of subjects. At the time of dissemination, 420 apartments in Hallmark House were occupied; surveys were mailed to a randomly selected 150; usable returns were received from 75. While no consensus on acceptable response rates appears in the literature (Bailey, 1982; Miller, 1977; Dillman et al., 1974), this return falls within the expected range for a one-mailing survey. More important, there is reason to believe that this sample, small as it is, is reasonably representative of the resident population. The questionnaire contained items on the race, gender, and type of apartment of each respondent. Comparison of observed distributions on these to the actual (on apartment type) or those estimated by the building's resident manager (on race and sex)[1] revealed no statistically significant disjunctures, as demonstrated in Table 1. Accordingly, it seems reasonable to treat these respondents as a random sample of Hallmark residents and to address the data they offer on attachments to the immediate neighborhood and the larger city.

ATTACHMENT TO THE DEFENDED NEIGHBORHOOD

Most empirical studies of community attachment predate, or are simultaneous with, the development of the nested typology, so the specific level of community to which their findings speak is unclear. Since most reference the "local community" or the "neighborhood," it seems reasonable to apply them to the most personally immediate levels of community in the nest—the face-block and the defended neighborhood.

In their study of the persistence of community attachment in mass society, Kasarda and Janowitz (1974) specified two theories which they labeled "linear development" and "systemic." The former predicts the regular decline of attachment with increases in the size and diversity of

TABLE 1
Sample Adequacy and Response Bias Tests

Test Variables:		In Building No.	In Building % of Total	Surveyed No.	Surveyed % of Total
I. Apartment Type					
	Studio	304	72.3	51	68.0
	One-Bedroom	104	24.8	21	28.0
	Two-Bedroom	12	2.9	3	4.0
		420	100.0	75	100.0
		χ^2 = .770;	d.f.=2; n.s.		
II. Race					
	Black		60.0	48	63.9
	Non-Black		40.0	27	36.1
			100.0	75	100.0
		χ^2 = .500;	d.f.=1; n.s		
III. Gender					
	Female		50.0	41	54.8
	Male		50.0	34	45.2
			100.0	75	100.0
		χ^2 = .653;	d.f.=1; n.s.		

the community of residence. The latter predicts the growth of attachment with immersion in and experience with the social system extant in the community, whatever its structural character. Their analyses provided strong support for the systemic theory and comparatively little for the other. These results were paralleled by Hunter's (1974) findings on community attachments among a sample of Chicagoans. In his study, attachment to the local community was largely a function of a person's local social status, and not his or her general status, which in turn was presumed a function of immersion in the local systems which confer status and worth. These studies converge to suggest that one's degree of social connection to nearby friends, neighbors, and facilities determines one's emotional attachment to the defended neighborhood.

Which kinds of connections are the most critical generators of community attachment? According to Homans (1950), any social system is a set of individuals linked in a web of sentiments, activities, and interactions; no causal direction is or need be implied among these linkages. Foley (1954) applied this perspective to a selected neighborhood in Rochester, New York, to uncover the extent to which these elements were empirically linked. In replicating Foley, Hunter (1975) sought to answer the same question in the same setting 25 years later and thus to identify temporal changes in the social bases of community life. Further, Hunter imposed causal assumptions on Homans's model to specify the relative weights of informal neighboring and common facility use in forging community attachments. In both studies, informal neighboring far outweighed frequent use of neighborhood facilities in generating attachments. In Homansian terms, interaction was far more critical than activity in generating sentiment in the local community system.

Because neighboring occurs in a context, community attachments may have a contextual component worth addressing. Many studies (Schorr, 1963; Caplow et al., 1964; Keller, 1968; Laumann, 1972; Granovetter, 1973) have suggested that intense local neighboring, and thus, indirectly, intense local attachment, approaches the interactional choice of "last resort;" the resourceless are most likely to center their social lives on neighbors. Resources like income, education, and occupational status play a minor role in generating neighboring and attachment in the Hunter and Kasarda and Janowitz efforts, but neither studied less tangible psychological resources in this regard. Fischer (1982) has shown that one of the few differentiators of city dwellers from others, after controlling for social status, is the higher fear of crime among the former. Both Lofland (1973) and Merry (1981) note that fear correlates with a decreased sense of personal efficacy, and Merry ties the latter to withdrawal from neighborly interaction. Newman (1980) offers further confirmation. Neighboring and community attachment may be constrained if both must occur in a context perceived as threatening.

Part of the Hallmark House questionnaire was designed with these arguments in mind. Questions on attachment to the building, informal neighboring, and facility use were included to address the Hunter/Foley argument in a high-rise defended neighborhood. Questions on fear of crime were added to capture the perceived context. Measurement procedures for these were as follows.

ATTACHMENT

Each respondent was asked whether he or she would feel "very sorry," "somewhat sorry," or "not sorry at all" to move out of Hallmark House, were that imperative, with the responses as listed indicating decreasing levels of attachment. This question is virtually identical to that used by Kasarda and Janowitz. Hallmark House residents are relatively attached to their vertical neighborhood: 44.6% would be unhappy to leave, while only 10.8% would welcome a departure.

NEIGHBORING

Foley and Hunter used a six-question index of informal neighboring among their Rochester subjects; that same index was used here, with a reliability level reaching $\alpha = .80$.

FACILITY USE

Each respondent was asked how frequently he or she made use of the services located on the ground floor of Hallmark House. Intercorrelations here varied widely, with the strongest pattern in the data linking use of the self-service laundry, the dry cleaner, and the confectionary. Responses to these items were summed to create an index that reaches a reliability of $\alpha = .61$.

FEAR AND SAFETY

Five questions on crime and fear were included in the questionnaire. Two asked respondents whether crime was decreasing, relatively constant, or increasing (a) in the city and (b) in the area around Hallmark. Two others asked whether respondents felt very, moderately, or not at all safe walking alone in the Hallmark area (a) by day and (b) at night. The fifth tapped satisfaction with building security arrangements. Consistent with findings from other research (Skogan and Maxfield, 1981), most Hallmark residents see crime increasing in the city (76.4%) but remaining constant near the building (a plurality of 47.1%); most feel unsafe (51.4%) walking near Hallmark at night, but very or moderately safe (39.7% and 45.3%, respectively) doing so by day. Most (78.7%) are satisfied with building security. While perceptions of crime in the city do not generally correlate with fears about the building or the neighborhood, the latter are sufficiently related to be combined into an index of perceived safety, with a reliability of $\alpha = .76$.

The panels of Table 2 display findings on the attachment process in Hallmark House. The first compares frequencies of neighboring in Hallmark with comparable findings from the Foley and Hunter efforts. While the rank order of frequencies here is similar to what it was in the Rochester studies,[2] the table nonetheless demonstrates that neighboring of any specific type is uniformly less frequent in Hallmark. For all but fleeting conversational contacts, it is rare on an absolute scale as well.

The second panel compares the correlations among attachment, neighboring, and facility use produced by the two Rochester studies and this one. Since measures of the first and third differ across studies, comparisons like this are risky and merit attention only if the differences they identify are comparatively strong. At the zero-order level, the three studies converge with regard to some of the social bases for attachment to the local community. In all three, informal neighboring and local facility use are positively, if modestly, related; in all three, attachment and facility use are independent. Where something distinctive emerges is in the link between neighboring and attachment: In Rochester, it is moderately strong and positive, while in Hallmark House it is nonexistent. The latter, of course, is a major anomaly.

The introduction of an intervening variable, displayed in the third panel of Table 2, helps explain this apparent anomaly. Recall that Hallmark House is a high-rise complex sited to maximize resident convenience to the facilities of downtown Newark and of the larger New York/New Jersey megalopolis. For the Hallmark resident who seeks to maximize such convenience, high rates of informal neighboring in the building may be more curse than blessing, more an imposition by strangers with whom one shares little than an affirmation of social commonalities. Fischer (1982) has shown that city dwellers have a strong propensity for forging close social relationships with nonkin, nonneighbor acquaintances. That suggests that informal neighboring will attach a city dweller to a defended neighborhood only if opportunities for such neighboring are actively sought in the choice of a residence. Panel three of Table 2 offers evidence to support this line of reasoning by including among the correlates of neighboring, facility use, and attachment those linking each to respondent satisfaction with the sociability potential[3] of the building. In Hallmark, informal neighboring and frequent facility use vary positively, but neither has much to do with attachment to the defended neighborhood. Both, however, make a resident more satisfied with the building as a locus for interaction, and this associates positively with attachment. All things considered, Table 2

TABLE 2
Comparative Sentiments, Activities, and Interactions in Defended Neighborhoods

I. Informal Neighboring

	Comparative Frequencies (% Responding "Often" or "Sometimes")		
	Rochester$_1$ (Foley)	Rochester$_2$ (Hunter)	Hallmark House
o Have informal chats ...	73.9	79.7	66.6
o Exchange favors ...	58.5	56.5	23.0
o Exchange things ...	41.2	51.3	14.7
o Visit informally ...	38.7	47.4	24.0
o Ask for advice on personal matters ...	26.1	30.8	20.3
o Have planned get-togethers ...	17.2	26.0	13.4
N	(446)	(154)	(75)

II. Comparative Correlations (Rochester$_1$/Rochester$_2$/Hallmark)

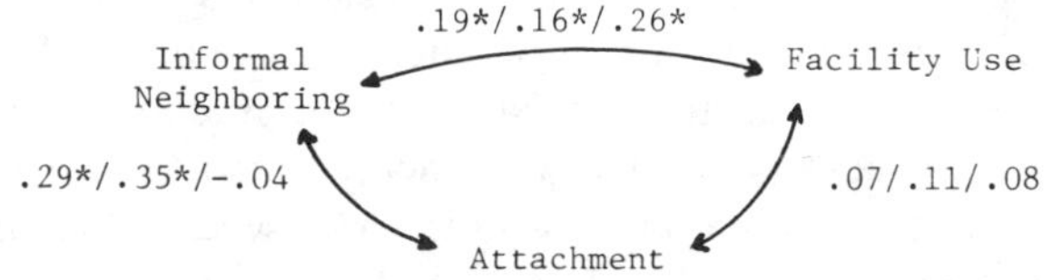

III. Hallmark House: Expanded Schematic

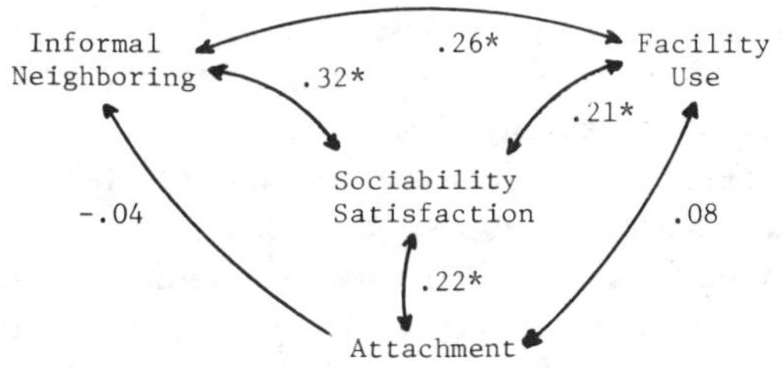

*Significant at $p \leqslant .05$.

suggests that the social bases for attachment in Hallmark House are similar to those identified by Foley and Hunter in Rochester—but only for those who want neighborhood-like sociability in the high-rise context. That is by no means everyone.

What role does perceived security in the immediate neighborhood play in the attachment process? Evidence on this is offered in Table 3 in two path models and their standardized coefficients. That in the upper panel formalizes the argument made above and highlights both the importance of neighboring in attachment formation and the low level of attachment predictability generated by processes endogenous to the neighborhood. The second model, which includes perceived safety as an attachment predictor, shows an exogenous process to be critical. Attachment predictability is tripled with this addition, and yet fear in these data is independent of facility use, neighboring, and sociability satisfaction; none is "conditioned" on fear in the sense suggested by the literature. Rather, a factor exogenous to the neighborhood—its perceived criminological context—is the strongest predictor of community attachment in Hallmark House, while the endogenous process of neighborly interaction makes a secondary, independent contribution to attachment.

Table 3 offers no support for the argument that the resourceless are the most attached to the neighborhood. Rather, the evidence points the other way. To the extent that perceived safety taps the resource of a sense of efficacy, it is the resourceful who are most attached.[4] Among the Hallmark residents, at least, attachment to the defended neighborhood is not the psychological substitute of the desperate, least able to cope with the exigencies of urban life; rather, it is more of an affirmation by the confident of their connections to a secure, worthwhile living environment.

These results offer both replication and extension of earlier work. Replication comes in the assessment of interactions and activities as generators of community sentiments. Allowing for the additional complexity of translating the former into the latter in the high-rise context, these results demonstrate that in Hallmark House, as in Hunter's Rochester neighborhood, informal neighboring is more critical than common facility use in generating community attachment. Extension comes when perceptions of safety in the neighborhood's environs are added to the analysis. While endogenous social processes forge common bonds of sentiment among community members, it is clearly an error to treat the defended neighborhood as isolated from its surroundings and attachment to it as internally generated. Neighborhood context and one's perceived safety in it are as important as—in these data, more important than—those endogenous social processes in building attachment to the defended neighborhood.

TABLE 3
Alternative Models of Attachment

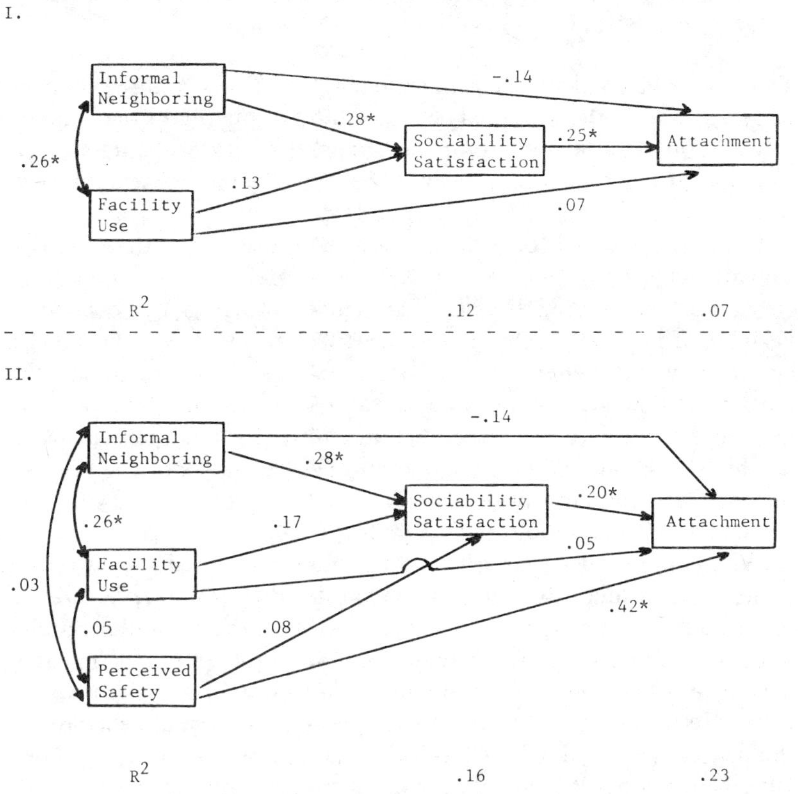

*Significant at $p \leqslant .05$.

ATTACHMENT TO THE COMMUNITY OF LIMITED LIABILITY

According to Janowitz (1967), the community of limited liability is distinct from the block and the neighborhood in terms of both interactions and attachments. It is an entity wherein

> the individual, responding to the general cultural norms, is likely to demand more from his community than he will invest. But more

> significantly, his relation to the community is such—his investment is such—that when the community fails to serve his needs, he will withdraw. Withdrawal implies either departure . . . or merely lack of involvement [Janowitz, 1967: 211-212].

This cost-benefit calculus for attachment is something far different from what operates in the defended neighborhood. It highlights the community of limited liability as a more instrumental entity, with attachments to it the product of forces beyond the scope of the more expressive face-block and defended neighborhood.

Uncovering those forces is the aim of the analysis that follows. Toward that end, the city of Newark is defined as a combined community of limited liability;[5] attachment to it is the dependent variable of interest. In this analysis, we seek to identify (a) whether a community sentiment carryover process exists such that attachment to the defended neighborhood generates attachment to the larger community, and (b) whether interactions and activities not focused in the neighborhood, and adherence to Janowitz's "general cultural norms," produce attachment to the larger city, net of any carryover of sentiments. A word about each is in order.

While empirical research has not to date addressed the carryover issue, it is a plausible notion. Much of the urban revitalization movement is predicated on it. As the process takes hold and neighborhood attachments among the revitalizers are forged, those people may develop a vested interest in the quality of city life and play more involved roles in its economy, polity, and society, becoming more attached to it in the process (Allen, 1980). Theories of balance in psychology (Heider, 1958; Newcomb, 1961) and of cognitive dissonance reduction (Festinger, 1957) would predict this. The strongest counterexample in the literature is the old West End of Boston (Gans, 1962), where intense neighborhood attachment was accompanied by mistrust of and detachment from actors in the larger city. Note, however, that the Italian West Enders were stigmatized in the eyes of other Boston actors, a status not held generally by middle-class persons like the Hallmark residents. The amount of attachment carryover among the latter is not predictable a priori, but it seems likely that some will exist.

Beyond carryover, there are other candidate variables that might predict attachment to the city while having no link to attachment to the defended neighborhood. Homans's (1950) perspective on the social system seems expandable to cover attachment to the larger community.

Local facility use translates, on a citywide scale, into use of urban, and not suburban, facilities for the satisfaction of life needs; similarly, informal neighboring translates into participation in formal organizations in the broader community, for Fischer (1982) has shown that city dwellers forge most of their close personal ties with coworkers and fellow organization members, not kin or neighbors. Janowitz's discussion of instrumental attachment to the community of limited liability suggests that, unlike the case in the defended neighborhood, the former would be a stronger predictor of attachment than the latter.

Janowitz does not specify the general cultural norms operative in forging attachment to a community of limited liability, but the literature suggests that urban alienation deserves special scrutiny in this regard. While there is no empirical basis for believing city dwellers more alienated than others (Fischer, 1973, 1982), general alienation might still constrain the formation of attachments to a community. Seeman (1975) has noted that three of the critical facets of alienation are powerlessness, normlessness, and isolation. The anticipated connection between each and attachment seems self-evident: More of any of the former should result in less of the latter.

The Hallmark House questionnaire was partly designed to test these arguments. It included items to measure city attachment, facility use, participation in formal organizations, interest in politics, and normlessness. Measurement procedures for each were as follows.

ATTACHMENT

This measure comes from a question identical, but for its reference to the city, to that asked about the building. Among the respondents, 28.4% would be happy to leave Newark were departure required, while 23.0% would be unhappy to leave. A comparison with the findings on attachment to the building suggests that the defended neighborhood commands more allegiance than the community of limited liability.

CITY FACILITY USE

Eight questions were used to tap this concept. Each listed a common, everyday activity; for each, respondents noted whether they usually performed it in Newark or some other community. City-user proportions varied widely, but five activities (shopping for groceries, clothing, furniture, and home accessories and going out for dining or entertainment) correlated sufficiently to be combined into an index of city facility use, with reliability of $\alpha = .65$.

ORGANIZATIONAL PARTICIPATION

To measure this, each respondent was asked whether he or she belonged to and had ever been a leader in each of six types of organizations. For purposes of index construction, respondents received for each question a score of 2 for leadership, 1 for membership, and 0 for inactivity. These were summed across organizations to generate one index with reliability of $\alpha = .66$.

NORMLESSNESS

This was operationalized as a seven-question index. The seven include the items of the original anomie scale offered by Srole (1956) and extensively used by others. The index attains reliability of $\alpha = .76$.

POLITICAL INTEREST

Powerlessness is measured indirectly here, by presuming a negative correlation between it and interest in politics and actually questioning the latter. Three survey items, asking respondents their levels of interest in national, state, and local politics, were summed to create an index with reliability of $\alpha = .86$.

Table 4 displays correlations among these variables and thus preliminary evidence on determinants of attachment to the city. Key findings can be summarized in three points. First, although its causal direction is not specifiable, there is evidence of attachment carryover across the two broad levels of community. The relevant correlation is strong, positive, and significant: Those most intensely attached to Hallmark are most intensely attached to the larger city. Second, organizational participation, normlessness, and political interest cluster as anticipated from the literature. Activists are more interested in politics and less anomic than the organizationally detached. While the relevant coefficients are not strong, they are consistent. Note, however, that only one of these correlates well with attachment of either type: The anomic are more, not less, attached to the city. To the extent that this

TABLE 4

City Attachment: Simple Correlations

	City Facility Use	Organizational Participation	Normlessness	Political Interest	Attachment: Hallmark	Attachment: Newark
City Facility Use	1.0	.00	-.05	-.02	-.26*	-.37*
Organizational Participation	---	1.0	-.24*	.38*	.14	.02
Normlessness	---	---	1.0	-.06	.17	.28*
Political Interest	---	---	---	1.0	.07	-.02
Attachment: Hallmark House	---	---	---	---	1.0	.52*
Attachment: Newark	---	---	---	---	---	1.0

*Significant at $p \leq .05$.

index taps perceived personal efficacy, as Nettler (1957) suggests, this finding implies that those least willing or able to deal with life in cost-benefit terms are most likely to forge sentimental attachments to the cost-benefit community. Finally, use of the city is a negative correlate of both types of attachment, but especially of that to the city. Further, it is stronger in this regard than is organizational participation, lending support to Janowitz's notion of instrumentalism and the cost-benefit calculus. The negative direction of this association, of course, is not what Homans's perspective would have led us to anticipate.

Formal tests of these arguments with multiple regression are offered in Table 5, and the tests do little more than reinforce the interpretations offered above. No signs of coefficients are changed by the regression; the only three significant correlates of attachment to the city remain its only significant regression predictors; and the rank order of these coefficients remains what it was for the correlations.[6]

In this as in any case study, context probably affects findings. The fact that Hallmark House lies adjacent to Newark's symbolic center, its City Hall, makes the link between the two levels of community immediately apparent. Comparable data from a neighborhood farther from the central city might reduce the magnitude of attachment overlap observed here. Similarly, serious decay in contemporary Newark probably inflates the negative effect of city facility use on city attachment. To grant this is not, however, to suggest that these findings would disappear in an alternative study site. Few citizens in any urban area can long hold that the fate of their neighborhood is unrelated to that of their city. The play of political and economic events would soon invalidate such a belief. By the same token, central city decline is not unique to Newark; rather, it is a general, albeit less severe, experience throughout the Snowbelt. In this region, the contrast between city and suburban amenities increasingly favors the latter. The citizen who chooses to use, or is constrained to use, city facilities cannot help but be aware of this trend and reflect it in his or her emotional attachments. All things considered, magnitudes of coefficients from this study might change in a comparable effort from another context, but their direction and substantive meaning probably would not.

Attachment to the community of limited liability emerges as a particularly complex emotion. It is, in part, a product of attachment to the defended neighborhood which is, in turn, an affirmation of life in a secure, supportive, immediate environment. In equal part, however, it is a product of disenchantment with the general quality of urban life and

TABLE 5
City Attachment: Regression Results

Independent Variables:	B	$S.E._B$	Beta	T
Attachment: Hallmark	.421	.123	.390	3.433**
City Facility Use	-.117	.051	-.248	-2.263*
Normlessness	.034	.015	.195	2.193*
Political Interest	-.029	.042	-.079	-.683
Organizational Participation	.017	.045	.044	.716

Multiple R = .582; R^2 = .339

*Significant at p ⩽ .05; **significant at p ⩽ .01.

the perceived normlessness of postindustrial society. Unlike its counterpart at the more immediate levels of the nested community, attachment to the broader levels is a two-faced phenomenon.

ATTACHMENT FORMATION IN THE NESTED COMMUNITY

The analyses of the two types of attachment suggest that they are different phenomena, responsive to analytically and empirically distinct determinants. That suggestion deserves a formal test of its own, a test that "plays off" the predictors of neighborhood against those of larger community attachment as determinants of each kind of emotional link. Strong support for the hypothesis of distinctive attachment formation processes at each level of the nested community would come with a discovery that predictors of one type play no role in predicting the other. Such findings might suggest a model of the overall attachment process to guide future empirical research. Conducting such a test by means of multiple regression analysis is the task of what follows.

The analysis of attachment to the community of limited liability found use of city facilities, normlessness, and attachment carryover to be its primary determinants; all are retained for this test. The analysis of attachment to the defended neighborhood found that perceived safety, informal neighboring, and sociability satisfaction played direct or indirect roles in its production. The first is retained here, but length of residence is substituted for the second and third. It is significantly correlated with both (r = .20 and .21, respectively) and its use offers two additional advantages: (1) Length of residence is correlated with perceived safety (r = –.23), while neighboring and satisfaction are not, so the substitution imposes a more rigorous condition that both must meet to attain significance as attachment predictors; and (2) length of residence was the critical predictor of attachment in the study by Kasarda and Janowitz (1974), so a limited replication becomes possible with its use as such here. If length of residence emerges as a predictor of attachment to the defended neighborhood but not the community of limited liability, the hypothesis of distinctness will be even more strongly upheld.

Table 6 offers the relevant regression results. Significant predictors of attachment to each level of community are highlighted, and values of R^2 are presented for each equation evaluated.[7]

The equations evaluated in Table 6 explain moderate and near identical proportions of variance in their respective dependent variables. Further, the regression results offer strong support for the hypothesis of distinct attachment-generating processes for different levels of the nested community, and this occurs even with the substitution of the length of residence variable. As suggested by previous research, length of residence in Hallmark taps the relative immersion of residents in networks of interaction in the building and, thus, leads to attachment to it; in fact, the coefficient produced here is quite compatible with that generated by Kasarda and Janowitz. Length of residence, however, has no independent effect on attachment to the community of limited liability, as expected in a setting where the emotional "investment" is so little dependent on informal interaction and sociability.

Attachment to the community of limited liability remains a very complex phenomenon. Note that the effect on it of perceived normlessness, even though inflated slightly by the exclusion of other measures correlated with it, still cannot top that of city facility use. This, too, we would expect, given the nature of a community of limited liability.

CONCLUSION

It is obviously risky to generalize very far from a case study, even one explicitly designed to test theoretical propositions. Peculiarities of the

TABLE 6
Modeling the Attachment Process: Regression Results

	B	$S.E._B$	Beta	T
I. Dependent: Attachment to Newark				
Attachment: Hallmark	.412	.143	.402	2.875**
City Facility Use	-.131	.055	-.279	-2.376*
Normlessness	.044	.020	.259	2.231*
Length of Residence	-.008	.023	-.044	-.346
Perceived Safety	-.004	.042	-.012	-.087
Multiple R = .610; R^2 = .372				
II. Dependent: Attachment to Hallmark House				
Perceived Safety	.153	.036	.515	4.300**
Length of Residence	.057	.021	.331	2.744**
Normlessness	.028	.019	.171	1.494
City Facility Use	-.016	.054	-.034	-.288
Multiple R = .587; R^2 = .345				

*Significant at $p \leqslant .05$; **significant at $p \leqslant .01$.

research setting can have effects on findings that might not be replicated in other settings. As we have suggested, that is probably true of this study of attachments to community. Granting that, there are some fairly definite conclusions to be drawn from this effort. It seems clear first of all that defended neighborhoods of both the horizontal and vertical types are containers of parallel interactional processes that forge emotional attachments in similar ways. Second, it seems clear that the environs of the defended neighborhood—in particular, its perceived criminological context—play a role at least as critical as, and possibly more critical than, those interactional processes in forging community attachments. Finally, attachment to the community of limited liability, while in part a product of attachment carryover, is in no small measure a function of social processes and perspectives characteristic of life in the larger city, outside of the immediate neighborhood. Attachments to the different levels of the nested community are not completely isolated emotions; after allowing for their connection, however, it appears that they are largely formed by level-specific dynamics.

Throughout this discussion, we have generally distinguished between social processes (like neighboring or facility use) and perceived social contexts (like neighborhood safety or societal normlessness) as generators of attachment. In this study, their effects on attachment differ across levels of the nested community; in the defended neighborhood, attachment seems more heavily contextual than processual, while in the community of limited liability the reverse seems to hold. The differences, however, go beyond this. Among the Hallmark respondents, attachment to the defended neighborhood is more a function of interactional and expressive than instrumental social processes, and attachment itself is an affirmation of life in a secure, supportive environment. Attachment to the community of limited liability, on the other hand, is more responsive to instrumental than expressive social processes and, as an emotion, seems more a reaction against, rather than an affirmation of, the quality of contemporary urban life.

Treated in this fashion, the findings from this study can be generalized into a rough model of the overall process of attachment to different levels of the nested community. That model may be idiosyncratic to Hallmark House, although the findings on which it is based are consistent with what the literature suggests is a general phenomenon. Whether and to what extent they hold as such is a worthwhile question for future studies of nested communities and the differential ties that bind people to them.

NOTES

1. In an informal interview, the resident manager at Hallmark House was asked to estimate the racial and gender breakdowns of the building's population. His estimates are used as the basis for the tests on race and gender in Table 1. At the time of the interview, he had held his position for seven years, so his estimates are reasonable standards for comparisons.

2. Spearman's rho between the third and both the first and the second columns in the table amounts to .71.

3. Each respondent was asked to indicate his or her satisfaction with, among other things, "ease of making friends in the building." Those responses are the measures of satisfaction with sociability discussed here.

4. Other evaluations of this model were conducted with more conventional resource measures, like income and occupational status. Their results offered no significant additions to the model presented in Table 3. Inclusion of such measures incremented R^2 only slightly and none emerged as significant predictors of any variables in the model as presented. This is generally congruent with what Hunter found in Rochester.

5. For this study, that seems a reasonable operationalization. Hallmark's location in the heart of the city, amid government, corporate, and other high-rise residential buildings and away from more conventional neighborhoods, effectively makes its "larger context" inseparable from that of the city as a whole. At the same time, the severe separation that other citizens and elites of Essex County draw between their communities and Newark makes the latter an oppositionally defined reality (Suttles, 1968, 1972) for its residents.

6. Evaluations of alternatives to this model that included respondents' background characteristics produced the same general lack of results reported earlier for attachment to the neighborhood. In that physical structure and rent schedule at Hallmark House constrain this sample toward homogeneity of background, this lack of results is not very remarkable.

7. In these analyses, we have assumed that attachment carryover works from the immediate to the more expanded levels of community, and not the reverse. In Newark, that seems reasonable. In recent times, resident leaders most active in promoting the city's image to the outside and in pushing for internal redevelopment have generally come from "careers" as leaders or activists in tightly knit, cohesive neighborhoods. Further, this may not be peculiar to Newark. Others, most recently Crenson (1983), have documented similar patterns in other cities. The directional issue is not resolved by these cases, of course, but they do make the assumption made here seem the more reasonable of the alternatives.

8. It also occurs when attachment to the city is entered as an independent variable in the equation predicting attachment to the building. This alternative specification increases the predictability of R^2 in said equation to .440, but it does not change the significance of either length of residence or perceived security as predictors. Further, the actual attenuation in their respective coefficients is marginal and their rank order is unchanged.

REFERENCES

ALLEN, I. (1980) "The ideology of dense neighborhood redevelopment: cultural diversity and transcendent community experience." Urban Affairs Q. 15 (June): 409-428.

BAILEY, K. D. (1982) Methods of Social Research. New York: Free Press.

CAPLOW, T., S. STRYKER, and S. E. WALLACE (1964) The Urban Ambience. Totowa, NJ: Bedminister.

CRENSON, M. A. (1983) Neighborhood Politics. Cambridge, MA: Harvard Univ. Press.

DILLMAN, D. A., J. A. CHRISTENSEN, E. H. CARPENTER, and R. M. BROOKS (1974) "Increasing mail questionnaire response: a four state comparison." Amer. Soc. Rev. 39 (October): 744-756.

FESTINGER, L. (1957) A Theory of Cognitive Dissonance. Stanford, CA: Stanford Univ. Press.

FISCHER, C. S. (1973) "On urban alienations and anomie: powerlessness and social isolation." Amer. Rev. 38: 311-326.

———(1982) To Dwell Among Friends: Personal Networks in Town and City. Chicago: Univ. of Chicago Press.

FOLEY, D. L. (1952) Neighbors or Urbanites? Rochester: Univ. of Rochester Press.
GANS, H. J. (1963) The Urban Villagers. New York: Free Press.
GRANOVETTER, M. (1973) "The strength of weak ties." Amer. J. of Sociology 78: 1360-1380.
GREER, S. A. (1972) The Urbane View. New York: Oxford Univ. Press.
GUEST, A. M. and B. A. LEE (1983) "The social organization of local areas." Urban Affairs Q. 19: 217-240.
HEIDER, F. (1958) The Psychology of Interpersonal Relations. New York: John Wiley.
HOMANS, G. (1950) The Human Group. New York: Harcourt Brace Jovanovich.
HUNTER, A. (1974) Symbolic Communities. Chicago: Univ. of Chicago Press.
———(1975) "The loss of community: an empirical test through replication." Amer. Soc. Rev. 40: 537-552.
———and G. SUTTLES (1972) "The expanding community of limited liability," pp. 44-81 in G. Suttles (ed.) The Social Construction of Communities. Chicago: Univ. of Chicago Press.
JANOWITZ, M. (1967) The Community Press in an Urban Setting. Chicago: Univ. of Chicago Press.
KASARDA, J. D. and M. JANOWITZ (1974) "Community attachments in mass society." Amer. Soc. Rev. 39: 328-339.
KELLER, S. (1968) The Urban Neighborhood: A Sociological Perspective. New York: Random House.
LAUMANN, E. O. (1972) Bonds of Pluralism: The Form and Substance of Urban Social Networks. New York: Wiley-Interscience.
LOFLAND, L. H. (1973) A World of Strangers. New York: Basic Books.
MERRY, S. E. (1981) Urban Danger: Life in a Neighborhood of Strangers. Philadelphia: Temple Univ. Press.
MILLER, D. C. (1977) Handbook of Research Design and Social Measurement. New York: McKay.
NETTLER, G. (1957) "A measure of alienation." Amer. Soc. Rev. 22: 670-677.
NEWCOMB, T. (1961) The Acquaintance Process. New York: Holt, Rinehart & Winston.
NEWMAN, O. (1982) Community of Interest. Garden City, NY: Anchor/Doubleday.
OLSON, P. (1982) "Urban neighborhood research: its development and current focus." Urban Affairs Q. 17: 491-518.
SCHORR, A. (1963) Slums and Social Insecurity. Washington, DC: Social Security Administration, Dept. of Health, Education and Welfare.
SEEMAN, M. (1975) "Alienation studies," pp. 91-124 in A. Inkeles et al. (eds.) Annual Review of Sociology I. Palo Alto, CA: Annual Reviews.
SIMMEL, G. (1905) "The metropolis and mental life," pp. 47-60 in R. Sennett (ed.) Classic Essays on the Culture of Cities. New York: Appleton-Century-Crofts.
SKOGAN, W. C. and M. G. MAXFIELD (1981) Coping with Crime: Individual and Neighborhood Reactions. Beverly Hills, CA: Sage.
SLOVAK, J. S. (1984) "Symbolic communities and suburban voting: a case study." J. of Urban Affairs 6: 69-80.
SMITH, M. P. (1979) The City and Social Theory. New York: St. Martin's.
SROLE, L. (1956) "Social integration and certain corollaries: an exploratory study." Amer. Soc. Rev. 21: 709-716.

SUTTLES, G. (1968) The Social Order of the Slum. Chicago: Univ. of Chicago Press.
———(1972) The Social Construction of Communities. Chicago: Univ. of Chicago Press.
WIRTH, L. (1938) "Urbanism as a way of life." Amer. J. of Sociology 44: 1-44.

Jeffrey S. Slovak is Associate Professor of Sociology at Rutgers University in Newark. His interests lie in the area of community studies and in the sociology of urban police. Other of his articles on the former topic have appeared in Social Forces *and in the* Journal of Urban Affairs.

RESEARCH NOTE

OFFICER ORIENTATIONS TOWARD THE COMMUNITY
The Impact of Police Bureaucracy

MICHAEL STEINMAN
University of Nebraska—Lincoln

This study examines why police officers have positive or negative orientations toward the communities they serve. Orientations are measured by respondent agreement or disagreement with two statements: "I often encounter situations where my professional standards are in conflict with the expectations of the community" and "The people in this city don't seem to appreciate, on the whole, what good police services are all about." The hypothesis is that officer orientations are much more affected by factors related to their memberships in a department than by their direct, off-duty community involvements and their personal histories. Data were obtained in a survey of rank-and-file officers in two urban departments.

PROFESSIONALIZATION AND BUREAUCRATIZATION

Police officers have considerable discretion because of the work they do and management's limited ability to supervise their conduct. Officers use their discretion to set priorities, enforcing laws that are more "important" or those laws that are easily enforced (Brown, 1981; Muir, 1977). Departments make priorities, too. However, the existence of officer discretion weakens these priorities.

Individual officer decisions are important to a community wanting to control its police. Most of this century's police reforms have sought more control by rationalizing individual work (professionalization) and overall coordination (bureaucratization). The former has meant officer exposure to good policing techniques, the law, and due process, resulting in a more professional self-image (Banton, 1964; Harris, 1978). The latter has led to more care about lines of authority and communica-

AUTHOR'S NOTE: *I am indebted to Susan Welch for her comments on this study.*
URBAN AFFAIRS QUARTERLY, Vol. 21 No. 4, June 1986 598-606

tion, written job descriptions, and more objective personnel standards (Caiden, 1977; Price, 1977; Steinman, 1984).

While professionalization and bureaucratization have produced benefits, they have also created problems. Thompson's (1961) and Lipsky's (1980) studies of specialist-hierarchical relations and street-level bureaucrats discuss them (see also Blumberg, 1979; Gouldner, 1957-1958; and Goldstein, 1977).

Thompson and Lipsky examine the professional self-images and commitments to goal achievement exhibited by low-ranking service delivery personnel. Lipsky notes that they often lack resources and experience frustration knowing they face only parts of their clients' larger problems. They will communicate with anyone about anything to do their jobs well.

Others in service delivery bureaucracies have hierarchical orientations. They value following orders and loyalty. They use only formal lines of communications, expecting superiors (they hope themselves) to monopolize them and organization resources.

The interaction of these two types is associated with personnel problems. Specialists stress "doing," while bureaucrats stress "obeying." The former tend to concentrate on goal accomplishment and the latter tend to worry about subordinate compliance. As a result, bureaucrats often use managerial procedures to assert control rather than to facilitate job performance. Specialists may view this as managerial interference and respond with their own informal work norms.

Wilson (1968) observed that police officers tend to view managerial rules as threats, even though the rules are meant to promote professionalization. Rules can represent "a failure of confidence and a withdrawal of support." They tell officers they do not know what they are doing.

What does this mean for management? Its job is to get officers to work in "acceptable" ways. It means that management may alienate officers when it pushes too hard for control. What does this mean for getting police work consistent with community expectations? Officers learn about these expectations from management as well as from their own street experience. It means that officer alienation from management may produce alienation from communities served.

HYPOTHESES

Many factors influence the behavior of police officers. This study hypothesizes that department factors are more important than any others. They affect every officer: how he or she does the job, the course of the officer's career, and daily satisfaction. Department factors include management, formal procedures, peers, training, evaluations, encouragement, and constraints. Officers find ways of living with these factors. Officers with positive views of them are expected to see their communities as more supportive and appreciative.

Department morale and reputation affect officer pride and self-confidence. Living with the department's identity on and off duty, an officer with a positive self-image may be more open to community expectations.

Departments reflect community expectations in their priorities, budgets, and the kinds of people chosen to run them. These factors affect every officer's work. They may change over time; but officers deal with them daily and may see them as symbols of community trust or distrust.

This study's dependent variable is the degree to which officers think they are supported and appreciated by their communities. There are three sets of explanatory variables. The first describes officers' relations with and commitments to their departments. This set is expected to have the greatest relationship to the dependent variable.

The second set of explanatory variables includes officers' direct, off-duty involvement in, and evaluations of, their communities. This set is expected to be related to the dependent variable but not as closely as the first. Again, department factors are expected to be most important.

The third set of explanatory variables contains individual officer characteristics. Factors such as age, education, marital status, military service, and places of birth and residence do not have a direct bearing on department membership. Thus, they are expected to be unrelated. However, they may shape how officers see their community and must be considered.

This study does not assume that individual officer responsiveness equals police accountability. An officer may treat a citizen as he or she wants to be treated and still act unaccountably, both to the larger community as well as to the local definition of professional behavior. Nevertheless, this study assumes that police accountability is less of a problem when officers think their community appreciates and supports them.

METHODOLOGY

THE SETTING

Data were generated from a survey of rank-and-file uniformed officers in Minneapolis and St. Paul, Minnesota. The survey was done in December 1982 and January 1983. Every officer received a questionnaire. Of St. Paul's officers, 68% (n = 184) completed their questionnaires. In Minneapolis, 100 officers (24% of that city's rank and file) also completed the questionnaire.

The two departments differed in several ways. St. Paul's appeared more collegial. Officers worked out of only two precincts and headquarters. Their chief rose from the ranks and symbolized continuity. Budget problems created the only observable department tension. It was caused by state deficit problems and led to some early retirements. Most officers realized that the budgetary problems were not the city's fault.

There was more tension in Minneapolis. The chief was from the East Coast and in his third year. His accent, personal style, and policies were unfamiliar and threatening for some officers. Although his reputation was that of a solid professional, his tenure was controversial. As a result, budget processes and union negotiations had a confrontational tone.

The appointment of Minneapolis's chief represented a major departure. The job had historically been rotated among high-ranking officers for brief terms. The current chief had a more permanent appointment, and unhappy officers could not anticipate the next rotation to be rid of him. There were also command officers who previously had served as chief.

Finally, Minneapolis officers work out of four precincts and headquarters, and their union is more active than St. Paul's.

THE DEPENDENT VARIABLE

Responses to all attitudinal survey items ranged from "strongly agree" to "strongly disagree" on a 5-part Likert-type scale. Responses to the following statements were used to create a summary dependent variable, the community-orientation scale: (1) "The people in this city don't seem to appreciate, on the whole, what good police services are all about"; and (2) "I often encounter situations where my professional standards are in conflict with the expectations of the community." The community-orientation scale was created by giving each respondent one point if he or she disagreed with each statement. There is a reasonable variation in the scales from both cities with an imbalance toward a higher point total. Responses to the statements were highly correlated in both Minneapolis (Pearson's r = .387**) and St. Paul (Pearson's r = .404**).[1] It is reasonable to view attitudes as precursors to behavior.

INDEPENDENT VARIABLES

The questionnaire contained over 70 items measuring the two sets of attitudinal explanatory variables. Since working with so many items is unwieldy and methodologically unwise, a factor analysis was done on those with initial bivariate correlations of more than .15 with the dependent variable. In Minneapolis 23 items had the requisite correlation; 11 did in St. Paul.[2]

Factor analysis yielded three factors in the Minneapolis data. Two include variables describing views of the departments: perceptions of its operations and of relations with superiors. The third combines variables describing commitments to the department and evaluations of the community. While this combination might seem unusual, it underscores this study's central assumption that attitudes about department and community are related.

Four factors emerged in St. Paul with the same explanatory perspectives as the three from Minneapolis. They describe respondents' relations with superiors, views of department operations, commitments to the department, and evaluations of St. Paul.

Simple additive factor scales were created from the items in each factor loading at .4 or above. These scales were used as independent variables in a multiple regression analysis. Variables describing respondents' personal characteristics were also used in this analysis; they showed no, or very minimal, relationships with the dependent variable. Results are reported for only four: age, education, place of birth (community served or elsewhere), and military service. There were too few women and minority officers to test for gender and minority status.

FINDINGS

In Minneapolis, 50% (n = 50) of respondents agreed that the people of that city do not appreciate what good police services are; 37% (n = 68) of

St. Paul respondents replied the same way. In addition, 40% (n = 40) of Minneapolis and 36% (n = 67) of St. Paul respondents reported often encountering conflict between their own and the community's standards. These findings are interesting because they show that tensions exist between large groups of officers and communities served in both cities. Minneapolis's higher percentages suggest that morale problems are important there. However, the presence of large percentages in both departments suggests the possible impact of specialist-managerial problems more generally.

Bivariate analysis, linking the community-orientation scale with explanatory variables, shows the importance of officers' relations with, and commitments to, their departments. For example, respondents in both departments who see rare disagreement with their administrators over professional standards tend to receive higher scores in the dependent variable (Pearson's r = –.237* in Minneapolis; Pearson's r = –.231** in St. Paul). So do those who think their departments are good places in which to spend their careers (Pearson's r = –.190* in Minneapolis; Pearson's r = –.185 in St. Paul) and those who would not rather work in another department (Pearson's r = .255* in Minneapolis; Pearson's r = .158 in St. Paul).

Two other independent variables concerning respondents' evaluations of their communities met the .15 cutoff in both cities. Respondents describing their cities as "fine" places to live tend to have higher dependent variables scores (Pearson's r = –.252* in Minneapolis; Pearson's r = –.152 in St. Paul) as do those who do not want to live elsewhere (Pearson's r = .158 in Minneapolis and .196* in St. Paul). However, items covering officers' direct off-duty community involvements failed to correlate at the .15 level with the dependent variable. Examples of these are being an active member of various community groups (church, veterans, recreational, civic, etc.), discussing public affairs with non-police friends, and voting regularly.

Items describing respondents' personal characteristics (education, age, military service, marital status, fathers' occupations, and places of birth and residence) were not highly related to the dependent variable. Education had the strongest relationship (Pearson's r = .143 in Minneapolis and and .109 in St. Paul); those with higher levels of achievement had higher community-orientation scores.

The findings confirm that department variables correlate most often with officer perceptions of community appreciation and support. Respondents' evaluations of their communities are also associated with the dependent variable. This supports the belief that officers' views of

TABLE 1
The Impact of Factors and Personal Characteristics on the Community-Orientation Scale

	Minneapolis (n=93)			St. Paul (n=166)		
Independent Variables	b	Beta	Standard Error of b	b	Beta	Standard Error of b
Commitments to city and department.	.14	.18*	.09	NA	NA	NA
Views of how department works.	.32	.19*	.17	-.01	-.02	.04
Relations with superiors.	.10	.15*	.07	.37	.19**	.15
Level of educational achievement.	.20	.20**	.10	.11	.12*	.08
Age.	.00	.02	.01	.01	.07	.01
Military service.	-.01	-.03	.23	.03	.02	.15
Place of birth.	.07	.04	.20	-.15	-.09	.13
Evaluations of city.	NA	NA	NA	-.05	-.04	.11
Commitments to department.	NA	NA	NA	.46	.20**	.18
Multiple R	.391			.343		
Multiple R^2	.153			.118		

1. Multiple regression analysis.
*s ⩽ .10 ⩾ .05; **s ⩽ .05.

their communities are associated with their departmental experiences.

Table 1 reports the results of a multiple regression analysis identifying the independent effects of the factor scales created from the factor analysis and some individual characteristic items on community orientation. The Minneapolis data reveal the significant impacts of factors describing officers' evaluations of their city and their commitments to their department, their views of department operations, and their relations with superiors. Factors from St. Paul with significant impacts on community orientation are relations with superiors and commitments to the department. Officer education also had a significant impact in this analysis: Officers with more education tended to have a more positive community orientation.

Thus, department factors are the most important influences on officer orientations toward the communities they serve. Although St. Paul's department was smaller, less fragmented into precincts, and more content with its chief, its officers' community orientations were stilll influenced by department factors.

Most factors with an independent, direct relationship to the community-orientation scale revealed the importance of department membership. In addition, officers in both cities with more education had more positive community orientations. Other officer characteristics had no significant relationship.

CONCLUSION

While officers' off-duty community involvements and their personal characteristics are not very important in shaping their community orientations, their departments are. Officers face considerable uncertainty on the street. Perceptions of department support and appreciation may help them see community support and appreciation.

Barnard (1938) and Simon (1957) studied the problems of persuading the members of organizations to comply with organizational policies. Both stressed the importance of personal incentives: An organization must seem to offer rewards for complying with formal policy. Officers aware of department support may be more apt to respect community expectations as reflected in department policy.

Brown (1981: 89) observed that supervisors sometimes stress compliance with minor rules to assure themselves that officers can be trusted. If officers see such rules as petty and irrelevant, they may not view their departments as supportive. This may make it harder to match officer behavior with community expectations. Goldstein (1977: 264-265) recommends that departments show officers that they understand what is required to do a good job. He suggests the elimination of unnecessary demands (e.g., daily inspections). He may be right. If departments ignore this advice, they may seem irrelevant, at best, or dysfunctional, at worst, to their officers.

NOTES

1. * represents level of significance $\leq .01$; ** represents level of significance $\leq .001$.

2. I would be happy to send the results of bivariate and factor analyses to those requesting them. Send requests to 504 Oldfather, University of Nebraska, Lincoln, NE 68588-0328. Each factor had an eigenvalue of more than 1. Their coefficients were produced from an oblique rotation.

REFERENCES

BANTON, M. (1964) The Policeman in the Community. New York: Basic Books.

BARNARD, C. I. (1938) The Functions of the Executive. Cambridge, MA: Harvard Univ. Press.

BLUMBERG, A. S. (1979) Criminal Justice. New York: New Viewpoints.

BROWN, M. K. (1981) Working the Street: Police Discretion and the Dilemmas of Reform. New York: Russell Sage.

CAIDEN, G. E. (1977) Police Revitalization. Lexington, MA: Lexington Books.

GOLDSTEIN, H. (1977) Policing a Free Society. Cambridge, MA: Ballinger.

GOULDNER, H. (1957-1958) "Cosmopolitans and locals." Admin. Sci. Q. 2: 281-306, 444-480.

HARRIS, R. N. (1978) "The police academy and the professional self-image," in P. K. Manning and J. Van Maanen (eds.) Policing: A View from the Street. Santa Monica, CA: Goodyear.

LIPSKY, M. (1980) Street-Level Bureaucracy. New York: Russell Sage.

MUIR, W. K., Jr. (1977) Police: Streetcorner Politicians. Chicago: Univ. of Chicago Press.

PRICE, B. R. (1977) Police Professionalism. Lexington, MA: Lexington Books.

SIMON, H. A. (1957) Administrative Behavior. New York: Free Press.

STEINMAN, M. (1984) "Rationalizing police operations: some explanatory factors." J. of Criminal Justice 12, 3: 221-233.

THOMPSON, V. (1961) "Hierarchy, specialization, and organization conflict." Admin. Sci. Q. 5 (March): 485-521.

WILSON, J. Q. (1968) Varieties of Police Behavior. Cambridge, MA: Harvard Univ. Press.

Michael Steinman is Associate Professor in the Political Science Department at the University of Nebraska in Lincoln. His research interests combine literatures in organization theory, public policy, and police behavior. He has had his work published in a variety of journals dealing with public administration and police management.

RESEARCH NOTE

CONSTITUENCY OF THE ANTIGROWTH MOVEMENT

A Comparison of the Growth Orientations of Urban Status Groups

DON E. ALBRECHT
Texas A&M University
GORDON BULTENA
ERIC HOIBERG
Iowa State University

This study tested the "status-growth hypothesis," which holds that antigrowth values are more pervasive among middle- and upper-class persons than those in blue-collar positions. Businessmen, however, were expected to be an exception to this pattern by displaying a strong attachment to progrowth orientations. The respondents were metropolitan residents in Iowa. Contrary to expectations, antigrowth sentiment was most pervasive among blue-collar respondents. Businessmen, as predicted, displayed the staunchest commitment of any occupational group to a growth ideology and to policies that promote urban expansion.

INTRODUCTION

There has been substantial controversy recently in the United States over the desirability of continued urban, industrial, economic, and population growth. That concerted challenges have arisen to a long-standing and pervasive "growth ethic" suggests that, as a nation, we may be undergoing a profound shift in values—perhaps of a paradigmatic nature (Catton and Dunlap, 1980). Americans have long equated growth with progress—the "more is better" philosophy. But accumulating evidence of environmental degradation and a deteriorating quality of life for many Americans have stirred public concern about the potential dysfunctions of growth. Growth-inducing policies are now often portrayed in the literature as endangering our national survival,

URBAN AFFAIRS QUARTERLY, Vol. 21 No. 4, June 1986 607-616

threatening revered social values, and as the root cause of various social and personal pathologies (Anderson, 1976; Meadows et al., 1972; Catton, 1980).

A prominent target of the contemporary antigrowth movement is the unplanned peripheral expansion of cities, which has been fueled partly by the financial interests of local elites (Maurer and Christenson, 1982; Molotch, 1976). But while providing benefits to some groups, urban sprawl has also given rise to many social and economic costs, including unsightly development, the loss of prime farmland and open space, and infrastructure problems. As a result of these adverse impacts, and the perceived threats of growth to privileged lifestyles, forceful opposition has emerged in some states and communities to the perpetuation of growth-including policies (Applebaum, 1976; Miner, 1977; Finkler et al., 1976).

Despite occasional evidence of local disenchantment with growth and with its use as a tool for solving social problems, the locus of antigrowth sentiment in the general population remains obscure. Findings are presented here from a study that tested the popular argument (status-growth hypothesis) that antigrowth sentiment tends to be concentrated in the middle and upper social classes and that laborers and blue-collar workers hold predominately progrowth orientations.

THE STATUS-GROWTH HYPOTHESIS

A prevalent view is that the middle and upper social classes are the primary fountainhead of today's antigrowth philosophies and that the working class and the poor remain staunchly devoted to continued growth (Wiener, 1973; Morrison, 1976). The presumed working-class support of economic expansion is usually attributed to the negative impacts of antigrowth controls upon their job security, housing costs, and opportunities for social mobility (Neuhaus, 1971; Frieden, 1980; England and Bluestone, 1973). There is a paucity of scientific evidence, however, as to the growth orientations of different class groups. Scattered findings, consistent with the status-growth hypothesis, suggest that lower-class persons are generally more accepting of continued growth than are middle- and upper-class persons (Coughenour and Christenson, 1980; Buttel, 1978). However, evidence from a related body of literature on the general environmental concerns of Americans provides only mixed support for the status-growth hypothesis. In a recent review, Van Liere and Dunlap (1980) conclude that whereas better-educated persons tend, comparatively, to be the most concerned about environmental quality, income and occupational differences hold little or no importance for explaining environmental concern.

REFINEMENT OF THE STATUS-GROWTH HYPOTHESIS

In previous tests of the status-growth hypothesis, investigators usually have aggregated respondents into broad categories (e.g., "high," "medium," and "low" status). However, this analytical procedure serves to mask possible variations within status categories and, thus, could be obscuring important exceptions to the status-growth hypothesis. Buttel and Larsen (1980), for example, have argued that middle- and upper-class support of environmental goals is drawn primarily from the "noncorporate" sectors of society; that is, from the professional ranks of educators, doctors, lawyers, scientists, government officials, and students.

It would seem, contrary to the status-growth hypothesis, that some segments of the middle and upper social classes are unlikely to subscribe to the emergent antigrowth philosophies. The self-interests of businesspersons, in particular, typically are not well served by a substantial slowing of population, industrial, and economic growth in their communities. In fact, businesspersons (including bankers, developers, speculators, real estate agents, and contractors) constitute a principal advocacy group today for expansionist policies (Molotch, 1976).

HYPOTHESES

This study examined patterns of commitment by Iowans to a general growth ideology and to some policies for constraining urban sprawl. Consistent with the status-growth hypothesis, it was predicted that persons in the higher income (H_1), educational (H_2), and occupational (H_3) brackets would be the most supportive of both the general philosophy of controlling growth and of public policies that are designed to constrain urban sprawl. In a refinement of the status-growth hypothesis, it was predicted that businesspersons would be more progrowth than persons in other white- and blue-collar occupations (H_4).

SAMPLE AND PROCEDURES

SAMPLE

Respondents in this study were randomly selected from the eight Standard Metropolitan Statistical Areas in Iowa. These cities were sampled, relative to population size, using a random-digit dialing technique. Phone calls were made to the selected numbers to obtain the names and addresses of household members. An adult in each household was randomly selected to participate in the study. In 1980, mail questionnaires were sent to the selected persons, of whom 73% (N = 468) responded.

MEASUREMENT OF VARIABLES

"Socioeconomic status" was measured by three variables: family income, educational attainment, and occupation of the head of household. Education was the number of years of schooling completed. Occupational status was the self-placement by respondents into one of five categories of laborer, skilled blue-collar, clerical/sales, business, or professional. Annual family income was measured by eight income categories, ranging from "under $5,000" to "$40,000 or more."

Two growth orientations were examined. First, support of a general growth ethic was measured by a subset of four items from the New Environmental Paradigm Scale (Dunlap and Van Liere, 1978; Albrecht, et al., 1982). These items, which used a fourfold Likert response format, were as follows: (1) "We are approaching the limit of the number of people the earth can support"; (2) "To maintain a healthy economy we will have to develop a steady state economy where industrial growth is controlled"; (3) "The earth is like a spaceship with only limited room and resources"; (4) "There are limits to growth beyond which our industrialized society cannot expand." Cumulative scores on these items ranged from 4 (rejection of growth limits—progrowth) to 16 (acceptance of limits—antigrowth). The average score was 12.4. The reliability of the four items (Cronbach's alpha) was .62.

A five-item "urban growth control" scale was used to measure the respondents' acceptance of antigrowth policies in their local communities. These items were as follow: (1) "Establish a minimum-lot-size requirement of at least 3 to 6 acres for subdivisions on the urban fringe";

(2) "Strengthen local zoning laws to limit further residential and industrial development on the urban fringe"; (3) "Prohibit the expansion of key facilities (e.g., water and sewer) so that new development cannot occur on the urban fringe"; (4) "Limit the number of new housing units on the urban fringe"; (5) "Require the development of most vacant lots within the city limits before there is further expansion outwards." A fourfold Likert response format measured the relative acceptance of these policies.

Scale scores ranged from 5 (complete rejection of growth controls—progrowth) to 20 (complete acceptance of controls—antigrowth). The average scale score was 14.6. The reliability of the five-item scale (Cronbach's alpha) was .80.

FINDINGS

STATUS-GROWTH HYPOTHESIS

Consistent with the status-growth hypothesis, it was predicted that persons in the higher education, income, and occupation categories would be the most accepting of antigrowth views (i.e., score highest on the two scales). Analysis of the data revealed that education and income were not significantly related to scores on the scale measuring views about general growth. Occupational status was correlated with these scores ($r = -.25$), but not in the expected direction: Surprisingly, persons in the lower occupational ranks (laborers and skilled blue-collar workers) collectively made stauncher commitments to growth limitation than did white-collar, business, and professional workers.

Contrary to expectations, the three status characteristics were inversely related to scores on the urban growth control scale. Persons in the higher income ($r = -.21$), education ($r = -.22$), and occupation ($r = -.30$) categories consistently were the least willing to endorse constraints being imposed on the expansion of their local communities.

Growth Orientations of Business Persons

The primary interest in this analysis was in testing a refinement of the status-growth hypothesis. Namely, it was predicted that businesspersons would be more accepting generally of the desirability of continued growth and more opposed to the imposition of controls on local urban growth than would persons in the other occupational groups. It was found that only 17% of the businesspersons displayed a high level of support for general growth limitations, as compared to 32% of the professionals, 33% of the clerical/sales workers, 48% of the skilled blue-collar workers, and 43% of the laborers (Table 1).

The predicted strong progrowth orientations of businesspersons were substantiated for the urban growth control items. The number of businesspersons who vigorously rejected urban growth controls (56% scored "low" on this scale) was more than double that recorded for any of the other four occupational categories. Surprisingly, laborers were the most supportive of the urban growth control items (Table 1).

SUMMARY AND DISCUSSION

There is widespread controversy in the United States over the likely impacts and desirability of further economic and population growth. The recent appearance of staunch antigrowth sentiment marks a sharp departure from the longstanding commitment of Americans to a growth ethic.

Consistent with the literature about antigrowth values, it was posited (status-growth hypothesis) that the income, education, and occupational statuses of Iowans living in metropolitan areas would be related positively to support for limiting growth generally and for urban growth controls. The data, however, failed to confirm these anticipated relationships. On the contrary, the greatest endorsement of growth generally and of urban growth controls came from persons in the lower- rather than higher-status ranks, especially occupational ranks. However, a modification of the status-growth hypothesis was confirmed in that businesspersons were shown to be less supportive of growth controls than were persons in the other occupational categories. These findings call into question the conventional view that working-class persons view growth as antithetical to their interests and thus constitute a potential bastion of opposition to efforts to constrain growth. Rather, for this urban Iowa sample, more support was forthcoming for growth controls from blue-collar than from white-collar workers.

One explanation of these findings may be in the ways that members of various status groups perceive themselves being affected by antigrowth

TABLE 1

Relationship of Occupational Status to the Growth Limitations Scale and the Urban Growth Control Scale

	Occupational Status				
Orientation	Professional	Business	Clerical or Sales	Skilled Blue-Collar	Laborer
	(Percent)				
Support of General Growth Limitation					
Low	17	42	31	12	14
Medium	51	41	36	40	43
High	32	17	33	48	43
	100	100	100	100	100
TOTAL (N)	(142)	(41)	(48)	(60)	(58)
Mean Score, Growth Limitation[a]	12.3	11.3	12.1	13.0	13.0
Support of Urban Growth Controls					
Low	27	56	26	19	17
Medium	48	31	48	51	38
High	25	13	26	30	45
	100	100	100	100	100
TOTAL (N)	(140)	(39)	(50)	(59)	(58)
Mean Score,[b] Urban Growth Control	14.5	12.3	14.5	15.2	15.9

a. The mean score (raw scale score) for businesspersons was significantly lower than the mean scores of the other occupational groups (i.e., laborers, skilled blue-collar workers, and professionals). These differences were tested using ANOVA and the .05 probability level.

b. The mean score (raw scale score) for businesspersons was significantly lower than the mean scores of each of the other four occupational groups.

policies. The status-growth hypothesis reflects the assumption that lower-class persons are generally opposed to growth controls because such controls may have potentially harmful effects on their job security and social mobility. However, Buttel and Flinn (1978) have noted that lower-class persons may more often be victims than beneficiaries of growth, especially in their disporportionate exposure to problems of air and water pollution, vulnerability to neighborhood disruption from urban renewal, and residential displacement by development projects. That some types of growth may be seen by the poor as antithetical to their interests is suggested by our finding of comparatively greater lower- than upper-class endorsement of urban growth controls.

The self-interests of middle- and upper-class persons, especially those with business and/or speculative investments, are seemingly well served by growth. Whereas many businesspersons directly benefit from growth, others making speculative investments may profit as well. Although we were unable to test for relationships between the respondents' financial investments and growth orientations, we compared the growth scale scores of white-collar workers (exclusive of businesspersons) at different income levels. Consistent with a self-interest model, professionals and white-collar workers with larger incomes displayed markedly greater commitment to growth than did their counterparts with lesser incomes.

There is a need in future research to more finely disaggregate occupational categories in testing for orientations toward growth. Variance within occupational groups may be explained by the sector of the economy in which respondents are employed. In this regard, Molotch (1976) has argued that the most intense interest in growth among businesspersons comes from the financial and real estate sectors.

Greater attention should also be paid to how citizens react to various types of growth policies, such as population, economic, and industrial controls. The present research examined general growth orientations and suburban growth, but different results may have been obtained for other types of growth. A further consideration in assessing class differences is the "abstractness" of the issues under investigation. It has been shown (Neiman and Loveridge, 1981) that class conflicts tend to be less apparent when issues are cast at a general or national level than when they are locality relevant.

The importance of contextual variables for growth orientations needs to be more fully explored. The longstanding population and economic stagnation in many smaller cities can be expected to foster more pervasive support of the traditional growth ethic than where there has been a recent history of rapid expansion and possibly adverse growth-related impacts. Our findings of less than enthusiastic support of growth in Iowa's metropolitan population is of particular interest in this regard. Seemingly, the state's historical record of relatively stable population and economic patterns should be reflected in a staunch commitment in the population to the virtues of future growth. The lack of consensus for this growth suggests that antigrowth sentiment isn't confined to communities with booming economies. Growth limitations may also be promulgated out of a desire to preserve established lifestyles as well as social and environmental amenities from the perceived disruptive impacts of unfettered development.

REFERENCES

ALBRECHT, D., G. BULTENA, E. HOIBERG, and P. NOWAK (1982) "Measuring environmental concern: the new environmental paradigm scale." J. of Environmental Education 13: 39-43.

ANDERSON, C. H. (1976) The Sociology of Survival: Social Problems of Growth. Homewood, IL: Dorsey.

APPLEBAUM, R. P. (1976) "City size and urban life: a preliminary inquiry into some consequences of growth in American cities." Urban Affairs Q. 12: 139-170.

BUTTEL, F. H. (1978) "Economic growth and the welfare-state: implications for the future of environmentalism." Social Sci. Q. 58: 692-699.

———and W. L. FLINN (1978) "Social class and mass environmental beliefs: a reconsideration." Environment and Behavior 10: 433-450.

BUTTEL, F. H. and O. W. LARSEN, III (1980) "Whither environmentalism? The future path of the environmental movement." Natural Resources J. 20: 323-344.

CATTON, W. R., Jr. (1980) Overshoot: The Ecological Basis of Revolutionary Change. Urbana: Univ. of Illinois Press.

———and R. E. DUNLAP (1980) "A new ecological paradigm for postexuberant sociology." Amer. Behavioral Scientist 24: 15-47.

COUGHENOUR, M. C. and J. A. CHRISTENSON (1980) "Farm structure, social class, and farmers' policy preferences." Presented at the Symposium on Farm Structure and Rural Policy, Iowa State University.

DUNLAP, R. E. and K. D. VAN LIERE (1978) "The 'new environmental paradigm': a proposed measuring instrument and preliminary results." J. of Environmental Education 9: 10-19.

ENGLAND, R. and B. BLUESTONE (1973) "Ecology and social conflict," in H. E. Daly (ed.) Toward a Steady State Economy. San Francisco: Freeman.

FINKLER, E., W. J. TONER, and F. J. POPPER (1976) Urban Nongrowth: City Planning for People. New York: Praeger.

FRIEDEN, B. J. (1980) "The consumer's stake in environmental regulation." Annals of the Amer. Academy of Pol. and Social Sci. 451: 36-44.

MAURER, R. C. and J. A. CHRISTIANSEN (1982) "Growth and nongrowth orientations of urban, suburban and rural mayors: reflections on the city as a growth machine." Social Sci. Q. 63: 350-358.

MEADOWS, D. H., D. L. MEADOWS, J. RANDERS, and W. W. BEHRENS, III (1972) The Limits to Growth: A Report for the Club of Rome's Project on the Predicament of Mankind. New York: Universe Books.

MINERS, D. D. (1977) "Perspectives of growth management." Soil Conservation Society of America, Land Use: Tough Choices in Today's World. Ankeny, IA.

MOLOTCH, H. (1976) "The city as a growth machine: toward a political economy of place." Amer. J. of Sociology 82: 309-332.

MORRISON, D. E. (1976) "Growth, environment, equity and scarcity," Social Sci. Q. 57: 292-306.

NEIMAN, M. and R. O. LOVERIDGE (1981) "Environmentalism and local growth control: a probe into the class bias thesis." Environment and Behavior 13, 6: 759-772.

NEUHAUS, R. (1971) In Defense of People: Ecology and the Seduction of Radicalism. New York: Macmillan.

VAN LIERE, K. D. and R. E. DUNLAP (1980) "The social bases of environmental concern: a review of hypotheses, explanations and empirical evidence." Public Opinion Q. 44: 181-197.

WIENER, A. J. (1973) "The future of economic activity with questions and answers." Annals 408: 47-61.

Don E. Albrecht is Research Scientist in the Department of Rural Sociology and the Texas Real Estate Research Center at Texas A&M University. His current research interests include the influence of resource availability on society, agricultural change, and residential mobility. Some of his recent publications have appeared in Rural Sociology, Sociological Inquiry, Southern Rural Sociology, Journal of Forestry, *and the* Journal of Leisure Research.

Gordon Bultena is Professor in the Department of Sociology and Anthropology at Iowa State University, Ames. His research has dealt with public response to planned environmental change and the adoption of innovative conservation practices. He has recently published in Rural Sociology, Water Resources Bulletin, Journal of Soil and Water Conservation, *and* Leisure Sciences.

Eric Hoiberg is Associate Professor in the Department of Sociology and Anthropology at Iowa State University, Ames. His research interests include human ecology, environmental sociology, and adoption/diffusion. He has recently published articles in Sociological Quarterly, Rural Sociology, Journal of Soil and Water Conservation, *and the* Journal of Environmental Education.

THE CORPORATE CENTER STRATEGY
The State in Central Cities

Fainstein, Susan S., Norman I. Fainstein, Richard Child Hill, Dennis Judd, & Michael Peter Smith, *Restructuring the City: The Political Economy of Urban Redevelopment* (New York: Longman, 1983), 296 pp.

Friedland, Roger, *Power and Crisis in the City: Corporations, Unions, and Urban Policy* (New York: Schocken Books, 1983), 248 pp.

Mollenkopf, John, *The Contested City* (Princeton: Princeton University Press, 1983), 328 pp.

Swanstrom, Todd, *The Crisis of Growth Politics: Cleveland, Kucinich, and the Challenge of Urban Populism* (Philadelphia: Temple University Press, 1985), 307 pp.

These four important books contribute to the development of a more adequate view of the state and urban redevelopment. While there has recently been an explosion of theoretical work on the state and capitalism, very little of that theorizing has targeted the city or the local state. This theoretical neglect of the local state can be corrected by drawing on the rich empirical analyses presented by the eight authors of the books listed above. All of these authors deal with the redevelopment of central cities, with the "corporate center strategy" and the large-scale state assistance required to implement and to ameliorate the consequences of that major urban restructuring strategy. While each of the books overlaps to some extent with at least one of the others, each contributes a different piece of the state-urban economy puzzle. The list below provides a summary of these contributions.

THE STATE AND THE CENTRAL CITY: AN OVERVIEW

Key Dimensions	*Relevant Authors*
(1) The state responds to the needs of capital (the "corporate center" strategy).	*the Fainsteins, Hill, Judd, Smith, Friedland*
(2) Capital responds to political entrepreneurs.	*Mollenkopf, the Fainsteins*
(3) Unions collaborate with capital.	*Friedland, Mollenkopf*
(4) Minority displacement.	*the Fainsteins, Hill, Judd, Smith, Friedland*
(5) Minority resistance and riots.	*the Fainsteins, Hill, Judd, Smith, Friedland*
(6) The local state and the national state.	*the Fainsteins, Hill, Judd, Smith, Friedland*
(7) State redistributive policies.	*Friedland, the Fainsteins, Swanstrom*
(8) Organizing populist resistance to the corporate center strategy.	*Swanstrom*
(9) The global context shapes capital flight.	*Hill*

It is clear from this listing that a *comprehensive* analysis of the "corporate center" strategy of central city restructuring would include not only the way in which this state strategy was a response to the needs of capital, but also such dimensions as political entrepreneurs, minority displacement and resistance, unions, state levels, the global context, populist resistance, and state redistributive policy. Cities have become arenas of struggle between different levels of the state, different worker groups, and different fractions of capital.

Pluralist theories of urban politics take a beating in these four parallel but distinctive analyses of urban development. In the pluralist paradigm, individual voters and an array of interest groups compete for influence in urban politics within a social system in which there is a general value consensus. Government is seen as a mosaic of agencies which are readily accessible to democratic influence. The structure of political power results from contention among an array of private individuals and interest groups with their own resources and power. Yet these four books show how the pluralist view is contradicted by the empirical realities of urban redevelopment.

In this review essay I will show how the pluralist view is called into question in each case. I will accent the corporate center strategy.

In *The Contested City* John Mollenkopf looks at data on urban programs and urban redevelopment, particularly for Boston and San Francisco. Mollenkopf argues that neo-Marxist analysis and pluralist analysis are wrong: "This study rejects the two dominant traditions for explaining the structure of political power: the notion that some controlling 'power structure' or capitalist elite intervenes to determine what decisions are made, or, alternatively, that they result from the contention among private interest groups" (p. 9). Mollenkopf, in contrast with all the other authors reviewed here, views politics and government as "independent driving forces" which can override economic interests and diverse interest groups. Economic factors are mediated through and influenced by the political system. Particularly important are the "political entrepreneurs" at the federal and local levels. Democratic presidents have led the progrowth coalition at the national level, since urban development and other social programs have been used by the Democratic party to cement various groups together (e.g., minorities, unions, city machines) to build that modern party. Republican presidents, as a result, have resisted various urban development programs. Democratic leaders also played a critical role as political entrepreneurs building growth coalitions at the local city level. At the city level, no single elite is in control; public actors take the *initiative* in creating the growth-oriented urban programs. Mollenkopf notes that while political entrepreneurs may be dependent on business interests for campaign contributions, they frequently at *against* the interests of business elites.

To document his political entrepreneur theory, Mollenkopf reviews the cases of Boston and San Francisco, where, he argues, four mayors and two prominent urban renewal administrators used their expert political skills, together with help from national political entrepreneurs, to build huge redevelopment programs. The political entrepreneurs were not "class-conscious," but were seeking concrete solutions to the general societal problem of decaying cities. Mollenkopf traces the decline of large-scale urban redevelopment programs both to the Republican opposition in the Eisenhower, Nixon, and Ford years and to the opposition from the central-city poor and working-class elements of the Democratic coalition which did not benefit from urban renewal.

In my judgment, the most valuable part of the *The Contested City* is not the discussion of political entrepreneurs, which, as I will show below, is flawed, but rather the brilliant discussion of certain trends in U.S. cities since the 1930s. Mollenkopf tracks the huge array of governmental programs which were developed during the Roosevelt, Truman, and Johnson years and shows how programs such as the 1930 Public Works Administration rebuilt urban areas, including billions of dollars for bridges, roads, airports, and sewer projects. Mollenkopf is the first to emphasize the massive recapitalization of U.S. industry in cities under the War Production Board and allied wartime agencies. Additions to U.S. physical plant in 1942-1944 amounted to about $37 billion, only a little less than the *total* value of all U.S. manufacturing facilities in 1939! About $14 billion went to build military facilities and housing, while $23 billion went for new manufacturing facilities. These plant investments disproportionately favored certain cities, with Detroit, Chicago, New York, and Pittsburgh among the top cities, as one might expect, but with Sunbelt cities like Houston, Dallas, and Los Angeles also receiving huge per capita infusions of federal investment capital. My own research on wartime expenditures in the greater Houston area indicates that a substantial portion of that city's industrial base—particularly the petrochemical industry—was laid during World War II with huge infusions of federal investment capital. Yet this infusion of capital was directed and influenced by corporate executives and elites working behind and through federal war production agencies. This wartime operation of business elites through national-level government agencies presents some problems for Mollenkopf's excessively political analysis.

The empirical data on U.S. cities and governmental agencies do not support an "independent state" view of the state under capitalism, both at the national and at the local level. Even in Mollenkopf's two major examples, Boston and San Francisco, there is substantial evidence of small business elites *initiating* and *guiding* urban development. Political entrepreneurs are important and should not be neglected, but they are not independent forces. In Boston a group of banking, retail, and industrial capitalists, called "The Vault," played a major role in shaping the city government's fiscal and redevelopment activities. The mayor of the city (Collins) implemented their advice and was a broker who worked with union groups, but he was hardly an example of an independent political entrepreneur who initiated the idea of downtown redevelopment. In San Francisco a number of capitalist elite groups, including the 1946 Bay Area Council, formulated the basic ideas about redevelopment and guided later development. An "independent state" theory, at the very least, does not fit Boston and San Francisco very well; and in many Sunbelt cities, such as Dallas, Houston, and Los Angeles, downtown redevelopment programs fit an orthodox "instrumentalist" state theory, since local capitalists working through agencies such as the Chamber of Commerce or the (Dallas) Citizens' Council have directed government in the area of redevelopment and in many other spheres. Independent political entrepreneurs are of modest importance at the local level in these latter cities.

The other three books recognize the importance of the state and political entrepreneurs, but they also point up the dominant power of capitalist elites in urban development. One of the best theoretical assessments of urban redevelopment programs can be found in the concluding chapter of *Restructuring the City*. Susan and Norman Fainstein track out the historical development of urban renewal; they note the shift from an early concern for housing working-class families (a labor-business coalition backed the 1949-1954 urban renewal legislation) to the reality of massive clearance followed by high-rise commercial, governmental, and luxury apartment construction. As the renewal programs evolved in cities across the nations, they were used by local white authorities to displace minority residents and to bring whites back into central city areas. The heavy redevelopment emphasis on expanding office and luxury retail facilities in downtown areas, to attract corporations and suburbanites, illustrates this point.

However, the availability of federal funds for redevelopment was only a necessary condition. Local business action was necessary to bring programs to particular cities. In virtually every case, urban growth coalitions, involving close cooperation between local government officials and a business elite, have been behind central city redevelopment programs. In San Francisco, Boston, and Detroit business groups were dominant, while in New Haven and New Orleans mayors helped to organize business coalitions.

Local governments depend heavily on taxes paid by affluent urbanites, so they try to attract and keep affluent whites. Since private enterprises provide most jobs, city governments must attract new private investment using subsidies and tax concession. Business elites finance and dominate the political system as well as the mass media. Given these conditions, local governments facing central city decline have tried to bring corporations and the affluent back, to displace and remove low-income and minority households, and to maintain residential segregation. Attempts to restructure central cities along these lines regularly bring local growth coalitions into conflict with their poor and working-class residents. There may be conflict over constuction of manufacturing plants (with blue-collar jobs) and of office towers (with white-collar jobs). Since local governments are composed of and mostly represent business elites and affluent urbanites, they "significantly advance lower-class and working-class interests in redevelopment only when compelled to do so by political movements, protest, and social disorder" (p. 257). Such mobilization did eventually force changes in the massive clearance approach to urban renewal. But citizen protest is resisted. In response, capital mobilizes its own agents to influence local governments. Millions have been spent to stop rent control movements in numerous cities, to promote elite projects (such as BART in San Francisco and the Superdome in New Orleans), and to overthrow populist and progressive elected governments, as happened with the Kucinich government in Cleveland.

The Fainsteins suggest that we have seen three types of local governments since the 1950s: In the 1950s, *directive* governments planned large-scale redevelopment in the interest of upper- and middle-income groups, with no real opposition; from the mid-1960s to the mid-1970s, many urban governments were *concessionary,* forced by protests of the era to consider the needs of their low-income populations; from the mid-1970s to the 1980s, the *conserving* governments in cities paid more attention to low-income needs than in the 1950s, but also paid more attention to facilitating private enterprise. This typology fits certain northern cities with protest movements, but does not fit the histories of numerous other cities, particularly cities in the Sunbelt.

In an opening essay the Fainsteins frame a set of questions originating from the case studies:

(1) What conditions give rise to state-sponsored redevelopment action?
(2) What class and political conflict conditions shape that redevelopment action?
(3) Who wins and who loses in that action?

An article on New Haven by the Fainsteins raises these basic issues. An old manufacturing city in decline, in the 1950s and 1960s New Haven became the leader in state-assisted redevelopment programs. Working-class neighborhoods and old business areas were demolished and replaced with highways, office buildings, garages, and a hotel. Government and university leaders initially took the lead, with substantial support from some (but not all) local capitalists. The government-university-business coalition projects were challenged in the 1960s. Pressures from black communities brought some reforms, including jobs for black professionals and social service contracts for advocacy organizations. Low-income groups had forced some changes, but they were not able to translate their protests into a dominating political position.

Hill's essay on Detroit is one of the best in *Restructuring the City,* in part because it is the only piece that sets the decline of a major city within a *global* context—in this case, the global reorganization of the auto industry. One of the major needs in the area of urban political economy is for more attention to be given to the impact of shifts in the capitalist world system on cities. In the Detroit area, capital and job losses between 1968 and 1977 were colossal; about 200,000 jobs were lost. The response to decline was a downtown redevelopment plan, as in New Haven, but with a significant difference. Business and government leaders worked together "to transform this aging industrial city into a modern corporate image," with a financial and professional services center for auto and related firms, a research and development center, and a luxury shopping complex. A coalition of industrial, commercial, financial, and real estate capitalists was the basic force behind this corporate-center strategy. One result of their actions is the now-ailing Renaissance Center complex. Substantial public aid was provided for a range of business-oriented redevelopment projects. Yet the price to citizens was austerity in the form of reduced social consumption services (so as to lower taxes). Hill's assessment of this restructuring strategy is essentially negative, because it is a *local* strategy for a city that is primarily whipsawed by the national and international reorganization of the auto manufacturing industry.

The article on New Orleans by Michael Peter Smith and Marlene Keller deals with an older southern city which has also seen a business-government growth coalition trying to rebuild a city with severe poverty and race problems. After attempts at massive urban redevelopment (e.g., a riverfront expressway) failed, the growth coalition decided to pursue revitalization projects in selected areas of the city, such as office towers in the central business district. Projects aimed at tourists, such as the 1984 World's Fair buildings, were also subsidized from public funds. Because of the huge population of poor people, government officials had sought out and secured hundreds of millions of dollars in federal monies to keep the city afloat. Reagan cutbacks then had a severe impact on social service and other programs in the city. The huge investments in office construction, in a World's Fair, and in other business-oriented projects did not bring the jobs that the growth coalition had promised. Again urban redevelopment had many losers, with life becoming even harder for low-income residents. Smith and Keller accent the major social costs of redevelopment schemes. Similarly, Judd's analysis of Denver points up major conflicts over urban growth.

In 1955, several dozen downtown business leaders began developing a coordinated strategy for downtown redevelopment. Early projects were traditional slum clearance projects. In 1961-1978, the Skyline redevelopment project involved $.6 billion and a dozen new office and hotel buildings in the downtown area. As in most other central cities, these were office, commercial, and hotel projects. In his analysis, Judd also accents the social costs and uneven benefits of Denver's growth, not only the urban sprawl, water problems, and air pollution, but also the racial segregation, poverty, and poor housing. Judd notes the conflict between neighborhoods, including minority neighborhoods, and downtown business interests. A part of a corporate center strategy, central city housing has, as in other urban areas, displaced minority residents.

Taken together, these essays in *Restructuring the City* highlight several of the key dimensions cited in the list above, most notably the local and national states responding to the needs of capital (the corporate center strategy) and the conflict generated by minority displacement and "rewhiteizing" of central city neighborhoods. It is also very clear in these case studies that Mollenkopf's political entrepreneurs are generally not independent driving forces, but rather are one group of local actors typically drawn from, or dependent upon, local business elites. Together they make up the local growth coalitions emphasized by Harvey Molotch.

In *Power and Crisis in the City* Roger Friedland gives particular attention to the role of large multinational corporations and major unions in shaping urban policies. In his view "corporate and union powers shaped local policy responses to local constraints on local economic growth and social control" (p. 207). Friedland shows how the corporate center redevelopment strategy works in cities with powerful corporations; massive slum clearance facilitated office development. Friedland argues that national corporate elites dominated the origins of urban growth programs, with unions playing "second fiddle." Urban renewal programs were conceived by a coalition of liberal and business groups, yet they soon became programs serving office-centered downtown redevelopment. A broad array of capitalistic organizations dominated national urban policy formation, including the National Association of Real Estate Boards and its Urban Land Institute, the Chambers of Commerce, and numerous local corporate organizations from San Francisco to Boston.

Looking at the local level, Friedland quotes the classic conservative analysis of urban renewal of Banfield and Wilson, which note that "the business elite of the city met privately, agreed upon more or less comprehensive plans for the redevelopment of the central city, and presented the plans to the press, the politicians and the public."

In some cities, corporate executives have participated in these growth coalitions. In others, they have not been active. It is not so much the participation of particular corporate executives that reflects the power of large corporations, but rather is these organizations' broad control over economic and mobilization resources. Powerful corporations not only shape particular local government policies but also shape the structure of the policymaking process itself by shaping economic conditions. Among these are economic growth (new office towers, garages, apartment complexes) and the public costs of economic transformation (loss of industrial jobs, damage to neighborhoods). City governments were used to change the face, the infrastructure, of central cities to facilitate private (office-centered) growth. Friedland points up major differences in corporate and union power to shape local policies and policymaking processes. Unions have power in cities primarily because they can mobilize voters, but corporations control the economic resources which can severely constrain the policy and fiscal successes of local governments. If corporations feel unions are too active in influencing government, for example, they can disinvest and leave a community with fewer jobs.

Among the four books, Friedland gives the most attention to the black ghetto revolts, which threatened the policies of urban economic growth and the strategy of corporations. The redistributive (state) response to the black revolts varied: In cities dominated by corporations, blacks got substantial federal War on Poverty funds, but less local public employment expenditures than in cities where unions were more powerful. In cities with significant union strength, public sector expansion helped unions sustain the electoral support of black constituencies. Those excluded from the growth process, including blacks engaging in rioting, forced governments to respond with state employment and other redistributive services. The growth coalition's central city growth program, with its huge governmental subsidies, had failed to create the forecasted benefits for central city residents. The hostile response of excluded citizens forced federal and local governments to spend large amounts on public services. Friedland makes the important point that urban renewal agencies hurt people, but rarely faced the victims directly. It was other government agencies, the police, public housing, and social service agencies, which had to deal with the casualties of redevelopment. The police and social service agencies are more visible and politicized, while the renewal agencies were generally hidden from the city electorates and worked in close relationship with private investors. Public spending, particularly federal aid to cities, helped to purchase political peace for a while, but eventually cities suffered the heavy fiscal strain of expenditures for policing and social services and of expenditures to aid investors and developers. Friedland's analysis thus accents both the importance of large corporations in the corporate center strategy and also the state redistributive policies highlighted in the list above.

Swanstrom's book, *The Crisis of Growth Politics,* is a case study of "growth politics" in one troubled northern city, Cleveland, Ohio. By "growth politics" Swanstrom means the efforts by local governments to enhance the economic attractiveness of cities for capitalist investors with mobile wealth. In *conservative* growth politics the planning and implementation of growth are left primarily to the private sector; this type of politics rejects redistributive policies benefiting urban folk below the upper-income level. *Liberal* growth politics, in contrast, is a balancing act, providing incentives for wealthy investors interested in growth and also providing some redistributive action for the nonwealthy. Liberal growth politics can be seen in the mayoral regimes of Stokes in Cleveland and of Lindsay in New York. More recently, the swing toward conservative growth politics, with an emphasis on cutting back social and welfare programs, can be seen in the Koch regime in New York. Examining Cleveland in lush detail, Swanstrom shows how, in the 1950s and 1960s, the federal urban renewal program was used to benefit downtown corporate interests at the expense of neighborhoods and minorities. In the 1960s and 1970s, Cleveland's private utility used its monopoly over the production of electricity to try to destroy the local public utility. In the 1970s, the city government gave large tax abatements to assist local developers. And the 1970s, the populist Kucinich fought against business interests.

Swanstrom profiles the rise and fall of Cleveland's populist mayor, Dennis Kucinich, a man who *rejected* the politics of growth, who abandoned costly urban development policies aimed at attracting corporations downtown, and who, instead, pressed for distributing the limited resources of city government to the people in the form of redistributive government services. Kucinich implemented his populist rhetoric by *killing* state aid for downtown redevelopment. He axed $41 million in federal aid for a downtown "people mover" and a $153.5 million government subsidy for a Republic Steel dock project. He also killed a tax abatement program, which he demonstrated provided little benefit to city residents but good profits for developers. Kucinich also got involved in protecting Cleveland's money-saving public utility (Muny Light) against an orchestrated attack on it by a local private utility and allied local banks. However, Kucinich's aggressive populism was not an alternative political program of well-thought-out economic democracy backed by organization; Kucinich was unable to develop a political organization that could give him control of the city council or public bureaucracy. He was inept at coalition politics and even got into conflict with his natural allies, the neighborhood groups.

In December 1978, the local banks "precipitated the city's default for political reasons: to facilitate the sale of the public utility and help defeat a radical populist mayor" (p. 228). The city government did not go into default for economic reasons; it was forced into default by local banks for *political* reasons. The city was still a good investment for local banks, but local bankers were so upset over Kucinich's actions, particularly in regard to Muny Light, that they gave him the ultimatum of selling Muny or city default. Kucinish refused, and the banks retaliated. A key aspect here, in contrast to European cities, is that local governments in the United States are heavily dependent for credit on private banking firms. Thus, city governments can be manipulated by finance capitalists.

A couple of other contributions by Swanstrom are worth noting here. He makes a useful distinction between two factions within local growth coalitions. Growth coalitions are viewed as alliances between mobile wealth (large industrial corporations) and immobile wealth (real estate interests, banks, utilities, newspapers). The immobile fraction, in particular, seeks to make money off of rising land prices (an "externality") which come from large corporations locating in an area. In addition, he makes the important point that the federal government's important role in shaping cities is often more indirect than direct; that, for example, accelerated depreciation laws render "older buildings in central cities relatively less attractive for investment" and accelerate "the decentralization of jobs and the flight of industry out of central cities" (p. 28). Most prominently, however, Swanstrom adds dimension 8 to the list above; that is, he provides a clear example of people organizing successfully (for a time) to fight a corporate center development strategy.

In conclusion, I would like to emphasize that each of these books accents certain dimensions of the state and local economy drama, key dimensions that need to be integrated into a comprehensive theory of the local state. That task will require a recognition of the relevant structural conditions, such as the need of large corporations for office buildings, for the state-linked corporate center strategy. And it will require a recognition of the different levels (local, regional, national) of the state, as well as of factions (Democratic Party entrepreneurs, multinational corporations, unions) within the national growth coalition, and factions (mobile wealth, immobile wealth) within the local growth coalition. In addition, the dimension of community (class, race, territorial) struggles is accentuated here, particularly in the discussions of minority displacement and protest, and of Dennis Kucinich's populism. Government redistributive policy, thus, was in part a response to government investment and urban redevelopment policy. And we must not forget the global context in which state development program responses to the needs of capital take place. That context involves a high velocity of investment flows in and out of particular places, a velocity which makes many local growth coalition efforts to get mobile wealth to locate in a place ephemeral, as Hill's discussion of Henry Ford's Renaissance Center redevelopment ("white elephant") project makes very clear.

—*Joe R. Feagin*
University of Texas at Austin

INDEX

to

URBAN AFFAIRS QUARTERLY

Volume 21

Number 1 (September 1985) pp. 1-136
Number 2 (December 1985) pp. 137-288
Number 3 (March 1986) pp. 289-456
Number 4 (June 1986) pp. 457-634

Authors:

ADAMS, CAROLYN TEICH, "Homelessness in the Postindustrial City: Views from London and Philadelphia," 527.

ALBRECHT, DON E., GORDON BULTENA, and ERIC HOIBERG, "Constituency of the Antigrowth Movement: A Comparison of the Growth Orientations of Urban Status Groups," 607.

ALEXANDER, JAMES R., "Public Property and Private Power [Book Review]," 129.

APPELBAUM, RICHARD P., "Swedish Housing in the Postwar Period," 221.

BULTENA, GORDON, see Albrecht, D. E.

BUSS, TERRY, see Clarke, S. E.

CLARKE, SUSAN E., F. STEVENS REDBURN, and TERRY BUSS, "The Local Impacts of Economic Change [Symposium Contribution]," 139.

DIETZ, THOMAS, see Frey, R. S.

DiGREGORIO, DENISE A., see Shlay, A. B.

FAINSTEIN, NORMAN I., see Fainstein, S. S.

FAINSTEIN, SUSAN S. and NORMAN I. FAINSTEIN, "Economic Restructuring and the Rise of Urban Social Movements [Symposium Contribution]," 187.

FEAGIN, JOE R., "The Corporate Center Strategy: The State in Central Cities [Book Review]," 617.

FLEMMING, ROY B., "Suburbanization, Segregation, and Politics [Book Review]," 448.

FORESTER, JOHN, "Planners and the Public [Book Review]," 126.

FREY, R. SCOTT, THOMAS DIETZ, and JANE MARTE, "The Effect of Economic Dependence on Urban Primacy: A Cross-National Panel Analysis," 359.

GITTELL, MARILYN, "The American City: A National Priority or an Expendable Population [Symposium Contribution]," 13.

GORDON, MARGARET T., "The Urban Condition: 'Plates' Beneath City Surfaces and a New Research Agenda [Symposium Contribution]," 25.

GUEST, AVERY M. and R. S. OROPESA, "Informal Social Ties and Political Activity in the Metropolis," 550.

HAAS, AIN, see Maher, T.
HAINES, VALERIE A., "Energy and Urban Form: A Human Ecological Critique," 337.
HOIBERG, ERIC, see Albrecht, D. E.
HUDSON, RAY and DAVID SADLER, "Communities in Crisis: The Social and Political Effects of Steel Closures in France, West Germany, and the United Kingdom [Symposium Contribution]," 171.
HULA, RICHARD C., "Markets and Redevelopment: The Case of Neighborhood Housing Service," 461.
HUNTER, ALBERT, "Crossing Urban Boundaries: The Mission of *Urban Affairs Quarterly* [Symposium Contribution]," 5.
JOHNSON, ARTHUR T., "Economic and Policy Implications of Hosting Sports Franchises: Lessons from Baltimore," 411.
KEATING, W. DENNIS, "Urban Displacement Research: Local, National, International [Book Review]," 132.
KIRBY, ANDREW, "Nine Fallacies of Local Economic Change [Symposium Contribution]," 207.
KRIVO, LAUREN J. and JAN E. MUTCHLER, "Housing Constraint and Household Complexity in Metropolitan America: Black and Spanish-Origin Minorities," 389.
LEE, BARRETT A., see London, B.
LEVINE, BETTY, see Maher, T.
LIELL, JOHN, see Maher, T.
LINEBERRY, ROBERT L., "Urban Affairs: A Look into the Past and the Future [Symposium Contribution]," 20.
LIPTON, S. GREGORY, see London, B.
LOGAN, JOHN, see Schneider, M.
LOGAN, JOHN R., see Molotch, H.
LONDON, BRUCE, "Ecological and Political-Economic Analyses of Migration to a Primate City: Bangkok, Thailand ca. 1970," 501.
LONDON, BRUCE, BARRETT A. LEE, and S. GREGORY LIPTON, "The Determinants of Gentrification in the United States: A City-Level Analysis," 369.
LORENCE, JON, see Nelson, J. I.
MAHER, TIMOTHY, AIN HAAS, BETTY LEVINE, and JOHN LIELL, "Whose Neighborhood: The Role of Established Residents in Historic Preservation Areas," 267.
MARLIN, MATTHEW R., "Reevaluating the Benefits and Costs of Industrial Revenue Bonds," 435.
MARTE, JANE, see Frey, R. S.
MOLOTCH, HARVEY and JOHN R. LOGAN, "Urban Dependencies: New Forms of Use and Exchange in U.S. Cities [Symposium Contribution]," 143.
MUTCHLER, JAN E., see Krivo, L. J.
NELSON, JOEL I. and JON LORENCE, "Employment in Service Activities and Inequality in Metropolitan Areas," 106.
OROPESA, R. S., see Guest, A. M.
PASCARELLA, THOMAS A. and RICHARD D. RAYMOND, "Rejoinder to Matthew R. Marlin's 'Reevaluating the Benefits and Costs of Industrial Revenue Bonds,'" 443.
PETERSON, PAUL E., see Wong, K. K.
RAFFEL, JEFFREY A., "The Impact of Metropolitan School Desegregation on Public Opinion: A Longitudinal Analysis," 245.

RAYMOND, RICHARD D., see Pascarella, T. A.
REDBURN, F. STEVENS, see Clarke, S. E.
SADLER, DAVID, see Hudson, R.
SCHNEIDER, MARK and JOHN LOGAN, "Suburban Municipalities: The Changing System of Intergovernmental Relations in the Mid-1970s," 87.
SHLAY, ANNE B. and DENISE A. DiGREGORIO, "Same City, Different Worlds: Examining Gender- and Work-Based Differences in Perceptions of Neighborhood Desirability," 66.
SLOVAK, JEFFREY S., "Attachments in the Nested Community: Evidence from a Case Study," 575.
STEINMAN, MICHAEL, "Officer Orientations Toward the Community: The Impact of Police Bureaucracy," 598.
VAN TIL, JON, "Comment on 'Energy and Urban Form,' " 355.
WARREN, ELIZABETH, "The Dispersal of Subsidized Housing in Chicago: An Index for Comparisons," 484.
WHITT, J. ALLEN and GLENN YAGO, "Corporate Strategies and the Decline of Transit in U.S. Cities," 37.
WIRT, FREDERICK M., "State of the Art in Urban Research: 1923 [Book Review]," 282.
WOLMAN, HAROLD, "The Reagan Urban Policy and Its Impacts," 311.
WONG, KENNETH K. and PAUL E. PETERSON, "Urban Response to Federal Program Flexibility: Politics of Community Development Block Grant," 293.
YAGO, GLENN, see Whitt, J. A.

Articles:

"Attachments in the Nested Community: Evidence from a Case Study," Slovak, 575.
"Comment on 'Energy and Urban Form,' " Van Til, 355.
"Constituency of the Antigrowth Movement: A Comparison of the Growth Orientations of Urban Status Groups," Albrecht et al., 607.
"Corporate Strategies and the Decline of Transit in U.S. Cities," Whitt and Yago, 37.
"The Determinants of Gentrification in the United States: A City-Level Analysis," London et al., 369.
"The Dispersal of Subsidized Housing in Chicago: An Index for Comparisons," Warren, 484.
"Ecological and Political-Economic Analyses of Migration to a Primate City: Bangkok, Thailand ca. 1970," London, 501.
"Economic and Policy Implications of Hosting Sports Franchises: Lessons from Baltimore," Johnson, 411.
"Editors' Note," 291.
"The Effect of Economic Dependence on Urban Primacy: A Cross-National Panel Analysis," Frey et al., 359.
"Employment in Service Activities and Inequality in Metropolitan Areas," Nelson and Lorence, 106.
"Energy and Urban Form: A Human Ecological Critique," Haines, 337.
"Homelessness in the Postindustrial City: Views from London and Philadelphia," Adams, 527.
"Housing Constraint and Household Complexity in Metropolitan America: Black and Spanish-Origin Minorities," Krivo and Mutchler, 389.

"The Impact of Metropolitan School Desegregation on Public Opinion: A Longitudinal Analysis," Raffel, 245.

"Informal Social Ties and Political Activity in the Metropolis," Guest and Oropesa, 550.

"Markets and Redevelopment: The Case of Neighborhood Housing Service," Hula, 461.

"Officer Orientations Toward the Community: The Impact of Police Bureaucracy," Steinman, 598.

"The Reagan Urban Policy and Its Impacts," Wolman, 311.

"Reevaluating the Benefits and Costs of Industrial Revenue Bonds," Marlin, 435.

"Rejoinder to Matthew R. Marlin's 'Reevaluating the Benefits and Costs of Industrial Revenue Bonds,'" Pascarella and Raymond, 443.

"Same City, Different Worlds: Examining Gender- and Work-Based Differences in Perceptions of Neighborhood Desirability," Shlay and DiGregorio, 66.

"Surban Municipalities: The Changing System of Intergovernmental Relations in the Mid-1970s," Schneider and Logan, 87.

"Swedish Housing in the Postwar Period," Appelbaum, 221.

"Urban Response to Federal Program Flexibility: Politics of Community Development Block Grant," Wong and Peterson, 293.

"Whose Neighborhood? The Role of Established Residents in Historic Preservation Areas," Maher et al., 267.

Book Review Essays:

"The Corporate Center Strategy: The State in Central Cities," Fegin, 617.

"Planners and the Public," Forester, 126.

"Public Property and Private Power," Alexander, 129.

"State of the Art in Urban Research: 1923," Wirt, 282.

"Suburbanization, Segregation, and Politics," Flemming, 448.

"Urban Displacement Research: Local, National, International," Keating, 132.

Contributions to Symposia:

"The American City: A National Priority or an Expendable Population," Gittell, 13.

"Communities in Crisis: The Social and Political Effects of Steel Closures in France, West Germany, and the United Kingdom," Hudson and Sadler, 171.

"Crossing Urban Boundaries: The Mission of *Urban Affairs Quarterly*," Hunter, 5.

"Economic Restructuring and the Rise of Urban Social Movements," Fainstein and Fainstein, 187.

"Editor's Introduction," 3.

"The Local Impacts of Economic Change," Clarke et al. 139.

"Nine Fallacies of Local Economic Change," Kirby, 207.

"Urban Affairs: A Look into the Past and the Future," Lineberry, 20.

"The Urban Condition: 'Plates' Beneath City Surfaces and a New Research Agenda," Gordon, 25.

"Urban Dependencies: New Forms of Use and Exchange in U.S. Cities," Molotch and Logan, 143.